Lecture Notes in Computer Science 3005

Commenced Publication in 1973
Founding and Former Series Editors:
Gerhard Goos, Juris Hartmanis, and Jan van Leeuwen

Springer
*Berlin
Heidelberg
New York
Hong Kong
London
Milan
Paris
Tokyo*

Günther R. Raidl et al. (Eds.)

Applications of Evolutionary Computing

EvoWorkshops 2004: EvoBIO, EvoCOMNET,
EvoHOT, EvoIASP, EvoMUSART, and EvoSTOC
Coimbra, Portugal, April 5-7, 2004
Proceedings

 Springer

Volume Editors

see next page

Coverillustration: "Embrace" by Anargyros Sarafopoulos
http://ncca.bournemouth.ac.uk/main/staff/Anargyros/
Anargyros Sarafopoulos is a lecturer in computer animation and visualisation at the
National Centre for Computer Animation at Bournemouth University, where he applies genetic programming to the procedural representation of regular textures and
images using graph grammars and iterated function systems (IFS)

Library of Congress Control Number: 2004102415

CR Subject Classification (1998): F.1, D.1, B, C.2, J.3, I.4, J.5

ISSN 0302-9743
ISBN 3-540-21378-3 Springer-Verlag Berlin Heidelberg New York

Springer-Verlag is a part of Springer Science+Business Media

springeronline.com

© Springer-Verlag Berlin Heidelberg 2004
Printed in Germany

Typesetting: Camera-ready by author, data conversion by PTP-Berlin, Protago-TeX-Production GmbH
Printed on acid-free paper   SPIN: 10993293   06/3142   5 4 3 2 1 0

Volume Editors

Günther R. Raidl
Institute of Computer Graphics
and Algorithms
Vienna University of Technology
Favoritenstrasse 9-11/186
1040 Vienna, Austria
raidl@ads.tuwien.ac.at

Stefano Cagnoni
Dept. of Computer Engineering
University of Parma
Parco Area delle Scienze 181/a
43100 Parma, Italy
cagnoni@ce.unipr.it

Jürgen Branke
Institute AIFB
University of Karlsruhe
76128 Karlsruhe, Germany
branke@aifb.uni-karlsruhe.de

David W. Corne
Department of Computer Science
University of Exeter
North Park Road
Exeter EX4 4QF, UK
d.w.corne@ex.ac.uk

Rolf Drechsler
Institute of Computer Science
University of Bremen
28359 Bremen, Germany
drechsle@informatik.uni-bremen.de

Yaochu Jin
Honda Research Institute Europe
Carl-Legien-Str.30
63073 Offenbach/Main, Germany
yaochu.jin@honda-ri.de

Colin G. Johnson
Computing Laboratory
University of Kent
Canterbury, Kent, CT2 7NF, UK
c.g.johnson@ukc.ac.uk

Penousal Machado
Dep. de Engenharia Informática
University of Coimbra
Polo II, 3030 Coimbra, Portugal
machado@dei.uc.pt

Elena Marchiori
Dept. of Mathematics and
Computer Science
Free University of Amsterdam
de Boelelaan 1081a
1081 HV, Amsterdam,
The Netherlands
elena@cs.vu.nl

Franz Rothlauf
Department of Information Systems 1
University of Mannheim
Schloss, 68131 Mannheim, Germany
rothlauf@uni-mannheim.de

George D. Smith
School of Computing Sciences
University of East Anglia
UEA Norwich
Norwich NR4 7TJ, UK
gds@sys.uea.ac.uk

Giovanni Squillero
Dip. di Automatica e Informatica
Politecnico di Torino
Corso Duca degli Abruzzi 24
10129 Torino, Italy
squillero@polito.it

Preface

Evolutionary Computation (EC) deals with problem solving, optimization, and machine learning techniques inspired by principles of natural evolution and genetics. Just from this basic definition, it is clear that one of the main features of the research community involved in the study of its theory and in its applications is multidisciplinarity. For this reason, EC has been able to draw the attention of an ever-increasing number of researchers and practitioners in several fields.

In its 6-year-long activity, EvoNet, the European Network of Excellence in Evolutionary Computing, has been the natural reference and incubator for that multifaceted community. EvoNet has provided logistic and material support for those who were already involved in EC but, in the first place, it has had a critical role in favoring the significant growth of the EC community and its interactions with longer-established ones. The main instrument that has made this possible has been the series of events, first organized in 1998, that have spanned over both theoretical and practical aspects of EC.

Ever since 1999, the present format, in which the EvoWorkshops, a collection of workshops on the most application-oriented aspects of EC, act as satellites of a core event, has proven to be very successful and very representative of the multi-disciplinarity of EC. Up to 2003, the core was represented by EuroGP, the main European event dedicated to Genetic Programming. EuroGP has been joined as the main event in 2004 by EvoCOP, formerly part of EvoWorkshops, which has become the European Conference on Evolutionary Computation in Combinatorial Optimization.

EvoWorkshops 2004, of which this volume contains the proceedings, was held in Coimbra, Portugal, on April 5–7, 2004, jointly with the seventh edition of EuroGP and the fourth edition of EvoCOP. EvoWorkshops 2004 consisted of the following individual workshops:

- EvoBIO, the 2nd European Workshop on Evolutionary Bioinformatics;
- EvoCOMNET, the 1st European Workshop on Evolutionary Computation in Communications, Networks, and Connected Systems;
- EvoHOT, the 1st European Workshop on Hardware Optimization Techniques;
- EvoIASP, the 6th European Workshop on Evolutionary Computation in Image Analysis and Signal Processing;
- EvoMUSART, the 2nd European Workshop on Evolutionary Music and Art; and
- EvoSTOC, the 1st European Workshop on Evolutionary Algorithms in Stochastic and Dynamic Environments.

EvoBIO was concerned with the exploitation of evolutionary computation and advanced hybrids of evolutionary computation with other techniques in addressing the very wide range of problems that occur in the analysis and understanding of biological data. In this area, evolutionary computation is playing an increasingly important role in pharmaceutical, biotechnology, and associated industries, as well as in scientific discovery.

EvoCOMNET, the 1st European Workshop on Evolutionary Computation in Communications, Networks, and Connected Systems, addressed the application of evolutionary computation techniques to problems in communication, networks, and connected systems. New communication technologies, faster networks, new types of interpersonal and interorganizational communication as well as the integration and interconnection of production centers and industries have a great impact on the structure of companies and business processes and are the driving forces on our road towards a connected, networked society. EvoCOMNET is a platform for the dissemination of the research and application of EC techniques in facing these new challenges through designing and building more efficient communication systems, networks, and connected systems. The papers presented at the workshop illustrated both the continuing success of EC and the potential of more recent developments to solve real-world problems.

EvoHOT highlighted the latest developments in the field of EC applications to hardware optimization. The works presented show how problems can be examined with complementary approaches, starting from their particular practical aspects or from the evolutionary computation theory. The different subjects tackled cover a broad spectrum. They include classical problems, such as minimization of disjoint sums-of-products based on binary decision diagrams and the multilayer floorplan layout problem, together with some very specific problems, like the implementations of median circuits when limited resources are available, the optimization of mask and illumination geometries, and the optimization of a manipulator trajectory. The behavior of evolutionary techniques on such problems was carefully analyzed, showing the effect of multiobjective optimization and how specific problems can be evaluated and characterized.

EvoIASP, the first European event specifically dedicated to the applications of evolutionary computation to image analysis and signal processing, has been a traditional appointment since 1999. This year it addressed topics ranging from optimization of low-level image and signal processing techniques to complex object-recognition systems and analysis of financial time series, which reflects the breadth of the possible applications in the fields covered by the workshop.

The second edition of EvoMUSART focused on the use of evolutionary computation techniques for the development of creative systems. There is a growing interest in the application of these techniques in fields such as art, music, architecture, and design. The goal of EvoMUSART was to bring together researchers who use evolutionary computation in this context, providing the opportunity to promote, present, and discuss the latest work in the area, fostering its further developments and collaboration among researchers.

The topic of EvoSTOC was the application of evolutionary algorithms in stochastic environments. This included optimization problems changing over time, the treatment of noise, and the search for robust solutions. These topics recently gained increasing attention in the evolutionary computing community, and EvoSTOC was the first workshop to provide a platform to present and discuss the latest research in the field.

EvoWorkshops 2004 has confirmed its tradition in providing researchers in these fields, as well as people from industry, students, and interested newcomers, with an opportunity to present new results, discuss current developments and applications, or just get acquainted with the world of EC, besides fostering closer future interaction between members of all scientific communities that may benefit from EC techniques.

EvoWorkshops 2004 had the highest number of submissions ever, even after EvoCOP, which had been by far the largest of the EvoWorkshops in the previous years, became an independent conference. The acceptance rates are an indicator of the high quality of the papers presented at the workshops and included in these proceedings.

Workshop	submitted	accepted	acceptance ratio
EvoBIO	21	13	61.9%
EvoCOMNET	27	6	22.2%
EvoHOT	11	6	54.5%
EvoIASP	33	15	45.4%
EvoMUSART	17	9	52.9%
EvoSTOC	14	6	42.9%
Total	123	55	44.7%

We would like to give credit to all members of the program committees, to whom we are very grateful for their quick and thorough work. EvoWorkshops 2004 was sponsored, for the last time, by EvoNet, whose activity as an EU-funded project has come to an end with the organization of this year's events. However, the figures reported above show that EvoWorkshops, as well as the main conferences with which it is jointly organized, has reached a degree of maturity and scientific prestige that will allow the activity promoted by EvoNet in the past six years to go on, and possibly further expand, in the years to come. The organization of the event was made possible thanks to the active participation of many members of the EvoNet working groups, but especially to the invaluable restless work of Jennifer Willies, EvoNet's administrator.

April 2004   Günther R. Raidl   Stefano Cagnoni   Jürgen Branke
              David W. Corne   Rolf Drechsler   Yaochu Jin
              Colin Johnson   Penousal Machado   Elena Marchiori
              Franz Rothlauf   George D. Smith   Giovanni Squillero

Organization

EvoWorkshops 2004 was organized by EvoNet jointly with EuroGP 2004 and EvoCOP 2004.

Organizing Committee

EvoWorkshops Co-chairs: Günther R. Raidl, Vienna University of Technology, Austria

Stefano Cagnoni, University of Parma, Italy

Local Chair: Ernesto Costa, University of Coimbra, Portugal

EvoBIO Co-chairs: David Corne, University of Exeter, UK

Elena Marchiori, Free University Amsterdam, The Netherlands

EvoCOMNET Co-chairs: Franz Rothlauf, University of Mannheim, Germany

George D. Smith, University of East Anglia, UK

EvoHOT Co-chairs: Giovanni Squillero, Politecnico di Torino, Italy

Rolf Drechsler, University of Bremen, Germany

EvoIASP Chair: Stefano Cagnoni, University of Parma, Italy

EvoMUSART Co-chairs: Colin G. Johnson, University of Kent, UK

Penousal Machado, University of Coimbra, Portugal

EvoSTOC Co-chairs: Jürgen Branke, University of Karlsruhe, Germany

Yaochu Jin, Honda Research Institute Europe, Germany

Program Committees

EvoBIO Program Committee

Jesus S. Aguilar-Ruiz, University of Seville, Spain
Wolfgang Banzhaf, University of Dortmund, Germany
Jacek Blazewicz, Institute of Computing Science, Poznan, Poland
Carlos Cotta-Porras, University of Malaga, Spain
Bogdan Filipic, Jozef Stefan Institute, Ljubljana, Slovenia
David Fogel, Natural Selection, Inc., USA
Gary B. Fogel, Natural Selection, Inc., USA
James Foster, University of Idaho, USA

Steven A. Frank, University of California, Irvine, USA
Jin-Kao Hao, LERIA, Université d'Angers, France
William Hart, Sandia National Labs, USA
Jaap Heringa, Free University Amsterdam, The Netherlands
Francisco Herrera, University of Granada, Spain
Daniel Howard, QinetiQ, UK
Kees Jong, Free University Amsterdam, The Netherlands
Antoine van Kampen, AMC University of Amsterdam, The Netherlands
Douglas B. Kell, University of Wales, Aberystwyth, UK
William B. Langdon, UCL, UK
Bob MacCallum, Stockholm University, Sweden
Brian Mayoh, Aarhus University, Denmark
Andrew C.R. Martin, University of Reading, UK
Peter Merz, Eberhard-Karls-Universität, Tübingen, Germany
Martin Middendorf, Leipzig University, Germany
Jason H. Moore, Vanderbilt University Medical Center, USA
Pablo Moscato, University of Newcastle, Australia
Martin Oates, British Telecom Plc., UK
Jon Rowe, University of Birmingham, UK
Jem Rowland, University of Wales, Aberystwyth, UK
Vic J. Rayward-Smith, University of East Anglia, UK
El-ghazali Talbi, Laboratoire d'Informatique Fondamentale de Lille, France
Eckart Zitzler, Swiss Federal Institute of Technology, Switzerland

EvoCOMNET Program Committee

Stuart Allen, Cardiff University, UK
Dave Corne, University of Exeter, UK
Bryant Julstrom, St. Cloud State University, USA
Joshua Knowles, Université Libre de Bruxelles, Belgium
Geoff McKeown, UEA Norwich, UK
Martin Oates, University of Reading, UK
Günther R. Raidl, Vienna University of Technology, Austria
Giovanni Squillero, Politecnico di Torino, Italy
Andrew Tuson, City University, London, UK

EvoHOT Program Committee

Gabriella Kókai, Friedrich-Alexander University, Erlangen-Nürnberg, Germany
Ernesto Sanchez, Politecnico di Torino, Italy
Lukáš Sekanina, Brno University of Technology, Czech Republic
George D. Smith, University of East Anglia, UK
Tan Kay Chen, National University of Singapore, Singapore
Massimo Violante, Politecnico di Torino, Italy

EvoIASP Program Committee

Giovanni Adorni, University of Genoa, Italy
Lucia Ballerini, University of Örebro, Sweden
Bir Bhanu, University of California, USA
Dario Bianchi, University of Parma, Italy
Alberto Broggi, University of Parma, Italy
Ela Claridge, University of Birmingham, UK
Laura Dipietro, MIT, USA
Marc Ebner, University of Würzburg, Germany
Terry Fogarty, South Bank University, UK
Daniel Howard, QinetiQ, UK
Mario Köppen, FhG IPK, Berlin, Germany
Evelyne Lutton, INRIA, France
Peter Nordin, Chalmers University of Technology, Sweden
Gustavo Olague, CICESE, Mexico
Riccardo Poli, University of Essex, UK
Conor Ryan, University of Limerick, Ireland
Giovanni Squillero, Politecnico di Torino, Italy
Kiyoshi Tanaka, Shinshu University, Japan
Ankur M. Teredesai, Rochester Institute of Technology, USA
Andy Tyrrell, University of York, UK
Hans-Michael Voigt, GFaI, Germany
Mengjie Zhang, Victoria University of Wellington, New Zealand

EvoMUSART Program Committee

Mauro Annunziato, Plancton Art Studio, Italy
Paul Brown, Birkbeck College, University of London, UK
Amílcar Cardoso, CISUC Centre for Informatics and Systems,
    University of Coimbra, Portugal
John Gero, Key Centre of Design Computing and Cognition,
    University of Sydney, Australia
Andrew Gartland-Jones, University of Sussex, UK
Carlos Grilo, School of Technology and Management of Leiria, Portugal
Matthew Lewis, Ohio State University, USA
Bill Manaris, College of Charleston, USA
Eduardo R. Miranda, University of Plymouth, UK
Ken Musgrave, Pandromeda, Inc., USA
Luigi Pagliarini, Academy of Fine Arts, Rome, Italy
Juan Romero, University of Coruña, Spain
Celestino Soddu, Politecnico de Milano, Italy
Tim Taylor, University of Edinburgh, UK
Stephen Todd, IBM, UK
Tatsuo Unemi, University of Zurich, Switzerland
Geraint Wiggins, City University, London, UK

EvoSTOC Program Committee

Tim Blackwell, University of London, UK
Dirk Büche, University of Applied Sciences, Aargau, Switzerland
Ernesto Costa, University of Coimbra, Portugal
Kalyanmoy Deb, IIT Kanpur, India
Anna I. Esparcia-Alcazar, Universitat Politecnica de Valencia, Spain
Marco Farina, STMicroelectronics, Italy
Michael Guntsch, University of Karlsruhe, Germany
Hajime Kita, Kyoto University, Japan
Dirk Mattfeld, University of Bremen, Germany
Daniel Merkle, University of Leipzig, Germany
Markus Olhofer, Honda Research Institute Europe, Germany
Khaled Rasheed, University of Georgia, USA
Christopher Ronnewinkel, SAP, Germany
Christian Schmidt, University of Karlsruhe, Germany
Lutz Schönemann, University of Dortmund, Germany
Stephen Smith, Carnegie Mellon University, USA
Jürgen Teich, University of Paderborn, Germany
Lars Willmes, NuTech Solutions, Germany

Sponsoring Institutions

- EvoNet, the Network of Excellence in Evolutionary Computing
- University of Coimbra, Coimbra, Portugal

Table of Contents

EvoBIO Contributions

EvoCOMNET Contributions

EvoHOT Contributions

EvoIASP Contributions

EvoMUSART Contributions

EvoSTOC Contributions

Author Index

A Memetic Algorithm for Protein Structure Prediction in a 3D-Lattice HP Model

Andrea Bazzoli and Andrea G.B. Tettamanzi

Università degli Studi di Milano
Dipartimento di Tecnologie dell'Informazione
Via Bramante 65, I-26013 Crema (CR), Italy
andrea.tettamanzi@unimi.it

Abstract. This paper presents a memetic algorithm with self-adaptive local search, applied to protein structure prediction in an HP, cubic-lattice model. Besides describing in detail how the algorithm works, we report experimental results that justify important implementation choices, such as the introduction of speciation mechanisms and the extensive application of local search. Test runs on 48-mer chains show that the proposed algorithm has promising search capabilities.

1 Introduction

After the successful completion of the Human Genome Project, the focus of biological investigation has shifted to the study of proteins and their interactions, which are a key to understanding the metabolism of cells. Since the biological activity of a protein depends on its 3D (tertiary) structure, determining that structure has become one of the most central problems in Bioinformatics.

A number of computational methods have been developed over the years, in order to simulate the folding process of linear chains of amino-acid residues (primary sequences) to their tertiary conformations, also called native states. These methods, however, are computationally very expensive, and their applicability is limited to relatively short polymer sequences.

An alternative approach is to "predict" the 3D structure given the primary sequence, by using some suitable heuristics, which can be statistical (like comparative modeling) or optimization-based.

1.1 Problem Statement

The protein structure prediction (PSP) problem can be stated as an optimization problem, whereby the minimum of a specific energy function is sought in the space of all possible conformations. As a matter of fact, according to Anfinsen's hypothesis [1], the native state of a protein can be seen as the one with the lowest energy.

Given the considerable number of amino acids in a protein, all-atom energy functions are often prohibitive on today's computers. For this reason, researchers

G.R. Raidl et al. (Eds.): EvoWorkshops 2004, LNCS 3005, pp. 1–10, 2004.

have developed a great variety of simplified protein models, which speed up the calculations by somewhat reducing the number of degrees of freedom (and therefore parameters) involved. Although their descriptions are inevitably less precise, these models offer nonetheless a global perspective of protein structures, which has proven helpful in confirming or questioning important theories.

One remarkable simplified energy function stems from the so-called HP model [4], where amino acids are considered as single beads either hydrophobic (H) or hydrophilic (P), and protein conformations are embedded in a lattice as self-avoiding, connected paths. Given the number n_H of its hydrophobic (H-H) contacts between non-consecutive amino acids, the energy of a protein is typically defined to be $-n_H$.

1.2   Related Work

PSP in the HP model has been demonstrated to be an NP-hard problem [2]. Therefore, global optimization heuristics, and in particular evolutionary algorithms, have been reasonably used in order to solve it [5]. Unger and Moult [12] developed a genetic algorithm where only feasible (self-avoiding) conformations are allowed, and a Monte Carlo acceptance criterion biases crossover and mutation toward decreasing energies. The limits of this approach were discussed by Patton and colleagues [10], who also proposed a standard genetic algorithm based on the penalization of illegal (colliding) shapes. They designed a new conformational representation, called Preference Order Encoding, which further promotes feasibility within the population of solutions. Krasnogor et al. [5] analyzed three main factors affecting the efficacy of an evolutionary algorithm for PSP: the encoding scheme, the way illegal shapes are considered by the search, and the energy (fitness) function used. In the off-lattice, HP model of Piccolboni and Mauri [11], protein conformations are represented through a distance matrix, which was suggested to have considerable advantages over internal coordinates.

Section 2 describes in detail a memetic algorithm for PSP, while its results on a set of ten 48-mer sequences are presented in Section 3. A critical discussion of this work and its further developments is provided in Section 4.

2   Outline of the Approach

Memetic Algorithms (MAs) [8] are a powerful combination of local search with standard evolutionary algorithms. Their name stems from the term "meme", which Richard Dawkins used in his book [3] to identify a cultural gene, evolving at a much faster pace than a natural gene. Central to MAs is the use of an improvement operator, based on local-search methods, alongside the standard "blind" mutation and recombination operators.

This paper presents a MA for PSP. We used a self-adaptive strategy, as the local search can act toward either exploitation or diversification of fitness, according to its degree of convergence within the population. Our algorithm is strongly based on a previous work of Krasnogor and Smith [6], where the authors successfully compared self-adaptation against other local-search approaches.

We describe now the implementation of our algorithm, with a number of graphs illustrating the main experiments we realized for tuning its parameters. All these graphs, except that of Fig. 4, show the average results of 30 independent MA runs. We always used the same 48-mer sequence (see below, Sequence no. 1 of Table 1), whose native structure has an energy of -32.

2.1 Encoding of Protein Structures

In order to find a convenient representation for lattice protein structures, we compared two integer-gene encodings on the basis of their impact on global search performance. Both use internal coordinates, i.e., they specify the sequence of directions that one must follow on the lattice to locate the successive amino acids of a polymer chain.

The first method is the classical relative-move encoding [10]. A widely known problem for this type of encoding is that, with increased chain length, randomly initialized populations tend to be dominated by infeasible shapes.

To overcome this problem, we decided to use the Preference Order Encoding (POE), introduced by Patton et al. [10].

2.2 Fitness

When PSP under the HP model is approached with evolutionary algorithms, it is natural to choose a fitness function that promotes, through its maximization, the formation of a hydrophobic core. Therefore, we selected a simple evaluation method that rewards H-H contacts and penalizes infeasible shapes. According to this method, the fitness f of a given protein structure s is determined as follows:

$$f(s) = n_H(s) - \rho \cdot n_L(s),$$

where $n_H(s)$ is the number of hydrophobic contacts in the protein, while $n_L(s)$ is the number of lattice sites occupied by two or more amino acids; the impact of the term $\rho \cdot n_L(s)$ tends to vanish under the POE, therefore ρ can be set to 1 for simplicity.

2.3 Genetic Operators

After some experiments, we chose 1-point crossover to be the recombination operator for our MA, as it proved to work better than both 2-point and uniform crossover.

Offspring mutation is applied at a very low rate, so it plays a minor role in the search process. When acting upon a protein's encoding, it blindly changes only one of its genes.

More clever mutation operators are used in the local-search process, and will be described in the following section.

2.4   Local Search

Our algorithm differs from a classical evolutionary algorithm in that the whole parent pool undergoes at each generation a step of local search (LS), which allows the algorithm to be classified as "memetic". We chose a self-adaptive strategy highly similar to the one proposed by Krasnogor and Smith [6], whereby the local search can be applied either to optimize or diversify fitness values, depending on their spread over the population (see Fig. 1 and 2). The probability of applying LS is kept fixed for the whole run, while the temperature parameter T is updated at each generation to the inverse of σ, the standard deviation of fitness within the population[1]. The temperature determines, according to a Boltzmann distribution, the chances of accepting a bad LS move, that is, a move causing a fitness decrease. So, when the population has a large variety of fitness values (high σ), the local search works toward optimization and bad moves tend to be rejected. Conversely, if fitness values become concentrated in a short range (low σ), much more bad moves are accepted and the local search acts as a diversification process. After some testing, the k coefficient was set to 0.96, a value relatively severe with bad moves; it remains to be studied to which extent this can be generalized to other problem instances.

```
LocalSearch(parents) {
    T = 1/σ;
    while(i ≤ NUM_PARENTS) {
        /* p_LS: probability of applying local search */
        if(Random(0, 1) < p_LS) {
            LSmoves(parents[i]);
        }
        i = i + 1;
    }
}
```

Fig. 1. Pseudo-code for the LocalSearch function.

We designed a set of four LS moves, which are a 3D-cubic extension of those developed by Miller et al. [7] for a square-lattice model, and are implemented as macromutations of POE strings. As shown in Fig. 3, our moves result in at most two monomers shifting to a new lattice site, so conformational changes are made as local as possible; nonetheless, when a LS move leads to a collision, the POE implicitly forces a structural rearrangement that generally involves more amino acids [10]. Each time the Mutate function is called, a random extraction determines which of the four LS moves will be applied.

Testing these operators was an opportunity for verifying a sort of continuity of the fitness landscape: as illustrated in Fig. 4, little conformational changes, caused by LS moves, induce relatively small fitness variations; on the other hand, single-gene mutations, which imply the rotation of entire protein substructures, have also a higher impact on fitness.

---

[1] This technique is similar to the *reheating* proposed in [8].

```
LSmoves(ind) {
    /* allow at most MV consecutive moves */
    while(move < MV) {
        old = ind;
        Mutate(ind);
        Δ = Fitness(old) − Fitness(ind);
        /* Δ ≤ 0: always accept move
           Δ > 0: conditionally accept move */
        if(Δ > 0) {
            if(Random(0, 1) > e^(− kΔ/T) ) {
                /* reject move and exit */
                ind = old;
                return;
            }
        }
        move = move + 1;
    }
}
```

Fig. 2. Pseudo-code for the LSmoves function.

Although the maximum number of chained moves M V was fixed at 5, our experimental results with a simple version of the MA indicate that local search ends, on average, after just 2.4 moves. This value is even lower, when the algorithm is enhanced with speciation mechanisms that promote genotypic diversity (see below). To confirm the advantages of LS hybridization over the classical approach [6], we compared the simple MA against a standard evolutionary algorithm without local search but with thrice as many generations. The results clearly encourage to use self-adaptive local search, which allows to find better solutions, while keeping a lower global convergence. In a similar experiment, our iterated-LS method outperformed the 1-step approach of Krasnogor and Smith [6]. Hence, investing most of the computation time in local search is an issue worth considering, when designing an evolutionary algorithm for HP-model PSP.

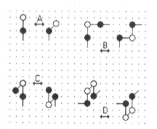

Fig. 3. The four LS moves available to the memetic algorithm. A: end move, B: corner move, C: end-corner move, D: crankshaft move. Shifting monomers are white, fixed monomers are black (adapted from Nunes et al. [9]).

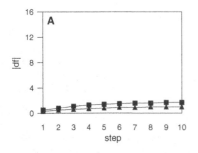 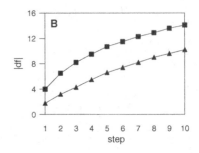

Fig. 4. Comparison between single-gene mutation (squares) and local-search moves (triangles), with respect to the fitness change they induce. A series of ten random perturbations was applied to a given protein structure and, at every step, the total fitness distance ($|df|$) from the initial conformation was measured. Each graph shows the average results of 1000 independent executions of this procedure. The starting proteins were drawn from a MA population, at the beginning of a run (A) and after 400 generations (B).

2.5   Speciation

While self-adaptive local search can, if needed, diversify the fitness in a population, it does little to avoid premature convergence at a genotypic level. Therefore, we believe the global evolutionary process may unduly get stuck in relatively narrow hyperplanes of the conformational space, which nonetheless guarantee a wide range of fitness values. In order to avoid such trapped conditions, we decided to promote speciation among protein structures by means of suitable selection, mating and replacement operators. They are all based on a simple scoring function, which estimates the degree of similarity between two conformations through a gene-by-gene comparison of their POE sequences. Fig. 5 presents the species-oriented selection, a two-step process which starts by structurally comparing a parent to a random set of other ones; that parent and its most similar individuals in the set, together forming a species, then undergo a classical tournament based on fitness, whose winner will be selected for reproduction. This procedure is repeated for all parents. Even simpler schemes allow the search to further emphasize speciation, through crossover of similar individuals and crowding-based replacement from the offspring population to the mating pool.

   According to a great deal of experimental results, we can draw the following conclusions about the introduction of the speciation operators in the memetic algorithm: first, when species-selection is coupled with crowding-replacement, the search is undoubtedly more powerful (see Fig. 6), although both techniques, used alone, involve a clear deterioration of performance. Second, the size of the species set (SPC) in the selection function must be kept to 1, that is, each parent has to compete with just one rival, because a higher number would imply a premature convergence of the population. Third, by crossing similar individuals, the search seems to be unable to sustain the coevolution of separate species, even when

```
SpeciesSelection(par_id) {
    /* structural comparison. SMP = size of sample set */
    sample_set = RandomSet(parents, par_id, SMP);
    SortBySimilarity(sample_set, par_id);

    /* fitness-based selection. SPC = size of species set. */
    species_set = SimilarityCut(sample_set, SPC);
    winner = Tournament(species_set, par_id);
    mating_pool[free_slot] = parents[winner];
}
```

Fig. 5. Pseudo-code for the SpeciesSelection function.

selection and replacement are biased toward speciation, for the average fitness rapidly converges to a poor local maximum, as if the population were dominated by a single genotype. An analogous behavior often concerns the replacement operator, when the crowding factor is increased beyond a value of 15–20: instead of obtaining, as expected, a higher spread of fitness, the net effect is to favor its global convergence. Therefore, the above results suggest to foster, but not to exasperate, speciation, although it would be useful to investigate in greater depth how speciation affects the distribution of genotypes in the population.

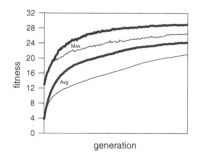

Fig. 6. Impact of speciation on search performance. A bold line represents a memetic algorithm where the operators of selection and replacement are species-oriented. A thin line refers to fitness-proportional selection and 100% replacement. The two topmost graphs plot the course of the maximum fitness, while the other two indicate the average fitness. Runs were 200-generation long. Note that, using standard operators, global convergence is lower, but increases at a much faster pace.

3   Experiments and Results

The experimental work described in Section 2, and many other tuning trials, led us to choose the following operators and parameters for what is, at the moment, the final configuration of our memetic algorithm:

- Preference Order Encoding
- same population size (1000) for parents, mating pool and offspring
- local search ($p_{LS} = 1.0$, M V =5, k = 0.96)
- unit penalty for each collided site ($\rho = 1$)
- intra-species selection (SM P $= 5$, SPC $= 1$)
- random mating
- 1-point crossover with probability 0.9
- single-gene mutation with probability 0.048 for each protein
- crowding replacement from offspring population to mating pool (step 1), with a crowding factor of 10
- 100% replacement from mating pool to parents (step 2)
- unit elitism of the best solution.

Table 1. The 48-mer test sequences with the lowest-energy conformations found for them by the MA (adapted from Yue et al. [13]). For all except proteins no. 7 and no. 9, actual native conformations are shown. Protein structures are represented by absolute-move encoding, which uses the directions of the lattice Cartesian axes (F = Forward, B = Backward, L = Left, R = Right, U = Up, D = Down).

1.	HPHHPPHHHHPHHHPPHHPPHPHHHPHPHHPPHHPPPHPPPPPPPPHH
	RUURFLLDRDLLULBRDDBURUFUUFLDBUBDDBURFURRBDDFULD
2.	HHHHPHHPHHHHHPPHPPHHPPHPPPPPPHPPHPPPHPPHHPPHHHPH
	RDLDRBLUURDRRDLDFUUFUBRURBDLLUBDBDDFRULLBUFLDDR
3.	PHPHHPHHHHHHPPHPHPPHPHHPHPHPPPHPPHHPPHHPPHPHPPHP
	RDRBLURFUBUULDFDLBRBRRUFFLFDRBRBLDRFLDDBUBUBLFD
4.	PHPHHPPHPHHHPPHHPHHPPPHHHHHPPHPHHPHPHPPPPPHPPHPHP
	RURFUFDRBBBULDDDFRDBUUFLFDDFURBUFLLBLFDRBDBUBUB
5.	PPHPPPHPHHHHPPHHHHHPHHPHHHPPHPHPHPPHPPPPPPHHPHHPH
	RBDFRBRBLBRRULLFFRBUFLBBBRFULLDLDRBDLFFURUURFLD
6.	HHHPPPHHPHPHHPHHPHHPHPPPPPPPHPHPPHPPPHPPHHHHHHPH
	RRULBDLLDFRBBRDLFFLBLBRDRRFURBRULBULFURDFDLFRDL
7.	PHPPPPHPHHHPHPHHHHPHHPHHPPPHPHPPPHHHPPHHPPHHPPPH
	RFURDBRBBLLDBRFFULDDFURFRBBDLDBLURBDRUFRULBBUFL
8.	PHHPHHHPHHHHPPHHHPPPPPHPHHPPHHPHPPPHHPHPHPHHPPP
	RRBDLDDFURFFUBLUFFUBRDBRDDFDBLLULUBRRRDBLDFRBDD
9.	PHPHPPPPHPHPHPPHPHHHHHHPPHHHPHPPHPHHPPHPHHHPPPPH
	RURRFDLBRBULUBDRDLFLDBBRFFDRURBLDLLLFRFRULLBUBR
10.	PHHPPPPPPHHPPPHHHHPPHPHPHHPPHPPHPPHHPPHHHHHHHPPHH
	RRDRBBLFULLBURDRRFRULBLUBLFUFDLDRFLURRDBURFFDBD

We then checked this algorithm with a set of ten 48-mer sequences previously used in a work of Yue et al. [13]. Such polymer chains are shown in Table 1, together with the absolute-move encoding [5] of the best conformations found for them by the MA. 30 runs of 6000 generations were performed for each sequence, with every single run taking about half an hour on a 1.8-GHz Linux PC. Table 2 presents the results of these test executions; since all best solutions are feasible, they are denoted by their HP-model energy, instead of their positive fitness.

As the reader can observe, our algorithm finds native conformations for eight of the ten sequences, and achieves nearly optimal solutions for the remaining two. This is an indication of a certain robustness, especially if we consider that all tuning tests were made uniquely with Sequence no. 1. Sequences no. 7 and no. 9 proved to be particularly difficult, because the algorithm never found any of their native states, even when running for 12000 generations.

The same table also shows no general correlation between the chances of finding native energies for a chain and its minimal native-state degeneracy (g_N), that is, a lower bound on the number of its native conformations [13]. This fact can suggest the existence of structural patterns very hard to form with the genetic operators we have designed so far: should these patterns be critical for the correct folding of a protein chain, it would be unlikely that the MA found its native structures.

Further results confirm that initialization actually contributes to the outcome of a search, although the best-fitness values fall in a short range. Hence, we recommend to distribute computational power among a number of independent runs, or, much harder, to design operators that guarantee a fair sampling of the solution space.

Table 2. Native energy (E_N), lowest energy of a MA solution (E_{MA}), number of successes out of 30 runs (n_{succ}) — i.e., number of runs where a native energy was found — and lower bound on native degeneracy (g_N) for the ten HP sequences shown in Table 1. Adapted from Yue et al. [13].

seq	E_N	E_{MA}	n_{succ}	g_N
1	-32	-32	7	1.5×10^6
2	-34	-34	1	14×10^3
3	-34	-34	1	5×10^3
4	-33	-33	4	62×10^3
5	-32	-32	7	54×10^3
6	-32	-32	3	52×10^3
7	-32	-31	0	59×10^3
8	-31	-31	2	306×10^3
9	-34	-33	0	10^3
10	-33	-33	2	188×10^3

4   Conclusions and Future Work

Although the above results are quite encouraging, we believe that providing the MA with more problem-specific knowledge would further enhance its search capabilities, with a minimal impact on robustness. For example, if we could figure out an even approximate picture of the energy landscape, based on the fraction or distribution of hydrophobic residues in a polymer sequence, a number of ad-hoc genetic operators, and an adaptive method to apply them, might be developed.

Making this MA, and evolutionary algorithms in general, perform true simulations of protein folding, would be another challenging problem. If that were possible, generations would represent the successive time-steps of a folding reaction, and their populations might indicate the most likely protein structures at those instants, from both a thermodynamic and kinetic point of view. To achieve this goal, genetic operators should be made aware of the particular folding phase they are applied in, so that their output conformations would not be out of the physical context. This way, evolutionary algorithms could represent a valid alternative to well established methods, such as Molecular Dynamics or Monte Carlo, for faithful simulations of protein folding.

References

1. C. B. Anfinsen, E. Haber, M. Sela, and F. H. White Jr. The kinetics of formation of native ribonuclease during oxidation of the reduced polypeptide chain. In *Proceedings of the National Academy of Sciences of the USA*, volume 47, pages 1309–1314, 1961.
2. B. Berger and T. Leight. Protein folding in the hydrophobic-hydrophilic (HP) model is NP-complete. *Journal of Computational Biology*, 5(1):27–40, 1998.
3. R. Dawkins. *The Selfish Gene*. Oxford University Press, New York, 1976.
4. K. A. Dill. Theory for the folding and stability of globular proteins. *Biochemistry*, 24:1501–1509, 1985.
5. N. Krasnogor, W. E. Hart, J. Smith, and D. A. Pelta. Protein structure prediction with evolutionary algorithms. In *GECCO '99: Proceedings of the Genetic and Evolutionary Computation Conference*, volume 2, pages 1596–1601. Morgan Kaufmann, 1999.
6. N. Krasnogor and J. Smith. A memetic algorithm with self-adaptive local search: TSP as a case study. In *GECCO 2000: Proceedings of the Genetic and Evolutionary Computation Conference*, pages 987–994. Morgan Kaufmann, 2000.
7. R. Miller, C. A. Danko, M. J. Fasolka, A. C. Balazas, H. S. Chan, and K. A. Dill. Folding kinetics of proteins and copolymers. *Journal of Chemical Physics*, 96:768–780, 1992.
8. Pablo Moscato. On evolution, search, optimization, genetic algorithms and martial arts: Towards memetic algorithms. Technical Report C3P 826, California Institute of Technology, Pasadena, CA, 1989.
9. N. L. Nunes, K. Chen, and J. S. Hutchinson. Flexible lattice model to study protein folding. *Journal of Physical Chemistry*, 100(24):10443–10449, 1996.
10. A. L. Patton, W. F. Punch III, and E. D. Goodman. A standard GA approach to native protein conformation prediction. In *Proceedings of the Sixth International Conference on Genetic Algorithms*, pages 574–581. Morgan Kaufmann, 1995.
11. A. Piccolboni and G. Mauri. Application of evolutionary algorithms to protein folding prediction. In N. Kasabov, editor, *Proceedings of the ICONIP '97*, Berlin, 1998. Springer Verlag.
12. R. Unger and J. Moult. A genetic algorithm for 3D protein folding simulations. In *Proceedings of the Fifth International Conference on Genetic Algorithms*, pages 581–588. Morgan Kaufmann, 1993.
13. K. Yue, K. M. Fiebig, P. D. Thomas, H. S. Chan, E. I. Shakhnovich, and K. A. Dill. A test of lattice protein folding algorithms. In *Proceedings of the National Academy of Sciences of the USA*, volume 92, pages 325–329, 1995.

An Improved Genetic Algorithm for the Sequencing by Hybridization Problem

Carlos A. Brizuela, Luis C. González, and Heidi J. Romero

Computer Science Department, CICESE Research Center
Km 107 Carr. Tijuana-Ensenada, Ensenada, B.C., México
{cbrizuel, gurrola, hjromero}@cicese.mx, +52–646–1750500

Abstract. This paper presents a genetic algorithm for a computational biology problem. The problem appears in the computational part of a new deoxyribonucleic acid (DNA) sequencing procedure denominated sequencing by hybridization (SBH). The proposed genetic algorithm is an improvement over a recently proposed algorithm in the literature. The improvement is achieved by modifying the crossover operator towards an almost deterministic greedy crossover which makes the algorithm both more effective and more efficient. Experimental results on real DNA data are presented to show the advantages of using the proposed algorithm.

1 Introduction

The DNA sequencing is one of the most important problems in molecular biology. It refers to the identification of an unknown short DNA sequence of $100 \leq n \leq 500$ base pairs. Among the existing methods for sequencing we are going to concentrate in a relatively new one denominated sequencing by hybridization (SBH) [1]. The SBH problem is composed of two stages: the biochemical experiment and the computational stage. For the biochemical experiment we are given an unknown DNA sequence, composed by a sequence of nucleotides from a set of four of them: A (adenine), C (cytosine), G (guanine), and T (thymine), respectively. From this sequence we need to detect all oligonucleotides (short sequence of nucleotides) of length l, usually 8 to 30 nucleotides, which properly ordered compose the unknown sequence. The detection is performed using a DNA chip (or DNA array) which contains all fragments (oligonucleotides) of length l, i.e. 4^l fragments. A single strand of the unknown DNA sequence treated with a fluorescent substance is deposited on the DNA chip. During the biochemical experiment, complementary fragments (A-T and C-G) of length l come together, i.e. hybridize. After the hybridization experiment and by reading a fluorescent image of the chip, we can obtain the spectrum, which is the set of oligonucleotides composing the unknown DNA sequence. Here, the second stage of SBH starts, i.e. given the spectrum and the length of the unknown DNA sequence, find the order of the oligonucleotides such that consecutive elements always overlap on $l-1$ nucleotides. When the hybridization is performed without errors the spectrum includes all length l oligonucleotides originally in the

G.R. Raidl et al. (Eds.): EvoWorkshops 2004, LNCS 3005, pp. 11–20, 2004.

unknown DNA sequence. However, many factors do not allow the experiment to be run error free. If the spectrum does not include one or more oligonucleotides originally in the DNA sequence, then we have an experiment with negative errors. On the other hand, if the spectrum includes oligonucleotides that are not present in the original sequence then we have an experiment with positive errors.

There have been many attempts in trying to find an efficient method to approximately solve the computational part of the SBH problem. For the ideal experiment case it has been shown that the problem can be solved in polynomial time [8] by reducing it to finding an Eulerian path in a directed graph. However, when only negative or only positive or both errors are present, the problem becomes strongly NP-hard [5]. A Tabu Search based algorithm for the latter case is proposed in [4], then the same authors propose a sophisticated heuristics [2] that improves the results in [4]. At the same time a genetic algorithm [6] is proposed to effectively and efficiently deal with positive and negative errors. In a previous work, Blazewicz and colleagues [3] present a branch and bound method to deal with positive and negative errors. This algorithm obtains its best performance with only positive errors, however, it has problems handling negative errors produced by repetitions of length l oligonucleotides. In a more recent work [9], still a different technique is employed to effectively handle negative errors generated by repetitions of length l oligonucleotides. The work presented here is an improvement over the genetic algorithm proposed by Blazewicz et al. [6] by a modification of the crossover operator.

The remainder of the paper is organized as follows. Section 2 briefly describes the problem we are dealing with. Section 3 explains the methodology proposed to approximately solve the problem. Section 4 presents the experimental setups and results. Finally, section 5 states the conclusions and points out some future research.

2   Problem Statement

The computational part of the SBH problem consists of a set $\mathbf{S} = \{s_1, s_2, \cdots, s_k\}$ of equal length (l) strings s_i's over an alphabet $\Sigma = \{A, C, G, T\}$ and, a number n representing the length of the unknown sequence. Each s_i is always a fragment of the original sequence N, whenever the experiment is error free ($|\mathbf{S}| = n - l + 1$). However, in general, s_i may represent a fragment that is not in the original sequence (positive errors), furthermore, there may be fragments in the original sequence N that do not appear as a string s_i in $\mathbf{S}$ (negative errors). The problem is to find a sequence L of length no greater than n such that the number of used strings s_i's is maximized, and therefore the differences between N and L minimized. The justification for maximizing the number of used strings s_i's, is the assumption that most of the information from the hybridization experiment is correct. This problem was proven to be strongly NP-hard [5].

3   The Proposed Algorithm

In this section the proposed algorithm is described in detail. The algorithm is based on the one proposed by Blazewicz and colleagues [6]. The main difference is in the crossover operator, and this is explained in section 3.2. Next, the encoding method and the objective function computation are explained.

3.1   Encoding

Each individual is represented by a permutation of indices of oligonucleotides in the spectrum. Specifically, the adjacency-based coding is used: value i at locus j in the chromosome means that oligonucleotide i follows oligonucleotide j.

Therefore, feasible solutions are represented by subcycle free permutations, except for a single cycle of length $|\mathbf{S}|$. Figure 1 shows a feasible individual $i1{=}[4\ 2\ 3\ 0\ 1]$, for a given spectrum $\mathbf{S} = \{CTG,ACT,GGA,GAC,TGA\}$. In this chromosome, the number 4 at locus 0 indicates that the oligonucleotide at position 0 in the spectrum (CTG), is followed by the oligonucleotide at position 4 in the spectrum (TGA). In this way, following the indices in the spectrum, the sequence of oligonucleotides that this individual represents is: CTG,TGA,ACT,GGA,GAC (0,4,1,2,3,0). Notice that this solution defines a set of candidate sequences not a single sequence, as it will be explained in the computation of the objective function. Once we understand how to encode the solutions, we can explain the general algorithm.

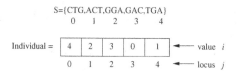

Fig. 1. Adjacency based representation for the SBH problem, $|\mathbf{S}| = 5$

Algorithm 1. Sequencing GA

Input: S and n
Output: A candidate sequence **L** of length $\leq n$
1 **for** $i = 1$ to Pop_Size
2   **do** Generate_Individual(i)
3   Evaluate Objective_Function(i)
4 **do** Select individuals to update the population
5   Keep the best individual found
6 **for** $i = 1$ to Num_Of_Iter
7   **do** Crossover

8	Apply Generational Replacement
9	**for** $j = 1$ to *Pop_Size*
10	**do** Evaluate Objective_Function(j) of individual j
11	**do** Select Individuals to update the population
12	Keep the best individual found

The algorithm input is given by the spectrum **S** and the length n of the original unknown sequence. *Pop_size* is the GA population size. The function Generate_Individual(i) randomly and uniformly generates an individual. Subcycles must be avoided in the individuals, this is to ensure the use of as many as possible oligonucleotides in the spectrum. Evaluate Objective_Function(i) computes the fitness for each individual i. The fitness of each individual is the maximum number of oligonucleotides, that, maximally overlapped, generates a sequence of nucleotides not longer than n. Figure 2 shows the way the objective function is computed. First, we start at position zero of the resulting cycle (0,4,1,2,3,0). We begin overlapping oligonucleotides, once we have 3 oligonucleotides (CTG, TGA and ACT) and an $n' \leq 6 \leq n$, we can add the next oligonucleotide (GGA), in this case the resulting sequence (using 4 oligonucleotides) is CTGACTGGA (0,4,1,2,3,0), however, the last oligonucleotide has to be eliminated since it makes the sequence to have a length (n') greater than n. We repeat this process starting at each position. This can be done given that the permutation of indices in the individual generates a cycle of length $|\mathbf{S}|$. After having selected all the positions, we choose the sequence employing the maximum number of oligonucleotides. For this example, this sequence is generated starting at position 2 (2,3,0,4,1,2), the corresponding sequence is GGACTGA. This sequence uses 4 oligonucleotides (being the maximum number that this individual represents) and its length is exactly n. Notice that for this particular case, the resulting sequence is identical to the original sequence, but this is not always the case. For each individual its fitness value is normalized based on the maximum number of oligonucleotides in any valid sequence ($n - l + 1$), and then linearly scaled.

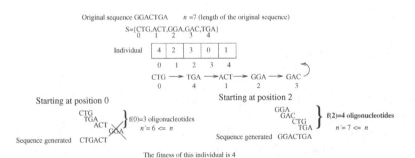

Fig. 2. Fitness function computation for individual $i1 = [4\ 2\ 3\ 0\ 1]$ and $\mathbf{S} = \{CTG, ACT, GGA, GAC, TGA\}$

The individuals are selected (steps 4 and 11) according to the stochastic remainder method without replacement [7]. The population for the next generation is constructed based on the already selected individuals, which are randomly paired, to undergo crossover, elitism is also applied (steps 5 and 12). The stopping criterion is given by a maximum number of iterations, Num_Of_Iter (step 6).

3.2 Crossover Operator

The crossover operator is an improvement over the one proposed by Blazewicz et al. [6]. In [6] the selection of oligonucleotides for constructing new individuals is based on a probabilistic choice. In our case, the best successor in the parents is always selected as long as a subcycle is not generated. Otherwise, the best successor not generating a subcycle, is selected among the remaining oligonucleotides in the spectrum. Details of the operator are supplied below. We will show, by means of computational experiments results, that this strategy is faster and generates better solutions than the one proposed in [6].

Algorithm 2. Crossover

Input: Two subcycle free permutations
Output: A subcycle free permutation
1 **set** the first oligonucleotide randomly (for child 1)
2 **for** $i = 1$ to $Spectrum\_Size - 2$
3   **if** it does not produce subcycle
4   **do** pick up the best successor in the parents of the chromosome
5   **otherwise**
6   **do** pick up the best overlapping oligonucleotide from the spectrum such that a subcycle is not introduced
7 **set** the last oligonucleotide

$Spectrum\_Size$ indicates the number of elements in the spectrum. The first oligonucleotide and its locus in a chromosome is set randomly. Next, the best oligonucleotide between the corresponding successors in the parents is selected as long as it does not produce a subcycle. Otherwise, the best oligonucleotide from the spectrum, that do not produce a subcycle, is chosen. The best oligonucleotide is the one which overlaps on the highest number of nucleotides with the previously selected one. In all cases, if there is more than one best choice, the first found is chosen. Finally, the last oligonucleotide for completing the cycle is set.

Figure 3 shows how this operation is performed. Suppose again that the spectrum is given by **S**={CTG,ACT,GGA,GAC,TGA}. The first oligonucleotide randomly selected is GAC, oligonucleotide 3, and its randomly selected locus is 2 (Fig. 3A). Notice that for completing the cycle, oligonucleotide 2 will be the last one to be selected in the chromosome. We look at parent 1 and parent 2 for the successors of oligonucleotide 3, which are 4 and 0, respectively (Fig. 3B). The best successor (best overlapping oligonucleotide) is oligonucleotide 0 (Fig. 3C). Next, we look at the parents for the best successor of oligonucleotide 0, which is oligonucleotide 2, but this oligonucleotide generates a subcyle (Fig. 3D), so we look at the spectrum for the best successor which is oligonucleotide 4 (Fig. 3E). For oligonucleotide 4, both successors in the parents generate a subcycle, so we look at the spectrum, given that oligonucleotide 2 will be the last one, we have only one option, oligonucleotide 1 (Fig. 3F). Finally, for completing the cycle, we set oligonucleotide 2 (Fig. 3G).

The main difference between the crossover proposed by Blazewicz et al. [6], and the algorithm proposed here, is in lines 3 and 5, where Blazewicz et al. [6] use a 20% - 80% probabilistic rule for choosing the oligonucleotides.

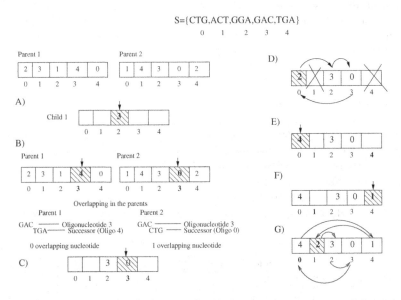

Fig. 3. Almost deterministic greedy crossover for $S = \{CTG,ACT,GGA,GAC,TGA\}$

4   Experimental Setup and Results

The proposed algorithm has been applied to real DNA sequences. All spectra used in the experiment have been derived from the DNA sequences coding human proteins (taken from GenBank, National Institute of Health, USA). Their accession numbers are given by D00726, D11428, D13510, X00351, X02160, X02874, X02994, X04772, X05299, X05451, X05908, X06537, X06985, X07820, X07982, X07994, X12654, X13440, X13452, X13561, X14322, X14618, X14758, X14894, X15005, X15610, X51408, X51535, X51841, X52104, X53799, X54867, X55762,

X57548, X58794, Y00093, Y00264, Y00649, Y00651 and Y00711, respectively. Each derived spectrum was modified with the introduction of 40% of errors (20% negative and 20% positive). Given that $100 \leq |\mathbf{S}| \leq 500$, the spectrum instances contain from 40 to 200 errors (e.g. for $|\mathbf{S}| = 500$, 100 randomly chosen oligonucleotides are erased, and 100 randomly generated oligonucleotides are introduced in the spectrum). The spectra have been sorted alphabetically, thus no information about the original order of oligonucleotides from its original sequences is known. The length of oligonucleotides in all cases is $l=10$ and the length of the sequences have been set to $109 \leq n \leq 509$. For each case, 40 different instances were generated, the parameters for the instances are shown in Table 1. The sequences produced by the algorithm have been compared with the original sequences using a pairwise alignment algorithm. Parameters for the algorithm have been set to $Pop\_Size = 50$ and $Num\_Of\_Iter = 20$, as it is used in [6]. Since the proposed algorithm does not use a mutation operator, an increment in the number of iterations will not improve significantly the results. These values led to good quality solutions and short computation times [6]. All the experiments have been performed on a PC station with Athlon XP 2.0 GHz processor, 512 MB RAM and Linux Mandrake 9.1 operating system.

Table 1. The instances generated for the experiments

Instances	Length (n)	Spectrum Size ($|S|$)	Number of Errors
40	109	100	40
40	209	200	80
40	309	300	120
40	409	400	160
40	509	500	200

Table 2 presents comparative results of the algorithm proposed by Blazewicz et al. [6] (Blazewicz GA) and our proposed algorithm (Sequencing GA). Here, quality is the number of oligonucleotides in the spectrum used by the GA for composing a solution. Notice that, the optimal quality is the number of proper (not corresponding to positive errors) oligonucleotides in the spectrum for a given case. The number of original sequences found is the number of times (over 30 runs) the algorithm is able to generate the original sequence. Finally, similarity score indicates the percentage of similarity between the sequence generated by the GA and the original sequence (if both sequences are identical, then the similarity score is 100%). In order to compute the last two criteria, we compared the solutions generated by the GA with the original sequence, using a pairwise alignment algorithm. The standard deviation percentage is also presented for each criterion. All entries are average values for 40 instances over 30 runs each.

In all criteria, we see that the Sequencing GA outperforms the Blazewicz GA. The average quality of solutions generated by both algorithms are similar, however for the number of original sequences found and the similarity score, the

Table 2. Comparison results for the Blazewicz GA and the Sequencing GA

Spectrum Size	100	200	300	400	500
Optimal Quality	80	160	240	320	400
Average Quality					
Sequencing GA	**79.51**	**159.24**	**238.61**	**317.94**	**397.01**
Blazewicz GA	79.26	158.42	236.84	315.28	392.67
(%) Standard Deviation					
Sequencing GA	**0.11**	**0.06**	**0.06**	**0.07**	**0.05**
Blazewicz GA	0.15	0.14	0.08	0.12	0.13
Average of Original Sequences Found					
Sequencing GA	**19.03**	**13.70**	**13.76**	**11.53**	**8.90**
Blazewicz GA	15.40	9.93	5.66	3.63	2.86
(%) Standard Deviation					
Sequencing GA	**6.54**	**9.98**	**11.39**	**11.99**	**18.03**
Blazewicz GA	13.16	14.22	28.69	37.89	40.69
Average Similarity Score (%)					
Sequencing GA	**98.85**	**96.41**	**94.26**	**87.77**	**86.37**
Blazewicz GA	97.12	88.72	84.13	77.40	70.24
(%) Standard Deviation					
Sequencing GA	**0.55**	**1.54**	**2.47**	**3.70**	**5.82**
Blazewicz GA	1.36	3.55	4.61	7.39	8.90

Sequencing GA presents clear improvements over the Blazewicz GA. An interesting point is in the entries corresponding to the standard deviation, in most cases, the standard deviation of the Sequencing GA are half the ones obtained by the Blazewicz GA.

The figures 4 A) and 4 B) show the average behavior of the Blazewicz GA and the Sequencing GA at each particular instance (40 instances) over 30 runs. Fig. 4 A) shows the similarity score for all instances of $|\mathbf{S}| = 500$. The similarity score obtained by the Sequencing GA is better than the one obtained by the Blazewicz GA.

Figure 4 B) shows the number of original sequences found by both algorithms for each instance of $|\mathbf{S}| = 500$ over 30 runs. The Sequencing GA shows a clear superiority with respect to the Blazewicz GA.

Finally, figure 5 shows comparison results regarding computation time for both algorithms. In this figure we can see that the Sequencing GA needs less computational effort than the Blazewicz GA for getting better results.

The reason for success of the proposed algorithm is conjectured to be the deterministic choices it makes for selecting successors in the crossover operator. It explodes the problem structure by using a deterministic greedy procedure selecting, almost always, the best successor. Using an almost deterministic crossover makes the selection of the successors faster than the crossover operator proposed in Blazewicz et al. [6], and selecting in almost all cases the best successor helps to improve the solution quality.

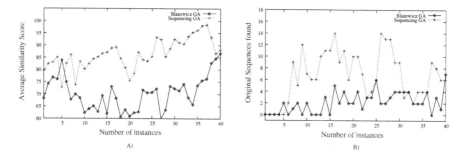

Fig. 4. A) Average similarity score over 30 runs for instances of $|\mathbf{S}| = 500$. B) Number of original sequences found over 30 runs for instances of $|\mathbf{S}| = 500$

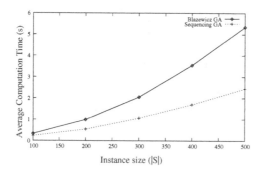

Fig. 5. Average computation time for the Blazewicz GA and the Sequencing GA

5   Conclusions

An efficient and effective genetic algorithm for the computational part of the SBH problem has been proposed. The procedure is based on a recently proposed algorithm for the same problem. An almost deterministic greedy crossover operator is introduced to improve the solution quality and to reduce the computational effort. Experimental results carried out on real DNA data show that the proposed algorithm can handle positive and negative errors producing high quality solutions. The algorithm achieved average results, for all instances, of more than 99% of the optimal number of used oligonucleotides.

As a future research we would like to further explore the rationale for success of the algorithm as well as its robustness to greater values of positive, but specially of negative errors.

Acknowledgments. The authors thank the anonymous referees for their comments that have been very helpful in writing this final version.

References

1. W. Bains and G.C. Smith. A novel method for nucleic acid sequence determination. *Journal of Theoretical Biology*, 135:303–307, 1988.
2. J. Blazewicz, P. Formanowicz, F. Guinand, and M. Kasprzak. A heuristic managing errors for DNA sequencing. *Journal of Bioinformatics*, 18(5):652–660, 2002.
3. J. Blazewicz, P. Formanowicz, M. Kasprzak, W.T. Markiewicz, and J. Weglarz. DNA sequencing with positive and negative errors. *Journal of Computational Biology*, 6:113–123, 1999.
4. J. Blazewicz, P. Formanowicz, M. Kasprzak, W.T. Markiewicz, and J. Weglarz. Tabu search for DNA sequencing with false negatives and false positives. *European Journal of Operational Research*, 125:257–265, 2000.
5. J. Blazewicz and M. Kasprzak. Complexity of DNA sequencing by hybridization. *Journal of Theoretical Computer Science*, 290:1459–1473, 2003.
6. J. Blazewicz, M. Kasprzak, and W. Kuroczycki. Hybrid Genetic Algorithm for DNA Sequencing with Errors. *Journal of Heuristics*, 8:495–502, 2002.
7. D.E. Goldberg. *Genetic Algorithms in Search, Optimization, and Machine Learning*. Addison-Wesley, 1989.
8. P.A. Pevzner. l-tuple DNA Sequencing: Computer Analysis. *Journal of Biomolecular Structure and Dynamics*, 7:63–73, 1989.
9. J. Zhang, L. Wu, and X. Zhang. Reconstruction of DNA sequencing by hybridization. *Journal of Bioinformatics*, 19(1):14–21, 2003.

Evolutionary Search of Thresholds for Robust Feature Set Selection: Application to the Analysis of Microarray Data

Carlos Cotta[1], Christian Sloper[2], and Pablo Moscato[3]

[1] Dept. Lenguajes y Ciencias de la Computación, University of Málaga,
ETSI Informática, Campus de Teatinos, 29071 – Málaga, Spain
[2] Department of Informatics, University of Bergen, HIB, 5020 Bergen, Norway
[3] Newcastle Bioinformatics Initiative,
School of Electrical Engineering and Computer Science,
The University of Newcastle, Callaghan, NSW, 2308, Australia
Contact ccottap@lcc.uma.es

Abstract. We deal with two important problems in pattern recognition that arise in the analysis of large datasets. While most feature subset selection methods use statistical techniques to preprocess the labeled datasets, these methods are generally not linked with the combinatorial properties of the final solutions. We prove that it is $NP-$hard to obtain an appropriate set of thresholds that will transform a given dataset into a binary instance of a robust feature subset selection problem. We address this problem using an evolutionary algorithm that learns the appropriate value of the thresholds. The empirical evaluation shows that robust subset of genes can be obtained. This evaluation is done using real data corresponding to the gene expression of lymphomas.

1 Introduction

The problems discussed in this paper are central to pattern recognition and data mining tasks. Although their relevance is not restricted to Bioinformatics, they are of particular importance for this latter field, and more precisely in the analysis of microarray data. Consider the following typical situation: data from microarray experiments have been collected; these data contain gene-expression patterns for several samples from different classes. For simplicity, let us assume that the data samples are obtained from some healthy individuals and from some individuals affected by some illness. It is obviously interesting –for the purposes of prognosis, development of genic therapies, etc.– to determine which genes are related to this illness. This problem could be formalized as follows [1]:

$k-$FEATURE SET (decision version)

- **Input:** A set X of m examples (which are composed of a binary value specifying the value of the target feature and a vector of n binary values specifying the values of the other features) and an integer $k > 0$.

G.R. Raidl et al. (Eds.): EvoWorkshops 2004, LNCS 3005, pp. 21–30, 2004.

- **Question:** Does there exist a set S of non-target features (i.e., $S \subseteq \{1, \cdots, n\}$) such that:
  - $|S| \leq k$,
  - No two examples in X that have identical values for all the features in S have different values for the target feature ?

Given a set of measurements obtained by means of a microarray experiment on m samples/conditions, the 0-1 values on each one of the features would correspond to under or over expressed genes. It is clear that a decision should be made as to a given threshold on the measured value such that all measures below to that value are assumed to correspond to a '1' while the others would correspond to '0'. We will return to this issue later on in the paper.

Notice at this point the nature of the data being analyzed. Despite the enormous advances that are taking place in the microarray technology, the data we are dealing with is inherently noisy, since measurements can have errors. This implies that robust feature identification methods are essential. In other words, we must seek gene subsets such that their discriminatory power is kept even if some genes of this subset are later shown to have either measurement errors or spurious correlation with the target feature. This robust feature subset selection problem will be formalized in the next section. We will analyze the complexity of the problem, both as an stand-alone combinatorial problem, and in connection with the discretization of the original data. As it will turn out, both problems are intrinsically hard, and hence heuristic approaches are required to tackle them. We will show how an evolutionary algorithm jointly with a reduction approach inspired by kernelization rules often used in the design of fixed-parameter algorithms can provide good solutions for this problem.

2 The $(\alpha, \beta) - k$−Feature Set Problem

As mentioned before, we aim at obtaining subsets of features (i.e., genes – both terms are interchangeably used) of robust discriminatory power. To this end, we will now introduce a generalization of the k−FEATURE SET problem which accounts for finding these possibly larger, though more robust feature sets from the data.

$(\alpha, \beta) - k$−FEATURE SET

- **Input:** An instance of the k−FEATURE SET problem and integers $\alpha, \beta \geq 0$.
- **Question:** Does there exist a set S of non-target features ($S \subseteq \{1, \cdots, n\}$) such that:
  - $|S| \leq k$,
  - for any pair of examples in X that have different values for the target feature, there are at least α different values for the features in S,
  - for any pair of examples in X that have the same value for the target feature, there are at least β equal values for the features in S.

For the sake of clarity, let us appropriately reformulate this problem by making its structure explicit:

$(\alpha, \beta) - k-$FEATURE SET

- **Instance**: A set of m examples $X = \{x^{(1)}, \ldots, x^{(m)}\}$, such that for all i, $x^{(i)} = \{x_1^{(i)}, x_2^{(i)}, \ldots, x_n^{(i)}, t^{(i)}\} \in \{0,1\}^{n+1}$, and three integers $k > 0$, and $\alpha, \beta \geq 0$.
- **Question**: Does there exist an $(\alpha, \beta) - k-$feature set S, $S \subseteq \{1, \cdots, n\}$, with $|S| \leq k$ and such that:
  - for all pairs of examples $i \neq j$, if $t^{(i)} \neq t^{(j)}$ there exists $S' \subseteq S$ such that $|S'| \geq \alpha$ and for all $l \in S'$ $x_l^{(i)} \neq x_l^{(j)}$?
  - for all pairs of examples $i \neq j$, if $t^{(i)} = t^{(j)}$ there exists $S' \subseteq S$ such that $|S'| \geq \beta$ and for all $l \in S'$ $x_l^{(i)} = x_l^{(j)}$?

We note that in the definition above the set S' is not fixed for all pairs of examples, but it is a function of the pair of examples chosen, so we mean $S' = S'(i,j)$.

The basic idea of this problem is to achieve robustness via some redundancy in example discrimination. Thus, we seek to have at least α genes for differentiating between any two samples of different classes. Similarly, we want to have at least β genes with consistent values for any two samples of the same class.

Let us now study the complexity of this problem. First of all, we consider its classical complexity within the P vs NP paradigm. The following theorem establishes that the problem is $NP-$hard:

Theorem 1. The $(\alpha, \beta) - k-$FEATURE SET problem is $NP-$hard.

Proof. The proof is simple, and based on the fact that this problem generalizes the basic $k-$FEATURE SET problem. This latter problem was shown to be $NP-$hard by Davies and Russell [1]. Notice now that the $k-$FEATURE SET problem can be expressed as an $(1,0) - k-$FEATURE SET problem. Ergo, the $(\alpha, \beta) - k-$FEATURE SET problem is in general $NP-$hard. □

This $NP-$hardness result implies that there currently exists no polynomial-time algorithm for this problem. A possibility for dealing with this complexity barrier is resorting to the realm of parameterized complexity [2]. This paradigm tries to study the complexity of a combinatorial problem once some parameter has been extracted from it. This parameter may represent some structural property of the problem, or a property of the solutions sought. The basic idea here is trying to see whether the complexity of the problem can be isolated within this parameter, thus allowing for efficiently solving the problem for fixed values of the parameter [1]. This is known as fixed-parameter tractability (FPT) [4].

In this case, the cardinality of the feature subset is the natural parameter, since this cardinality is always intended to be kept as small as possible. Unfortunately, it can be shown that the problem is also probably intractable from a parameterized point of view:

---

[1] The $k-$VERTEX COVER problem is a good example of this situation. The brute-force approach is $\Omega(n^{k+1})$ while a clever algorithm can solve it in $O(1.286^k + n)$, i.e., in linear time for any fixed k [3].

Theorem 2. The $(\alpha, \beta) - k-$FEATURE SET problem is not fixed-parameter tractable for parameter k.

Proof. Again the proof relies on results for the basic $k-$FEATURE SET problem. Cotta and Moscato [5] have recently proved that this latter problem is $W[2]$-complete. $W[2]$ is a parameterized class comprising substantially harder problems than FPT. Under the currently open –but widely believed conjecture in parameterized complexity– that $FPT \neq W[1]$, and being $W[1] \subseteq W[2]$ we can not expect that a clever fixed-parameter algorithm can be found for the $(\alpha, \beta) - k-$FEATURE SET problem.   □

Once both the classical intractability and the parameterized intractability of the problem have been established, it becomes evident that heuristic algorithms are the most appropriate choice for tackling this problem. For example, evolutionary algorithms could be used here. However, recall that solving this $(\alpha, \beta) - k-$FEATURE SET problem is not our final goal. On the contrary, it is a problem that arises in an intermediate stage, once we have determined the thresholds for discretizing to 0/1 the values of the gene expression levels. Since it is likely that many different choices of thresholds have to be tested, we must strive for finding a fast resolution method for dealing with this subsidiary problem. The next section will describe a greedy heuristic coupled with reduction rules for this purpose.

3   Fast Heuristic Resolution of the $(\alpha, \beta) - k-$Feature Set Problem

In order to approach the heuristic resolution of this problem in its optimization version, we will use the underlying relationship between it and the RED-BLUE DOMINATING SET problem. To illustrate this relationship, let us begin by considering the $(1, 0) - k-$FEATURE SET problem, i.e., the basic $k-$FEATURE SET problem. An instance I of this problem is reducible to RED-BLUE DOMINATING SET by using the following procedure: let $G(V_1 \cup V_2, E)$ be a bipartite graph such that

- there is a red vertex $g_i \in V_2$ for each feature/gene in I, i.e., $|V_2| = n$.
- there is a blue vertex $p_{jk} \in V_1$ for each pair of examples $x^{(j)}$ and $x^{(k)}$ such that $t^{(j)} \neq t^{(k)}$.
- there is an edge (g_i, p_{jk}) whenever $x_i^{(j)} \neq x_i^{(k)}$.

It can be clearly seen that I is a yes-instance if, and only if, there exists a red dominating set $D \subseteq V_2$ such that $|D| \leq k$. This construction can be generalized to the $(\alpha, 0) - k-$FEATURE SET problem by requesting that D be $\alpha-$dominating, i.e., that at least α vertices in D dominate each vertex in V_1 [6]. The final generalization to the $(\alpha, \beta) - k-$FEATURE SET problem is easy from here: a tripartite graph $G(V_1 \cup V_2 \cup V_3, E)$ is constructed such that V_1, V_2, and the edges among vertices in them are defined as above, and

- there is a blue vertex $c_{jk} \in V_3$ for each pair of examples $x^{(j)}$ and $x^{(k)}$ such that $t^{(j)} = t^{(k)}$.

- there is an edge (g_i, c_{jk}) whenever $x_i^{(j)} = x_i^{(k)}$.

According to this construction, an instance I would be a yes-instance if, and only if, $D \subseteq V_2$ α-dominates V_1, β-dominates V_3, and $|D| \leq k$.

Once this translation mechanism has been performed, the resulting graph has to be solved. Obviously, finding the generalized dominating set is NP-hard as well, so a greedy heuristic will be utilized. This greedy heuristic will be jointly applied with some reduction rules. These rules are aimed at simplifying the problem instance, without altering its solution space, i.e., any solution of the original instance will be a solution of the simplified instance, and vice versa. As shown in [7], the application of reduction rules can in some cases turn large instances of NP-hard problems into trivial instances or small instances solvable by hand or by enumeration.

Let r_v be an integer associated with each vertex $v \in V_1 \cup V_3$; initially, $r_p = \alpha$ for each $p \in V_1$, and $r_c = \beta$ for each $c \in V_3$; let $G(v) = \{g \in V_2 \mid (g, v) \in E\}$ be the set of vertices (genes) dominating vertex $v \in V_1 \cup V_3$; conversely, let $N(g) = \{v \in V_1 \cup V_3 \mid (g, v) \in E\}$ be the vertices in $V_1 \cup V_3$ dominated by gene $g \in V_2$. Now, the rules considered for this problem are the following:

R1. For each $v \in V_1 \cup V_3$ such that $r_v = |G(v)|$ do
    i. For each $g \in G(v)$, mark g as belonging to the solution.
    ii. Delete v from G.
R2. For each $v \in V_1 \cup V_3$ such that $r_v \leq 0$ delete v from G.
R3. For each $v_1, v_2 \in V_1 \cup V_3$, $v_1 \neq v_2$ such that $r_{v_1} \geq r_{v_2}$ and $G(v_1) \subseteq G(v_2)$, delete v_2 from G.

In these rules, the following actions are taken whenever a gene is marked, or a vertex is deleted:

Gene marking [g]: For each $v \in N(g)$ do
    i. $r_v \leftarrow r_v - 1$.
    ii. $G(v) \leftarrow G(v) \setminus \{g\}$.

Vertex deleting [v]: For each $g \in G(v)$ do $N(g) \leftarrow N(g) \setminus \{v\}$

These rules greatly simplify the original instance by marking genes that are bound to appear in the final solution, and removing subsumed vertices, i.e., vertices that will be dominated for sure upon domination of another vertex. The application of these rules is interleaved with the use of a greedy insertion rule for adding a new gene to the solution any time the graph cannot be further simplified. More precisely, the process would be as follows:

1. **while** $V_1 \cup V_3 \neq \emptyset$ **do**
    a) Apply reduction rules.
    b) Let $g \in V_2$ be the gene for which $|N(g)|$ is maximal. Mark g as belonging to the solution.

Notice that the fact that indispensable genes are directly added to the solution, and that subsumed vertices are deleted from every $N(g)$, makes the greedy selection be more meaningful than otherwise.

4   Threshold Selection for Robust Feature Selection

As anticipated in Sect. 1, the $(\alpha, \beta) - k-$FEATURE SET problem is a subsidiary problem that emerges once thresholds for discretizing gene-expression values have been set. We will now discuss the computational complexity of this latter problem, i.e., setting the threshold value for each gene such that an $(\alpha, \beta) - k-$FEATURE SET problem is obtained:

$(\alpha, \beta)-$THRESHOLD SELECTION

- **Input:** A $m \times n$ $\mathbb{R}-$matrix M, class identifiers $t[i] \in \mathbb{N}$ for every row i, $1 \leq i \leq m$, and two integers $\alpha, \beta \geq 0$.
- **Question:** Does there exist an array of n thresholds (one for each of the columns in M) such that each entry in the ith column of M greater than the ith threshold is given the value 1, and 0 otherwise, and such that
  1. $\forall i, j, t[i] \neq t[j]$, the number of columns where $M_{i,l} \neq M_{j,l}$ (disagree) is at least α, and
  2. $\forall i, j, t[i] = t[j]$, the number of columns where $M_{i,l} = M_{j,l}$ (agree) is at least β ?

We note that this is a necessary but not a sufficient condition to create a yes-instance of the $(\alpha, \beta) - k-$FEATURE SELECTION problem. Notice also that for the sake of generality we have considered natural class identifiers rather than simply binary tags.

Theorem 3. $(\alpha, \beta)-$THRESHOLD SELECTION is $NP-$complete.

Proof. The membership of this problem to NP is straightforward: given a solution –i.e., a list of n thresholds– the corresponding binary matrix can be computed in $O(mn)$, and its feasibility can be checked in $O(m^2n)$, which is polynomial in the input size. As to the $NP-$hardness of the problem, it can be established by reduction from $k-$VERTEX COVER. To avoid certain difficult cases we will reduce from a slightly modified version $k-$VERTEX COVER$_M$. The modification only guarantees that the vertex cover has cardinality greater or equal to 3, and it should be clear that this variation is $NP-$complete.

$k-$VERTEX COVER$_M$

- **Input:** A graph $G = (V, E)$ where the minimum vertex cover of G has at least 3 vertices, and an integer $k > 0$.
- **Question:** Does $G = (V, E)$ have a vertex cover of size k ?

Given a instance of a $k-$VERTEX COVER$_M$ $G = (V, E)$, let $n = |V|$ and $m = |E|$. We will construct an instance of $(\alpha, \beta)-$THRESHOLD SELECTION. Let $\alpha = 1$ and $\beta = (n - k)$ and construct a $(m + 2) \times n$ matrix M as follows:

$$\forall i \leq m, \forall j \leq n \qquad M_{i,j} = \begin{cases} 1 \text{ if } v_j \in e_i \\ 0 \text{ otherwise} \end{cases}$$

$$\forall j, \quad M_{(m+1),j} = 0$$

$$\forall j, \quad M_{(m+2),j} = 1$$

The target values are set as follows:

$$T[i] = \begin{cases} 0 \text{ if } i \leq m \\ 1 \text{ if } i \geq m+1 \end{cases}$$

We will now argue that this instance of (α, β)–THRESHOLD SELECTION has a solution if and only if k–VERTEX COVER$_M$ has a vertex cover of size at most k.

($\Rightarrow$) Given a k–VERTEX COVER$_M$ $S \subseteq V(G')$ we can find a yes-instance of (α, β)–THRESHOLD SELECTION. In the matrix M set the thresholds as follows:

$$Threshold[i] = \begin{cases} 0.5 \text{ if } v_i \in S \\ 1.5 \text{ otherwise} \end{cases}$$

We argue that this assignment of thresholds to each of the columns satisfy the requirements for α and β.

Claim (1). β is satisfied for all pairs of rows.

Proof. Since $|S| \leq k$ at least $(n - k)$ columns have threshold 1.5. This sets all values in these columns to 0. Thus any pair of rows agree in at least $(n - k)$ places.

Claim (2). For all pairs of examples (i, j) for which $t[i] \neq t[j]$, the number of columns for which $M_{i,k} \neq M_{j,k}$ is at least α.

Proof. It is sufficient to argue that an arbitrary row representing an edge has at least one 1 and at least one 0 entry in the columns representing the vertex cover S. By definition a vertex cover must be incident to all edges. Thus there is at least one 1 in every row. Further, since every solution S is of at size at least 3 and every row contains at most 2 ones it follows that every row has at least one 0.

($\Leftarrow$) Given a valid assignment of thresholds for each of the columns of M we can find a vertex cover in S. We remark that setting thresholds in a 0-1 matrix leaves only three possibilities: (1) setting an entire column to 0, (2) leaving the column with no changes, and (3) setting the entire column to 1. For purposes regarding agreement/disagreement (1) and (3) can be considered equivalent. Note that a changed column can never have any disagreements. To achieve at least $(n - k)$ agreements between row $(m+1)$ and row $(m+2)$ we must change at least $(n-k)$ columns.

We will argue that the at most k remaining unchanged columns represent a vertex cover in G. Since no changed column has any disagreements we must find the required disagreements in these remaining columns. Thus, each row (representing an edge) must have at least one 1 to disagree with row $(m + 1)$ (which are all 0). This is clearly a vertex cover.   □

This NP–completeness result does obviously imply the NP–hardness of the corresponding optimization version of the problem, i.e., finding the thresholds for obtaining the smallest (α, β)–feature subset. Hence, we will tackle this problem using a metaheuristic approach.

5   Learning Thresholds with Evolutionary Algorithms

The problem we will now address can be viewed as a continuous optimization problem. Let l_i and u_i be the lower bound and the upper bound for the expression values of gene g_i. We therefore have a search space $\mathcal{S} = \mathcal{D}_1 \times \cdots \times \mathcal{D}_n$, where $\mathcal{D}_i = [l_i, u_i]$. Let $x \in \mathcal{S}$ be a vector of thresholds for each gene. When this vector is applied on the matrix of gene-expression values, a binary matrix is obtained. Together with the class-identifiers, this matrix constitutes an instance of the (α, β)–FEATURE SELECTION problem (its optimization version) that can be solved via the heuristic approach described in Sect. 3. The size $s(x)$ of the so-obtained gene subset indicates the absolute quality of vector x. We would be interested in finding $x \in \mathcal{S}$ such that $s(x)$ is minimal.

This continuous optimization problem has been attacked using an evolutionary algorithm specialized for this task: an evolution strategy (ES). To be precise, a (16, 100)-ES with binary tournament selection, flat recombination, and independent self-adaptive stepsizes for each variable has been used. The stepsizes are mutated following the guidelines shown in [8], i.e., a global learning rate $\tau = 1/\sqrt{2n}$, and a local learning rate $\tau' = 1/\sqrt{\sqrt{2n}}$. The fitness function (to be minimized) is defined as

$$Fitness(x) = s(x) + \left(1 - \frac{\min_{v \in V_1 \cup V_3}\{|G(v)|\}}{n+1}\right) . \tag{1}$$

The rationale behind this fitness function is the following: first of all, notice that the second term is always smaller than 1, and hence, minimizing $s(x)$ is sought in the first place. In case two sets of thresholds induce gene subsets of the same size, the one that maximizes the minimum degree of a vertex in $V_1 \cup V_3$ is preferred. The underlying idea is that this way, the density of the graph is increased, and the chances that a small gene subset dominates $V_1 \cup V_3$ are higher.

The experiments have been done using both simulated data and data from real microarray experiments. Due to space constraints, we will focus here on the latter, which is taken from [9]. This dataset corresponds to different types of diffuse large B-cell lymphoma, and comprises gene-expression profiles for 2984 genes. There exist two classes in these data, each one containing 4 samples. Figure 1 (left) shows the matrix of gene-expression values. The evolutionary algorithm has been run on this dataset using different values for α and β. Concretely, we have considered $\alpha = \beta \in \{100, 200, 300\}$. For each value, 10 runs have been performed, for a maximum number of 50,000 fitness evaluations.

For $\alpha = \beta = 100$, the ES manages to find a gene subset of exactly 100 genes in all runs. A subset of this size is the optimal solution for this parameter setting, although we notice that this optimum is not unique. Figure 1 (middle-left) shows the original data after being normalized to $[-1, +1]$ using the thresholds obtained in one of the runs as the zero-level, and Fig. 1 (middle-right and right) shows the selected genes in this same run. As it can be seen, the gene subset selected exhibits a clearly distinctive expression profile in each of the classes, thus providing a robust mechanism for classifying samples.

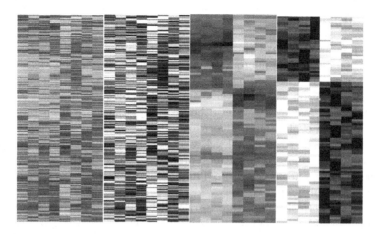

Fig. 1. (Left) Original dataset used in the experimentation. (Middle-left) The original dataset after applying the thresholds obtained in a typical run for $\alpha = \beta = 100$. (Middle-right) Genes selected in a typical run for $\alpha = \beta = 100$. (Right) Genes selected in a typical run for $\alpha = \beta = 100$ (thresholds applied).

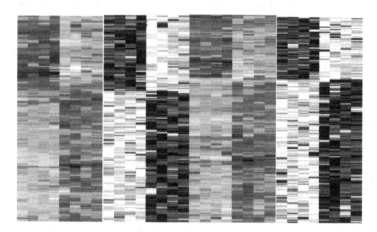

Fig. 2. (Left) Genes selected in a typical run for $\alpha = \beta = 200$. (Middle-left) Genes selected a typical run for $\alpha = \beta = 200$ (thresholds applied). (Middle-right) Genes selected in a typical run for $\alpha = \beta = 300$. (Right) Genes selected a typical run for $\alpha = \beta = 300$ (thresholds applied).

For $\alpha = \beta = 200$ and $\alpha = \beta = 300$, the ES finds gene subsets of 227.3 and 360.5 genes on average respectively. Figure 2 shows the outcome of average runs of the algorithm. Again, the results are very satisfactory, since well-differentiated expression profiles are found for each class. As a comparison, a plain greedy heuristic using 0.0 as the discretization threshold for all genes produces subsets of 129, 292, and 452 genes for $\alpha = \beta = 100$, 200, and 300 respectively, i.e., above 25% larger gene subsets on average.

6   Conclusions

We have presented both a theoretical and an applied study of two problems arising in the analysis of microarray data. We have shown that these problems are inherently hard, suggesting the need for heuristics. Since no pre-existing algorithms were available (recall these are novel problems that depart for classical feature selection tasks), a two-level heuristic approach has been proposed: on the first level, an evolutionary algorithm explores different thresholds for gene-expression values; on the second level, a greedy algorithm coupled with reduction rules solves a subsidiary combinatorial problem. The evaluation of this combined heuristic has been encouraging, providing robust subsets of genes for identifying different classes of lymphoma.

On the theoretical line, future work will be directed to determine whether some subclasses of the general $(\alpha, \beta)-$THRESHOLD SELECTION problem can be found to be in the FPT class. From an applied standpoint, we plan to study several computational issues of the evolutionary algorithm proposed. In particular, we intend to test the performance of the algorithm in parallel environments. The fact that this application is computationally intensive lead us to believe that it can greatly benefit from the use of distributed programming techniques.

Acknowledgements. Carlos Cotta is partially supported by Spanish MCyT, and FEDER under contract TIC2002-04498-C05-02. We thank Mike Fellows and Luke Mathieson for useful discussions, and Evosolve (UK Registered Charity No. 1083684) for supporting previous work.

References

1. Davies, S., Russell, S.: NP-completeness of searches for smallest possible feature sets. In Greiner, R., Subramanian, D., eds.: AAAI Symposium on Intelligent Relevance, New Orleans, AAAI Press (1994) 41–43
2. Downey, R., Fellows, M.: Parameterized Complexity. Springer-Verlag (1998)
3. Chen, J., Kanj, I., Jia, W.: Vertex cover: further observations and further improvements. In: Proceedings of the 25th International Workshop on Graph-Theoretic Concepts in Computer Science. Number 1665 in Lecture Notes in Computer Science, Springer-Verlag (1999) 313–324
4. Downey, R., Fellows, M.: Fixed parameter tractability and completeness I: Basic theory. SIAM Journal of Computing **24** (1995) 873–921
5. Cotta, C., Moscato, P.: The k-FEATURE SET problem is $W[2]$-complete. Journal of Computer and Systems Science **67** (2003) 686–690
6. Harant, J., Pruchnewski, A., Voigt, M.: On dominating sets and independent sets of graphs. Combinatorics, Probability and Computing **8** (1999) 547–553
7. Weihe, K.: Covering trains by stations or the power of data reduction. In Battiti, R., Bertossi, A., eds.: Proceedings of Algorithms and Experiments (ALEX 98), Trento, Italy (1998) 1–8
8. Bäck, T.: Evolutionary Algorithms in Theory and Practice. Oxford University Press, New York (1996)
9. Alizadeh, A., et al.: Distinct types of diffuse large B-cell lymphoma identified by gene expression profiling. Nature **403** (2001) 503–511

Evolving Regular Expression-Based Sequence Classifiers for Protein Nuclear Localisation

Amine Heddad, Markus Brameier, and Robert M. MacCallum

Stockholm Bioinformatics Center
Stockholm University
106 91 Stockholm
Sweden
{heddad,brameier,maccallr}@sbc.su.se

Abstract. A number of bioinformatics tools use regular expression (RE) matching to locate protein or DNA sequence motifs that have been discovered by researchers in the laboratory. For example, patterns representing nuclear localisation signals (NLSs) are used to predict nuclear localisation. NLSs are not yet well understood, and so the set of currently known NLSs may be incomplete. Here we use genetic programming (GP) to generate RE-based classifiers for nuclear localisation. While the approach is a supervised one (with respect to protein location), it is unsupervised with respect to already-known NLSs. It therefore has the potential to discover new NLS motifs. We apply both tree-based and linear GP to the problem. The inclusion of predicted secondary structure in the input does not improve performance. Benchmarking shows that our majority classifiers are competitive with existing tools. The evolved REs are usually "NLS-like" and work is underway to analyse these for novelty.

1 Introduction

Many bioinformatics tools aim to increase our knowledge about the growing number of proteins for which little experimental information is available. One important approach is to transfer annotations from characterised proteins to less well studied proteins. This is usually achieved through similarity searches against databases of whole sequences (e.g. with BLAST[1] or FASTA[22]) or domain libraries (e.g. INTERPRO[19]), or with more localised motif or subsequence searching (e.g. PROSITE[3] and PRATT[12]). On the other hand, there are many tools which directly predict aspects of protein function without reference to previously known proteins. For example, protein functional categories can be predicted to some extent with neural networks trained on sequence-derived properties[11]. A number of groups have developed methods to predict the subcellular compartment(s) in which a protein does its job[21,7]. Subcellular location is important low-resolution functional information which can guide experimental work and speed progress.

In eukaryotic cells, the nucleus is one such compartment of great importance. Most control mechanisms converge on the nucleus, where the paradigm states

G.R. Raidl et al. (Eds.): EvoWorkshops 2004, LNCS 3005, pp. 31–40, 2004.

that genes (which usually encode proteins) are turned on and off in response to changing conditions. Proteins are manufactured on ribosomes outside the nucleus, and must get back to the nucleus if they are needed there. Most are actively transported in an energy-consuming process through the so-called nuclear pore complex[16]. Import through the nuclear pore is controlled by proteins called importins which bind to short recognition sequences on the cargo proteins called nuclear localisation signals (NLS). A number of NLS subtypes have been identified experimentally[5], and regular expressions (REs, basically the same thing as PROSITE patterns) have been developed for them[6].

Clearly, one way to determine nuclear localisation for a protein is to scan its sequence against a library of known NLS motifs[6]. This will not be sufficient, of course, for proteins which do not contain these particular motifs but perhaps contain some other kind of NLS which has not yet been discovered. Here we need a more generalised approach like, for example, neural network-based predictors which take amino acid frequencies as input[23,20]. Predictors which use only this global information perform less well than pattern-based methods, however. Hybrids methods using both global and pattern information, such as PSORT II[21], may perform better. PSORT II may be disadvantaged, however, because it uses only a small set of NLS REs.

Here, we make hybrid predictors that are not restricted to a predefined set of NLS patterns. Our approach is to use genetic programming[14] (GP) to evolve classifiers which can, if required, simultaneously consider global information (e.g. amino acid frequencies) and local sequence motifs. These motifs are not predefined, but are evolved at the same time as the other classification rules. Koza et al presented the first GP system for evolving sequence classifiers for subcellular location[15]. They used a low-level automaton-like implementation, and because of this, perhaps, they did not present, analyse or distribute the evolved classifiers. By choosing higher-level implementations for pattern matching in GP we make the eventual post-analysis more straightforward.

In this paper, we have benchmarked a number of implementation variations: including two different genetic programming systems, and have experimented with predicted secondary structure as an extra input. Simple combinations of multiple predictors are shown to improve performance. Our results are competitive with both PSORT II and PredictNLS[6]. A web interface is provided for the community and work is continuing to propose biological explanations and possibly novel NLSs for proteins that our methods confidently and uniquely predict as nuclear. URL: http://www.sbc.su.se/~maccallr/nucpred

2   Methods

2.1   Data for Supervised Learning

Swiss-Prot[2] is an expert-maintained protein "knowledgebase" and is the source of our training data. We extracted two sets of proteins (and their sequences) from Swiss-Prot release 40 (8 Jan 2003) according to the following definitions:

nuclear – subcellular location annotation matches 'nuclear' (4135 proteins)

non-nuclear – eukaryotic proteins where the subcellular location annotation contains 'cytoplasmic', 'mitochondrial', 'chloroplast', 'peroxisomal', 'extracellular', 'endoplasmic reticulum' but not 'nuclear' (6055 proteins)

In both sets above, proteins are excluded where the subcellular location is annotated as 'by similarity', 'probable', 'possible', 'potential', or 'predicted'. Because we do not discard proteins with multiple locations (as some others have done), our two sets should strictly be described as "proteins which have a role in nucleus" and "proteins which have no role in the nucleus". Two separate non-redundant benchmark sets, A and B, were generated from these proteins, as detailed in the supplementary information available at http://www.sbc.su.se/~maccallr/supplementary/heddad2004/. These benchmark sets are both divided into a 10-fold cross-validation set (A has 1368 nuclear and 1231 non-nuclear proteins; B has 760 nuclear and 1147 non-nuclear proteins) and a final validation set (A 456 nuclear, 412 non-nuclear; B 178 nuclear, 293 non-nuclear).

2.2   Fitness Evaluation

We use a correlation coefficient called MCC (first used by Matthews in the area of computational biology[18]) as the fitness measure for our classifiers evolved by genetic programming. MCC conveniently takes into account both over-prediction and under-prediction and imbalanced data sets. It is defined as:

$$MCC = \frac{tp \times tn - fn \times fp}{\sqrt{(tn + fn)(tn + fp)(tp + fn)(tp + fp)}}$$

True positives (tp) are correctly predicted nuclear proteins, true negatives (tn) are correctly predicted non-nuclear proteins, and so on.

2.3   PerlGP Implementation

In PerlGP[17], evolved code is expanded from a tree-based genotype into a string before being evaluated with Perl's eval() function. The trees of each individual are built (and later, mutated) according to a grammar and are strongly typed. In this application, we want the evolved code to look like the example given in Figure 3; that is to say, the solution should be some arithmetic expression containing constants and RE matches against a protein sequence. The matches() function feeds the number of separate RE matches into the arithmetic expression. If the result of the expression for a given sequence is greater than zero, it is predicted/classified as nuclear, otherwise it is non-nuclear.

The grammar for the arithmetic is fairly standard, the operators are + - * pdiv(x,y) plog(x), where pdiv and plog are protected functions. The RE grammar is given in Figure 1 in PerlGP syntax, and includes character classes, nesting/grouping and quantifiers.

```
$F{REGEXP} = [ '{REGEXP}{REGEXP}', '({REGEXP}){QUANT}'
               '{AAS}{REPEAT}', '[{HAT}{AAS}]{REPEAT}' ];
$F{AAS}    = [ '{AA}', '{AAS}{AAS}' ];

$T{REGEXP} = [ '.' ]; $T{HAT} = [ '', '^' ]; $T{REPEAT} = [ '', '+' ];
$T{QUANT}  = [ '{1,1}', '{1,3}', ... '{3,8}' ];
$T{AAS}    = $T{AA} = [ 'A', 'C', 'D', 'E', 'F', ... 'V', 'W', 'Y' ];
```

Fig. 1. Grammar definition (simplified and abbreviated) for the generation of regular expressions in the PerlGP implementation. The F and T hash tables contains function (branching) and terminal (non-branching) nodes respectively. Note that this is very close to the Backus-Naur format for grammars, the main difference being that ⟨*type*⟩ is written here as {TYPE} and ::= becomes =.

Secondary structure predictions and "dual REs". PSIPRED[13] was used with default parameters to predict the secondary structural state for each amino acid in the protein: helix (H), strand (E for extended) and coil (C). We provided GP with a function to perform parallel matching with two REs against two sequences of the same length but with different alphabets (amino acid and predicted secondary structure). The first RE is matched against the first sequence and the positions of matching fragments are noted. The second RE is then matched against fragments of the second sequence corresponding to those found in the first, and the number of matches are returned. This can be applied in either order: sequence→structure or structure→sequence.

2.4   Linear GP Implementation

We have modified a linear GP (LGP) system[4] to the needs of this study. In LGP the program representation basically consists of variable-length sequences of instructions from an imperative programming language. Operations manipulate variables (registers) and constants and assign the result to a destination register, e.g., $r_0 := r_1 + 1$. In this modification, each GP individual has two parts (see Fig. 5 for example code). In the first, a set of REs is defined, and registers are loaded with the results of matching them against the protein sequence input string. In the second, the registers are manipulated with arithmetic operations. For each data instance, the final value of r[0] is used for classification as described in Section 2.3. Regular expression support is provided by the PCRE library [9].

2.5   GP Parameters

Both implementations were run with non-migrating populations of 2000 individuals and a tournament selection scheme. In LGP, the number of evolved REs was 10, and the maximum program length (second part) was 50 instructions. Full details of parameters are available in the supplementary web material (URL given in Section 2.1).

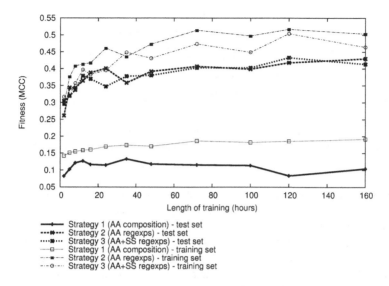

Strategy 1 (AA composition) - test set
Strategy 2 (AA regexps) - test set
Strategy 3 (AA+SS regexps) - test set
Strategy 1 (AA composition) - training set
Strategy 2 (AA regexps) - training set
Strategy 3 (AA+SS regexps) - training set

Fig. 2. Best-of-tournament training fitness and testing performance obtained at the end of separate 10-fold cross-validation experiments (dataset A) with different run-times. Test set performance is calculated from the pooled "left-out" data, and individuals were selected on the basis of training fitness only. Training fitnesses are calculated as the mean training fitness over the 10 cross-validation runs.

3   Results and Discussion

3.1   PerlGP

Strategies. Three approaches for generating GP individuals were tested:

– Strategy 1 evolves expressions containing only trivial REs which count the occurrences of single amino acids.
– Strategy 2 evolves expressions containing full REs for amino acid sequence.
– Strategy 3 as Strategy 2 plus "dual REs" using an additional input of predicted secondary structure.

Because the size of the search space differs between strategies, we tried to allow sufficient run-time in each case so that we could characterise the learning (and over-training) dynamics. Figure 2 shows the final fitnesses for a set of 10-fold cross-validation runs with different run-times using data from Set A. Relying only on amino-acid composition, strategy 1 performs poorly compared to the approaches able to detect local sequence motifs. Strategy 1 also exhibited over-training after around 40 hours. Strategies 2 and 3 did show a gap between training and testing performance but we conclude from Figure 2 that "pathological" over-training (where test set performance is no longer showing the same trends as the training fitness) has not yet occurred.

Since proteins are three-dimensional objects which usually interact with each other and the cellular machinery at their surfaces, we expect signal sequences to

```
$nuclear = (((((matches($seq, qr/[K][R]/)
        + matches($seq, qr/([KR])([KR]+)[RKHM]/))
        + matches($seq, qr/([KRH])([RQ]+)[RKYM]+/))
        + matches($seq, qr/(([RKHD]){1,4}([R])[FKMT]+)[KRH]/))
        - matches($seq, qr/AKV/))
        - matches($seq, qr/[^W]+/));
```

Fig. 3. Example of an evolved nuclear localisation predictor. If the result is greater than zero, the protein with sequence $seq is predicted to be nuclear.

be present on the surface of proteins. Although the actual 3D structure is only available for some proteins in our data sets, the predicted secondary structure can be obtained for all (see Section 2.3). Geometric considerations lead us to hypothesise that signal motifs should be more common in coil regions than in helix and strand, where they would be less accessible (strand in particular). Strategy 3 was introduced to see if GP could take advantage of this possible source of extra information. Based on test set performance (see Fig. 2) we conclude that it does not, but many of the evolved expressions (not shown) do behave as expected and restrict the sequence pattern search to predicted coil regions. Others have recently shown surface/non-surface predictions to be of use in composition-based predictions[20].

Many of the evolved expressions from strategy 2 contain REs which broadly agree with the patterns derived for actual NLSs, in that they contain a lot of arginine (R) and lysine (K). One of the more compact solutions is shown in Figure 3. We are currently working to gain a deeper understanding of the relationship between our evolved REs and already-known NLS motifs.

Majority classifiers. Perhaps one disadvantage of evolutionary computation compared to more deterministic optimisation strategies is that runs often fall into local minima and explore mutually exclusive regions of solution space. This can often be turned into an advantage however by combining the "knowledge" of separately evolved classifiers into one "meta-classifier".

A new set of 10×10-fold cross-validation runs using strategy 2 were performed. Dataset B is now used, after we found that dataset A is liable to over-estimate performance (see Section 2.1 and supplementary information). The smaller dataset and a few other optimisations mean that training for 36 hours is now sufficient. The mean MCC on the test set proteins is now just 0.29. From past experience we suspect that majority voting by different classifiers will produce better results. For each test-set partition of the cross-validation set, we can do a majority vote using the 10 different evolved predictors which were not trained on that data. This means that for each protein, 5 or more of the 10 classifiers must predict "nuclear" in order to classify a protein as such. Using this approach, the MCC for goes up to 0.38 from a mean of 0.29 for the individual predictors.

Final validation set. If we want to combine all 100 evolved predictors then we must use the final validation set (see Section 2.1) because none of these sequences (or their close relatives) have been used in the cross-validation training runs. We restarted each of the 100 populations and performed a single tournament using the entire cross-validation set as the "training set" and chose the best-of-tournament individuals (on training data) for the final validation set performance calculations. The mean MCC for individual predictors on this set is 0.33. When 50 or more predictors out of 100 vote nuclear then the MCC again rises to 0.47. Of course, thresholds other than 50 can be used, and this is described below.

Comparison with other methods. We give the name "NucPred" to the strategy 2 approach, and define the NucPred score as the fraction of predictors (usually 100) which vote nuclear. In Figure 4 we show the performance of NucPred, in terms of sensitivity and specificity, at different score thresholds and compare this with the performance of the two most widely used existing methods: PSORT II and PredictNLS. On this data (validation set B), the NucPred approach does a little better than all other at all sensitivities. However, previous results trained and validated on dataset A showed NucPred to be equal to PSORT II and slightly worse than PredictNLS, so the exact ranking of methods is difficult. The best performance at high specificity on validation set B is obtained using combinations of NucPred and PredictNLS (see Figure 4 for details).

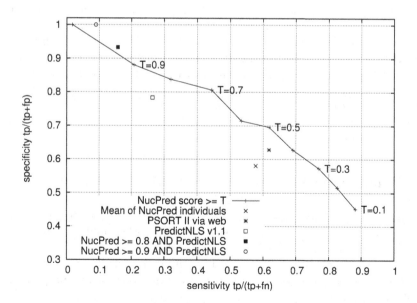

Fig. 4. Performance of NucPred, PSORT II and PredictNLS on validation set B (471 sequences). Specificity and sensitivity are shown for different thresholds of NucPred score (fraction of predictors voting "nuclear").

3.2   Linear GP

Our work evolving Perl-based classifiers has shown that string matching code can be produced at a high level (using REs), providing an alternative to low level approaches where the matching mechanism is evolved as part of the solution[15, 10]. This should reduce search space complexity and solutions will also be more human-readable. However, the PerlGP solutions often contain duplicate REs which are wastefully matched more than once against the same sequence. With our linear GP (LGP) system[4], it is possible to perform the RE matches once and use their results many times during calculation of the final output (see Section 2.4 and Fig. 5 for further details). Additionally, no crossover is allowed between REs in the individuals, so duplications of complex REs are highly improbable. The LGP system has a mechanism for removing ineffective code prior to evaluation[4]. This is particularly useful because it automatically identifies which of the evolved REs are not used, and does not perform the (relatively expensive) match for them. We were also interested in measuring the performance of simpler forms of RE than were used with the Perl system.

Cross-validation set B was used to generate LGP classifiers (500 generations). Combinations of two strategies were tested: building REs with and without character sets (a character set, e.g. "[FWV]", means match either F,W or V); and loading the registers with the number of RE matches (multiple) or simply zero or one signifying non-match or match (boolean).

Classification performance figures for the final validation set are shown in Tables 1&2. The LGP performance is very close to the PerlGP results for both individual predictors (mean $MCC = 0.33$) and majority voting ($MCC = 0.46$). The sensitivity-specificity curves (not shown) for the best performing LGP configurations are also similar to the one in Figure 4. The relative performances of the RE strategies were interesting: individuals using REs without character sets (essentially just short sequences of amino acids) performed almost identically to those with character sets. Boolean matching in general does not perform well although, as expected, the use of character sets helps. Boolean matching may also encourage more "interesting" REs to evolve (data not shown). An example classifier is shown in Figure 5.

4   Final Remarks

We have, with relative ease, evolved classifiers which use global and local sequence information and which are least as good as other published methods. Direct comparison is always difficult because of differences in test set construction. Further improvements can be gained by building a multi-location predictor[21, 7] since, for example, proteins predicted to be integral membrane proteins are unlikely to be nuclear.

In both of the GP implementations we used, the RE matching is performed by efficient C-coded routines. We have not performed run-time profiling, but we suspect that the RE matching is the principal drain on CPU in our two

```
void gp(double *r, char *seq)
{
  r[3] = match("SA", seq);
  r[4] = match("[RK]R", seq);
  r[5] = match("[P]GP", seq);
  r[6] = match("[FWV]", seq);
  r[10] = match("[QS]", seq);

  r[3] = r[3] + r[5];
  r[8] = r[6] + r[3];
  r[0] = r[4] - r[8];
  r[0] = r[10] + r[0];
  r[0] = r[4] * r[0];
}
```

Fig. 5. Example best-of-run individual from linear GP using character sets and multiple matching. Only effective REs and register operations are shown (5 REs were not used).

Table 1. Mean MCC, sensitivity and specificity for 100 individuals measured on validation set B. Sensitivity and specificity are defined in Figure 4.

char. sets	matching	MCC	sens.	spec.
no	boolean	0.21	0.49	0.56
yes	boolean	0.25	0.40	0.56
no	multiple	0.31	0.55	0.60
yes	multiple	0.33	0.59	0.57

Table 2. Majority voting by 100 individuals on validation set B.

char. sets	matching	MCC	sens.	spec.
no	boolean	0.26	0.32	0.63
yes	boolean	0.32	0.48	0.61
no	multiple	0.45	0.59	0.70
yes	multiple	0.46	0.65	0.66

approaches and for the evolution of REs in general. Interestingly, the results from the "no character set" LGP runs suggest that this classification problem may not require RE matching at all – it may be sufficient (and much more efficient) to pre-calculate all the frequencies of all k-tuplets ($1 \leq k \leq 3$) and store them in hash tables. Structural biology, however, suggests that longer sequences are involved in the nuclear import recognition process[8].

Acknowledgements. We thank Andrea Krings for the PredictNLS data, Arne Elofsson and Erik Granseth for helpful discussion, the PDC for cluster administration, the Swedish Foundation for Strategic Research (SBC funding) and the Knut and Alice Wallenberg Foundation (cluster funding).

References

1. S. F. Altschul, T. L. Madden, A. A. Schaffer, J. H. Zhang, Z. Zhang, W. Miller, and D. J. Lipman. Gapped BLAST and PSI-BLAST: a new generation of protein database search programs. *Nucleic Acid Research*, 25:3389–3402, 1997.
2. A. Bairoch and R. Apweller. The SWISS-PROT protein sequence data bank and its supplement TrEMBL. *Nucleic Acid Research*, 25:31–36, 1997.
3. A. Bairoch, P. Bucher, and K. Hofmann. The PROSITE database, its status in 1997. *Nucleic Acid Research*, 25:217–221, 1997.
4. M. Brameier and W. Banzhaf. A comparison of linear genetic programming and neural networks in medical data mining. *IEEE-EC*, 5:17–26, February 2001.
5. D. Christophe, C. Christophe-Hobertus, and B. Pichon. Nuclear targeting of proteins: how many different signals. *CS*, 12(5):337–341, May 2000.

6. M. Cokol, R. Nair, and B. Rost. Finding nuclear localization signals. *EMBO Rep*, 1(5):411–415, Nov 2000.

7. O. Emanuelsson, H. Nielsen, S. Brunak, and G. von Heijne. Predicting subcellular localization of proteins based on their N-terminal amino acid sequence. *Journal of Molecular Biology*, 300(4):1005–1016, Jul 2000.

8. M. R. M. Fontes, T. Teh, D. Jans, R. I. Brinkworth, and B. Kobe. Structural basis for the specificity of bipartite nuclear localization sequence binding by importin-alpha. *Journal of Biological Chemistry*, 278(30):27981–27987, Jul 2003.

9. P. Hazel. PCRE - Perl Compatible Regular Expressions library. www.pcre.org.

10. D. Howard and K. Benson. Promoter prediction with a GP-automaton. In *Applications of Evolutionary Computing, EvoWorkshops2003: EvoBIO, EvoCOP, EvoIASP, EvoMUSART, EvoROB, EvoSTIM*, volume 2611 of *LNCS*, pages 44–53, University of Essex, England, UK, 14-16 April 2003. Springer-Verlag.

11. L. J. Jensen, R. Gupta, H.-H Staerfeldt, and S. Brunak. Prediction of human protein function according to Gene Ontology categories. *Bioinformatics*, 19(5):635–642, Mar 2003.

12. I. Jonassen, J. F. Collins, and D. G. Higgins. Finding flexible patterns in unaligned protein sequences. *Protein Science*, 4(8):1587–1595, Aug 1995.

13. D. T. Jones. Protein secondary structure prediction based on position- specific scoring matrices. *Journal of Molecular Biology*, 292:195–202, 1999.

14. J. R. Koza. *Genetic Programming: On the Programming of Computers by Natural Selection*. MIT press, Cambridge, MA, 1992.

15. J. R. Koza, F. H. Bennett III, and D. Andre. Using programmatic motifs and genetic programming to classify protein sequences as to cellular location. In V. W. Porto, N. Saravanan, D. Waagen, and A. E. Eiben, editors, *Evolutionary Programming VII*, pages 437–447, Berlin, 1998. Springer. LNCS 1447.

16. I. G. Macara. Transport into and out of the nucleus. *Microbiology and Molecular Biology Reviews*, 65(4):570–594, Dec 2001.

17. R. M. MacCallum. Introducing a Perl Genetic Programming System: and Can Meta-evolution Solve the Bloat Problem? In *Genetic Programming, Proceedings of EuroGP'2003*, volume 2610 of *LNCS*, pages 369–378, 2003.

18. B. W. Matthews. Comparison of the predicted and observed secondary structure of T4 phage lysozyme. *Biochem. Biophys. Acta*, 405:442–451, 1975.

19. N. J. Mulder et al. The InterPro Database, 2003 brings increased coverage and new features. *Nucleic Acid Research*, 31(1):315–318, Jan 2003.

20. R. Nair and B. Rost. Better prediction of sub-cellular localization by combining evolutionary and structural information. *Proteins: Structure, Function and Genetics*, 53(4):917–930, Dec 2003.

21. K. Nakai and P. Horton. PSORT: a program for detecting sorting signals in proteins and predicting their subcellular localization. *Trends in Biochemical Science*, 24(1):34–36, Jan 1999.

22. W. R. Pearson. Rapid and sensitive sequence comparison with FASTP and FASTA. *Methods in Enzymology*, 183:63–98, 1990.

23. A. Reinhardt and T. Hubbard. Using neural networks for prediction of the sub-cellular location of proteins. *Nucleic Acid Research*, 26(9):2230–2236, May 1998.

Analysis of Proteomic Pattern Data for Cancer Detection

Kees Jong, Elena Marchiori, and Aad van der Vaart

Department of Mathematics and Computer Science
Vrije Universiteit Amsterdam, The Netherlands
`cjong,elena,aad@cs.vu.nl`

Abstract. In this paper we analyze two proteomic pattern datasets containing measurements from ovarian and prostate cancer samples. In particular, a linear and a quadratic support vector machine (SVM) are applied to the data for distinguishing between cancer and benign status. On the ovarian dataset SVM gives excellent results, while the prostate dataset seems to be a harder classification problem for SVM. The prostate dataset is futher analyzed by means of an evolutionary algorithm for feature selection (EAFS) that searches for small subsets of features in order to optimize the SVM performance. In general, the subsets of features generated by EAFS vary over different runs and over different data splitting in training and hold-out sets. Nevertheless, particular features occur more frequently over all the runs. The role of these "core" features as potential tumor biomarkers deserves further study.

1 Introduction

Surface-enhanced laser desorption/ionization time-of-flight mass spectronomy (SELDI-TOF MS) is a recent laboratory technology which offers high-throughput protein profiling. It measures the concentration of low molecular weight peptides in complex mixtures, like serum (cf. e.g. [1]). Because it is relatively inexpensive and noninvasive, it is a promising new technology for classifying disease status.

SELDI-TOF MS technology produces a graph of the relative abundance of ionized peptides (y-axis) versus their mass-to-charge (m/z) ratios (x-axis). (Cf. Figure 1) The m/z ratios are proportional to the peptide masses, but the technique is not able to identify individual peptides, because different peptides may have the same mass and because of limitations in the m/z resolution. Currently the graph is represented by 15000 measuring points. There is no obvious relation between neighbouring measurement points, apart from the fact that they refer to peptides of similar masses and that the resolution is such that the graph should be considered a smoothed version of the true mass density.

Given proteomic profiles for a sample of healthy and diseased individuals it is desired to build a classifier for tumor diagnostics and to identify the protein masses that are potentially involved in the disease. Because of the large number

G.R. Raidl et al. (Eds.): EvoWorkshops 2004, LNCS 3005, pp. 41–51, 2004.

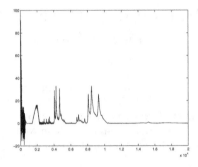

Fig. 1. A typical protein profile produced by SELDI-TOF MS.

of features (the m/z ratios) and the small sample size (the specimens), the second problem is tackled using heuristic algorithms for feature selection.

In this paper we analyze two datasets obtained by applying SELDI-TOF MS to serum samples. The first dataset concerns measurements from women with or without ovarian cancer, was previously analized in [3,4]. The second dataset contains samples from patients with prostate cancer and patients with benign prostate conditions, was analyzed in [2]. Both datasets are publically available from the NCI/CCR and FDA/CBER Clinical Proteomics Program Databank (http://clinicalproteomics.steem.com/).

As preliminary analyses we first investigate the extent to which single m/z ratios can be used to discriminate the two classes of healthy and cancer state samples. Secondly we report the error rate of support vector machine (SVM) classifiers using the full protein profiles. It turns out that the ovarian cancer dataset is "easy" for a linear SVM classifier, whereas the prostate cancer dataset is "harder".

We perform a further analysis of the prostate cancer dataset by means of a feature selection algorithm based on EAs. We introduce an EA for feature selection, called **EAFS** (Evolutionary Algorithm for Feature Selection), in order to identify small subsets of features that discriminate the healthy and cancer groups. The results over multiple data splittings (into training, test and validation set) and multiple EA runs show that the method is slightly unstable. However, specific features occur most frequently in the solutions of multiple runs. Further study is needed in order to assess the role of these "core" features as potential tumor biomarkers.

2   Data Analysis with All Features

The "ovarian dataset" (8-7-02) consists of 253 samples, with 91 controls and 162 ovarian cancers, which include early stage cancer samples. The "prostate dataset" contains 322 samples, with 69 cancers and 253 healthy (or benign) samples.

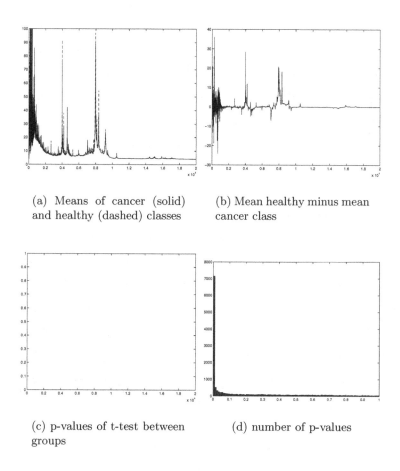

(a) Means of cancer (solid) and healthy (dashed) classes

(b) Mean healthy minus mean cancer class

(c) p-values of t-test between groups

(d) number of p-values

Fig. 2. Mean values analysis of ovarian cancer data set

We analyze the two datasets in order to assess how difficult it is to separate healthy and cancer groups. Figure 2 shows properties of the mean values of the two classes for the ovarian dataset. Parts (a) and (b) of the figure indicate that the healthy and cancer classes differ only in a few regions substantially in mean. Because the variances in the two samples vary significantly with m/z ratio, the t-test applied for each m/z ratio separately is nevertheless significant for a much larger number of m/z ratios. In fact, as shown in part (c), there are many p-values equal to zero all across the full range of m/z-values, and "most" p-values are close to zero, as shown in part (d), which is a histogram with 100 bins. This seems to suggest that it is not difficult to find a good classifier for the ovarian dataset. The same information on the prostate data set is given in Figure 3. We can see there are fewer features with significant difference in mean in the prostate than in the ovarian dataset (part (d) of the figures). Thus finding a good classifier for the prostate dataset seems to be a more difficult task.

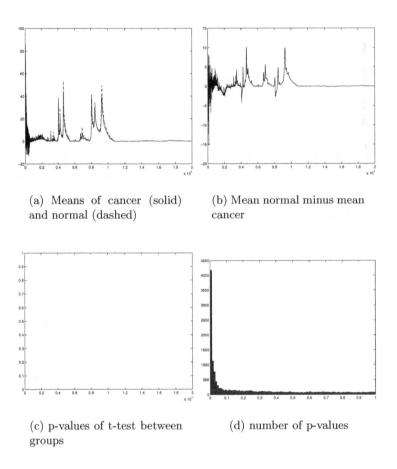

(a) Means of cancer (solid) and normal (dashed)

(b) Mean normal minus mean cancer

(c) p-values of t-test between groups

(d) number of p-values

Fig. 3. Mean values analysis of prostate cancer data set

We classify the data using all the features and a SVM classifier. The choice of SVM is motivated by their good performance also in the presence of many features. In SVM classification [6], the samples of the two classes are mapped into a feature space where they are separated by means of a maximum margin hyperplane, that is, the hyperplane that maximizes the sum of the distances between the hyperplane and its closest points in each of the two classes (the margin). The inner product in the feature space can be computed in the input space by means of a so-called kernel function. This choice is shown to affect positively the generalization performance of the classifier. When the classes are not linearly separable in the feature space, a variant of SVM, called soft-margin SVM, is used. This SVM variant penalizes misclassification errors and employs a parameter (the soft-margin constant C) to control the cost of misclassification. In our experiments we use soft-margin SVM classifiers with C=100, and two types of kernel functions, linear and quadratic.

Table 1. Average results over 25 runs of SVM with linear and quadratic kernel, on ovarian and prostate data

	Lin., Ovar.	Poly., Ovar.	Lin., Pros.	Poly., Pros.
Test Error	**0.0028** (0.0061)	0.0040 (0.0065)	0.0600 (0.0201)	**0.0590** (0.0246)
Sens.	0.9987 (0.0044)	**0.9988** (0.0042)	0.8884 (0.0596)	**0.8936** (0.0719)
Spec.	**0.9947** (0.0153)	0.9912 (0.0169)	0.9539 (0.0205)	**0.9552** (0.0261)
Pos.Pred.Val.	**0.9969** (0.0090)	0.9951 (0.0097)	0.8361 (0.0630)	**0.8475** (0.0867)

Table 1 contains the results obtained by applying an SVM classifier with linear and quadratic kernel to the ovarian and prostate cancer datasets. Experiments are conducted using the SVM software package LibSVM. We perform 25 runs, where in each run the data is randomly partitioned into training (60%) and test (40 %) sets, a classifier is induced by the SVM learning algorithm applied to the training set, and its classification error rate on the test set is measured. Each entry of the table contains the average result over 25 runs (with standard deviation written between brackets) for a specific pair of SVM classifier and dataset.

In all the runs the SVM classification error on the training set is zero. The table contains the average test error rate, sensitivity (number of cancer samples correctly classified divided by total number of cancer samples), specificity (number of healthy samples correcty classified divided by total number of healthy samples), and positive predictive value (number of cancer samples correctly classified divided by total number of samples classified as cancer).

On the ovarian dataset, the SVM classifier with linear kernel gives excellent results, being able to output the correct diagnosis in many runs, in particular cancer samples are almost always detected (pred. pos. val. and sensitivity are close to 1). Thus the ovarian dataset can be considered easy for a linear SVM classifier. Other methods applied to this dataset obtain also very good results. In [3] a commercial package that uses a genetic algorithm (GA) based feature selection method is applied. The GA searches in the space of all subsets of features. It uses a fitness function that scores a feature subset according to its ability to cluster samples in consistent groups, that is, groups containing samples with equal class. The authors report almost perfect classification for a specific data splitting in training and test sets. The paper does not mention results obtained by cross-validation. A more thorough analysis of the ovarian dataset is performed in [4], where 10-fold cross validation is applied, and different classification and feature selection methods are considered. Features are first "smoothed" by means of a discretization algorithm. Perfect classification is achieved using an SVM classifier with quadratic kernel, when all features are used but also when a small subset of 17 features is used. This feature subset is generated using a feature selection algorithm that iteratively constructs sets of features using the best-first-search and a scoring criterion, for selecting a best feature subset, which considers the correlation between pairs of features and between feature and class.

On the prostate dataset, sensitivity and predicted positive values are lower than specificity, possibly due to the unbalanced distribution of the two classes, where cancer samples are about 1/3 of the healthy ones. The results indicate that the prostate data set is somewhat harder to classify than the ovarian one, when using SVM with a linear or quadratic kernel and all the features. In [2] the GA-based commercial package described above is applied to this dataset. The authors identify a subset of 7 features that allow their classification method to obtain 0.95 sensitivity, 0.78 specificity, and 0.1992 test error rate.

In summary, on the ovarian dataset a soft-margin SVM linear classifier provides a good diagnostic tool, while for the prostate dataset the sensitivity achieved is still too low hence does not allow a direct use of this classifier in diagnostics. An early stage tumor diagnostic tool should have sensitivity equal to 1 and specificity very close to 1.

3   An EA-Based Method for Feature Selection

In this section we describe a novel method for feature selection based on evolutionary algorithms (EA). Given a dataset and a learning algorithm, the goal of feature selection is to find a "small" subset of features that minimizes the generalization error (that is, the classification error on new examples) of the classifier induced by the learning algorithm when run only on the selected features.

The data is randomly partitioned into a training, a test and a validation sets (in the experiments these sets contain 60%, 30% and 10% of the data, respectively). The training and test sets are used in the feature selection algorithm and the validation set is used for assessing the performance of the resulting classifier on new data. In the standard wrapper model for feature selection, one searches for a feature subset that minimizes the test error of the classifier trained on data restricted to that feature subset. In [5], Ng shows that the main source of error in standard wrapper algorithms, when many irrelevant features are present, comes from over-fitting hold-out or cross-validation data. He proposes an exact algorithm which is more tolerant to the presence of many irrelevant features. The algorithm, called ordered-fs, works in two phases. First, for each feature set size $i \in [1, m]$, where m is the maximum number of features permitted, the algorithm finds a feature set of size i that minimizes the classifier training error. Next, the resulting m classifiers are run on the test set, and the one yielding minimum error is chosen.

The EA-based method we propose, called EAFS, is inspired by the ordered-fs algorithm. The core of EAFS (illustrated below) consists of an EA which evolves a number of populations, where each population consists of individuals representing feature subsets of a given size. The populations interact by means of highly fit individuals which are used as seed for generating new individuals of other populations. Genetic operators are used for moving in the search space in order to minimize the SVM training error. At the end of the evolutionary process, the best SVM classifier of each population is run on the test set and the one yielding minimum error on this set is selected. Thus the test set is used only to determine the optimal size of the feature set. The selection of an optimal feature set of a given size is based only on the training set.

```
//the core of EAFS
{
  generate initial population
  while (termination criterion not satisfied)
  {
    select a population
    select to parents from that population
    generate offspring using uniform crossover
    apply mutation to offspring
    find populations with right number of features
    replace worst individuals with offspring
    determine fitness (error SVM on training set)
    if (offspring has very good fitness)
        apply migration operator
  }
}
```

Feature subsets are represented by bit strings of length equal to the total number of features. A bit value equal to 1 means the corresponding feature is considered by the learning algorithm, while a 0 means it is discarded. Individuals of each population are initialized by means of n-tournament selection which uses a feature ranking obtained from t-tests on all single features. The fitness of a feature subset F is equal to the training error of the SVM classifier restricted to the features of F. Mutation removes a feature from F and adds a new one, where both features are randomly selected. Standard GA uniform crossover is used. While mutation does not affect the size of a feature subset, this is not the case for crossover. Thus if the feature set size of an offspring is different from the one of its parents, it migrates to another population. At each iteration of the EA, a population is selected and used to generate two offspring. The EA uses tournament selection and a steady state replacement mechanism, where offspring replace the worse individuals of the population. When the EA terminates its execution, the best individual of each population is chosen and the one yielding the lowest error on the test set provides the output. In the sequel, we focus only on the application of EAFS to the prostate dataset, and will not compare EAFS to other EA-based feature selection algorithms.

4   Results

We used the following experimental setup: 20 populations, each one consisting of 10 individuals, 600 iterations, tournament selection of size 5, crossover and mutation rate of 0.95. These values have been chosen after a small number of runs (using only training and test sets). We consider 24 random splitting of the dataset in training (60%), test (30%) and validation (10%) sets. For each "split" of the data we run EAFS 25 times. This amounts to a total of 600 runs. Table 2 gives the results of EAFS with linear kernel. The values are the averages over all the 600 runs. Standard deviation is reported between brackets. Table 3 contains the results using a quadratic kernel. EAFS with a quadratic kernel SVM achieves best performance, but obtains sensitivity lower than that of SVM with all the features. However, a fair comparison is not possible due to the different cross validation approaches used.

Table 2. Results of EAFS with linear SVM

	Training	Test	Validation
Error	0.0617 (0.0254)	0.0880 (0.0313)	0.1116 (0.0515)
Sensitivity	0.7853 (0.0926)	0.7037 (0.1193)	0.6315 (0.2069)
Specificity	0.9827 (0.0118)	0.9658 (0.0238)	0.9484 (0.0456)
Pos. Pred. Value	0.9309 (0.0451)	0.8437 (0.0957)	0.7424 (0.2178)

Table 3. Results of EAFS with quadratic SVM

	Training	Test	Validation
Error	0.0463 (0.0287)	0.0774 (0.0283)	0.1096 (0.0579)
Sensitivity	0.8360 (0.1096)	0.7502 (0.1249)	0.6779 (0.2177)
Specificity	0.9874 (0.0109)	0.9674 (0.0216)	0.9441 (0.0525)
Pos. Pred. Value	0.9502 (0.0431)	0.8547 (0.0948)	0.7671 (0.1936)

In order to investigate whether the data "split" influences the performance of EAFS significantly, we perform a one-way Analysis of Variance to compare the 24 samples of 25 validation errors resulting from the 24 "splits". The difference is statistically significant, with zero p-values for both the linear and quadratic case. The "splits" explain about 24 % of the variance in the validation errors in the linear case and about 35 % in the quadratic case, indicating that 76 % and 65 % is due to the randomness inherent in EAFS. A correction for the effect of "split" on the error standard deviations in Tables 2 and 3 would reduce these somewhat, but not substantially (e.g. 0.0515 becomes 0.045). Figure 4 gives a visual impression of the variation due to the splitting and EAFS. The three graphs show boxplots of the training, test and validation errors of the 600 runs (top to bottom), organized by "split" (left) or "run".

An important aspect of these graphs is summarized in the Figure 5, which shows boxplots of the standard deviations of the 24 samples of validation errors corresponding to the 24 "splits". The linear SVM suffers from one extreme split, but is otherwise more stable across relative to the splitting of the data.

We analyze now the features obtained in all the runs.

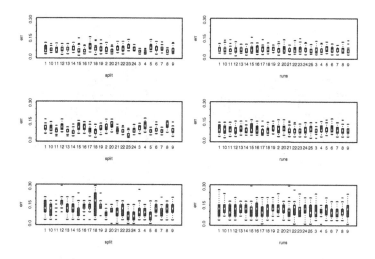

Fig. 4. Boxplot of training, test and validation errors (top to bottom), organized by split (left) and run (right)

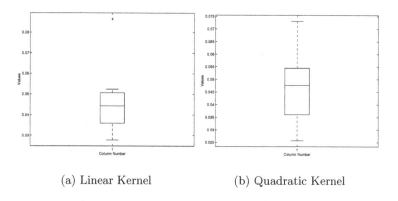

(a) Linear Kernel   (b) Quadratic Kernel

Fig. 5. Boxplots of standard deviation within the 24 runs.

Figure 6 shows histograms of the final feature set sizes found over the 600 runs. The algorithm shows no preference for the largest possible feature set size. We can see that EAFS with linear SVM has a peak on feature size 5, while EAFS with quadratic SVM prefers somewhat bigger feature sizes, with a peak on feature size 13.

Over all the runs EAFS with linear SVM finds 3935, while with quadratic SVM finds 3797 features. Figure 7 shows histograms of the features occurring in the solutions found over the 600 runs. It is clear that EAFS is not stable, yet the

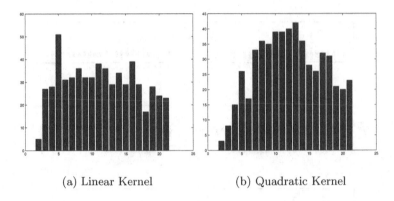

(a) Linear Kernel   (b) Quadratic Kernel

Fig. 6. Histograms of obtained feature set sizes

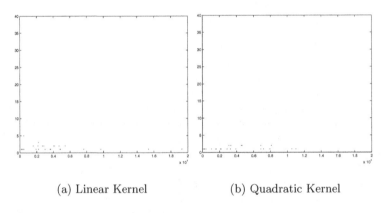

(a) Linear Kernel   (b) Quadratic Kernel

Fig. 7. Histograms of number of feature occurrence in final solutions

histograms indicate the presence of few frequency peaks . By considering features occurring in these peaks, 47 features occurring in at least 10 runs are extracted. We perform 100 runs of the linear SVM restricted to the 47 features, with rando mly chosen training and test set, and obtain 0.93 sensitivity (0.058 standard deviation) and 0.98 specificity (0.016 standard deviation). These significantly better results may be due to the fact that the selection of these features implicitly uses (almost) the entire dataset.

5   Conclusion

This paper analyzed two proteomic pattern datasets. We applied SVM classifiers for tumor diagnostics, and used them in **EAFS**, an EA-based feature selection algorithm for the identification of potential tumor markers identification. The results do not allow us to draw strong conclusions. On the ovarian dataset SVM with all the features exhibits excellent performance, while on the prostate dataset it obtains relatively low sensitivity. Results of **EAFS** show that its performance on the prostate dataset depends on the data splitting and EA run. Moreover, feature subsets generated by **EAFS** vary per run, with a small core of features occurring more often. This latter phenomenon was observed to happen also in the other methods discussed in this paper.

Future work includes: the incorporation of a pre-processing phase into **EAFS**; the investigation of other types of classifiers; the use of knowledge-based mutation operators; and the use of multiple **EAFS**'s runs with different splitting of training and test sets for extracting a "core" set of features from the resulting **EAFS**'s solutions.

Acknowledgment. We would like to thank Guus Smit and Connie Jime nez from the Department of Biology of the Vrije Universiteit Amsterdam for helpful discussions on the subject of this paper.

References

1. H.J. Issaq et al. SELDI-TOF MS for diagnostic proteomics. *Anal. Chem.*, 75(7):148A–155A, 2003.
2. Petricoin E.F. et al. Serum proteomic patterns for detection of prostate cancer. *Journal of the National Cancer Institute*, 94(20):1576–1578, 2002.
3. Petricoin E.F. et al. Use of proteomic patterns in serum to identify ovarian cancer. *The Lancet*, 359(9306):572–7, 2002.
4. H. Liu, J. Li, and L. Wong. A comparative study on feature selection and classification methods using gene expression profiles and proteomic patterns. *Genome Informatics*, 13:51–60, 2002.
5. Andrew Y. Ng. On feature selection: learning with exponentially many irrelevant features as training examples. In *Proc. 15th International Conf. on Machine Learning*, pages 404–412. Morgan Kaufmann, San Francisco, CA, 1998.
6. V.N. Vapnik. *Statistical Learning Theory*. John Wiley & Sons, 1998.

Self-Adaptive Scouting—Autonomous Experimentation for Systems Biology

Naoki Matsumaru[1], Florian Centler[1], Klaus-Peter Zauner[2], and Peter Dittrich[1]

[1] Bio Systems Analysis Group
Jena Centre for Bioinformatics (JCB) and
Department of Mathematics and Computer Science
Friedrich-Schiller-University Jena, D-07743 Jena, Germany
[2] School of Electronics and Computer Science
University of Southampton, SO17 1BJ, United Kingdom

Abstract. We introduce a new algorithm for autonomous experimentation. This algorithm uses evolution to drive exploration during scientific discovery. Population size and mutation strength are self-adaptive. The only variables remaining to be set are the limits and maximum resolution of the parameters in the experiment. In practice, these are determined by instrumentation. Aside from conducting physical experiments, the algorithm is a valuable tool for investigating simulation models of biological systems. We illustrate the operation of the algorithm on a model of HIV-immune system interaction. Finally, the difference between scouting and optimization is discussed.

1 Introduction

Perplexing complexity is prevalent in biology across the scale from single cells to ecosystems. Unraveling the intricate and manifold interplay of components in biological systems necessitates comprehensive information. Acquiring this information is challenging because the complexity of living systems entails extensive factor interaction. As an implication of these interactions the results of biological experiments have in general a narrow scope. Thus it is often impossible to synthesize quantitative system-level models form data in the existing literature, because measurements were obtained in disparate or unreported contexts.

Consequently, experiments are the limiting resource for quantitative systems biology. Automated high-throughput methods and recent sensor technologies are well suited to address this problem. To realize their potential, however, computational techniques have to be brought to bear not only to discover regularities in existing data, but rather the experimental procedure itself has to be embedded in a closed-loop discovery process. Only the latter affords the intervention of the computer during the experimental process required for full utilization of both the material subject to investigation and equipment time [1,2].

With the advent of large-scale biological models the need to apply autonomous experimentation also to simulations became apparent. For example, a differential equation model of the epidermal growth factor receptor signaling

G.R. Raidl et al. (Eds.): EvoWorkshops 2004, LNCS 3005, pp. 52–62, 2004.

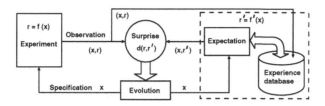

Fig. 1. Scouting combines the notion of information being equivalent to surprise value [11] with evolutionary computation for autonomous exploration. See text for details

pathway contains 94 time varying state variables and 95 parameters [3]; or a recent model of E. coli contains more than 1200 metabolites and reactions [4]. Aside from the combinatorial explosion of the parameter space with increasing number of parameters, the analysis of the dynamic behavior of such systems is further complicated by the the rich interactions among the parameters that is typical for biological systems.

In the present context, the work by Kulkarni and Simon [5] is of particular interest. They developed a program that attempts to generate experiments, in which unexplained phenomena are enhanced. Notably, the program does not start out with a pre-set goal as is common in optimization experiments but decides on its objectives dynamically. This work demonstrated that an algorithm can successfully navigate an immense search space by emulating the interplay of adjusting hypotheses and modifying experiments, which is characteristic of human experimenters [6]. Recently, evolutionary computation has been applied to autonomous experimentation [7] and was employed in conjunction with computer-controlled fluidics to characterize protein response with regard to chemical signals [8]. This method, named scouting, has also been suggested for detecting and localizing unusual chemical signatures [9]. A drawback of the scouting algorithm so far was that several application-dependent parameters need to be set by the user to achieve good performance.

We developed self-adaptive scouting combining the scouting algorithm with two parameter adaptation strategies. In the following, first the improved scouting algorithm with self-adaptive mutation strength and population size is presented. Then, we illustrate the operation of the new algorithm on a simulation model of HIV-immune system interaction [10]. Finally, the crucial difference between scouting and optimization is discussed in Section 4.

2   The Self-Adaptive Scouting Algorithm

The scouting algorithm is an evolutionary experimentation method for designing experiments dynamically, and experiments are scheduled to achieve maximal information gain at each step. In accordance with communication theory, information is quantified as the surprise value of arriving data [11]. No a priori knowledge about the system under investigation is required. An overview of the algorithm is depicted in Fig. 1. Given an experiment $\mathbf{f}$, the scouting algorithm interacts with it by sending specifications **x** of the experiment and receiving observed responses **r**. During the scouting run, every experiment performed contributes to an experience database, which stores the observations (pairs of **x** and **r**). This database together with a prediction mechanics (labeled as expectation) forms an empirical model **f'** of the experiment given, and this model is used to formulate an expected response **r'** from the experiment. The deviation **d(r, r')** between the expected and the real response constitutes the surprise for the specification. In the evolution step, the specification is an individual offspring and the surprise value is used as the fitness in generating the next offsprings. As a result of this algorithm, experiments are performed densely in regions where unexpected observations occur.

2.1   Adaptive Mutation Strength

In the evolution step of the algorithm, an offspring is created from the parent by adding a normally distributed value with mean 0 and standard deviation σ. Varying σ controls the strength of the mutation. Given the current surprise value s and the current mutation strength σ, the mutation strength is adapted as follows:

$$\sigma \leftarrow \sigma \cdot e^{(\bar{s}-s)/\bar{s}}, \tag{1}$$

where $\bar{s}$ is the average surprise value over all past experiments. As a result of this adaptation, the region from which offspring are chosen shrinks if the current surprise is above the average surprise. A surprise value below the average, on the other hand, causes the region to expand—eventually leading to random search.

We also investigated standard step size adaption methods from evolution strategies (ES), e.g., ref. [12,13] and found that those adaptation methods fail to keep up with the dynamics of our fitness landscape[1].

2.2   Adaptive Population Size

Originally, the population size λ had to be given by the user and determines the number of offspring generated from one parent (i.e., a $(1, \lambda)$-strategy in ES-terminology). If the population size is constant, we found that some individuals with high fitness are discarded because there was one individual with even higher fitness selected as the parent for the next generation. Conversely, it also happened that individuals with low fitness were selected as a parent.

The second adaptation scheme is developed to avoid this situation. We introduced an adaptive generation change. Whenever the surprise value is higher

---

[1] In the scouting algorithm, the fitness is obtained as the deviation between an expectation computed from the experience database and an observation. Since every experiment is stored in the experience database, the expectation improves continuously and the fitness landscape changes rapidly. In a deterministic setting (e.g., where the experiment is a simulation without randomness) even the individual with the highest fitness will have zero fitness when it is evaluated a second time (cf. [14, 15]).

than a threshold, the specification of the experiment is selected as a parent. The threshold at generation g is denoted as $\Theta^{(g)}$ and defined as the average surprise value of the second-best individuals in the past generations:

$$\Theta^{(g)} := \frac{1}{g-1} \sum_{k=1}^{g-1} s_{2;\lambda_k}^{(k)} \quad \text{for } g > 1, \qquad \Theta^{(1)} := 0. \tag{2}$$

Following Beyer and Schwefel [16], we use the notation of order statistics (e.g., ref. [17]) by identifying the surprise value of the second-best individual out of λ_k individuals of generation k by $s_{2;\lambda_k}^{(k)}$. The population size at generation k is λ_k. For a generation with only one member, we define this individual to be the "second-best": $s_{2;1}^{(k)} := s_1^{(k)}$, where $s_i^{(k)}$ is the surprise value of the ith individual of generation k (in the order of experiments performed).

The threshold is calculated as described above because the second-best surprise value separates the best, which is selected as the parent for the next generation, from the other offspring. The second-best surprise value works implicitly as a threshold in each generation. Furthermore, this method guarantees the threshold to be above the average surprise value $\bar{s}$, so that the mutation strength σ can become both bigger and smaller using the scheme of Sec. 2.1.

2.3 Pseudo Code

The complete scouting algorithm is presented here in more detail as pseudo code. During initialization (line 1–5), the minimum mutation strength σ_{min} and the number of experiments to perform t_{max} is set by the user. The mutation strength σ is initialized with 1. The number of the current experiment t and the number of the current generation g is set to 0. In line 6–9, an initial experiment specification is randomly chosen, the experiment performed, and stored with response $\mathbf{r}$ in the experience database DB. $\mathbf{x}_i^{(g)}$ is the experiment specification of the ith individual of generation g. Within the **while**-loop, a new generation is started by choosing the parent $\mathbf{x}^{(g)}$ of generation g to be the last individual of the last generation (line 13). The new generation is then populated within the **repeat**-loop. In line 16, a new experiment specification is created as a mutated copy of the parent individual (see Sec. 2.1), and the expectation $\mathbf{r}'$ is computed from the experience database. This is done here, as in ref. [8], by averaging over the (up to) 5 closest experiment entries from the experience database with inverse cubic distance weighting. The response $\mathbf{r}$ is derived by performing the experiment, and the result is stored in the experience database. Finally, the surprise value is calculated in line 21, and the mutation strength is adapted in line 22 (see Sec. 2.1). In generation g, the mean surprise value over all experiments is calculated as follows:

$$\bar{s} := \frac{1}{g} \sum_{k=1}^{g} \frac{1}{\lambda_k} \sum_{i=1}^{\lambda_k} s_i^{(k)}. \tag{3}$$

The **repeat**-loop is left and a new generation started, once the surprise value of an experiment is above the threshold $\Theta^{(g)}$ (see Sec. 2.2).

Algorithm: Self-adaptive Scouting

```
1  σ_min  ← minimum_resolution              # minimum resolution
   t_max  ← maximum_experiments             # number of exp. to perform
   σ      ← 1                               # mutation strength
   t      ← 0                               # time (experiments)
5  g      ← 0                               # time (generations)
   x_{λ_0}^{(0)} ← random_specification      # choose initial experiment
   r      ← f(x_{λ_0}^{(0)})                 # conduct experiment
   t      ← t + 1                           # increment time (experiments)
   DB     ← InsertIntoDB(DB, (x_1^{(0)}, r))  # initialize experience db

10 while t < t_max do
       g   ← g + 1                          # start a new generation
       λ_g ← 0                              # number of individuals
       x^{(g)} ← x_{λ_{(g-1)}}^{(g-1)}       # choose the parent
       repeat
15         λ_g    ← λ_g + 1                  # add a new individual by
           x_{λ_g}^{(g)} ← Mutate(x^{(g)}, σ)  # mutating the parent
           r'     ← Predict(DB, x_{λ_g}^{(g)})  # compute expectation
           r      ← f(x_{λ_g}^{(g)})          # conduct experiment
           t      ← t + 1                   # increment time (experiments)
20         DB     ← InsertIntoDB(DB, (x_{λ_g}^{(g)}, r)) # experience database
           s_{λ_g}^{(g)} ← d(r, r')           # compute surprise
           σ      ← Max(σ_min, σ · exp(1 - s_{λ_g}^{(g)}/s̄))  # adapt mutation strength
       until s_{λ_g}^{(g)} > Θ^{(g)} or t ≥ t_max
   end
```

3 Scouting an HIV-Immune System Model

Now we demonstrate the behavior of our new algorithm by applying it to a concrete model of immunological control of HIV by Wodarz and Nowak [10]. The model is a 4-dimensional ordinary differential equation (ODE) system. A mathematical analysis reveals that the model has two asymptotically stable fixed points. Using scouting, we will now explore how the model behaves depending on its initial state given a fixed parameter setting.

3.1 Definition of the Experiment

The experiment is a dynamic simulation of the the immunological control model taken from [10], which contains 4 variables: uninfected CD4$^+$ T cells x, infected CD4$^+$ T cells y, cytotoxic T lymphocyte (CTL) precursors (CTLp) w, and CTL effectors z. The dynamics is given by the ODE system: $\dot{x} = \lambda - dx - \beta xy, \dot{y} = \beta xy - ay - pyz, \dot{w} = cxyw - cqyw - bw, \dot{z} = cqyw - hz$. Uninfected CD4$^+$ T

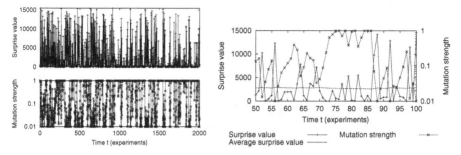

Fig. 2. Surprise value $s_i^{(g)}$ and mutation strength σ while exploring the behavior of the HIV immunology model with the self-adaptive scouting algorithm. A surprise value higher than the average decreases the mutation strength. The mutation strength is increased, when the surprise value is less than the average (see Eq. 1). This mutation strength adjustment helps the scouting algorithm to concentrate the samples on surprising regions

cells are produced at a rate λ, decay at a rate dx, and become infected at a rate βxy. Infected cells decay at a rate ay and are killed by CTL effectors at a rate pyz. The production of CTLp at rate $cxyw$ requires uninfected CD4$^+$ cells, virus load represented by y, and CTLp themselves. CTLp decay at a rate bw and differentiate in CTL effectors at a rate $cqyw$. CTL effectors decay at a rate hz. Here we set the parameters as in ref. [10]: $\lambda = 1, d = 0.1, \beta = 0.5, a = 0.2, p = 1, c = 0.1, b = 0.01, q = 0.5, h = 0.1$.

Given a specification $\mathbf{x} = (x_1, x_2, x_3, x_4)$, we perform the experiment and obtain the response $\mathbf{r} = (r_1, r_2, r_3, r_4)$ in the following way: (1) We set the initial state of the ODE system as follows: $x_{t=0} = x_1, y_{t=0} = x_2, w_{t=0} = x_3 \times 0.05, z_{t=0} = x_4$. (2) We integrate the ODE numerically (using lsode built in octave [18]) for a duration of t_1 (here, $t_1 = 500$) and obtain the response as the final state: $r_1 = x_{t=t_1}, r_2 = y_{t=t_1}, r_3 = w_{t=t_1}, r_4 = z_{t=t_1}$.

3.2 Scouting the Model

For scouting, we set the range of specification $\mathbf{x}$ of the experiment to $[0, 1]^4$ and the minimum mutation strength $\sigma_{min} = 0.01$. We allow a total number of $t_{max} = 2000$ experiments in a scouting run. Every experiment integrates numerically the ODE representing the HIV immunology model.

Figure 2 shows the progress of the surprise value $s_j^{(g)}$ (left top) and mutation strength σ (left bottom) of a typical run of (self-adaptive) scouting. On the right-hand side, experiments 50–100 are shown in detail. Surprise value and mutation strength are plotted together with the average surprise value $\bar{s}$ to illustrate the mutation strength adaptation. The difference between the current surprise value and the average surprise determines the adaptation of the mutation strength according to Eq. 1.

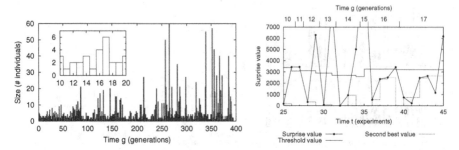

Fig. 3. Population size λ_g and threshold $\Theta^{(g)}$. See text for details

The time evolution of the population size λ_g is plotted on the lefthand side of Fig. 3. For the purpose of explaining the population size adaptation, the right-hand side of the graph shows in detail the surprise value of every individual experiment from generation 10–17, the second-best surprise, and the threshold. Generation 17 consists of 6 individuals $\mathbf{x}_{40} \ldots \mathbf{x}_{45}$ ($\mathbf{x}_i$ denotes the ith experiment conducted). Because the surprise of the 6th offspring is greater than the threshold, the individual $\mathbf{x}_{45}$ is selected to be the parent of generation 18. The surprise experienced by the experiment $\mathbf{x}_{43} = \mathbf{x}_4^{(17)}$ is the second-best surprise value in the generation. This value is used to calculate the threshold for the following generation. Since the first offspring of generation 15 ($\mathbf{x}_{35} = \mathbf{x}_1^{(15)}$) yields a higher surprise than the threshold, the population size of generation 15 is 1. The second-best surprise value for this generation is, in this case, the best one.

Figure 4 shows the 2000 specifications sampled by the scouting algorithm. The 4-dimensional data is projected on 6 graphs showing every possible combination of the four dimensions. Each point represents an initial state of the ODE model. The sampling points seem to spread equally except for the last graph with CTL precursors and effectors as axes. The pattern appearing in the last graph matches with the border of the two basins of attraction of the two asymptotically stable fixed points of the ODE model. The respective dynamical behavior of the model is shown in Fig. 5. As seen in Fig. 4, scouting has explored the borderline between the two modes of behavior more accurately, thus the borderline can be described much more precisely than for cases where systematic or random sampling would have been used. To illustrate this, a 2-dimensional projection of systematic sampling given by a full 7^4 factorial design is shown in Fig. 6. In this design of experiments, each of the 4 factors $x_1, \ldots, x_4$ is explored equidistantly on 7 levels [19]. With approximately the same number of experiments as in the scouting method, the borderline can only roughly be approximated.

4   Scouting Is Not Optimization

It is important to note that scouting as described here is not a classical optimization method. Generally, the aim of optimization algorithms is finding the

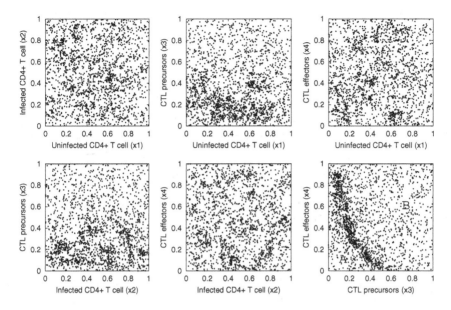

Fig. 4. Six different 2-dimensional projections of 2000 sampled locations (specifications) of a typical scouting run on the HIV immunology model developed by Woodarz and Nowak [10]. This model is described as an ODE with four variables. The scouting algorithm initializes the variables, which are plotted as dots, and observes the states of the model after 500 time steps as the response. When the locations are plotted with CTL precursors and effectors as axes (lower rightmost plot), a pattern of dense area shows up. The pattern matches with the border of two modes of behavior of the model, which are shown in Fig. 5

best solution among all possible solutions. More formally, given an objective function $F\colon Y \to Q$, which assigns to each solution from the search space Y a certain quality $\mathbf{q} \in Q$, an optimization algorithm tries to find the solution $\mathbf{y} \in Y$ such that $F(\mathbf{y})$ gets maximized. The result of optimization is a single best-so-far solution $\mathbf{y}$. For scouting, an experiment $f\colon X \to R$ is given, where X is the search space consisting of all possible experiment specifications and R the set of all possible responses. In contrast to optimization, the objective here is not to find a single best experiment $\mathbf{x} \in X$ (or a pareto set), but to gain as much information about f as possible by conducting experiments. The result of scouting is an experience database, which embodies the complete knowledge acquired about f and can be considered as an empirical model.

Trivially, every computational problem can be formulated as an optimization problem, e.g., by defining the objective function to be optimum when its argument is the solution of the problem. For example, a sorted sequence $\mathbf{y} = (y_1, \ldots, y_n)$ optimizes the objective function $F(\mathbf{y}) = \sum_{i<j}(y_i < y_j)$. Most sorting algorithms, however, contradict the typical picture of optimization where a sequence of evaluations of the objective function leads to a solution. Bubble sort, for instance, might be better regarded as a greedy strategy that seeks a

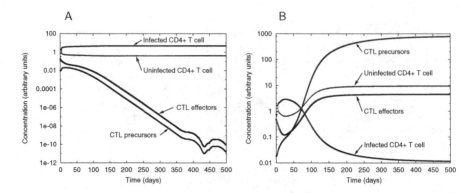

Fig. 5. The HIV immunology model has two modes of behavior: (A) immune system damaged and (B) CTL response established. The labels correspond to those in Fig. 4

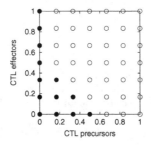

Fig. 6. Two-dimensional projection of systematic sampling. Initial state leading to a damaged immune system are marked by •; initial states establishing CTL response are indicated by ∘. Experiments with no initial infected $CD4^+$ T cells are excluded. Comparing to the lower rightmost panel in Fig. 4, the borderline of the two modes of behavior of the model can be approximated only roughly

local optimum to achieve the global optimum. The same is true for scouting with respect to the (implicit) aim of maximizing the total information about the experiment f. Every step (or every generation) of the scouting algorithm can be viewed as a step of a greedy strategy that tries to maximize the local information gain in terms of maximal surprise in the next experiment.

5 Concluding Remarks

We introduced an algorithm capable of exploring unknown phenomena without the need for manual adjustments aimed at an application domain. We described how the two parameters crucial for the exploration, the mutation strength and the population size, can be adapted automatically, and why existing techniques for evolutionary optimization were not applicable. Our experience with the algorithm provides some evidence that it can be applied usefully for exploring complex systems. However, the next important step is to quantify the performance of scouting systematically. A suitable assessment measure may be the predicting strength of the experience database after a given number of samples. The process of evolution underlies the complexity observed throughout the realms of biology—it may also hold the key to tackle this complexity.

Acknowledgments. This article is based upon work supported by BMBF (Federal Ministry of Education and Research, Germany) under grant No. 0312704A to PD, and NASA under Grant No. NCC2-1189 to KPZ.

References

1. Langley, P., Simon, H.A., Bradshaw, G.L., Żytkow, J.M.: Scientific discovery: Computational exploration of the creative processes. MIT Press, Cambridge, MA (1987)
2. King, R.D., Whelan, K.E., Jones, F.M., Reiser, P.G.K., Bryant, C.H., Muggleton, S.H., Kell, D.B., Oliver, S.G.: Functional genomic hypothesis generation and experimentation by a robot scientist. Nature **427** (2004) 247–252
3. Schoeberl, B., Eichler-Jonsson, C., Gilles, E.D., Müller, G.: Computational modeling of the dynamics of the MAP kinase cascade activated by surface and internalized EGF receptors. Nature Biotechnology **20** (2002) 370–375
4. Goryanin, I.: Progress in computational systems biology. Talk held on the Symposiumon Integrative Bioinformatics, Bielefeld, 4-5 August 2003 (2003)
5. Kulkarni, D., Simon, H.A.: Experimentation in machine discovery. In Shrager, J., Langley, P., eds.: Computational Models of Scientific Discovery and Theory Formation. Morgan Kaufmann Pubishers, San Mateo, CA (1990) 255–273
6. Gooding, D.: Experiment and the Making of Meaning. Kluwer Academic Publishers, Dordrecht (1990)
7. Pfaffmann, J.O., Zauner, K.P.: Scouting context-sensitive components. In Keymeulen, D., Stoica, A., Lohn, J., Zebulum, R.S., eds.: The Third NASA/DoD Workshop on Evolvable Hardware—EH-2001, Long Beach, 12-14 July 2001, IEEE Computer Society, Los Alamitos (2001) 14–20
8. Matsumaru, N., Colombano, S., Zauner, K.P.: Scouting enzyme behavior. In Fogel, D.B., El-Sharkawi, M.A., Yao, X., Greenwood, G., Iba, H., Marrow, P., Shackleton, M., eds.: 2002 World Congress on Computational Intelligence, May 12-17, Honolulu, Hawaii, IEEE, Piscataway, NJ (2002) CEC 19–24
9. Centler, F., Dittrich, P., Ku, L., Matsumaru, N., Pfaffmann, J., Zauner, K.P.: Artificial life as an aid to astrobiology: Testing life seeking techniques. In Banzhaf, W., Christaller, T., Dittrich, P., Kim, J.T., Ziegler, J., eds.: Advances in Artificial Life, ECAL 2003. Volume 2801 of LNAI., Berlin, Springer (2003) 31–40
10. Wodarz, D., Nowak, M.A.: Specific therapy regimes could lead to long-term immunological control of HIV. PNAS **96** (1999) 14464–9
11. Cherry, C.: Chapter 5. In: On Human Communication: A Review, a Survey, and a Criticism. 2nd edn. MIT Press, Cambridge, MA (1966)
12. Rechenberg, I.: Evolutionsstrategie'94. frommann-holzboog, Stuttgard (1994)
13. Hansen, N., Ostermeier, A.: Completely derandomized self-adaptation in evolution strategies. Evolutionary Computation **9** (2001) 159–195

14. Weicker, K., Weicker, N.: On evolution strategy optimization in dynamic environments. In Angeline, P.J., Michalewicz, Z., Schoenauer, M., Yao, X., Zalzala, A., eds.: Proceedings of the Congress on Evolutionary Computation. Volume 3., Mayflower Hotel, Washington D.C., USA, IEEE Press (1999) 2039–2046

15. Arnold, D.V., Beyer, H.G.: Random dynamics optimum tracking with evolution strategies. In Guervós, J.J.M., Adamidis, P., Beyer, H.G., nas, J.L.F.V., Schwefel, H.P., eds.: Parallel Problem Solving from Nature VII (PPSN-2002). Volume 2439 of LNCS., Granada, Spain, Springer Verlag (2002) 3–12

16. Beyer, H.G., Schwefel, H.P.: Evolution strategies - a comprehensive introduction. Natural Computing 1 (2002) 3–52

17. Arnold, B., Balakrishnan, N., Nagaraja, H.: A First Course in Order Statistics. New York. Wiley (1992)

18. Eaton, J.W.: GNU Octave Manual. Network Theory Limited, Bristol, UK (2002)

19. Hinkelmann, K., Kempthorn, O.: Design and Analysis of Experiments. Wiley, New York (1994)

An Improved Grammatical Evolution Strategy for Hierarchical Petri Net Modeling of Complex Genetic Systems

Jason H. Moore and Lance W. Hahn

Center for Human Genetics Research, Department of Molecular Physiology and Biophysics, 519 Light Hall, Vanderbilt University, Nashville, TN, USA 37232-0700
{Moore, Hahn}@phg.mc.Vanderbilt.edu

Abstract. DNA sequence variations impact human health through a hierarchy of biochemical and physiological systems. Understanding the hierarchical relationships in the genotype-phenotype mapping is expected to improve the diagnosis, prevention, and treatment of common, complex human diseases. We previously developed a hierarchical dynamic systems approach based on Petri nets for generating biochemical network models that are consistent with genetic models of disease susceptibility. This strategy uses an evolutionary computation approach called grammatical evolution for symbolic manipulation and optimization of Petri net models. We previously demonstrated that this approach routinely identifies biochemical network models that are consistent with a variety of complex genetic models in which disease susceptibility is determined by nonlinear interactions between two DNA sequence variations. However, the modeling strategy was generally not successful when extended to modeling nonlinear interactions between three DNA sequence variations. In the present study, we evaluate a modified grammar for building Petri net models of biochemical systems that are consistent with high-order genetic models of disease susceptibility. The results indicate that our hierarchical model-building approach is capable of identifying perfect Petri net models when an appropriate grammar is used.

1 Introduction

Epistasis or gene-gene interaction was recognized by Bateson [1] and other early geneticists [e.g. 2,3] as playing an important role in the mapping between genotype and phenotype. Today, this idea prevails and epistasis is believed to be a ubiquitous component of the genetic architecture of common human diseases [4]. In fact, it has been hypothesized that results from studies of single genes do not replicate across multiple independent samples because the effect of any given gene on disease susceptibility is dependent on the context of other interacting genes [5]. As a result, the identification of genes with genotypes that confer an increased susceptibility to a common disease will require a research strategy that embraces, rather than ignores, the complexity of these diseases.

G.R. Raidl et al. (Eds.): EvoWorkshops 2004, LNCS 3005, pp. 63–72, 2004.

New analytical strategies such as multifactor dimensionality reduction, or MDR, are able to model combinations of DNA sequence variations that are associated with discrete clinical endpoints [6-8]. However, the multilocus models of disease susceptibility generated by these methods are often difficult to interpret due to the dimensionality of the information. If we are to successfully use genetic information at the public health level to improve the diagnosis, prevention, and treatment of common diseases we will need to understand how DNA sequence information influences human health through hierarchical networks of biochemical and physiological systems. To this end, we have developed a hierarchical dynamic systems approach to generating models of biochemical and physiological networks that are consistent with high-dimensional models of disease susceptibility [9]. With this approach, discrete dynamic systems modeling is carried out using Petri nets. A limitation of Petri nets is that the modeling process is typically carried out by trial and error. In response to this limitation, Moore and Hahn [9] developed a machine intelligence strategy that uses an evolutionary computation approach called grammatical evolution for the symbolic manipulation and optimization of Petri net models. This approach routinely generates Petri net models that are consistent with a variety of genetic models in which disease susceptibility is dependent on nonlinear interactions between two DNA sequence variations [9,10]. However, when applied to higher-order genetic models, the strategy did not consistently yield perfect Petri nets [11]. In fact, only one perfect model was discovered out of 100 independent runs. The goal of the present study is to develop a strategy that is able to discover Petri net models of biochemical systems that are consistent with nonlinear interactions between three DNA sequence variations.

A. Model 1

| | CC | | | Cc | | | cc | | |
	BB	Bb	bb	BB	Bb	bb	BB	Bb	bb
AA	.06	.06	.01	.04	0	.10	.02	.08	0
Aa	.02	.06	0	.09	.01	.06	.03	.07	.01
aa	.01	.07	.04	.01	.08	.02	.01	0	.10

B. Model 2

| | CC | | | Cc | | | cc | | |
	BB	Bb	bb	BB	Bb	bb	BB	Bb	bb
AA	.05	.06	.03	.09	.02	.06	.06	.03	.01
Aa	.02	.08	.04	.06	.02	.08	.03	.08	0
aa	.07	0	.02	.01	.10	.02	.09	.01	.10

Fig. 1. Penetrance functions for nonlinear gene-gene interaction models 1 (a) and 2 (b). High-risk genotype combinations are shaded while low-risk combinations are unshaded.

2   The Nonlinear Gene-Gene Interaction Models

Our two high-order, nonlinear, gene-gene interaction models are based on penetrance functions. Penetrance functions represent one approach to modeling the relationship between genetic variations and risk of disease. Penetrance is simply the probability (P) of disease (D) given a particular combination of genotypes (G) that was inherited (i.e. P[D|G]). A single genotype is determined by one allele (i.e. a specific DNA sequence state) inherited from the mother and one allele inherited from the father. For most genetic variations, only two alleles (encoded by *A* or *a*) exist in the biological population. Therefore, because the ordering of the alleles is unimportant, a genotype can have one of three values: *AA*, *Aa* or *aa*. Figures 1a and 1b (above) illustrate the penetrance functions used for Models 1 and 2, respectively. Each model was discovered using a modified version of the software of Moore et al. [12]. What makes these models interesting is that disease risk is dependent on each particular combination of three genotypes. Each single-locus genotype has effectively no main effect on disease risk when the allele frequencies are equal and the genotypes are consistent with Hardy-Weinberg proportions.

3   An Introduction to Petri Nets for Modeling Discrete Dynamic Systems

Petri nets are a type of directed graph that can be used to model discrete dynamical systems [13]. Goss and Peccoud [14] demonstrated that Petri nets could be used to model molecular interactions in biochemical systems. The core Petri net consists of two different types of nodes: places and transitions. Using the biochemical systems analogy of Goss and Peccoud [14], places represent molecular species. Each place has a certain number of tokens that represent the number of molecules for that particular molecular specie. A transition is analogous to a molecular or chemical reaction and is said to fire when it acquires tokens from a source place and, after a possible delay, deposits tokens in a destination place. Tokens travel from a place to a transition or from a transition to a place via arcs with specific weights or bandwidths. While the number of tokens transferred from place to transition to place is determined by the arc weights, the rate at which the tokens are transferred is determined by the delay associated with the transition. Transition behavior is also constrained by the weights of the source and destination arcs. A transition will only fire if two preconditions are met: 1) if the source place can completely supply the capacity of the source arc and, 2) if the destination place has the capacity available to store the number of tokens provided by the full weight of the destination arc. Transitions without an input arc, act as if they are connected to a limitless supply of tokens. Similarly, transitions without an output arc can consume a limitless supply of tokens. The firing rate of the transition can be immediate, delayed deterministically or delayed stochastically, depending on the complexity needed. The fundamental behavior of a Petri net can be controlled by varying the maximum number of tokens a place can hold, the weight of each arc, and the firing rates of the transitions.

4 Our Petri Net Modeling Strategy

The goal of identifying Petri net models of biochemical systems that are consistent with observed population-level gene-gene interactions is accomplished by developing Petri nets that are dependent on specific genotypes from two or more genetic variations. Here, we make transition firing rates and/or arc weights genotype-dependent yielding different Petri net behavior. Each Petri net model is related to the genetic model using a discrete version of the threshold model from population genetics [15]. With a classic threshold or liability model, it is the concentration of a biochemical or environmental substance that is related to the risk of disease, under the hypothesis that risk of disease is greatly increased once a particular substance exceeds some threshold concentration. Conversely, the risk of disease may increase in the absence of a particular factor or with any significant deviation from a reference level. In such cases, high or low levels are associated with high risk while an intermediate level is associated with low risk. Here, we use a discrete version of this model for our deterministic Petri nets. For each model, the number of tokens at a particular place is recorded and if they exceed a certain threshold, the appropriate risk assignment is made. If the number of tokens does not exceed the threshold, the alternative risk assignment is made. The high-risk and low-risk assignments made by the discrete threshold from the output of the Petri net can then be compared to the high-risk and low-risk genotypes from the genetic model. A perfect match indicates the Petri net model is consistent with the gene-gene interactions observed in the genetic model. The Petri net then becomes a model that relates the genetic variations to risk of disease through an intermediate biochemical network.

5 The Grammatical Evolution Algorithm

5.1 Overview of Grammatical Evolution

Evolutionary computation arose from early work on evolutionary programming [16,17] and evolution strategies [18,19] that used simulated evolution for artificial intelligence. The focus on representations at the genotypic level lead to the development of genetic algorithms by Holland [20,21] and others. Genetic algorithms have become a popular machine intelligence strategy because they can be effective for implementing parallel searches of rugged fitness landscapes [22]. Briefly, this is accomplished by generating a random population of models or solutions, evaluating their ability to solve the problem at hand, selecting the best models or solutions, and generating variability in these models by exchanging model components between different models. The process of selecting models and introducing variability is iterated until an optimal model is identified or some termination criteria are satisfied. Koza [23] developed an alternative parameterization of genetic algorithms called genetic programming where the models or solutions are represented by binary expression trees. Koza [24] and others [25] have applied genetic programming to modeling metabolic networks.

Grammatical evolution (GE) has been described by O'Neill and Ryan [26] as a variation on genetic programming. Here, a Backus-Naur Form (BNF) grammar is specified that allows a computer program or model to be constructed by a simple genetic algorithm operating on an array of bits. The GE approach is appealing because only a text file specifying the grammar needs to be altered for different applications. There is no need to modify and recompile source code during development once the fitness function is specified. The end result is a decrease in development time and an increase in computational flexibility. It is for this reason that Moore and Hahn [9] selected GE as the evolutionary computation method for the discovery of Petri net models.

5.2 A Grammar for Petri Net Models in Backus-Naur Form

Moore and Hahn [9] developed a grammar for Petri nets in BNF. Backus-Naur Form is a formal notation for describing the syntax of a context-free grammar as a set of production rules that consist of terminals and nonterminals [27]. Nonterminals form the left-hand side of production rules while both terminals and nonterminals can form the right-hand side. A terminal is essentially a model element while a nonterminal is the name of a possibly recursive production rule. For the Petri net models, the terminal set includes, for example, the basic building blocks of a Petri net: places, arcs, and transitions. The nonterminal set includes the names of production rules that construct the Petri net. For example, a nonterminal might name a production rule for determining whether an arc has weights that are fixed or genotype-dependent. We show below the production rule that was executed to begin the model building process for the study by Moore and Hahn [11] and then describe the modifications evaluated in the present study.

```
<root> ::= <pick_a_gene> <pick_a_gene> <pick_a_gene> <net_iterations>
<expr> <transition> <transition> <place_noarc>
```

When the initial <root> production rule is executed, a single Petri net place with no entering or exiting arc (i.e. <place_noarc>) is selected and a transition leading into or out of that place is selected. The arc connecting the transition and place can be dependent on the genotypes of the genes selected by <pick_a_gene>. The nonterminal <expr> is a function that allows the Petri net to grow. The production rule for <expr> is shown below.

```
<expr> ::= <expr> <expr>      0
         | <arc>              1
         | <transition>       2
         | <place>            3
```

Here, the selection of one of the four nonterminals (0, 1, 2, or 3) on the right-hand side of the production rule is determined by a combination of bits in the genetic algorithm chromosome.

The base or minimum Petri net that is constructed using the <root> production rule consists of a single place, two transitions, and an arc that connects each transition to the place. Multiple calls to the production rule <expr> by the genetic algorithm chromosome can build any connected Petri net. In addition, the number of times the Petri net is to be iterated is selected with the nonterminal <net_iterations>. Many other production rules define the arc weights, the genotype-dependent arcs and transitions, the number of initial tokens in a place, the place capacity, etc. All decisions made in the building of the Petri net model are made by each subsequent bit or combination of bits in the genetic algorithm chromosome. The complete grammar is too large for detailed presentation here but can be obtained from the authors upon request.

For the present study, we modified the grammar such that the initial Petri net must have at least one arc and/or transition that is dependent on genotypes from each DNA sequence variation in the genetic model. We also evaluated a grammar that specifies a Petri net in which at least two arcs and/or transitions are dependent on genotypes from each DNA sequence variation.

5.3 The Fitness Function

Once a Petri net model is constructed using the BNF grammar, as instructed by the genetic algorithm chromosome, the model fitness is determined. As described in detail by Moore and Hahn [10,11], this is carried out by executing the Petri net model for each combination of genotypes in the genetic dataset and comparing the final token counts at a defined place to a threshold constant to determine the risk assignments. The optimal threshold is determined by systematically evaluating different threshold constant. Fitness of the Petri net model is determined by comparing the high risk and low risk assignments made by the Petri net to those from the given nonlinear gene-gene interaction model (e.g. see Figure 1). Fewer inconsistencies are associated with a better fitness. Ideally, the risk assignments made by the Petri net are perfectly consistent with those in the genetic model.

5.4 The Genetic Algorithm Parameters

Details of the genetic algorithm are given by Moore and Hahn [11]. Briefly, each genetic algorithm chromosome consisted of 14 32-bit bytes. In implementing the grammar, it is possible to reach the end of a chromosome with an incomplete instance of the grammar. To complete the instance, chromosome wrap-around was used [26]. In other words, the instance of the grammar was completed be reusing the chromosome as many times as was necessary.

We ran the genetic algorithm a total of 100 times with different random seeds for each gene-gene interaction model. Each run consisted of a maximum of 800 generations. The genetic algorithm was stopped when a model with a classification error of zero was discovered. We used a parallel search strategy of 10 demes, each with a population size of 2000, for a total population size of 20,000. A best chromosome migrated from each deme to all other demes every 25 generations. The recombination probability was 0.6 while the mutation probability was 0.02.

6 Results

The grammatical evolution algorithm was run a total of 100 times using each grammar for each of the two high-order, nonlinear gene-gene interaction models. For genetic model one, the modified grammatical evolution strategy yielded five perfect Petri net models when grammar one was used and 13 when grammar two was used. For genetic model two, eight and nine perfect Petri net models were discovered using grammars one and two, respectively. These results are in contrast to the grammar of Moore and Hahn [11] that yielded no perfect Petri nets for the first genetic model and only one perfect Petri net for the second genetic model.

Table 1 below summarizes the mode (i.e. most common) and range of the number of places, arcs, transitions, and conditionals that define the genotype-dependencies of the elements in the best Petri net models found across the 100 runs for each model using each of the grammars. For each gene-gene interaction model, most Petri net models discovered using either grammar consisted of one place and a minimum of four transitions, five arcs, and six elements that are conditional on genotype. In general, these Petri net models were larger than those described by Moore and Hahn [11] due to the improved grammar. Figure 2 illustrates example Petri net architectures that were discovered by the grammatical evolution algorithm using each grammar for each genetic model.

Table 1. Summary of the distribution (mode and range) of the number of different Petri net elements identified across 100 grammatical evolution runs using both grammars for the two nonlinear gene-gene interaction models.

	Mode (range) number of Petri net elements			
	Grammar 1		Grammar 2	
Petri net	Model 1	Model 2	Model 1	Model 2
Place	1 (1-2)	1 (1-2)	1 (1-2)	1 (1-2)
Arc	5 (5-8)	5 (5-7)	8 (8-9)	8 (8-10)
Transition	4 (2-6)	4 (2-6)	6 (3-8)	5 (3-8)
Conditional	7 (3-10)	6 (3-10)	10 (7-14)	9 (7-12)

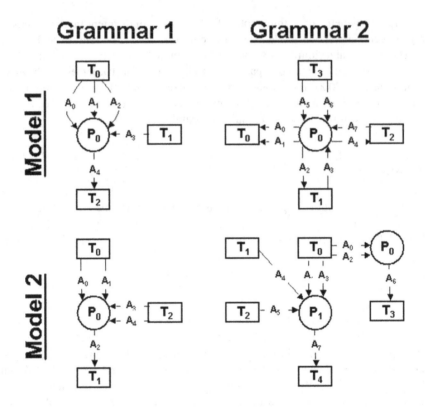

Fig. 2. Examples of Petri net architectures discovered using each grammar for each genetic model.

7 Discussion

Moore and Hahn [9,10] have previously developed a grammatical evolution approach to the discovery of discrete dynamic systems models that were consistent with genotype-specific distributions of disease risk for combinations of DNA sequence variations. These initial studies demonstrated that the grammatical evolution approach routinely identified Petri net models that are perfectly consistent with the high-risk and low-risk assignments for each combination of genotypes with no classification error when the genetic models consisted of two DNA sequence variations. However, Moore and Hahn [11] showed that this approach had limited success when extended to models of three DNA sequence variations. The reduced performance was largely due to an exponential increase in the number of genotype combinations from nine with two DNA sequence variations to 27 with three. The goal of the present study was to determine whether modification of the grammar used in Petri net construction could improve the performance. Indeed, we showed that a grammar requiring each DNA sequence variation to impact at least two Petri net elements significantly improved the performance. In fact, across 100 runs for each model the algorithm discovered 9-13 perfect models.

What is the next step for this modeling approach? Although the Petri net strategy identified perfect models, it did not do so routinely. The next step is to further optimize the grammatical evolution search in order to identify perfect models on every run. This will be necessary if this approach is to be extended to even higher-order genetic models. Additional changes to the grammar in addition to changes to the genetic algorithm parameters will be explored and evaluated.

It is increasingly recognized that nonlinear interactions among multiple genes are likely to play an important role in susceptibility to common, complex human diseases [4]. This is partly due to the inherent complexity of genetic and biochemical networks. Understanding how interactions at the biochemical level manifest themselves as interactions among genes at the population level, will provide a basis for understanding the role of genes in disease susceptibility. Making this hierarchical connection may ultimately lead to an understanding of complex biological systems that will facilitate new treatment and prevention strategies.

Acknowledgements. This work was supported by National Institutes of Health grants HL65234, HL65962, GM31304, AG19085, and AG20135. We would like to thank two anonymous referees for their very thoughtful c

References

1. Bateson, W.: Mendel's Principles of Heredity. Cambridge University Press, Cambridge (1909).
2. Wright, S.: The role of inbreeding, crossbreeding and selection in evolution. Proceedings of the 6th international Congress on Genetics 1 (1932) 356-66
3. Wright, S.: Physiological and evolutionary theories of codominance. American Naturalist 68 (1934) 25-53
4. Moore, J.H. The ubiquitous nature of epistasis in determining susceptibility to common human diseases. Human Heredity 56 (2003) 73-82
5. Moore, J.H., Williams, S.M.: New strategies for identifying gene-gene interactions in hypertension. Annals of Medicine 34 (2002) 88-95
6. Ritchie, M.D., Hahn, L.W., Roodi, N., Bailey, L.R., Dupont, W.D., Plummer, W.D., Parl, F.F. and Moore, J.H.: Multifactor dimensionality reduction reveals high-order interactions among estrogen metabolism genes in sporadic breast cancer. American Journal of Human Genetics 69 (2001) 138-147
7. Ritchie, M.D., Hahn, L.W., Moore, J.H.: Power of multifactor dimensionality reduction for detecting gene-gene and gene-environment interactions. Genetic Epidemiology 24 (2003) 150-7
8. Hahn, L.W., Ritchie, M.D., Moore, J.H.: Multifactor dimensionality reduction software for detecting gene-gene and gene-environment interactions. Bioinformatics 19 (2003) 376-82

9. Moore, J.H., Hahn, L.W. Grammatical evolution for the discovery of Petri net models of complex genetic systems. In: Cantu-Paz et al., editors, Genetic and Evolutionary Computation – GECCO 2003. Lecture Notes in Computer Science 2724 (2003) 2412-13

10. Moore, J.H., Hahn, L.W. Evaluation of a discrete dynamic systems approach for modeling the hierarchical relationship between genes, biochemistry, and disease susceptibility. *Discrete and Continuous Dynamical Systems: Series B* 4 (2003) 275-87

11. Moore, J.H., Hahn, L.W. Petri net modeling of high-order genetic systems using grammatical evolution. *BioSystems* 72 (2003) 177-86

12. Moore, J.H., Hahn, L.W., Ritchie, M.D., Thornton, T.A., White, B.C: Application of genetic algorithms to the discovery of complex genetic models for simulation studies in human genetics. In: W.B.Langdon, E. Cantu-Paz, K. Mathias, R. Roy, D. Davis, R. Poli, K. Balakrishnan, V. Honavar, G. Rudolph, J. Wegener, L. Bull, M.A. Potter, A.C. Schultz, J.F. Miller, E. Burke, and N. Jonoska, editors, Proceedings of the Genetic and Evolutionary Computation Conference. Morgan Kaufmann Publishers, San Francisco (2002)

13. Desel, J., Juhas, G.: What is a Petri net? Informal answers for the informed reader. In H. Ehrig, G. Juhas, J. Padberg, and G. Rozenberg, editors, Unifying Petri Nets, Lecture Notes in Computer Science 2128, pp 1-27. Springer (2001)

14. Goss, P.J., Peccoud, J.: Quantitative modeling of stochastic systems in molecular biology by using stochastic Petri nets. Proceedings of the National Academy of Sciences USA 95 (1998) 6750-5

15. Falconer, D.S., Mackay, T.F.C: Introduction to Quantitative Genetics, 4th edition, Longman, Essex (1996)

16. Fogel, L.J. Autonomous automata. Industrial Research 4 (1962) 14-19

17. Fogel, L.J., Owens, A.J., Walsh, M.J. Artificial Intelligence through Simulated Evolution. John Wiley, New York (1966).

18. Rechenberg, I. Cybernetic solution path of an experimental problem. Royal Aircraft Establishment, Farnborough, U.K., Library Translation No. 1122 (1965).

19. Schwefel, H.-P. Kybernetische Evolution als Strategie der experimentellen Forschung in der Stromungstechnik. Diploma Thesis, Technical University of Berlin (1965).

20. Holland, J.H. Adaptive plans optimal for payoff-only environments. In: Proceedings of the 2nd Hawaii International Conference on Systems Sciences. University of Hawaii, Honolulu (1969) 917-920.

21. Holland, J.H. Adaptation in Natural and Artificial Systems. University of Michigan Press, Ann Arbor (1975).

22. Goldberg, D.E.: Genetic Algorithms in Search, Optimization, and Machine Learning. Reading: Addison-Wesley (1989)

23. Koza, J.R.: Genetic Programming: On the Programming of Computers by Means of Natural Selection. The MIT Press, Cambridge London (1992)

24. Koza, J.R., Mydlowec, W., Lanza, G., Yu, J., Keane, M.A. Reverse engineering of metabolic pathways from observed data using genetic programming. Pacific Symposium on Biocomputing 6 (2001) 434-45

25. Kitagawa, J., Iba, H. Identifying metabolic pathways and gene regulation networks with evolutionary algorithms. In: Evolutionary Computation and Bioinformatics. Fogel, G.B., Corne, D.W., editors. Morgan Kaufmann Publishers, San Francisco (2003) 255-278.

26. O'Neill, M., Ryan, C.: Grammatical evolution. IEEE Transactions on Evolutionary Computation 5 (2001) 349-358

27. Marcotty, M., Ledgard, H.: The World of Programming Languages. Springer-Verlag, Berlin (1986)

Two-Step Genetic Programming for Optimization of RNA Common-Structure

Jin-Wu Nam[1,2], Je-Gun Joung[1,2], Y.S. Ahn[4], and Byoung-Tak Zhang[1,2,3]

[1] Graduate Program in Bioinformatics
[2] Center for Bioinformation Technology (CBIT)
[3] Biointelligence Laboratory, School of Computer Science and Engineering
Seoul National University, Seoul 151-742, Korea
[4] Altenia Corporation, Korea
{jwnam, jgjoung, ysahn, btzhang}@bi.snu.ac.kr

Abstract. We present an algorithm for identifying putative non-coding RNA (ncRNA) using an RCSG (RNA Common-Structural Grammar) and show the effectiveness of the algorithm. The algorithm consists of two steps: structure learning step and sequence learning step. Both steps are based on genetic programming. Generally, genetic programming has been applied to learning programs automatically, reconstructing networks, and predicting protein secondary structures. In this study, we use genetic programming to optimize structural grammars. The structural grammars can be formulated as rules of tree structure including function variables. They can be learned by genetic programming. We have defined the rules on how structure definition grammars can be encoded into function trees. The performance of the algorithm is demonstrated by the results obtained from the experiments with RCSG of tRNA and 5S small RNA.

1 Introduction

The universe of functionally important non-transcribed RNAs is rapidly expanding but their systematic identifications in genomes remain challenging. A number of non-coding RNA (ncRNA) genome screening approaches have been reported in the literature, including composition, sequence and structure similarity-based and comparative genomics [1], [2], [3]. For example, some focus on secondary structure prediction for a single sequence and some aim at finding a global alignment of multiple sequences. Yet other groups predict the structure based on free energy minimization or make comparative sequence analyses to determine the structure. However, these methods are limited to sets of short sequence or require the structural information of some known sequences [4]. Also these approaches usually use only positive data to learn a model and there are no doubts that these methods have a weak constitution for noise. To overcome these limitations, we have tried to develop a general method. One of these general methods is learning and optimization of RNA common structure [5]. Most ncRNAs have low sequence similarity but high structure similarity [6] making it suitable for using common-structure for identification of putative ncRNAs [4], [7].

G.R. Raidl et al. (Eds.): EvoWorkshops 2004, LNCS 3005, pp. 73–83, 2004.
© Springer-Verlag Berlin Heidelberg 2004

Searching for these common-structures is a crucial step to identify similar new functional ncRNAs in genome. Recently, some researches have various methods for finding common-structure. For instance, hidden Markov models and genetic algorithm have been applied to search common structure [7], [8]. However, these methods have two great limitations: first, they are not at the level to use as applications, and second, they are not based on learning from structure, thus, unable to find distant homologies.

On the other hand, some research groups have developed the structural grammar, which is context free type [9], [10], [11]. Using the structural grammar, we can easily and formally express RNA secondary structures. Macke et al. introduced the structure definition language, which is used in RNAMotif [12]. The language can not only easily represent various RNA secondary structure elements such as loop, bulge, stem and mispair, but also include some sequence features such as conserved motif and mismatch number. This structure definition language allows abstraction of the structural pattern into a 'descriptor' with a pattern language so that it can give detailed information regarding base pairing, length and motif. In addition, these structural grammar and structure definition language can be applied to learning the common-structure. The results of the learning represent RNA common-structural grammars (RCSGs). There are various approaches to learning the RCSGs but we apply genetic programming, a kind of evolutionary algorithms, with focus on two steps, structural learning step and motif learning step.

Genetic programming is an automated method for creating a working genetic program, which is called individual and generally represented by tree structure, from a high-level problem statement of a problem [13]. A genetic tree consists of elements from a function set and a terminal set. Function symbols appear as internal nodes. Terminal symbols are used to denote actions taken by the program. Genetic programming does this by genetically breeding a population of genetic programs using the principles of Darwinian natural selection and biologically inspired operations. Genetic programming uses crossover and mutation as the transformation operators, which can endow variation to genotype, to change candidate solutions into new candidate solutions [13].

We optimize the RCSG of fly tRNA and eukaryotic 5S small rRNA using our application of genetic programming and present the result of evaluation of our method for identifying mouse tRNA and 5S small rRNA.

2   Materials and Methods

2.1   Genetic Programming to Optimize RNA Common-Structural Grammar

To identify the putative ncRNAs in genome database, we have tried to find common-structure conserved among ncRNAs. We have implemented a program for learning the common-structure, which is devised by genetic programming. We call the program esRCSG, evolutionary search for RNA Common-Structural Grammar. The algorithm of esRCSG is summarized as a pseudo-code in Figure 1. The algorithm

```
begin                    /* Structural Learning */
    t = 0                /* generation */
    initialize P(t)      /* population */
    convert P(t)         /* tree to grammar*/
    evaluate P(t)
    while (not termination-condition) do
    begin
        S = S + above(P(t))                  /* Top group for Seq learning*/
        t = t+1
        select P(t) from P(t-1)       /* selection */
        crossover-mutate P(t) except Best  /* genetic operators */
        convert P(t)
        evaluate P(t)                 /* fitness function */
        if (local search)
            while (not termination-condition) do
                j = j + 1
                Pⱼ(t) = mutate P(t)
                    if (evaluate P(t) < evaluate Pⱼ(t) )
                        P(t) = Pⱼ(t)
    end
end
w = wordwise(training data)
begin                    /* Learning of Sequence */
    t = 0                /* generation */
    initialize S(t) from S with w    /* population */
    convert S(t)
    evaluate S(t)
    while (not termination-condition) do
    begin
        t = t+1
        select S(t) from S(t-1)            /* selection */
        mutate S(t) for only seq. except Best  /* genetic operators */
        convert S(t)
        evaluate S(t)
    end
end
```

Fig. 1. The pseudo-code for RCSG optimization algorithm. The algorithm consists of two steps: (1) learning RCSG from a set of training data, known miRNA precursors without sequence-related variables (such as "seq" and "mismatch"); (2) Optimizing RCSG which is learned in structural learning by incorporating the sequence-related variables. The "word-wise" method randomly splits sequences of training data set into 7-mer words. Initialization of this step is accomplished by incorporating the words into RCSGs that are learned in structural learning.

consists of two-step; a structural learning which optimizes only tree structure of grammar without sequence and a learning of sequence that specifies RCSGs of structural learning by incorporating a word, fragment of sequence, into the RCSGs. Both steps (1) (2) are implementations (or instances) of genetic programming and both share many of the procedures. The common procedures of (1) and (2) can be described as follows: (a) initialize the population with randomly generated trees; (b) convert all function trees into structural grammars; (c) calculate the fitness, specificity, sensitivity, and complexity for all grammars with the positive and negative training data set; (d) evaluate all structural grammars in terms of the sensitivity, specificity and complexity; (e) using ranking selection, select function trees that will generate offspring (next generation); (f) apply variations, such as mutation and crossover, with the selected function trees; (g) Iterate steps (b) through (f) for the user-defined number of generations. There are two differences between two steps; the structural learning includes a local search procedure; the learning of sequence uses the wordwise method and utilizes the word to initializes the population. In addition, structural learning step uses mutation and crossover as variation operators to change a tree structure but learning of sequence uses only mutation to change the sequence and the number of mismatch without changing tree structure.

Individual representation. In order to convert structural grammars into function trees, we have defined the function f1, f2 and root as shown in Figure 2a. These functions can be formulated by some expression rules (Figure 2a). Therefore, using the expression rules, we can represent the structural grammars (Figure 2c) as function trees (Figure 2b). Thus, we can use the function trees as individuals of genetic programming because one of the characteristics of genetic programming is that individuals are represented by tree structures.

To avoid creation of invalid structural grammars, function trees have some constraints on the order of the function and the terminal node. First, f2 function should not appear consecutively in the same depth of the tree, contiguous f2 functions can be considered as only one. Second, f2 function can only appear as terminal node to terminate recursive generation of function tree. Finally, variables 'minlen' and 'maxlen' should always come in pair and should not coexist with variable 'len.'

Population initialization. An initial population is randomly created with some constraints about function tree as described above. The initial population contains various function trees because there is no limitation in the number of nodes and the width of tree. That makes it possible to cover a wide range for searching start point. The broad coverage at start point is one of the major reasons the esRCSG is efficient for searching optimal solution.

Fitness function. The fitness function (Equation 1) is defined by using specificity, sensitivity and the complexity that are defined at Equation (4).

$$Fitness = spC * Specificity + stC * Sensitivity - Complexity \qquad (1)$$

$$spC + stC = 1 \qquad (2)$$

Two parameters, spC and stC were added as a way to regulate the effects of specificity and sensitivity. To normalize the fitness, the sum of spC and stC is always 1 (Equation 2). The parameters decide the trade-off between the specificity and the sensitivity on the fitness function.

The complexity, which is a negative factor to the fitness function, controls the growing of the tree structures. Without the complexity term, the size of the tree does not converge to a minimum description length where the tree has best efficiency and can grow infinitely in evolving the trees. To overcome that size problem, we make

$Comp_i^j$ include the node number and the depth of jth tree on ith generation (Equation 3). Equation (4) describes the definition of *Complexity* of jth tree on ith generation.

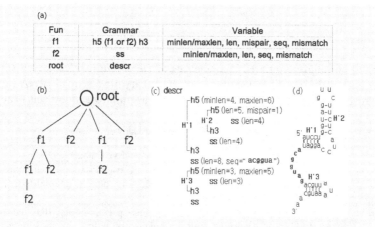

Fig. 2. (a): Function f1 generates recursively structural grammar, including one helix structure and either f1 or f2 as next deviation. Function f2 only represents ss (single strand), which means loop, bulge and single strand. Both f1 and f2 contain some variables, which measure structural information such as the length of helix (len), the number of pair (mispair) and mismatch, and sequence (seq). (b): A function tree to which can be converted into structural grammar (c): The child nodes of root in (b) conform to the first indentation of (c) and the nodes of second depth conform to the second indentation of (c). One helix that consists of the pair of h5-h3, h means helix, 5 and 3 mean 5' end and 3' end) (d): Secondary RNA structure is represented by structural grammar (c). H1, H2 and H3 in (c) and (d) are helix structures.

$$Comp_i^j = TreeDepth_i^j \times 10 + NodeNum_i^j \qquad (3)$$

$$Complexity_i^j = \frac{1}{(NS+PS)^2} \times \frac{Comp_i^j}{Comp_{i-1}^{best}} \qquad (4)$$

where *Complexity* is normalized by square of the number of training data set ($NS + PS$). *NS* is the number of negative training data set (see Table 1) and *PS* is the number of positive training data set (see Table 1). $Complexity_i^j$ depends on $Comp_{i-1}^{best}$ which is *Comp* of the best individual (tree) on (i-1)th generation. That dependency makes the trees have the minimum *Comp* as the progress of generation. Finally, the size of the best tree on last generation is converged into minimum length. This is the effect of the Occam's razor [14] of the complexity factor in our fitness function.

Variation. The variation operators are applied so that each descendent will have a different tree structure relative to the parents. The first operator to perturb the tree is the mutation. The mutation changes the value of the function variable by a random variable drawn from Poisson distribution. The crossover exchanges each sub-tree in two parent trees via single-point recombination to generate two new offspring trees. In the crossover, two parent function trees are selected at random from the population and then each single recombination point is selected at random from the each parent.

2.2 Dataset

We applied our algorithm to tRNA sequences of *Drosophila melanogaster* (available at http:// www.ncbi.nlm.nih.gov/entrez) and the eukaryotic 5S small rRNA (available at http://rose.man.poznan.pl/5SData/5SRNA.html) as training and test sets (Table 1).

Table 1. Training and Test Dataset.

	Positive Dataset		Negative Dataset
Training set		50 tRNAs	200 sequences; hairpins, pseudo-knots, IRE, consecutive hairpins, miRNA precursors, bulges, internal loops, rRNA, and fragment of mRNA
		50 rRNAs	200 sequences; hairpins, pseudo-knots, IRE, consecutive hairpins, miRNA precursors, bulges, internal loops, tRNA, and fragment of mRNA
Test set		100 tRNAs	290 sequences, negative data like training set
		100 rRNAs	290 sequences, negative data like training set

Negative data set consists of some classes; linear sequences that are extracted from mRNA and simple secondary structure elements such as IRE (Iron-responsive element), pseudo-knots, hairpins, bulges and internal loops. Also negative data set includes ncRNAs except itself. The negative data set is a negative rudder to decide the direction of learning. Hence, the negative data have to be collected carefully and the distribution by the classes of those has to be considered.

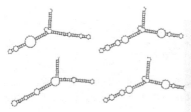

Fig. 3. The secondary structures of eukaryotic 5S small rRNA, these structures were drawn by RNAfold of Vienna package.

3 Results

3.1 RCSG of 5S Small rRNA by One-Step Learning

We show the result of 5S small rRNA, one of ncRNAs, preceding the result of tRNA. First, we looked into the secondary structure of four 5S small rRNAs within the positive training set, which are eukaryotic 5S small rRNAs. Figure 3 shows the secondary structure, which are predicted by RNAfold, of the rRNAs. As the results show, the common structure of 5S small rRNAs in training data should have two stem structures. To optimize RCSG of 5S small rRNA, esRCSG uses the positive training set (= 50) and negative training data set (= 200) as Table 1. The optimized RCSG is represented in the Figure 4(a) and is learned using only structural learning step. It is optimized under the parameters as Figure 4(b) and it is the best solution learned from four trainings (Sensitivity = 0.94;

(a) descr

```
ss(len=30)
    h5(len=7, mispair=5)
        h5(len=1, mispair=1)
            h5(mispair=2)
                ss (len=30)
            h3
            ss(minlen=5, maxlen=21 )
    h3
    h5(mispair=1)
        ss(minlen=5, maxlen=22 )
    h3
```

(b)

Data	50 5s small rRNAs
Population #	100 individuals
Generation #	30 iterations
spC	0.95
stC	0.05
Sensitivity	0.94
Specificity	0.98
Fitness	0.95

Fig. 4. (a): The optimal RCSG of 5S small rRNA for structural learning; (b): The setting of the parameters and the best values for training.

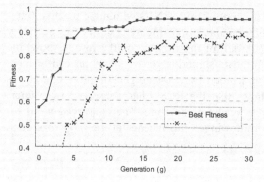

Fig. 5. The plot of the best fitness and the average in 5S small rRNA experiments.

Specificity = 0.98; Fitness = 0.95). However, the values of the variables of the best RCSG have broader range than we expected. It means that the RCSG may be not optimal actually. Thus, to probe the local optima, we have applied the local search, by decreasing the values of the variables gradually.

To analyze the change of the best fitness according to the iterations, we measure the best fitness for each generation (Figure 5). Based on the results, the best fitness reaches a saturation point (0.95) at about thirteenth generation. It is because the searching problem of RCSG for 5S small rRNA is not complex. In most experiments, the esRCSG is used to detect best RCSG before the fifteenth generation. Also, because we apply the elitism during the selection, we can guarantee the best fitness in the last generation. The average fitness also is increased during iteration of esRCSG gradually.

On the other hand, we have searched for the RCSG under several different parameter conditions by varying *spC* and *stC*. We found that the trade-off between specificity and sensitivity was considerably important in searching for the optimum solution, but the population size was not directly related with the problem. In the results, we detected the best solution at *spC* (= 0.95) and *stC* (= 0.05). To assess the optimized RCSG, we evaluated it with the test set of 5S small rRNAs. The sensitivity was 0.83 and the specificity was 0.86 in the results.

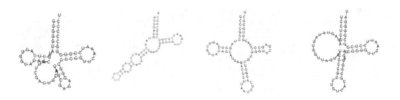

Fig. 6. The secondary structures of *drosophila melanogaster* tRNAs, these structures were drawn by RNAfold of Vienna package. We applied free energy minimum approach with rescale energy parameter to temperature 37°C.

3.2 RCSG of tRNAs by Two-Step Learning

First, we looked into the secondary structure of four tRNAs within the positive training set, which are tRNAs of *drosophila melanogaster*. Figure 6 shows the secondary structure, which are predicted by RNAfold, of the tRNAs. As the results show, the common structure of tRNAs in training data should have two stems instead of three stems. The RCSG of tRNAs, which is learned by two-step genetic programming, is represented as follow. The result shows that the RCSG has conserved two stems, bulge structure and conserved motif as common structure. The conserved motif includes 7 nucleotides, "gaucacu" with allowing 3 mismatches at the loop of second stem loop structure.

```
<Best RCSG for tRNA>
 descr
     h5 ( mispair=2 )
             h5 ( mispair=3 )
                     ss ( len=10 )
             h3
             h5 ( mispair=1 )
                     ss ( len=24, seq="gaucacu", mismatch=3 )
             h3
             ss (minlen = 2, maxlen = 15)
     h3
```

```
<Training>                                    <Test>
Step1_#Structural Learning results           Specificity = 0.946
      Fitness = 0.957                         Sensitivity = 0.840
      Specificity = 0.957
      Sensitivity = 0.931
Step2_#Sequence Learning results
      Fitness = 0.959
      Specificity = 0.964
      Sensitivity = 0.870
```

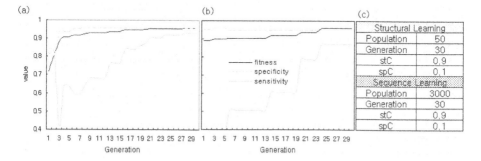

Fig. 7. The results of two-step genetic programming. (a): The plot of the obtained values during structural learning step, (b): The plot of the obtained values during sequence learning step, (c): The optimized parameters for two steps genetic programming.

Through two-step genetic programming, the sensitivity of the optimized RCSG is diminished but the fitness and specificity of the optimized RCSG increased. The results show sequence learning, the second step, is efficient to gain the specificity. High specificity is important in our study because higher specificity produces less false specificity, sensitivity with the test data as mentioned in the table 1. The results show positive and experimental errors. Next, to validate the optimized RCSG, we measured that the specificity and the sensitivity which are presented in the training rarely change in the test. It means that our algorithm is very efficient for identification of putative ncRNA. Figure 7 shows the change of the best fitness, specificity and sensitivity according to generation in both structural learning step (Figure 7a) and sequence learning step (Figure 7b). Also, we were able to conclude that the specificity converged more quickly than the sensitivity due to high spC (=0.9) parameter.

4 Conclusions

In this study, we suggested an efficient approach for searching of a RCSG with ncRNA sequences using genetic programming, which is of evolutionary computation. With fly tRNA sequences and eukaryotic 5S small rRNAs, our learning algorithm, application of genetic programming, learned distinctive RCSGs. The optimized

RCSGs well reflected common structures of training set and could be applied as common structure model for searching of putative ncRNAs.

We can derive two contributions from our new approach. The first contribution is that we have proven the possibility of learning common-structural grammar from structurally unknown sequences through genetic programming. We believe that our approach can be adapted for various applications such as RNA similarity search and putative RNA identification. The second contribution is that we have shown that it is possible to design and generate the RNA structural grammar automatically. Designing of the RNA structural grammar according to the RNA sequences is a difficult problem. Therefore, the system generating structural grammar may be considerably useful.

Acknowledgments. This research was supported by the National Research Laboratory (NRL) Program and the Systems Biology (SysBio) Program of the Ministry of Science and Technology and the BK21-IT Program of the Ministry of Education.

References

1. Rivas E. and Eddy S.R. A dynamic programming algorithm for RNA structure prediction including pseudoknots. *J. Mol. Biol.*, (1999) 285:2053-2068.
2. Zuker M. On finding all suboptimal foldings of an RNA molecule. *Science,* (1989) 244:48-52.
3. Eddy S.R. and Durbin R. RNA sequence analysis using covariance models. *Nucleic Acids Research*, (1994) 22:2079-2088.
4. Gorodkin J., Stricklin S.L. and Stormo G.D. Discovering common stem-loop motifs in unaligned RNA sequences. *Nucleic Acids Reearch*, (2001) 29:2135-2144.
5. Perriquet O., Touzet H. and Dauchet M. Finding the common structure shared by two homolous RNAs. *Bioinformatics*, (2003) 19:108-116.
6. Gary B. Fogel, V. William Porto, Dana G. Weekers, David B. Fogel, Richard H. Griffey, John A. McNeil, Elena Lesnik, David J. Ecker and Rangarajan Sampath. Discovery of RNA structural elements using evolutionary computation. *Nucleic Acids Research*, (2002) 30:5310-5317.
7. Jih-H. Chen, Shu-Yun Le and Jacob V. Maizel. Prediction of common secondary structures of RNAs : a genetic algorithm approach. *Nucleic Acids Research*, (2000) 28:991-999.
8. Sakakibara Y. Pair Hidden Markov models on tree structures *Bioinformatics*, (2003) 19:i232-240.
9. Cai L., Malmberg R.L., Wu Y. Stochastic modeling or RNA pseudoknotted structures: a grammatical approach. *Bioinformatics,* (2003) 19:i66-i73.
10. Sakakibara Y., Brwon M., Hughey, R., Mian I.S., Sjolander K., Underwood R.C. and Haussler D. Stochastic context-free grammars for tRNA modeling. *Nucleic Acids Research*, (1994) 22:5112-5120.
11. Knudsen B. and Hein J. RNA secondary structure prediction using stochastic context-free grammars and evolutionary history. *Bioinformatics*, (1999) 15:446-454.

12. Thomas J. Macke, David J. Ecker, Robin R. Gutell, Daniel Gautheret, David A. Case and Rangarajan Sampath. RNAMotif, an RNA secondary structure definition and search algorithms. *Nucleic Acids Research*, (2001) 29:4724-4735.

13. Koza J.R. *Genetic Programming: On the Programming of Computers by Means of Natural Selection.* MIT Press, (1992).

14. Zhang B.-T., Ohm P., and Mühlenbein H. Evolutionary neural trees for modeling and predicting complex systems. *Engineering Applications of Artificial Intelligence*, (1997) 10:473-483.

Evolutionary Algorithms for Optimal Control in Fed-Batch Fermentation Processes

Miguel Rocha[1], José Neves[1], Isabel Rocha[2], and Eugénio C. Ferreira[2]

[1] Departamento de Informática – Universidade do Minho
Campus de Gualtar, 4710-057 Braga PORTUGAL
{mrocha,jneves}@di.uminho.pt
[2] Centro de Engenharia Biológica - Universidade do Minho
Campus de Gualtar, 4710-057 Braga - PORTUGAL
{irocha,ecferreira}@deb.uminho.pt

Abstract. In this work, *Evolutionary Algorithms (EAs)* are used to achieve optimal feedforward control in a recombinant bacterial fed-batch fermentation process, that aims at producing a bio-pharmaceutical product. Three different aspects are the target of the optimization procedure: the feeding trajectory (the amount of substrate introduced in a bioreactor per time unit), the duration of the fermentation and the initial conditions of the process. A novel *EA* with variable size chromosomes and using real-valued representations is proposed that is capable of simultaneously optimizing the aforementioned aspects. Outstanding productivity levels were achieved and the results are validated by practice.

Keywords: Bio-engineering processes, Fed-batch fermentation optimization, Variable size chromosomes, Real-valued representations

1   Introduction

A number of valuable products such as recombinant proteins, antibiotics and amino-acids are produced using fermentation techniques and thus there is an enormous economic incentive to optimize such processes. However, these are typically very complex, involving different transport phenomena, microbial components and biochemical reactions. Furthermore, the nonlinear behavior and time-varying properties make bioreactors difficult to control with traditional techniques. Under this context, there is the need to consider quantitative mathematical models, capable of describing the process dynamics and the interrelation among relevant variables. Aditionally, robust optimization techniques must deal with the model's complexity, the environment constraints and the inherent noise of the experimental process.

Several optimization methods have been applied in this task. It has been shown that, for simple bioreactor systems, the problem can be solved analytically, from the Hamiltonian function, by applying the minimum principle of Pontryagin. However, besides having a problem of singular control, those methodologies become too complex when the number of state variables increases [14].

G.R. Raidl et al. (Eds.): EvoWorkshops 2004, LNCS 3005, pp. 84–93, 2004.

Numerical methods make a distinct approach to dynamic optimization. The gradient algorithms are based on the local sensitivities of the objective function for changes in the values of the control variables, which are used to adjust the control trajectories in order to iteratively improve the objective function [3]. In contrast, dynamic programming methods discretize both time and control variables to a predefined number of values. A systematic backward search method in combination with the simulation of the system model equations is used to find the optimal path through the defined grid. However, in order to achieve a global minimum the computational burden is very high [13].

An alternative approach comes from the use of Evolutionary Algorithms (EAs), which have been used in the past to optimize nonlinear problems with a large number of variables. Previous work has obtained interesting results in the optimization of feeding or temperature trajectories [8][1]. Comparisons with traditional methods have been addressed with favorable results [12][4]. Recent work [6] focused on the feed optimization in the fed-batch culture of insect cells, but uses EAs based on binary representations and only optimizes the maximum densities of a pre-defined set of nutrients.

In this work, a fed-batch recombinant E. coli fermentation process was studied, aimed at producing a bio-pharmaceutical product [10]. In fed-batch fermentations there is an addition of certain nutrients along the process, in order to prevent the accumulation of toxic products, allowing the achievement of higher product concentrations. The purpose is to apply real-valued representation based EAs, with novel features such as variable sized chromosomes, in order to optimize not only some of the fermentation's variables, namely the substrate feeding trajectory and the initial conditions, but also the duration of the fermentation.

2   The Fed-Batch Fermentation Process

Since the advent of the recombinant DNA technology, the bacterium E. coli is the microorganism of choice for the production of the majority of the valuable bio-pharmaceuticals, usually grown under fed-batch mode due to the effect of acetic acid, which is produced when glucose is present above certain concentrations.

During this process the system states change considerably, from a low initial to a very high biomass and product concentration. This dynamic behavior motivates the development of optimization methods to find the optimal input feeding trajectories in order to improve the process. The typical input in this process is the substrate inflow rate as a function of time. One way to evaluate the process performance is the productivity, defined as the units of product (recombinant protein) formed per unit of time. In this case, it is usually related with the final biomass obtained, when the duration of the process is pre-defined.

For the proper optimization of the process, a white box mathematical model was developed, based on differential equations that represent the mass balances of the relevant state variables. The general dynamical model [2] is accepted as representing the dynamics of an n components and m reactions bioprocess.

During the aerobic growth of the bacterium, with glucose as the only added substrate, the microorganism can follow three different metabolic pathways:

- Oxidative growth on glucose:

$$k_1 S + k_5 O \xrightarrow{\mu_1} X + k_8 C \tag{1}$$

- Fermentative growth on glucose:

$$k_2 S + k_6 O \xrightarrow{\mu_2} X + k_9 C + k_3 A \tag{2}$$

- Oxidative growth on acetic acid:

$$k_4 A + k_7 O \xrightarrow{\mu_3} X + k_{10} C \tag{3}$$

where S, O, X, C, A represent glucose, dissolved oxygen, biomass, dissolved carbon dioxide and acetate components, respectively. In the sequel, the same symbols are used to represent the state variables concentrations (in g/kg); μ_1 to μ_3 are time variant specific growth rates that nonlinearly depend on the state variables, and k_i are constant yield coefficients.

The associated dynamical model can be described by the following equations:

$$\frac{dX}{dt} = (\mu_1 + \mu_2 + \mu_3)X - DX \tag{4}$$

$$\frac{dS}{dt} = (-k_1\mu_1 - k_2\mu_2)X + \frac{F_{in,S}S_{in}}{W} - DS \tag{5}$$

$$\frac{dA}{dt} = (k_3\mu_2 - k_4\mu_3)X - DA \tag{6}$$

$$\frac{dO}{dt} = (-k_5\mu_1 - k_6\mu_2 - k_7\mu_3)X + OTR - DO \tag{7}$$

$$\frac{dC}{dt} = (k_8\mu_1 + k_9\mu_2 + k_{10}\mu_3)X - CTR - DC \tag{8}$$

$$\frac{dW}{dt} \simeq F_{in,S} \tag{9}$$

being D the dilution rate, $F_{in,S}$ the substrate feeding rate (in kg/h), W the fermentation weight (in kg), OTR the oxygen transfer rate and CTR the carbon dioxide transfer rate.

Real experiments served as the basis for the model derivation, being conducted in a fermentation laboratory with a 5-L bioreactor, being the experimental results consistent with the model [9]. This model was thus used for the optimization of several relevant features of the process. For optimization purposes, the model simulation was performed, by using the Euler numerical integration method, with a small step size d and a given duration for the process (T_f) measured in hours. Typical values of T_f and d were 25 and 0.005. The kinetic behavior, expressed in the rates μ_1 to μ_3, was given by a specific algorithm based on the state variables, that is out of the scope of the present work but can be found in [9].

3   Evolutionary Algorithms for Feeding Trajectory Optimization

The first approach to the problem was to develop an EA capable of optimizing the feeding trajectory, i.e., to determine the amount of substrate (glucose) to be fed into the bioreactor per time unit ($F_{in,S}$). Real-valued representations were used in order to encode the feeding amounts, since these have proven to be more appropriate than the classical binary ones, in tasks where the purpose is to optimize real valued parameters [5][7].

Thus, each gene will encode the amount of substrate to be introduced into the bioreactor in a given time unit and the genome will be given by the temporal sequence of such values. In this case, the size of the genome is determined based on the final time of the process (T_f) and the discretization step (d) considered in the simulation, being given by the expression: $\frac{T_f}{d}$.

However, this could produce a very large genome (a typical value would be 5000), which would difficult the EA's convergence. Thus, feeding values are defined only at certain equally spaced points, and the remaining values are linearly interpolated. The size of the genome becomes $\frac{T_f}{dp} + 1$, where p stands for the number of points within each interpolation interval. The values used in the experiments described in this section are: $T_f = 25$, $d = 0.005$ and $p = 200$.

There are physical constraints on the amount of substrate that can be introduced per time unit, due to limitations in the feeding pump capacity. Thus, there is the need to impose limits in the gene values, in this particular case defined in the range $[0.0; 0.4]$. In the initial population, each individual is assigned, for each of its genes, a random value in the appropriate range.

The evaluation process, for each individual in the population, measures the quality of the feeding trajectory in terms of the fermentation's productivity. This calculation is achieved by firstly running a simulation of the defined model, given as input the feeding values in the genome. In each simulation, the relevant state variables are initialized with the following values: $X_0 = 5$, $S_0 = 0$, $A_0 = 0$, $W_0 = 3$. The fitness value is then calculated from the final and initial values of the state variables X and W, by the expression $X_f * W_f - X_0 * W_0$ (measured in g).

Regarding the recombination step, both mutation and crossover operators were taken into account. Two mutation operators were used, namely:

- Random Mutation, which replaces one gene by a new randomly generated value, within the range $[min_i, max_i]$ [7]; and
- Gaussian Mutation, which adds to a given gene a value taken from a gaussian distribution, with a zero mean and a standard deviation given by $\frac{max_i - min_i}{4}$ (i.e., small perturbations will be preferred over larger ones).

where $[min_i; max_i]$ is the range of values allowed for gene i. In both cases, an innovation is introduced: the mutation operators are applied to a variable number of genes (a value that is randomly set between 1 and 10 in each application). This operator obtained interesting results in the training of Artificial Neural Networks [11], and its good performance in this context was verified empirically

On the other hand, the following crossover operators were chosen:

- Two-Point and Uniform, two standard Genetic Algorithm operators [7], applied in the traditional way;
- Arithmetical, each gene in the offspring will be a linear combination of the values in the ancestors' chromosomes [7];
- Sum, inspired in Differential Evolution [4], where the offspring genes denote the sum/ subtraction of the ones in the parents.

All operators were constrained to respect the limits of the gene's values, so when a value would be out of range it was replaced by the nearest boundary.

In terms of the EAs setup, the population size was set to 200. The selection procedure is done by converting the fitness value into a linear ranking in the population, and then applying a roulette wheel scheme. In each generation, 50% of the individuals are kept from the previous generation, and 50% are bred by the application of the genetic operators.

The implementation of the proposed EA was based on a general purpose package, developed by the authors in the Java programming language. All experiments reported were run on a PC with a Pentium IV 2.4 GHz processor.

A first set of experiments was conducted in order to find the best set of genetic operators to tackle this problem. All possible combinations of a crossover and a mutation operator were tested, as well as alternatives with one single mutation operator. It must be noticed that, in the proposed EA, genetic operators are selected whenever a new individual is created, based on a given probability. In this case, both crossover and mutation operators were considered to have equal oportunities of breeding offspring. Each run of the EA is stopped after 500 iterations and the results are given in terms of the mean of thirty runs, with the associated 95% confidence intervals. The results are given in Table 1, where the most promising method seems to be the combination of the arithmetical crossover with a random mutation, although there are alternatives with overlapping confidence intervals.

Table 1. Comparison of *EAs* with different genetic operators on the problem of feeding trajectory optimization.

Crossover	Gaussian Mutation	Random Mutation
None	111.6 ± 2.6	128.4 ± 6.1
Two-Point	184.4 ± 4.4	185.3 ± 2.3
Uniform	182.3 ± 2.3	198.3 ± 3.6
Arithmetical	191.3 ± 4.3	200.6 ± 3.1
Sum	103.7 ± 3.2	100.2 ± 3.3

An alternative that contemplates the use of all genetic operators described above was also attempted. In this case each crossover operator is responsible for breeding 12.5% of the offspring and each mutation operator 25%. Testing this alternative a result of 210.4 ± 1.9 was obtained, which is better than all the previous attempts, being the difference statiscally significant. To further evaluate this alternative, the number of generations was increased to 3000, being obtained a new result of 224.4 ± 1.4.

These results are similar to those obtained by two different approaches. The first uses a gradient based algorithm, implemented by the MATLAB optimization toolbox function fmincon (version 2.1); the latter is based on the genetic algorithm toolbox for MATLAB (version 1.7), developed by Polheim at University of Sheffield. However, the computational time taken to achieve results in both cases is clearly superior (between 10 to 100 times) than the ones of the proposed Java-based EA s. As a consequence, more experiments were made possible and statistical significance could be reached. Since that is not the case with the other approaches the results are not given here. Furthermore, it was possible to develop new algorithms to tackle other kinds of , such as the ones described in the following.

The best of the thirty runs will be analyzed in detail, to get an insight of the EA's behavior. The fitness value was 228.0, obtained with the values of $X_f = 50.1$ and $W_f = 4.85$. It is known that a value of $W = 5$ is a physical limit (maximum weight allowed by the fermentation vessel), so the optimal result should set the value of W_f to 5. The value obtained is near, but is still sub-optimal, which can be due to an optimization insufficiency, but can also mean that the initial conditions and/or the duration of the process are not correctly set.

4 Optimization of Initial Conditions

The initial conditions of the experiments were set based on the practicioner's experience and wisdom. However, there is no guarantee that the initial values of the state variables are optimal. So, it was decided to incorporate the initial values of significant state variables in the optimization procedure.

Once each variable has different physical constraints it was necessary to define a genome where the limits are distinct in each position. The variables chosen to be optimized, aditionally to the feeding trajectory, were the initial values of X, W, S and A, with their range of variability given by $X_0 \in [1; 5]$, $W_0 \in [2; 4]$, $S_0 \in [0; 5]$ and $A_0 \in [0; 5]$. In the experiment performed to evaluate this approach, the fitness function, the genetic operators and the EA's setup was kept from the previous section and each run of the EA was stopped after 3000 generations.

The mean of the results obtained was 234.4 (± 1.4), which means a considerable improvement over the previous results. As before the best run will be examined in detail to illustrate the EA s behavior, being the fitness obtained 236.5, with $X_f = 50.3$ and $W_f = 5.0$. As explained before this value for W is highly desirable and an important condition to reach the optimality of the process. The initial values of the state variables, in the best run, were $X_i = 5.0$, $S_i = 0.45$, $A_i = 0.01$ and $W_i = 3.15$. It is believed that the slight difference of values in the W initial's value is determinant to the result obtained, since it is almost unchanged in the other runs.

5   Optimization of the Final Time

The duration of the fermentation is not imposed by any theoretical result, yet is chosen by empirical knowledge, making it possible to optimize its value. In this section, an EA will be proposedfor this task, based on the ones defined above, but considering variable size chromosomes and new genetic operators.

The genetic operators defined in Section 3 were kept: the mutations were unchanged and the crossovers were updated to cope with parents of different sizes. In this case, each of the offspring keeps the size of one parent and for the genes where only one parent is defined (the one with greater length), their value is passed into the corresponding offspring. In the creation of the initial population the individuals are given chromosomes with distinct sizes, randomly selected in a range defined by two parameters: a minimum and a maximum size. Furthermore, two novel mutation operators were defined, in order to allow for the change of the size of individuals during the evolution process:

– G row: consists in the introduction of a new gene into the genome, in a random position, being its value the average of the values of the two neighboring genes.
– Shrink: a randomly selected gene is removed from the genome.

Both operators are only applied when the maximum and minimum size constraints are obbeyed. With the introduction of the new genetic operators, the probabilities used in the experiments are the following: each of the four crossover operators has a probability value of 10%, the random and gaussian mutation keep their probabilities of 25% and the new mutation operators have a probability of 5% each.

Two different experiments were conducted: in the first, only the final time and feeding trajectory are optimized, being the genome made out of the feeding trajectory; in the latter, the initial conditions are also considered a target of optimization, being the initial parameters encoded into the first group of four genes (fixed size), as before, and the remaining of the genome used to code the feeding trajectory (variable size).

The fitness function also has to suffer a slight modification. Indeed, once the time is variable it makes sense to evaluate the productivity of the process per time unit. The fitness of an individual is thus given by the following expression:

$$\frac{X_f * W_f - X_0 * W_0}{T_f}$$

The minimum and maximum duration of the fermentation are set to 20 and 50 hours, respectively. The remaining parameters of the EA are kept unchanged. The results obtained are displayed in Table 2 and compared with the previous ones. In the table, the first column indicates the purpose of the EA, where F stands for feeding trajectory, I for initial conditions and T for final time optimization. The results are given in terms of the newly defined fitness, in order to make a comparison possible, being shown, in the second column, the mean of the thirty runs and the confidence interval and in the third column the best result obtained over all the runs.

Table 2. Comparison of the results obtained by the *EAs* for feeding trajectory, initial conditions and duration optimization.

Optimization aim	Mean and conf.interval	Best result
F	8.98 ± 0.06	9.12
F+I	9.38 ± 0.06	9.46
F+T	9.16 ± 0.09	9.32
F+T+I	9.44 ± 0.05	9.50

From the results, it is possible to conclude that the final time optimization implies some significant improvement over the results of the feeding trajectory optimization. The mean of duration obtained was 26.2 hours, a value slightly higher than the value of 25 (set empirically). The best run results in a process duration of 26 hours, obtaining the values of $X_f = 51.7$ and $W_f = 4.98$. So, comparing with previous results, the final biomass is increased, taking advantage of the extra hour and the final value of W is very near its physical limit.

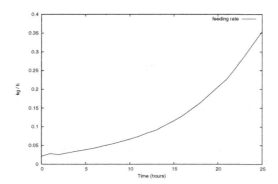

Fig. 1. Feeding trajectory obtained by the *EA* which combines feeding, initial conditions and final time optimization (best run).

A further and more significant improvement is obtained when the initial parameter optimization is added. The duration of the process obtained in all runs was 25 hours, the default value, showing the correctness of the practicioner's choice. Analyzing the results of the best run, the values of X_f and W_f are 50.7 and 5.0, respectively. The initial parameters took values similar to those obtained in the previous section, being worth to notice that $W_i = 3.15$. The feeding trajectory obtained is depicted in Figure 1. It can be noticed the smoothness of the result obtained, without resorting to specially tailored genetic algorithms, such as the ones proposed in [12]. The smoothness is important since it makes easier the physical implementation of the proposed solution.

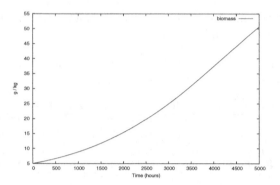

Fig. 2. Biomass trajectory obtained by the *EA* which combines feeding, initial conditions and final time optimization (best run).

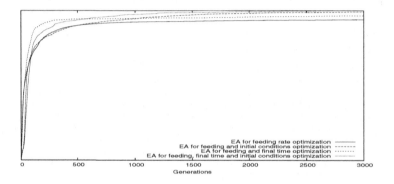

Fig. 3. Plot of the convergence of the different *EAs*.

Making a comparison of the different EA s, their computational performance is quite similar, although the EA s for final time optimization can be dependent on the minimum and maximum values defined. The convergence of the different algorithms is plotted in Figure 3, where it is visible that good results are obtained in about 1000 generations, which means about 15 minutes of computation time.

6   Conclusions and Further Work

In this work an EA, based on real-valued representations and variable size chromosomes was proposed in order to optimize both the feeding trajectory, the initial conditions and the duration of a fermentation process. The results, although based on a simulation model, show that the EA is capable of simultaneously optimizing all the aforementioned aspects, a result that is never been obtained in any study known by the authors. The settings reached by the EA s are quite near the values used in real experiments, being the result of both theoretical knowledge and years of practice. It is remarkable that the EA s are capable of setting, in tens of minutes, a number of parameters that takes years for a practicioner to learn. Therefore, the results of the EA are quite encouraging and its application to these kind of bioprocesses highly recommended.

The quantitative model that serves as a base for the simulations done in this work is based on differential equations. Other types of models have been proposed in literature, namely Fuzzy Rules or Artificial Neural Networks [13]. The testing of the proposed EAs in these settings is desirable. Another area of future research is the consideration of on-line adaptation, being the model of the process updated during the fermentation process, a task that can be also performed by EAs In this case, the good computational performance of the proposed EAs are a benefit, if there is the need to re-optimize the feeding given a new model and values for the state variables measured on-line.

References

1. P. Angelov and R. Guthke. A Genetic-Algorithm-based Approach to Optimization of Bioprocesses Described by Fuzzy Rules. *Bioprocess Engin.*, 16:299–303, 1997.
2. G. Bastin and D. Dochain. *On-line Estimation and Adaptive Control of Bioreactors*. Elsevier Science Publishers, Amsterdam, 1990.
3. A.E. Bryson and Y.C. Ho. *Applied Optimal Control - Optimization, Estimation and Control*. Hemisphere Publication Company, New York, 1975.
4. J.P. Chiou and F.S. Wang. Hybrid Method of Evolutionary Algorithms for Static and Dynamic Optimization Problems with Application to a Fed-batch Fermentation Process. *Computers & Chemical Engineering*, 23:1277–1291, 1999.
5. F. Herrera, M. Lozano, and J. Verdegay. Tackling Real-Coded GAs: Operators and Tools for Behavioral Analysis. *Artif. Intel. Review*, 12:265–319, 1998.
6. R. Marteijn, O. Jurrius, J. Dhont, C. de Gooijer, J. Tramper, and D. Martens. Optimization of a Feed Medium for Fed-Batch Culture of Insect Cells Using a Genetic Algorithm. *Biotechnol Bioeng*, 81:269–278, 2003.
7. Z. Michalewicz. *Genetic Algorithms + Data Structures = Evolution Programs*. Springer-Verlag, USA, third edition, 1996.
8. H. Moriyama and K. Shimizu. On-line Optimization of Culture Temperature for Ethanol Fermentation Using a GA. *Journ. Chem. Tec. Biotec.*, 66:217–222, 1996.
9. I. Rocha. *Model-based strategies for computer-aided operation of recombinant E. coli fermentation*. PhD thesis, Universidade do Minho, 2003.
10. I. Rocha and E.C. Ferreira. On-line Simultaneous Monitoring of Glucose and Acetate with FIA During High Cell Density Fermentation of Recombinant E. coli. *Analytica Chimica Acta*, 462(2):293–304, 2002.
11. M. Rocha, P. Cortez, and J. Neves. Evolutionary Approaches to Neural Network Learning. In *Proc. Portug. Conf. Artif. Intel.-EPIA'2003*. Springer, 2003.
12. J.A. Roubos, G. van Straten, and A.J. van Boxtel. An Evolutionary Strategy for Fed-batch Bioreactor Optimization: Concepts and Performance. *Journal of Biotechnology*, 67:173–187, 1999.
13. A. Tholudur and W.F. Ramirez. Optimization of Fed-batch Bioreactors Using Neural Network Parameters. *Biotechnology Progress*, 12:302–309, 1996.
14. V. van Breusegem and G. Bastin. Optimal Control of Biomass Growth in a Mixed Culture. *Biotechnology and Bioengineering*, 35:349–355, 1990.

Discrete Branch Length Representations for Genetic Algorithms in Phylogenetic Search

Jian Shen and Robert B. Heckendorn

University of Idaho, Moscow ID 83843-1010, USA,
{shen7547,heckendo}@uidaho.edu
http://marvin.ibest.uidaho.edu/~heckendo.html

Abstract. Likelihood analysis for phylogenetics is a well suited domain for optimization by genetic algorithm. A major factor in the performance of genetic algorithms is representation and operators. In this paper we present promising preliminary results on using a discrete set of edge lengths in the phylogenetic trees. We find that discretizing the edge lengths changes the fundamental character of the search and can produce higher quality trees. Our results suggest a search that is more robust to traps in local optima and an opportunity to better control the balance between topology search and edge length search.

1 Introduction

Rapid advances have been made in the field of phylogenetic inferencing using molecular data in the last decade. Most notable is a shift from the purely algorithmic methods to methods based on stochastic optimality criterion. Phylogenetic inferencing is then a search through potential trees, defined by their topologies and branch lengths, for trees that maximize a stochastic score. Unfortunately the total number of distinct unrooted, strictly bifurcating trees for T taxa is intractably large [1]:

$$B(T) = \prod_{i=3}^{T}(2i - 5) \ .$$

Therefore, heuristic search methods must be used to search for the optimal tree for any phylogenetic inference problem with nontrivial number of taxa.

Genetic algorithms (GA), are known for their ability to search very complex fitness landscapes and their unique way of perturbing the current solution by mimicking the recombination and mutation of biological evolution. GAs are a natural choice for heuristic search in the large and complicated tree space. Matsuda [2], Lewis [3], Katoh et al. [4], Lemmon [5], and Brauer et al. [6] have all applied the genetic algorithms to phylogenetic inference. They show that genetic algorithms are a feasible approach to phylogenetic search.

Considering that it is rare that a GA discovers the best known phylogenetic tree [6], there are plenty of opportunities for improving the effectiveness of GAs in phylogenetic inferencing. A critical factor in GA performance is the

G.R. Raidl et al. (Eds.): EvoWorkshops 2004, LNCS 3005, pp. 94–103, 2004.
© Springer-Verlag Berlin Heidelberg 2004

representation of the problem domain and the associated evolutionary operators. Furthermore, empirically determined parameters of GA such as mutation rate can also significantly affect its performance.

In this study, a genetic algorithm is applied to a maximum likelihood measure for inferring phylogenetic relationships using DNA sequence data. Maximum likelihood (ML) is one of the best for phylogenetic inference [1]. It provides a consistent statistical framework that accommodates a wide range of evolutionary factors. It is robust against some violations of its statistical assumptions, and resistant against long-branch attraction [7]. It makes full use of the original character matrix, avoiding the problem of information loss during character transformation which is common for many other popular approaches such as distance matrix methods. But the calculation of ML score is much more computationally intensive than many other methods. Coupled with the hard problem of tree-space searching, the maximum likelihood method is a perfect candidate for applying genetic algorithms.

This paper proposes a new representation for the branch lengths of phylogenetic trees in a GA and associated mutation operator, and studies the affect on performance. Instead of rigorously optimizing branch lengths for each new tree, GAs usually incorporate the branch length optimization into the major genetic evolving cycle by slightly mutating a small proportion of branch lengths of a new tree randomly. Conventionally, the tree topologies are considered a discrete set, while the branch lengths are considered continuous real numbers. Branch lengths for a tree are initially set to a small real number and mutated by multiplying it by a small positive factor. The question is whether this continuous representation of branch lengths could be a possible bottleneck for the efficiency of GA search by causing premature optimization of branch length. If branch lengths are limited to take on values only from a small discrete set of predefined values, and mutation limited to adjacent values in the set could the GA be able to more efficiently search the tree-space, and discover better solutions? Another benefit might be that the discrete encoding would help the GA avoid being trapped in some local optima. Also the granularity and specific values of the discrete encoding become another useful tuning parameter in creating a high performance search of the tree space. Finally, a limited discrete encoding theoretically reduces search space and practically allows us to **precalculate** some evolutionary model computations and compress the representation of cached values.

In this paper we will present preliminary data using GAs to produce phylogenetic trees for two sets of taxa. One, the closely related set of 48 taxa of Drosophila and a more distantly related set of 55 green plants. For both data sets we will compare the performance in terms of number of evaluations and quality of answer for GAs with discretized branch lengths and continuous branch length representations.

2   Materials and Methods

2.1   The Common Genetic Algorithm

In order to do the performance comparison between the two representations, two versions of an otherwise identical program are implemented, with branch lengths in one version being represented by continuous real number, while branch lengths in the other version represented as a fixed set of discrete real numbers. A common program framework (thereafter simply referred to as "the program") implements a typical steady state genetic algorithm which uses Maximum Likelihood to do phylogenetic inferencing using DNA sequence data.

Specifically, the program implements the widely used HKY85 nucleotide substitution model. Since the purpose of the study is to evaluate the effects of a new branch-length representation on GA performance, instead of finding a phylogenetic tree with absolute best Maximum Likelihood score, several simplifications are made in the program. The transition/transversion rate ratio, κ, a parameter of HKY85 model, is fixed at 4.0, instead of being optimized through the genetic evolutionary process. Also the four base frequencies are set to the empirical frequencies calculated from the given DNA sequence data. Models of rate heterogeneity are not implemented.

Before the GA starts to evolve, a population of 64 individuals are created, each of which encodes a potential solution to the problem, in our case, a phylogenetic tree including all given taxa. Each individual directly maps the topology and labeling of a phylogenetic tree as a simple node-based rooted binary tree data structure. Each internal node maintains three pointers, one pointing to the parent node, and the other two connected to its child nodes. A leaf node also contains the taxon name to which it corresponds. Every node, except the root, keeps a real value which indicates the length of the branch leading from the node to its parent. At the beginning of the GA run, all individuals/trees are created randomly. Given an individual/tree and taxa sequences, the ML score can be calculated. The maximum likelihood method itself supplies no ancestry information, but due to the pulley principle [8], the location and existence of a tree root has no effect on ML score evaluation.

Instead of explicitly generating a new population, a steady state GA only maintains one population, and continuously creates new children through genetic evolutionary cycle of selection, crossover, and mutation. Each newly created child replaces one individual in the population. Our implementation replaces the worst individual, the one with the lowest ML score, with the new child. The creation of a new child and evaluation of its ML score is referred to as an evaluation, which is used as the metric to measure GA speed in this study.

For each evaluation, two parent individuals are chosen from the population using tournament selection. Tournament selection first randomly chooses N individuals from a population, and with probability p of picking the best individual among them, and with probability of $1 - p$ of picking the second best individual [9]. The program uses tournament selection of size 10 and of probability 0.8.

Next, the two parent individuals are crossed over with probability of 0.8 to produce a new child. If no crossover occurs, one of the two parents is duplicated as the child. The crossover operation is similar to subtree pruning/regrafting (SPR). A subtree is first cut off from one parent. Next, all leaf nodes that appear on this subtree are pruned from the other parent. Lastly, the subtree is regrafted to a random branch of the pruned parent, producing a new valid phylogenetic tree. This SPR-like crossover operation is basically the same as that used in Lewis' GAML software [3]. Because each individual is directly represented as a binary tree, about half of the branches are exterior branches (branches that lead to a leaf node). Therefore, if we randomly cut off a branch to get the subtree, about half of the time we get a trivial subtree with only one leaf node. The program employs the 90/10 rule commonly used in genetic programming to overcome this problem. The 90/10 rule stipulates that when choosing a branch from a tree, 90% of time, an interior branch should be picked, while 10% for an exterior branch.

The last phase of the evolutionary cycle is for the child to go through topological mutation and branch length mutation. The child will be topologically mutated with probability of 0.2. The topological mutation is exactly the same as SPR branch-swapping. The length of every branch on the child tree will be mutated with a probability of 0.05. The details of branch length representation and mutation for two versions of the program will be discussed later. Now, the newly created child tree is ready to be put back into the population by replacing the the worst individual.

2.2   Branch Length Representations and Mutation

Almost all previous GAs for solving phylogenetic problems have a continuous real number representation for branch length. The continuous branch-length representation version of this program implements this conventional approach. Theoretically, the branch length can be in the range from 0 to ∞, indicating the expected number of substitutions. Commonly, all initial branch lengths are set to a certain small real number, and branch length mutation operator mutates the branch length by multiplying the old branch length by a small positive factor. Typically, this multiplicative factor is drawn from a gamma distribution with mean of 1.0 and a very high value of the shape parameter [3]. Our continuous version sets all initial branch lengths to 0.05. Instead of a gamma-distributed multiplicative factor, a random multiplicative factor is drawn from a uniform distribution within range [0.9, 1.1].

The discrete branch-length version of the program implements our new branch length representation scheme and simple mutation operator. Instead of allowing an arbitrary real value in the range of $[0, \infty)$, only a small fixed set of predefined real values are allowed for each branch length. The justification for this approach comes from two simple observations: 1) The set of optimal branch lengths of a given phylogenetic tree is typically only falls in a certain limited range; 2) Phylogenetic trees found by a GA, though maybe having a high quality tree topology and a set of near-optimal branch lengths, normally do not have the optimal set of branch lengths [6]. In this discrete branch-length scheme, the lower and upper bounds and the total number of allowable branch length levels are easily configurable. For our experiment, the set of discrete branch lengths has 2048 different levels with a lower bound of 10^{-4} and upper bound of 0.5. Although we could have used a more complex distribution, our initial experiments used an uniform distribution within the bounds (lower and upper bounds inclusive). Every branch length is initialized to the predefined value that is closest to 0.05. The branch length mutation operator changes the current branch length level to an adjacent level.

2.3   Hypothesis Testing

A statistical experiment was designed to prove or disprove that the discrete representation and incremental mutation operator produces a more efficient search of the data sets and parameters we tried than the continuous representation. Two data sets are used for the same experiment. The first is sequences of the chloroplast gene rbcL from 55 taxa of green plants, the same data set used by Paul Lewis in his 1998 paper [3]. The second data set is sequences from 48 taxa of Drosophila in a study of Schawaroch [10]. The aligned sequences are available at NCBI Entrez site, Popset database, gi:20805521.

We measure the quality of phylogenetic trees by the ML score and the agreement subtree distance [11], a metric for measuring tree topological dissimilarity. In order to use the dissimilarity metric we must have a reference tree which we assume to be the correct tree. In our experiments, the reference tree is the one found by the DNAML program in the software package Phylip 3.6a [12].

The overall hypothesis can be divided into two parts: 1) the discrete representation GA with incremental mutation produces trees with higher ML scores than the continuous representation; 2) the discrete representation GA with incremental mutation produces trees more similar to the reference tree (with lower agreement subtree metric) than the continuous version. The null hypothesis assumes both quality metrics to be equal between the two versions, and the significance levels are all set to 0.05.

MANOVA (multiple analysis of variance) tests are used to test our hypothesis. Like ANOVA, MANOVA is a procedure for testing the significance of differences between means of two or more populations. MANOVA can compare multiple response variables simultaneously. For this experiment, there are two treatments: continuous and discrete, and two dependent variables: ML score and agreement subtree distance. Each GA run is dependent on a random seed. A set of 50 random seeds are created. And both versions run 50 times using this set of 50 random seeds. For each GA run, we want it to keep evolving until the population converges, and no further improvements seem likely. So, the stopping criterion is that the best ML score for the population increases by less than 10^{-3} for 100 generations. Each generation is defined as the number of evaluations that equal to the size of the population. For example, for a population of 64, as in our experiments, that would be 6400 evaluations. During our experiments we logged the total number of evaluations, the best ML score, and the best phylogenetic tree at a specified interval for further analysis on GA convergence behavior.

3   Results and Discussion

The same statistical experiment is applied on our two data sets. The results are extremely similar, thus mutually verifying the experimental results. The following discussion pertains to the 55-taxa green plants dataset, but the discussion is equally applicable to the 48-taxa Drosophila dataset.

The MANOVA test on the results of 50 random runs of both versions of GA reveals that the performances of the two versions of GA are significantly different. The overall hypothesis that the two versions produce trees with same quality is rejected at a significance level of 0.05. All four MANOVA statistics, i.e., Wilks' Lambda, Pillai's Trace, Hotelling-Lawley Trace, and Roy's Greatest Root, have a P-value of < 0.0001.

Specifically for the 55-taxa green plants dataset, the continuous version has a mean for best ML score of -26390.34, while the discrete version a mean ML score of -26265.99. The MANOVA test rejects the null hypothesis with P-value of < 0.0001, strongly supporting the alternative hypothesis that the discrete version with incremental mutation produces trees with better ML score than continuous version does.

For tree topological comparison, the agreement subtree distance metric for each best tree discovered by each GA run is calculated against the reference tree produced by DNAML program from Phylip3.6a3. The agreement subtree distance metric is the total number of taxa that must be pruned off the comparing trees before they have the exactly same topology. For the green plants dataset, the continuous version has an agreement subtree metric mean of 18.48, while the discrete version a mean of 9.02. The MANOVA test again rejects the null hypothesis with P-value of < 0.0001. Therefore, the discrete GA with incremental mutation produces trees with better topology than the continuous version does. Table 1 summaries some of the experiment results.

Table 1. Results of MANOVA Test

	Mean(Continuous)	Mean(Discrete)	P-value
Green Plants			
ML Score	-26390.34	-26265.99	< 0.0001
Agreement Metric	18.48	9.02	< 0.0001
Wilk's Lambda			< 0.0001
Drosophila			
ML Score	-9260.66	-9208.46	< 0.0001
Topology Metric	16.68	10.90	< 0.0001
Wilk's Lambda			< 0.0001

After establishing that the discrete version is able to discover higher quality solutions than the continuous version, the speed of convergence, i.e., the mean of total number of evaluations needed for each version is compared, which reveals that discrete version does nearly one-third more evaluations than the continuous version. For green plants dataset, the continuous version takes 296,110 evaluations on average, while the discrete version takes 541,619. Since the two versions produce trees with different qualities, a simple assertion that one version is faster than the other is at best uninformative, and should be replaced by a careful study of the convergence patterns of both versions.

By plotting the convergence curves for best ML scores and agreement subtree metric for both versions, the GA convergence behavior can be seen clearly. Figures 1 and 2 plot the means of best ML score and agreement subtree metric with error bars for 50 runs of each GA version on 55-taxa green plants dataset respectively. Since these runs do not stop at the same point, step-curves which indicate the percentage of active runs out of a total of 50 are also plotted on the same graph but with a different scale. Before both versions stop, they've already lingered on a plateau of ML score and agreement subtree metric for about 200,000 evaluations. This suggests that the stringent stopping criterion does allow both versions of GA to evolve to a convergent population and it is highly unlikely that either version still has potential to improve solutions significantly.

Each of ML score curves in Figure 1 has its distinct characteristics, the pattern of which strongly suggests that one of them might have prematurely converged. The continuous version improves the ML score very rapidly in the early stage of search, and then abruptly transforms a nearly vertical increasing curve into a straight flat line as early as about 50,000 evaluations, one sixth of the entire GA lifetime. The final solutions found by the continuous version are apparently inferior to that found by discrete version. Combining these facts, it is likely that the continuous version is trapped in a local optimum. The discrete version, in its early search stage, does not increase the best ML score as quickly as the continuous one. Instead, it has a 45 degree steadily increasing curve. The ML score, though being inferior to that of continuous version from the very beginning, finally surpasses the continuous version at about 300,000 evaluations, at which point about 50% of the continuous GA runs are still active. After 400,000 evaluations, the discrete version also enters a plateau.

As for the tree topology in Figure 2, a different scenario is perceived. The agreement subtree metric curves for the two versions have very similar shape, characterized by a rapid increase in earliest search phase followed by a slow approach toward an asymptote. Interestingly, the discrete version starts out with better tree topologies, even though these trees apparently do not have as good ML scores as those discovered by continuous version during the same phase of search. This implies that the tree-space is truly a complicated space filled with local optima. Furthermore, the complication of the search space is partly caused by the intermingling of the tree topologies and the set of branch lengths that maximizes its score under criterion in use. The convergence patterns of the two versions of GA suggest that a tree with better topology yet un-optimized set of branch lengths probably has a lower score than a tree with worse topology but fully optimized branch lengths. Therefore, it is possible that a tree with better topology will be discarded and the heuristic search trapped in a local optima.

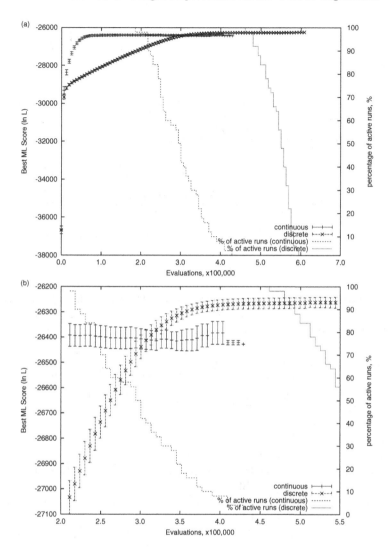

Fig. 1. Comparison between Continuous version and Discrete version GA. The progress of mean of best ML score with error bars for 55-taxa green plants dataset (percentage of active runs also shown). (a) the overview of the entire search process; (b) detailed view of the phase of search where two curves cross

Another reason for the improved performance of the discrete version might be as follows. The whole search space can be thought of as directly rendered by huge amount of tree topologies, each of which literally creates a sub-search-space with its dimensions and shape determined by a set of branch lengths and other parameters. For the continuous GA, the sub-search-space created by a tree topology is conceptually considered as a smooth continuous space, therefore, a continuous real number representation and a mutation operator of randomly

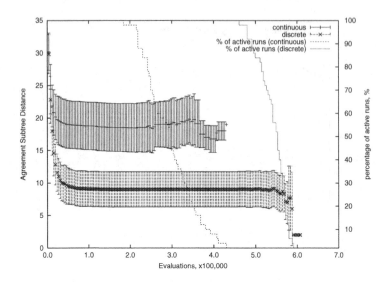

Fig. 2. Comparison between Continuous version and Discrete version GA. The progress of mean of agreement subtree metric with error bars for 55-taxa green plants dataset (percentage of active runs also shown)

multiplying small factor, should serve well to explore the optimum of this subspace. Unfortunately, this approach seems to be easily trapped in local optima, because topologies, that are discovered earlier in the search, have much better a chance to develop an optimalized set of branch lengths, consequently suffocating candidates having better topologies but unoptimized branch lengths.

The discrete version only samples a finite set of points on each sub-searchspace. Instead of a clear view of a continuous smooth subspace, the discrete version has a rather coarse, blurred vision of each subspace. The associated mutation operator for discrete version enables a much faster examination of each subspace by moving quickly among predefined branch lengths. Since the set of predefined branch lengths, though a good approximation, is unlikely to be an exact optimal set of any tree topology. The disadvantage is that a tree topology is never truly optimized. However, the early convergence problem could be substantially postponed, and better tree topologies have a better chance to stand out. The tradeoff for discrete version GA is that it achieves a better macroperspective on the whole search space by sacrificing the resolutions of the microview on sub-search-spaces. The net result is for the discrete version GA may be able to explore a larger portion of the search space in a more effective way.

4   Conclusions and Future Work

We found that discretizing the edge lengths and using incremental mutation changed the fundamental character of the search and can produce higher quality trees. Our results suggested a search that is more robust to traps in local optima and an opportunity to better control the balance between topology search and edge length search. Our experiments are only preliminary. We are now exploring various distributions of discrete edge lengths and mutation operators. One of our goals is to vary the coarseness of our edge distribution in order to control the careful layered assembly of a tree topology from disparate groups to closely-knit clades in much the same way as simulated annealing.

References

1. Felsenstein, J.:   Inferring Phylogeny.   Sinauer Associates, Sunderland, Massachusetts (2004)
2. Matsuda, H.: Protein phylogenetic inference using maximum likelihood with a genetic algorithm (1996)
3. Lewis, P.O.: A genetic algorithm for maximum-likelihood phylogeny inference using nucleotide sequence data. Mol. Biol. Evol. **15** (1998) 277–283
4. Katoh, K., Kuma, K.I., Miyata, T.: Genetic algorithm-based maximum-likelihood analysis for molecular phylogeny. J. Mol. Evol. **53** (2001) 477–484
5. Lemmon, A.R., Milinkovitch, M.C.: The metapopulation genetic algorithm: An efficient solution for the problem of large phylogeny estimation. PNAS **99** (2002) 10516–10521
6. Brauer, M.J., Holder, M.T., Dries, L.A., Zwickle, D.J., Lewis, P.O., Hillis, D.M.: Genetic algorithms and parallel processing in maximum-likelihood phylogeny inference. Mol. Biol. Evol. **19** (2002) 1717–1726
7. Gaut, B., Lewis, P.O.: Success of maximum likelihood phylogeny inference in the four-taxon case. Mol. Biol. Evol. **12** (1995) 152–162
8. Felsenstein, J.: Evolutionary trees from dna sequences: A maximum likelihood approach. J. Mol. Evol. **17** (1981) 368–376
9. Goldberg, D., Deb, K.: A comparative analysis of selection schemes used in genetic algorithms. In Rawlins, G., ed.: Foundations of Genetic Algorithms - 1, Morgan Kaufmann Publishers, Inc. (1991) 69–93
10. Schawaroch, V.A.: Phylogeny of a paradigm lineage: Drosophila melanogaster species group (diptera: Drosophilidae). Biol. J. Linn. Soc. Lond. **76** (2002) 21–37
11. Goddard, W., Kubicka, E., Kubicki, G., McMorris, F.R.: The agreement metric for labeled binary trees. Mathematical Bioscience **123** (1994) 215–226
12. Felsenstein, J.: Phylip (phylogeny inference package) version 3.6a. Distributed by the author. Department of Genetics, Univeristy of Washington, Seattle (1993)

Iteratively Inferring Gene Regulatory Networks with Virtual Knockout Experiments

Christian Spieth, Felix Streichert, Nora Speer, and Andreas Zell

Centre for Bioinformatics Tübingen (ZBIT), University of Tübingen,
Sand 1, D-72076 Tübingen, Germany,
spieth@informatik.uni-tuebingen.de,
http://www-ra.informatik.uni-tuebingen.de

Abstract. In this paper we address the problem of finding gene regulatory networks from experimental DNA microarray data. We introduce enhancements to an Evolutionary Algorithm optimization process to infer the parameters of the non-linear system given by the observed data more reliably and precisely. Due to the limited number of available data the inferring problem is under-determined and ambiguous. Further on, the problem often is multi-modal and therefore appropriate optimization strategies become necessary. Therefore, we propose a new method, which will suggest necessary additional biological experiments to remove the ambiguities.

1 Introduction

In the past few years, DNA microarrays have become one of the key techniques in the area of gene expression analysis. This technology enables the monitoring of thousands of genes in parallel and can therefore be used as a powerful tool to understand the regulatory mechanisms of gene expression in a cell.

However, due to the huge number of components within the regulatory system, a large amount of experimental data is needed to infer genome-wide networks. This requirement is almost impracticable to meet today, because of the high costs of these experiments and due to the fact that the investigated processes are too short and do not allow for more sampling points in time. To bypass this problem, additional data has to be acquired like knock-out, over-expression experiment data or data sets with different starting conditions that decrease the uncertainties in the system.

In this paper we propose a methodology for reverse engineering large sets of time series data obtained by expression analysis. This is successively done by optimizing the parameters of systems of differential equations modelling the interactions in the network for the given data followed by a second phase, aimed to reduce the ambiguities by suggesting subsequent knock-out experiments. Information gained by these follow-up experiments are incorporated into the first phase to increase the probability of finding the correct network model. And although traditional knock-out experiments are expensive and time consuming, techniques like chemical knock-outs are subject of recent research and will

G.R. Raidl et al. (Eds.): EvoWorkshops 2004, LNCS 3005, pp. 104–112, 2004.
© Springer-Verlag Berlin Heidelberg 2004

become more flexible in future. Further on, time series in which single gene products are over-expressed can be accomplished comparably easily and result in information that can be used in our approach as well. Our approach is also able to use data sets with different starting concentrations of the relevant gene products, i.e. examining the genes of interest under different environment conditions.

Section 2 of this paper presents an overview over related work and lists associated publications. Detailed description of our proposed method will be given in section 3 and example applications will be shown in section 4. Finally, conclusions and an outlook on future research will be covered by section 5.

2   Related Work

Researchers are interested in understanding the mechanisms of gene regulatory processes and therefore in inferring the underlying networks. This has recently become one of the major topics in bioinformatics due to the increased amount of data available. The following section briefly describes the work that has been done in this area.

One kind of model to simulate regulatory systems found in the literature are Boolean or Random Boolean Networks (RBN) [10,19]. In Boolean Networks gene expression levels can be in one of two states: either 1 (on) or 0 (off). The quantitative level of expression is not considered. Two examples for inferring Boolean Networks are given by Akutsu [1] and the REVEAL algorithm [12].

In contrast to discrete methods like RBNs, qualitative network models allow for multiple levels of gene regulation. Two examples for this kind of approach are given by Thieffry and Thomas in [16]. Akutsu et al. suggest a heuristic for inferring such models in [2].

Quantitative models like the weighted matrix model by Weaver et al. [18] consider the continuous level of gene expression. The topology and the parameters of this model have been successfully inferred by the use of Genetic Algorithms in [3] and [4]. Inference methods based on linear models for gene regulatory networks are given for example in [5] and [6]. An example for mathematical models using S-Systems to infer regulatory mechanisms has been examined by Tominaga et al. [17].

3   Modelling

On an abstract level, the behavior of a cell is represented by a gene regulatory network of N genes. Each gene g_i produces a certain amount of RNA x_i when expressed and therefore changes the concentration of this RNA level over time: $\boldsymbol{x}(t+1) = h(\boldsymbol{x}(t))$, $\boldsymbol{x}(t) = (x_1, \cdots, x_n)$.

To model and to simulate regulatory networks we decided to use S-Systems since they are well-documented and examined. But there are alternatives as listed in section 2, which will be the subject of research in future applications.

S-Systems are a type of power-law formalism which has been suggested by Irvine and Savageau [9,14] and can be described by a set of nonlinear differential equations:

$$\frac{dx_i(t)}{dt} = \alpha_i \prod_{j=1}^{N} x_j(t)^{\mathcal{G}_{i,j}} - \beta_i \prod_{j=1}^{N} x_j(t)^{\mathcal{H}_{i,j}}$$ (1)

where $\mathcal{G}_{i,j}$ and $\mathcal{H}_{i,j}$ are kinetic exponents, α_i and β_i are positive rate constants and N is the number of equations in the system. The equations in (1) can be seen as divided into two components: an excitatory and an inhibitory component.

The equation system is integrated using a fourth-order Runge-Kutta algorithm (with adaptive step size controlling). The parameters of the S-System α, β, $\mathcal{G}$, and $\mathcal{H}$ are optimized with an enhanced Evolutionary Algorithm described in the following.

Evolutionary Algorithms have proved to be a powerful tool for solving complex optimization problems. Three main types of evolutionary algorithms have evolved during the last 30 years: Genetic Algorithms (GA), mainly developed by J.H. Holland [8], Evolutionary Strategies (ES), developed by I. Rechenberg [13] and H.-P. Schwefel [15] and Genetic Programming (GP) by J.R. Koza [11]. Each of these uses different representations of the data and different operators working on them. They are, however, inspired by the same principles of natural evolution. Evolutionary Algorithms are a member of a family of stochastic search techniques that mimic the natural evolution as proposed by Charles Darwin of mutation and selection.

Because ES are suited for optimizing problems based on real values, they meet our requirement best. The following listing describes the general principle of Evolutionary Strategies:

1. Create an initial set (population) $P_{t=0}$ of λ solutions (individuals).
2. Evaluate all individuals of this population P_t according to a given fitness function.
3. Select the μ best individuals of the population with respect to the calculated fitness value as the population of parents P_t'.
4. Mutate/recombine individuals of the parent generation to create a new population of λ offsprings P_t'' .
5. Replace the initial population by the new population of offsprings $P_{t+1} = P_t''$ (eventually merged with P_t).

Repeat steps 2 to 5 until a termination criterion is met.

In our application an ES individual encodes the parameters α, β, $\mathcal{G}$ and $\mathcal{H}$ and represents a possible solution of the model identification problem.

For evaluating the fitness of the individuals we used the following equation for calculation of the fitness values:

$$f = \sum_{i=1}^{N} \sum_{k=1}^{T} \left\{ \left(\frac{\hat{x}_i(t_k) - x_i(t_k)}{x_i(t_k)} \right)^2 \right\}$$ (2)

where N is the total number of genes in the system, T is the number of sampling points taken from the time series and $\hat{x}$ and x distinguish between estimated data and sampled data. The overall problem is to minimize the fitness value f. In theory, the solution, i.e. the inferred GRN, should be the best individual found by the ES after termination.

Due to the small number of data the system is highly under-determined and therefore finding the biologically correct model is very difficult. A large number of different sets of model parameters fit the given data with comparably good fitness values (in respect to the fitness function mentioned above) but with only small resemblance to the true system.

To cope with this issue, our proposed method consists of a framework holding m ES populations, which will be optimized separately to gain different models satisfying the constrains given by the fitness function. This framework combines the best individuals from each population to form a population of best-suited models, which will have comparably good fitness values due to the ambiguity of the data but different parameters. To choose the very best model, i.e. the model representing the real biological dependencies, each of the combined models is further examined by simulating virtual knock-out, over-expression or changed start condition experiments. These virtual experiments are performed in silico for every gene in each model, i.e. every gene in a model is knocked out to gather information about the impact of that gene on the network represented by the current model. After the genes are ranked for each model, a committee decision is made to determine which gene has to be knocked out in real world experiments to gain the strongest information benefit for the inference process. The rankings is presented to biological researchers to actually perform the corresponding experiments.

The whole process is repeated with incorporation of the new data until a minimum quality level of the resulting models is reached. These models can then be verified by biologists to find the overall best network model. The details of this iterative process are described in the following work flow.

3.1   Inference Work Flow

The following work flow illustrates the interactive process of computer scientists and biologists to infer a GRN from expression data:

Phase $i = 1a$. The first optimization phase is started with m different initial populations to reach a diverse set of individuals. After the first optimization, the algorithm collects the best l individuals of the m ES populations and evaluates each of the $l * m$ models by finding the gene having the strongest impact on the dynamics if knocked out in silico. This is done by simulating the network without the corresponding gene and evaluating the differences of the calculated time course to the dynamics of the complete network. In this first implementation, we use a simple relative squared error (Eq. 2) summed up at each sampling point over time. After this, the resulting list of genes is ranked and the top candidate gene is suggested for further investigation.

Phase $i = 1b$. Additional microarray experiments based on the knock-out proposals have to be accomplished yielding another set of expression data. These experiments can either be carried out using techniques like knock outs or by inhibiting single gene products chemically.

Phase $i = 2a$. The set of new data is incorporated in the next optimization step. The whole process is then repeated iteratively until a termination criterion is met.

4   Applications

To illustrate our method, we established two regulatory network systems, which were simulated to gain sets of expression data. After creating the data sets, we used our proposed algorithm to reverse engineer the correct model parameters. The following sections show this for a 5-dimensional and a 10-dimensional example, respectively.

4.1   Gene Regulatory Network with $N = 5$ Genes

Due to the fact that GRNs in nature are sparse systems, we created regulatory networks randomly with a maximum cardinality of $k <= 3$, i.e. each of the $N = 5$ genes depends on three or less other genes within the network. The dynamics of the example can be seen in Fig. 1.

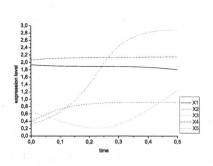

parameter	value	parameter	value
α_1	0.233	G_{11}	-2.000
α_2	2.330	G_{25}	-0.788
α_3	1.217	G_{31}	-0.496
α_4	1.602	G_{35}	2.072
α_5	3.153	G_{42}	-0.473
		G_{53}	-0.958
β_1	0.703	H_{12}	-0.591
β_2	2.012	H_{13}	1.462
β_3	2.737	H_{21}	-1.025
β_4	1.597	H_{22}	0.112
β_5	2.573	H_{53}	-0.023

Fig. 1. Artificial 5-dimensional gene regulatory network

Fig. 2. Model parameter of the target S-System

In Fig. 1, each x_i represents the RNA level of a certain gene. At this point, we do not differentiate between closely related molecules like mRNA and distantly related like proteins.

Inference. This time course data was then subject to our inference method as described in Section 3. In the following subsections each phase of the algorithm is explained using the 5-dimensional example. The results are then compared to a standard ES with identical optimization settings but without incorporating additional information.

Phase 1a. The optimization process was performed using a (μ,λ)-ES with $\mu = 5$ and $\lambda = 30$ together with a Covariance Matrix Adaptation (CMA) mutation operator [7] and no recombination to evolve individuals. This optimization was repeated $m = 20$ times with different starting populations to calculate 20 different populations, i.e. 20 different models. After evolving the models for 10,000 generations (total number of 300,000 fitness evaluations), the best individual of each population was taken to form a population of best individuals. For each of these individuals, virtual knock-out experiments were simulated and the top candidate genes were ranked. Tables 1 - 3 list the ranking of each gene for the corresponding algorithm phase, i.e. the number of votes in each network.

Table 1. Ranking of the genes (phase 1)

Gene	Votes
1	9
2	3
3	4
4	1
5	3
	20

Table 2. Ranking of the genes (phase 2)

Gene	Votes
1	-
2	1
3	4
4	4
5	11
	20

Table 3. Ranking of the genes (phase 3)

Gene	Votes
1	-
2	1
3	16
4	3
5	-
	20

Phase 1b. After ranking the importance of the gene within the network the biological knock-out experiments were performed in silico resulting in an additional set of expression data.

Phase 2–4. These phases were repeated until the correct model was found. Fig. 3 shows the averaged fitness values for each repetition phase, i.e. for the degree of additional knock-out information in comparison with the fitness values for a standard ES optimizer.

As can be seen in the figure, the fitness converges quickly to 0.0 for both algorithms, which corresponds to a very good model quality with respect to the fitness function. Unfortunately, the models found by the standard ES resemble the original parameters only little. This is illustrated by Fig. 4, where the euclidian distance between the inferred parameters and the parameters of the original system is shown. The standard ES converges to a local optimum, which has a comparably good fitness value but represents completely different dependencies. The proposed method on the other hand leads directly to the global optimum, i.e. the correct network by successively removing ambiguities.

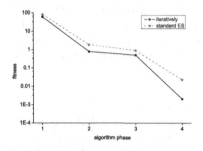 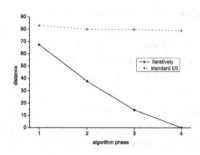

Fig. 3. Best fitness values for each phase   **Fig. 4.** Distance values for each phase

4.2   Gene Regulatory Network with $N = 10$ Genes

As a second and due to the increased number of participating genes more difficult test case, we created another regulatory network randomly with a maximum cardinality of $k <= 3$. The dynamics of the example can be seen in Fig. 5, where each gene expression level is again represented by the corresponding x_i.

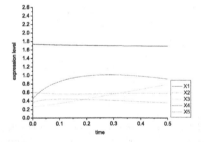 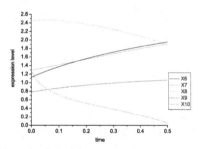

Fig. 5. Artificial 10-dimensional gene regulatory network

Inference.   The given time course data was then again inferred by our algorithm. The optimization process was performed using the same settings for the ES as in example 1 (see Section 4.1). The optimization was repeated $m = 20$ times with different starting populations to calculate 20 different populations, i.e. 20 different models. The resulting ranking tables are not shown here due to the limited space available.

The different phases of our algorithm were repeated until the termination criterium was reached, i.e. a total number of $500,000$ fitness evaluations per algorithm phase. Fig. 6 shows the averaged fitness values for each phase.

In this example, a standard ES was not able to find a solution for the optimization problem. Only the enhanced algorithm, which included additional information, found the correct system, as illustrated in Fig. 7.

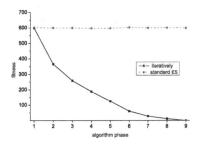 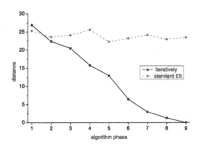

Fig. 6. Best fitness values for each phase   **Fig. 7.** Distance values for each phase

5   Discussion

The problem of inferring GRNs is a very difficult process due to the limited data available and the large number of unknown variables in the system. Most examples found in literature are artificial and very small, i.e. with a total number of ten genes or lower. And although the dimensionality of these examples is by far not relevant to biological processes, they show the first attempts of modelling regulatory networks from high-throughput experimental techniques.

In this paper we have shown a method to infer gene regulatory systems even in cases where standard approaches were not able to cope with the problem of under-determination. Our method yields promising results by incorporating additional knowledge into the inference procedure. The necessary information can be gathered by additional biological experiments like (chemical) knock-out and over-expression experiments or by altering environmental conditions to change the initial concentrations of the relevant gene products.

In future work we plan to include a-priori information into the inference process like partially known pathways or information about co-regulated genes, which can be found in literature. For better coverage of the solution space of the optimizer we will use a cluster-based niching algorithm which was developed in our group. Additional models for gene regulatory networks will be examined for simulation of the non-linear interaction system as listed in Section 3 to overcome the problems with those gene regulatory networks which cannot be modelled by S-Systems.

Further on, we will continue to test our method with real microarray data in close collaboration with biological researchers at our facility.

References

1. T. Akutsu, S. Miyano, and S. Kuhura. Identification of genetic networks from a small number of gene expression patterns under the boolean network model. In *Proceedings of the Pacific Symposium on Biocomputing*, pages 17–28, 1999.

2. T. Akutsu, S. Miyano, and S. Kuhura. Algorithms for identifying boolean networks and related biological networks based on matrix multiplication and fingerprint function. In *Proceedings of the fourth annual international conference on Computational molecular biology*, pages 8 – 14, Tokyo, Japan, 2000. ACM Press New York, NY, USA.

3. S. Ando and H. Iba. Quantitative modeling of gene regulatory network - identifying the network by means of genetic algorithms. In *Poster Session of Genome Informatics Workshop 2000*, pages 278–280, 2000.

4. S. Ando and H. Iba. Inference of gene regulatory model by genetic algorithms. In *Proceedings of the 2001 Congress on Evolutionary Computation*, pages 712–719. IEEE Press, 2001.

5. T. Chen, H. L. He, and G. M. Church. Modeling gene expression with differential equations. In *Proceedings of the Pacific Symposium on Biocomputing*, 1999.

6. P. D'haeseleer, X. Wen, S. Fuhrman, and R. Somogyi. Linear modeling of mRNA expression levels during CNS development and injury. In *Proceedings of the Pacific Symposium on Biocomputing*, volume 4, pages 41–52, 1999.

7. N. Hansen and A. Ostermeier. Adapting arbitrary normal mutation distributions in evolution strategies: the covariance matrix adaptation. In *Proceedings of the 1996 IEEE Int. Conf. on Evolutionary Computation*, pages 312–317, Piscataway, NJ, 1996. IEEE Service Center.

8. J. H. Holland. *Adaption in Natural and Artificial Systems: An Introductory Analysis with Applications to Biology, Control and Artificial Systems*. The University Press of Michigan Press, Ann Arbor, 1975.

9. D. H. Irvine and M. A. Savageau. Efficient solution of nonlinear ordinary differential equations expressed in S-systems canonical form. *SIAM Journal of Numerical Analysis*, 27(3):704–735, 1990.

10. S. A. Kauffman. *The Origins of Order*. Oxford University Press, New York, 1993.

11. J. R. Koza. *Genetic Programming: On the Programming of Computers by Means of Natural Selection*. MIT Press, Cambridge, MA, USA, 1992.

12. S. Liang, S. Fuhrman, and R. Somogyi. REVEAL, a general reverse engineering algorithm for inference of genetic network architectures. In *Proceedings of the Pacific Symposium on Biocomputing*, volume 3, pages 18–29, 1998.

13. I. Rechenberg. *Evolutionsstrategie - Optimierung technischer Systeme nach Prinzipien der biologischen Evolution*. Frommann-Holzboog, Stuttgart, 1973.

14. M. A. Savageau. 20 years of S-systems. In E. Voit, editor, *Canonical Nonlinear Modeling. S-systems Approach to Understand Complexity*, pages 1–44, New York, 1991. Van Nostrand Reinhold.

15. H.-P. Schwefel. *Numerical optimization of computer models*. John Wiley and Sons Ltd, 1981.

16. D. Thieffry and R. Thomas. Qualitative analysis of gene networks. In *Proceedings of the Pacific Symposium on Biocomputing*, pages 77–87, 1998.

17. D. Tominaga, N. Kog, and M. Okamoto. Efficient numeral optimization technique based on genetic algorithm for inverse problem. In *Proceedings of German Conference on Bioinformatics*, pages 127–140, 1999.

18. D. Weaver, C. Workman, and G. Stormo. Modeling regulatory networks with weight matrices. In *Proceedings of the Pacific Symposium on Biocomputing*, volume 4, pages 112–123, 1999.

19. A. Wuensche. Genomic regulation modeled as a network with basins of attraction. In *Proceedings of the Pacific Symposium on Biocomputing*, volume 3, pages 89–102, 1998.

Multiple Sequence Alignment Using SAGA: Investigating the Effects of Operator Scheduling, Population Seeding, and Crossover Operators

René Thomsen and Wouter Boomsma

Bioinformatics Research Center (BiRC)
Department of Computer Science
University of Aarhus
Ny Munkegade, Bldg. 540.
DK-8000 Aarhus C, Denmark
{thomsen,wb}@daimi.au.dk

Abstract. Multiple sequence alignment (MSA) is a fundamental problem of great importance in molecular biology. In this study, we investigated several aspects of SAGA, a well-known evolutionary algorithm (EA) for solving MSA problems. The SAGA algorithm is important because it represents a successful attempt at applying EAs to MSA and since it is the first EA to use operator scheduling on this problem. However, it is largely undocumented which elements of SAGA are vital to its performance. An important finding in this study is that operator scheduling does not improve the performance of SAGA compared to a uniform selection of operators. Furthermore, the experiments show that seeding SAGA with a ClustalW-derived alignment allows the algorithm to discover alignments of higher quality compared to the traditional initialization scheme with randomly generated alignments. Finally, the experimental results indicate that SAGA's performance is largely unaffected when the crossover operators are disabled. Thus, the major determinant of SAGA's success seems to be the mutation operators and the scoring functions used.

1 Introduction

During the last decades, the amount of available biological sequence data (DNA, RNA, and proteins) has increased exponentially. This wealth of new information requires automated methods that can assist practitioners in the process of analyzing and interpreting the data. Valuable tools in this context are multiple sequence alignment (MSA) programs, which allow for the comparison of multiple sequences.

Among the vast number of possible applications, MSAs can be used to (i) infer phylogenetic relationships of organisms, (ii) discover conserved motifs that might be of great importance on the levels of transcription, translation, or structure/function, and finally (iii) assist secondary and tertiary structure prediction methods.

G.R. Raidl et al. (Eds.): EvoWorkshops 2004, LNCS 3005, pp. 113–122, 2004.

Initially, the most popular methods for obtaining MSAs used dynamic programming (DP) because DP can guarantee a mathematically optimal alignment given the commonly used sum-of-pairs (SOP) scoring function [1]. However, DP-based methods can only handle a relatively small number of sequences because the size of the lookup table increases dramatically with the number of sequences in the alignment and their length. In fact, finding the optimal MSA solution wrt. the SOP score is known to be NP-hard [2].

In order to solve larger problem instances several heuristics have been introduced. The most popular heuristic is ClustalW [3], an algorithm that belongs to the class of progressive alignment methods [4]. These methods gradually construct an alignment by first estimating the evolutionary distance between all sequences to be aligned and then aligning the sequences in order of decreasing similarity. Although the progressive methods are very fast they typically suffer from entrapment in local optima because they optimize the alignment in a pairwise manner, not taking the entire alignment into account.

To overcome this problem several stochastic heuristics have been applied to MSA, such as simulated annealing [5] and evolutionary algorithms (EAs) [6,7]. Typically, these methods start with randomly generated candidate alignments that are gradually improved using several variation operators.

SAGA (Sequence Alignment by Genetic Algorithm) [6] introduced the idea of operator scheduling (OS) for MSA based on the assumption that the scheduling of the operators would improve the overall performance of the algorithm. However, our preliminary experiments with several OS schemes on MSA using the MSAEA [9] did not indicate any improvements for OS compared to choosing the operators randomly with a uniform probability. More specifically, these observations raised the question of whether OS has any effect at all when applied to EAs for MSA.

Moreover, Thomsen et al. [8,9] investigated the effects of seeding an EA with a ClustalW-derived solution. The experimental results indicated that seeding the EA resulted in a marked improvement in runtime needed to derive solutions of high quality. Furthermore, it was shown that the resulting alignments were significantly better than the ClustalW seed, making the EA useful as an alignment improver.

These findings motivated us to investigate the following aspects of SAGA: (i) operator scheduling compared to uniform choice of variation operators, (ii) seeding the initial population with a ClustalW-derived alignment compared to random initialization, and finally (iii) the effect of crossover operators compared to using mutation only. These investigations were conducted on selected MSA benchmark problems obtained from the BAliBASE sequence alignment database [10].

The experimental results show that operator scheduling does not improve the overall performance of SAGA compared to a uniform selection of operators. Moreover, the results indicate that SAGA is able to obtain better results using seeds compared to random initialization given the same number of fitness evaluations. Finally, the use of crossover operators did not generally increase the performance.

2 SAGA

In 1996 Notredame and Higgins introduced SAGA [6], one of the first evolutionary algorithms (EAs) for MSA. Basically, SAGA resembles a standard EA with a population of candidate alignments (individuals) that are subjected to variation and selection. During selection the individuals compete for survival and the most promising ones are transferred to the next generation. Contrary to other EAs solving MSA, SAGA provides a total of 25 variation operators (19 mutation and 6 crossover) with a variety of functionality, such as modifying gap regions (adding, deleting, moving gaps) and combining promising regions. A complete description of the operators is beyond of the scope of this paper, see [6] for a detailed description. The default initialization mode in SAGA is to randomly initialize all individuals by prefixing a randomly chosen number of gaps to each sequence.

SAGA differs from all other MSA algorithms regarding the utilization of the operators. It uses an operator scheduling (OS) strategy originally described by Davis in 1989 [11] to select which operators to use. The OS strategy works as follows: Each operator is assigned a probability for its application. Initially, these probabilities are all equal, but during the course of the run they are adapted based on the recent performance of the operator. Operators are rewarded when they create an individual with a fitness greater than any of the current individuals in the population. Furthermore, operators responsible for the individuals' parents and more distant ancestors are rewarded with some percentage of the original reward. This is motivated by the fact that a series of suboptimal solutions is often necessary in order to reach a new optimal solution and corresponding operators therefore should be rewarded. With certain intervals, a new probability setting is computed as a weighted sum of the previous setting and the distribution of rewards among the operators.

The motivation for using OS in SAGA is that it is difficult to determine in advance which of the 25 operators to apply. The problem gets more complicated since the utilization of each operator might depend on the actual alignment problem being solved and optimal usage of operators might change during the course of the optimization run. The idea is that by measuring the performance of operators during the run, operators can be continuously scheduled so that the best operators are used at all times.

SAGA provides three different ways of scoring alignments, (i) sum-of-pairs without weights (SOP), (ii) sum-of pairs using weights (WSOP), and (iii) Consistency based Objective Function For alignmEnt Evaluation (COFFEE) [12]. The three scoring functions are briefly described below (see [6] and [12] for more details).

The SOP and WSOP scoring functions are almost identical except for the additional sequence weights used in WSOP. Equation 1 shows how the total score of an alignment is calculated. N specifies the number of sequences in the alignment, S_i and S_j are two aligned sequences from the given alignment, and W_{ij} is the corresponding weight (a detailed description of the weighting scheme used is provided in [12]). When no weights are provided, i.e., using SOP, all weights are set to 100 (default setting in SAGA). The $COST$ function calculates the substitution scores for each pair of residues in sequence S_i and S_j using e.g, BLOSUM or PAM matrices. Furthermore, the $COST$ function includes affine gap penalties, e.g., penalties for gap opening and extension (GOP and GEP, respectively). Terminal gaps are only penalized for extension, not for opening. Moreover, SAGA transforms the (W)SOP scoring functions into minimization problems by scaling the entries of the substitution matrix.

$$(W)SOP = \sum_{i=2}^{N} \sum_{j=1}^{i-1} W_{ij} \times COST(S_i, S_j) \,. \tag{1}$$

The COFFEE score is defined as a maximization problem where the task is to maximize the consistency between the residue pairs in the alignment and the residue pairs observed in a library generated by pairwise alignments between all the sequences. Equation 2 shows how the score is calculated.

$$COFFEE = \sum_{i=1}^{N-1} \sum_{j=i+1}^{N} W_{ij} \times SCORE(A_{ij}) \,. \tag{2}$$

$SCORE(A_{ij})$ is the number of aligned pairs of residues that are shared between A_{ij} and the generated library, where A_{ij} is the pairwise projection of sequence S_i and S_j obtained from the evaluated candidate alignment.

For the experiments described in this study we used SAGA V0.95, which is publically available from `http://igs-server.cnrs-mrs.fr/~cnotred/`. The original termination criteria (terminate after 100 consecutive generations without performance improvements) was modified so that SAGA terminates when a certain number of fitness evaluations has occurred. This change was necessary in order to make a general comparison between different settings possible.

3   Experiments

3.1   BAliBASE Benchmarks

The BAliBASE database [10] contains 142 multiple sequence alignments, which are manually refined from the known 3D structures of proteins. This makes it possible to evaluate the quality of MSA algorithms regarding their ability to derive true (biological plausible) alignments. Table 1 shows the protein sequence data sets used in our experiments. All seven data sets were randomly selected from the first reference set of the BAliBASE database (version 2, `http://bess.u-strasbg.fr/BioInfo/BAliBASE2/`).

Table 1. BAliBASE data sets used in the experiments. NSEQ = number of sequences, LSEQ = length of sequences, SEQID = percent residue identity

Data set	NSEQ	LSEQ (min,max,avg)	SEQID
1idy	5	(49,58,53.6)	<25%
1aboA	5	(49,80,63.6)	<25%
kinase	5	(263,276,270.2)	<25%
1hfh	5	(116,132,121.2)	20-40%
1pfc	5	(108,117,112)	20-40%
1pii	4	(247,259,251.5)	20-40%
451c	5	(70,87,80)	20-40%

3.2 Evaluation Measures

The results from the SAGA runs were evaluated according to each of the scoring functions described in Section 2. Furthermore, the quality of the overall best found alignments were compared with the BAliBASE reference alignments using the BAliBASE evaluation measures described below.

The BAliBASE sum-of-pairs score (SPS) was calculated as follows: Given a candidate alignment (individual) of N sequences containing M columns, the i'th column in the alignment is designated by $A_{i1}, A_{i2}, \ldots, A_{iN}$. For each pair of residues A_{ij} and A_{ik} we defined p_{ijk} such that $p_{ijk} = 1$ if residues A_{ij} and A_{ik} from the candidate alignment were aligned with each other in the reference alignment. Otherwise, $p_{ijk} = 0$. The score for the i'th column is thus:

$$S_i = \sum_{j=1,j\neq k}^{N} \sum_{k=1}^{N} p_{ijk} \, . \tag{3}$$

The overall SPS for the candidate alignment is:

$$SPS = \sum_{i=1}^{M} \frac{S_i}{\sum_{i=1}^{M_r} S_{ri}} \, , \tag{4}$$

where M_r is the number of columns in the reference alignment and S_{ri} is the score S_i for the i'th column in the reference alignment.

The BAliBASE column score (CS) was calculated as follows: Given an alignment as described above, the score C_i for the i'th column is equal to 1 if all the residues in the column are aligned in the reference alignment. Otherwise, C_i is set to 0. The overall CS for the candidate alignment is:

$$CS = \sum_{i=1}^{M} \frac{C_i}{M} \, . \tag{5}$$

The ranges of SPS and CS are 0.0-1.0, where higher values indicate closer resemblance with the BAliBASE reference alignment. When calculating both scores we used the annotation files provided with BAliBASE to identify core blocks in the reference alignment, i.e., only the regions that were marked as being important were used in the calculation.

3.3   Experimental Setup and Data Sampling

In this study we used the default parameter settings provided with SAGA. The population size was set to 100 and the total number of fitness evaluations allowed was set to 200000 (max number of evaluations in the termination criterion). The SOP and WSOP scoring functions used the BLOSUM-45 substitution matrix and gap penalties were set to $GOP = 8$ and $GEP = 12$ (SAGA default settings).

Different configurations of SAGA were investigated regarding the seven alignment problems shown in Table 1 (see section 4 for more details). Each experiment was repeated 30 times with different random seeds, and the average of the 30 best alignment scores was recorded.

4   Results

The performance of SAGA was evaluated regarding the seven alignment benchmarks described in section 3.1. The experiments were designed to provide answers to the following three main questions: (i) does operator scheduling (OS) outperform simple uniform choice of operators?, (ii) what is the effect of using seeding compared to random initialization only?, and (iii) does crossover improve performance compared to using mutation only?

Table 2 summarizes the results from all the experiments. The Configuration column shows the choice of configuration for each particular experiment (see caption for Table 2 for information on the abbreviations used). The remaining columns show the BAliBASE CS and SPS measures (mean of 30 runs) for each of the tested alignments. The significance of the results was validated using the Wilcoxon Signed Rank Test (statistical p-values are provided in supplementary material).

Overall, the results from table 2 show that OS is not an advantage compared to a uniform choice of operator (the differences are not statistically significant $(p > 0.0625)$). Moreover, seeding improves the performance of SAGA in four of the seven test cases (the results are statistically significant with $p < 0.05$ for 1aboA, kinase, 1hfh, and 1pii). For the remaining test cases, the differences observed are not significant. The use of crossover operators improves the performance for kinase and 1hfh, while being a disadvantage for the 1aboA problem (the results are statistically significant with $p < 0.05$). For the four other test cases, using crossover does not make any performance difference.

In conclusion, SAGA using seeding, crossover, OS, and the SOP or WSOP scoring function (S,C,O, SOP/WSOP) or the same settings except OS (S,C,NO, SOP/WSOP) generally performed better than all other configurations. The small differences between these settings were not statistically significant according to the Wilcoxon Signed Rank Test.

Table 2. BAliBASE evaluation measures on tested benchmarks using different SAGA configurations. R (random initialization), S (ClustalW-seed), C/NC (crossover/no-crossover), O/NO (operator-scheduling/uniform-choice), SOP/WSOP/COFFEE (scoring functions)

Configuration	Data set						
	1idy CS/SPS	laboA CS/SPS	kinase CS/SPS	1hfh CS/SPS	1pfc CS/SPS	1pii CS/SPS	451c CS/SPS
R, C, O, SOP	0.380/0.565	0.484/0.721	0.353/0.606	0.878/0.944	0.991/0.997	0.805/0.895	0.622/0.746
R, C, O, WSOP	0.380/0.550	0.518/0.730	0.304/0.558	0.889/0.950	0.940/0.979	0.805/0.891	0.638/0.744
R, C, O, COFFEE	0.167/0.510	0.570/0.775	0.541/0.734	0.847/0.936	0.893/0.959	0.800/0.882	0.611/0.787
R, NC, O, SOP	0.380/0.540	0.566/0.769	0.272/0.565	0.853/0.931	0.990/0.997	0.775/0.877	0.620/0.717
R, NC, O, WSOP	0.380/0.550	0.562/0.765	0.272/0.558	0.857/0.936	0.940/0.979	0.768/0.873	0.666/0.732
R, NC, O, COFFEE	0.207/0.520	0.570/0.774	0.468/0.705	0.853/0.937	0.890/0.958	0.801/0.883	0.635/0.794
R, C, NO, SOP	0.380/0.550	0.508/0.732	0.362/0.617	0.894/0.951	0.989/0.996	0.805/0.896	0.620/0.744
R, C, NO, WSOP	0.380/0.550	0.496/0.725	0.298/0.569	0.897/0.955	0.940/0.979	0.809/0.893	0.641/0.765
R, C, NO, COFFEE	0.151/0.507	0.570/0.774	0.531/0.732	0.851/0.936	0.891/0.958	0.801/0.883	0.606/0.784
R, NC, NO, SOP	0.380/0.548	0.555/0.764	0.305/0.583	0.863/0.935	0.992/0.997	0.799/0.890	0.600/0.718
R, NC, NO, WSOP	0.380/0.550	0.544/0.758	0.278/0.566	0.859/0.935	0.940/0.979	0.804/0.890	0.627/0.739
R, NC, NO, COFFEE	0.203/0.533	0.569/0.775	0.450/0.692	0.822/0.924	0.890/0.958	0.802/0.884	0.639/0.796
S, C, O, SOP	0.380/0.595	0.566/0.768	0.621/0.792	0.896/0.953	0.985/0.995	0.810/0.899	0.589/0.698
S, C, O, WSOP	0.380/0.543	0.566/0.766	0.627/0.795	0.889/0.950	0.940/0.979	0.810/0.893	0.618/0.709
S, C, O, COFFEE	0.186/0.542	0.570/0.776	0.554/0.737	0.845/0.934	0.890/0.958	0.800/0.882	0.630/0.794
S, NC, O, SOP	0.380/0.596	0.567/0.767	0.531/0.755	0.883/0.947	0.988/0.996	0.810/0.897	0.620/0.711
S, NC, O, WSOP	0.380/0.541	0.568/0.769	0.529/0.752	0.894/0.953	0.940/0.979	0.810/0.892	0.630/0.715
S, NC, O, COFFEE	0.207/0.528	0.570/0.776	0.527/0.729	0.859/0.939	0.892/0.959	0.800/0.882	0.631/0.794
S, C, NO, SOP	0.380/0.594	0.567/0.767	0.608/0.787	0.909/0.959	0.985/0.995	0.810/0.899	0.585/0.696
S, C, NO, WSOP	0.380/0.548	0.567/0.768	0.616/0.800	0.903/0.957	0.940/0.979	0.810/0.892	0.615/0.707
S, C, NO, COFFEE	0.183/0.525	0.570/0.776	0.559/0.736	0.834/0.929	0.892/0.959	0.800/0.882	0.629/0.796
S, NC, NO, SOP	0.380/0.594	0.568/0.766	0.547/0.763	0.890/0.950	0.988/0.996	0.810/0.898	0.605/0.705
S, NC, NO, WSOP	0.380/0.550	0.568/0.767	0.581/0.782	0.878/0.945	0.940/0.979	0.810/0.892	0.624/0.712
S, NC, NO, COFFEE	0.218/0.552	0.570/0.776	0.518/0.726	0.816/0.921	0.893/0.959	0.800/0.882	0.633/0.795

Finally, the best configuration found in the previous experiments was compared to the alignments obtained from SAGA using default parameter settings (R,C,O,SOP), ClustalW and T-Coffee [13]. Table 3 shows the CS and SPS values for each of the seven testcases using one of the tested alignment programs. In five out of seven cases, SAGA with the best-found configuration outperformed the other alignment programs wrt. the BAliBASE evaluation measures (three times using CS and five times using SPS). For the remaining two cases, SAGA using random initialization obtained slightly higher scores than using the ClustalW seed for 1pfc. However, the differences are not statistically significant. SAGA was not able to improve the 451c problem. In fact, the resulting alignment had a worse score compared to the ClustalW seed. This case shows that an improvement of the SOP score does not always correlate with an improvement of the alignment quality, i.e., a better CS or SPS value. In conclusion, using SAGA with the new parameter settings outperformed SAGA using default values for five of the seven tested problems, indicating the importance of population seeding when the number of evaluations are fixed at 200000.

Table 3. BAliBASE evaluation measures on tested benchmarks using different MSA programs. *SAGA(seeding)* is SAGA with the best-found settings and ClustalW seeding (see previous table) and *SAGA(random)* is SAGA using default parameter settings and random initialization. All SAGA results represent mean values obtained from 30 runs

	MSA program			
Data set	SAGA (seeding) CS/SPS	SAGA (random) CS/SPS	ClustalW CS/SPS	T-Coffee CS/SPS
1idy	**0.380**/**0.595**	**0.380**/0.565	**0.380**/0.588	0.000/0.150
1aboA	**0.566**/**0.768**	0.484/0.721	0.540/0.755	0.150/0.570
kinase	0.621/**0.792**	0.353/0.606	**0.630**/0.788	0.600/0.769
1hfh	**0.896**/**0.953**	0.878/0.944	0.770/0.900	0.870/0.938
1pfc	0.985/0.995	**0.991**/**0.997**	0.750/0.903	0.940/0.979
1pii	0.810/**0.899**	0.805/0.895	0.740/0.855	**0.820**/**0.899**
451c	0.589/0.698	0.622/0.746	**0.700**/0.755	0.640/**0.786**

5   Discussion

In this paper, we investigated different aspects of SAGA, such as (i) scheduling operators to obtain optimal usage compared to uniform selection of all available operators, (ii) seeding the initial population with a ClustalW derived alignment compared to random initialization only, and finally (iii) using crossover operators compared to using mutation-based operators only.

Overall, the experimental results showed that operator scheduling (OS) did not perform any better than simply choosing the operators uniformly (see table 2). This observation differs from the intuitive notion that OS is useful when solving optimization problems with many variation operators. Preliminary experiments trying out other OS strategies confirmed the reported results. In all cases uniform selection of operators was as good or better than the tested methods. A possible explanation of why OS does not increase the performance is that repeated usage of an operator that is believed to be good does not necessarily result in a stepwise improvement of alignment quality. The main reason seems to be the stochastic nature of the variation operators which usually randomly select the sequences and/or gap-regions to be modified. However, more in-depth investigations on the search-spaces induced by the MSA scoring schemes are needed to fully understand why OS does not work very well on this particular problem.

Moreover, our study showed that in most cases the seeding approach was able to obtain similar or better scores than the random initialization approach (using the same parameter settings and number of evaluations). Again, this observation is in contrast to the original study by Notredame and Higgins [6] where seeding has been avoided because it was believed to bias the search to local optima. Furthermore, using random initialization without seeding typically required twice as many fitness evaluations as the seeding approach to obtain similar fitness and CS/SPS values (see supplementary material for more details).

Generally, the use of crossover did not improve the performance of SAGA on the tested data sets. On the kinase and 1hfh test cases using crossover operators resulted in slightly better CS/SPS scores whereas omitting crossover improved the results on the 1aboA test case. Whether to use crossover or not seems to depend on the actual data set in question. More experiments on other BAliBASE data sets might give some guidelines on when to apply or omit crossover operators.

Finally, the comparison to other MSA programs showed that SAGA is able to improve the initial alignment provided by ClustalW in five out of 7 cases (see table 3). Typically, the runtime needed by SAGA was between 40-240 seconds on a 1.8GHz Pentium-IV PC making it a valuable tool as an alignment improver. Furthermore, SAGA using the seeding approach is able to obtain the overall best scores in five out of seven cases compared to ClustalW, T-Coffee, and SAGA using default random initialization.

In conclusion, seeding SAGA with ClustalW solutions improved the convergence properties of SAGA (see convergence graphs in the supplementary material) thus lowering the total number of fitness evaluations needed to obtain alignments of good quality (wrt. CS and SPS measures). The results also indicate that the benefits of using OS and crossover operators are questionable, thus suggesting that simpler algorithms without these features may be sufficient to solve the MSA problem. Repeating the investigations described in this study on all the BAliBASE data sets will provide us with a better indication on whether the use of OS and crossover operators are needed in general.

6   Supplementary Material

Additional experimental results (fitness tables, convergence graphs, etc.) are publically available from http://www.daimi.au.dk/~thomsen/evobio2004/.

Acknowledgments. The authors would like to thank the Danish Research Council for financial support. The authors also thank Jakob Vesterstrøm for valuable comments on draft versions of the manuscript.

References

1. Gupta, S., J.D. Kececioglu, J., Schaffer, A.: Improving the practical space and time efficiency of the shortest-paths approach to sum-of-pairs multiple sequence alignment. Journal of Computational Biology **2** (1995) 459–472
2. Wang, L., Jiang, T.: On the complexity of multiple sequence alignment. Journal of Computational Biology **1** (1994) 337–348
3. Thompson, J., Higgins, D., Gibson, T.: Clustal W: Improving the sensitivity of progressive multiple sequence alignment through sequence weighting. Nucleic Acids Research **22** (1994) 4673–4680
4. Feng, D., Doolittle, R.: Progressive sequence alignment as a prerequisite to correct phylogenetic trees. Journal of Molecular Evolution **25** (1987) 351–360
5. Kim, J., Pramanik, S., Chung, M.: Multiple sequence alignment using simulated annealing. Computer Applications in the Biosciences (CABIOS) **10** (1994) 419–426
6. Notredame, C., Higgins, D.: SAGA: Sequence alignment by genetic algorithm. Nucleic Acids Research **24** (1996) 1515–1524
7. Chellapilla, K., Fogel, G.B.: Multiple sequence alignment using evolutionary programming. In: Proceedings of the First Congress of Evolutionary Computation (CEC-1999). (1999) 445–452
8. Thomsen, R., Fogel, G., Krink, T.: A Clustal alignment improver using evolutionary algorithms. In: Proceedings of the Fourth Congress on Evolutionary Computation (CEC-2002). Vol. 1. (2002) 121–126
9. Thomsen, R., Fogel, G., Krink, T.: Improvement of Clustal-derived sequence alignments with evolutionary algorithms. In: Proceedings of the Fifth Congress on Evolutionary Computation (CEC-2003). (2003)
10. Thompson, J., Plewniak, F., Poch, O.: BAliBASE: A benchmark alignment database for the evaluation of multiple alignment programs. Bioinformatics **15** (1999) 87–88
11. Davis, L.: Adapting operator probabilities in genetic algorithms. In: Proceedings of the Third International Conference on Genetic Algorithms (ICGA III). (1989) 61–69
12. Notredame, C., Holm, L., Higgins, D.: COFFEE: An objective function for multiple sequence alignments. Bioinformatics **14** (1998) 407–422
13. Notredame, C., Higgins, D., Heringa, J.: T-Coffee: A novel method for fast and accurate multiple sequence alignment. Journal of Molecular Biology **302** (2000) 205–217

Constructing Microbial Consortia with Minimal Growth Using a Genetic Algorithm

Frederik P.J. Vandecasteele[1,2], Thomas F. Hess[1], and Ronald L. Crawford[2]

[1] Dept. of Biol. and Agric. Engineering, University of Idaho, Moscow, ID 83844-0904
[2] Environmental Biotechnology Institute, University of Idaho, Moscow, ID 83844-1052
{vand8442, tfhess, crawford}@uidaho.edu

Abstract. The processes occurring in microbial ecosystems are typically governed by the actions of many different microorganisms that can all interact with each other in a highly nonlinear way. Historically, most work in microbiology has been focused on pure cultures of single organisms, while the study of groups of organisms (consortia) still forms a major challenge. Although genetic algorithms are capable of optimising noisy and nonlinear systems and they should therefore be very well suited for studying microbial ecology, they have only rarely been used in this field. In this work, a genetic algorithm was successfully used to construct microbial consortia exhibiting minimal growth from separate isolated fast growing strains. The technique developed here may open the way to new ecological insights.

1 Introduction

Over the years, a vast amount of work in microbiology has been focused on the isolation and characterisation of pure cultures of microorganisms. Such traditional work has clearly advanced the fields of microbial physiology, genetics and ecology. In nature however, microorganisms rarely occur as pure cultures. Rather, they live in complex ecological systems, which can have high levels of non-linear interaction. The actions of every member of an ecosystem can be advantageous, disadvantageous or neutral for one or more of the other members. These complex interactions make the study of ecosystems particularly challenging. In addition to this, experimental ecological data is often rather noisy in nature.

Here we describe a genetic algorithm approach to constructing microbial consortia with minimal growth from a set of separate isolated strains, an objective that can't be obtained with classical microbiological enrichment techniques. This work represents a novel way to address the relationship between an ecosystem's species composition and its function and the technique developed here can result in new fundamental ecological observations.

G.R. Raidl et al. (Eds.): EvoWorkshops 2004, LNCS 3005, pp. 123–129, 2004.
© Springer-Verlag Berlin Heidelberg 2004

2 Background

As a new approach in microbial ecology, we first proposed the use of genetic algorithms to efficiently construct microbial consortia from sets of isolated strains in [1] and [2]. With this approach, a GA is used to artificially construct microbial consortia from separate isolated strains that optimally perform a specifically chosen ecological function. In [1], a GA was used to search a set of 40 different microbial soil isolates for subsets that degrade a dye chemical as fast as possible. In [2], the same approach was used to assemble consortia with optimal biomass production from 20 different soil isolates. Both experiments involved representing candidate consortia as binary strings and experimentally evaluating their fitness.

Other applications of evolutionary computation in experimental microbiology (as opposed to simulation studies) exist [3,4,5,6,7,8]. However, such studies have mainly been concerned with growth medium optimisation, in which the objective typically is to find the levels of various growth conditions resulting in the best performance of a microbial system.

Other studies exist that involve artificial assemblies of ecosystems. Examples include ecosystems constructed in controlled environments (e.g. [9]), the field of restoration ecology (e.g. [10]) and some of the work concerning the relationship between richness and productivity of ecosystems (for a review, see [11]). However, such studies typically don't include a classical optimisation approach.

3 Materials and Methods

3.1 Isolation of Strains

Microbial isolates with morphologically distinct colony features were obtained by incubating a dilution of a surface layer soil sample on R2A agar and incubating the plates at different temperatures. From these isolates, 20 different fast growing strains were selected that had grown well in an overnight Luria Bertani (LB) broth, as judged by the turbidity of the culture medium. An equal volume of 40% glycerol was added to the cultures (final concentration 20% glycerol), after which they were aliquoted in cryovials and stored at -80 °C.

3.2 GA Settings

The GA used here followed the generational model and had a population size of 20. Each solution was represented as a string of 20 bits, encoding the presence or absence of the corresponding microorganism. In this way, each solution encoded for a specific microbial consortium. The first generation was randomly generated. Fitness values were linearly rescaled, with $\mu'=\mu$ and $f_{max}'=2\mu$. If this yielded negative values, the fitness values were rescaled so that $\mu'=\mu$ and $f_{min}'=0$. Roulette Wheel selection was used. Whenever at least one parent was selected more than two times, the selection scheme was rejected and selection was repeated. Single crossover was performed on each pair of selected individuals with a probability of 0.90. Mutation was performed by flipping bit values with a probability of 0.01 per bit. Elitism was applied by copying the parent solution with the highest fitness into the next generation. Eight generations in total were evaluated.

3.3 Fitness Evaluation

The objective of this optimisation effort was to obtain a microbial consortium with minimal growth after 24 hours, composed of fast growing member strains. To evaluate the fitness of the individuals in a generation, the corresponding microbial consortia were assembled and incubated in the lab. First, the separate strains were diluted from their stock vials by adding 20 μL of each vial to 3 mL of LB. The 20 consortia were then constructed in 20 standard glass test tubes by transferring 100 μL volumes of the right dilution tubes to the right consortium tubes. After this, LB was added to the consortium tubes to make up all volumes to 6 mL. Each consortium was now made in triplicate by vortexing its tube and transferring 2 mL to two new glass test tubes. This resulted in a final growth medium volume for each experiment of 2 mL. The 60 (3 x 20) tubes making up one generation were incubated at 37 °C and 200 rpm for 24 hours. Growth after 24 hours was assessed by transferring 200 μL of each test tube to a 96 well microtiter plate and measuring the optical density in each well using an automated spectrophotometric plate reader. Optical density (OD) (dimensionless units) is a measure of turbidity, which is proportional to the amount of microbial cells present in each sample and thus OD constitutes a measure of microbial growth. The fitness value of each individual in the GA was calculated as the inverse of the average optical density value of the corresponding consortium for the three replicates. When a solution encoded for zero consortium members, it received a fitness value of zero (no instances of this occurred).

4 Results and Discussion

4.1 Trends in Minimum, Maximum, and Average Growth

The trends in minimum, maximum and average growth (expressed as OD units) are shown in Figure 1. During the course of these eight generations of optimisation, there was a significant decrease in minimum and overall growth per generation (p= 0.0119 and p <0.0001, respectively). By generation 8, the minimum, maximum and average growth had decreased by 18%, 23% and 23%, respectively, as compared to the first, random generation. The overall decrease in growth per generation was 0.04 OD units.

4.2 Best and Median Consortia Repeated

To account for between generation experimental variability, the experiments for the best and median consortium of each generation were repeated, both in a single batch,

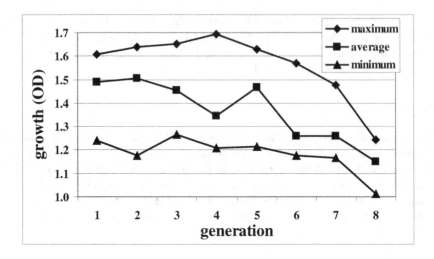

Fig. 1. Trends in Minimum, Maximum and Average Growth

with each consortium within a batch performed in triplicate. For each generation, the best consortium was the one with the lowest OD value and the solution that ranked at position 10 in a list sorted according to increasing OD values was chosen as the median consortium. There was a significantly decreasing trend in growth through the generations for both these batches ($p<0.0001$ for both), which confirmed the previously observed trends.

4.3   Gene Frequencies

For some strains, clear trends were visible in the average number of times they were present per consortium for each generation. While a number of these trends might be due to drift, they could also indicate some underlying ecological mechanisms. Some strains (e.g. strain 20) were clearly positively selected by the algorithm while others (e.g. strain 3) were eliminated from the population. This suggests that the respective negative or positive contribution of these strains to the growth of the consortia they are a member of was very pronounced regardless of their possible interactions with the other members of each consortium. On the other hand, the frequencies of some strains (e.g. strain 2) did not show a clear upward or downward trend. This might suggest that the effect of these strains on the growth of the consortia they are a member of was dependent on the presence or absence of other strains or that these strains have a neutral effect on overall growth. As an example, the trends of strains 2, 3 and 20 are given in Figure 2.

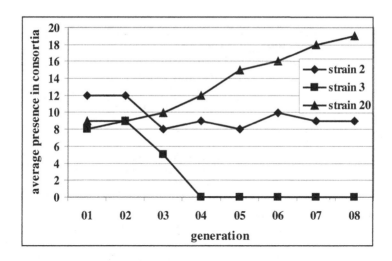

Fig. 2. Gene Frequencies of Three Strains

4.4 Composition of Generation 9

The composition of generation 9, the last calculated generation, is listed in Table 1:

Table 1. Composition of Generation 9

Individual	Structure	Individual	Structure
1	11000110101000111001	11	11000000001000111101
2	00010000001001001101	12	00010001001000111111
3	00010001001010001100	13	11010000001000111001
4	10010000001000111111	14	00010001001000111101
5	10011110101001111101	15	00011100111001011101
6	11000110001110011101	16	11010101001110101111
7	00010001001000111101	17	00010101111001011101
8	10010000001000011101	18	11110000000011001101
9	10011110001110011001	19	11000101001000101101
10	11000110101000111101	20	11010110101001111101

Several conserved regions within the chromosomes are apparent, while the population does not seem to be near convergence yet.

4.5 Best Individual in Each Generation

The structure of the best individual in each generation is given in Table 2:
It can be noted from the listed structures that conserved regions within the chromosomes were present.

Table 2. Best Individual in Each Generation

Generation	Structure
1	11110101101000111101
2	11010101101000111101
3	11001110101001101111
4	11010101001000111101
5	00010000001000111101
6	00010000001100111101
7	00010001001000111111
8	11000110101000111001

4.6 Proposed Ecological Mechanisms

We propose a number of hypothetical mechanisms by which the algorithm assembles consortia with low growth. It appears as if the GA has been quickly eliminating certain strains from the consortia. These could be strains that have a dominating overall positive effect on growth of the consortia of which they are a member. On the other hand, some strains seemed to be positively selected. These could be strains that have an overall negative effect on growth. Possibly, the algorithm is also seeking out clusters of organisms that together exhibit low growth. Ideally, this will ultimately result in the algorithm identifying a subset of organisms that together grow less than would each member individually. This could occur when such a set of organisms forms an ecological network where each strain is inhibited by the other strains. Such a find would be of fundamental ecological interest.

It should also be noted here that the objective of these experiments (minimal growth) can't be reached using classical enrichment techniques, the typical way of obtaining consortia in microbiology, because these techniques are based on a positive selection of faster growing strains under certain selective conditions.

5 Conclusion

This paper describes the successful use of a genetic algorithm to construct microbial consortia from separate isolated fast growing strains, with decreasing levels of growth through the generations. Within 8 generations (160 evaluations), a set of consortia was obtained of which the minimal growth had decreased by 18% and the average growth by 23% as compared to a first random set of consortia.

Even though this experiment may be considered to be somewhat of an academic exercise, the technique described here can lead to observations of fundamental ecological interest. In general, we have demonstrated that evolutionary computation can be used to design ecosystems to optimally perform certain specific predetermined functions. This technology can provide benefit to both industry (in e.g. fermentation and bioreactor applications) and fundamental ecology.

Acknowledgement. This research was supported by a fellowship from the Inland Northwest Research Alliance (INRA) Subsurface Science Research Institute which is funded by the Department of Energy under contract DE-FG07-02ID14277.

References

1. Vandecasteele, F.P.J.: Constructing Efficient Microbial Consortia Using a Genetic Algorithm. Biological Applications for Genetic and Evolutionary Computation (BioGEC) – 2003 Genetic and Evolutionary Computation Conference Workshop Program (2003) 69-71

2. Vandecasteele, F.P.J., Hess, T.F., Crawford, R.L.: Constructing Microbial Consortia with Optimal Biomass Production Using a Genetic Algorithm. 2003 Genetic and Evolutionary Computation Conference – Late-Breaking Papers (2003) 299-302

3. Davies, Z.S., Gilbert, R.J., Merry, R.J., Kell, D.B., Theodorou, M.K., Griffith, G.W.: Efficient Improvement of Silage Additives by Using Genetic Algorithms. Applied and Environmental Microbiology 66 (2000) 1435-1443

4. Marteijn, R.C.L., Jurrius, O., Dhont, J., de Gooijer, C.D., Tramper, J., Martens, D.E.: Optimization of a Feed Medium for Fed-Batch Culture of Insect Cells Using a Genetic Algorithm. Biotechnolgy and Bioengineering 81 (2003) 269-278

5. Patil, S.V., Jayaraman, V.K., Kulkarni, B.D.: Optimization of Media by Evolutionary Algorithms for Production of Polyols. Applied Biochemistry and Biotechnology 102-103 (2002) 119-128

6. Weuster-Botz, D., Pramatarova, V., Spassov, G., Wandrey, C.: Use of a Genetic Algorithm in the Development of a Synthetic Growth Medium for *Arthrobacter simplex* with High Hydrocortisone Δ^1-dehydrogenase Activity. Journal of Chemical Technology and Biotechnology 64 (1995) 386-392

7. Weuster-Botz, D., Wandrey, C.: Medium Optimization by Genetic Algorithm for Continuous Production of Formate Dehydrogenase. Process Biochemistry 30 (1995) 563-571

8. Zuzek, M., Friedrich, J., Cestnik, B., Karalic, A., Cimerman, A.: Optimization of Fermentation Medium by a Modified Method of Genetic Algorithms. Biotechnology Techniques 10 (1996) 991-996

9. Lawton, J.H., Naeem, S., Woodfin, R.M., Brown, V.K., Gange, A., Godfray, H.J.C., Heads, P.A., Lawler, S., Magda, D., Thomas, C.D., Thompson, L.J., Young, S.: The Ecotron: a Controlled Environmental Facility for the Investigation of Population and Ecosystem Processes. Philosophical Transactions of the Royal Society London B 341 (1993) 181-194

10. Jordan, W.R., Gilpin, M.E., Aber, J.D.: Restoration Ecology: a Synthetic Approach to Ecological Research. Cambridge University Press, Cambridge New York (1987)

11. Waide, R.B., Willig, M.R., Steiner, C.F., Mittelbach, G., Gough, L., Dodson, S.I., Juday, G.P., Parmenter, R.: The Relationship between Productivity and Species Richness. Annual Review of Ecology and Systematics 30 (1999) 257–300

2-Objective Optimization of Cells Overlap and Geometry with Evolutionary Algorithms

Adel Jedidi[2], Alexandre Caminada[1], and Gerd Finke[2]

[1] Lab. Systèmes et Transport, UTBM, 90010, Belfort, France
alexandre.caminada@utbm.fr
[2] Lab. LEIBNIZ, INPG, 46 avenue Félix Viallet, 38000 Grenoble, France
gerd.finke@imag.fr, adel.jedidi@free.fr

Abstract. Cellular network design is a very large and complex combinatorial optimization problem. It consists of antenna location and parameters settings. Until now, the design is done using radio quality criteria. Radio coverage, traffic capacity and field overlap are the main factors considered within optimization process to make decisions about network solutions. Nevertheless, such objectives do not lead to an efficient organization of network cells whereas this is a major assessment for radio expert planners. Absence of a clear geometrical structure of network cells prevents experts using many theoretical concepts on network design. This paper proposes an original model to evaluate the cell shape and a bi-criteria approach using an Evolutionary Algorithm to handle cells overlap and cells geometry as criteria for real-life network optimization.

1 Introduction

Locating sites to position base station transmitters (BS) and defining their antenna parameters represent the most difficult tasks in wireless network design [1][2][3]. First, sites are selected using one fixed setting for every BS. Then, an antenna parameter-tuning step is necessary to enhance the quality of service on the large geographical area where different BSs are deployed. This area has grid architecture and every bin simulates a possible position of a mobile station (MS). A concentrator approach [4] is then defined in order to concentrate MS on BS. This concentration is done during an optimization process regarding some radio constraints and objectives explicitly described in [1]. Generally, the final optimized network provides a good compromise between the different radio criteria. However, radio expert planners lack assurance about feasibility of such theoretically modeled and optimized networks. Design decision makers (experts) take more interest in the structure of networks, which are defined by the geometry of cells and their organization over the working area. Best field mapping is one of the relevant tools used to visualize network structure. It always shows, for theoretically optimized networks, a randomized cell shape and chaotic networks. Area irregularities and effects of radio signal propagation that are not taken into account during the standard optimization process appear in the resulting networks. The absence of a clear geometrical structure is limiting the network evolution because its traffic capacity and service quality cannot be guaranteed. This paper formulates in detail the shortcomings of the network geometry and tackles briefly its

G.R. Raidl et al. (Eds.): EvoWorkshops 2004, LNCS 3005, pp. 130–139, 2004.
© Springer-Verlag Berlin Heidelberg 2004

state-of-art. Then we propose a multi-objective scenario to allow the network planner to optimize cell geometry and cell overlap. Finally a Multi-Objective Evolutionary Algorithm for the optimization of BS parameterization is used to validate this model on real life networks and check the effect of cell shaping on bi-criteria network design.

2 Problem Statement

As mentioned earlier, network optimization is only based on radio criteria. Previous works in this field [1][2][3] usually consider coverage, overlapping cells and deployment cost as the main optimization objectives. The resulting design formulates precisely site locating and BS antenna settings. Radio experts who proceed to the evaluation of such design refuse most of the time the different BS parameterization. In fact, decision makers (radio experts), when visualizing different cells, realize the poor network geometry provided by optimizing BS parameters. Actually, the cell shape (see definition of cell in the next section) depends directly on location of bins where stations offer the best radio signal. Signal strength is controlled by the BS parameters. Optimizing station parameters without a criterion taking into account geometry of cells inevitably leads to bad network structures especially if there is no evident relationship between radio criteria and geometry. Some papers dealing with cellular network design [1][5] propose cell and network connectivity constraints to consider geometrical aspects in the BS parameter optimization (this work was done during the European IT project ARNO nr.23243, 1997-1999). Area irregularities may interrupt the propagation of electromagnetic waves. Bins assigned to one BS cell can be scattered because of irregular field strength rising. Connectivity constraints avoid BS antenna settings leading to different disconnected parts of the cell or the entire network. However, cells shape and organization cannot be handled by this constraint.

Theoretically, the cellular concept [6] is based on regular hexagonal lattices to represent the different cells. It facilitates the station antenna positioning and it is equipped with periodic frequency assignment reuse to get a total cellular radio network planning. Nevertheless, this simple concept and its derivatives (cell splitting and frequency set reuse) are not able to take into account constraints resulting from the topography of the covering area and its corresponding traffic density. Adaptive meshing as presented in [7] is based on the cellular concept and handles the traffic density. The goal of adaptive meshing is to homogeneously subdivide a given traffic resource between meshes. The meshes are subject to hard geometrical constraints of shape and topology. The adapted meshing is especially used as a solution to the problem of mobile network dimensioning and not for the design. Indeed, models used for adaptive meshing do not consider radio engineering and consequently no BS parameter optimization can be done.

From this brief state of art, we see that network geometry based on cellular concept and design of real life networks have been treated separately. The study presented in this paper uses cell geometrical and cell overlapping criteria all together to optimize the network design.

3 Optimization Formulation

3.1 Pre-optimization Step

To carry out this optimization, we propose to develop it in two steps. Since the cellular network design is a very large combinatorial optimization problem, a pre-optimization step meaningfully contributes to a reduction of the search space and to enhance the candidate solution quality for the optimization step. Indeed, BS parameters are picked from a set of settings fixed at the beginning of each optimization. In our case, all tilt, azimuth and antenna type values respectively cover a common interval for global stations. Combining these three parameters builds up one BS antenna setting. The pre-optimization step tries to eliminate BS antenna settings producing abnormal cells. The antenna parameter performance is evaluated using the cell shape model G described in [8] and other geometrical quality constraints such as connectivity, etc. The pre-optimization step acts as a filter of bad antenna settings in order to yield better solutions for the optimization process. All these solutions compose the parameter space L from which decision vector x is selected to define the network antenna configurations. Formally, considering a network with m stations, a possible configuration of its antenna settings for the optimization process may be written as follows:

$$x=(x_1, x_2,\ldots, x_m) \in L=L_1 \times L_2 \times \ldots \times L_m$$

where L_i is the list of the different antenna settings kept in the pre-optimization step for the ith BS. The choice of the final solutions (decision vectors) is subject to constraints and to a vector function, which consists of the different objectives to be optimized during the second step of optimization. The next section describes in detail these objectives and constraints.

3.2 Optimization Step

As mentioned in the beginning, the cellular network design is a multi-criteria and multi-constraint optimization problem. In our case, we restrict the criteria only to radio coverage, field overlap and geometry of cells, which is a new optimization criterion. Coverage is handled as a constraint, overlap and geometry as objectives. Our optimization will be based on a multi-objective evolutionary algorithm widely used to solve such problems.

- Radio coverage constraint. The radio coverage constraint consists of keeping sufficient field strength over the working area in order to establish communications between an MS ($b_{(i,j)}$) and at least one BS. The radio coverage being a hard constraint, we propose to manage this later in our MOEA by a specific transformation described in 4.2. If we note   the design threshold, the radio coverage constraint may be written as follows:

$$\exists k \in BTS \mid F_{(i,j)}^k \geq \tau \ \forall \ b_{(i,j)} \ \textit{from the working area} \tag{1}$$

- Cell geometry. The cell geometry is a new criterion in the network design that can be handled as a constraint or as an objective. Previous work on the same problem considered the first approach [8]. It uses a distance based penalty method incorporating a dynamic aspect that depends on the length of the search (i.e. generation number). Unfortunately, this technique uses parameters, which are problem dependent and consequently cannot be useful for an operational and automatic design tool. Typically, these parameters require a specific tuning to perform final optimization solutions. Hence we propose a parameter-less method (MOEA) taking the geometry as an objective given below:

$$G(C_k) = \frac{\sum_{b_{(i,j)} \in C_k} V^k(b_{(i,j)})}{8 \times Surface(C_k)} + \log_n^{-2}(Surface(C_k)) \tag{2}$$

- Cell overlap. Network design gives a high importance to overlap management. After BS positioning and parameterization of their antenna, the network is assigned a frequency plan. Interference quantity is highly dependent of field overlap. If there is too much cell overlap, interference will be very high. However, field overlap is necessary for handover management (communication continuity when MS moves between cells). Compromise solutions are necessary in order to balance between interference quantity and field overlap. In order to define the overlap management, the field strengths are sorted on each bin $b_{(i,j)}$ of a cell C_k from the best signal to the worst one:

$$\underbrace{F_{(i,j)}^k \geq F_{(i,j)}^{k_1} \geq ... \geq F_{(i,j)}^{k_h}}_{Necessary\ Fields} \geq \underbrace{F_{(i,j)}^{k_{h+1}} \geq ... \geq s_m \geq ...}_{Undesiarble\ Fields} \tag{3}$$

where h represents the target number of BS for the handover and s_m is the sensitive threshold beyond which fields are not taking into account. The overlap quantity to be minimized for each cell C_k is defined by the size of the set I_k as in [1].

$$I_k = \left\{ F_{(i,j)}^{k_l} / l \geq h+1\ and\ F_{(i,j)}^{k_l} \geq s_m, \forall b_{(i,j)} \in C_k \right\} \tag{4}$$

Notice that the set I_k can contain repeated points. Undesirable fields received on different bins of a cell may come from the same BS.

4   A MOEA for Network Design

Network design is restricted in this study to the choice of BS antenna parameter settings. The MOEA used to achieve such design considers objectives and constraints presented in the last section. It uses also the concept of Pareto dominance to provide the *Optimal Pareto Set* of *non-dominated* solutions [9]. A decision vector x (or a solution) is said to *dominate* another decision vector y iff:

$$\forall i \in \{1,2,...,n\}: f_i(x) \leq f_i(y) \quad \wedge$$
$$\exists j \in \{1,2,...,n\}: f_j(x) < f_j(y) \tag{5}$$

where $f(x)=(f_1(x),f_2(x),...,f_n(x))$ is the objective vector for a minimization problem.

In this paper, the objective vector is bi-dimensional ($n=2$) and is a function only of overlap and geometry. Previous work on the optimization of these two objectives used a population-based non-Pareto approach. This method also called Vector Evaluated Evolutionary Algorithm [10] separates the original population into two subpopulations. Each one evolves its individuals according to one criterion. Richardson

[11] noted that combining individuals of many sub-populations is equivalent to a linear combination of different criteria using "virtual" weighting coefficients. However, this method as mentioned in [12] has serious limitations especially in the case of a concave trade-off surface. Consequently, our MOEA will consider a non-dominated sorting procedure in conjunction with a sharing technique. This will yield more diversity and individuals are well spread along the best Pareto front. These techniques are presented in detail in the next section.

4.1 Problem Transformation

Standard Evolutionary Algorithms (SEA) need a modification in order to take into account several objectives. This modification occurs at the selection level. Conventionally, SEA select individuals according to their fitness function. MOEA, considering several criteria, measure performance in terms of an objective value vector. The assigned fitness expresses individual reproductive ability and must remain a scalar for the MOEA. Hence MOEA require for individual evaluation a new fitness function called in the literature the *dummy fitness* [13][14]. This latter is defined by a *Ranking Strategy* and uses the concept of *non-dominance*. The majority of MOEA that are based on the concept of Pareto dominance uses one of the following ranking procedures: the Non-Dominated Sorting (NDS) proposed by Goldberg in [15] or the Multi-Objective Ranking (MOR) proposed by Fonseca and Fleming in [16].

Once individuals have been ranked by any one of these two methods (NDS or MOR), they are assigned a new dummy fitness function giving an approximation of their reproduction probability. This fitness is as follows for an individual i:

$$
fitness(i) = \begin{cases} \dfrac{1}{r(i)} \ for \ a \ \text{minimization problem} \\[2mm] r(i) \ for \ a \ \text{maximization problem} \end{cases}
\tag{6}
$$

In our study, we have to minimize the overlap and maximize the total geometry of network cells. In order to homogenize the optimization direction, we propose to minimize the inverse of the function G. We adopt for that the first formulation in equation (6).

To prevent a premature convergence and to achieve the diversity, the literature distinguishes two useful methods: parameter-based methods and parameter-less ones [17]. Fitness sharing [9][10] is one of the most used parameter-based techniques in MOEA. This niche formation method prevents genetic drift by penalizing individuals, which are too close one to another. By this way, the population tends to distribute itself around the optima forming niches. This technique requires a definition of a *closeness* parameter called *niche radius* (*size*) and referred to in literature by σ_{share}. A *distance* measure operating in a genotypic or phenotypic space defines this neighborhood parameter value. Some papers [14][17][18] noted the similarity between the sharing function and the *Epanechnikov* kernel density estimator used by statisticians. Indeed, the kernel smoothing parameter used in the estimator is largely analogous to the fitness sharing niche size. The techniques developed in statistics have then been used to find a suitable niche radius, which remains the main difficulty for the fitness sharing parameter-based methods. Because of that, many researchers like Ziztler et al. [19],

Deb et al. [20], Knowles et al. [21] and Corne et al. [22] investigated parameter-less methods to overcome the inconvenience of determining the niche size value.

After this brief state-of-the-art, we present in the next section the techniques used in our MOEA to achieve the design of cellular networks.

4.2 A MOEA to Optimize BS Parameters Settings

Our optimization problem for BS parameter settings can be stated as follows:

$$Min \quad f(x) = (f_1(x), f_2(x)) \in O$$
$$subject \ to \ x = (x_1, x_2, ..., x_m) \in F \subseteq L \tag{7}$$

Where f is the objective vector, f_1 is the overlap quantity, f_2 is the inverse of the cell geometry function, x is the decision vector, $L = L_1 \times L_2 \times ... \times L_m$ is the parameter space, m is the number of stations, L_i is the list of validated settings for station i during pre-optimization step, F is the feasible parameter space (with respect to coverage constraint), O is the objective space.

The NDS procedure developed for our study is combined with a fitness sharing parameter-based method. This sharing is considered at the phenotypic level to maintain diversity in the objective space. Genotypic sharing is not very interesting in our problem because two different network BS parameterizations may have the same f evaluation and consequently diversity can be lost. The various steps of our Non-dominated Sorting Evolutionary Algorithm combined with sharing are the following for every generation:

1. Firstly, identify for each individual i in the population the front to which it belongs using the NDS ranking;
2. Assign the dummy fitness function $fitness(i)$ to all individuals of the population;

$$fitness(i) = \frac{1}{r(i)} \tag{8}$$

3. For each higher fitness value, an individual (non-dominated solution of current front) share its dummy fitness by dividing its value by a quantity proportional to its neighbor individual density and according to a given radius σ_{share}. The new degraded dummy fitness value is:

$$fitness(i) = \frac{\alpha}{r(i).m(i)} \tag{9}$$

where α is initialized to one for the first and global non-dominated solutions, $m(i)$ is the niche count quantified as follows:

$$m(i) = \sum_{j=1}^{P} Sh(d(i,j)) \tag{10}$$

where P is the number of individuals belonging to the current front, $Sh(d)$ is a non-linear decreasing sharing function of d and defined by:

$$Sh\big(d(i,j)\big) = \begin{cases} 1 - \left(\dfrac{d(i,j)}{\sigma_{share}}\right)^2 & if \quad d(i,j) \le \sigma_{share} \\ 0 & else \end{cases} \tag{11}$$

d is a *normalized Euclidian distance* defined in the phenotypic space and has this measure form for our problem:

$$d(i,j) = \sqrt{\left(\frac{f_1(i) - f_1(j)}{Max(f_1) - Min(f_1)}\right)^2 + \left(\frac{f_2(i) - f_2(j)}{Max(f_2) - Min(f_2)}\right)^2} \tag{12}$$

where for a population size N: $Max(f_k) = \underset{l=1,\dots,N}{MAX} f_k(l)$ and $Min(f_k) = \underset{l=1,\dots,N}{MIN} f_k(l)$, $k \in \{1,2\}$

4. Update the value α by the minimum fitness previously found by equation (9) in step 3.
5. The last individuals treated in step 3 are temporarily ignored from the population and the remaining ones form a new population. Go to step 3 and repeat the process until the global population has been visited.
6. All population individuals are then assigned a dummy fitness, genetic operators can be applied in the usual manner.

The niche size σ_{share} is specified by the formula defined by Deb in [10] and which can be calculated as follows: $\sigma_{share} = \dfrac{0.5}{\sqrt[n]{q}}$

where n is the objective vector size and q is the desired number of distinct Pareto-optimal solutions. Moreover, as mentioned in [10], the performance of the Non-Sorted Evolutionary Algorithm is not sensitive to niche radius value when this latter is obtained using $q=10$. Thus we use for our algorithm the same parameter value q, which gives a niche radius of 0.158 ($n=2$).

Notice that for the handling of the radio coverage constraint, we use a binary penalty function stated as below for an individual i:

$$Penalty(i) = \begin{cases} 1 & if \quad i \in F \\ -1 & else \end{cases} \tag{13}$$

where F is the feasible region in the parameter space. This penalty is included in the dummy fitness function of equation (15) and its new formulation may be written:

$$fitness(i) = Penalty(i).\frac{\alpha}{r(i).m(i)} \tag{14}$$

Notice that our problem being transformed to a maximization problem assigns the worst fitness to individuals that do not satisfy the radio coverage constraint. At the re-placement level, the selection operator only operates on individuals with positive dummy fitness. Consequently, all the selected solutions satisfy the radio coverage constraint.

5 Preliminary Experimental Tests

Experimental tests were carried out on a real life network A. Various runs with different MOEAs were tested in order to compare the convergence towards the Pareto front and the diversity of the obtained non-dominated solutions. The best MOEA offers to experts a solution range to choose the appropriate network configuration with an acceptable overlap and geometry compromise.

5.1 Experimental Conditions

Notice that an individual is a network configuration where BS antenna parameters are assigned values picked from a BS setting list. For our study, we distinguish four MOEAs that only differ in the used selection strategy. The first algorithm uses the *stochastic universal sampling* selection mechanism because of its low stochastic error. The second one uses the standard two-point tournament selection. It consists of picking at random two individuals in the population and in comparing them. The best one is sorted and both are re-introduced in the population. The third algorithm combines both elitism and sharing schemes to perform convergence and diversity of solutions across the final trade-off surface. The last algorithm uses a combination of SUS selection and elitism to speed up convergence toward the best Pareto front. Mutation consists of one replacement of the BS setting. The new BS parameters are randomly picked from the BS setting list. This latter is provided during the pre-optimization step (see 3.1). Crossover operators are not used at all in the MOEA.

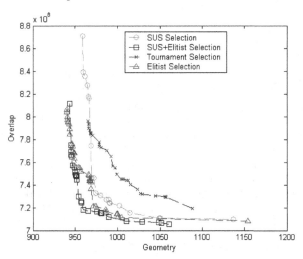

Fig. 1. Comparison of multiple Pareto fronts provided by MOEAs applied to network A.

5.2 Performance Evaluation

In the literature, the performance of a MOEA can be measured into two major criteria:

- *Diversity*: this criterion gives a spread measure of the different non-dominated so-lutions composing the trade-off surface.
- *Closeness* (*Generational distance*): this metric formulates the nearness (or dis-tance) of each non-dominated solution to the nearest point belonging to the true (or global) optimal Pareto front denoted by P^*. These distances (usually the Euclidian distances) can be averaged to provide a measure for a single MOEA accuracy.

The four MOEAs earlier mentioned use the same sharing strategy. Thus no spread metric is presented here to compare the different MOEA. The generational distance is usually used in comparison of a multiple MOEA performance applied to benchmarks (academic examples) where the global (optimal) Pareto front P^* is explicitly defined like in [10]. Moreover, this set should be sufficiently large and should be uniformly distributed across the trade-off surface. Unfortunately, we cannot provide obviously the set P^* for our optimization problem. Our evaluation (see Fig.1) is only based on a simple visualization of the different Pareto fronts provided by the multiple MOEA. This evaluation is similar to the concept of the *attainment surface* described in [17]. Fig.1 illustrates selection impact on Pareto fronts. SUS+Elitist selection seems to be the more suitable strategy to obtain the nearest non-dominated solutions to the global Pareto front. These solutions are well spread along the trade-off surface. The same sharing technique being used by all of the MOEAs, the diversity can also be checked for the non-dominated solutions provided by the other selection strategies. Notice that when the archive set is large, a random sorting procedure is applied to reduce its size. This technique may provide a bias of solutions. Thus further work will consider the clustering procedure presented in [19] to perform well diversity of non-dominated solutions.

6   Conclusion and Further Work

This paper has introduced a bi-criteria model for cells evaluation in the design of cel-lular networks. A Multi-Objective Evolutionary Algorithm was described to handle cell geometry and cell overlap provided by BS parameter settings. Four variant selec-tion MOEAs were tested on a real-world network. The obtained Pareto fronts offer a non-dominated solution range to radio experts in order to make decisions about the suitable network configuration. A sharing mechanism was added to the MOEA to maintain a maximum diversity in the offered solutions. Our study was only restricted to the design of BS antenna parameters. Further work will consider in addition the problem of locating sites to position new stations. This future work aims at respond-ing to the GSM traffic growth and to the deployment of the UMTS networks.

References

1. P. Reininger and A. Caminada, "Multicriteria Design Model for Cellular Network", *Annals of Operation Research 107*, 2001, pp. 251-265.
2. L.J. Ibbetson and L.B. Lopes, "An Automatic Base Site Placement Algorithm", *Vehicular Technology Conference*, N°46, pp. 760-765, 1997.
3. P. Calegari, F. Guidec, P. Kuonen and D. Wagner, "Genetic Approach to Radio Network Optimization for Mobile Systems", *IEEE VTC'97*, N°46, pp. 755-759.

4. G.D. Smith, P. Chardaire and J.W. Mann, "The Location of Concentrators using Genetic Algorithm", *School of Information Systems*, University of East Anglia, Norwich, August 1994.
5. J.K. Hao and M. Vasquez, "Heuristic Approach for Antenna Positioning in Cellular Networks", *Journal of Heuristics*, February 2000, pp. 443-472.
6. V.H. Mac Donald, "The Cellular Concept", *The Bell System Technical Journal*, Vol.58, N°1, pp. 14-41, January 1979.
7. T. Lissajoux, A. Koukam, D. Renaud, A. Caminada and J.C. Creput, "Evolutionnary Meshing for Mobile Network Dimensionning", *ALGOTEL*, June 1999.
8. A. Jedidi, A. Caminada, G. Finke, T. Dony, "Geometrical Constraint Handling and Evolutionary Algorithm for Cellular Network Design", *Int. Network Optimisation Conf. 2003*, *Paris*.
9. C.M. Fonseca and P.J. Fleming, "An Overview of Evolutionary Algorithms in Multiobjective Optimization", *Evolutionary Computation*, 1995, pp. 1-16.
10. K. Deb, "Evolutionary Algorithm for Multi-Criterion Optimization in Engineering Design", *In Proc. of Evolutionary Algorithms in Engineering and Computer Science*, EUROGEN'99.
11. J.T. Richardson, M. R. Palmer, G. Liepins and M. Hilliard, "Some Guidelines for Genetic Algorithms with Penalty Functions", 3rd *Int. Conf. on Genetic Algorithms*, pp. 191-197.
12. Y. Collette and P. Siarry, "Optimisation multiobjectif", *Edition Eyrolles*, 2002.
13. N. Marco, J.A. Désidéri and S. Lanteri, "Multi-Objective Optimization in CFD by Genetic Algorithms", *Report N°3686*, INRIA Sophia Antipolis, April 1999.
14. C.M. Fonseca and P.J. Fleming, "Multiobjective Genetic Algorithms Made Easy: Selection Sharing and Mating Restriction", 1st *Int. Conference on Genetic Algorithms in Engineering Systems: Innovations and Applications*, (Conf. Publ. N°446), 12-14 Sep. 1995, pp. 45–52.
15. D. E. Goldberg, "Genetic Algorithms in Search, Optimization and Machine Learning", *Addison-Wesley*, Reading, Massachusetts.
16. C.M. Fonseca and P.J. Fleming, "Genetic Algorithms for Multiobjective Optimization: Formulation, Discussion and Generalization", 5th *ICGA*, 1993, pp. 141-153.
17. R. C. Purshouse and P. J. Fleming, "Elitism, Sharing and Ranking Choices in Evolutionary Multi-Criterion Optimization", *Research Report N°815*, Departement of Automatic Control and Systems Engineering, University of Sheffield, UK, January 2002.
18. R. C. Purshouse and P. J. Fleming, "The Multi-objective Genetic Algorithm Applied to Benchmark Problems – An Analysis", *Research Report N°796,* Departement of Automatic Control and Systems Engineering, University of Sheffield, UK, August 2001.
19. E. Zitzler and L. Thiele, "Multiobjective Evolutionary Algorithms: A Comparative Case Study and the Strength Pareto Approach", *IEEE T. on Evo.Comp.*, Vol.3 , N°4, pp. 257-271.
20. K. Deb, A. Pratap, S. Agarwal and T. Meyarivan, "A Fast and Elitist Multiobjective Genetic Algorithm: NSGA-II", *IEEE Trans. on Evolution. Comp.*, Vol.6, Apr. 02, pp.182-197.
21. J.D. Knowles and D.W. Corne, "M-PAES: A Memetic Algorithm for Multiobjective Optimization", *In Proc. of CEC 2000*, pp. 325-332, IEEE Press, Piscataway, NJ.
22. D.W. Corne, N.R, Jerram, J.D. Knowles and M.J. Oates, "PESA-II: Region-base Selection in Evolutionary Multiobjective Optimization, *In Proc. of GECCO-2001*, pp. 283-290.
23. H. Meunier, E.G. Talbi and P. Reininger, "A Multiobjective Genetic Algorithm for Radio Network Optimization", *Int. Workshop on Emergent Synthesis IWES'99*, pp. 317-324.
24. M. Laumanns, E. Zitzler and L. Thiele, "A Unified Model for Multi-Objective Evolutionary Algorithms with Elitism", *In Proc. Of Evolutionary Computation*, 2000, Vol.1, pp. 46-53.

A Genetic Algorithm for Telecommunication Network Design

Silvana Livramento[1], Arnaldo V. Moura[1], Flávio K. Miyazawa[1],
Mário M. Harada[2], and Rogério A. Miranda[2]

[1] Computing Institute, University of Campinas, Brazil
{silvana.livramento,arnaldo,fkm}@ic.unicamp.br
http://www.ic.unicamp.br
[2] Research Center in Telecommunications - CPqD, Brazil
{harada,rogeriom}@cpqd.com.br
http://www.cpqd.com.br

Abstract. A Genetic Algorithm (GA) to solve a problem in telecommunication network design is described. The problem is to partition a large urban project area into smaller service sections, which can be controlled by a single standard communication switch. The GA incorporates geometric and topological information from the project area by operating directly with a grid of geographically dispersed demand points. Computational results show this to be a promising technique for partitioning the project area and positioning the control switches. Tests were realized with real instances taken from large areas in the city of São Paulo.

1 Introduction

Usually, and particularly in Brazil, an urban telecommunication network is organized as a large and sophisticated hierarchical system. At the topmost nodes one finds a set of very large control stations, which may encompass a whole city. At the lowest nodes there are small distribution switches, from which customers receive their individual lines. This article describes a Genetic Algorithm (GA) that focuses on the middle range of this hierarchy. The GA was developed as an automatic computational aid that can be used when designing the network[1].

In order to better understand the problem, the network is partitioned into two logical segments. The first part is formed by large capacity trunks, typically interconnected by optical, radio or satellite links. This first segment terminates in a substation, which may control from tens of thousand to a few hundred thousand individual lines, although these numbers may vary considerably. The second segment comprises the area controlled by one such substation, which we call a project area. Each project area, in turn, is subdivided into a number of smaller areas, called service sections, each service section typically controlling around five hundred individual lines. Within each service section is located a distribution switch, linked by optical fiber to the corresponding substation. Typically,

---

[1] This work has been partially supported by CNPq (Proc. 300301/98-7, 470608/01–3, 478818/03–3) and CPqD.

G.R. Raidl et al. (Eds.): EvoWorkshops 2004, LNCS 3005, pp. 140–149, 2004.

copper pairs (in bundled cables) run from the distribution switch to the individual demand points. A demand point may request more than one line. Further, since the project data also takes into account an estimate of future needs in the number of communication pairs, a demand point may well require a fractional number of lines. To resume, the segment of interest is formed by a project area in which a large set of demand points are geographically positioned. An estimate is also given for each demand point, indicating its present and future needs for communication lines. The network design problem is the problem of partitioning the project area into service sections and locating the distribution switches within each service section, while satisfying a number of project constraints and minimizing a known cost function. Details are given in the next section.

We propose a GA to solve the network design problem. The representation we adopt differs from others found in the literature, like vectors or graphs, which are not adequate to treat some important geometric aspects of the problem. As a consequence, the genetic operators will also differ from the usual ones. The result was a novel evolutionary formulation for the network design problem. The algorithm was tested using large real instances stemming from complex urban areas in the city of São Paulo. It produced very adequate solutions in a reasonable amount of computing time, when run on a typical desktop PC. Even though the algorithm was developed to treat the specific constraints that apply to the communication networks in the city of São Paulo, we believe that the same ideas can be adapted to other scenarios without much effort.

There are a number of other studies that deal with the network design problem, or one of its many variants [1,2,3]. Steiner trees, minimum spanning trees, or extensions thereof, have also been used to model the network design problem [4,5,6,7]. Another approach is to use extensions of the capacitated single commodity network design problem [8], or use generalizations of the facility location problem [9]. Other models use linear programming coupled with a Lagrangian relaxation technique [10]. In [11], a whole section is dedicated to evolutionary algorithms for telecommunication network design. It includes studies on reliability, leased-line networks, network planning, and optical network, among others. One restriction of many of these approaches is that they need a predefined set of possible positions of the distribution switches.

The paper is organized as follows. Section 2 introduces details of the network design problem. Section 3 presents the GA formulation and Section 4 discusses computational results. Lastly, we offer some closing remarks.

2   Problem Definition

The problem is given by a set T of triples $(x, y, d) \in \mathbb{R}^3$, where x and y are location coordinates of a demand point, and d represents its needs in terms of communication lines. A solution is a partition π of T, each member of π being a service section. Within the convex hull of each service section, we have to locate a distribution switch. Initially, we do not know how many service sections there ought to be.

The cost of a service section is the cost of its distribution switch plus an estimate of the cost for cables running from the switch to each demand point located within the section. So, the cost of a service section s is defined by

$$w_s = c_a + f \sum_{i \in s} [d_i \times dist(p_a, p_i)], \tag{1}$$

where c_a is the cost of a switch, p_i and d_i are the position and demand of point i, respectively, p_a is the location of the switch in s, $dist$ is the Euclidean distance, and $f = \sigma\beta$ is a constant, where σ represents the cables average cost per unit length, and $\beta > 1$ is a correction factor that is applied to the distance since, in reality, cabling does not follow the shortest path. The constants σ and β were obtained by averaging over existing networks in similar project areas. The cost of a solution π is the value $w(\pi) = \sum_{s \in \pi} w_s$. The objective is to find a solution π that minimizes $w(\pi)$. Throughout this paper we use C as the distribution switch capacity, K as the maximum load factor, k as the minimum load factor and D_s as the total demand in a section s, i.e. $D_s = \sum_{i \in s} d_i$. In any acceptable solution π we must have $k \times C \leq D_s \leq K \times C$, for each section s of π.

3   The Genetic Algorithm

In this section we present the GA and its particularities. For an introduction to GAs, see [12,13,14,15]. Finer details can be found in [16].

3.1   Representation

The first step when designing a GA is to devise a suitable representation for it. For the network problem, the usual vector representation is not adequate since we do not know the number of service sections in advance, nor do we know the position of its switches. We also have to ensure a reasonable geometry for the service sections, that being a subjective measure of roundness, to be judged adequate by experimented project engineers. We propose a different representation.

We circumscribe the project area by a rectangle and divide it into equal $\ell \times \ell$ cells, where the size ℓ is an external parameter. We assign a single demand point to each cell, with a demand equal to the sum of its demand points, and positioned at the weighted average location of all its interior points. See Figure 1. The resulting mesh is called the neighborhood mesh. It yields geometric, topological and neighborhood information about all demand points. Now, the problem reduces to partitioning the neighborhood mesh into service sections.

A chromosome encodes a mesh M and a vector S of sections. Each cell of M points to a position in S, indicating the section it belongs to. Each entry in S contains a pointer to a list of its cells, a pair of integers representing the position of its switch, and a number indicating its total demand. The mesh M and the vector S contain redundant information but, for efficiency reasons, we keep both.

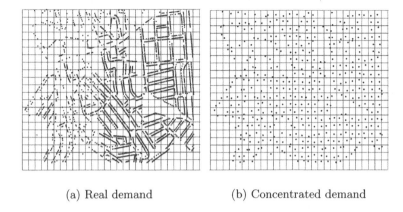

(a) Real demand   (b) Concentrated demand

Fig. 1. Neighborhood mesh.

3.2   Initial Population

In order to obtain the i-th individual in a population of size n, n being an external parameter, we start by rotating the mesh clockwise by $\pi/2 \times (i/n)$. Next, the mesh is recursively sectioned by vertical and horizontal cuts, until each resulting rectangular area comprises a total demand of at most $K \times C$. At each iteration, we section the largest side of each rectangle whose demand is above $K \times C$.

3.3   Crossover

The crossover point will be given by a cut through the neighborhood mesh. We defined four types of cuts: horizontal, vertical, southwest and northwest. Figure 2 illustrates two such cuts. Initially, depending on the cut type, a cell is chosen in the mesh. Next, the cut is augmented by randomly selecting one among three neighboring cells at the cut's present edge, repeating the cycle until a mesh boundary is reached. When selecting the next cell in a cut, we assign probabilities to each candidate cell. The probabilities depend on the type of the cut, on the position of the candidate cell and on whether it lies on the same service section as does the cell at the present edge of the cut. For details, see [16].

For the crossover operator, we select two parents by the roulette method [14], define cuts in each one and cross-interchange their halves, thereby creating two children. See Figure 3, where regions with different numbers mark distinct sections and empty cells have zero demand. Figures 3(a) and 3(b) represent the parent chromosomes. Figure 3(c) illustrates a northwest cut across the first parent; a similar cut was obtained across the other parent. Figure 3(d) illustrates one of the children created by the crossover operator. After crossover, sections divided by the cut may show a demand below the allowed minimum. To remedy this, a repair operation attempts to incorporate low demand sections into neighboring sections. This operation can be described as

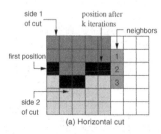 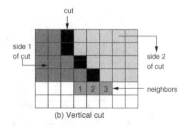

(a) Horizontal cut   (b) Vertical cut

Fig. 2. Two cut types.

CROSSREPAIR(π)
1    $S \leftarrow \{s : s$ is a section of $\pi\}$
2   **for** each $s \in S$
3   **do if** $D_s < k \times C$
4   **then repeat**
5   Distribute the cells at the border in s into neighboring
6   sections, without exceeding the allowed maximum.
7   **until** $(s \neq \emptyset)$ or (there are no such neighboring sections)

A section will remain with low demand, if it does not have enough neighboring sections capable to incorporate all its demand points.

3.4   Mutation

The mutation operator has a local search flavor. It needs three external parameters d_{min}, d_{med} and d_{max}, with $d_{min} \leq d_{med} \leq d_{max}$, all proportional to C. We start by randomly selecting a number of chromosomes to undergo mutation. This number is an external parameter. Each selected chromosome will undergo one of two types of mutation.

If the number of sections is above the minimum $\lceil (\sum_{s \in \pi} D_s)/(K \times C) \rceil$, we randomly select 40% of the sections, section s having a selection probability proportional to $(D_s - K \times C)^2$. For each selected section s, if $D_s < d_{min}$, we make s lose all its points to neighboring sections, and if $D_s > d_{max}$ we make it lose points until its demand falls below $K \times C$. When $d_{min} < D_s < d_{med}$, s will receive points from neighboring sections. These operations are described bellow.

LOSEPOINTS(s, D)	RECEIVEPOINTS(s, D)
1 **while** $D_s > D$	1 **while** $D_s < D$
2 **do for** each p in the border of s	2 **do for** each p in the border of s
3 **do** Put p at the neighboring	3 **do** Put in s the neighboring
4 section that has the lesser	4 points of p that are in a
5 demand	5 different section

This mutation operator adjusts the number of service sections in the solution.

If the selected chromosome already has the minimum number of sections, we attempt to lower the cost of the solution by applying the second kind of

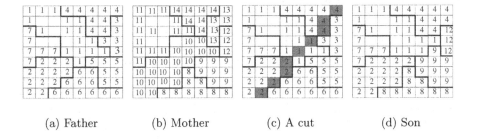

(a) Father   (b) Mother   (c) A cut   (d) Son

Fig. 3. Crossover operator.

mutation. This operator is described as follows, where $SwitchPos(s)$ gives the position of the switch in s and m corresponds to 40% of the number of sections.

POINTMUTATION(π, m)

1   $S \leftarrow \{s : s \text{ is a section of } \pi\}$
2   **for** $i \leftarrow 0$ to $m - 1$
3   **do**   Select $s \in S$ with probability $w_s / \sum_{s \in S} w_s$
4   **for** each p in the border of s
5   **do if** $\exists s_v \in S : dist(SwitchPos(s_v), p) < dist(SwitchPos(s), p)$
6   **then**   Remove p from s
7   Put p in s_v

3.5   Fitness Function

The roulette method needs a fitness function. First we attribute penalties for capacity violations. For a section s, the penalty associated to s is

$$\tau_s = \begin{cases} \gamma \times (k \times C - D_s) & \text{if } D_s < k \times C \\ \gamma \times (D_s - K \times C) & \text{if } D_s > K \times C \\ 0 & \text{if } k \times C \le D_s \le K \times C, \end{cases} \tag{2}$$

where $\gamma > 0$ is a parameter. The penalty of a solution π is $\tau(\pi) = \sum_{s \in \pi} \tau_s$.

The fitness of a solution π is given by $\varphi(\pi) = \left[N - (w(\pi) + \tau(\pi)) \right] / F$, where N is the minimum value that makes φ positive for all solutions in the population, and F is a uniform normalizing factor given by summing all parcels $\left[N - (w(\pi) + \tau(\pi)) \right]$ over the entire population.

3.6   Other Features

To select parents for crossover we use the roulette method based on the fitness function. The individuals selected to mutate are chosen randomly among the children generated by crossover only. We use elitism, i.e. the best individuals always survive. The number of elite individuals, of individuals that will generate children, and of those that will mutate are all external parameters.

4   Computational Results

The GA was implemented in C++ and tests were ran on a Pentium IV platform with a 2 GHz clock and 1GB of RAM. All test instances were real data, representatives of urban neighborhoods in the city of São Paulo, Brazil. Tables 1 and 2 give some numerical characteristics of the data. The cost of a switch and the average cost of a unit length of cable are given in the same monetary unit. The population size was set to 50 individuals, the elite rate was 10%, the crossover rate was 80% and the mutation rate 20%.

Table 2. Problem parameters.

Parameter	Sym.	Value
Distribution switch capacity	C	600
Distribution switch cost	c_a	2.3×10^5
Max. load factor	K	0.8
Min. load factor	k	0.3
Aver. cable cost per unit length	σ	0.0323
Distance correction factor	β	1.9
Coefficient of the penalty function	γ	800
Min. demand in mutation operator	d_{min}	216
Med. demand in mutation operator	d_{med}	480
Max. demand in mutation operator	d_{max}	504

Table 1. Data characteristics.

Inst.	Num. points	Demand
1	6276	10112.85
2	8482	11350.35
3	19007	34432.75
4	42453	90679.80

Table 3. Results of GA for all test cases.

Inst. area	Time (min)	Numb. of sections	Total cost ($\times 10^3$)	Demand			
				st. dev.	min.	max.	ave.
1	29	21	4,912.02	4.99	471.20	499.80	481.56
2	30	24	5,608.05	7.09	456.40	484.31	472.89
3	200	71	16,703.25	17.87	406.13	533.43	480.62
4	600	187	43,661.22	21.46	411.10	560.05	481.40

The intent of the algorithm is to minimize the total cost of the network, as well as to obtain a demand distribution among the various sections that is as uniform as possible. For each test instance, the algorithm was executed five times, each run lasting for 1000 iterations. The results depicted in Table 3 are averages over all five runs. For each instance, it is shown the computation time in minutes, the number of sections obtained, the total cost, using the same monetary unit as in Table 2, and some statistics about the total demand in each section: the standard deviation, the minimum, the maximum and the average.

In all tests, the algorithm found a solution with the minimum number of switches and with a very uniform demand distribution among them. Figure 4 illustrates this point by plotting the demand in all sections, for the first test case. Notice how all demand values are very close to the best value of 480.

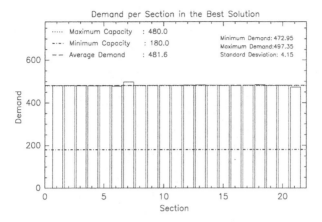

Fig. 4. Demand distribution per section, first test case.

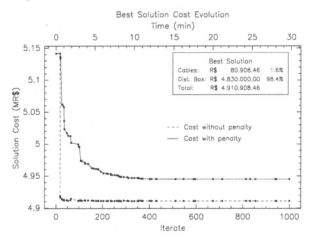

Fig. 5. Evolution of the algorithm, first test case.

Figure 5 illustrates the GA evolution when using the first test case. We notice a great cost improvement in the first iterations. This happens when the number of sections is reduced. After this point, the algorithm is working to reduce cable costs by exchanging demand points between sections. Figure 6 shows the solution obtained for the first test case. Each shaded area is a distinct section and the large black dots give the location of the corresponding switches. The geometric shape of these sections was deemed adequate for this stage of the design. From this point on, experienced engineers can make small local adjustments. In any case, the computational tool has already arrived at a quite satisfactory solution, saving many labor intensive hours involving expert engineers and trained technicians.

A tabu search (TS) was also implemented and tested over the same instances. Table 4 illustrates the results. When the number of demand points is small, TS

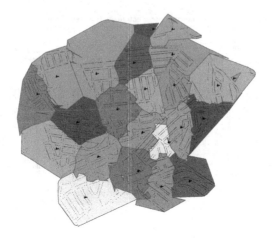

Fig. 6. Solution, first test case.

Table 4. TS results

Inst. area	Time (sec)	Numb. of sections	Total cost ($\times 10^3$)	Demand			
				st. dev.	min.	max.	ave.
1	20	21	4,907.80	63.70	324.00	529.20	481.56
2	30	24	5,606.27	68.63	263.00	527.10	472.89
3	100	72	16,822.34	79.18	212.55	592.20	476.10
4	400	200	46,533.83	102.67	11.10	583.80	450.10

obtained somewhat lower cable costs, but the GA produced a better demand distribution. For larger instances, the GA obtained the best solutions.

5   Conclusions

A GA to solve a complex optimization problem that arises in the context of telecommunication network design is described. The algorithm was developed to minimize the total project cost and to produce a demand distribution among the various service sections that is as uniform as possible. It is worth mentioning that neither the best number of sections, nor the set of demand points served by each section, nor the position of any switch was known in advance. Another important aspect of the algorithm is its ability to deal with geometric information that is present in the input data. This required new crossover and mutation operators, while other approaches to similar problems do not treat this aspect explicitly. All tests cases stem from real data, taken from urban neighborhoods of a large city. The algorithm performed quite well in all test cases, within acceptable computing time bounds. The demand distribution was very nearly uniform, and the algorithm obtained the minimum number of service sections in all cases.

References

1. A. Balakrishman, T. L. Magnanti, A. Shulman, and R. T. Wong. Models for planning capacity expansion in local access telecommunication networks. *Annals of Operations Research*, pages 33:239–284, 1991.

2. T. L. Magnanti, P. Mirchandani, and R. Vachani. The convex hull of two core capacitated network design problems. *Mathematical Programming*, 60:233–250, 1993.

3. D. Bienstock and O. Günlük. Computational experience with a difficult mixed-integer multicommodity flow problem. *Mathematical Programming*, 68:213–237, 1995.

4. H. P. L. Luna, N. Ziviani, and R. M. B. Cabral. The telephonic switching center network problem: Formalization and computational experience. *Discrete Applied Mathematics*, 18:199–210, 1987.

5. B. Gavish. Formulations and algorithms for the capacitated minimal directed tree. *Journal of the ACM*, 30:118–132, 1983.

6. B. Gavish. Topological design of telecommunication networks — local access design methods. *Annals of Operations Research*, 33:17–71, 1991.

7. D. S. Hochbaum and A. Segev. Analysis of a flow problem with fixed charges. *Networks*, 19:291–312, 1989.

8. G. R. Mateus, H. P. L. Luna, and Adriana B. Sirihal. Heuristics for distribution network design in telecommunication. *Journal of Heuristics*, 6:131–148, 2000.

9. E. Gourdin, M. Labbé, and H. Yaman. Telecommunication and location. Technical report, Service de Mathematiques de la Gestion, Universite Libre de Bruxelles, 2001. citeseer.nj.nec.com/587324.html.

10. G. R. Mateus and Jean-Michel Thizy. Exact sequential choice of locations in a network. *Annals of Operations Research*, 86:199–219, 1999.

11. David W. Corne, Martin J. Oates, and George D. Smith, editors. *Telecommunications Optimization: Heuristic and Adaptive Techniques*. Wiley, 2000.

12. Wolfgang Banzhaf, Peter Nordin, Robert E. Keller, and Frank D. Francone. *Genetic Programming: An Introduction*. Morgan Kaufmann Publishers, Inc., 1998.

13. D. A. Goldberg. *Genetic Algorithms in Search. Optimization and Machine Learning*. Addison-Wesley, January 1989.

14. Zbigniew Michalewicz. *Genetic Algorithms + Data Structures = Evolution Programs*. Springer, third, revised and extended edition edition, 1996.

15. Zbigniew Michalewicz and David B. Fogel. *How to solve it : modern heuristics*. Springer, 1999.

16. Silvana Livramento, Arnaldo V. Moura, Flávio K. Miyazawa, Mário M. Harada, and Rogério A. Miranda. Um algoritmo genético para projeto de rede de telecomunicações. Technical Report IC-03-024, Instituto de Computação - Unicamp, november 2003. In Portuguese.

A GA/Heuristic Hybrid Technique for Routing and Wavelength Assignment in WDM Networks

A. Cagatay Talay and Sema Oktug

Department of Computer Engineering, Istanbul Technical University,
34469 Istanbul, Turkey
{talay, oktug}@cs.itu.edu.tr

Abstract. The routing and wavelength assignment problem which is known to be NP-hard, in all-optical transport networks is considered. The present literature on this topic contains a lot of heuristics. These heuristics, however, have limited applicability because they have a number of fundamental problems including high time complexity, and lack of scalability with respect to optimal solutions. We propose a hybrid genetic algorithm/heuristic based algorithm. A cost model that incorporates a dependency on link wavelength requirements is adopted. The hybrid algorithm presented uses an object-oriented representation of networks, and incorporates four operators: semi-adaptive path mutation, single-point crossover, reroute, and shift-out. Experimental results of the test networks make clear that, when the network cost depends on heavily wavelength assignment, the proposed GA/Heuristic hybrid approach provides promising results compared to recent wavelength assignment heuristics.

1 Introduction

Recently, there has been considerable progress in the area of all-optical networks, in particular the networks based on wavelength division multiplexing (WDM) [1]. WDM technology has been shown to provide cost-effective transmission and switching. WDM based all optical networks or almost all optical networks offering multi-gigabit rate per wavelength may soon become economical as the underlying backbone in wide area networks.

When individual static traffic requirements are supposed to be routed independently on a single wavelength end-to-end, one aspect of the optical-path-layer design of multiwavelength all-optical transport networks is to determine the route, fibers, and wavelength each connection will use. This problem and its variants have attracted considerable interest, with a variety of solution approaches including heuristics, genetic algorithms (GAs), and ILP technique. Those heuristic algorithms have restricted applicability in a practical environment because they have a number of fundamental problems including high time complexity, lack of robustness and no performance guarantee with respect to the optimal solutions.

Nagatsu *et al.* [2] presented a heuristic where the initial routing is accomplished with Dijkstra's algorithm using the number of paths carried by each link as the link

G.R. Raidl et al. (Eds.): EvoWorkshops 2004, LNCS 3005, pp. 150–159, 2004.
© Springer-Verlag Berlin Heidelberg 2004

weights. Next, iterative rerouting, constrained by hop count, is used to equalize link weights. Finally, wavelengths are allocated to the paths, aiming for minimum network wavelength requirement (NWR). In [3], Nagatsu *et al.* then extended their heuristic to include preplanned path restoration in single-link failure conditions. Whereas in [4] Nagatsu and Sato modified the original heuristic to include multiple fiber links, with only a restricted number of wavelengths per fiber. Then, in [5], Nagatsu *et al.* combined the two earlier extensions into a single heuristic. For both [4, 5], their objective was to minimize the average number of ports on the network's optical cross-connects (OXCs).

Wuttisittikulkij and O'Mahony [6] developed a simple, fast and non-iterative heuristic, which works with *k*-lowest hop count paths to obtain a low NWR.

Tan and Sinclair [7] described a variety of GA-based solution approaches. The most successful of these, combined a traditional binary GA for route selection and with a heuristic for wavelength and fiber allocation, aiming for minimum NWR.

Wauters and Demeester [8] presented an integer-linear-programming approach that aims for maximum throughput, and two heuristics. The first algorithm is based on a version of Dijkstra's algorithm. The algorithm is modified such that when extending an already found part of a route, only those arcs that have a wavelength channel free on all links of the already found part of the route are considered. This algorithm produces a low cost allocation, and also keeps NWR low. Their second algorithm, called the heuristic routing and wavelength assignment (HRWA), is based on iterative application of a modified version of Yen's *k*-shortest path algorithm, and aims to produce the lowest cost allocation to achieve minimum NWR.

Our GA/Heuristic approach is to incorporate some advanced heuristics into an overall genetic algorithm. It adopts a problem-specific encoding based on object-oriented manner, and then employs problem-specific operators that together combine the best existing heuristics for the problem with an overall GA framework. It is almost possible to develop a problem-specific heuristic/GA hybrid that will outperform either the heuristic or traditional GA solutions. This is the approach employed in this work.

The paper is organized as follows: The cost model used is described in Section 2. Section 3 gives the detailed information about the GA/heuristic technique proposed here. Section 4 presents the simulation environment and results obtained. Finally, Section 5 concludes the paper.

2 Cost Model to Be Considered

Many researchers [2, 3, 6, 7, 9,10] have considered a low NWR as a design objective due to the technological limitations, and resulting cost implications, of carrying more than a small number of wavelengths over national or even international distances [9]. However, an objective that consists of a simplified assessment of the cost of the whole network including, at an appropriate level the cost of exceeding the minimum NWR, is arguably superior.

The original version of the cost model used here had been developed in [10]. Separate models for both links and nodes are required to determine the cost of a network. The intension is to approximate the relative contribution to purchase, installation and maintenance costs of the different network elements, while ensuring that the model is not too complex to use in the inner loop of a design procedure. Given the network path, the capacity of link (i,j) is taken to be:

$$V_{ij} = \lambda_{ij} V_\lambda \qquad (1)$$

where λ_{ij} is the total number of wavelengths in use on the link (i.e. across all its fibers) and V_λ is the granularity of the wavelength channels (i.e. 10Gbit/s). The wavelength-requirement capacity of link (i,j) can be formulated as:

$$V_{\lambda,ij} = \lambda_{req,ij} F_{ij} V_\lambda \qquad (2)$$

where $\lambda_{req,ij}$ is the wavelength requirement of the link (i,j) (i.e. the highest wavelength number of any fiber on the link) and F_{ij} is the number of fibers in use on link (i,j). The wavelength-requirement capacity is thus the capacity that would result if all the dark (unused) wavelengths on all (partially used) fibers of the link were filled, up to the current link wavelength requirement. Capacity is one of the elements in the link cost calculation. Consequently, wavelength requirement capacity allows the additional costs of uneven fiber loading and dark wavelengths to be assessed in equivalent capacity terms, and thus included at an appropriate level in the overall link cost. The capacity cost of link (i,j), $C_{V,ij}$, and the wavelength-requirement cost of link (i,j), $C_{\lambda,ij}$, are:

$$C_{V,ij} = V_{ij}^\alpha L_{ij} \qquad \text{and} \qquad C_{\lambda,ij} = V_{ij}^\beta L_{ij} \qquad (3)$$

where α and β are constants and L_{ij} is the length of link (i,j) in km. Increasing capacity necessarily implies increased cost due to wider transmission bandwidth, narrower wavelength separation and/or increasing number and speed of transmitters and receivers. With $\alpha=1$, linear dependence of cost on capacity is assumed, but with $\alpha<1$, the cost can be adjusted to rise more slowly with increases in the link capacity. The linear link length dependency approximates the increasing costs of, for example, duct installation, fiber blowing and/or the larger number of optical amplifiers with increasing distance. By setting $\beta\neq\alpha$, the link model can be adjusted to allow different dependency of cost on wavelength requirement capacity. The overall cost of link (i,j) is then taken to be:

$$C_{ij} = \gamma C_{V,ij} + (1-\gamma)C_{\lambda,ij} \qquad (4)$$

where γ is a constant ($0 \leq \gamma \leq 1$). Different values of γ allow the model to reflect the relative contributions to link cost of the capacity cost and the wavelength-requirement cost. With $\gamma=1$, the link only takes account of the capacity used, and ignores the link wavelength requirement; whereas, with $\gamma=0$, the actual capacity used is ignored, and the focus is entirely on the wavelength requirement. An intermediate value of γ, such as 0.5, is regarded as being more representative of the actual cost involved.

For the nodes, a node effective distance is used as a way of representing the cost of nodes in an optical network in equivalent distance terms. It can be regarded as the effective distance added to a path as a result of traversing a node. Although [11] uses it to influence the selection of paths in minimum cost network topology design, thereby reflecting the relatively high costs of optical switching, here it is only used as a part of the node cost model. The node effective distance of node i is taken to be:

$$N_i = K_0 + n_i K_n \qquad (5)$$

where n_i is the degree of node i, i.e. the number of links attached to it. Here the constants K_0 and K_n are taken as 200km and 100km, respectively. Thus, node effective distance increases, as the switch grows more complex. Node capacity is the sum of the effective capacity of all attached links, where V_i is the capacity of node i in Gbit/s and the effective capacity of link (i,j) is given by:

$$V_{e.ij} = \gamma W_{ij} + (1 - \gamma)V_{\lambda.ij} \qquad (6)$$

The node capacity is therefore dependent, to some extent, on the wavelength requirements of the links attached to it. The node cost can then be formulated as:

$$C_i = 0.5 N_i V_i \qquad (7)$$

The cost is thus derived as if a node is a star made by links, each of half the node effective length, and each having the same capacity as the node itself. Further, if all the links attached to a node are of the same capacity (have equally balanced fibers), the node costs would grow approximately with the square of the node degree, corresponding, for example, to the growth in the number of crosspoints in a simple optical space switch. Overall, the relative costs of nodes and links can be adjusted by setting the values of K_0 and K_n appropriately.

The network cost is then taken to be the sum of the costs of all individual links and nodes comprising the network. However, the metric used also includes a penalty, added for each individual traffic requirement unsatisfied, to avoid the false minimum of carrying no traffic at all, which would otherwise have a network cost of zero.

3 The Technique Proposed

We introduce an object-oriented approach to represent networks. The *NetworkModel* class category contains classes used to represent networks for topology design as well as routing, fiber and wavelength allocation, plus metrics to allow the assessment of designs. For example, the main *Network* class composed of *Nodes*, *Links*, and *PathLossSeqs* (path-loss sequences, [12]), plus several implementation classes used to represent the network's adjacency matrix [13, 14], connection matrix and the static traffic requirements.

The classes that implement GA framework are grouped into the GA class category, and illustrated in the main GA class diagram in Figure 1 with its *Population* of individuals and its *OperatorPool* of operators. An individual simply consists of a single *Network* object and some additional accounting information. Operators themselves are created by deriving classes from either unary operator (*UnaryOp*) or binary operator (*BinaryOp*) classes (not shown). In general, those derived from *UnaryOp* are analogous to mutation [15] in a traditional GA, but can be powerful heuristics that utilize arbitrary amounts of problem-specific information. Similarly, *BinaryOp* subclass is analogous to traditional cross-over [15], although once again, there is considerable potential for problem-specific heuristics. As in [16], the probabilities of individual operators being applied to an individual adapt through the course of a run using a credit-assignment algorithm described below.

As well as including the abstract classes representing operators (*Operator, UnaryOp* and *BinaryOp*) and routers (*Router, UnaryRouter* and *BinaryRouter*), the *Operators* class category includes a large number of concrete classes derived from these. The operators range from those of modest effect, analogous to traditional mutation or crossover, intended for use within a GA framework, through more powerful problem-specific operators, up to complete design heuristics, intended for use in isolation. Routers are those operators capable of completely routing a network, rather than merely modifying an existing routing (i.e. either simple routing, for topology design, or complete routing, fiber and wavelength allocation as appropriate).

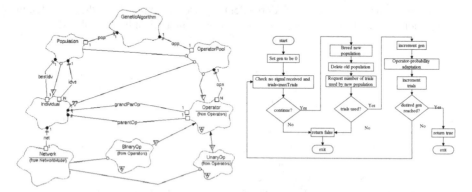

Fig. 1. GA class diagram

Fig. 2. Flowchart of the GeneticAlgorithm run() member function

3.1   The Genetic Algorithm Class

The Genetic Algorithm class is central to GA/heuristic hybrid approach. It supports a generational, rather than steady-state, algorithm [16], and depends heavily on two other classes: *Population*, which holds the population of evolving network designs, and *OperatorPool*, which not only manages the pool of genetic operators used for population evolution, but also runs the operator-probability adaptation mechanism.

The main *GeneticAlgorithm* class constructor takes three arguments: parameter databases built from both the network specification and parameter files, plus a pseudo-random number generator object. After extracting the GA's one parameter, the maximum number of trials, it uses the parameter databases and random number generator to build both population and operator-pool objects. Both of these, as well as the maximum number of trials, can subsequently be retrieved with the appropriate member functions. In addition, a GA object maintains one additional data member, the current number of trials, which is initialised to zero, and can also be accessed via a member function. A flowchart of the *run()* member function is given in Figure 2 below. This shows the overall generational nature of the process, represented by the main loop, including breeding of a new population and its replacement of the old, as well as the use of operator-probability adaptation. However, there are a number of decision points that can end the iteration. As well as receipt of the appropriate interprocess signal, exceeding the maximum number of trials or completing the desired number of generations, there is one further possibility. To appreciate this, first note that network objects both cache their last assessment result, and also count the number of trials they have used in self-assessment since their construction. This count is made available via a member function, and so the number of trials (i.e. assessments) used in constructing a population can be obtained by summing over all its constituent network objects. Consequently, if a new population is bred without consuming any trials, then not a single network has been changed in the breeding process: the GA is `spinning' (i.e. has converged to identical or almost identical population members), and the run is terminated.

3.2 Population Class

The Population class is not only responsible for containing a population of individuals, but also maintaining several important population statistics. There are two main *Population* class constructors. One of these, taking both network specification and parameter databases plus a random number generator, creates a full population. The other, omitting the network specification parameter database, creates an empty population, to which individuals can subsequently be added. The former constructor is used for initial population construction, whereas the latter is intended as part of breeding a new population from an old one. Both constructors extract and store several parameters: the population size, the window size (w) for best-in-window fitness, the selection function and, if the latter is tournament selection, the tournament size. The statistics stored include, at the end of the last generation, the highest fitness (i.e. assessment) of any individual in the population, the lowest fitness, the average fitness and the median fitness. Further, a record is maintained of the lowest fitness in each generation over a user-defined number of generations. In addition, a copy of the best individual (i.e. of lowest fitness) seen up to the end of the last generation is made.

3.3 Individual Class

The Individual class is simply a network class with some additional accounting in formation to support operator credit assignment. The main constructor takes two arguments: the parameter databases for network specification and parameters. From the latter database, a single parameter is taken to determine whether the individual constructs a *Network* or a *PhyNetwork* using the network database. However, construction of an individual from parameter databases in this way is computationally relatively expensive, and as a result, after the first, the remainder of the individuals in a population is actually created using the copy constructor. An individual stores a pointer to its network object, as well as pointers to both its parent and grandparent operators. These latter objects are used by the credit-assignment mechanism to ensure that two- and three-operator sequences are properly rewarded.

3.4 OperatorPool Class

A variety of operators have been incorporated GA that are used in this work. These are, Wavelength-allocation path mutation (WM), wavelength-allocation single-point crossover (WCO), wavelength-allocation path reroute operator (WRR) and wavelength-allocation path shift-out operator (WSO). In addition to containing and owning the set of operators utilized in a particular GA/heuristic hybrid algorithm, the operator pool is responsible for both breeding the population and managing the credit-assignment and operator-probability adaptation mechanisms.

The *OperatorPool* class provides only two member functions: *breed()* and *adaptOpProb()*. The former creates a new population from an old one. Until the new population is full, it first chooses an operator from the pool at random, according to their current probabilities. Next, for unary operators, it selects an individual from the old population using the designated selection function, creates a new individual from this, and then applies the chosen operator. Both the operator's children and trials counts are increased by 1 and the number of trials actually used (which may be 0, 1 or more), respectively. Then, the operator itself, as well as the individual's parent and grandparent operators, are awarded any credit earned, according to the applicable credit type. Finally, the new individual, possibly modified, is added to the new population. The second member function periodically adjusts the individual operator probabilities according to the algorithm discussed below.

3.5 Operator-Probability Adaptation

As a variety of operators are incorporated in different GA/heuristic hybrid algorithms, it might seem necessary to determine appropriate operator probabilities for each of the distinct combinations of operators used. However, this implies a large computational effort. Instead, the probabilities of individual operators being applied to an individual adapt during the course of a run using a credit-assignment algorithm, rather than being fixed throughout.

The operator-probability adaptation algorithm adopted is based on that of Davis [16]. Whenever an individual is created whose fitness exceeds that of the best individual found before the end of a generation, the improvement in fitness is credited to the operator responsible:

$$c'_u = c_u + (f_b + f_i), \quad f_i < f_b \tag{8}$$

where c'_u and c_u are the current and previous values of the accumulated credit of operator u, f_b is the best fitness found at the end of the previous generation, and f_i is the fitness of individual i. In addition, as it has already been mentioned, a decreasing fraction of the credit is awarded to the parent operator and grandparent operator, to ensure that two- and three-operator sequences are rewarded appropriately. After a few generations, a small proportion of the operator probabilities are reassigned according to the average credit earned per child. In addition, operators are given a minimum probability to ensure they do not lose the opportunity to gain some credit if they, having decayed to the minimum level, are later found to be useful to further evolve the population. Figure 3 gives the operator probabilities for another run, where the effect of the adaptation algorithm can be clearly seen.

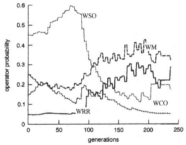

Fig. 3. Operator probability adaptation

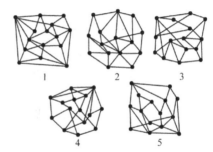

Fig. 4. Test network topologies

4   Experimental Results

The results obtained from the GA/heuristic hybrid approach are compared with three of the recent wavelength allocation algorithms: Wuttisittikulkij and O'Mahony's heuristic [6] (W&O), Wauters and Demeester's [8] modified Dijkstra based heuristic (W&D), and their HRWA heuristic (W&D2). Five test network topologies adopted from [17] are employed in experiments. The initial node locations and traffic requirements for the networks (Fig. 5) are generated using the approach described by Griffith et al. [18], after being modified to ensure reasonable node separations. Each network with 15 nodes, covers a 1000kmx1000km area and carries an overall traffic of 1500Gbit/s. The proposed hybrid method generates the best results over the other compared algorithms. The simulations for the GA/heuristic hybrid method have a population size of 500 networks. A maximum of 10000 generations, and tournament selection of size 4 are used. The operators' initial probabilities are 0.05 for WM, 0.25 for WCO, 0.15 for WRR, and 0.45 for WSO. The probabilities are selected after a few trial runs, aiming that would remain approximately constant for 50 or so generation. It could be argued that such starting values best promote high-quality solutions by approximately matching operator probabilities according to their effectiveness. Throughout the simulations, the operator probability adaptation algorithm parameters were set to the values suggested in Section 3.

Each hybrid is run five times with different initial random seeds (the best of five runs is selected). Simulations are repeated with different α and β values as shown in Tables 1-6. In addition, W&O, W&D1 and W&D2 are also run for the test networks for each setting of α, β and γ and the best result is considered. When necessary in heuristics k value is taken as 8. The results are given in Tables 1-6, with the lowest cost in each table for a given network shown in bold. For almost all network topologies, the lowest cost values are obtained by the proposed hybrid algorithm.

With $\gamma=1$, the network cost on capacity is focused rather than wavelength requirement. Here, the best heuristic among the others is W&D1, and this result could be justified considering that W&D1 uses shortest paths. However, the hybrid method provides the best results for all networks under this parameter setting.

Setting $\gamma=0$, means that the network cost depends entirely on wavelength requirement rather than capacity. Here, the best results are produced by W&O and the hybrid techniques. Such a result for W&O is rather natural since this technique is based on the optimization of wavelength requirement.

Table 1. Network cost for $\alpha=\beta=1$ and $\gamma=0.5$

Nt.	W&O	W&D1	W&D2	Hybrid
1	5.909	6.007	6.358	**5.579**
2	5.151	5.241	5.278	**4.886**
3	5.153	5.707	5.637	**4.976**
4	5.413	5.528	5.765	**5.117**
5	5.424	5.778	5.658	**5.108**

Table 2. Network cost for $\alpha=\beta=1$ and $\gamma=1$

Nt.	W&O	W&D1	W&D2	Hybrid
1	5.704	5.172	5.896	**4.994**
2	5.081	4.589	5.046	**4.436**
3	5.051	4.625	5.446	**4.394**
4	5.313	4.808	5.388	**4.645**
5	5.302	4.806	5.326	**4.640**

Table 3. Network cost for $\alpha=\beta=1$ and $\gamma=0$

Net	W&O	W&D1	W&D2	Hybrid
1	**6.036**	6.843	6.820	6.116
2	**5.213**	5.893	5.510	5.228
3	5.229	6.789	5.828	**5.228**
4	5.503	6.247	6.142	**5.499**
5	5.544	6.740	5.991	**5.523**

Table 4. Network cost for $\alpha=\beta=0.8$ and $\gamma=0.5$

Net	W&O	W&D1	W&D2	Hybrid
1	4.653	4.890	5.103	**4.450**
2	4.089	4.238	4.212	**3.909**
3	4.138	4.656	4.559	**3.866**
4	4.312	4.474	4.608	**4.062**
5	4.313	4.684	4.518	**4.040**

Table 5. Network cost for $\alpha=\beta=0.8$ and $\gamma=1$

Net	W&O	W&D1	W&D2	Hybrid
1	4.489	4.233	4.757	**4.014**
2	4.036	3.731	4.039	**3.531**
3	4.056	3.802	4.414	**3.541**
4	4.230	3.910	4.320	**3.716**
5	4.216	3.913	3.267	**3.716**

Table 6. Network cost for $\alpha=\beta=0.8$ and $\gamma=0$

Net	W&O	W&D1	W&D2	Hybrid
1	4.755	5.546	5.448	**4.742**
2	**4.128**	4.745	4.384	4.130
3	**4.200**	5.510	4.704	4.188
4	4.382	5.039	4.896	**4.378**
5	4.409	5.455	7.769	**4.361**

As a final notice, we should mention the amount of computing time required. Simulations were run on an Intel Pentium 4 2.6GHz computer with 512MB RAM. While a single run of GA1 takes about 41 seconds, running GA3 takes some 2 hours 35 minutes. When we run the other algorithms on the same environment we observed that, W&O takes 3 hours 10 minutes, W&D1 takes 1 hour 22 minutes and W&D2 takes nearly 2 hours 52 minutes for a single run.

5 Conclusions and Future Work

In this study, a GA/heuristic based hybrid technique is proposed. Object oriented network representation is employed. Two metrics for network effectiveness assessment are used: one is based on NWR, and the other is based on a simplified model of network cost. The results obtained with the hybrid technique are compared with those obtained from the recent wavelength-allocation heuristics. It is observed that the proposed hybrid technique has very promising results under various parameter settings.

Currently, as well as increasing network sizes, we are comparing our hybrid technique with the others considering the blocking ratio as the performance measure. Parallelism of the GA framework on such an application could be another future work issue.

References

1. Special issue on photonic packet switching systems, technologies and techniques. IEEE/OSA Journal of Lightwave Technology, Vol. 16, No. 12, (1998)
2. Nagatsu, N., Hamazumi, Y., and Sato, K.I.: Number of wavelengths required for constructing large-scale optical path networks. El. Com. Jpn. 1, Com., (1995), 78, 1-11
3. Nagatsu, N., Hamazumi, Y., and Sato, K.I.: Optical path accommodation designs applicable to large scale networks. IEICE Trans. Commun., (1995), E78-B, (4), 597-607
4. Nagatsu, N., and Sato, K.I.: Optical path accommodation design enabling cross-connect system scale evaluation. IEICE Trans. Commun., (1995), E78-B, (9), 1339-1343
5. Nagatsu, N., Okamoto, S., and Sato, K.I.: Optical path cross-connect system scale evaluation using path accommodation design for restricted wavelength multiplexing'. IEEE J. Sel. Areas Commun., (1996), 14, (5), 893-902
6. Wuttisittikulkij, L., and O'Mahony , M.J.: A simple algorithm for wavelength assignment in optical networks. Proceedings 21st European conference on Optical Commun., ECOC'95, Brussels, (1995), 859-862
7. Tan, L.G., and Sinclair, M.C.: Wavelength assignment between the central nodes of the COST 239 European optical network. Proceedings of the 11th UK Performance engineering workshop, Liverpool, UK, (1995), 235-247
8. Wauters, N., and Demeester, P.: Design of the optical path layer in multiwavelength cross-connected networks. IEEE J. Sel. Areas Commun., (1996), 14, (5), 881-892
9. Omahony, M.J., Simeonidou, D., Yu, A., and Zhou, J.: The design of a European optical network. J. Lightwave Technol., (1995), 13, (5), 817-828
10. O'Mahony, M., Sinclair, M.C.,Mikac, B.,: Ultra-High capacity optical transmission network: European research project COST 239, Inf. Tel. Automati v12, (1993), 33-45
11. Sinclair, M.C.: Minimum cost topology optimization of the COST 239 European optical network'. Proceedings of the international conference on Artificial neural networks and genetic algorithms, ICANNGA'95, Ales, France, (1995), 26-29
12. Lin, P.M., Leon, B.J. & Stewart, C.R.: Analysis of circuit-switched networks employing originating-office control with spill-forward, IEEE Transactions on Communications v26 n6, (1978), 754-765
13. Ahuja, R.K., Magnanti, T.L. & Orlin, J.B., Network Flows: Theory, Algorithms, and Appli-cations, Prentice Hall, (1993)
14. Sedgewick, R., Algorithms (2nd Ed.), Addison-Wesley, (1988)
15. Goldberg, D.E., Genetic Algorithms in Search, Optimization and Machine Learning, Addison-Wesley, (1989)
16. Davis, L. (Ed.), Handbook of Genetic Algorithms, Van Nostrand Reinhold, (1991)
17. Mikac, B. & Inkret, R.: Application of a genetic algorithm to the availability-cost optimization of a transmission network topology, Proc. 3rd Intl. Conf. on Artificial Neural Networks and Genetic Algorithms (ICANNGA'97), Univ.of East Anglia, Norwich, UK, (1997), 304-307
18. Griffit, P.S., Proestaki, A., and Sinclair, M.C.: Heuristic topological design of low-cost optical telecommunication networks. Proc. of the 12th UK Perf. Eng. workshop, Edinburgh, UK, (1996), 129-140

Ant Colony Optimization
for the Maximum Edge-Disjoint Paths Problem*

Maria Blesa[1] and Christian Blum[2]

[1] Universitat Politècnica de Catalunya
Dept. Llenguatges i Sistemes Informàtics, E-08034 Barcelona, Spain
mjblesa@lsi.upc.es

[2] Université Libre de Bruxelles
IRIDIA, B-1050 Brussels, Belgium
cblum@ulb.ac.be

Abstract. Given a graph G representing a network topology, and a collection $T = \{(s_1, t_1) \ldots (s_k, t_k)\}$ of pairs of vertices in G representing connection request, the maximum edge-disjoint paths problem is an NP-hard problem which consists in determining the maximum number of pairs in T that can be routed in G by mutually edge-disjoint $s_i - t_i$ paths. We propose an *Ant Colony Optimization* (ACO) algorithm to solve this problem. ACO algorithms are inspired by the foraging behavior of real ants, whose distributed nature makes them suitable for the application in network environments. Our current version is aimed for the application in static graphs. In comparison to a multi-start greedy approach, our algorithm has advantages especially when speed is an issue.

1 Introduction

One of the basic operations in communication networks consists in establishing routes for connection requests between physically separated network endpoints that wish to establish a connection for information exchange. In many situations, either because of technical constraints or just to improve the communication, it is required that no two routes interfere with each other, which implies not to share network resources such as links or switches.

The maximum edge-disjoint paths problem (EDP) can be stated as follows. Let $G = (V, E)$ be an edge-weighted undirected graph representing a network

---

* Partially supported by the FET Programme of the EU under contract number IST-2001-33116 (FLAGS), and by the Spanish CICYT projects TIC-2001-4917-E and TIC-2002-04498-C05-03 (TRACER). M. Blesa acknowledges support by the Catalan Research Council of the Generalitat de Catalunya (grant no. 2001FI-00659). C. Blum acknowledges support by the *Metaheuristics Network*, a Research Training Network funded by the Improving Human Potential program of the CEC, grant HPRN-CT-1999-00106. The information provided is the sole responsibility of the authors and does not reflect the Community's opinion. The Community is not responsible for any use that might be made of data appearing in this publication.

in which the nodes represent the hosts and switches, and the edges represent the links. The edge-weights $w(e) > 0$, $\forall\, e \in E$, correspond to distances. Let $T = \{(s_j, t_j) \mid j = 1, \ldots, |T|; s_j \neq t_j \in V\}$ be a list of commodities, i.e., pairs of nodes in G, representing endpoints demanding connection requests. T is said to be realizable in G if there exist mutually edge-disjoint paths from s_j to t_j in G, for every $j = 1, \ldots, |T|$. Deciding whether a given set of pairs is realizable in a given graph is one of Karp's original NP-complete problems [1]. The problem remains NP-complete even when the underlying graph is a two-dimensional mesh. The EDP problem is a generalization of the edge-disjoint Menger problem and a simpler version of the unsplittable flow.

The combinatorial optimization version of the problem consists in satisfying as many of the requests as possible, which is equivalent to finding a realizable subset of T of maximum cardinality. A solution S to the combinatorial optimization problem is a set of edge-disjoint paths for a (sub)set of the commodities, and the objective function value $f(S)$ of a solution S is defined as $f(S) = |S|$.

The EDP problem has a multitude of applications in areas such as real-time communications, VLSI-design, scheduling, bin packing, load balancing, and recent applications to routing and admission control in modern networks, namely large-scale, high-speed and optical networks [2,3,4]. Concerning real-time communications, the EDP problem is very much related to survivability and information dissemination, since disjoint paths help to increase the effective bandwidth, reduce congestion, increase the velocity and the probability of receiving the information, as well as to minimize the effect of possible failures [5,6].

In this paper, we present an Ant Colony Optimization (ACO) algorithm [7] for the EDP problem. ACO is a recent metaheuristic for solving hard combinatorial optimization problems. To the best of our knowledge, our algorithm is the first metaheuristic approach to tackle this problem. Our choice of ACO is motivated by the successful application to adaptive routing in communication networks [8]. ACO approaches provide many advantageous features that are useful when applications in dynamic environments are concerned, such as for example the usage of only local information. Our current approach is developed for the EDP problem in static graphs.

In Sect. 2 we present a (multi-start) greedy for the EDP problem. In Sect. 3 we present our Ant Colony Optimization approach. The benchmark instances used to test the performance of our approach are introduced in Sect. 4. In Sect. 5 we analyze the results obtained and point out possible lines for future research.

2   A Greedy Approach

Greedy algorithms often provide quite good solutions in a reasonable computation time. We propose a multi-start greedy algorithm, which is based on the simple greedy algorithm (SGA) proposed in [9] for the development of approximation algorithms for very specific types of graphs. The SGA starts with an empty solution S. Then, it naturally approximates the problem by proceeding through the list of commodities in the order given as input. For routing each commodity $T_j \in T$, it considers the graph G without the edges that are already

Algorithm 1 : Multi-start simple greedy algorithm (MSGA) for the EDP problem

input: a problem instance (G, T, N_{perm})
$S_{best} \leftarrow \emptyset, \pi \leftarrow (1, 2, \ldots, |T| - 1, |T|)$
for $i = 1$ to N_{perm} **do**
    $S_i \leftarrow \emptyset, \hat{E} \leftarrow E$ // Simple greedy algorithm [9]
    for $j = 1, \ldots, |T|$ **do**
        if $s_{\pi(j)}$ and $t_{\pi(j)}$ can be connected by a path in $G = (V, \hat{E})$ **then**
            $P_{\pi(j)} \leftarrow$ shortest path from $s_{\pi(j)}$ to $t_{\pi(j)}$ in $G = (V, \hat{E})$
            $S_i \leftarrow S_i \cup P_{\pi(j)}, \hat{E} \leftarrow \hat{E} \setminus \{e \mid e \in P_{\pi(j)}\}$
        end if
    end for
    if $f(S_i) > f(S_{best})$ **then**
        $S_{best} \leftarrow S_i$
    end if
    if $i < N_{perm}$ **then** $\pi \leftarrow$ GenerateRandomPermutation($|T|$)
end for
output: S_{best}

in the solution S under construction. The shortest path between s_j and t_j (w.r.t. the edge-weights) is assigned as path for the commodity $T_j = (s_j, t_j)$.

We extend this simple greedy algorithm to a multi-start version (see Algorithm 1) in which the input list of commodities is permuted randomly N_{perm} times. SGA is then applied to each of these permutations. We refer to this greedy approach as multi-start greedy algorithm (MSGA). In Algorithm 1, $e \in P_j$ denotes the fact that edge e is on path P_j, S_i denotes the solution under construction in the embedded SGA, and S_{best} denotes the best solution found so far. The method GenerateRandomPermutation($|T|$) provides the next permutation π of the commodities for every iteration of the external loop.

3   ACO Approach

In ACO algorithms [7], artificial ants incrementally construct a solution by adding appropriately defined solution components to a partial solution under construction. Each of the construction steps is a probabilistic decision based on local information, which is represented by the pheromone information. The exclusive use of local information makes ACO algorithms a natural choice for the application to the EDP problem.

Each problem instance $\mathcal{P} = (G, T)$ of the EDP problem can be naturally decomposed into $|T|$ subproblems $\mathcal{P}_j = (G, T_j)$, with $j \in \{1, \ldots, |T|\}$, by regarding the task of finding a path for a commodity $T_j \in T$ as a problem itself. As a consequence, we use a number of $|T|$ ants each of which is assigned to exactly one of the subproblems. Therefore, the construction of a solution consists of each ant building a path between the two endpoints of her commodity. Obviously, the subproblems are not independent as the set of $|T|$ paths constructed by the ants should be mutually edge-disjoint.

Ant solutions. A solution S constructed by $|T|$ ants is a set of (not necessarily edge-disjoint) paths that contains a path for each commodity. We henceforth refer to them as ant solutions. From each ant solution a valid EDP solution can be produced by iteratively removing the path which has most edges in common with other paths, until all remaining paths are mutually edge-disjoint.

The objective function $f(\cdot)$ of the problem is characterized by having many plateaus when it is applied to ant solutions, as many ant solutions have the same number of disjoint paths. Thus, a consequence of decomposing the EDP problem is the need to define an objective function $f^a(\cdot)$ that differentiates between ant solutions. Therefore, referring to $f(S)$ as a first criterion, we introduce a second criterion $C(S)$, which is defined as follows:

$$C(S) = \sum_{e \in E} \left(\max \left\{ \left(\sum_{P_j \in S} \delta^j(S,e) \right) - 1, 0 \right\} \right), \text{ where } \delta^j(S,e) = \begin{cases} 1 : e \in P_j \in S \\ 0 : \text{otherwise.} \end{cases}$$

This second criterion tries to quantify the degree of non-disjointness of an ant solution. $C(S)$ increases when increasing the usage of common edges in S, and it is zero when the paths in S are edge-disjoint. Based on the idea that "the fewer edges are shared in a solution, the closer the solution is to disjointness", we define a function $f^a(\cdot)$ such that, for two ant solutions S and S', it holds that

$$f^a(S) > f^a(S') \Leftrightarrow \underbrace{(f(S) > f(S'))}_{1^{st} \text{ criterion}} \text{ or } \underbrace{((f(S) = f(S') \text{ and } (C(S) < C(S')))}_{2^{nd} \text{ criterion}}. \quad (1)$$

Pheromone models. The problem decomposition as described above implies that we use a pheromone model τ^j for each subproblem $\mathcal{P}_j$. Each pheromone model τ^j consists of a pheromone value τ_e^j for each edge $e \in E$. The set of $|T|$ pheromone models is henceforth denoted by $\tau = \{\tau^1, \ldots, \tau^{|T|}\}$. The pheromone values are bounded by $\tau_{\min}$ and τ_{max}, which prevent the algorithm from converging to a solution. These bounds are set to 0.001 and 0.999, respectively.

Algorithm framework and components. Algorithm 2 is a high level description of our ACO algorithm. Three different solutions are kept in the algorithm. S_{ibest} is the iteration-best solution, i.e., the best ant solution generated in the current iteration. S_{pbest} is the currently best solution, i.e., the best ant solution generated since the last escape action (see below). S_{gbest} is the the best-so-far solution, i.e., the best ant solution found since the start of the algorithm.

To control the improvement of the criteria we introduce the counters c_{crit1} and c_{crit2}, which count respectively the number of successive iterations without improvement of the first and the second criterion, and the boolean variable all_update, which is set to true if c_{crit1} exceeds a limit $cl_{\max}$.

First, all the variables are initialized. In particular, the pheromone values are set to their initial value $\tau_{\min}$ by the procedure InitializePheromoneValues(τ). Second, N_{sols} ant solutions are constructed per iteration. To construct a solution, each ant applies the function ConstructPath$((s_{\pi(j)}, t_{\pi(j)}), \tau^{\pi(j)})$. At each iteration, the first of those N_{sols} ant solutions is constructed by sending the ants in the order in which the commodities are given in T. For each further ant solution construction in the same iteration, this order is randomly generated by the function GenerateRandomPermutation($|T|$). Third, the value of the variables S_{ibest}, S_{gbest} and S_{pbest} is updated. Finally, the pheromone values are updated.

Algorithm 2 ACO for the EDP problem

INPUT: a problem instance (G, T)
$S_{gbest} \leftarrow \emptyset$, $S_{pbest} \leftarrow \emptyset$, $c_{crit1} \leftarrow 0$, $c_{crit2} \leftarrow 0$, $all\_update \leftarrow$ FALSE
InitializePheromoneValues(τ)
while termination conditions not met **do**
   $\pi \leftarrow (1, 2, \ldots, |T| - 1, |T|)$
   for $i = 1$ to N_{sols} **do**
      $S_i \leftarrow \emptyset$
      for $j = 1$ to $|T|$ **do**
         $P_{\pi(j)} \leftarrow$ ConstructPath$((s_{\pi(j)}, t_{\pi(j)}), \tau^{\pi(j)})$
         $S_i \leftarrow S_i \cup \{P_{\pi(j)}\}$
      end for
      if $i < N_{sols}$ **then** $\pi \leftarrow$ GenerateRandomPermutation($|T|$)
   end for
   Determine $S_{ibest} \in \{S_i \mid i = 1, \ldots, N_{sols}\}$ s.t. $f^a(S_{ibest}) \geq f^a(S), \forall S \in \{S_i \mid i = 1, \ldots, N_{sols}\}$
   if $f(S_{ibest}) > f(S_{gbest})$ **then** $S_{gbest} \leftarrow S_{ibest}$ **end if**
   if $f^a(S_{ibest}) > f^a(S_{pbest})$ **then**
      $c_{crit2} \leftarrow 0$
      if $f(S_{ibest}) > f(S_{pbest})$ **then**
         $S_{update} \leftarrow$ ExtractDisjointPaths(S_{ibest})   // First phase
         $c_{crit1} \leftarrow 0$, $all\_update \leftarrow$ FALSE
      else
         $c_{crit1} \leftarrow c_{crit1} + 1$
      end if
      $S_{pbest} \leftarrow S_{ibest}$
      if all_update **then** $S_{update} \leftarrow S_{pbest}$ // Second phase
   else
      $c_{crit2} \leftarrow c_{crit2} + 1$
   end if
   if all_update **then**
      if $c_{crit2} > c2_{max}$ **then**
         $S_{pbest} \leftarrow$ DestroyPartially(S_{pbest})   // Escape mechanism
         $S_{update} \leftarrow$ ExtractDisjointPaths(S_{pbest})
         $c_{crit2} \leftarrow 0$, $c_{crit1} \leftarrow 0$
      end if
   else
      $all\_update \leftarrow (c_{crit1} > c1_{max})$
   end if
   UpdatePheromoneValues(τ, S_{update}, all_update)
end while
OUTPUT: the EDP solution generated from the best solution S_{gbest}

The pheromone update depends on the search phase in which our algorithm is at the moment of the update. Our algorithm works in two phases based on the two criteria of function $f^a(\cdot)$ as outlined in Eqn. 1 (this is in some sense similar to the approach in [10]). First, it tries to improve only the first criterion. If for a number of $c1_{max}$ iterations the first criterion could not be improved, the algorithm tries to improve the second criterion. In case of success the algorithm jumps back to the first phase trying to improve again the first criterion. Otherwise, if for a number of $c2_{max}$ iterations the second criterion could not be improved, some of the paths from the EDP solution that can be produced from S_{pbest} are deleted from S_{pbest}. This action can be seen as a backtracking move in order to escape from the current area in the search space. The algorithm is iterated until some opportunely defined termination conditions are satisfied. The algorithm returns the EDP solution generated from S_{gbest}.

The components of our algorithm are outlined more in detail in the following.

· InitializePheromoneValues(τ) sets the pheromone values $\tau_e^j \in \tau^j \in \tau$ to τ_{min}.

· ConstructPath($(s_{\pi(j)}, t_{\pi(j)}), \tau^{\pi(j)}$): An ant first chooses randomly to start either from $s_{\pi(j)}$ or from $t_{\pi(j)}$. Then, the ant iteratively moves from node to node using edges that are not already in the path $P_{\pi(j)}$ under construction, and that are not labelled forbidden by a backtracking move. Backtracking is done when the ant finds itself in a node in which either all the incident edges have been used, or all labelled forbidden. With this strategy the ant will find a path between source and target, if there exists one. Otherwise, the ant returns an empty path. In the following, the current node is denoted by v_c, the goal node is denoted by v_g, and the set of edges in G which are not used yet in the path and not labelled as forbidden is denoted by $\mathcal{I}^*_{v_c}$. At each construction step, the choice of where to move to has a certain probability to be done deterministically. This is a feature we adopt from a particularly effective ACO variant called Ant Colony System (ACS) which was proposed by Dorigo and Gambardella in [11]. We draw a random number d_{rate} between 0 and 1. If $d_{rate} \leq 0.8$ (where 0.8 was chosen by parameter tuning, see Sect. 4), the next edge e^* to join path $P_{\pi(j)}$ is chosen deterministically:

$$e^* = \{v_c, u\} \leftarrow \text{argmax} \ \{\tau_e^j \cdot \mathbf{p}(D_e)^\beta \cdot \mathbf{p}(U_e)^\gamma \mid e \in \mathcal{I}^*_{v_c}\} \ , \tag{2}$$

where $\mathbf{p}(D_e)$ is a value that determines the influence of the distance from v_c via u to the goal vertex v_g, and $\mathbf{p}(U_e)$ is a value that determines the influence of the overall usage of edge e for the same solution. The length of the shortest path between two vertices u and v in G is henceforth denoted by $\sigma(u, v)$. $\mathbf{p}(D_e)$ and $\mathbf{p}(U_e)$ are defined as follows:

$$\mathbf{p}(D_{e=\{v_c,u\}}) \leftarrow \frac{(\sigma(u,v_g)+w(e))^{-1}}{\sum_{e^0 = \{v_c, u^0\} \in \mathcal{I}^*_{v_c}} (\sigma(u^0,v_g)+w(e^0))^{-1}}$$

$$\mathbf{p}(U_e) \leftarrow \frac{U(e)^{-1}}{\sum_{e^0 \in \mathcal{I}^*_{v_c}} U(e^0)^{-1}} \ , \quad \text{in which} \quad U(e) = \begin{cases} 2 : e \text{ already used in } S_i \\ 1 : \text{otherwise} \end{cases}$$

If $d_{rate} > 0.8$, e^* is chosen according to the following transition probabilities:

$$\mathbf{p}(e \mid \mathcal{I}^*_{v_c}) = \begin{cases} \dfrac{\tau_e^j \cdot \mathbf{p}(D_e)^\beta \cdot \mathbf{p}(U_e)^\gamma}{\sum_{e^0 \in \mathcal{I}^*_{v_c}} \tau_{e^0}^j \cdot \mathbf{p}(D_{e^0})^\beta \cdot \mathbf{p}(U_{e^0})^\gamma} & : \text{ if } e \in \mathcal{I}^*_{v_c} \\ 0 & : \text{ otherwise.} \end{cases} \tag{3}$$

The high probability of doing a deterministic step leads the search already at the start of the algorithm to relatively good areas in the search space. Although there is also the danger that the algorithm gets stuck in sub-optimal regions. The use of the pheromone information τ_e^j ensures the flexibility of the algorithm, whereas the use of $\mathbf{p}(D_e)^\beta$ ensures a bias towards short paths, and $\mathbf{p}(U_e)^\gamma$ ensures a bias towards disjointness of the $|T|$ paths constituting a solution. Finally, after every ant has constructed its path and the solution S is completed, some amount of pheromone from the edges that were used by the ants evaporates as follows:

$$\tau_e^j \leftarrow \begin{cases} (1 - e_{rate}) \cdot \tau_e^j & : e \in P_{\pi(j)} \in S, \ j = 1, \dots, |T| \\ \tau_e^j & : \text{otherwise} \ . \end{cases}$$

The reason for this pheromone evaporation is the desire to diversify the search in each iteration. After parameter tuning we chose a setting of $e_{rate} = 0.05$.

· ExtractDisjointPaths(S_{pbest}) produces a valid EDP solution S_{update} from the ant solution S_{pbest} by iteratively removing the path which has most edges in common with other paths, until all remaining paths are mutually edge-disjoint. The solution S_{update} is then used for updating the pheromone values in the phase of the algorithm in which it tries to improve the 1st criterion (i.e., the number of disjoint paths). In addition, the pheromone values associated to commodities for which there is no path in S_{update} are reset to τ_{min}.

· DestroyPartially(S_{pbest}): When neither the attempt of improving the first criterion, nor the attempt of improving the second criterion is successful (i.e., all_update is true and $c_{crit2} > c2_{max}$) an escape mechanism is employed. This escape mechanism consists in removing one quarter of the disjoint paths of the EDP solution that corresponds to solution S_{pbest}. Finally, the pheromone values that correspond to the commodities of the removed paths are reset to τ_{min}.

· UpdatePheromoneValues(τ, S_{update}, all_update): Only the solution S_{update} is used for updating the pheromone values. This solution is obtained from solution S_{pbest}, in a way that depends on the current search phase (1st or 2nd) of the algorithm. When all_update is false (i.e., the algorithm tries to improve the first criterion), S_{update} is obtained from S_{pbest} as described in function ExtractDisjointPaths(S_{pbest}) above. In this case only the pheromone values of commodities for which disjoint paths exist are updated. When all_update is true (i.e., the algorithm tries to improve the second criterion), S_{update} is equal to S_{pbest}. In this case, the pheromone values of all commodities are updated. This introduces a bias towards ant solutions sharing fewer edges, which in turn might eventually lead to an improvement in terms of the first criterion. The pheromone values for all $j \in \{1, \ldots, |T|\}$ for which $P_j \in S_{update}$ are updated as follows:

$$\tau_e^j \leftarrow \max\left\{\tau_e^j + \rho \cdot \left(1 - \tau_e^j\right), \tau_{max}\right\} \quad \forall e \in P_j , \tag{4}$$

where $\rho \in (0, 1]$ is a constant value called learning rate. This rate ρ is set to 0.1 when all_update does not hold, i.e., in the first search phase, and it is set to 0.05 otherwise. The update rule as outlined above can be regarded as the update rule of ACS when implemented in the hyper-cube framework [12].

4   Benchmark and Experiments

So far there is no set of benchmark instances available for the EDP problem. To experimentally evaluate our ACO approach we have considered three graphs representing different communication networks. The graphs graph3 and graph4 are similar to real telecomunication networks of the Deutsche Telekom AG, Germany.[1] Using the network topology generator BRITE [13], we have generated the graph bl-wr2-wht2.10-50 which represents a two-level top-down hierarchical topology. Table 1 shows other features of these three chosen graphs.

---
[1] We would like to thank Martin Oellrich for providing these graphs.

Table 1. Our new set of benchmark graphs. The graph bl-wr2-wht2.10-50 has 10 nodes placed randomly (AS-level topology) and, for each of these nodes, 50 nodes which are placed according to *heavy-tailed* distributions (router-level topology). The nodes of the topologies in both levels are interconnected using the Waxman probability model [14].

Graph	$|V|$	$|E|$	Degree (min., avg., max.)			Diameter	Represents...
graph3	164	370	1	4.512	13	16	Deutsche Telekom's subnetwork
graph4	434	981	1	4.521	20	22	Deutsche Telekom's subnetwork
bl-wr2-wht2.10-50	500	1020	2	4.08	13	23	Internet topology (generated)

Instances and platform. Henceforth we refer to the combination of a graph and a set of commodities as an *instance*. For each graph, we generated 20 different instances with 10, 25, 50, and 75 randomly generated commodities. This makes a sum of 80 instances for each graph, and 240 instances altogether. Furthermore, all the algorithms in this paper were implemented in C++ and compiled using GCC 2.95.2 with the -o3 option. The experiments have been run on a PC with Intel(R) Pentium(R) 4 processor at 3.06GHz and 900 Mb of memory running under Linux. Moreover, they were all implemented on the same data structures. Information about the shortest paths in the respective graphs is provided to all of them as input. Notice however that, while the multi-start greedy algorithm MSGA needs to partially recompute this informatio, ACO does not.

Results. First of all, the execution of the ACO approach requires the setting of values of the algorithm parameters. The values of parameters d_{rate}, β and γ were set —with respect to tuning experiments— to $d_{rate} = 0.8$ and $\beta = \gamma = 1.0$.

We applied MSGA as well as our ACO approach to all 240 instances exactly once. Hereby, MSGA was applied with $N_{perm} = 10$ restarts. For each instance, the computation time of MSGA was used as a maximum CPU time limit for the ACO algorithm on that instance. We present the results as averages over the 20 instances of each combination of graph and commodity number in Table 2.

First, we observe that in 9 out of 12 cases the ACO approach beats MSGA. Furthermore, in general the ACO approach needs less computation time than MSGA. This advantage in computation time decreases with growing number of commodities. Exceptions for this evaluation are the results for the combinations of graph4 with commodity numbers 50 and 75, which might be due to the high degree of some vertices of graph4. Apart from graph4, the average results for 50 and 75 commodities show a clear advantage of ACO in contrast to MSGA, both in quality and time. In general, the robustness of both algorithms is comparable.

A second analysis that we can apply to our algorithms concerns the development of the best solutions found over time. When observing the run-time behavior of our algorithms we notice that the ACO approach finds relatively good solutions (which might be sufficient in practice) already after a very short computation time. In general, already the first solutions produced by ACO are quite good, whereas the greedy approach reaches the same solution quality only much later in time (see Fig. 1(a)). This property of our ACO approach is a desirable feature in the context of communication networks. Fig. 1(b) illustrates the usefulness of the two phases of our ACO approach trying to improve the first crite-

Table 2. Comparison of the results obtained by MSGA and ACO. The first and second columns give the name of the graph and the number of commodities. For both algorithms there are three columns reporting on the results obtained for the 20 instances of each combination of graph and number of commodities: The first column shows the average of the values (in boldface if the result better in quality or the same but faster), the second column provides the standard deviation, and the third column reports on the average time needed to find the best solution values. The last column shows the computation time of MSGA, which was used as computation time limit for ACO.

Graph	nb.pairs	MSGA Best $|S|$	σ	Best t	ACO Best $|S|$	σ	Best t	$\bar{t}$
graph3	10	9.850	0.357	0.629	**9.850**	0.357	0.015	6.535
graph3	25	**23.150**	1.276	3.629	22.450	1.396	2.998	8.841
graph3	50	33.400	2.223	6.342	**33.85**	2.555	3.862	12.190
graph3	75	36.400	2.577	7.024	**39.45**	3.008	6.518	15.599
graph4	10	10	0	15.734	**10**	0	0.842	134.270
graph4	25	24.6	0.490	25.317	**24.75**	0.433	6.135	161.338
graph4	50	**45.85**	2.455	79.901	44.95	2.334	106.276	188.478
graph4	75	**57.1**	3.491	87.597	55.050	3.653	123.629	218.371
bl-wr2-wht2.10-50	10	8.950	0.92	61.504	**9**	0.894	9.070	240.559
bl-wr2-wht2.10-50	25	14.9	1.729	94.546	**16.150**	1.492	40.535	267.923
bl-wr2-wht2.10-50	50	22.200	2.657	129.614	**24.75**	2.165	48.880	313.972
bl-wr2-wht2.10-50	75	25.35	3.439	121.549	**29.35**	3.245	76.097	354.434

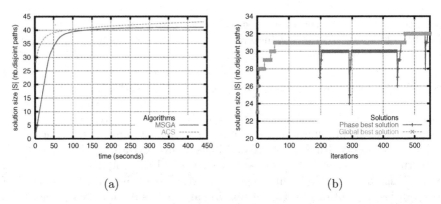

(a)   (b)

Fig. 1. (a) A representative example of the run-time behavior of ACO in comparison to MSGA. In general, the ACO approach reaches good solutions much faster. (b) The first 500 iterations of a representative run of ACO. The best solution found is quickly improved. At about iteration 450 the algorithm destroys part of the S_{pbest} solution (with $f(S_{pbest}) = 30$), which produces an instantaneous worsening in the quality; however, this helps in achieving an improvement soon afterwards.

rion, respectively the second criterion. In the future we intend to experimentally prove the usefulness of the two-phases approach.

5 Conclusions and Further Work

We have proposed an Ant Colony Optimization (ACO) approach to tackle the maximum edge-disjoint paths problem. To the best of our knowledge, this is the first application of a metaheuristic to this problem. Our approach is based on a decomposition of the maximum edge-disjoint paths problem into subproblems. We have compared our algorithm to a multi-start greedy approach. The results showed that our ACO approach has in general advantages over the multi-start greedy in terms of solution quality as well as computation time. Especially in the run-time behavior, the ACO approach is superior to the multi-start greedy approach. Already in early stages of a run the ACO algorithm provides relatively good solutions. In general, our ACO approach is well suited for the implementation in communication networks, as (in contrast to the greedy approach) it only uses local information for building paths. In the future, we intend to investigate different greedy approaches and to deepen the analysis of our ACO approach.

References

1. R. Karp. *Compexity of Computer Computations*, chapter Reducibility among combinatorial problems, pages 85–103. Plenum Press, New York, 1972.
2. B. Awerbuch, R. Gawlick, F. Leighton, and Y. Rabani. On-line admission control and circuit routing for high performance computing and communication. In *35th. IEEE Symposium on Foundations of Computer Science*, pages 412–423, 1994.
3. P. Raghavan and E. Upfal. Efficient all-optical routing. In *26th. Annual ACM Symposium on Theory of Computing*, pages 134–143, 1994.
4. A. Aggarwal, A. Bar-Noy, D. Coppersmith, R. Ramaswami, B. Schieber, and M. Sudan. Efficient routing and scheduling algorithms for optical networks. In *5th. ACM-SIAM Symposium on Discrete Algorithms*, pages 412–423, 1994.
5. J. Hromkovič, R. Klasing, E. Stöhr, and H. Wagener. Gossiping in vertex-disjoing paths mode in *d*-dimensional grids and planar graphs. In *1st Annual European Symposium on Algorithms*. LNCS, 726:200–211, 1993. Springer Verlag.
6. D. Sidhu, R. Nair, and S. Abdallah. Finding disjoint paths in networks. *ACM SIGCOMM Computer Communication Review*, 21(4):43–51, 1991.
7. M. Dorigo, G. Di Caro, and L. Gambardella. Ant algorithms for discrete optimization. *Artificial Life*, 5(2):137–172, 1999.
8. G. Di Caro and M. Dorigo. AntNet: Distributed stigmergetic control for communications networks. *Journal of Artificial Intelligence Research*, 9:317–365, 1998.
9. J. Kleinberg. *Approx. algorithms for disjoint paths problems*. PhD thesis, 1996.
10. L. M. Gambardella, E. D. Taillard and G. Agazzi. *New Ideas in Optimization*, pages 63–76. McGraw-Hill, London, UK, 1999.
11. M. Dorigo and L. Gambardella. Ant Colony System: A cooperative learning approach to the traveling salesman problem. *IEEE Transactions on Evolutionary Computation*, 1(1):53–66, 1997.
12. C. Blum and M. Dorigo. The hyper-cube framework for ant colony optimization. *IEEE Transactions on Systems, Man, and Cybernetics - Part B*, 2004. To appear.
13. A. Medina, A. Lakhina, I. Matta, and J. Byers. BRITE: Boston University Representative Internet Topoloy Generator. http://cs-pub.bu.edu/brite/, 2001.
14. B. Waxman. Routing of multipoint connections. *IEEE Journal on Selected Areas in Communications*, 6(9):1671–1622, 1988.

Using Genetic Programming to Design Broadcasting Algorithms for Manhattan Street Networks*

Francesc Comellas and Cristina Dalfó

Departament de Matemàtica Aplicada IV, Universitat Politècnica de Catalunya
Avda. Canal Olímpic s/n, 08860 Castelldefels, Catalonia, Spain
{comellas,cdalfo}@mat.upc.es
http://www-mat.upc.es/~comellas/

Abstract. Broadcasting is the process of disseminating a message from a node of a communication network to all other nodes as quickly as possible. In this paper we consider Manhattan Street Networks (MSNs) which are mesh-structured, toroidal, directed, regular networks such that locally they resemble the geographical topology of the avenues and streets of Manhattan. With the use of genetic programming we have generated broadcasting algorithms for 2-dimensional and 3-dimensional MSNs.

1 Introduction

The study of a class of directed torus networks known as Manhattan Street Networks has received significant attention since they were introduced by Maxemchuk in 1985 [1] as an unidirectional regular mesh structure resembling locally the topology of the avenues and streets of Manhattan. Most of the work has been devoted to the computation of the average distance and the generation of routing schemes for the 2-dimensional case [2,3]. The study of spanning trees [4] in a Manhattan Street Network (MSN) has allowed the computation of the diameter and the design of a multi-port broadcasting algorithm. More recently, Varvarigos in [5] evaluated the mean internodal distance, provided a shortest path routing algorithm and constructed edge-disjoint Hamiltonian cycles in the general 2-dimensional case. The multidimensional natural extension of the MSN has been considered by Banerjee et. al, see [6,7], with the determination of the average distance of a 3-dimensional MSN, and a conjecture for higher dimensions. Chung and Agrawal [8] studied the diameter and provided routing schemes for a 3-dimensional construction based on 2-dimensional MSNs, although the result is not strictly a 3-dimensional MSN. In this paper, and with the use of genetic programming, we provide algorithms to broadcast efficiently (in some cases optimally) in 2-dimensional and 3-dimensional MSN.

In the next section we give some general definitions, preliminary results and introduce the notation. Section 3 describes the genetic programming method

* Research supported by the Ministry of Science and Technology, Spain, and the European Regional Development Fund (ERDF) under project TIC2002-00155.

G.R. Raidl et al. (Eds.): EvoWorkshops 2004, LNCS 3005, pp. 170–177, 2004.
© Springer-Verlag Berlin Heidelberg 2004

and some details of the implementation considered. In Section 4 we present and discuss the results obtained for 2-dimensional and 3-dimensional MSNs. Finally, in the last section we summarize the results and give some open problems.

2   Notation and Known Results

We model a network using graphs. A directed graph (digraph), $G = (V, E)$, consists of a non empty finite set V of elements called vertices and a set E of ordered pairs of elements of V called arcs. The number of vertices $N = |G| = |V|$ is the order of the digraph. If (x, y) is an arc of E, it is said that x is adjacent to y or that y is adjacent from x, and it is usually written $x \to y$. The out-degree of a vertex $\delta^+(x)$ is the number of vertices adjacent from x, the in-degree of a vertex $\delta^-(x)$ is the number of vertices adjacent to x. A digraph is regular of degree Δ or Δ-regular if the in-degree and out-degree of all vertices equal Δ. A digraph is strongly connected if there is a (directed) path from any vertex to every other. The distance between two vertices x and y, $d(x, y)$, is the number of arcs of a shortest path from x to y, and its maximum value among all pairs of vertices, $D = \max_{x,y \in V} d(x, y)$, is the diameter of the digraph.

A digraph G is vertex symmetric if its automorphism group acts transitively on its set of vertices. Loosely speaking we say that the digraph looks the same from any vertex. The interest in vertex symmetric digraphs comes from the fact that in the associated network each node is able to execute the same communication software without modifications and in this way these graphs may be considered for easy implementation of parallelism. We refer to [9] for other basic concepts in graph theory not defined here.

Broadcasting is one of the most studied problems in communication networks and refers to the sending of a message from one node of the network to all the other nodes as quickly as possible, subject to the constraints that each call involves only two nodes, a node which already knows the message can only inform one of the nodes to which it is connected (one-port model) and each call requires one unit of time.

More precisely, given a digraph $G = (V, E)$ and a vertex $u \in V$, broadcasting is the process of disseminating a piece of information from vertex u (called the originator) to every vertex reachable from u in G. The set of transmissions used to disseminate the information is called a broadcast scheme or broadcast protocol. A broadcast algorithm is a set of rules which generate the scheme. We assume that communication is synchronized under the constant time model. That is, each transmission takes one unit of time and all transmissions at any given integer time occur simultaneously.

Therefore, given a connected digraph G and a vertex u, the broadcast time of u, denoted $b(u)$, is the minimum number of time units required to broadcast a message originating at u. The broadcast time of the graph G is defined $b(G) = \max\{b(u)|u \in G\}$. For any vertex u in a connected graph with $|V|$ vertices, $b(u) \geq \lceil \log_2 |V| \rceil$, since during each time unit the number of vertices informed can at most double. For a vertex symmetric graph, the broadcast time is equal to the broadcast time of any of its vertices.

For grid graphs and in the undirected case, optimal broadcasting algorithms are known, for example, for 2-grids ($b(M_{m \times n}) = m + n - 2 = D$), 2-torus ($b(T_{m \times n}) = D$, if m and n are even and $b(T_{m \times n}) = D + 1$ otherwise), see [10]. Here we present the first optimal one-port broadcasting algorithms for Manhattan Street Networks.

The vertices of a 2-dimensional $N \times N$ Manhattan Street Networks with N^2 vertices are labeled with pairs (u_1, u_2) where $0 \leq u_1 \leq N-1$ and $0 \leq u_2 \leq N-1$. The edges of this graph are $\{(u_1, u_2) \to ((u_1 \pm 1) \bmod N, u_2)$ and $\{(u_1, u_2) \to (u_1, (u_2 \pm 1) \bmod N)$ where the sign is plus or minus depending on whether u_1 and u_2 are even or odd, as Figure 1 illustrates.

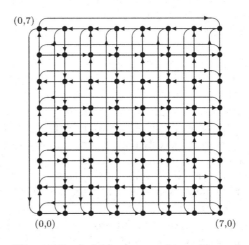

Fig. 1. The 8×8 Manhattan Street Network.

The vertices of a 3-dimensional $N \times N \times N$ Manhattan Street Networks with N^3 vertices are labeled (u_1, u_2, u_3) where $0 \leq u_1 \leq N - 1$, $0 \leq u_2 \leq N - 1$ and $0 \leq u_3 \leq N - 1$. The edges of this graph are $\{(u_1, u_2, u_3) \to ((u_1 \pm 1) \bmod N, u_2, u_3)$, $\{(u_1, u_2, u_3) \to (u_1, (u_2 \pm 1) \bmod N, u_3)$ and $\{(u_1, u_2, u_3) \to (u_1, , u_2, (u_3 \pm 1) \bmod N)$ where the sign is plus or minus depending on whether u_1, u_2 and u_3 are even or odd, see Figure 2. Therefore the MSNs considered in this study are modeled by directed regular graphs with indegree and outdegree two or three which are vertex symmetric.

The following result is used in Section 4 to justify the optimality of the broadcast scheme produced using genetic programming.

Lemma 1. For a graph G with diameter D, $b(G) \geq D$. Moreover, if there exist three vertices u, v_1 and v_2 such that v_1 and v_2 are at distance D of u, then $b(G) \geq D + 1$

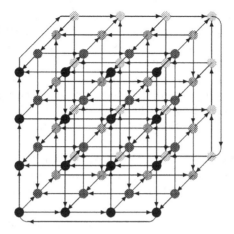

Fig. 2. The 4×4×4 Manhattan Street Network (most wraparound connexions are not shown for clarity).

P roof. Given a graph G with diameter D let us assume that there exists a broadcasting protocol for it. By recurrence on i, we see that at step i of this protocol, at most one vertex at distance i from the originator could be informed. Hence the first assertion. Moreover, if there exist two vertices at distance D from the originator, only one could be informed at time D and we would need at least one more step to finish the broadcasting process. Then, $b(G) \geq D + 1$.

The diameter of a 2-dimensional MSN has been computed in [4] by considering spanning trees. We have obtained the same result [11] from the study of the distribution of vertices at each distance:

The diameter of a N×N Manhattan Street Network is $N + 1$ for $N > 4, N = 0$ (mod 4) and N for $N > 4, N = 2$ (mod 4).

The diameter of a multidimensional MSN is not known in the general case.

3 Using Genetic Programming to Generate Broadcasting Algorithms

Optimal broadcasting algorithms, obtained by examination, are known for some networks: cycles, cliques, grids, 2-dimensional undirected tori and hypercubes [10]. However, for other simple networks like the multi-dimensional undirected torus or the butterfly network, existing broadcasting algorithms are not optimal. In these cases, genetic programming has proven useful by generating new and better broadcasting schemes, see [12].

With respect to MSNs, Chung and Agrawal [4], based on the study of spanning trees, provided an optimal multi-port broadcasting algorithm in the 2-dimensional case. It is interesting to produce one-port broadcasting algorithms for general MSNs but they are not easy to construct by inspection, and even in the 2-dimensional case it would be quite demanding to check all the possibilities. For this reason, we have adapted an existing genetic programming package to construct these algorithms for 2-dimensional and 3-dimensional MSNs of any size. Genetic programming was used by Comellas and Giménez in [12] to generate efficiently several known optimal broadcasting algorithms and a new algorithm for wrapped undirected butterflies. Their software package (C++) can be obtained from the website of the first author [1]. This package is based on GPQUICK, a GP implementation written by Andy Singleton [13] who made it publicly available for non commercial purposes.

GPQUICK is a steady state genetic algorithm which uses tournament selection. It also uses node mutation (switching nodes), constant mutation (small adjustments to constant values) and shrink mutation (promote a sub-subtree to replace a subtree) 10% of the time each, a copy with reevaluation on new cases 10% of the time, and subtree crossover 70% of the time. The default population size is 2000. GPQUICK uses the genetic algorithm to evolve S-expressions, see [14], which represent solutions of the problem. An S-expression consists of a function followed, in some cases, by arguments. Each argument is also an S-expression. Functions with no arguments are called terminals. A special function, PROGn, is used to join together n other functions into a procedural program. For example, to generate broadcasting algorithms it is possible to represent "If the message has reached the node from an horizontal node, move it next using a vertical link" as the following S-expression (IfProc_Hor MoveVert), where IfProc_Hor is a conditional function and MoveVert a terminal. The GPQUICK package was adapted by modifying the file chrome.cxx and its header file and creating a new file, specific for this family of graphs and needed to process the functions and terminals.

Functions and terminals: The graphical representation of a MSN suggests the choice of the function set and terminal set which is as follows:
    Function set: {IfProc_Ori, IfProc_Ver, IfProc_Hor, IfProc_Across, If_turn_0, If_turn_1, If_turn_2, Prog6, Prog5, Prog4, Prog3, Prog2, Prog1}
    Terminal set: {MoveHor, MoveVer, MoveAcross, Null}
Notice that IfProc_Across, If_turn_2 and Move_Across are only used to generate 3-dimensional algorithms. The Null terminal does not perform any action, but it is important as a way to allow a better performance of the mutation operator.

Fitness: As in [12] the fitness of a solution is computed by counting the number of vertices reached when executing the associated broadcasting algorithm on the graph. The length of the algorithm (number of nodes of the corresponding S-expression) decrements de fitness.

As a broadcasting algorithm is an inherently parallel process and the program which tests it is sequential, it is possible a situation in which two (or more) nodes could inform the same node at a given broadcasting step. Then the actual node that will transmit the message is the node which received it first. Moreover, the

---

algorithm is executed in the order that is written. Therefore the program can generate algorithms containing conditional functions which will never be used.

4   Results

We compiled the GPQUICK package using DJGPP[2] on a PC (Pentium4 CPU at 1.50 GHz) under Windows XP. The CPU time to find the MSN algorithms ranged from a few minutes in the case of a 2-dimensional MSN of size 8×8, to several hours for a 3-dimensional MSN of size $24 \times 24 \times 24$.

2-Dimensional MSN

One of the algorithms generated by GPQUICK (MSN of size 12×12) is:

```
(Prog5 (IfProc_Horiz (If_turn_0 MoveHoriz))
       (IfProc_Horiz (If_turn_1 MoveVert))
       (IfProc_Ori (If_turn_1 MoveVert))
       (IfProc_Vert (Prog5 Null
                           Null
                           (If_turn_0 MoveVert)
                           (If_turn_1 MoveHoriz)
                           Null))
       (IfProc_Ori (If_turn_0 MoveHoriz)))
```

The algorithm can be written as follows:

ALGORITHM BROADCAST 2-DIM MSN

1. The originator sends the message vertically and then, in the following round, horizontally.
2. If a vertex receives the message from a vertical neighbor it first sends it vertically and then, in the following round, horizontally.
3. If a node receives the message from a horizontal neighbor it first sends it horizontally and then, in the following round, vertically.

This algorithm can be used to broadcast in any MSN and differs noticeably from the standard broadcasting algorithm for the undirected case in which, after a first change of direction, there can be other changes of direction.

We have proved [11] that this algorithm always informs every node of a MSN with diameter D in time $D + 1$ for a MSN of size $N \times N$, $N \geq 4$, $N = 0 \pmod{4}$, or time $D + 2$ when $N = 2 \pmod{4}$. Because in the first case the MSN has four vertices at distance D the algorithm is optimal.

We notice that extensive tests using GPQUICK with MSNs of different sizes have produced broadcasting algorithms which are equivalent to the former algorithm (in some cases with the horizontal and vertical calls reversed or swapped).

In Figure 3 we show the execution of the broadcast algorithm for a 8×8 MSN (diameter 9). The last four vertices reached (at time 10) are shown in different size.

---

[2] http://www.delorie.com/djgpp/

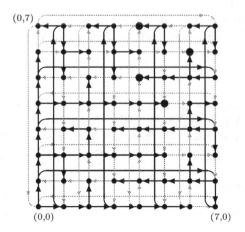

Fig. 3. Optimal broadcasting in a 8×8 Manhattan Street Network.

3-Dimensional MSN

Now the program provides the following algorithm (MSN of size 8×8×8):

```
(Prog6 (IfProc_Across (If_turn_0 MoveAcross))
       (IfProc_Vert (If_turn_0 MoveVert))
       (Prog6 (IfProc_Ori (If_turn_2 MoveHoriz))
              (IfProc_Vert (If_turn_1 MoveAcross))
              (IfProc_Across (If_turn_1 MoveHoriz))
              (IfProc_Ori (If_turn_1 MoveVert))
              (IfProc_Ori (If_turn_0 MoveAcross))
              (IfProc_Across (If_turn_2 MoveVert)))
       Null
       (IfProc_Horiz
       (Prog3 (If_turn_1 MoveAcross)
              (If_turn_0 MoveHoriz)
              (If_turn_1 MoveVert)))
   Null)
```

The algorithm can be written as follows:

ALGORITHM BROADCAST 3-DIM-MSN

1. The originator sends the message across then, in the following round, vertically and finally horizontally.
2. If a vertex receives the message from a vertical neighbor it first sends it vertically then, in the following round, across and in the final round horizontally.
3. If a node receives the message from a horizontal neighbor it first sends it horizontally then, in the following round, across and in the final round vertically.
4. If a node receives the message from an across neighbor it first sends it across then, in the following round, horizontally and in the final round vertically.

Tests of this algorithm for 3-dimensional MSNs of sizes $6 \times 6 \times 6$ up to $100 \times 100 \times 100$ show that the algorithm broadcasts always in time $\frac{3N}{2} + 2$ when $N = 0$ (mod 4) and $\frac{3N}{2} + 3$ when $N = 2$ (mod 4).

5   Conclusions and Open Problems

Genetic programming has proved to be a useful tool capable to generate efficient broadcasting algorithms for 2-dimensional and 3-dimensional Manhattan street networks producing, in some cases, optimal algorithms. Because the GP package considered uses a robust genetic algorithm, it is possible to generate new communication schemes without expending much time tuning it. On the other hand, the choice of the size of the network and the function and terminal sets is non-critical (we have seen that considering extra functions, for example, affects the running time to find an acceptable solution, but not its quality).

It is an open problem to verify the universality and optimality of the broadcasting algorithm for 3-dimensional MSNs and to determine their diameter.

References

1. Maxemchuk, N.F: The Manhattan Street Network. Proc. of the IEEE Global Telecommunication Conf., New Orleans, LA, USA, (1985) 255–261
2. Khasnabish, B.: Topological properties of Manhattan Street Networks. Electronics Lett. **25** (1989) 1388–1389
3. Maxemchuk, N.F: Routing in the Manhattan Street Network. IEEE Trans. Commun. **35** (1987) 503–512
4. Chung, T.Y., Agrawal, D.P.: On network characterization of and optimal broadcasting in the Manhattan Street Network. Proc. IEEE INFOCOM '90, Vol. 2 (1990) 465–472
5. Varvarigos, E.A: Optimal communication algorithms for Manhattan Street Networks. Discrete Appl. Math. **83** (1998) 303–326
6. Banerjee, S., Jain, V., Shah, S.: Regular multihop logical topologies for lightwave networks. IEEE Comm. Surveys and Tutorials, First Quarter, Vol. 2, No. 1 (1999)
7. Banerjee, D., Mukherjee, B., Ramamurthy, S.: The multidimensional torus: analysis of average hop distance and application as a multihop lightwave network. IEEE International Conference on Communications, Vol. 3 (1994) 1675–1680
8. Chung, T.Y., Agrawal, D.P.: Design and analysis of multidimensional Manhattan Street Networks. IEEE Trans. Commun. **41** (1993) 295–298
9. Chartrand, G., Lesniak, L.: Graphs & Digraphs. 2nd edition, Wadworth and Brooks Cole Advanced Books and Software, Monterey, California, USA, (1986)
10. Fraigniaud, P., Lazard, E.: Methods and problems of communication in usual networks. Discrete Appl. Math. **C-53** (1994) 79–133
11. Comellas, F., Dalfó, C.: Optimal broadcasting in Manhattan Street Networks. (Submitted)
12. Comellas, F., Giménez, G.: Genetic programming to design communication algorithms for parallel architectures. Parallel Process. Lett. **8** (1998) 549–560
13. Singleton, A: Genetic Programming with C++. BYTE, February 1994, 171-176
14. Koza, J.R.: Genetic Programming: On the Programming of Computers by Means of Natural Selection. MIT Press, Cambridge, MA, USA (1992)

A Scenario-Based Approach to Protocol Design Using Evolutionary Techniques

Sérgio G. Araújo, Antônio C. Mesquita, and Aloysio C.P. Pedroza

Electrical Engineering Dept.
Federal University of Rio de Janeiro
C.P. 68504 - CEP 21945-970 - Rio de Janeiro - RJ - Brazil
Tel: +55 21 2260-5010 - Fax: +55 21 2290-6626
{granato,aloysio}@gta.ufrj.br   mesquita@coe.ufrj.br

Abstract. An evolutionary approach to design communication protocols from scenario-based specifications is presented. It enables to automatically generate finite-state models of protocol entities from Message Sequence Charts. By converting the Message Sequence Charts into input/output sequences, the problem reduces to evolving finite-state machines with the specified input/output behaviors. The proposed approach does not overgeneralize the entity behavior producing, by construction, minimal, deterministic and completely specified finite-state machines.

1 Introduction and Related Works

Distributed systems play a significant role in the implementation of computer-based applications. The masking of the data/process location for the user, through reliable communication protocols, is the main concept behind these systems. Nevertheless, their modeling and implementation remain, today, a complex task. During the last two decades, several methods to formally describe telecommunication systems and services have been proposed with limited dissemination in industry. As an alternative, much attention has been given to the more intuitive semi-formal approaches, such as interaction scenarios. Scenario-based modeling is particularly well suited for operational descriptions, which are critical in reactive systems, and can be introduced in iterative and incremental design processes [1].

State-oriented specifications and interaction-oriented descriptions techniques provide orthogonal views of systems. Automata represent projections of the complete system behavior onto individual *components*, while Message Sequence Charts (MSCs) represent projections of the complete system behavior onto particular *services*. Because automata usually reveal, to a certain degree, how a particular behavior is achieved, their typical position in the system development process is closer to design and implementation than to requirements capture [2].

G.R. Raidl et al. (Eds.): EvoWorkshops 2004, LNCS 3005, pp. 178–187, 2004.

Clearly, the application of system scenarios, typically used in reverse engineering, within a forward engineering approach calls for precise conversion between models. So, a number of strategies for translating scenarios to automata have been proposed in the recent literature [2, 3]. The SCED algorithm [3] employs the domain-specific assumption that the capability of outputting a specific message uniquely identifies the state of a component. SCED may produce automata with more general behavior than the scenarios themselves as a consequence of the merging of scenarios into state-transition paths. While examples in a typically inductive system can be either positive or negative, scenarios consistently represent positive data and, thus, do not give sufficient information about the target system for inference [4]. Krüger [2] derived an automaton from a given MSC specification by successively applying four transformation steps: 1. *Projection* of MSCs onto the component, 2. *Normalization* to determine the transition-path segments defined by the projected MSCs, 3. *Transformation* into an automaton by turning every message into a transition and by adding intermediate states, and 4. *Optimization* of the resulting automaton. In contrast to SCED the automaton produced by Krüger's approach is neither deterministic nor minimal by construction requiring a distinct optimization step.

On the other hand, Evolutionary Algorithms (EAs) and variations have been used in the synthesis of sequential machines enabling to efficiently explore the solutions space of this category of design problems. Early attempts [5] used some of the EAs concepts to evolve an automaton that predicts outputs based on known input sequences. Lacking the crossover genetic operator [10] the approach has shown, however, poor performances. Recent works have been successful in synthesizing sequential systems with the aid of Genetic Algorithms (GAs) [6, 7, 8]. An approach to synthesize synchronous sequential logic circuits from partial input/output (I/O) sequences is presented in [6]. By using a *technology-based* representation, essentially a netlist of gates and flip-flops, the method was able to synthesize a variety of small FSMs, such as serial adders and 4-bit sequence detectors. Others methods [7, 8] used a technology-independent *state-based* representation in which the next-state and the output corresponding to each current-state/input pair of the state-transition table are coded in a binary string defined as the *chromosome*.

In this work an approach based on evolutionary techniques for the construction of protocol specification models from scenarios is proposed. The method is efficient in generating minimum automata by construction and differently from other approaches [3] does not overgeneralize the entity behavior.

2 Definitions

2.1 MSC and FSM

Message Sequence Charts (MSCs) are scenario notations widely used for requirements capture in the telecommunications domain [1]. A MSC is a graphical scenario consisting of *vertical axes* and *arrows*. The vertical axes represent the system reactive instances, or communicating entities, and the arrows, directed from a sending to a receiving instance, denote a communication event.

Since MSCs usually describe a partial behavior of the system, a question arises about how complete the information contained in the MSCs is and how to transit between possible and mandatory behaviors. It is convenient by this time to correctly understand the *interpretations* of the MSCs with respect to the system under development. Krüger [2] defines four such interpretations: 1. *Existential*: the behavior can, but does not need to occur during the system execution, 2. *Universal*: the behavior must occur in all executions, 3. *Exact*: explicitly prohibits other behaviors than the ones specified through the MSCs and 4. *Negation*: used to describe forbidden or undesirable protocol behaviors. The exact interpretation not only requires what *can* or *must* happen (the behavior explicitly represented by the MSCs); it also makes precise what *must not* happen (everything else).

Finite-state machines (FSMs) are commonly used for specifying communication protocols [9]. At the same time, the FSM is the mostly used target model in construction schemes starting from scenarios [1]. The Mealy FSM model M is formally defined as a 7-tuple $\{Q,V,t,q_0,V',o,D\}$ where $Q \neq \emptyset$ is a finite set of states of M, V is a finite input alphabet, t is the state transition function, $q_0 \in Q$ is the initial state, V' is a finite output alphabet, o is the output function and D is the specification domain, which is a subset of $Q \times V$. t and o together characterize the behavior of the FSM, i.e., $t(q,v)$: $Q \times V \rightarrow Q$ and $o(q,v)$: $Q \times V \rightarrow V'$. If $D = Q \times V$, then t and o are defined for all possible state/input combinations and therefore the FSM is said to be *completely specified*.

2.2 Evolutionary Computation

Evolutionary Computation (EC) consists of the design and analysis of probabilistic algorithms inspired by the principles of Darwinian natural selection. The parallel search performed by EC differs from conventional problem solving techniques in that it does not depend on decomposition. Therefore, EC solutions are best applied to highly non-linear problems for which deterministic solutions are not available.

Genetic Algorithm (GA) and Genetic Programming (GP) are among the most widely used instances of EC. The *chromosome* is the basic component of the GA. It represents a point of the search space of the problem. The fitness value measures how close the individual is to the solution. By iteratively applying the genetic operators (fitness evaluation, fitness-based selection, reproduction, crossover and mutation) to a randomly started population of individuals, it gradually evolves in order to breed at least one offspring with the desired behavior. GA, which usually works with strings (chromosomes) of *fixed length*, is widely used in optimization problems. GP [10] is a branch of GA, the main difference being the solution representation. Unlike GA, GP can easily code chromosomes of *variable length*, which increases the capacity in structure creation.

Programs, or structures, may be produced by combining context-free grammar (CFG) with GP, known as G³P (Grammar-Guided GP). GP Kernel (GPK) [11] is a complex G³P system and was used in this work to evolve trees, each encoding an automaton, from a Backus-Naur form (BNF) provided as input.

3 Methodology

The proposed methodology searches a deterministic FSM, possibly minimal with respect to the number of states, consistent with a given sample of I/O behaviors extracted from MSCs. The I/O behaviors, in the following called *training sequences* (*TSs*), are derived from the projection of the MSC specification onto the entity to be modeled. The execution flow of the methodology is drawn in Fig. 1a: the GP box outputs a population of FSMs for fitness evaluation based on *TSs*; if at least one individual reproduces the I/O behavior given by the *TSs*, the algorithm stops. The resulting FSM describes the protocol entity.

The model adopted for fitness evaluation (shaded box of Fig. 1a) uses the *black-box* approach (Fig. 1b), in which the entity to be evolved interacts with the cooperating entities through an event-driven interface. It is assumed, as in most protocol synthesis approaches [12], that the communication system has reliable FIFO channels. In each generation the system probes a population of FSMs with input sequences and records the corresponding output sequences. These output sequences are compared with the *correct* output sequences, i.e., the outputs of the *TSs*, and a fitness value is assigned to each candidate solution.

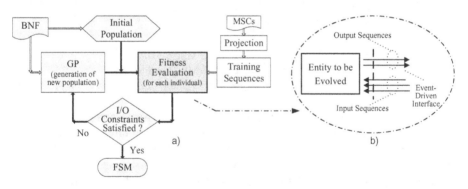

Fig. 1. a) Execution flow of the methodology; b) Model for fitness evaluation

3.1 Derivation of Training Sequences from MSCs

A trace or *training sequence* (*TS*) is defined as a finite sequence of *correct* I/O pairs < v_1/v_1', v_2/v_2'... v_L/v_L' >, where $v \in V$, $v' \in V'$ and L is the length of the sequence. The derivation method is based on the exact interpretation of the MSC specification. The derivation of *TSs* from a set of MSCs is a two-step procedure:

Step 1. Generation of *TSs* with positive mandatory information by projecting all the MSCs onto the object for which the state machine will be synthesized. A projection is carried out by traversing the vertical line of that object, from top to bottom; sequential ordered incoming and outgoing events are grouped into *TS* I/O pairs. Sequential composition of traces from two MSCs containing the object of interest is achieved by means of condition symbols; the random combination of traces in such a way allows the generation of diverse, lengthy *TSs*.

Fig. 2 depicts the MSC specification of a refined connection-oriented protocol. These MSCs have two condition symbols, ACTIVE and IDLE, used to link the MSCs.

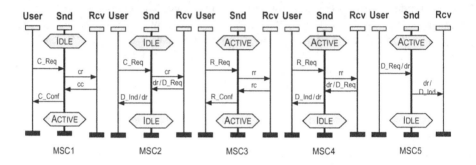

Fig. 2. Connection-oriented protocol MSC specification

The following *TSs* were generated from the procedures described in the first step, by selecting the sender entity as the target object:

ST$_1$: <C_Req/cr, cc/C_Conf, D_Req/dr> (MSC1 and MSC5);
ST$_2$: <C_Req/cr, cc/C_Conf, R_Req/rr, rc/R_Conf> (MSC1 and MSC3);
ST$_3$: <C_Req/cr, dr/D_Ind, C_Req/cr, cc/C_Conf, dr/D_Ind> (MSC1, MSC2 and MSC5).

The *TSs* produced in step 1 does not cover unspecified (non-expected) input events, resulting in incomplete information for state-machine inference. The concept of *completeness* is essential to achieve equivalence between the synthesized FSM and the unknown one from which the sample traces are taken. Completeness implies that there exists a transition for every input event in every state; this assumption assures that the traces will eventually give sufficient information about the state machine for inference [13]. Moving from partial machines to completely specified ones is accomplished in basically two ways: requiring that the state machine remains in the present state without producing any output (i.e., reacting with the *null* output) for any unspecified input or forcing a transition to an added "error state". The implementation of the former on traces is straightforward, as seen in the next step.

Step 2. Insertion of negative information into the *TSs*, obtained in the first step, by randomly adding unspecified input events between I/O pairs of such *TSs*; in this case, the pair is completed with the *null* output forcing the automaton to perform a self-loop. The unspecified input event set (V_U) is inferred from the "exact" MSCs, as follows: $V_U = V - V_E$, where V_E is the expected input event set obtained from the

MSC specification. It is assumed that unspecified input events occur with uniform distribution, i.e., $P(E_i) = 1/N$, for $E_i \in V_U$, $i = 1,...,N$.

This step ensures that each state of the entity is able to respond to every input of its input alphabet, i.e., the construction process yields a completely specified FSM. The following *TSs* were obtained at the end of the second step:

$ST_{1:}$ <C_Req/cr, **rc/Null**, cc/C_Conf, **cc/Null**, **rc/Null**, D_Req/dr>;

$ST_{2:}$ <C_Req/cr, **C_Req/Null**, cc/C_Conf, **cc/Null**, R_Req/rr, **D_Req/Null**, rc/R_Conf>;

$ST_{3:}$ <**R_Req/Null**, C_Req/cr, **rc/Null**, **R_Req/Null**, dr/D_Ind, **rc/Null**, **cc/Null**, C_Req/cr, **R_Req/Null**, cc/C_Conf, **cc/Null**, dr/D_Ind>.

3.2 Length of the Training Sequences (*TSs*)

The *TSs* must be long enough to exercise all paths of the FSM that describes the protocol entity. Ref. [6] gives an approximation formula to estimate the length of the *TSs* that yields a correct FSM, based on the *waiting times in sampling* problem solution. This formula defines the length of the input sequence as $L = E(S) \times E(I)$, where $E(S)$ and $E(I)$ are the *expected value of the number of state transitions* and the *expected value of the number of inputs*, respectively. The expected value of the number of state transitions to traverse all states of a given FSM can be computed using $E(S) = S (S + {}^{S}/_{2} + ... + {}^{1}/_{S})$. Likewise, the expected value of the number of inputs to traverse all paths from a given state is evaluated by $E(I) = I (1 + {}^{1}/_{2} + ... + {}^{1}/_{I})$. However, since the number of states S required to describe the protocol entity is unknown, it must be overestimated a priori.

3.3 Chromosome Coding and BNF Definition

The chromosome, which encodes a FSM, uses state-based representation (SBR). The resulting string (chromosome) with S states and I inputs is shown in Fig. 3.

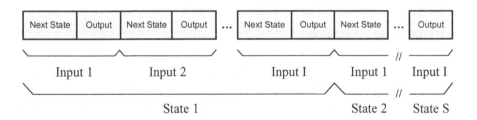

Fig. 3. Chromosome coding using SBR

Unlike other approaches [7, 8], in the present one the length of the chromosome is allowed to vary. GP algorithm was used, since this is the most efficient way to implement an evolutionary process with variable length chromosomes known to date. The BNF that allows the variable length chromosome coding is defined as:

```
s             :=   <expr>;
<expr>        :=   <state>|<expr> <state>;
<state>       :=   <next_st><out> <next_st><out> <next_st><out>
                   <next_st><out> <next_st><out> <next_st><out>;
<next_st>     :=   "0"|"1"|"2"|"3"|"4"|"5";
<out>         :=   "0"|"1"|"2"|"3"|"4"|"5"|"6";
```

where *<expr>* allows the chromosome to vary in length, while *<state>* fixes the number of input events (six, in the above BNF definition, each yielding a next-state/output pair, i.e., *<next_st> <out>*).

3.4 Fitness Evaluation

The number of states used to implement the FSM weights the fitness value assigned to a given FSM behavior. The fitness function F has the form:

$$F = \left(\sum_{i=1}^{N} w_i H_i \right) * \left(1 + K(S) * GR \right) \tag{1}$$

where N is the number of fitness cases (*TSs*), w_i is a weighting factor for fitness case i (*TS_i*), H_i is the number of *output hits* due to the fitness case i, $K(S)$ is a weighting factor that considers the effect of the number of states S used to implement the FSM and GR is the gradient of the overall output hits of the best individual. H_i is computed as follows. Initially, the FSM must be in the reset state. In the sequence, for each input of the TS_i, its output is compared with the *correct* output and an output hit is signed in case of a match. $K(S)*GR$ raises F for FSM implementations with lower number of states. However, as the fitness value tends to get trapped into local optima for an inadequate FSM, GR goes to zero allowing fair competition among FSMs regardless of their sizes.

4 Experimental Results

As an example, the synthesis of a protocol entity specification for the sender side, PS_s, of the connection-oriented protocol from given interaction scenarios, is discussed. The training sequences, *TS*, were produced from the MSC specification of Fig. 2 using the derivation method presented in Subsection 3.1. The *TS* length was evaluated using six inputs (*I*) and an estimated value of five for the parameter S, as described in Subsection 3.2, leading to a 168-input/output *TS*. In fact, eighteen ($N = 18$) 32 bits-*TSs* ($w_i = 1$) were used corresponding to more than three 168-length *TSs*.

The problem consists in finding a minimum-state deterministic FSM consistent with the derived *TSs*. The population size, M, and the maximum number of generations, G_{MAX}, were chosen as 500 and 3,000, respectively. The two-point crossover and mutation probabilities were set to $p_c = 0.65$ and $p_m = 0.05$, respectively. Linear rank selection was used considering the elitist strategy. The population of FSMs was created using the BNF described in Subsection 3.3 allowing FSM implementations with up to six states. The factor $K(S)$ was defined by the set of values $K(S) = \{0.01, 0.008, 0.006, 0.004, 0.002, 0.000\}$ for $S = \{1, 2, 3, 4, 5, 6\}$ respectively. GR was continuously evaluated over 50 generations, except for the first 50 generations and at the end of the evolution where it was set to 1; in this last case because GR tends naturally to zero. To improve the population diversity the mutation probability, p_m, was increased to 0.15 whenever $GR = 0$.

Fig. 4 depicts the fitness curve of the best FSM, its number of states and GR for a typical run. In this figure, it can be observed that at the first 50 generations the number of states of the best FSM fluctuate significantly due to the high population diversity. The same behavior is observed between generations 153 and 205, this time as GR is set to zero. Finally it can be observed that, in general, each increase in the fitness value of the best FSM is correlated with an increase followed by a decrease in the number of its states. This is particularly perceptible at the first 50 generations and between generations 260 and 350. The state-transition graph (STG) of the 4-state resulting FSM, which successfully describes the PS_s after 576 output hits at generation 435, is given in Fig. 5.

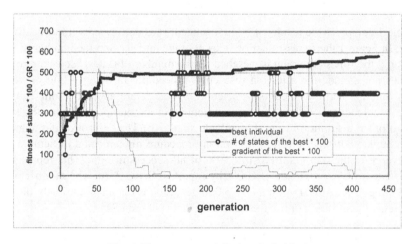

Fig. 4. Fitness curve of the best individual

It should be mentioned that the proposed system does not generate the minimal FSM in all successful runs, i.e., runs that achieve all output hits within the specified G_{MAX}. In some trials the fitness value of the best individual got stuck into local optima for a great number of generations. In these cases the system provokes the premature selection of FSMs with the highest possible number of states yielding to non-optimal solutions. To minimize the early selection of large FSMs, a "selection restriction" procedure was implemented. According with this procedure, individuals with two or more extra states by report to a previous best-fitted individual were disqualified to the selection step.

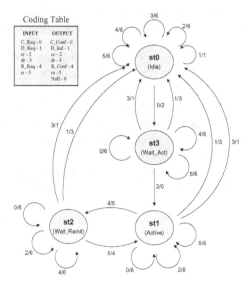

Chromosome: 320106060606 160316012516 260310012614 360310013636

Fig. 5. PS_S, using STG, of the fittest FSM

Table 1 compares the results of 50 independent runs performed with three different setups. In <u>Setup 1</u> the fitness function does not take into account the number of states. In <u>Setup 2</u> the fitness function is weighed by the number of states, according to eq. 1, but does not include the selection restriction procedure. In <u>Setup 3</u> both a weighed fitness function and the selection restriction procedure are applied. From Table 1 it can be conclude: (a) Without an explicit control in the number of states the system tends to breed a solution using all available states, (b) The control of the number of states coupled with the selection restriction procedure implemented in Setup 3 allow to converge to the minimum FSM in 59% of all successful runs. This represents an improvement of, approximately, 400% by report to Setup 2. (c) The number of runs not yielding to the global optimum in 3,000 generations remained basically the same, regardless of controlling or not the number of states of the FSM.

Table 1. Comparison among three different setups for 50 independent runs

SETUP	Runs not yielding to global optimum in 3,000 generations	Runs yielding to global optimum in 3,000 generations		
		4 states	*5 states*	*6 states*
1. $F = \sum_{i=1}^{N} w_i H_i$	20	0	3	27
2. Eq. (1)	18	4	15	13
3. Eq. (1) with selection restriction	21	17	9	3

5 Conclusion

An evolutionary approach to the design of communication protocols specified by Message Sequence Charts was presented. As in other construction approaches [2, 3] the assumption that a set of MSCs specifies the system behavior *completely* was adopted. However, the methodology relaxes the exact MSC interpretation by adding behaviors not explicitly specified by the MSCs and, contrary to [3], avoids the over-generalization of the synthesized automata.

State-based representation is not efficient for systems with large number of states. However, the benefit of using it in the protocol synthesis is that it guarantees the completeness of the synthesized specifications.

The resulting automata are minimal in many cases, deterministic and completely specified by construction. The application of an analytic method, such as that used in [2], on MSC specification of Fig. 2 yields, in the first steps, a non-deterministic FSM. Moreover, contrary to SCED approach, the proposed approach is not sensitive to the order of traces in its input.

References

1. Amyot, D., Eberlein, A.: An Evaluation of Scenario Notations and Construction Approaches for Telecommunication Systems Development, Telecommunications Systems Journal, 24:1, 61-94 (2003)
2. Krüger, I. H.: Distributed System Design with Message Sequence Charts, PhD Thesis, Technische Universität München (2000)
3. Koskimies, K., Männistö, T., Systä, T., Toumi, J.: Automated Support for Modeling OO Software, IEEE Software, 15, 1, pp. 87-94 (1998)
4. Systä, T.: Static and Dynamic Reverse Engineering Techniques for Java Software Systems, PhD Thesis, University of Tempere (2000)
5. Fogel, L.: Autonomous Automata, Industrial Research, 4:14-19 (1962)
6. Manovit, C., Aporntewan, C., Chongstitvatana, P.: Synthesis of Synchronous Sequential Logic Circuits from Partial Input/Output Sequences, ICES'98, pp. 98-105 (1998)
7. Collins, R., Jefferson, D.: Representation for Artificial Organisms, in Proceedings of the 1st Int. Conf. on Simulation of Adaptive Behavior, MIT Press (1991)
8. Chongstitvatana, P., Aporntewan, C.: Improving Correctness of Finite-State Machine Synthesis from Multiple Partial Input/Output Sequences, in Proceedings of the 1st NASA/DoD Workshop on Evolvable Hardware, pp. 262-266 (1999)
9. Bockmann, G., Petrenko, A.: Protocol Testing: A Review of Methods and Relevance for Software Testing, ISSTA'94, ACM, Seattle, U.S.A., pp. 109-124 (1994)
10. Koza, J.: Genetic Programming: On the Programming of Computers by Means of Natural Selection, MIT Press (1992)
11. Hörner, H.: A C++ Class Library for Genetic Programming, Release 1.0 Operating Instructions, Viena University of Economy (1996)
12. Probert, R., Saleh, K.: Synthesis of Protocols: Survey and Assessment, IEEE Transactions on Computers, Vol. 40, No 4, pp. 468-476 (1991)
13. Koskimies, K., Mäkinen, E.: Automatic Synthesis of State Machines from Trace Diagrams, Software Practice and Experience, 24(7), 643-658 (1994)

A Slicing Structure Representation for the Multi-layer Floorplan Layout Problem

Johan Berntsson and Maolin Tang

School of Computing Science and Software Engineering
Queensland University of Technology
QLD 4001, Australia
{j.berntsson, m.tang}@qut.edu.au

Abstract. This is a preliminary study in which we use a genetic algorithm to solve the multiple layer floorplanning problem. The original contribution is a three dimensional slicing structure representation which, to the best of our knowledge, is the first 3D floorplan representation in the literature. In this paper we give some background on VLSI design and the floorplanning problem before describing the slicing structure representation and the genetic algorithm extensions. We present results for benchmark problems and obtain improvements on previously published results for single layer floorplanning.

1 Introduction

The rapid increase in VLSI integrated circuit complexity has been made possible by the development of Electronic Design Automation (EDA) tools that can simplify the design process by presenting abstractions of hardware at several levels from system specification design to packing. One of these phases is physical design, where the logical layout of a circuit (a list of components and connections) is transformed to a physical layout. Floorplanning is the problem of placing a set of large sub-circuits (blocks) without overlap on a layout surface to meet a set of design goals and constraints. It is an essential step in the hierarchical physical design of deep sub-micron VLSI circuits, and is often solved by simulated annealing, force-directed heuristics or aggregate methods to place the blocks on each layer in a feasible (non-overlapping) configuration, which is usually subject to secondary goals such as minimizing wire length to cut down signal delays.

As the VLSI complexity increases, interconnect is increasingly dominating the overall design and must be taken into account in the whole process, especially in earlier stages such as floorplanning. Instead of solving the floorplanning problem layer by layer and leaving interlayer connections for the later partitioning and routing stages, a floorplanner that treats the multi-layer interconnect as an integral part of the floorplanning problem should be able to place tightly interconnected modules more closely, thus making it easier to meet their timing goals in the routing phase. The semiconductor industry has expressed the need for such a 3D floorplanner [1], and theoretical aspects of multi-layer floorplanning have been investigated [2].

G.R. Raidl et al. (Eds.): EvoWorkshops 2004, LNCS 3005, pp. 188–197, 2004.
© Springer-Verlag Berlin Heidelberg 2004

1.1 Releated Work

The floorplanning problem is a generalization of the quadratic assignment problem, which is an NP-hard problem [3]. The reported approaches can be divided into three general cases: constructive, knowledge-based, and iterative [4]. The constructive approach starts from a seed module, and adds modules to the floorplan until all modules have been selected. The knowledge-based approach uses a database with expert knowledge to guide the floorplan development. The iterative approach starts from an initial floorplan which undergoes a series of transformations until the optimization goal is reached. The iterative class includes force directed relaxation methods, simulated annealing, and evolutionary algorithms.

A number of representations have been proposed for the floorplan problem, among them direct representation, slicing structures, and non-slicing representations [4]. A slicing structure divides the floorplan by vertical and horizontal segments into a finite number of non-overlapping rectangles and fit one block into each segment [5]. Slicing floorplans are easy to use for optimization, but they are only a subset of all possible floorplans and in recent years much research has been directed to devising more exact representations of the topology using directed acyclic graphs such as B*-trees [6], TCG [7], and Twin-Binary Sequences [8], or by using direct representations with parameters for the orientation and location of each block. These representations can handle any floorplan, but they rely on complicated and often computationally intensive procedures to handle common requirements in floorplanning design such as soft modules and pre-placed blocks [9].

The slicing structure representation has been extensively used for iterative algorithms since its simplified structure makes it possible to develop efficient representations and operators for manipulation. Although slicing structures cannot represent all possible floorplans, empirical evidence suggest that the slicing floorplan can be quite efficient in packing blocks tightly [10]. The reduction of the solution space can be advantageous as long as the remaining solutions are good enough, and it has been argued that this is the case when the floorplan contains soft modules that have flexible shapes [10]. The enveloping area can be estimated in polynomial time by the shape curve method, which can handle combinations of soft, hard, and pre-placed modules [11]. Flexibility in module sizes is common in early stages of design, making slicing structures suitable for the floorplanning problem.

Research in using Genetic Algorithms (GA) with slicing structure representations has been reported for sequential GA [12,13,14] and parallel GA [15]. These GAs encode the slicing structure as Polish (postfix) expression strings in the genome, and define crossover operators that produce children that are Polish expressions by identifying and swapping subtrees in the parents. Tests with non-trivial benchmark problems give solutions of good quality compared to other iterative methods. The main drawback is that they are slow, and more recently progress has been made in reducing the runtime by developing more efficient representation and recombination operators, such as crossover operators that actively search for fit subtrees in each parent [9]. Another approach is to use a normalized postorder genome representation that guarantees a one-to-one mapping between genotype and phenotype. By using an algorithm that constructs normalized expressions from a permutation list of blocks, and then applying well-known methods for enclosing area estimation of Polish expressions, the authors are able to beat a simulated annealing algorithm both in quality and number of evaluations when optimizing for minimal dead space [16].

One recent paper uses a simplified multi-level floorplan representation with GA optimization [17], where the floorplan is coded as a set of 2D slicing plans, one for each layer. The present work is significantly different, in that the floorplan is a true 3D representation which can represent building blocks not only in each layer, but also between different layers.

2   Problem Formulation

Input: A set of n rectangular blocks $\{B_1, B_2, \ldots, B_n\}$ and a list of triplets $\{A_1, r_1, s_1\}, \{A_2, r_2, s_2\}, \ldots, \{A_n, r_n, s_n\}$, where A_i is the area, and r_i and s_i are the lower and upper bounds on the aspect ratio of block B_i. $r_i < s_i$ if the block is soft (flexible), and $r_i = s_i$ if the block is hard. The blocks are divided into two sets S_1 and S_2 such that $S_1 \cup S_2 = \{B_1, B_2, \ldots, B_n\}$ and $S_1 \cap S_2 = \emptyset$, where S_1 represents the blocks with fixed orientation and S_2 represents the blocks with free orientation. Symbols p and q represent the upper and lower bounds on the shape of each layer, and m represents the maximum allowed number of layers.

Output: A feasible floorplan solution consisting of enveloping rectangle R_i for layer i, $1 \leq i \leq j$. Each R_i is subdivided by horizontal and vertical cuts into p_i non-overlapping rectangles. The rectangles are labelled $R_1, R_2, \ldots, R_j$. The floorplan is subjected to the following constraints:

1. $j \leq m$
2. $n = \sum_{i=1}^{j} p_i$
3. $p \leq \frac{H_i}{W_i} \leq q, 1 \leq i \leq j$, where H_i and W_i are the height and width of the enveloping rectangle for layer i.
4. $A_i = w_i * h_i$ for all $R_i \in S_1$, where h_i and w_i are the height and width of B_i.
5. $r_i \leq \frac{h_i}{w_i} \leq s_i$ or $\frac{1}{s_i} \leq \frac{h_i}{w_i} \leq \frac{1}{r_i}$ for all $R_i \in S_2$

Goal: Minimize overall area $A = \sum_{i=1}^{j} H_i * W_i$

3   Representation

In the 3D floorplanner, a floorplan is encoded in normalized Polish expressions that use the symbols 'H', 'V', and 'Z', representing horizontal, vertical, and lateral cuts, respectively. The integers $1 \ldots n$ represent the blocks in a problem. By using normalized Polish expressions we guarantee a unique mapping between the Polish expression and its corresponding binary tree. An example can be found in Fig 1, which shows the binary tree for the Polish expression "3 1 6 8 Z H Z 2 7 Z V 5 4 H V."

To evaluate the floorplan it is necessary to break down the 3D slicing structure. We have defined a splicer algorithm which accepts a 3D floorplan and the maximum number of layers, and returns a slicing structure for each layer. The three trees on the right side of Fig 1 shows the same Polish expression divided into three layers.

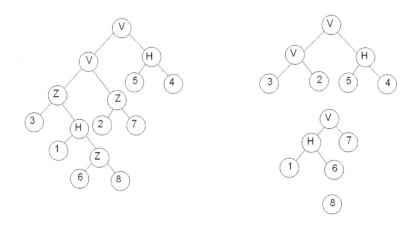

Fig. 1. The 3D floorplan tree for "3 1 6 8 Z H Z 2 7 Z V 5 4 H V", and its three 2D layers

The basic task of the splicer algorithm, outlined below, is to examine the binary tree for the 3D slicing floorplan, and remove 'Z' nodes, leaving only a 2D slicing tree with 'V' and 'H' nodes. All 'Z' nodes in the current layer are replaced with their left child while their right child is inserted into the next layer. Since the maximum number of layers is fixed, the function wraps around and starts reinserting nodes in the first layer when it reaches the top layer.

If the next layer is empty, the right child becomes the next layer; otherwise a new root node joins the current content of the next layer and the right subtree. We consider subtrees to be the natural building blocks for iterative methods to work with, and take special care to keep the their topological relationships intact when splitting the full 3D slicing structure into separate 2D structures for each layer. The ID ('V' or 'H') of the new root node is defined as the common ancestor in the original 3D floorplan between the most previously inserted subtree and the subtree to be inserted. In this way the relative location between subtrees is maintained. Fig 2 shows the slicing structures corresponding to the examples used in Fig 1. Block 6 and 1, originating from the left-most 'Z' node in Fig 1, are put to the right of block 7 which originates from the right-most 'Z' node, since the common ancestor of both subtrees is the leftmost 'V' node in the 3D tree from Fig 1.

Once all 'Z' nodes have been removed from the current layer the next layer becomes the current layer, and the algorithm iterates until no new layers are generated.

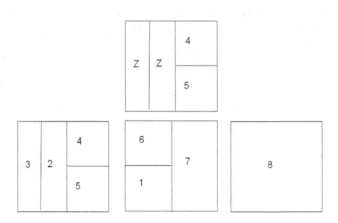

Fig. 2. The 3D slicing floorplan (top), and the three slicing floorplan layers (bottom). Structures marked 'Z' in the 3D floorplan denotes subtrees branching upwards.

```
Function Splicer
[Input: m = number of layers, 3DTree = Floorplan Tree]
[Output: array of 2D floorplans]
layerNumber = 0
currentLayer = 3DTree
do {
  nextLayer = 0
  subtrees = FindZSubtrees(currentLayer)
  foreach(tree in subtrees) {
    currentLayer.ReplaceNode(tree.root, tree.left);
    subtrees.Append(FindZSubtrees(tree.left))

    if(nextLayer == 0) {
      nextLayer=tree.right
    } else {
      node = CommonAncestor(tree.right, lastLayer);
      while (node = 'Z') node = node.parent;
      nextLayer = Node(node.ID, tree.right, nextLayer)
    }
    lastLayer = nextLayer
  }

  2DTree[layerNumber % m ] = currentLayer
  currentLayer = nextLayer
```

```
  layerNumber = layerNumber + 1
} while(currentLayer != 0)
return 2DTree[]

Function FindZSubtrees
[Input: binary 3D Floorplan tree]
[Output: array of subtrees]
Find all subtrees with a 'Z' node root without 'Z'
node ancestors.
```

4 The Genetic Algorithm

The GA used to evaluate the 3D floorplan representation is based on a recently published normalized Polish expression GA. Below we briefly describe our extensions to handle the new 3D representation, and the reader is referred to [16] for an in-depth description of the GA.

The genome consists of an array of records, each of which corresponds to a block in the problem, and consists of three fields:

1. A block ID: this identifies the block from the data set
2. An chain type ID: this can be set to one of three operator chains; 1=VHVHV..., 2=HVHVHV..., and 3=ZHZV...
3. Chain field length: this defines the maximum length of the operator chain associated with this field.

The phenotype (a normalized Polish expression) is constructed using this algorithm:

1. Examine the first record; copy the rectangle ID to the phenotype
2. Generate the chain of alternating operators specified by the chain type ID
3. Copy operators from the chain to the phenotype until the end of the chain is reached or more operators would invalidate the expression
4. Go to 1 if there are more records to process, or else complete the expression by continuing to copy alternating operators until the expression is valid.

The genome is initialized like in the original implementation for 2D floorplans, with the exception of the chain type which is set to 1, 2 or 3 with equal probability. The genome is order based, and uses permutation CX crossover [18] to assign blocks to leaves in the slicing tree. There are three mutation operators that modify the genome.

1. Swap positions of two block IDs
2. Change the chain type (type 1 becomes 2, 2 becomes 3, 3 becomes 1)
3. Mutate the length by increasing or decreasing the chain length with equal probability.

4.1   Genome Decoder

The objective function first decodes the genome representation to a 3D Polish expression, and uses the splicer algorithm to generate a 2D Polish expression for each layer. The enveloping rectangle for each of these expressions is calculated using the curve method. The objective function also checks that the width to height ratio of the enveloping rectangles lies in the allowed $0.5 \leq \frac{h}{w} \leq 2$ range, and the GA will reapply the selection and recombination operators until a valid offspring has been produced.

4.2   Fitness Evaluation

For evaluating the new representation we have defined objective functions to test for total area minimization, and for balanced area minimization where each layer will be of similar size. Initially we tried several alternative fitness functions, including minimizing for area or waste, and optimizing on all layers or for the largest layer only. We found that most variations tend to put a small number of blocks on the higher layers that fit together with almost no waste, and put the remaining blocks in the bottom layer. The best result was achieved when calculating the fitness as an aggregate multi-objective problem with two objectives, using the equation

$$fitness = p * \frac{\sum_{i=1}^{n} A_i}{\sum_{i=1}^{j} H_i * W_i} + \frac{\sum_{i=1}^{n} A_i}{j * \max(H_i) * \max(W_i)}$$

where p is a control parameter that balances between the two objectives.

1. For the total overall area minimization, dividing the total block area with the sum of each layer's enveloping rectangle area gives a reasonably even distribution of blocks among the available layers while efficiently reducing waste.
2. For balanced area minimization, we define the fitness value as the sum of each block's area divided by the number of layers times the area of the bounding rectangle of the total floorplan. Fig 3 illustrates how the bounding rectangle for the full floorplan is related to the enclosing rectangle for each layer.

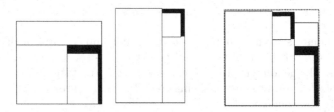

Fig. 3. Two layers with enclosing rectangles (left) and the combined multi-layer floorplan (right). The bounding rectangle is marked with a dashed line.

5   Results

The present goal of our research is a "proof of concept" of the proposed 3D slicing structure, and we limit the objective function to optimization of the floorplan area. The GA can easily find the optimal solutions for the soft block version of the benchmarks used, and we use the more difficult hard version to be able to make meaningful comparisons. The number of layers is set to 4, and the GA is a generational GA with elitism 1, population size 200, maximum number of generations 2000, 2-tournament selection, crossover probability 0.9, and mutation probability 0.1.

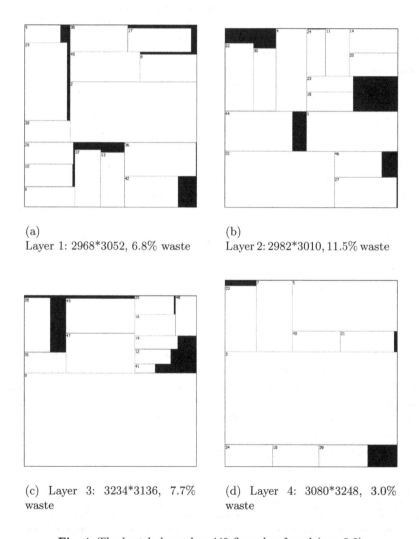

(a)
Layer 1: 2968*3052, 6.8% waste

(b)
Layer 2: 2982*3010, 11.5% waste

(c) Layer 3: 3234*3136, 7.7% waste

(d) Layer 4: 3080*3248, 3.0% waste

Fig. 4. The best balanced ami49 floorplan found ($p = 0.3$)

Table 1. Area minimization results with MCNC benchmarks

Problem p	Best 3D Bounding	Area	Waste	Best 2D Bounding	Area	Waste
ami33 1.0	1190*665	1193346	3.09%	1337*903	1207311	4.21%
ami33 0.3	651*504	1223530	5.48%			
ami33 0.0	658*504	1315944	12.1%			
ami49 1.0	2296*5572	13891500	3.76%	7084*5250	37191000	4.69%
ami49 0.3	3248*3136	38179820	7.16%			
ami49 0.0	4354*2394	41073760	13.7%			

No benchmarks have been published for multi-layer floorplanning, and to be able to verify the potential of 3D floorplanning we have compared the performance of our 3D floorplanner with the best reported results on MCNC benchmarks [19]. Table 1 show the results when we test for total area minimization only ($p = 1.0$), and we improve on the previously known best result by using multiple layers.

The total area minimization objective tends to put blocks that fit well together in the upper layers and put the rest of the blocks in the bottom layer which makes the upper layers smaller. In real-world floorplanning it is more important to generate layers of similar size, and we have also tested the benchmarks with multiple objectives ($p < 1.0$). The balanced area objective sacrifices some packing efficiency for an even distribution of layer size, and too much emphasis gives poor results (e.g. $p = 0.0$). We have found that $p = 0.3$ is a good trade-off between the objectives, and the bounding rectangle for the 3D solutions is approximately one quarter of the 2D case, which shows that each layer is of similar size. Although the waste is slightly higher than when using the total area minimization only, we believe that a balanced floorplan is more suited for multi-layer benchmarking and we will use the multiobjective area minimization in future research.

6   Conclusion

We have presented a 3D slicing floorplan representation for the multi-layer floorplan problem and applied it to a genetic algorithm. The packing efficiency is in line with the theoretical predictions for 3D slicing floorplans [2], and motivates further research. For real VLSI design efficient packing is not enough, and in future research we intend to use netlists to find the blocks that are tightly interconnected, and use this knowledge to place densely interconnected modules closer. This will reduce overall wire length and associated delays, making it easier to meet timing specifications.

References

1. J. Parkhurst, N. Sherwani, S. Maturi, D. Ahrams, and E. Chiprout: "SRC Physical Design Top Ten Problems," in Proceedings of the 1999 international symposium on Physical design, ACM Press, 1999, pp. 55-58.

2. S. Salewski and E. Barke: "An Upper Bound for 3D Slicing Floorplans," in Proceedings of the Asia South Pacific Design Automation/VLSI Design Conference, IEEE Computer Society, 2002, pp. 567-572.
3. M. Garey and D. S. Johnson: Computers and Intractability: A Guide to NP-Completeness, Freeman, 1979.
4. S. M. Sait and H. Youssef: VLSI physical design automation : theory and practice, IEEE Press, 1995.
5. R. H. J. M. Otten: "Automatic Floorplan Design," in Proceedings of the 19th Design Automation Conference, 1982, pp 261-267.
6. Y. C. Chang, Y. W. Chang, G. M. Wu and S. W. Wu: "B*-trees: a new representation for non-slicing floorplans," in Proceedings of the 37th Design Automation Conference, ACM Press, 2000, pp 458-463.
7. J. M. Lin, and Y. W. Chang: "TCG: a transitive closure graph-based representation for non-slicing floorplans," in Proceedings of the 38th conference on Design automation, ACM Press, 2001, pp 764-769.
8. E. F. Y. Young, C. C. N. Chu, and Z. C. Shen: "Twin binary sequences: a nonredundant representation for general nonslicing floorplan," in IEEE Transactions on Computer-Aided Design of Integrated Circuits and Systems, vol. 22, 2003, pp 457-469.
9. C. T. Lin, D. S. Chen, and Y. W. Wang: "An efficient genetic algorithm for slicing floorplan area optimization," in Proceedings of the 2002 IEEE International Symposium on Circuits and Systems, vol 2, IEEE Press, 2002, pp 879-882.
10. F. Y. Young, and D. F. Wong: "How good are slicing floorplans?," in Proceedings of the 1997 international symposium on Physical design, ACM Press, 1997, pp 144-149.
11. F. Y. Young, and D. F. Wong: "Slicing floorplans with pre-placed modules," in Proceedings of the 1998 IEEE/ACM international conference on Computer-aided design, ACM Press, 1998, pp 252-258.
12. I. Tazawa, S. Koakutsu, and H. Hirata: "An immunity based genetic algorithm and its application to the VLSI floorplan design problem," in Proceedings of IEEE International Conference on Evolutionary Computation, IEEE Press, 1996, pp 417-421.
13. V. Schnecke, and O. Vornberger: "Genetic design of VLSI-layouts," in Proceedings of the First International Conference on Genetic Algorithms in Engineering Systems, 1995, pp 430-435.
14. H. Esbensen, and E. S. Kuh: "EXPLORER: an interactive floorplanner for design space exploration," in Proceedings of the European Design Automation Conference, 1996, pp 356-361.
15. J. P. Cohoon, S. U. Hegde, W. N. Martin, and D. S. Richards: "Distributed genetic algorithms for the floorplan design problem," in IEEE Transactions on Computer-Aided Design of Integrated Circuits and Systems, vol. 10(4), 1991, pp 483-492.
16. C. L. Valenzuela, and P. Y. Wang: "VLSI placement and area optimization using a genetic algorithm to breed normalized postfix expressions," in IEEE Transactions on Evolutionary Computation, vol. 6(4), 2002, pp 390-401.
17. S. Salewski, M. Olbrich, and E. Barke: "LIFT: Ein Multi-Layer IC Floorplanning Tool," in EIS-Workshop, 2003, pp 157-162.
18. Z. Michalewicz: Genetic Algorithms + Data Structures = Evolution Programs, Springer-Verlag, 1992.
19. MCNC Floorplanning benchmarks,
http://www.cse.ucsc.edu/research/surf/GSRC/MCNCbench.html

Disjoint Sum of Product Minimization by Evolutionary Algorithms

Nicole Drechsler, Mario Hilgemeier, Görschwin Fey, and Rolf Drechsler

Institute of Computer Science
University of Bremen
28359 Bremen, Germany
{nd,mh,fey,rd}@informatik.uni-bremen.de

Abstract. Recently, an approach has been presented to minimize Disjoint Sum-of-Products (DSOPs) based on Binary Decision Diagrams (BDDs). Due to the symbolic representation of cubes for large problem instances, the method is orders of magnitude faster than previous enumerative techniques. But the quality of the approach largely depends on the variable ordering of the underlying BDD.

This paper presents an Evolutionary Algorithm (EA) to optimize the DSOP representation of a given Boolean function. The EA is used to find an optimized variable ordering for the BDD representation. Then the DSOP is derived from the optimized BDD using structural and symbolic techniques. Experiments are performed to adjust the parameters of the EA. Experimental results are given to demonstrate the efficiency of the approach.

1   Introduction

A DSOP is a representation of a Boolean function as a sum of disjoint cubes. DSOPs are used in several applications in the area of CAD, e.g. the calculation of spectra of Boolean functions [7,8,22] or as a starting point for the minimization of Exclusive-Or-Sum-Of-Products (ESOPs) [17,20]. In [9,21] some techniques for minimization of DSOPs have been introduced. They are working on explicit representations of the cubes and therefore are only applicable to small instances of the problem.

BDDs in general are an efficient data structure for representation and manipulation of Boolean functions. They are well-known and widely used in logic synthesis [16,10] and formal verification [2,15] of integrated circuits. BDDs are well-suited for applications in the area of logic synthesis, because the cubes in the ON-set of a Boolean function are implicitly represented in this data structure.

A hybrid approach for the minimization of DSOPs relying on BDDs in combination with structural methods has recently been introduced in [11]. It has been shown that BDDs are applicable to the problem of DSOP minimization. Given a BDD of a Boolean function, the DSOP can easily be constructed: each one-path, i.e. a path from the root to the terminal 1 vertex, corresponds to a cube in the DSOP, and moreover, different one-paths lead to disjoint cubes. For

G.R. Raidl et al. (Eds.): EvoWorkshops 2004, LNCS 3005, pp. 198–207, 2004.
© Springer-Verlag Berlin Heidelberg 2004

the construction of the BDD the variables of the Boolean function are considered in a fixed order. The permutation of the variables largely influences the number of one-paths in the BDD and thus the number of cubes in the corresponding DSOP. Additionally, the importance of choosing a "good" variable order to get a small DSOP has theoretically been supported.

In this context EAs have been shown to be a promising approach, i.e. they work very well for BDD minimization and other variants of permutation problems (see e.g. [6,14]).

In this paper we present an EA for determining a good ordering for a BDD. The BDD is optimized in such a way that the corresponding DSOP is minimized. The parameters of the EA are studied in detail. Experimental results are given that show improvement over the best known heuristics.

The paper is organized as follows: Section 2 briefly introduces the necessary notion of BDDs and one-paths and shows how the DSOP representation is related to BDDs. In Section 3 the EA is discussed in detail. Experimental results are given in Section 4. Finally, conclusions are drawn.

2 Preliminaries

2.1 Binary Decision Diagrams

A BDD is a directed acyclic graph $G_f = (V, E)$ that represents a Boolean function $f : \mathbf{B}^n \longrightarrow \mathbf{B}^m$. The Shannon decomposition $g = x_i g_{x_i} + \overline{x}_i g_{\overline{x}_i}$ is carried out in each internal node v labeled with $\mathrm{label}(v) = x_i$ of the graph, therefore v has the two successors $\mathrm{then}(v)$ and $\mathrm{else}(v)$. The leaves are labeled with 0 or 1 and correspond to the constant Boolean functions. The root node $\mathrm{root}(G_f)$ corresponds to the function f. In the following, BDD refers to a reduced ordered BDD (as defined in [1]) and the size of a BDD is given by the number of nodes.

Definition 1. A one-path in a BDD $G_f = (V, E)$ is a path

$$p = (v_0, ..., v_{l-1}, v_l),$$

$$v_i \in V, (v_i, v_{i+1}) \in E$$

with $v_0 = \mathrm{root}(G_f)$ and $\mathrm{label}(v_l) = 1$. p has length $l + 1$.
$\mathcal{P}_1(G_f)$ denotes the number of all different one-paths in the BDD G_f.

2.2 BDD and DSOP

Consider a BDD G_f representing the Boolean function $f(x_1, ..., x_n)$. A one-path $p = (v_0, ..., v_l)$ of length $l + 1$ in G_f corresponds to an $(n - l)$-dimensional cube that is a subset of $ON(f)$[1]. The cube is described by:

$$m_p = \bigcap_{i=0}^{l-1} l_i, \text{where}$$

---

[1] $ON(f)$ is the ON-set of the Boolean function f, i.e. the variable assignments that evaluate f to value 1.

$$l_i = \begin{cases} \overline{\text{label}(v_i)}, & \text{if } v_{i+1} = \text{else}(v_i) \\ \text{label}(v_i), & \text{if } v_{i+1} = \text{then}(v_i) \end{cases}$$

Two paths p_1 and p_2 in a BDD are different iff they differ in at least one edge. Since all paths originate from $\text{root}(G_f)$, there is a node v where the paths separate. Let $\text{label}(v) = x_i$. Therefore one of the cubes includes x_i, the other $\overline{x}_i$. Hence, the cubes m_{p_1} and m_{p_2} are disjoint.

Now the DSOP can easily be built by summing up all cubes corresponding to the one-paths.

Remark 1. Let G_f be a BDD of $f(x_1, ..., x_n)$ and $\mathcal{M}_1$ be the set of one-paths in G_f. Then G_f represents the DSOP

$$\sum_{p \in \mathcal{M}_1} m_p,$$

where m_p is the cube given above.

From this it is clear that the number of cubes in the DSOP represented by G_f is equal to $\mathcal{P}_1(G_f)$. Thus, as opposed to the usual goal of minimizing the number of nodes in a BDD, here the number of one-paths is minimized.

Known techniques to minimize the number of nodes can be used to minimize the number of paths by changing the objective function. One such technique is sifting [19]: A variable is chosen and moved to any position of the variable order based on exchange of adjacent variables. Then it is fixed at the best position (i.e. where the smallest BDD results), afterwards another variable is chosen. No variable is chosen twice during this process.

For the evaluation of our fitness function, in the following the improved path-minimization algorithm based upon sifting from [11] is used. This algorithm employs structural techniques to reduce the number of cubes in the DSOP.

3   Evolutionary Algorithm

In this section we describe the Evolutionary Algorithm (EA) that is applied to the problem given above. In Sections 3.1 to 3.4 the submodules of our EA (like the evolutionary operators) and the overall structure of the algorithm are described. Finally, the detailed choices for the parameter settings are discussed.

The DSOP of a Boolean function that is represented by a BDD directly depends on the chosen variable ordering. Finding a good or even optimal variable ordering is a permutation problem that is optimized by an evolutionary approach.

3.1   Representation

A population is a set of individuals that represent solutions of the given optimization problem. In this application an individual represents the ordering position of each variable:

We use an integer encoding to represent the ordering of the variables. (A binary encoding would require special repair operators to avoid the creation of invalid solutions similar to the TSP, see e.g. [23].) Each integer vector of length n represents a permutation of the variables and thus it is a feasible ordering.

The length of the strings is given by the number of variables n, because for each variable the ordering position has to be stored.

3.2   Objective Function and Selection

The objective function assigns to each individual a fitness that measures the quality of the variable ordering. First the BDD is constructed using the variable ordering given by the individual, then the number of reduced one-paths are counted [11].

The selection is performed by roulette wheel selection and we also make use of steady-state reproduction [4]: The best individuals of the old population are included in the new one of equal size. This strategy guarantees that the best element never gets lost and a fast convergence is obtained. (EA practice has shown that this method is usually advantageous.)

3.3   Evolutionary Operators

Different types of crossover operators and mutations for permutation problems are used. For the crossover operators two parents are selected by the method described above. For more details about the evolutionary operators we refer to [13,3,18,5,14].

Notice that a simple exchange of the parts between the cut positions (as often applied to binary encoded EA problems) is not possible, since this would often produce invalid solutions.

PMX [13]: Choose two cut positions randomly in the parent elements. Construct the children by choosing the part between the cut positions from one parent and preserve the absolute position and order of as many variables as possible from the second parent.

OX [3]: Choose two cut positions randomly in the parent elements. Construct the children by choosing the part between the cut position from one parent and preserve the relative position and order of as many variables as possible from the second parent.

CX [18]: Choose a single position i in the parent elements at random. Copy the values of this position into the children at exactly the same position: child1$[i]$ = parent1$[i]$ and child2$[i]$ = parent2$[i]$. Then, position j in parent1 is determined, such that parent1$[j]$ = parent2$[i]$. Set $i := j$ and continue the procedure as described above, until the new position j has already been copied in the children elements. Then a "cycle" has been found and the remaining positions in child1 (child2) are taken from parent1 (parent2).

MERGE [14]: It produces the first child in the following way. Alternating between the parents, MERGE takes one variable index from each parent (in the order they appear in the parents) until the double permutation length is reached. After doing this, MERGE checks from left to right if an index has been used already. If this is the case, that index number is removed. The second child is produced by exchanging even and odd positions in the index list.

INV: The inversion operator INV inverts the order of the index list for a randomly chosen part of the chromosome. It produces one child from each parent.

Additionally, three different mutation operators are used:

Mutation (MUT): Select one individual and choose two different positions at random. Swap the values of these two positions.

2-time Mutation (MUT2): Perform MUT two times on the same parent.

Mutation with neighbor (MUT-N): Perform MUT at two adjacent positions.

3.4   Flow of the Algorithm

Using the operators introduced above our EA works as follows:

- Initially a random population of permutations (variable ordering) is generated.
- The crossover operators described in Section 3.3 are applied to selected elements and create $|pop|/2$ offspring. The parent elements are chosen according to their fitness (see Section 3.2). The offspring are then mutated by the mutation operators with a given probability.
- The fitness of the offspring is calculated as described in Section 3.2. The worse half of the population is then replaced by new individuals.
- The last two steps are iterated until the termination criterion holds.

Experiments have shown that it is sufficient to consider 24 individuals in a population. For larger population sizes the execution times are getting "too high".

To get a good parameter setting of the EA, several experiments and operator studies have been performed. Due to the page limitation we can not discuss these experiments in detail. The following weighting of the evolutionary operators has been selected with respect to the given test suite: PMX, OX, CX, MERGE, and INV are performed with probabilities 1%, 43%, 1%, 11%, and 43%, respectively. The mutation probabilities are all set to 1%.

The termination criterion depends on the best fitness value of the considered population: The algorithm stops if no improvement is obtained for $50 * \log_{10} best\_fitness$ iterations. The idea is: if the considered fitness value is higher, more optimization potential can be expected.

4   Experimental Results

Experiments were carried out on a Pentium II system at 450 MHz with 256 MB of physical memory. The machine was running under Linux. Control programs for the experiments were written in Python. The EA was based on the C++ library for evolutionary algorithms GAME [12] (version 2.43).

The experimental results show the quality of the proposed evolutionary method. The EA is applied to several benchmark functions, most of them taken from LGSynth93. The experiments are summarized in the following tables.

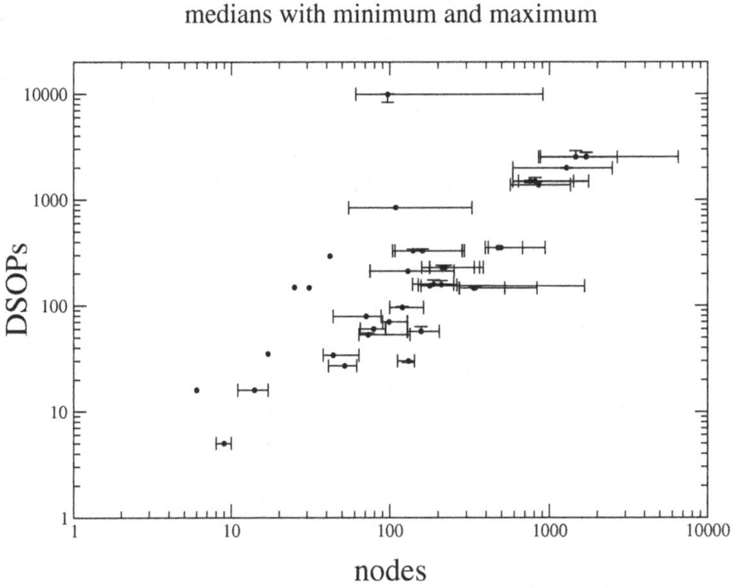

medians with minimum and maximum

Fig. 1. Representation of benchmark suite

In Table 1 the EA for all considered benchmarks is analyzed. To get an impression of the (local) minimum number of cubes per function, the EA is applied 25 times to the 37 benchmarks in the test suite. Each time a randomly chosen seed for the random number generator was used. In column **hybrid** the number of cubes resulting from the method proposed in [11] for each function is given. Columns **EA** summarize the results from the EA proposed in this paper. **min.** and **max.** show the minimal and maximal DSOP of all test runs, respectively. In column **median** the median values and in column Δ the differences between hybrid and **min.** are shown.

As can be seen, no DSOP number calculated by the EA in column **min.** is worse than the number of DSOPs found previously [11]. In more than 60% of the test cases the minima in column **hybrid** could be improved. E.g. for benchmark cordic the size of the DSOP is improved by more than 50%.

Table 1. Descriptive statistics and comparison of EA minima to hybrid algorithm

function	hybrid	DSOP EA min.	median	max.	Δ
s1196	2861	2504	2516	2877	357
s1238	2861	2504	2521	2776	357
s1488	369	352	352	353	17
s1494	369	352	352	353	17
s208	53	53	53	55	0
s27	16	16	16	16	0
s298	70	70	70	70	0
s344	330	330	330	344	0
s349	330	330	330	340	0
s382	238	230	230	239	8
s386	61	57	57	63	4
s400	238	230	230	241	8
s444	243	230	230	240	13
s510	170	153	153	155	17
s526	162	156	157	173	6
s526n	162	156	159	175	6
s641	1700	1444	1486	1609	256
s713	1700	1445	1486	1511	256
s820	155	146	146	146	9
s832	155	146	146	149	9
alu4	1545	1372	1372	1372	173
b12	60	60	60	60	0
clip	262	212	212	212	50
inc	66	27	27	27	39
majority	5	5	5	5	0
misex1	34	34	34	34	0
misex2	30	29	30	30	1
rd53	35	35	35	35	0
rd73	147	147	147	147	0
rd84	294	294	294	294	0
sao2	96	96	96	98	0
t481	1009	841	841	841	168
xor5	16	16	16	16	0
5xp1	82	79	79	79	3
9sym	148	148	148	148	0
cordic	19763	8311	9885	9978	11452
misex3	2255	1973	1986	1993	282

Fortunately, it can be observed that the differences between the minimum and maximum are relatively small. I.e. the performance of the proposed evolutionary method is very stable and nearly independent of the random number generator.

This small spread in the results can also be observed in Figure 1, where it is demonstrated by small or invisible range bars of the median DSOP values

Table 2. Comparison of different operator weightings

function	median EA_P	median EA	Δ	minimum EA_P	minimum EA	Δ
s1196	2534	2516	18	2504	2504	0
s1238	2544	2521	23	2504	2504	0
s1488	352	352	0	352	352	0
s1494	352	352	0	352	352	0
s208	53	53	0	53	53	0
s27	16	16	0	16	16	0
s298	70	70	0	70	70	0
s344	330	330	0	330	330	0
s349	330	330	0	330	330	0
s382	230	230	0	230	230	0
s386	57	57	0	57	57	0
s400	230	230	0	230	230	0
s444	236	230	6	230	230	0
s510	153	153	0	153	153	0
s526	160	157	3	156	156	0
s526n	162	159	3	156	156	0
s641	1496	1486	10	1444	1444	0
s713	1497	1486	11	1458	1445	13
s820	146	146	0	146	146	0
s832	146	146	0	146	146	0
alu4	1372	1372	0	1372	1372	0
b12	60	60	0	60	60	0
clip	212	212	0	212	212	0
inc	27	27	0	27	27	0
majority	5	5	0	5	5	0
misex1	34	34	0	34	34	0
misex2	30	30	0	29	29	0
rd53	35	35	0	35	35	0
rd73	147	147	0	147	147	0
rd84	294	294	0	294	294	0
sao2	97	96	1	96	96	0
t481	841	841	0	841	841	0
xor5	16	16	0	16	16	0
5xp1	79	79	0	79	79	0
9sym	148	148	0	148	148	0
cordic	9932	9885	47	9882	8311	1571
misex3	1986	1986	0	1973	1973	0

(ordinate). The figure also shows the size range of the benchmarks in the test suite.

In Table 2 a comparison of different operator weightings is given. The operator weighting used for the EA proposed in here (column **EA**) is shown in parallel with the results using a different kind of operator weighting (column EA_P). The problem specific weightings from [14] were used as reference (PMX:

98%, Inversion: 1%, MUT1: 7%, MUT2: 7%). The comparison of the results shows the advantage of the proposed setting for DSOP minimization.

Finally, the runtimes of the EA are shortly discussed. In principle, compared to specialized heuristics, the runtimes of EAs are relatively large. In this application they are in general smaller than 200 CPU seconds. And for small benchmark functions, the EA converges in a few CPU seconds. The quality of the results and the relatively short runtimes show the efficiency of the chosen termination criterion.

5   Conclusions

An approach based on Evolutionary Algorithms to minimize the DSOP representation of a Boolean function was presented. The experimental results show the quality of the proposed evolutionary method. For more than 60% of the test cases the results from the specialized heuristic could be improved. Even the runtimes of the EA are in an acceptable range. The experiments underlined the robustness of the approach.

References

1. R.E. Bryant. Graph-based algorithms for Boolean function manipulation. *IEEE Trans. on Comp.*, 35(8):677–691, 1986.
2. R.E. Bryant. Binary decision diagrams and beyond: Enabling techniques for formal verification. In *Int'l Conf. on CAD*, pages 236–243, 1995.
3. L. Davis. Applying adaptive algorithms to epistatic domains. In *Proceedings of IJCAI*, pages 162–164, 1985.
4. L. Davis. *Handbook of Genetic Algorithms*. van Nostrand Reinhold, New York, 1991.
5. R. Drechsler. *Evolutionary Algorithms for VLSI CAD*. Kluwer Academic Publisher, 1998.
6. R. Drechsler, B. Becker, and N. Göckel. A genetic algorithm for variable ordering of OBDDs. *IEE Proceedings*, 143(6):364–368, 1996.
7. B.J. Falkowski. Calculation of rademacher-walsh spectral coefficients for systems of completely and incompletely specified boolean functions. In *IEEE Proceedings on Circuits*, pages 1698–1701, 1993.
8. B.J. Falkowski and C.-H. Chang. Paired haar spectra computation through operations on disjoint cubes. In *IEEE Proceedings on Circuits, Devices and Systems*, pages 117–123, 1999.
9. B.J. Falkowski, I. Schäfer, and C.-H. Chang. An effective computer algorithm for the calculation of disjoint cube representation of boolean functions. In *Midwest Symposium on Circuits and Systems*, pages 1308–1311, 1993.
10. F. Ferrandi, A. Macii, E. Macii, M. Poncino, R. Scarsi, and F. Somenzi. Symbolic algorithms for layout-oriented synthesis of pass transistor logic circuits. In *Int'l Conf. on CAD*, pages 235–241, 1998.
11. G. Fey and R. Drechsler. A hybrid approach combining symbolic and structural techniques for disjoint SOP minimization. In *Workshop on Synthesis And System Integration of Mixed Information technologies (SASIMI)*, pages 54–60, 2003.

12. N. Göckel, R. Drechsler, and B. Becker. GAME: A software environment for using genetic algorithms in circuit design. In *Applications of Computer Systems*, pages 240–247, 1997.
13. D.E. Goldberg and R. Lingle. Alleles, loci, and the traveling salesman problem. In *Int'l Conference on Genetic Algorithms*, pages 154–159, 1985.
14. M. Hilgemeier, N. Drechsler, and R. Drechsler. Minimizing the number of one-paths in BDDs by an evolutionary algorithm. In *Congress on Evolutionary Computation*, pages 1724–1731, 2003.
15. Th. Kropf. *Introduction to Formal Hardware Verification*. Springer, 1999.
16. Y.-T. Lai, S. Sastry, and M. Pedram. Boolean matching using binary decision diagrams with applications to logic synthesis and verification. In *Int'l Conf. on CAD*, pages 452–458, 1992.
17. A. Mishchenko and M. Perkowski. Fast heuristic minimization of exclusive-sums-of-products. In *Int'l Workshop on Applications of the Reed-Muller Expansion in Circuit Design*, pages 242–250, 2001.
18. I.M. Oliver, D.J. Smith, and J.R.C. Holland. A study of permutation crossover operators on the traveling salesman problem. In *Int'l Conference on Genetic Algorithms*, pages 224–230, 1987.
19. R. Rudell. Dynamic variable ordering for ordered binary decision diagrams. In *Int'l Conf. on CAD*, pages 42–47, 1993.
20. T. Sasao. EXMIN2: A simplification algorithm for Exclusive-OR-Sum-of products expressions for multiple-valued-input two-valued-output functions. *IEEE Trans. on CAD*, 12:621–632, 1993.
21. L. Shivakumaraiah and M.Thornton. Computation of disjoint cube representations using a maximal binate variable heuristic. In *Southeastern Symposium on System Theory*, pages 417–421, 2002.
22. M. Thornton, R. Drechsler, and D.M. Miller. *Spectral Techniques in VLSI CAD*. Kluwer Academic Publisher, 2001.
23. D. Whitley, T. Starkweather, and D. Fuquay. Scheduling problems and traveling salesman: The genetic edge recombination operator. In *Int'l Conference on Genetic Algorithms*, pages 133–140, 1989.

Genetic Algorithms to Improve Mask and Illumination Geometries in Lithographic Imaging Systems

Tim Fühner[1], Andreas Erdmann[1], Richárd Farkas[2], Bernd Tollkühn[1], and Gabriella Kókai[2]

[1] Fraunhofer Institute of Integrated Systems and Device Technology (FhG-IISB),
Schottkystr. 10, 91058 Erlangen, Germany,
{fuehner, andreas.erdmann, tollkuehn}@iisb.fraunhofer.de
[2] University of Erlangen-Nuremberg, Department of Computer Science II,
Martensstr. 3, 91058 Erlangen, Germany,
gabriella.kokai@informatik.uni-erlangen.de

Abstract. This paper proposes the use of a genetic algorithm to optimize mask and illumination geometries in optical projection lithography. A fitness function is introduced that evaluates the imaging quality of arbitrary line patterns in a specified focus range. As a second criterion the manufacturability and inspectability of the mask are taken into account. With this approach optimum imaging conditions can be identified without any additional a-priori knowledge of the lithographic process. Several examples demonstrate the successful application and further potentials of the proposed concept.

1 Introduction

Optical projection lithography transfers the layout of a mask into a photoresist on the top surface of a silicon wafer [1]. The resolution of a microlithographic process is defined in terms of the size Δx of the minimum half-pitch or half-period of dense pattern of lines and spaces which can be produced by this process. In the context of microelectronic processing the Rayleigh-criterion for the resolution capability of a certain process is written as $\Delta x = k_1 \frac{\lambda}{\text{NA}}$, where λ specifies the wavelength of the used light and NA is the numerical aperture of the projection system. k_1 is usually referred to as the "k-factor" of a process, which depends on the spatial coherence, on the mask technology, and on the properties of the photoresist. This Rayleigh criterion dictates the fundamental trend of optical lithography towards smaller wavelengths and larger numerical apertures. Until mid of the nineties standard lithographic processes employed k-factors above 0.6. The mask was designed as a pattern of dark and bright features with spatial dimensions of the features to be printed on the wafer.

In contrast to this technologically rather simple imaging process, nowadays' k-factors of 0.3 to 0.4 require sophisticated techniques to improve resolution capabilities, some of which are shortly introduced in this paper.

G.R. Raidl et al. (Eds.): EvoWorkshops 2004, LNCS 3005, pp. 208–218, 2004.
© Springer-Verlag Berlin Heidelberg 2004

Furthermore, this paper proposes the utilization of a genetic algorithm (GA) to optimize mask and illumination source geometries, as the ever increasing complexity in the imaging process often prevents conventional (analytical) approaches from being applicable.

The paper is organized as follows. Section 2 briefly reviews the basics of the lithographic projection system and of optical resolution enhancement techniques. Details of the optimization procedure, such as problem definition, data representation, fitness function, and a few details on the GA, are described in Section 3. Section 4 presents first results, obtained with the proposed method. This paper concludes with a short summary and an outlook on future work.

2   Introduction to Mask Layout and Illumination

Figure 1(a) shows a schematic drawing of a lithographic projection stepper/scanner. The imaging system consists of an illumination optics (light source, condenser) and a projection optics (projection lens, aperture stop). The condenser system is designed to ensure a homogeneous illumination of the mask. The projection system images the mask into the image plane close to the wafer surface. The projection lens transmits only a certain angular range of light which is diffracted by the mask, whose sine is bounded by the numerical aperture $NA = sin(\theta)$ of the projection system.

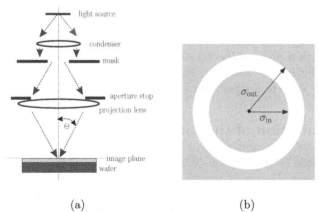

(a)   (b)

Fig. 1. (a) Principle sketch of an optical projection system used in lithograhpy steppers and scanners; (b) Annular illumination source: σ_{out} denotes the radius of the illumination disk, σ_{in} the radius of the inner cover disk.

Standard lithographic projection equipment employs the Köhler illumination. In this specific geometry of the illumination system the light source is projected into the entrance pupil of the projection lens. The mask is considered to be illuminated by mutually incoherent plane waves which emerge from different points of the light source. The lithographic projection system is modeled with standard Fourier optics [2]. The spatial coherence of the system is taken into account by the Hopkins [3] theory. Polarization effects, which become important in high numerical aperture systems, require a vector extension of the scalar theory [4], [5]. The images which are shown in this paper were computed with the in-house lithography simulator of the Fraunhofer Institute IISB [6].

2.1 Optical Resolution Enhancement Techniques

The term "resolution enhancement techniques" (RET) covers modifications of the geometry of the illumination and of the mask which improve the resolution of lithographic processes. This subsection reviews the most important aspects of these RET, which are necessary to understand the optimization problems presented in the remaining part of this paper. For a more detailed understanding of RET the reader is referred to Alfred Wong's excellent book [7].

Off-Axis Illumination (OAI). The geometry of illumination sources has a great impact on the imaging process. The investigations in this paper were performed for standard and annular illuminations Figure 1(b).

Optical Proximity Correction (OPC). Small sub-resolution assist features can strongly improve the performance of OAI for more isolated features. These assist feature are too small to be printed at the specified threshold intensity of the photoresist, but strongly improve the performance of the isolated feature. Additional assists at larger distances from the main feature can result in further improvements of the imaging performance.

Phase Shift Masks (PSM). In contrast to binary masks (BIM), which consist only of bright and dark areas, phase shift masks (PSM) modify the phase of the light by shifting the phase in its bright areas. This technique makes use of the fact that, with a phase-shift of 180° of the adjoining features' diffracted light, superposed fields are subtracted rather than added as in the case of unaltered phases. This leads to a significant enhancement of the resolution.

3 Optimization of the Lithographic Process

Implementation of the previously described techniques in real fabrication processes involves a number of problems. First of all, RET techniques are in most cases feature specific; e.g., OAI shows a good performance for dense features, but is only of limited use for isolated features. Moreover, there are many restrictions which result from manufacturability challenges. Thus, determination of the optimum mask design and source shape is a complex and demanding task.

3.1 Optimization Parameters

The optimization problem of one-dimensional mask with line/space patterns is specified in two different ways [8]. In the first case, the mask is represented by continuous variables which describe certain features on the mask.

Figure 2(a) depicts a main feature with sub-resolution assists, which are symmetrically positioned on the left and on the right side of the main feature. Simulations are performed using different numbers of assist features. Photomasks in optical lithography are commonly generated by so-called e-beam writers, that is, the desired structures are directly written onto the photoresist coated mask-substrate, which is subsequently processed. The electron beam can only be positioned on discrete grid point. Thus, the second, discrete representation of the mask geometry (demonstrated in Figure 2(b)) resembles this method. The mask is divided into pixels with size Δx that is determined by the resolution of the mask writer. Each pixel takes pre-defined complex transmission values t_i (binary (BIM): $t_1 = 0.0 + 0.0j$, $t_2 = 1.0 + 0.0j$; phase-shift (PSM): $t_1 = 0.0 + 0.0j$, $t_2 = 1.0 + 0.0j$, $t_3 = -1.0 + 0.0j$).

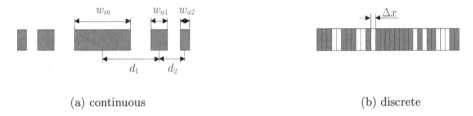

(a) continuous   (b) discrete

Fig. 2. Continuous and discrete representation of the mask geometry: gray areas symbolize intransparent chromium covered areas of the mask; w_m width of main feature, w_{ai} – width of assist feature i, d_i distance of assist feature i, Δx – grid resolution.

Additionally, the geometry of the illumination source is optimized. In this work the source is restricted to annular-type illumination. As shown in Figure 1(b), the source is presented by continuous values of the inner and outer radii of the annular illumination: σ_{in} and σ_{out}.

Thus, in the continuous case the optimizer typically has to deal with 3 (one main feature and one assist) to 5 (one main feature and two assists cf. Figure 2(a)) mask parameters and 2 illumination parameters, all of which are real numbers. In the discrete representation case the continuous mask parameters are replaced by more than 100 discrete parameters, taking 2 (BIM) or 3 (PSM) transmission states.

3.2   Fitness Function

For the purpose of this paper, the photoresist is assumed to operate as an intensity threshold detector. After development the photoresist is removed at all positions where the image intensity exceeds a certain threshold value. The threshold intensity can be determined for certain reference features or according to a specific resist process. In this paper, all intensity and threshold values are normalized with respect to the intensity which is obtained with a fully transparent mask.

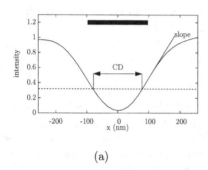

(a)

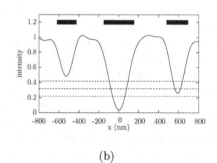

(b)

Fig. 3. Evaluation of lithographic images: (a) main feature: critical dimension (CD), i.e., size of feature at a specified threshold intensity (dashed line), the (average) slope is evaluated at the nominal edges of the feature; (b) global evaluation: band criterion, which ensures that side lobes are only printed where required.

The evaluation of lithographic processes has to take several effects into account, these include a good imaging performance, but also manufacturability issues. Following criteria should be met (for a detailed discussion see also [8]):

CD criterion (ΔCD): The critical dimension (CD) specifies the size of the printed main feature. The deviation between the size of the printed feature at the threshold intensity CD_p and the target CD_t provides the first component of the fitness function.

Slope criterion (SC): This criterion ensures, that good solutions should be tolerant against variations in exposure doses. Thus, the slope of the normalized intensity curve at the edges of the target feature is to be maximized (cf. Figure 3(a)).

Band criterion (BC): In order to ensure that only the desired features are printed, those solutions whose side lobes exhibit low an intensity are punished. On the other hand, the feature's intensity should not exceed a certain value to avoid exposed spots within areas that are to be printed. Therefor a band around the threshold value (as shown in Figure 3(b)) has been introduced. Solutions that violate this criterion are punished. The band size in this work is set to $\pm 30\%$.

Mask manufacturability criterion (MC): For manufacturability reasons it is disadvantageous to have a large number of regions with alternating transmission. Therefore, for the discrete mask representation this criterion assigns a higher fitness to masks with less fragmented regions of the same transmission value.

In order to provide a stable process minor variations of the focus position should have little impact on the imaging performance. Therefore, the former criteria are evaluated for different focus settings.

All of these objectives are combined into one fitness function, yielding a scalar pay-off value:

$$\mu(\boldsymbol{x}) : \boldsymbol{x} \mapsto \frac{w_{\text{MC}} \cdot \mu_{\text{MC}}(\boldsymbol{x}) + \sum\limits_{i=1}^{n_f} \frac{w_{\Delta\text{CD}} \cdot \mu_{\Delta\text{CD}}(\boldsymbol{x}) + w_{\text{SC}} \cdot \mu_{\text{SC}}(\boldsymbol{x}) + w_{\text{BC}} \cdot \mu_{\text{BC}}(\boldsymbol{x})}{n_f}}{w_{\text{MC}} + w_{\Delta\text{CD}} + w_{\text{SC}} + w_{\text{BC}}}, \qquad (1)$$

where μ_{MC}, $\mu_{\Delta\text{CD}}$, μ_{SC}, and μ_{BC} denote the results of the former criteria and w_{MC}, $w_{\Delta\text{CD}}$, w_{SC}, and w_{BC} symbolize the corresponding weights. The number of focus settings, which each solution is evaluated for, is denoted by n_f.

The complete evaluation process (which takes a few milliseconds) works as follows: (1) The phenotypic representation is directly used for the manufacturability criterion, (2) the so-called aerial image is calculated [6], (3) slope and band criteria are evaluated, and (4) a threshold model is used to determine the resulting structure in the resist, which is used to evaluate the CD criterion.

4 Genetic Algorithm

The optimization routine used in this work is a simple generational genetic algorithm, using a single population throughout the entire evolution. The main reasons for chosing a GA are: Placement of sub-resolution resists can rarely be done intuitively. Therefore, finding start values is very time consuming, rendering most (local) optimizers inapplicable. Furthermore, the large number of parameters (especially in the binary mask representation) proved to be hard for most analytic optimizers, since no properties of the search space can be utilized. Last but not least, parallelization of GAs is a relatively uncomplicated task, yielding a scalable procedure suited for cluster-computing. The GA was developed at Fraunhofer IISB and has been integrated into the in-house simulation toolkit [9]. Chromosomes in are coded as bit strings. The genetic operators are two-point-crossover, single-point mutation, and as selection operator fitness-proportional roulette wheel selection, binary tournament selection, and restricted tournament selection are applied. In order to maintain the currently best solution, elitism is performed, additionally.

Restricted Tournament Selection. In contrast to conventional selection operators, where each individual is competing against one another, with restricted tournament selection individuals only replace solutions which have a similar bit string [10]. Thus, this selection operator is not only well suited for multi-modal optimization tasks, but will also maintain a high level of diversity within the population. Two individuals A and B are randomly selected, recombination and mutation are performed, yielding offsprings A' and B'. For each of the both children, w individuals are randomly selected (window). First w individuals are compared to child A', the individual with the shortest distance to A' (A'') is compared with A'''s fitness. If A' exhibits a higher fitness than A'' it replaces A''. The same procedure is applied to B'.

Chromosome Representation. Continuous values, such as the parameters for the continuous mask geometry representation and the inner and outer radii of the illumination system (cf. Section 3.1) are modeled as follows: The parameter's domain, that is, upper and lower bounds of the parameter (u and l) and the required number of decimal places (d), is specified in advance. The number of bits taken by this parameter in the chromosome can then be calculated by shifting the parameter's domain ($u-l$) by the required number of decimal places, and computing the required (up-rounded) exponent of radix two ($\ell := \lceil \log_2(u - l)10^d + 1) \rceil$).

Any real number x can now be encoded by subtracting the offset (lower bound l) and dividing it by the range of the parameter ($u - l$); yielding numbers ranging from 0 to 1. The result is then scaled by the maximum number that can be represented by this parameter's part of the bit string ($2^\ell - 1$): $a_{10}(x) := \frac{x-l}{u-l} \cdot (2^\ell - 1)$. The binary representation ($a_2(x) := \text{bin}(a_{10}(x))$), finally, yields the parameter's bit encoding in the chromosome. Thus, decoding of the parameter is performed as follows: $x := \frac{\text{dec}(a_2)}{2^\ell - 1}(u - l) + l$.

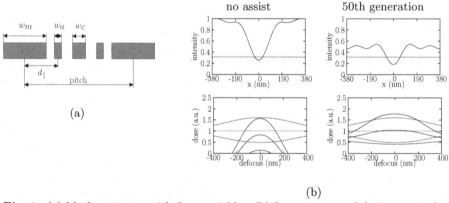

(a)

(b)

Fig. 4. (a) Mask geometry with four variables; (b) Improvement of the image performance obtained with the continuous mask representation, upper row: images at 250 nm lower row: process windows of the semidense feature (solid lines) compared to process widows of dense features (dashed lines), left column: isolated line without assist, right column: after 50 generations.

Parameters for the discrete mask representation are converted in a straightforward manner. For binary masks each grid point can only take two transmission values. Thus, only one bit is required. However, phase shift masks involve three values. In this case, two bits are required. Although this representation causes the occurrence of four values (where only three are valid, and consequently one setting punished by the fitness function), it proved to be feasible. Any other encoding scheme, such as expanding the allele alphabet by an additional value, did not improve the convergence behavior.

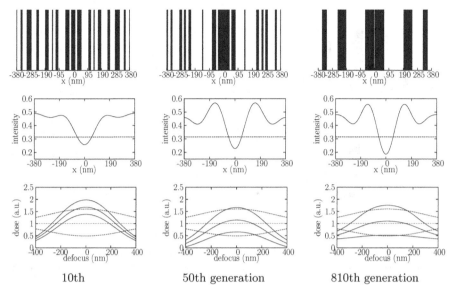

10th   50th generation   810th generation

Fig. 5. Improvement of the image performance obtained with the GA for the discrete mask representation, upper row: mask geometry, center row: images at 250 nm defocus, lower row: process windows.

5   Results

The optimization courses presented in this section have been conducted using a light's wavelength of $\lambda = 93$ nm and a numerical aperture of NA $= 0.7$. In a first experiment the objective of the optimization is to find the optimum mask for parameters for a lines/spaces pattern with a linewidth of 110 nm and a pitch between the lines of 760 nm. A reference process window (exposure dose vs. defocus) is defined by a dense lines and spaces pattern (same linewidth, pitch $= 220$ nm) with a threshold intensity of 0.314. This experiment was performed using the continuous mask representation: Three assist features have been placed between the two main features, one of which is placed in the center between both features, the remaining two assists have identical sizes and the same distance from the main feature. The goal was to find optimal width and distance parameters as depicted in Figure 4(a). The ranges for the four parameters are set as follows: width of main feature: $w_m \in [40$ nm, 100 nm$]$, width of center assist $w_c \in [40$ nm, 80 nm$]$, width of the other two assists $w_a \in [40$ nm, 80 nm$]$, and distance of theses assists $d_a \in [40$ nm, 300 nm$]$. For this example the illumination parameters are not varied but fixed to $\sigma_{\text{in}} = 0.5$, $\sigma_{\text{out}} = 0.7$.

The number of individuals is 51; experiments with larger population numbers did not improve the convergence behavior – yet, in case of restricted tournament selection a remarkable slowdown could be observed. Crossover probability is set to 0.6, mutation probabilities are 0.001 and 0.005, and the number of generations is 500. As shown in Table 1 several settings are tested. In order to verify the reproduceability of the results, five runs are conducted for each setting; each run

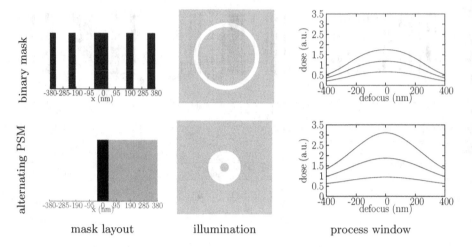

Fig. 6. Optimized imaging performance for 90 nm isolated lines for the discrete mask representation, upper row: binary mask (BIM), lower row: alternating phase shift mask (PSM).

Table 1. GA settings for both the continuous and discrete mask representation. Five runs are performed for each setting. The window size specifies the number of compared individuals with restricted tournament selection (see Section 4). The maximum, minimum, and average fitness of the five runs' best solution are listed.

selection operator	window size	mutation rate	Continuous average fitness	lowest fitness	best fitness	Discrete average fitness	lowest fitness	best fitness
roulette wheel		0.001	55.58	55.33	56.42	28.24	26.94	28.88
roulette wheel		0.005	55.93	55.35	56.42	28.60	26.51	29.80
binary tournament		0.001	55.52	55.35	55.67	24.37	22.84	25.49
binary tournament		0.005	55.60	54.78	56.42	29.45	28.52	29.80
restricted tournament	20	0.001	56.16	55.60	56.42	28.91	28.10	29.80
restricted tournament	20	0.005	56.42	56.42	56.42	29.68	28.99	30.08
restricted tournament	50	0.001	56.42	56.42	56.42	29.64	29.01	29.80
restricted tournament	50	0.005	56.35	56.11	56.42	29.57	28.77	29.80

takes about 5 – 6 minutes on a five node cluster with each machine having two 2.66 GHz Pentium 4 processors. Although with all settings the GA results do not differ significanctly, it is noticeable that restricted tournament selection proved to provide reproduceable results.

The improvement of the imaging performance after a certain number of generations is depicted in Figure 4(b). In the first row aerial images at a defocus of 250 nm are presented. The dashed line indicates the threshold intensity which is used for the image evaluation. The lower row shows process windows for the optimized mask (pitch = 760 nm, solid lines) compared to dense lines/spaces (dashed lines pitch= 220 nm). On the left, simulation results for the mask with no assist features are shown. The minimum intensity almost reaches the threshold value. Also, the overlap between the process windows of semidense and dense patterns is very small, i.e., semidense and dense patterns can only be printed simultaneously within a small range of dose and focus settings. After 50 generations the GA has already provided mask patterns that result in a highly improved imaging performance (result: $[w_m, w_a, w_c, d_1] = [125\,\text{nm}, 50\,\text{nm}, 55\,\text{nm}, 215\,\text{nm}]$). Both quality and overlap are noticeably improved.

The same problem is approached with the discrete mask representation. As illustrated in Figure 5, in the first generations the GA is assembling clusters of lines. In the 10th generation the mask mainly consists of thin lines and spaces. However after a number of iterations the manufacturability criterion leads to larger regions. It appears, that in the following steps the GA is combining these clustered patterns. As the clustering phase requires some time, the number of generations has to be increased. In this example the GA was run with 2000 generations, computing time (using the same computer set-up as in the previous example) scaled up to about 45 minutes. After 800 generations the GA yields a mask geometry which guarantees a good imaging performance and which resembles the mask obtained from the continuous optimization approach. The different settings tested with this experiment are listed in Table 1.

The discrete representation of mask geometries can be used to compare different mask types and illumination options. This is demonstrated in Figure 6, which shows the best mask layouts, annular illumination settings, and resulting process windows. The only information the GA was provided with, was the size of the addressable grid on the mask ($\Delta x = 5\,\text{nm}$), the complex transmission values of the mask (binary: $1+0j$, $0+0j$; PSM: $1+0j$, $-1+0j$, $0+0j$), and the type of illumination (annular). In case of binary masks the optimization of the fitness function results in a typical sub-resolution assisted mask configuration and strong off-axis illumination. For the PSM the algorithm suggests a standard phase edge design and coherent illumination. The process window for the PSM is considerably larger than for binary masks.

6   Conclusions and Future Work

The proposed optimization procedure using a genetic algorithm identifies optimal imaging conditions without any additional a-priori knowledge about lithographic processes. It is applied to automatically place sub-resolution assists for lines/space patterns with a specified range of pitches. The procedure identifies the best mask layout and illumination conditions for the generation of isolated lines with different mask types. Especially for the binary mask representation utilization of the restricted tournament selection operator appears advantageous. Further development of the GA will aim at improving the convergence behavior by implementing so-called "competent GA" enhancement techniques [11]. This can be particularly useful to speed up the the first phase (finding manufacturable masks) of the binary representation case.

Further work will also be necessary to improve the description of the mask and source geometries. Additional imaging criteria such as the mask error enhancement factor (MEEF) and the aberration sensitivity have to be included in a generalized form of the merit function. Moreover, the proposed optimization procedure has to be combined with more advanced lithography simulation models.

References

1. H. Levinson. Optical Lithography. In P. Rai-Choudhury, editor, *Handbook of Microlithograph, Micromachining and Microfabrication*, volume 1. SPIE Press, 1997.
2. J.W. Goodman. *Introduction to Fourier Optics*. McGraw-Hill, 1992.
3. H.H. Hopkins. On the diffraction theory of optical images. In *Proc. Roy. Soc. A 217*, page 408, 1953.
4. M. Mansuripur. Distribution of light at and near the focus of high numerical aperture objectives. *J. Opt. Soc. Am. A3*, page 2086, 1986.
5. D.G. Flagello and T.D. Milster. High numerical aperture effects in photoresist. *Applied Optics 36*, page 8944, 1997.
6. A. Erdmann and W. Henke. Simulation of optical lithography. In *Optics and Optoelectronics – Theory, Devices and Applications, Proc. SPIE 3729*, page 480, 1999.
7. A. K. Wong. Resolution Enhancement Techniques in Optical Lithography. In *Tutorial Texts in Optical Engineering*, **TT47**. SPIE Press, 2001.
8. A. Erdmann, R. Farkas, T. Fühner, B. Tollkühn, and G. Kókai. Mask and Source Optimization for Lithographic Imaging Systems. In *Proc. SPIE 5182*, 2003. in print.
9. B. Tollkühn, T. Fühner, D. Matiut, A. Erdmann, G. Kókai, and A. Semmler. Will Darwin's Law Help Us to Improve Our Resist Models. In *Proc. SPIE 5039*, page 291, 2003.
10. G.R. Harik. Finding multimodal solutions using restricted tournament selection. In Larry Eshelman, editor, *Proceedings of the Sixth International Conference on Genetic Algorithms*, pages 24–31, San Francisco, CA, 1995. Morgan Kaufmann.
11. D.E. Goldberg. *Evolutionary design by computers*, chapter 4. The Race, the Hurdle, and the Sweet Spot: Lessons from Genetic Algorithms for the Automation of Design Innovation and Creativity. Morgan Kaufmann, San Francisco, CA, 1999.

Multi-objective Genetic Manipulator Trajectory Planner

Eduardo José Solteiro Pires[1]*, Paulo B. de Moura Oliveira[1], and
José António Tenreiro Machado[2]

[1] Universidade de Trás-os-Montes e Alto Douro, Dep. de Engenharia Electrotécnica,
Quinta de Prados, 5000–911 Vila Real, Portugal,
{epires,oliveira}@utad.pt, http://www.utad.pt/~{epires,oliveira}
[2] Instituto Superior de Engenharia do Porto, Dep. de Engenharia Electrotécnica,
Rua Dr. António Bernadino de Almeida, 4200-072 Porto, Portugal,
jtm@dee.isep.ipp.pt, http://www.dee.isep.ipp.pt/~jtm

Abstract. This paper proposes a multi-objective genetic algorithm to
optimize a manipulator trajectory. The planner has several objectives
namely the minimization of the space and join arm displacements and
the energy required in the trajectory, without colliding with any obstacles
in the workspace. Simulations results are presented for robots with two
and three degrees of freedom, considering the optimization of two and
three objectives.

1 Introduction

In the last decade genetic algorithms (GAs) have been applied in a plethora of
fields such as in control, system identification, robotics, planning and scheduling,
image processing, pattern recognition and speech recognition [1]. This paper
addresses the planning of trajectories, that is, the development of an algorithm
to find a continuous motion that takes the manipulator from a given starting
configuration to a desired end position in the workspace without collision with
any obstacle.

Several single-objective methods for trajectory planning, collision avoidance
and manipulator structure definition have been proposed. A possible approach
consists in adopting the differential inverse kinematics, using the Jacobian matrix, for generating the manipulator trajectories [2,3]. However, the algorithm
must take into account the problem of kinematic singularities that may be hard
to tackle. To avoid this problem, other algorithms for the trajectory generation
are based on the direct kinematics [4,5,6,7,8].

Chen and Zalzala [2] propose a GA method to generate the position and the
configuration of a mobile manipulator. The authors study the optimization of the
least torque norm, the manipulability, the torque distribution and the obstacle
avoidance, through the inverse kinematics scheme. Davidor [3] also applies GAs
to the trajectory generation by searching the inverse kinematics solutions to pre

---

* This paper is partially supported by the grant Prodep III (2/5.3/2001) from FSE.

G.R. Raidl et al. (Eds.): EvoWorkshops 2004, LNCS 3005, pp. 219–229, 2004.
© Springer-Verlag Berlin Heidelberg 2004

defined end effector robot paths. Kubota et al [4] study a hierarchical trajectory planning method for a redundant manipulator with a virus-evolutionary GA running simultaneously, two processes. One process calculates some manipulator collision-free positions and the other generates a collision free trajectory by combining these intermediate positions. Rana and Zalzala [5] developed a method to plan a near time-optimal, collision-free, motion in the case of multi-arm manipulators. The planning is carried out in the joint space and the path is represented as a string of via-points connected through cubic splines. Chocron and Bidaud [9] proposes an evolutionary algorithm to perform a task-based design of modular robotic systems. The system consists in a mobile base and an arm that may be built with serially assembled links and joints modules. The optimization design is evaluated with geometric and kinematic performance measures. Kim and Khosha [10] presents the design of a manipulator that is best suited for a given task. The design consists of determining the trajectory and the length of a three degrees of freedom (dof) manipulator. Han et al [11] describe a design method of a modular manipulator that uses the kinematic equations to determine the robot configuration and, in a second phase, adopts a GA to find the optimal length.

Multi-objective techniques using GAs have been increasing in relevance as a research area. In 1989, Goldberg [12] suggested the use of a GA to solve multi-objective problems and since then other investigators have been developing new methods, such as multi-objective genetic algorithm (MOGA) [13], non-dominated sorted genetic algorithm (NSGA) [14] and niched Pareto genetic algorithm (NPGA) [15], among many other variants [16].

In this line of thought, this paper proposes the use of a multi-objective method to optimize a manipulator trajectory. This method is based on a GA adopting the direct kinematics. The optimal manipulator front is one that minimizes both the path trajectory length and the energy required to perform a task, without any collision with the obstacles in the workspace. Following this introduction, the paper is organized as follows: section 2 formulates the problem and the GA-based method for its resolution. Section 3 presents several simulations results involving different robots, objectives and workspace settings. Finally, section 4 outlines the main conclusions.

2 Problem and Algorithm Formulation

This study considers robotic manipulators that are required to move from an initial point up to a given final configuration. In the experiments are used two and three dof planar manipulators (i.e. 2R and 3R robots) with link lengths of one meter and rotational joints free to rotate 2π rad. To test a possible collision between the manipulator and the obstacles, the arm structure is checked in order to verify if it is inside any obstacle. The trajectory consists in a set of strings representing the joint positions between the initial and final robot configurations.

2.1   Representation

The path for a iR manipulator $(i = 2, 3)$, at generation T, is directly encoded as vectors in the joint space to be used by the G A as:

$$[\{q_1^{(\Delta t, T)}, .., q_i^{(\Delta t, T)}\}, \{q_1^{(2\Delta t, T)}, .., q_i^{(2\Delta t, T)}\}, .., \{q_1^{((n-2)\Delta t, T)}, .., q_i^{((n-2)\Delta t, T)}\}] \tag{1}$$

where i is the number of dof and Δt the sampling time between two consecutive configurations.

The values of joints $q_l^{(j\Delta t, 0)}$ $(j = 1, \ldots, n - 2;\ l = 1, \ldots, i)$ are randomly initialized in the range $]-\pi, +\pi]$ rad. It should be noted that the initial and final configurations have not been encoded into the string because they remain unchanged throughout the trajectory search. Without losing generality, for simplicity, it is adopted a normalized time of $\Delta t = 0.1$ sec, because it is always possible to perform a time re-scaling.

2.2   Operators in the Multi-objective Genetic Algorithm

The initial population of strings is generated at random. The search is then carried out among these populations. The three different operators used in the genetic planning are selection, crossover and mutation, as described in the sequel.

In what concerns the selection operator, the successive generations of new strings are reproduced on the basis of a Pareto ranking [12] with $\sigma_{\text{share}} = 0.01$ and $\alpha = 2$. To promote population diversity the count metric is used. This metric uses all solutions in the population independently of their rank to evaluate every fitness function. For the crossover operator it is used the simulated binary crossover (SBX)[14]. After crossover, the best solutions (among the parents and children) are chosen to form the next population. The mutation operator replaces one gene value with a given probability using the equation:

$$q_i^{(j\Delta t, T+1)} = q_i^{(j\Delta t, T)} + N(0, 1/\sqrt{2\pi}) \tag{2}$$

at generation T, where $N(\mu, \sigma)$ is the normal distribution function with average μ and standard deviation σ.

2.3   Evolution Criteria

Three indices $\{q, p, E_a\}$ (3) are used to qualify the evolving trajectory robotic manipulators. Some of these criteria are used by the planner to find the optimal Pareto front. Before evaluating any solutions all the values such that $|q_i^{(j+1, T)} - q_i^{(j, T)}| > \pi$ are eliminated from the strings.

$$q = \sum_{j=1}^{n} \sum_{l=1}^{i} \left(\dot{q}_l^{(j\Delta t, T)} \right)^2 \tag{3a}$$

$$p = \sum_{j=2}^{n} d\left(p_j, \, p_{j-1}\right)^2 \tag{3b}$$

$$E_a = (n-1)T \, P_a = \sum_{j=1}^{n} \sum_{l=1}^{i} |\tau_l \cdot \Delta q_l^{(j\Delta t, T)}| \tag{3c}$$

The joint distance q (3a) is used to minimize the joints manipulator traveling distance. For a function $y = g(x)$ the curve length is $\int[1 + (dg/dt)^2]dx$ and, consequently, to minimize the distance curve length it is adopted the simplified expression $\int(dg/dt)^2 dx$. The cartesian distance p (3b) minimizes the total arm trajectory length, from the initial point up to the final point, where p_j is the robot j intermediate arm cartesian position and $d(\cdot, \cdot)$ is a function that gives the distance between the two arguments. Finally, the energy in expression E_a (3c), where τ_l are the robot joint torques, is computed assuming that power regeneration is not available by motors doing negative work, that is, by taking the absolute value of the power.

3   Simulation Results

In this section results of various experiments are presented. In this line of thought, subsections 3.1 and 3.2 show the optimization of trajectories for the 2R and 3R robots respectively, for two objectives (2D). Finally, subsection 3.3 shows the results of a three dimensional (3D) optimization for a 2R robot.

3.1   2R Robot Trajectory with 2D Optimization

The experiments consist on moving a 2R robotic arm from the starting configuration defined by the joint coordinates $A \equiv \{-1.149, 1.808\}$ rad up to the final configuration $B \equiv \{1.181, 1.466\}$ rad in a workspace without obstacles. The objectives used in this section are joint distance q (3a) and cartesian distance p (3b).

The simulations results achieved by the G A, with a $T_t = 15000$ generations and $pop_{size} = 300$ strings, converge to two optimal fronts. One of the fronts (fig. 1(a)) corresponds to the movement of the manipulator around its base in the clockwise direction. The other front (fig. 1(b)) is obtained when the manipulator moves in the counterclockwise direction. The solutions a and b represent the best solution found for a given objective.

In 71.4% of the total number of runs the algorithm the Pareto optimal front was found. In all simulations of the two cases the solutions converged to a front type which can be modelled approximately by the equation ($\kappa, \alpha, \beta \in \mathbb{R}$):

$$p(q) = \kappa \frac{q + \alpha}{q + \beta} \tag{4}$$

Table 1. Statistics of the fronts parameters

	Pareto front			Local front		
	κ	α	β	κ	α	β
Median	77.80	−66.31	−70.74	82.50	34.73	−173.02
Average	77.76	−66.16	−70.71	83.27	29.88	−173.09
Standard Deviation	0.53	1.05	0.70	2.63	20.87	3.41

The achieved median, average and standard variation for the parameters κ, α and β of (4) are shown in table 1, both for the Pareto optimal and local fronts.

To study the diversity of the front solution, the approximated front was split into several intervals, limited by normal straight lines r_m (fig. 2), such that the front length is identical for all intervals. For any two consecutive normal straight lines is associated an interval I_m ($m = 1, \ldots, 19$), and the solutions located between these lines are counted. Figure 3 shows the solution distribution achieved by one simulation run. From the chart, it can be seen that the solutions are distributed by all intervals. However, the distribution is not uniform. This is due to the use of a sharing function in the parameter domain in spite of the objective domain. Moreover, the algorithm does not incorporate any mechanism to promote the development of well distributed solutions in the objective domain.

The results obtained for solutions a and b, of the Pareto optimal front in figure 1(a), are presented in figures 4 to 6. Comparing figures 4(a) and 6(a) with figures 4(b) and 6(b) it is clear that the joint/cartesian distance for the optimal solutions a and b, respectively, is significantly different due to the objective considered. Between these extreme optimal solutions several others were found, that have a intermediate behavior, and which can be selected according with the importance of each objective.

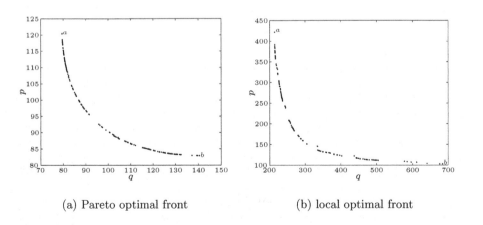

(a) Pareto optimal front   (b) local optimal front

Fig. 1. Optimal fronts for the 2R robot

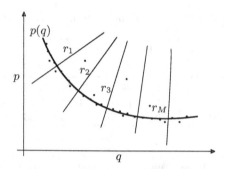

Fig. 2. Normal straight lines to the front obtained with $p(q)$ function

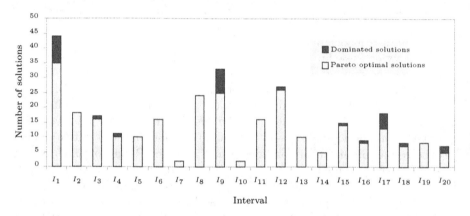

Fig. 3. Solution distribution achieved in one experiment for the $2R$ robot

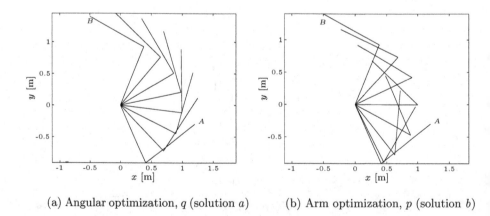

(a) Angular optimization, q (solution a)   (b) Arm optimization, p (solution b)

Fig. 4. Successive $2R$ robot configurations

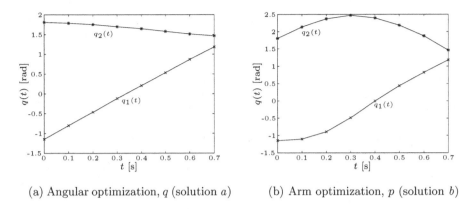

(a) Angular optimization, q (solution a)   (b) Arm optimization, p (solution b)

Fig. 5. Joint positions versus time for the $2R$ robot

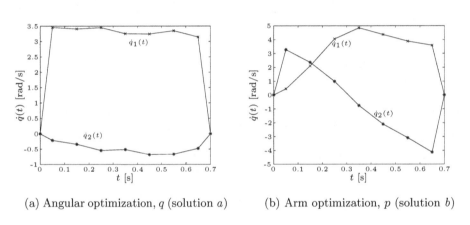

(a) Angular optimization, q (solution a)   (b) Arm optimization, p (solution b)

Fig. 6. Joint velocities versus time for the $2R$ robot

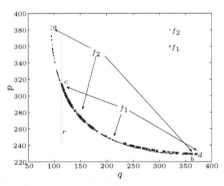

Fig. 7. Pareto optimal fronts, angular distance $vs.$ cartesian distance optimization: $f_1 = \widehat{ab}$ – workspace without obstacles; $f_2 = \widehat{cd}$ – workspace with one obstacle

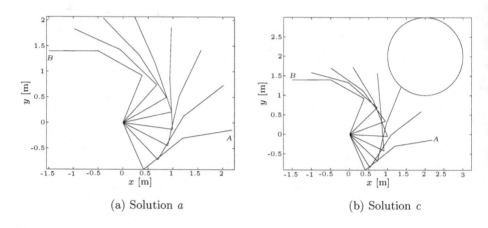

(a) Solution a (b) Solution c

Fig. 8. Successive $3R$ robot configurations

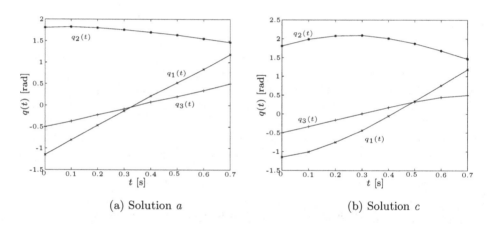

(a) Solution a (b) Solution c

Fig. 9. Joint position of trajectory *vs.* time for the $3R$ robot

3.2 $3R$ Robot Trajectory with $2D$ Optimization

In this subsection a 3R robot trajectory is optimized in a workspace which
may include a circle obstacle with center at $(x,y) = (2,2)$ and radius $\rho = 1$. The initial and final configurations are $A \equiv \{-1.15, 1.81, -0.50\}$ rad and
$B \equiv \{1.18, 1.47, 0.50\}$ rad, respectively. The T_t and pop_{size} parameters used are
identical to those adopted in the previous subsection. The trajectories witch
collide with the obstacle are assigned a very high fitness value.

For an optimization without any obstacle in the workspace is obtained the
$f_2 = \widehat{ab}$ front (fig. 7). However, when the obstacle is introduced the front is
reduced to the $f_1 = \widehat{cd}$. Thus, only the objective q if affected by the introduction
of the obstacle (figures 8 and 9). The solutions a to d represent the best solution
found for a given objective experiment.

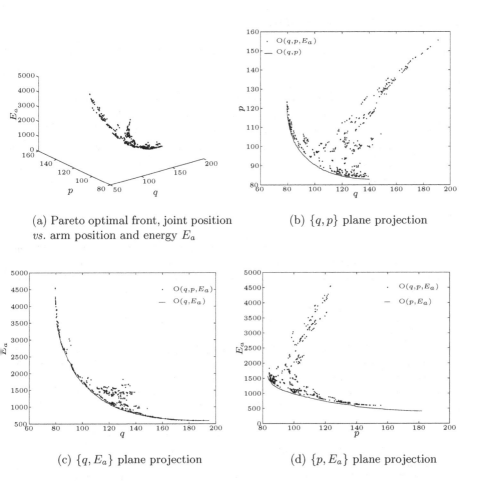

(a) Pareto optimal front, joint position
vs. arm position and energy E_a

(b) $\{q, p\}$ plane projection

(c) $\{q, E_a\}$ plane projection

(d) $\{p, E_a\}$ plane projection

Fig. 10. Pareto optimal front $\{q, p, E_a\}$ and Pareto optimal front plane projections: $\{q, p\}$, $\{q, E_a\}$ and $\{p, E_a\}$

3.3   2R Robot Trajectory with 3D Optimization

Here, the 2R manipulator trajectory is optimized considering three objectives, namely the joint distance, the cartesian distance and the energy required by the manipulator to perform the task. Figure 10(a) shows the optimization results achieved with $T_t = 30000$ generations and $pop_{\text{size}} = 600$ string.

Figure 10 shows the $\{q, p\}$, $\{q, E_a\}$ and $\{p, E_a\}$ planner projections of the 3D optimization. Additionally, in each figure is included the correspondeding 2D optimization obtained previously.

4   Summary and Conclusions

A multi-objective GA robot trajectory planner, based on the kinematics, was proposed. The algorithm is able to reach a determined goal with a reduced ripple both in the space trajectory and the time evolution. Moreover, any obstacles in the workspace do not represent a difficulty for the algorithm to reach the solution. Since the GA uses the direct kinematics the singularities do not constitute a problem. Furthermore, the algorithm determines the robot non-dominated front in order to the given objectives, maintaining a good solution distribution along the front. The results shows that the algorithm reaches the Pareto optimal front or a very close one.

References

1. Bäck, T., Hammel, U., Schwefel, H.P.: Evolutionary computation: Comments on the history and current state. IEEE Trans. on Evolutionary Comp. **1** (1997) 3–17
2. Chen, M., Zalzala, A.M.S.: A genetic approach to motion planning of redundant mobile manipulator systems considering safety and configuration. Journal Robotic Systems **14** (1997) 529–544
3. Davidor, Y.: Genetic Algorithms and Robotics, a Heuristic Strategy for Optimization. World Scientific (1991)
4. Kubota, N., Arakawa, T., Fukuda, T.: Trajectory generation for redundant manipulator using virus evolutionary genetic algorithm, Albuquerque, New Mexico, IEEE Int. Conf. on Robotics and Automation (1997) 205–210
5. Rana, A., Zalzala, A.: An evolutionary planner for near time-optimal collision-free motion of multi-arm robotic manipulators. Volume 1., UKACC International Conference on Control (1996) 29–35
6. Wang, Q., Zalzala, A.M.S.: Genetic control of near time-optimal motion for an industrial robot arm, Minneapolis, Minnesota, IEEE Int. Conf. On Robotics and Automation (1996) 2592–2597
7. Pires, E.S., Machado, J.T.: Trajectory optimization for redundant robots using genetic algorithms. In: Proc. of the Genetic and Evolutionary Computation Conference (GECCO-2000), Las Vegas, USA, Morgan Kaufmann (2000) 967
8. Pires, E.J.S., Machado, J.A.T.: A GA perspective of the energy requirements for manipulators maneuvering in a workspace with obstacles. In: Proc. of the 2000 Congress on Evolutionary Computation, Piscataway, NJ, (2000) 1110–1116
9. Chocron, O., Bidaud, P.: Evolutionary algorithms in kinematic design of robotic system, Grenoble, France, IEEE/RSJ Int. Conf. on Intelligent Robotics and Systems (1997) 279–286
10. Kim, J.O., Khosla, P.K.: A multi-population genetic algorithm and its application to design of manipulators, Raleight, North Caroline, IEEE/RSJ Int. Conf. on Intelligent Robotics and Systems (1992) 279–286
11. Han, J., Chung, W.K., Youm, Y., Kim, S.H.: Task based design of modular robotic manipulator using efficient genetic algorithm, Albuquerque, New Mexico, IEEE Int. Conf. on Robotics and Automation (1997) 507–512
12. Goldberg, D.E.: Genetic Algorithms in Search, Optimization, and Machine Learning. Addison – Wesley (1989)
13. Fonseca, C.M., Fleming, P.J.: An overview of evolutionary algorithms in multi-objective optimization. Evolutionary Computation Journal **3** (1995) 1–16

14. Deb, K.: Multi-Objective Optimization using Evolutionary Algorithms. Wiley-Interscience Series in Systems and Optimization. (2001)
15. Horn, J., Nafploitis, N., Goldberg, D.: A niched pareto genetic algorithm for multi-objective optimization, Proc. of the First IEEE Conf. on Evolutionary Computation (1994) 82–87
16. Coello, C., Carlos, A.: A comprehensive survey of evolutionary-based M.-O. optimization techniques. Knowledge and Information Systems **1** (1999) 269–308

Exploiting HW Acceleration for Classifying Complex Test Program Generation Problems

Ernesto Sanchez, Giovanni Squillero, and Massimo Violante

Politecnico di Torino
Dipartimento di Automatica e Informatica
Corso Duca degli Abruzzi 24 I-10129, Torino, Italy
{edgar.sanchez, giovanni.squillero, massimo.violante}@polito.it
http://www.cad.polito.it/

Abstract. This paper presents a complete framework to examine, evaluate and characterize an evolutionary test-program generation problem. Our methodology is based on a local analysis of the relationships between genotype and fitness. Furthermore we propose the adoption of a hardware accelerator device for speeding up program cultivation. A commercial, complex microprocessor was used as case study. Experimental analysis allows discovering the characteristics of the specific task and foreseeing the behavior of the test-program generation.

1 Introduction

Hardware optimization problems (HOPs), ranging from electronic-design automation to test-program generation, get more and more difficult as hardware complexity grows. Generally, these problems can be defined as NP *optimization problems.* Hence, traditional approaches [1], usually based on systematic and nearly exhaustive exploration of the search spaces, are rarely applicable on modern problems. As a result, in the quest for methods able to optimize the search process, an increasing number of methodologies that exploit heuristics and innovative methods are investigated.

Evolutionary Computation (EC) is one of the new and successful methods to solve this kind of problems. In fact, literature reports an increasing number of methodologies based on EC techniques.

Unfortunately, we lack a mathematical theory able to characterize the adopted methodology. Current studies are not yet mature enough to be used as a theoretical foundation on which to build an analysis of the evolutionary technique for HOPs. Moreover, HOPs are special because they require a deep specific knowledge about the hardware under analysis. Moreover the evaluation of the fitness function is usually a computationally complex task.

In this paper we focus on a test-program generation problem. Test-programs can be used in the design of microprocessors for several different proposes, from design validation to postproduction test [2-3]. The adoption of an EC-based solution for test-program generation is particularly challenging because the computational complexity of the fitness evaluation (requiring from minutes to several hours on a fast

G.R. Raidl et al. (Eds.): EvoWorkshops 2004, LNCS 3005, pp. 230–239, 2004.

workstation) have prevented any systematical modeling. Only naïve approaches, like that presented in [4], have been successful proposed.

The main goal of this paper is to present a complete framework to examine, evaluate and characterize the test-program generation problem using an evolutionary computation (EC) technique supported by a hardware-accelerator device. The use of a hardware accelerator device greatly speeds up the fitness evaluation, allowing us to execute a large number of experiments and to perform a more systematic analysis of the problem than otherwise possible.

As a case study we tackle a SPARCv8 pipelined processor using μGP, an evolutionary computation tool. The μGP is a known evolutionary approach to test-program generation for microprocessors [5].

The paper is organized as follows. Section 2 outlines the methodology used. Section 3 drafts the framework description and section 4 describes the hardware accelerator devised. In section 5 a case study is analyzed. The results and conclusions are presented in section 6 and section 7. Finally section 8 presents the future works.

2 Methodology

We lack theoretical studies on EC that allow us to understand how to approach HOPs. Often these problems present unknown fitness landscapes. In addition, HOPs are characterized by complex relationships between genotype and fitness, unlike popular test problems such as 1-max.

We devised a local analysis of the relationships occurring among genotype, phenotype, experimental results and fitness. A local analysis allows us to characterize the local behavior of the evolutionary methodology.

Starting from a reference individual, successive sets of individuals are generated at increasing genotypic distances. These are thoroughly characterized, both from an individual and a statistical point of view.

The reference individual is chosen this way: an initial evolutionary round is launched, to infer a typical fitness range. An intermediate fitness value is then chosen as a desired fitness. A new experiment is launched, but is terminated as soon as the desired fitness has been reached. The resulting best individual is chosen as reference.

We use this unorthodox method to choose the reference individual in an attempt to characterize what can be viewed as a typical work situation the evolutionary method faces. On one side, choosing a random individual as the reference just tells us what an evolutionary core sees in the first stages of its computation, telling us more about random methods; on the other side, an individual whose fitness is already very high might be part of a local fitness maximum, so we might only get information about the fitness landscape around that maximum.

3 Framework Description

In the experiment, the μGP engine was used to maximize the toggle activity (TA) on all pipeline registers of the processor under evaluation. This metric can be used both for test and validation.

Pipelines are composed of a set of stages interleaved by *boundary registers* holding the partial results of the performed computations, and they are very regular designs. Moreover, the combinational logic in each stage is not very deep. Hence, it is possible to conjecture that the *toggle activity* on the boundary registers is related to the activity of the combinational logic the registers feed.

When toggle activity on pipeline boundary registers is adopted to drive test-program cultivation, it can be easily measured by resorting to logic simulation.

The architecture of the experimental system is shown in Figure 1: the microprocessor assembly language is described in an instruction library. The Evolutionary Core (μGP engine) cultivates a population of individuals, where each individual represents a program. Then, the execution of each program is simulated with an external tool, the simulator, and the feedback, the evaluation function, is used to drive the generation process.

The approach is potentially able to maximize any evaluation function, provided that a way exists to evaluate it for each candidate program.

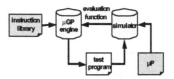

Fig. 1. Experimental System Architecture

3.1 Evolutionary Core

The μGP is an evolutionary approach for generating programs stemming from the genetic programming (GP) paradigm. Evolved programs are realistic assembly programs tweaked for a target microprocessor, that take full advantage of the assembly syntax, exploit the different addressing modes and instruction set asymmetries [5].

Programs are internally represented as *graphs* composed of different types of nodes, encoding the different types of instructions, such as sequential operations, jumps, branches, etc.

Each node is mapped to a different instruction, according to the instruction library, which encodes all the syntactically correct instructions, listing for each instruction the type of valid operands (e.g., a numeric value used as immediate value, a register together with its addressing mode, a label representing the target of a jump).

Test-programs are generated by an evolutionary algorithm implementing a $\mu+\lambda$ strategy modifying graph topologies and mutating parameters inside graph nodes. A population of μ individuals is stored, each individual representing a test-program. In each step, λ new individuals are generated. Each new individual is generated by applying one or more genetic operators. After creating new λ individuals, the best μ programs in the population of $(\mu+\lambda)$ are selected for surviving.

3.2 Simulator

The simulator computes experimental results corresponding to the execution of the generated program on the processor under evaluation.

As previous sections describe, logic simulations are needed to measure the toggle activity provoked by candidate test-programs. When complex microprocessor cores are tackled, even logic simulation performed by means of efficient RTL simulators may entail several minutes for each program, and therefore the number of test-programs that can be evaluated in reasonable time is very limited. For example, evaluating the toggle activity of pipeline registers during the execution of a 2K instruction program with a simulator would require approximately 10 minutes.

To overcome this problem we devised a method to exploit FPGA-based hardware accelerator that is able to compute the evaluation function described before in a fraction of the time simulations require. This will be detailed in section 4.

3.3 Evaluation Function

The task of the evaluation function is to collapse the obtained experimental results, feeding back a numerical fitness value to μGP engine. The evaluation function is a critical part of the evolutionary loop, because it has to report meaningful information to the evolutionary core to allow it to select best programs.

4 Hardware Accelerator

The basic idea behind our approach consists in equipping the considered processor core with suitable logic to measure toggle activity and then mapping it on an FPGA-based device that emulates the core during program execution. The additional logic allows easily gathering the information needed for computing the evaluation function.

The architecture of the developed hardware accelerator is presented in Figure 2.

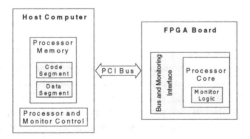

Fig. 2. Architecture of the hardware accelerator

The accelerator is composed of three modules:

- *FPGA Board*: it is a board equipped with an SRAM-based FPGA device whose purpose is to emulate the considered processor core during the execution of candidate test-programs. The adopted FPGA device hosts three logic blocks: the *Processor Core*, the *Monitor Logic,* aiming at recording if, during program execution, a set of user-selected registers toggled their contents (from 0 to 1 and from 1 to 0) and the *Bus and Monitoring Interface* whose purpose is to implement the connection channel between the emulated processor and the software processes running on the host computer.

- *PCI Bus:* it is the bridge between the host computer and the FPGA board.
- *Host Computer:* it is a Pentium-class PC that we use for implementing two software processes. The first process *(Processor Memory)* decodes all the bus cycles initiated by the emulated processor and executes the requested data transfer on the processor code and data segments. Conversely, the second process *(Processor and Monitor Control)* implements the synchronization mechanism between Host Computer and the FPGA Board.

In order to exploit the described hardware accelerator, the processor core, which is assumed to be available as a RT-level VHDL model, is instrumented by adding the *Monitor Logic* and the *Bus and Monitoring Interface*. Then, the resulting design is synthesized, placed and routed on the selected FPGA device.

For each candidate test-program the content of the processor Code and Data Segments are initialized. The processor is then started by first asserting its reset signal, and then by continuously applying clock pulses. For each clock pulse the bus cycle the processor is executing is performed and the memory is updated accordingly. The whole process is repeated until program completion is reached. At the end of program execution, the status of the *Monitor Logic* regarding the toggle activity is read back and forwarded to the μGP.

5   Case Study

The processor used in our experiments is a synthesizable VHDL model of a 32-bit pipelined processor conforming to the IEEE-1754 (SPARCv8) architecture. The processor is specifically designed for embedded applications and it is available under the GNU LGPL license. It is fully synthesizable and can be implemented on both FPGAs and ASICs [6].

The pipeline was instrumented with the monitor logic (all the 742 bits of the 105 registers in the pipeline were monitored) and the processor was mapped on the adopted FPGA board (we used the Alphadata ADM-XRC 1000E board).

A hardware accelerator saves us a large amount of time. For example, evaluating the toggle activity of pipeline registers during the execution of a 2K instructions program with a simulator would require approximately 10 minutes. Exploiting the hardware acceleration based on the proposed instrumentation, however, a single simulation requires about 2 seconds, achieving a speed-up of 300 times with respect to logic simulation.

In our technique, μGP is used as the evolutionary core. It is asked to maximize the toggle activity of all bits of user-selected registers inside the pipeline, i.e., the number of flip-flops that toggled at least once from 0 to 1 and at least once from 1 to 0 during the execution of a program.

5.1 Experimental Characterization

In our setup, genotypes are defined as µGP individuals, internally represented as graphs; the phenotype is an assembly program corresponding to an individual; experimental results are extracted as a matrix that reports the TA of the pipeline registers over the program execution. Finally the fitness reports the total number of bits that underwent TA. This correspondence is represented in Figure 3.

As mentioned in the previous sections, there is not clarity about the search space of the test-program generation problem. Additionally, the relationship among genotype - phenotype - fitness maps are unknown. This situation leads us to construct some definitions based upon distance.

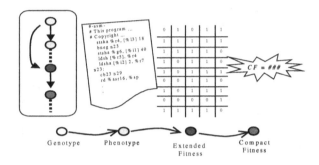

Fig. 3. Genotype - phenotype – *Simulation Results - fitness* map

5.2 Definitions

A reference individual (the Reference) was chosen as generator element. Its phenotype is used as the reference program. From this program we obtained the reference experimental results and the corresponding fitness.

Starting from the left of Figure 3, the individual genotype is originally represented by a graph; individual distance or *Genotype Distance* (ΔG) is defined as the number of simple mutations required to obtain a given individual starting from the Reference. In this case the available mutations are: Add node (adds a random node), Sub node (eliminates a random node) and Mod node (Modifies a node parameter).

The phenotype is an assembly program obeying the processor assembly syntax; *Program Distance* (ΔP) is the quantity of different instructions from the Reference program. It is worth noting that a Genotype Distance of 1 does not always leads to a Program Distance of 1. For example, when adding a node that calls a subroutine, µGP adds the necessary information to jump to the subroutine and to come back to the main program.

As described in section 3 (Monitor Logic), the fitness function is computed counting the pipeline register bits that exhibit TA. Each time a program is evaluated, a matrix that represents the TA is available; the complete matrix is called the *Simulation Results* (SR). However µGP requires only a number, then the number of bits that show TA is passed as fitness. *SR Distance* (ΔSR) is defined as the number of different bits in the TA matrix with respect to the Reference.

It is known that the maximum possible fitness equals the number of the pipeline register bits, which is 742.

6   Experimental Evaluation

Experimental results are presented here; the initial sub section describes the data gathering process, and the final sub section reports data analysis.

6.1   Experiments Characterization

Initial experiments determine a Reference individual. µGP default parameters are used ($\mu = 30$, $\lambda = 20$ and 100 generations). To select the Reference individual, a specific fitness value is chosen looking at the obtained fitness excursion. This excursion goes through 68% up to 84% of the maximum. We choose 80% as the desired fitness value, as outlined in the methodology.

The desired fitness value is used as a termination point for a new experiment. This experiment is finished when the chosen fitness is reached. The final best individual is selected as the Reference.

Starting from the Reference, 4 sets of new individuals are generated at incremental Genotype Distance. Each set of individuals is characterized by the same number of simple mutations with respect to the Reference. For every individual into each set the defined distances from the Reference are computed.

The average of Program Distance, Simulation Results Distance and fitness are computed for each set of individuals. Observing that the data distribution is not Gaussian, to represent its dispersion we chose to show the 20% interval centered around the median value, from 40% to 60%.

The relationship between genotype distance and program distance is shown in figure 4a. There is a smooth correlation between the distances but it is not so strict as we may desire. This means that simple genetic mutations may not be so simple when seen from a phenotype point of view.

Figure 4b shows a representation of the Simulation Results Distances vs Genotype Distances. This graph illustrates that few genetic mutations lead to programs that produce similar simulation results.

Figure 4c presents the correlation between simple mutations and fitness. It is possible to see that there is not a strong correlation between the data, implying that programs producing similar simulation results do not exhibit similar fitness.

For the sake of completeness, and to further clarify the relationships between different elements of the analysis, we include the graphs of the remaining relationships.

Figure 5 shows the relationship among Program Distance, Simulation Results Distance and fitness. A poor correlation exists among these parameters.

Figure 6 illustrates the relationship between fitness and Simulation Results Distance. It is interesting to note that a strong negative correlation exists between simulation results distance and fitness.

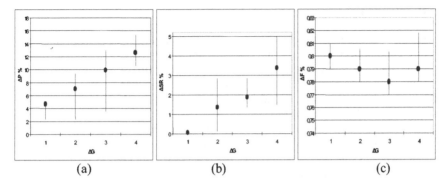

Fig. 4. (a) Program Distance (%) vs Genotype Distance. (b) Simulation Results Distance (%) vs Genotype Distance. (c) Fitness (%) vs Genotype Distance

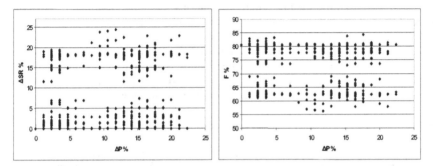

Fig. 5. (a) Simulation Results Distance (%) vs Program Distance (%). (b) Fitness (%) vs Program Distance (%)

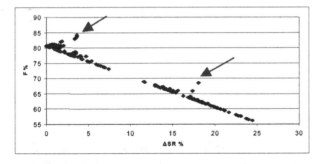

Fig. 6. Fitness (%) vs Simulation Results Distance (%)

This leads us to think the experiment is near a local maximum, as we could expect because the Reference already shows a high fitness.

It seems plausible, looking at the dots pointed by the upper arrow, that the Reference is located near a local maximum in the space of the SR distances. On the other hand, lower arrow could represent another local maximum.

A high density of individuals is found around the Reference, while others describe a descending line.

6.2 Results Analysis

The evaluation function must be able to represent faithfully the problem; in this way the correlation between genotype and fitness is improved.

As the pictures show, there is a poor genotype – fitness relationship. Simple mutations can produce important and irregular fitness variations.

A weak relationship was found between the program distances and both the experimental results and the fitness.

There could be two causes: firstly, small genotype changes, i.e. simple mutations, do not lead to small phenotype changes. Secondly there is loose relation between program distances and experimental results; looking at figure 6 it is possible to see a big dispersion in the first column.

A better correlation between genotype distance and fitness could be obtained by carefully selecting the evaluation function.

To obtain better results using the current setup, the evolutionary process could be launched several times using small populations and high number of generations, similar to a multi-start hill climber. Another possibility is to use an island model configuration for the evolutionary core.

Additional experiments were launched modifying the genetic population parameters. In all of them the same number of individuals is evaluated, while the number of generations decreases as the population increases. In this way we use the same time budget for each experiment. Final results are shown in table 1.

Table 1. Experimental results

Experiment	μ	λ	Max. Fitness
1	2	8	87.60%
2	8	32	84.36%
3	32	128	82.88%
4	100	400	78.57%

It is possible to observe that small populations attain better performance. In fact the best result was obtained by a population of $\mu=2$, $\lambda=8$.

7   Conclusions

This paper presented an empirical methodology to locally analyze and characterize the evolutionary approach to test-program generation, based on the adoption of a hardware accelerator device to speed up program evaluation. Without the hardware accelerator system, schematizing such problems would be unfeasible because of the huge quantity of experiments required.

The methodology was applied to a case study consisting in measuring the pipeline register TA on a SPARCv8 processor.

We performed a local analysis of the relationships among genotype, phenotype, simulation results and fitness, to characterize the local behavior of the evolutionary process.

The framework we used is composed of an evolutionary core named μGP, a FPGA-based device that emulates a microprocessor core during program execution and an evaluation function to collapse the experimental results into a single numeric fitness value.

We performed a statistical analysis of the obtained experimental results that both allowed us to discover a potential pitfall in our experimental setup and guided us in the choice of μGP parameters to obtain the best possible result for a given time budget.

8   Future Works

To explore new routes in the characterization methodology of test-program generation problem, several approaches can be tried.

First of all, it is possible to change the instruction library trying to improve the correlation between genotype distance and fitness. This way simple mutations will change and their effects could be different. On the other hand, we could carefully build a new evaluation function to partially restore the correlation between genotype distances and fitness. This would lead to a better performance on the evolutionary core.

Even though the current fitness function leads the genetic core to stimulate different pipeline stages using the TA metric, it could be possible to generate faster and smaller test-programs employing a different fitness function, based on detailed information about the hardware, able to gather experimental data about specific logic paths in the pipeline.

A final approach could be to use the evolutionary core in an island model configuration.

Acknowledgments. The authors wish to thank Massimiliano Schillaci for his invaluable help.

References

[1]   M. Abramovici, M. Breuer, A. Friedman. "Digital system testing and testable design". John Wiley & Sons, Inc. 1990.

[2]   C.A. Papachristou, F. Martin, M. Nourani, "Microprocessor Based Testing for Core-Based System on Chip", ACM/IEEE Design Automation Conference, 1999, pp. 586-591

[3]   J. Shen and J.A. Abraham, "Native Mode Functional Test Generation for Processors with Applications to Self Test and Design Validation", International Test Conference, 1998, pp. 990-999

[4]   F. Corno, G. Cumani, M. Sonza Reorda, G. Squillero, "Fully Automatic Test-program Generation for Microprocessor Cores", IEEE Design, Automation and Test in Europe, 2003, pp. 1006-1011

[5]   F. Corno, G. Squillero, "An Enhanced Framework for Microprocessor Test-Program Generation", EUROGP2003: 6th European Conference on Genetic Programming, Essex (UK), April 14-16, 2003, pp. 307-315

[6]   SPARC International, The SPARC Architecture Manual

Evolutionary Design Space Exploration for Median Circuits

Lukáš Sekanina

Faculty of Information Technology, Brno University of Technology
Božetěchova 2, 612 66 Brno, Czech Republic
sekanina@fit.vutbr.cz

Abstract. This paper shows that it is possible to (1) discover novel implementations of median circuits using evolutionary techniques and (2) find out suitable median circuits in case that only limited resources are available for their implementation. These problems are approached using Cartesian genetic programming and an ordinary compare–swap encoding. Combining the proposed approaches a method is demonstrated for effective exploration of the design space of median circuits under various constraints.

1 Introduction

Starting in 1992 when Higuchi et al evolved multiplexers in a programmable logic array [5], the evolutionary circuit design has become an important part of applications of evolutionary computing. In contrast to evolvable hardware, evolutionary circuit design deals in principle with a static fitness function and its objective is to discover novel solutions automatically, possibly without an assistance of human designers. A number of innovative and fault-tolerant digital as well as analog circuits have been evolved and demonstrated up to now (see examples in [4,14,18]).

Sorting networks have recently been recognized as potentially suitable objects for the evolutionary design and optimization [6,8]. They are also interesting from a hardware viewpoint because of their regular and combinational nature suitable for pipeline processing. For instance, Koza et al have used genetic programming to evolve a 7-sorting network directly in a field programmable gate array [11].

This paper deals with median circuits whose effective hardware implementations are crucial for high-performance signal processing. As far as we know, no research results are available dealing with their evolutionary design. Because the median circuits can easily be derived from sorting networks, it seems that their evolutionary design is useless. However, this paper shows that interesting median circuits can be evolved from scratch. The objective of this research is twofold: (1) to explore whether novel implementations of median circuits can be discovered using evolutionary techniques and (2) to find out suitable median circuits in case that only limited resources are available for their implementation. These problems will be approached using Cartesian genetic programming (which is applied

G.R. Raidl et al. (Eds.): EvoWorkshops 2004, LNCS 3005, pp. 240–249, 2004.
© Springer-Verlag Berlin Heidelberg 2004

in this context first time) and an ordinary compare–swap encoding (known from evolving sorting networks).

This paper is organized as follows. Sorting networks and median circuits are introduced in Section 2. Cartesian genetic programming is utilized for designing median circuits in Section 3. Section 4 presents the results obtained using the compare–swap encoding. Section 5 deals with designing median circuits under hardware constraints. Finally conclusions are given in Section 6.

2   From Sorting Networks to Median Circuits

A compare–swap of two elements (a, b) compares and exchanges a and b so that we obtain $a \leq b$ after the operation. A sorting network is defined as a sequence of compare–swap operations that depends only on the number of elements to be sorted, not on the values of the elements [9].

Although a standard sorting algorithm such as quicksort usually requires a lower number of compare operations than a sorting network, the advantage of the sorting network is that the sequence of comparisons is fixed. Thus it is suitable for parallel processing and hardware implementation, especially if the number of sorted elements is small. Figure 1 shows an example of a sorting network.

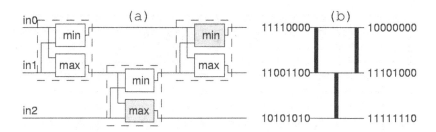

Fig. 1. (a) A 3-sorting network consists of 3 components, i.e. of 6 subcomponents (elements of maximum or minimum). A 3-median network consists of 4 subcomponents. (b) Alternative symbol. This sorting network can be tested in a single run if 2^3 bits can be stored in a single data unit.

Having a sorting network for N inputs, the median is simply the output value at the middle position (we are interested in odd N only in this paper). For example, efficient calculation of the median value is important in image processing where median filters are widely used with $N = 3\text{x}3$ or 5x5 [14].

The number of compare–swap components and the delay are two crucial parameters of any sorting network. Since we will only be interested in the number of compare–swap components in this paper (we will deal with delay in future research), the following Table 1 shows the number of components of some of the best currently known sorting networks, i.e. those which require the least number of components for sorting N elements. Some of these networks ($N = 13$–16) were discovered using evolutionary techniques [1,6,8,11]. The evolutionary approach was based on the encoding that will be described in Section 4. Evolutionary techniques were also utilized to discover fault-tolerant sorting networks [15].

Note that the compare–swap consists of two subcomponents: maximum and minimum. Because we need the middle output value only in the case of the median implementation, we can omit some subcomponents (dead code at the output marked in gray in Fig. 1) and so to reduce the implementation cost in hardware. Hence in the case of K components, we can obtain $2K - N + 1$ subcomponents (Table 1, line 3 with median*).

However, in addition to deriving median networks from sorting networks, specialized networks have been proposed to implement cheaper median networks. Table 1 (line 2) also presents the best-known numbers of subcomponents for optimal median networks. These values are derived from the table on page 226 of Knuth's book [9] and from papers [2,10,19]. Note that popular implementation of the 9-median circuit in an FPGA proposed by Smith is also area-optimal (in terms of the number of components) [16].

Table 1. Best known minimum-comparison sorting networks and median networks for some N. $c(N)$ denotes the number of compare–swap operations, $s(N)$ is the number of subcomponents. The last line holds for median networks derived from sorting networks using dead code elimination.

N	3	4	5	6	7	8	9	10	11	12	13	14	15	16	25
sortnet, $c(N)$	3	5	9	12	16	19	25	29	35	39	45	51	56	60	144
median, $s(N)$	4	-	10	-	20	-	30	-	42	-	> 52	-	> 66	-	174
median*, $s(N)$	4	-	14	-	26	-	42	-	60	-	78	-	98	-	264

The zero–one principle helps with evaluating sorting networks (and median circuits as well). It states that if a sorting network with N inputs sorts all 2^N input sequences of 0's and 1's into nondecreasing order, it will sort any arbitrary sequence of N numbers into nondecreasing order [9]. Furthermore, if we use a proper encoding, on say 32 bits, and binary operators AND instead of minimum and OR instead of maximum, we can evaluate 32 test vectors in parallel and thus reduce the testing process 32 times. Figure 1 illustrates this idea for 3-median. Note that it is usually impossible to obtain the general solution if only a subset of input vectors is utilized during the evolutionary design [7].

3   CGP for Designing Median Circuits

As far as we know, Cartesian Genetic Programming (CGP) has not been utilized to evolve median circuits or sorting networks yet. Our initial hypothesis is that novel and more efficient median circuits can be evolved using smaller building blocks (such as subcomponents minimum and maximum) instead of using compare–swap components.

3.1   Cartesian Genetic Programming

Miller and Thomson have introduced CGP that has recently been applied by several researchers especially for the evolutionary design of combinational circuits [12]. In CGP, the reconfigurable circuit is modeled as an array of u (columns) $\times$ v (rows) of programmable elements (gates). The number of circuit inputs and outputs is fixed. Feedback is not allowed. Each gate input can be connected to the output of some gate placed in the previous columns or to some of circuit inputs. L-back parameter defines the level of connectivity and thus reduces/extends the search space. For example, if $L=1$ only neighboring columns may be connected; if $L=u$, the full connectivity is enabled. The designer has to define for a given application: the number of inputs and outputs, L, u, v and the set of functions performed by programmable elements. Figure 2 shows an example and a corresponding chromosome. Miller and Thomson originally used a very simple variant of evolutionary algorithm to produce configurations for the programmable circuit [12]. Our algorithm is based on this evolutionary technique.

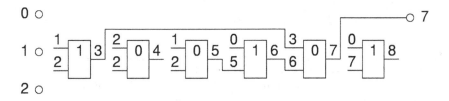

Fig. 2. An example of evolved 3-median circuit. CGP parameters are as follows: $L = 6$, $u = 6$, $v = 1$, functions Minimum (0) and Maximum (1). Gates 4 and 8 are not utilized. Chromosome: 1,2,1, 2,2,0, 1,2,0, 0,5,1 3,6,0, 0,7,1, 7. The last integer indicates the output of the circuit.

3.2   Experimental Setup

In order to evolve N-median circuits we utilized CGP with the following setting: $u = p$, $v = 1$, $L = p$, N inputs and a single output. p is the number of programmable elements depending on the problem size (for example, $p = 23$ for $N = 7$). Each of elements can be configured to operate as logical AND (minimum) or logical OR (maximum). Thus median circuits are rather constructed from subcomponents than from compare–swap components.

The evolutionary algorithm operates with population of 128 individuals. According to CGP, every individual consists of $u \times v \times 3 + 1$ integers. Four best individuals are considered as parents and every new population is generated as their clones. Elitism is supported. The initial population is generated randomly; however, the circuits with the maximum number of utilized elements are preferred. The evolution was typically stopped (1) when no improvement of the best fitness value occurs in the last 50k generations, or (2) after 600k generations.

Mutation works as follows: either the circuit output is mutated with the proba-bility 25% or one of the used elements is mutated – gate inputs are changed with the probability 85%, function is changed with the probability 15%. Only one mu-tation is performed per circuit; however, when the best fitness value stagnates for 10k generations, two mutations are employed. The proposed parameters were chosen as suitable after the experimental testing.

During fitness calculation all possible input combinations are supplied at the circuit inputs (i.e. 2^N vectors). The fitness value of every candidate circuit is incremented by one if the circuit returns the correct median value for a given input vector.

3.3   Results

Table 2 shows that it is very difficult to evolve a perfect median circuit (with the fitness value 2^N) for more than 5 inputs. Furthermore, we were not able to reach optimal $s(N)$ for $N = 9$ and 11. The algorithm usually traps in local optima, which is very close to the perfect fitness value 2^N. It seems that the cir-cuit evolution landscapes exhibit vast neutrality – similarly to Yu's and Miller's observations for even-parity problem [17].

Table 2. Summary of experiments performed to evolve small median circuits using CGP. N – # of inputs; p – # of columns in CGP; runs – # of runs performed; perfect – # of runs leading to the perfect fitness; perfect+opt $s(N)$ – # of runs with the perfect fitness and the optimal $s(N)$; best $s(N)$ – best obtained $s(N)$; best known $s(N)$

N	p	runs	perfect	perfect+opt $s(N)$	best $s(N)$	best known $s(N)$
3	8	50	50	15	4	4
5	16	100	11	1	10	10
7	23	2000	22	1	20	20
9	50	2000	35	0	36	30
11	90	200	2	0	71	42
13	120	200	none	-	-	-

Table 2 indicates that it is necessary to utilize much more programmable elements (the column denoted as p) than the resulting circuit requires in order to evolve a circuit with the perfect fitness. This requirement on redundancy was initially discussed by Miller et al [13]. For instance, 50 elements were used to evolve the 36-element median circuit for $N = 9$. However, we performed 200 runs with $p = 43$ for $N = 9$, but no circuit has appeared with the perfect fitness 512. The best circuits evolved using CGP are depicted in Fig. 3.

CGP has not allowed us to discover median circuits with lower $s(N)$ than the best known solutions exhibit. Furthermore, the approach produced median circuits only for small N. On the other hand, the obtained circuits are (1) totally different from the known median circuits that are based on the compare–swap approach and (2) much cheaper than those median circuits derived from classical sorting networks (see Table 1, line 3 with median*).

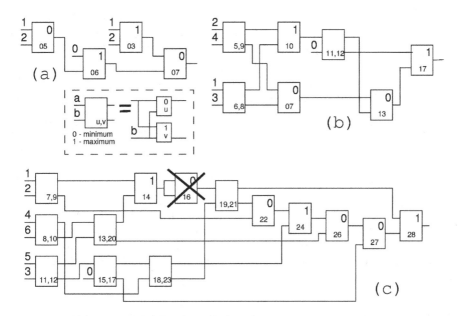

Fig. 3. Median circuits evolved using CGP: (a) 3-median, (b) 5-median and (c) 7-median circuits consist of the same number of subcomponents as the best–known conventional circuits. The evolved 7-median circuit contains one redundant subcomponent.

4   A Compare–Swap Approach

The compare–swap approach is usually applied in order to evolve sorting networks. This approach works at the level of compare–swap components. Candidate solutions are represented as sequences of pairs (a, b) indicating that a is compared/swapped with b. More complicated representations have been developed in order to minimize the delay of the network (for instance, see [1]). We applied the compare–swap approach to evolve area-efficient median circuits.

4.1   Experimental Setup

Each chromosome consists of a sequence of integers that represents a median circuit. We used variable-length chromosomes of maximum length ml; a sentinel indicates the end of valid sequence.

A typical setting of the evolutionary algorithm is as follows. Initial population of 200 individuals is seeded randomly using alleles $0 - (N - 1)$. New individuals are generated using mutation (1 integer per chromosome). Four best individuals are considered as parents and every newly formed population consists of their clones. The evolutionary algorithm is left running until a fully correct individual is found or 3000 generations are exhausted. We also increase mutation rate if no improvement is observable during the last 30 generations. Fitness calculation is performed in the same way as for CGP.

Because we would like to reduce the number of compare–swap components and because the fitness function does not consider the number of compare–swap operations, we utilized the following strategy. First, we defined a sufficient value ml for a given N (according to Table 1) and executed the evolutionary design. If a resulting circuit exhibits the perfect fitness, ml is decremented by 2, otherwise ml remains unchanged and the evolution is executed again. This is repeated until a predefined number of runs are exhausted. Because this approach works at the level of compare–swap components (i.e. $c(n)$), it was necessary to eliminate dead code to obtain $s(N)$.

4.2   Results

In contrary to CGP, perfectly operating median circuits were evolved up to $N = 25$ (see examples in Fig. 4). Table 3 shows that area-optimal circuits are up to $N = 11$. In spite of the best efforts of the author of this paper none specific values of $s(N)$ nor $c(N)$ were found in literature for median circuits with $N = 13 - 23$.

Table 3. The best median circuits evolved using the compare–swap approach

N	3	5	7	9	11	13	15	17	19	21	23	25
$c(N)$	3	7	13	19	26	34	44	55	65	80	94	109
$s(N)$	4	10	20	30	42	56	74	94	112	140	166	194
best known $s(N)$	4	10	20	30	42	?	?	?	?	?	?	174

Table 4. The number of correct calculations of output values for median circuits when reducing the number of compare–swap components $c(N)$ from 21 till 2

$c(N)$	2	3	4	5	6	7	8	9	10	11
5-median	24	26	27	28	30	32	32	32	32	32
7-median	90	96	98	102	104	108	112	116	122	126
9-median	346	366	372	384	390	402	410	420	430	442
$c(N)$	12	13	14	15	16	17	18	19	20	21
5-median	32	32	32	32	32	32	32	32	32	32
7-median	127	128	128	128	128	128	128	128	128	128
9-median	458	470	484	496	500	506	510	512	512	512

While evolved median circuits are area-optimal for $N = 3 - 11$ and perhaps close to optimal for $N = 13 - 19$, the evolved median circuits for $N = 21 - 25$ seem to be area wasting. The reason is that the best known value $s(25)$ is 174 [2]; however, we reached $s(25) = 194$.

The evolution takes several days on a common PC for $N \geq 23$. Hence we tried to reduce the training set in our experiments; however, no solution has appeared producing correct outputs for all possible input combinations.

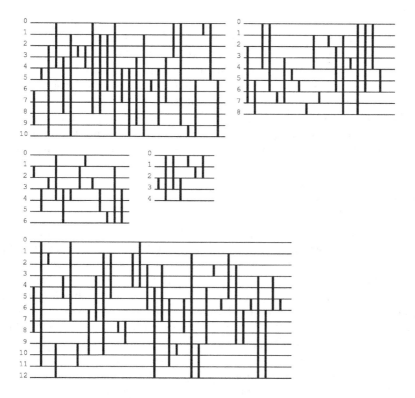

Fig. 4. Some of median circuits evolved using the compare–swap approach

It was much easier to evolve perfect median circuits using the compare–swap encoding than using CGP. Similarly to the results obtained from CGP, the median circuits are not optimized for delay.

5   Reducing Resources

The proposed evolutionary approach allows designers to explore much larger portion of the design space than conventional methods. This is demonstrated on the following experiment. The objective is to find out how many input combinations of all possible inputs lead to wrong output values if the number of circuit elements (compare–swap operations) is continually reduced. It is useful to know this characteristic from the fault tolerance point of view or when only limited resources are available for the implementation. Drechsler and Günther performed similar research for multiplexer circuits [3].

In order to evolve median circuits under hardware constraints, we utilized the experimental background from the previous section. Table 4 shows how reduction of the resources influences the number of outputs calculated correctly for median circuits of 5, 7 and 9 inputs. For instance, we need 13 compare–swap components to obtain the perfect fitness (128) for the 7-median circuit. If we reduce the number of components to 10, we obtain correct outputs for 122 input combinations. Using 5 components only, 102 out of 128 outputs are calculated correctly. It will probably be very difficult to design these "under-dimensioned" circuits by means of a conventional approach. Our method requires a few minutes to find a solution using a common personal computer.

The method could be useful for designing area/energy-consumption efficient median filters for image preprocessing. In this application, most input combinations should be processed correctly. Rare mistakes are not critical because our eye is not able to see them.

6   Conclusions

Two approaches for designing median circuits were proposed, implemented and analyzed in this paper. We were able to evolve better median circuits than those median circuits that can be created by means of dead code elimination from the best-known sorting networks. In some cases (up to $N=11$), the evolved median circuits are area-optimal. CGP has been applied in order to obtain median circuits directly without the need to eliminate same gates. However, the approach is suitable only for smaller N. Finally, we explored the design space of "reduced" median circuits and showed that these circuits operate correctly for most input vectors.

Combining the proposed approaches we provide a method for effective exploration of the design space of median circuits under various constraints.

Apart from hardware implementations of evolved circuits, our future research will be devoted to (1) designing larger median circuits by means of some developmental strategies, (2) investigating fault tolerance of evolved median circuits and (3) reducing latency.

Acknowledgment. The research was performed with the Grant Agency of the Czech Republic under No. 102/03/P004 Evolvable hardware based application design methods and No. 102/04/0737 Modern Methods of Digital System Synthesis and the Research intention No. MSM 262200012 – Research in information and control systems

References

1. Choi, S. S., Moon, B. R.: More Effective Genetic Search for the Sorting Network Problem. In: Proc. of the Genetic and Evolutionary Computation Conference GECCO'02, Morgan Kaufmann, 2002, p. 335–342
2. Devillard, N.: Fast Median Search: An ANSI C Implementation. 1998
   http://ndevilla.free.fr/median/median/index.html
3. Drechsler, R., Günther, W.: Evolutionary Synthesis of Multiplexer Circuits under Hardware Constraints. In: Proc. of the GECCO Workshop on Genetic Programming and Evolvable Hardware, Morgan Kaufmann Publishers, San Francisco 2000, p. 513–518

4. Gordon, T., Bentley, P.: On Evolvable Hardware. Soft Computing in Industrial Electronics, Physica-Verlag, Heidelberg 2001, p. 279–323

5. Higuchi, T. et al.: Evolving Hardware with Genetic Learning: A First Step Towards Building a Darwin Machine. In: Proc. of the 2nd International Conference on Simulated Adaptive Behaviour, MIT Press, Cambridge MA 1993, p. 417–424

6. Hillis, W. D.: Co-evolving parasites improve simulated evolution as an optimization procedure. Physica D 42 (1990) 228–234

7. Imamura, K., Foster, J. A., Krings, A. W.: The Test Vector Problem and Limitations to Evolving Digital Circuits. In: Proc. of the 2nd NASA/DoD Workshop on Evolvable Hardware, IEEE CS Press, 2000, p. 75–79

8. Juillé, H.: Evolution of Non-Deterministic Incremental Algorithms as a New Approach for Search in State Spaces. In Proc. of 6th Int. Conf. on Genetic Algorithms, Morgan Kaufmann, 1995, p. 351–358

9. Knuth, D. E.: The Art of Computer Programming: Sorting and Searching (2nd ed.), Addison Wesley, 1998

10. Kolte, P., Smith, R., Su, W.: A Fast Median Filter Using AltiVec. In Proc. of the IEEE Conf. on Computer Design, Austin, Texas, IEEE CS Press, 1999, p. 384–391

11. Koza, J. R., Bennett III., F. H., Andre, D., Keane, M. A.: Genetic Programming III: Darwinian Invention and Problem Solving. Morgan Kaufmann, 1999

12. Miller, J., Thomson, P.: Cartesian Genetic Programming. In: Proc. of the 3rd European Conference on Genetic Programming, LNCS 1802, Springer Verlag, Berlin 2000, p. 121–132

13. Miller, J., Job, D., Vassilev, V.: Principles in the Evolutionary Design of Digital Circuits – Part I. In: Genetic Programming and Evolvable Machines, Vol. 1(1), Kluwer Academic Publisher (2000) 8–35

14. Sekanina, L.: Evolvable Components: From Theory to Hardware Implementations. Natural Computing Series, Springer Verlag, Berlin 2003

15. Shepherd, R., Foster, J.: Inherent Fault Tolerance in Evolved Sorting Networks. In Proc. of GECCO 2003, LNCS 2723, Springer Verlag, 2003, p. 456–457

16. Smith, J. I.: Implementing Median Filters in XC4000E FPGAs. Xcell 23, Xilinx, 1996 http://www.xilinx.com/xcell/xl23/xl23_16.pdf

17. Yu, T., Miller, J.: Finding Needles in Haystacks Is Not Hard with Neutrality. In: Proc. of the 5th European Conference on Genetic Programming, Kinsale, Ireland, LNCS 2278, Springer-Verlag, 2002, p. 13–25

18. Zebulum, R., Pacheco, M., Vellasco, M.: Evolutionary Electronics – Automatic Design of Electronic Circuits and Systems by Genetic Algorithms. CRC Press, Boca Raton 2002

19. Zeno, R.: A reference of the best-known sorting networks for up to 16 inputs. 2003, http://www.angelfire.com/blog/ronz/

Genetic Optimization of Morphological Filters with Applications in Breast Cancer Detection

Lucia Ballerini[1] and Lennart Franzén[2]

[1] Dept. of Technology, Örebro University, Sweden
lucia@cb.uu.se
[2] Dept. of Pathology, Örebro University Hospital, Sweden
lennart.franzen@orebroll.se

Abstract. In this paper we apply genetic algorithms to morphological filter optimization. The validation of the method is illustrated by performing experiments with synthetic images, whose optimal filter is known. Applications to microscopic images of breast tissue are reported. The medical problem consists in the discrimination between cancerous tissue and normal one.

1   Introduction

Breast cancer is the most common form of cancer among women. The final diagnostic decision is based on the microscopic examination of tissue samples performed by the pathologist. This analysis is time consuming and requires the visual interpretation of complex images. Automation of this analysis would be of great help to the pathologists, as they have many images to assess each day.

The aim our research is to analyze histological samples of intact tissue taken with a biopsy. We are interested in developing methods that can improve the automated classification between cancerous and normal tissue [1,2]. The specific aim of this paper is to investigate the use of mathematical morphology to characterize tissue images.

Mathematical morphology is a methodology for studying geometric structures in images and it has been receiving growing attention in recent years. This is evident by the many industrial applications that have been developed and are currently being developed. These range from measurements of particles in microscopic images to analyses of identifiable features in earth resources satellite systems [3]. We decided to use mathematical morphology because it quantifies many aspects of the geometrical structure of images a way that agrees with human intuition and perception. This seems suitable for our problem, in fact the pathologist can not always explain why he reaches a particular diagnosis, but he takes his decisions based on experience acquired by observation of past cases.

Mathematical morphology has produced an important class of non linear image processing and analysis operators [4]. Morphological operators are simple, and the morphological filters arising from these operators have proved to be powerful tools and have found a range of applications, giving excellent results in areas such as noise reduction, edge detection and object recognition [3].

G.R. Raidl et al. (Eds.): EvoWorkshops 2004, LNCS 3005, pp. 250–259, 2004.
© Springer-Verlag Berlin Heidelberg 2004

However, design methods existing for these morphological filters tend to be computationally intractable or require some expert knowledge of mathematical morphology [5,6]. In this paper we investigate the use of Genetic Algorithms (GA) to morphological filter optimization, with the goal of finding filters able to differentiate normal and cancerous tissue and therefore classify breast images.

The paper is organized as follow: in Section 2 we review previous work using evolutionary algorithms in mathematical morphology optimization and we briefly discuss the difference with our method. In Section 3 are reported the definitions of mathematical morphology operators used in the work. The method is explained in Section 4. Experiments with synthetic images and medical images are described in Section 5 and 6 respectively.

2   Related Work

The use of genetic algorithms in the optimization of morphological filters has already been reported.

Harvey et al. [7] describe a technique for the optimization of multidimensional grayscale soft morphological filters that seeks to optimize the structuring element and the choice of the soft morphological operations. They also extend their technique to the optimization of grayscale soft morphological filters in the spatio-temporal domain, for applications in automatic film restoration [8].

Huttunen et al. [9] propose a method based on GA for finding an optimal soft morphological filter for specific situation. They also propose some optimal parameters for mean absolute error and mean square error criteria.

Yoda et al. [10] use GA to search mathematical morphology procedure, i.e. erosion and dilation operators, to extract object shape. They introduce the concept of era to deal with the over and under extraction problems. Binary images of sheet of music are used for experiments.

Zmuda et al. [11] describe a system based on evolutionary learning, called MORPH, that semi-automates the generation of morphological programs, by first synthesizing morphological sequences that extract novel features which increase program population diversity and then combining these sequences into larger programs. They extend their system to create HELPR, a hybrid evolutionary learning algorithm that synthesizes a complete multiclass pattern recognition system [12].

Quintana et al. [13] present a genetic programming approach to obtain mathematical morphology algorithms. The algorithms are constructed using the basic mathematical morphology operators, but differently to previous approaches, they explore the utilization of irregular structuring elements of various sizes.

All these methods require an example of ideal output of the target filter.

The method presented by Asano [14] is somehow the most close to our method because it does not require an example of ideal output. It is based on the optimization of the 'morphological opening/closing spectrum' (MOCS): filter parameters are adjusted to reduce the portions of smaller sizes in MOCS, since they are regarded as the contributions of noise-like high-frequency components.

Another method that does not require the goal image is described by Loncaric et al. [15]. They use GA to select the optimal structuring element for shape description and matching based on morphological signature transform (MST). They introduce a new patch-type crossover and a crossover rate based on population entropy.

The novelty of our method is that we do not have a goal image, and we do not use morphological filters for noise reduction or segmentation, but for image classification. Our approach is based on performing the same operation sequence on images belonging to different classes. The goal is to find a structuring element (or a sequence of them) that leaves unaltered images of one class while changing the others. Our fitness is based on the correlation between original images and their filtered versions.

3   Mathematical Morphology

Morphological operations are defined in terms of set theory [16]. One of the basic operation of morphological image processing is the opening.

The basic effect of an opening operator is to remove some of the foreground (bright) pixels from the edges of regions of foreground pixels. As with other morphological operators, the exact operation is determined by the structuring element. The effect of the operator is to preserve foreground regions that have a similar shape to this structuring element, or that can completely contain the structuring element, while eliminating all other regions of foreground pixels.

The opening of a a binary image S by a binary structuring element E (also an image) is defined to be the union of all translations of E which are subset of S. In effect, the template E is moved around inside S and the opening, $S \circ E$, consists of all the points of S which lie in some translated copy of E. Thus the opening can be expressed as a fitting process such that:

$$S \circ E = \cup \{(E)_z | (E) \subseteq S\} \qquad (1)$$

In other words, the opening of set S by structuring element E, is defined as

$$S \circ E = (S \ominus E) \oplus E\} \qquad (2)$$

where $\ominus$ and $\oplus$ are the erosion and dilation operation, defined as:

$$S \ominus E = \{z | (E)_z \subseteq S\} \qquad (3)$$
$$S \oplus E = \{z | (E)_z \cap S \neq \varnothing\}.$$

For more details on mathematical morphology and its applications see [17,18].

4   Proposed Method

The whole 'image classification' is divided in two steps. The first step is the learning phase, in which GA are used to extract sets of structuring element parameters. One set is extracted from every image class we want to classify. The second step is the implementation phase, in which the parameters obtained by GA are used to filter all the images and classify them based on their correlation.

In this section we describe the learning phase, while the implementation phase will be described together with the experiments.

The main issues in applying GA to any problem are selecting an appropriate encoding representation of the solutions, defining an adequate evaluation function (fitness), and choosing the values of the parameters used by the algorithm (e.g. population size, crossover, etc.).

In the case of morphological filters there are two basic items: the sequence of morphological operations and the structuring elements. It is well known that the opening operation with appropriate structuring elements is able to pass certain shapes and block others [16]. For this reason, in the present study we carried out experiments using the opening operator, and coding the sequence of structuring elements.

Each chromosome is composed of a list of fields, as shown in Fig. 1. In each field an elementary structuring element is encoded, defined by its shape and size. The possible shapes are chosen according to the experiment. We used squares, disks and other 'regular' shapes. The shape is coded by an integer number corresponding to the shape, i.e. "1" for a disk, "2" for a square, and so on. More details will be described in Section 5 and 6. The size is the dimension of the structuring element, i.e. radius for a disk, width for a square, etc. The size is also encoded as integer number. The maximum size is user defined. The numbers representing size and shape are codified in the chromosomes using the Gray code.

Fig. 1. Examples of coding a sequence of N structuring elements

Our goal is to find a filter that changes one image (or images belonging to the same class), while keeping as much as possible unaltered another image (or images belonging to another class). For simplicity, let us call good the image we want to keep and bad the one we want to change.

The evaluation is done by using similarity ($0 \leq S \leq 1$: a normalized correlation coefficient) between the original and the processed image [10]:

$$S = \frac{(f \cdot g)}{\sqrt{(f \cdot f)} \sqrt{(g \cdot g)}} \tag{4}$$

where:

$$(f \cdot g) = \frac{1}{N} \cdot \frac{1}{M} \sum_{i=1}^{N} \sum_{j=1}^{M} f(i,j) \cdot g(i,j) \tag{5}$$

The objective fitness function, that we minimize, is related to how similar is the good image to its corresponding filtered version and how different is the bad image from its filtered version, i.e.:

$$fitness = -S(good) + S(bad). \tag{6}$$

5 Experiments with Synthetic Images

The experiment used synthetic binary images containing circles or squares, as shown in Fig. 2. This experiment is carried out to see if the proposed method is able to select a filter that keeps one shape while deleting the other one.

Fig. 2. Examples of synthetic test image.

Circle and square dimensions satisfy the condition: $l < 2r < \sqrt{2}l$, where l is the square width and r the circle radius. This is done to force the algorithm to choose the appropriate shape of the structuring element. Without this condition any structuring element larger than the smaller shape could perform the task.

In this experiment, we used the opening operator and we optimize only one structuring element. Each chromosome was composed of one field, containing shape (circle or square) and size of the structuring element.

We trained the algorithm two times, using respectively the following fitnesses:

$$fitness_1 = -S(circles) + S(squares) \tag{7}$$
$$fitness_2 = -S(squares) + S(circles)$$

Not surprising, a circle shaped structuring element is selected at the end of the first training and a square shaped one in the second trial. The filters are able to complete remove the shape corresponding to the structuring element used. The correlation between the original and the filtered image is 1 for the image containing the searched shape and 0 for the other one.

These results are obtained with a population of 100 individuals, and running the GA for 100 iterations. Mutation and crossover probability are respectively 0.01 and 0.7. Gray code, two point crossover, roulette wheel selection, elitism are the GA options used. The implementation is done using the MATLAB Genetic Algorithm Toolbox developed by Chipperfield et al. [19].

6   Applications to Medical Images

6.1   Breast Tissue Images

The tissue specimens were fixed in 4% buffered formaldehyde, mounted in paraffin and cut into 4 μm thick sections. Immunohistochemical staining was then performed as follows. A primary antibody (Cam 5.2; Becton Dickinson Immuncytometry Systems, USA) was used to bind to the low molecular weight keratin of the epithelial cells. Detection of the primary antibody was performed using Dako ChemMate(tm) Envision(tm) Detection Kit (DAKO A/S, Denmark). For visualization of the binding site, Vector SG Substrate Kit (Vector Laboratories, USA) ware used. These procedures stained the epithelium black. The specimens were then stained with the Feulgen reaction which stained the nuclei red.

After preparation, the tissue samples were observed using a Leica DM RXE microscope. A magnification of 10 $\times$ was used in all experiments. The microscope was connected to a Leica DC 200 digital camera, allowing the images to be recorded onto a personal computer. Color images were 1280 $\times$ 1024 pixel matrices, with a resolution of 1.03 $\times$ 1.03 μm.

From each sample 10 images were acquired. Samples were collected from different patients and classified by the pathologist in four distinct classes. A total of 200 images has been employed in the present study.

For this research we considered two malignant conditions, namely ductal cancer and lobular cancer and a benign condition called fibroadenosis. Images of normal tissue were also acquired. Examples of images of different tissues are shown in Fig. 3.

6.2   Image Preprocessing

The original color images have been transformed to binary images through a segmentation procedure. This procedure is fully automatic and it has been applied to all the images used in the present study.

First the intensity non uniformities present in the images are corrected using the iterative spline fitting algorithm described in [20].

Then a fuzzy clustering method, the fuzzy c-means algorithm, has been used to separate different colors. This algorithm is an optimal approach that minimizes the objective function in an iterative procedure. It is widely used in image processing, especially for color image segmentation [21]. Using the fuzzy c-means, images were segmented in regions having three different values, based on color. One value has been used for the epithelial cells (black in the original images), another value for to the nuclei (red in the original images) and the third value for the remaining structures.

In these images there are numerous isolated nuclei that are not of interest for our study. Therefore a conditional dilation process has been used to remove them [16]. A morphological dilation has been applied to the regions belonging to epithelial cells, with the condition that only the regions containing nuclei that touch the starting regions should be connected. In the final binary images (see Fig. 4), the white objects are the epithelial cells together with their nuclei.

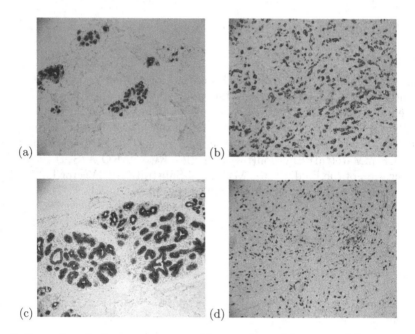

Fig. 3. Examples of microscopic image of breast tissue: (a) normal, (b) ductal carcinoma, (c) fibroadenosis, (d) lobular carcinoma.

6.3   Filter Optimization and Image Classification

On the binary images we applied the proposed method with the goal of classifying them in two classes: cancerous and not cancerous tissue.

In the training phase, we used the opening operator and we optimized four structuring elements. The chromosomes were composed of four fields, containing shape and size of the four structuring elements. The shapes we considered are: circle, square, diamond and octagon. Combination of morphological operators as well as the utilization of multiple structuring elements can improve the performance of morphological-based filters. So, in this experiment the filter sought was a sequence of opening using the four structuring elements codified in the chromosomes. The algorithm was trained using one image containing normal tissue and one image with cancerous tissue, shown in Fig. 4. The fitness used is:

$$fitness = -S(normal) + S(cancer) \qquad (8)$$

The GA options used are: roulette wheel selection, two point crossover, elitism. The genetic operators have been applied straightforward on our chromosome representation. We performed several experiments using the following GA parameter: population size = 300, iteration number = 300, mutation probability varying between 0.01 and 0.05, crossover probability varying between 0.5 and 0.7. Each GA run takes about 2 hours using the MATLAB Genetic Algorithm Toolbox [19].

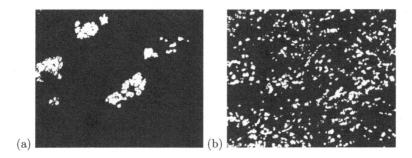

Fig. 4. Example of segmented images to which the GA are directly applied: (a) normal tissue, (b) cancerous tissue. White objects are epithelial cells and their nuclei.

The structuring elements most frequently selected at the end of training phase have diamond or octagon shapes. Examples of evolved sequences of structuring elements are shown in Fig. 5.

Fig. 5. Examples of evolved sequences of structuring elements

In the implementation phase, the filter obtained is then used to classify the 200 images contained in our data set. The correlation between the image before and after the filtering is used as a feature for the classification. The means and standard deviations of the correlation for the four groups of images used in this study are listed in Table 1. It can be noted that these values can easily be used to distinguish tissues having different pathologies. The mean correlation between original and filtered images is considerably lower in both ductal and lobular carcinoma than in normal tissue. Fibroadenosis mean value is lower that the value obtained for normal tissue, but still considerably higher than values obtained for the cancerous tissue.

The classification is done by setting a threshold on the correlation. Classification results reported in Table 2 are obtained using 0.5 as threshold value.

The overall correct classification is 87%, but it is worth to note all the images of cancerous tissue classified as non cancerous were collected from a sample that presents a cell organization very different from all the other cases.

Moreover we should note that these results are achieved by training the algorithm on only two images (normal and ductal cancer) and using the filter obtained on a very larger number of images containing also different pathologies as fibroadenosis and lobular cancer. Fibroadenosis is not a cancerous alteration and in most of the case has been correctly classified. Lobular cancer has been correctly identified in 100% of cases.

Table 1. Correlations between original and filtered image: mean ± standard deviation of each image class.

Class	correlation
normal tissue	0.714 ± 0.143
fibroadenosis	0.608 ± 0.170
ductal cancer	0.344 ± 0.214
lobular cancer	0.178 ± 0.108

Table 2. Classification results.

True class	Classified as normal	cancer
normal tissue	71	9
fibroadenosis	33	7
ductal cancer	10	30
lobular cancer	0	40

7 Conclusions

In this paper an application of GA to mathematical morphology is presented along with experimental results on synthetic and medical images. The optimized morphological filters have been used for image classification based on correlation measure.

The encouraging results obtained so far suggested that the method could be extended in many directions. First of all, we used only the opening operator. other morphological operators can be investigated. Second, we used only a small subset of the possible structuring elements, all of them having regular shape. Experiments with many other structuring elements can be performed, especially including irregular shaped ones. As concern the fitness function, we used a simple sum of the two similarities. Other techniques to combine the two objectives can be investigated.

Larger set of images could be used during the training. Moreover, the images used in the presented study were selected by a pathologist as representative examples of different alterations. In normal practice images may present mixed alterations, and different grades of cancer. We believe that the proposed method can conveniently deal also with these images, in fact the correlation can be an index somehow related to the presence and extent of cancerous tissue. A more accurate method to help the pathologist in the important recognition task of different grades of cancer can be a convenient extension of our method.

Finally, the classification is done by using a simple threshold on the correlation. Other classification rules can be used, and the correlation can be combined with other features extracted from the images.

Acknowledgments. We would like to thank the anonymous reviewers for their valuable comments.

References

1. Ballerini, L., Franzén, L.: Granulometric feature extraction for cancerous tissue classification in breast images. In: Proc. VIIP2003, 3rd IASTED International Conference on Visualization, Imaging, and Image Processing, Benalmádena, Spain (2003)

2. Ballerini, L., Franzén, L.: Fractal analysis of microscopic images of breast tissue. WSEAS Transactions on Circuits **2** (2003) 270–275
3. Serra, J., Soille, P., eds.: Mathematical morphology and its applications to image processing. Computational Imaging and Vision. Kluwer Academic Publishers, Dordrecht (1994)
4. Serra, J.: Image Analysis and Mathematical Morphology. Academic Press, London (1982)
5. Schonfeld, D., Goutsias, J.: Optimal morphological pattern restoration from noisy binary images. IEEE Transactions on Pattern Analysis and Machine Intelligence **13** (1991) 14–29
6. Schonfeld, D.: Optimal structuring elements for the morphological pattern restoration of binary images. IEEE Transactions on Pattern Analysis and Machine Intelligence **16** (1994) 589–601
7. Harvey, N.R., Marshall, S.: The use of genetic algorithms in morphological filter design. Signal Processing: Image Communication (1996) 55–71
8. Hamid, M.S., Harvey, N.R., Marshall, S.: Genetic algorithm optimization of multidimensional grayscale soft morphological filters with applications in film archive restoration. IEEE Transactions on Circuits and Systems for Video Technology **13** (2003) 406–416
9. Huttunen, H., Kuosmanen, P., Koskinen, L., Astola, J.: Optimization of soft morphological filters by genetic algorithms. In: Proc. SPIE Image Algebra and Mophological Image Processing V, San Diego, CA (1994)
10. Yoda, I., Yamamoto, K., Yamada, H.: Automatic acquisition of hierarchical mathematical morphology procedures by genetic algorithms. Image and Vision Computing **17** (1999) 749–760
11. Zmuda, M.A., Tamburino, L.A., Rizki, M.M.: An evolutionary learning system for synthesizing complex morphological filters. IEEE Transactions on Systems, Man and Cybernetics **26** (1996) 645–653
12. Rizki, M.M., Zmuda, M.A., Tamburino, L.A.: Evolving patter recognition systems. IEEE Transactions on Evolutionary Computation **6** (2002) 594–609
13. Quintana, M., Poli, R., Claridge, E.: Genetic programming for mathematical morphology algorithm design on binary images. In Sasikumar, M., ed.: Proceedings of the International Conference KBCS-2002, Mumbai, India, (2002) 161–170
14. Asano, A.: Unsupervised optimization of nonlinear image processing filters using morphological opening/closing spectrum and genetic algorithm. IEICE Trans. Fundamentals **E83-A** (2002) 275–282
15. Loncaric, S., Dhawan, A.P.: Near-optimal mst-based shape description using genetic algorithm. Pattern Recognition **28** (1995) 571–579
16. Gonzalez, R., Woods, R.: Digital image processing. 2nd edn. Prentice hall, Upper Saddle River, New Jersey (2001)
17. Serra, J.: Morphological filtering: an overview. Signal Processing **38** (1994) 3–11
18. Soille, P.: Morphological Image Analysis. Springer-Verlag, Berlin (1999)
19. Chipperfield, A., Fleming, P., Pohlheim, H., Fonseca, C.: Genetic algorithm toolbox for use with MATLAB. Technical report, Department of Automatic Control and Systems Engineering, University of Sheffield, Sheffield, England (1995)
20. Lindblad, J., Bengtsson, E.: A comparison of methods for estimation of intensity nonuniformities in 2D and 3D microscope images of fluorescence stained cells. In: Proc. 12th Scandinavian Conference on Image Analysis, Bergen, Norway (2001) 264–271
21. Chi, Z., Yan, H., Pham, T.: Fuzzy algorithms: with application to image processing and pattern recognition. World Scientific, Singapore (1996)

Image Segmentation by a Genetic Fuzzy c-Means Algorithm Using Color and Spatial Information

Lucia Ballerini[1], Leonardo Bocchi[2], and Carina B. Johansson[1]

[1] Dept. of Technology, Örebro University
Fakultetsgatan 1, 70182 Örebro, Sweden
lucia@cb.uu.se,Carina.Johansson@tech.oru.se
[2] Dept. of Electronics and Telecommunications, University of Florence
Via S.Marta 3, 50139 Firenze, Italy
leo@asp.det.unifi.it

Abstract. This paper describes a new clustering algorithm for color image segmentation. We combine the classical fuzzy c-means algorithm (FCM) with a genetic algorithm (GA), and we modify the objective function of the FCM for taking into account the spatial information of image data and the intensity inhomogeneities. An application to medical images is presented. Experiments show that the proposed algorithm provides a useful method for image segmentation, without the need of a prefiltering step for background estimation. Moreover, the segmentation of noise images is effectively improved.

1 Introduction

Applications with color images are becoming increasingly prevalent nowadays. Segmentation is usually the starting point for any subsequent analysis. Many image segmentation techniques are available in the literature with regard to gray tone images [1]. The literature on color image segmentation is not that rich as it is for gray tone images even if colors are very important image features [2].

In many real life application, where prior knowledge about the colors of the object may be difficult to gather, clustering technique can be used for segmentation [3]. The fuzzy c-means clustering algorithm (FCM) is one of the best known and the most widely used clustering technique [4,5]. However FCM suffers from some limitations. In fact, there may be a number of problem associates with this approach such as cluster center initialization, existence of local minima, and the selection of several parameters. Various authors proposed the use of Genetic Algorithms (GA) [6] to overcome some of these limits and reported promising results [7,8]. Moreover FCM exploits the homogeneity of data only in the feature space and does not adapt to their local characteristics. This is a major drawback of the use of FCM in image segmentation, because it does not take into account the spatial distribution of pixels in images.

We propose a modification of the FCM in order to deal with these limitations. Our method not only combines the FCM algorithm with a GA, but at the same time optimizes other parameters for taking into account the spatial relation

G.R. Raidl et al. (Eds.): EvoWorkshops 2004, LNCS 3005, pp. 260–269, 2004.
© Springer-Verlag Berlin Heidelberg 2004

between neighbor pixels and the uneven illumination of microscopic images. In fact the use of GA, as optimization, conveniently allows the addition of new terms in the objective function.

The outline of the paper is as follow: in Section 2 a description of the fuzzy c-means algorithm is given, along with its standard implementation, a brief discussion of its limitation and some improvements proposed in literature, with further consideration for GA implementations. The method is described in Section 3, first we explain how we include neighborhood information and background estimation by adding terms in the objective function of the FCM, then we describe the GA minimization. In Section 4 we present an application of our method to color image segmentation, in particular to histological images of bone implants.

2   Fuzzy c-Means Clustering Algorithm

The standard FCM algorithm is based on the minimization of the following objective function:

$$J_m(U,V) = \sum_{i=1}^{c} \sum_{k=1}^{n} u_{ik}^m \|\mathbf{x}_k - \mathbf{v}_i\|^2 \tag{1}$$

where:

- $\mathbf{x}_1, \mathbf{x}_2, ..., \mathbf{x}_n$ are n data sample vectors;
- $V = \{\mathbf{v}_1, \mathbf{v}_2, ..., \mathbf{v}_c\}$ are cluster centers;
- $U = [u_{ik}]$ is a $c \times n$ matrix, where u_{ik} is the ith membership value of the kth input sample $\mathbf{x}_k$, such that $\sum_{i=1}^{c} u_{ik} = 1$
- $m \in [1, \infty)$ is an exponent weight factor that determines the amount of "fuzziness" of the resulting classification.

If we assume that the norm operator $\| \cdot \|$ represents the standard Euclidean distance, the objective function is the sum of the squared Euclidean distances between each input sample and its corresponding cluster center, with the distance weighted by the fuzzy membership.

The standard FCM algorithm is iterative and consists of the following steps:

1. Fix the number of clusters c and choose the exponent weight m. Initialize the membership u_{ik} randomly or based on an approximation.
2. For $i = 1, 2, ..., c$, calculate the cluster centers V using:

$$\mathbf{v}_i = \frac{\sum_{k=1}^{n} u_{ik}^m x_{ik}}{\sum_{k=1}^{n} u_{ik}^m} \tag{2}$$

3. For $i = 1, 2, ..., c$ and $k = 1, 2, ..., n$, update the membership u_{ik} using:

$$u_{ik} = \frac{1}{\sum_{j=1}^{c} \left(\frac{\|\mathbf{x}_k - \mathbf{v}_i\|}{\|\mathbf{x}_k - \mathbf{v}_j\|} \right)^{2/(m-1)}} \tag{3}$$

4. Repeat steps 2. and 3. until the value of J_m is no longer decreasing, i.e. change in U is smaller than a pre-specified value ϵ.

As pointed out by several authors [9,10], the FCM algorithm always converges to strict local minima of J_m starting from an initial guess of u_{ik}, but different choices of initial u_{ik} might lead to different local minima.

Various methods have been proposed to improve and further automate the fuzzy clustering, in particular to reduce computational time and to look for a global minimum. Cannon et al. [4] suggested an approximate version of the algorithm that reduce the computational overhead. Al-Sultan et al. [11] introduce a simulated annealing algorithm to solve the fuzzy clustering problem globally. Some implementations provide methods for the initial values of the cluster centers [9]. Several works on validity criteria can be found in literature [3,12].

Bezdek et al. [7,8] introduces a general approach based on GA for optimizing a broad class of clustering criteria. Since the cluster centers are the only variable used by the GA, they reformulate the objective function, by substituting (3) in (1), The resulting reformulated FCM functional is:

$$R_m(V) = \sum_{k=1}^{n} \left(\sum_{i=1}^{c} \|\mathbf{x}_k - \mathbf{v}_i\|^{1/(1-m)} \right)^{(1-m)} \tag{4}$$

They demonstrate [13] that this functional is fully equivalent to the original one for each clustering criterion (hard, fuzzy and probabilistic). Their experiments show that GA can ameliorate the difficulty of choosing an initialization. GA are generally able to find the lowest known value of the objective function, avoid the less desirable solutions on data sets with several local extrema, and always avoid degenerate partitions.

Other works that combine GA with FCM have been proposed. The common structure of these methods is the use of GA for finding prototypes in FCM, while they differ in the cluster properties which are codified in the chromosomes (center [14], radius [15], number [16], or partition matrices [17,18]), or in the selection of the objective function (the FCM functional [7,8] or the partition coefficient [14], or the cluster validity index [16]).

3   Proposed Method

Our task is to use the FCM algorithm for color image segmentation. In particular we are interested in the segmentation of microscopic images of histological sections. A sample image is shown in Fig. 1. The black part is the implant, the purple/bluish area is bone, the light part is non-bone areas. A more accurate description of sample preparation and image acquisition can be found in Section 4.

We implemented a genetic version of FCM algorithm (in the following referred as GA-FCM): the GA operate on cluster centers using as fitness function the reformulated FCM functional (4). Our results were quite similar to that one obtained by previous authors. We noticed that GA helped to overcome the difficulties related to initialization and local minima of the FCM, but, the final image segmentation was not completely acceptable in our case.

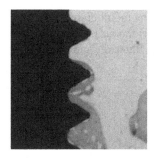

Fig. 1. Example of histological section with implant insertion (original is in color), full image (left) and particular (right)

In fact, the results obtained using the FCM algorithm, both in the classical version and in the genetic implementation, are negatively affected by the presence of noise in the image. We have considered two possible sources of noise: the first one is a low-frequency noise that appears as a non-uniform background; the second one is a high-frequency noise, that comes into sight as isolated points of contrasting color. The presence of non-uniform background is commonly caused by uneven illumination of the field of view of the microscope. Isolated dark points, in our images, can be the cell nuclei. They are present both in the soft tissue and in the bone.

3.1   Noise Removal

As already noticed in literature, the FCM applied in image segmentation operate "myopically" by classifying each pixel of the image using only information about the current point [19]. Classical attempts to introduce spatial context in the segmentation procedures are based on relaxation labeling methods, or more recently, on the idea of fuzzy-connectedness [20]. Few authors address this problem by incorporating spatial continuity in the FCM algorithm. Tolias et al. [19] add or subtract a small positive constant to the membership value of a pixel based on the correlation with its 8-connected neighborhood. Liew et al. [21] introduce a dissimilarity index that allows spatial interaction between image voxels of 3-D magnetic resonance images.

We modify the membership function in order to take into account the properties of a local neighborhood in a way that the membership of each pixel results as a weighted sum of the pixel membership and the memberships of the pixels in the 3×3 neighborhood S. In order to obtain an isotropic behavior, weights need to depend only on the distance of the selected pixel from the center. Therefore, assuming S_1 as the 4-connected neighborhood of the pixel k and S_2 as the 4-diagonal neighborhood of the pixel (see Fig. 2), the membership function to a generic cluster i ($i = 1, 2, ..., c$) is modified as follows:

$$\mu_{ik} = a_0 u_{ik} + a_1 \sum_{j \in S_1} u_{ij} + a_2 \sum_{j \in S_2} u_{ij} \tag{5}$$

where u_i is the membership function of the FCM algorithm. This modified membership function can be also described as the convolution product of the original membership function and the matrix A_i defined as:

$$A_i = \begin{pmatrix} a_{2,i} \, a_{1,i} \, a_{2,i} \\ a_{1,i} \, a_{0,i} \, a_{1,i} \\ a_{2,i} \, a_{1,i} \, a_{2,i} \end{pmatrix} \tag{6}$$

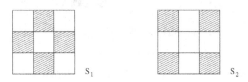

Fig. 2. Neighborhood used for sets S_1 and S_2

3.2   Background Model

The approach which is commonly used to deal with the presence of inhomogeneities in the background involves a two step procedure: in the first step the background level is estimated and removed. Afterward the segmentation procedure is applied. The methods described in the literature are mainly developed for magnetic resonance images [22]; a comparison of methods for estimation of intensity non-uniformities in microscope images is done in [23].

We propose to integrate the background removal process and the FCM algorithm: the GA is used to minimize the objective functional (Eq. 4) by varying both the cluster centers and a suitable description of the background. This allows the GA to search for the background parameters which provide the best discrimination between clusters.

We assume the background can be approximated as a function $b(x, y)$, whose values are in RGB color space, that linearly varies on the image:

$$b(x, y) = \left\{ d_o^R + d_x^R x + d_y^R y, d_o^G + d_x^G x + d_y^G y, d_o^B + d_x^B x + d_y^B y \right\} \tag{7}$$

where d_o, d_x and d_y are unknown coefficients, which will be determined as part of the minimization process.

Therefore, we apply the FCM algorithm to the difference image:

$$B(x, y) = I(x, y) - b(x, y) \tag{8}$$

As the FCM algorithm is insensitive to the addition of a constant level to the image, we remove the first term in each component of (7) assuming $d_o^R = d_o^G = d_o^B = 0$.

A method for estimating background variations using FCM has been proposed [24]. It is worth to note that our line of reasoning is independent of this reference and that the GA optimization allows us a simpler implementation.

3.3   Genetic Optimization

In our work, the parameters that undergo genetic optimization are:
- the cluster centers $\{\mathbf{v}_1, \mathbf{v}_2, ..., \mathbf{v}_c\}$. These vectors are the coordinates of a cluster center in data space. If we use the RGB color space, their structural representation is: $\{v_1^R, v_1^G, v_1^B, v_2^R, v_2^G, v_2^B, ..., v_c^R, v_c^G, v_c^B\}$
- the convolution matrices $\{A_1, A_2, ..., A_c\}$, represented using 3-component vectors $\{\mathbf{a}_1, \mathbf{a}_2, ..., \mathbf{a}_c\} = \{a_{0,1}, a_{1,1}, a_{2,1}, a_{0,2}, a_{1,2}, a_{2,2}, ..., a_{0,c}, a_{1,c}, a_{2,c}\}$
- the background slope coefficients. Accordingly to the RGB color space we use, their representation is: $\{d_x^R, d_y^R, d_x^G, d_y^G, d_x^B, d_y^B\}$.

All parameters are codified in the chromosomes using a Gray-code.

The fitness function is obtained by substituting (8) and (5) into (4).

$$R_m = \sum_{k=1}^{n} \left(\sum_{i=1}^{c} (A_i * \|B_k - \mathbf{v}_i\|)^{1/(1-m)} \right)^{(1-m)} \tag{9}$$

The standard Euclidean distance is used as norm operator, and $m = 2$ is used as fuzzifier value in all our experiments.

The domains of the parameters are:
- centroids are real values that can vary in the color space, $[0, 255]$
- A components are smaller than unit, with the additional constraint that the geometric mean of $\mathbf{a}_i$ is a constant, and equal to unity.
- slope coefficients are constrained in a range $[-0.1, +0.1]$

4   Application to Medical Images

In this section we describe the application of our method to color images segmentation. Our image set is composed of 54 images of histological sections. In the following we describe the sample preparation, and we present the results of the segmentation.

4.1   Image Acquisition

Screw shaped implants (3.75 mm in diameter and 8 mm long) were prepared from titanium rods by machining/turning. The implants were de-greased and sterilized before insertion in the hind legs of mature New Zealand white rabbits. The healing time was 6 weeks. The implants were retrieved together with surrounding bone tissue and immersed in 4% neutral buffered formaldehyde. Sample processing involved dehydration in ethanol and infiltration in resin following embedment of the samples in light curing resin. The cured blocks were divided in the long axis of the implants in modified band saws. Un-decalcified cut and ground samples were processed resulting in 10 μm thin sections [25, 26]. The sections were histologically stained in a mixture of Toluidinblue and pyronin G prior to cover-slipping. The samples were investigated and the image acquisition were performed in an Olympus BX 40 light microscope connected to a microscope digital camera system i.e. Olympus DP11.

Color images are 1368 × 1712 pixel matrices with a resolution of approximately 14 × 14 μm. An example has been previously shown in Fig. 1.

4.2 Image Segmentation

The proposed method has been applied for the segmentation of these images. The results has been compared with results obtained using GA-FCM. All the algorithms have been implemented using the GAucsd-1.4 package [27].

The number of clusters was set to three, which correspond to segmenting images in three color classes: dark (implant), bluish (bone), light (not bone). To be able to compare results, the image background has been estimated using the kernel density estimator described in [23] and the GA-FCM has been applied on the background corrected images. The proposed method has been directly applied to the original images of the same data set.

In the experiments with GA-FCM the following GA parameter are used: population size 560, total generations 120, mutation rate 0.00013 and crossover rate 0.6. The average computational time for each GA run is about 1 hour, on a Pentium III PC running at 500MHz. An example of the obtained segmentation, for a sub-image of size 256, in 3 clusters (implant, bone, soft tissue), is shown in Fig. 3 (left).

The application of the proposed method is computationally more expensive. In our experiments, we first used the same representation precision of the GA-FCM to be able to have an accurate comparison of segmentation results.

In the design of the following experiments our goal is to have a more tractable execution time while keeping reasonably good results, using different encoding. The number of bits for each feature has a lesser effect on the time for calculating the fitness values, but it is worth to note that the GA parameters are chosen according to the genome length, and the total computational time is greatly influenced by these parameters, especially by the population size and the generations.

In the first set of experiments, we used a genome length of 216 bits, obtained encoding the centroid components with 12 bits, the background slopes with 6 bits each, while neighbor information parameters have been encoded with 8 bits each. We have selected the other GA parameters accordingly to the genome size: population size 4000, total generations 300, crossover rate 0.59 and mutation rate 0.00002. Segmentation results, shown in Fig. 3 (right), appear to be improved as concerns both the rejection of dark spots in the tissue and the correct segmentation of bright areas near the implant surface. However, the method requires a higher computational load with respect to the GA-FCM method (about 10 times longer).

To reduce computational time, we have reduced the genome length by encoding the parameters with lesser bits. The second set of experiments has been carried out using an overall genome length of 171 bits (9 bits to encode centroids, while background slopes and neighbor information has been encoded with 6 bits). This is the minimum length which can produce acceptable results, as reported in Fig. 4 (left). In this case, the other parameters of the GA are: population size 1500, total generations 200, crossover rate 0.60 and mutation rate 0.00003.

To further improve performance, we introduced dynamic parameter encoding (DPE) [27]. Using this strategy, the genome length can be reduced to 96 bits,

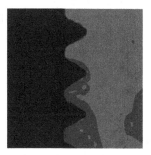 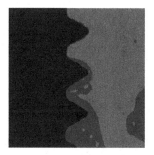

Fig. 3. Segmentation obtained with GA-FCM method (left) and with the proposed method (right)

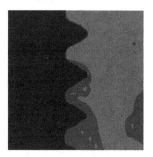 

Fig. 4. Segmentation obtained with reduced genome length (left) and DPE (right)

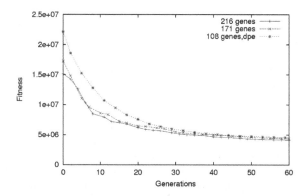

Fig. 5. Evolution of fitness functions averaged over 10 runs

by encoding each parameter with only 4 bits. The GA simulation parameters have been changed to population size 400, total generations 100, crossover rate 0.60 and mutation rate 0.0002. Results obtained with this implementation are reported in Fig. 4 (right). Also, the average execution time is comparable to the GA-FCM method, as the smaller number of evaluations (40000 against 67000) is compensated by the higher complexity of the algorithm.

A comparison of the evolution of fitness functions in the reported experiments is shown in Fig. 5. The graphic shows that, in the long term, the three methods give very similar fitness values, although the number of genes is halved in the last experiment.

5   Conclusions

We have presented a modified fuzzy clustering algorithm specially optimized for image segmentation. It takes into account two important image properties, the intensity inhomogeneity and the spatial pixel correlation. The genetic implementation has been very convenient for including additional terms in the FCM objective functionals, as a spatially weighted membership and a background estimation model. The method, except for the choice of GA parameters, is completely automatic and optimizes the segmentation while simultaneously compensating for background inhomogeneity and reducing noise effects. Our experiments confirm that genetic guided clustering algorithms provide reliable image segmentation results. Further validation studies are necessary, however, to better understand the trade-off between computational time and best possible segmentation results, and therefore to choice the optimal GA parameters.

Acknowledgments. We would like to thank Research Technicians Petra Johansson and Maria Hoffman, Department of Biomaterials/Handicap Research, Göteborg University, Göteborg, Sweden, for preparation of sections and providing the pictures.

References

1. Pal, N.R., Pal, S.K.: A review on image segmentation techniques. Pattern Recognition **26** (1993) 1277–1294
2. Skarbek, W., Koschan, A.: Colour image segmentation - a survey -. Technical Report 94-32, Technical University of Berlin, Berlin, Germany (1994)
3. Jain, A.K.: Cluster analysis. In Young, T.Y., Fu, K.S., eds.: Handbook of Pattern Recognition and Image Processing. Academic Press (1986) 33–57
4. Cannon, R.L., Dave, J.V., Bezdek, J.C.: Efficient implementation of the fuzzy c-means clustering algorithms. IEEE Transactions on Pattern Analysis and Machine Intelligence **PAMI-8** (1986) 248–255
5. Chi, Z., Yan, H., Pham, T.: Fuzzy algorithms: with application to image processing and pattern recognition. World Scientific, Singapore (1996)
6. Goldberg, D.E.: Genetic Algorithms in Search, Optimization, and Machine Learning. Addison-Wesley, Reading, MA (1989)
7. Bezdek, J.C., Hathaway, R.J.: Optimization of fuzzy clustering criteria using genetic algorithms. In: Proc. 1st IEEE Conf. Evolutionary Computation. (1994) 589–549
8. Hall, L.O., Ozyurt, I.B., Bezdek, J.C.: Clustering with a genetically optimized approach. IEEE Transactions on Evolutionary Computation **3** (1999) 103–112

9. Lim, Y.W., Lee, S.U.: On the color image segmentation algorithm based on the thresholding and the fuzzy c-means techniques. Pattern Recognition **23** (1990) 1935–952

10. Xie, X.L., Beni, G.: A validity measure for fuzzy clustering. IEEE Transactions on Pattern Analysis and Machine Intelligence **13** (1991) 841–847

11. Al-Sultan, K.S., Selim, S.Z.: A global algorithm for the fuzzy clustering problem. Pattern Recognition **26** (1993) 1357–1361

12. Dubes, R.C.: Cluster analysis and related issues. In Chen, C.H., Pau, L.F., Wang, P.S.P., eds.: Handbook of Pattern Recognition and Computer Vision. World Scientific (1993) 3–32

13. Hathaway, R.J., Bezdek, J.C.: Optimization of clustering criteria by reformulation. IEEE Transactions on Fuzzy Systems **3** (1995) 241–254

14. Nascimento, S., Moura-Pires, F.: A genetic approach to fuzzy clustering with a validity measure fitness function. Lectures Notes in Computer Science **1280** (1997) 325–335

15. Klawonn, F., Keller, A.: Fuzzy clustering with evolutionary algorithms. Intelligent Systems **13** (1998) 975–991

16. Maulik, U., Bandyopadhyay, S.: Fuzzy partitioning using a real-coded variable-length genetic algorithm for pixel classification. IEEE Transactions on Geoscience and Remote Sensing **41** (2003) 1075 –1081

17. Babu, G.P., Murty, M.N.: Clustering with evolution strategies. Pattern Recognition **27** (1993) 321–329

18. Meng, L., Wu, Q.H., Yong, Z.Z.: A faster genetic clustering algorithm. Lectures Notes in Computer Science **1803** (2000) 22–33

19. Tolias, Y.A., Panas, S.M.: Image segmentation by a fuzzy clustering algorithm using adaptive spatially constrained membership functions. IEEE Transactions on Systems, Man and Cybernetics **28** (1998) 359 –369

20. Udupa, J.K., Samarasekera, S.: Fuzzy connectedness and object definition: Theory, algorithms, and applications in image segmentation. Graphical Models and Image Processing **58** (1996) 246–261

21. Liew, A.W.C., Leung, S.H., Lau, W.H.: Fuzzy image clustering incorporating spatial continuity. Vision, Image and Signal Processing, IEE Proceedings- **147** (2000) 185 –192

22. Gonzalez, R., Woods, R.: Digital image processing. 2nd edn. Prentice hall, Upper Saddle River, New Jersey (2001)

23. Lindblad, J., Bengtsson, E.: A comparison of methods for estimation of intensity nonuniformities in 2D and 3D microscope images of fluorescence stained cells. In: Proc. 12th Scandinavian Conference on Image Analysis, Bergen, Norway (2001) 264–271

24. Pham, D.L., Prince, J.L.: An adaptive fuzzy c-means algorithm for image segmentation in the presence of intensity inhomogeneities. Pattern Recognition Letters **20** (1999) 57–68

25. Johansson, C.B.: On tissue reactions to metal implants. PhD thesis, University of Göteborg, Göteborg, Sweden (1991)

26. Johansson, C.B., Morberg, P.: Importance of ground section thickness for reliable histomorphometrical results. Biomaterials **16** (1995) 91–95

27. Schraudolph, N.N., Grefenstette, J.J.: A user's guide to GAucsd 1.4. Technical Report CS92-249, Computer Science and Engineering Department, University of California, San Diego, La Jolla, CA (1992)

Bond-Issuer Credit Rating with Grammatical Evolution

Anthony Brabazon[1] and Michael O'Neill[2]

[1] Dept. Of Accountancy, University College Dublin, Ireland.
Anthony.Brabazon@ucd.ie
[2] Biocomputing-Developmental Systems
Dept. Of Computer Science & Information Systems
University of Limerick, Ireland.
Michael.ONeill@ul.ie

Abstract. This study examines the utility of Grammatical Evolution in modelling the corporate bond-issuer credit rating process, using information drawn from the financial statements of bond-issuing firms. Financial data, and the associated Standard & Poor's issuer-credit ratings of 791 US firms, drawn from the year 1999/2000 are used to train and test the model. The best developed model was found to be able to discriminate in-sample (out-of-sample) between investment-grade and junk bond ratings with an average accuracy of 87.59 (84.92)% across a five-fold cross validation. The results suggest that the two classifications of credit rating can be predicted with notable accuracy from a relatively limited subset of firm-specific financial data, using Grammatical Evolution.

1 Introduction

The objective of this study is to determine whether Grammatical Evolution (GE) [1], using information drawn from the financial statements of bond-issuing firms, is capable of accurately modelling the corporate bond rating process. Most large firms employ both share and debt capital to provide long-term finance for their operations. The debt capital may be provided by a bank, or may be obtained by selling bonds directly to investors. When a company issues traded debt (bonds), it must obtain a credit rating for the issue from at least one recognised rating agency (Standard and Poor's (S&P), Moody's and Fitches'). The credit rating represents an agency's opinion, at a specific date, of the creditworthiness of a borrower in general (a 'bond-issuer' credit-rating), or in respect of a specific debt issue (a 'bond' credit rating). Therefore it serves as a surrogate measure of the risk of non-payment of interest or capital of the bond. These ratings impact on the borrowing cost, and the marketability of issued bonds.

Although several studies have examined the potential of both statistical and machine-learning methodologies for credit rating prediction [2,3,4,5,6], many of these studies used relatively small sample sizes, making it difficult to generalise strongly from their findings. This study by contrast, uses a large dataset of 791 firms, and introduces GE to this domain. In common with the related corporate failure prediction problem [7], a feature of the bond-rating problem is that there is no clear theoretical framework for guiding the choice of explanatory variables, or model form. Rating agencies assert that their credit rating process involves consideration of both financial and non-financial information about the firm and its industry, but the precise factors utilised, and the related weighting of these factors, are not publicly disclosed by the rating agencies. In the absence of an underlying theory, most published work on credit rating prediction employs a data-inductive modelling approach, using firm-specific financial data as explanatory variables, in an attempt to 'recover' the model used by the rating agencies. This produces a high-dimensional combinatorial problem, as the modeller is attempting to uncover a 'good' set of model inputs, and model form, giving rise to particular potential for an evolutionary automatic programming methodology such as GE. In this initial application of GE to modelling credit ratings, we restrict attention to the binary classification case, discriminating between investment grade vs junk grade ratings. This will be extended to the multi-class case in future work.

The rest of this paper is organized as follows. The next section provides a concise overview of the bond rating domain. We then outline Grammatical Evolution, followed by the data set and methodology utilized. The remaining sections provide the results of the study followed by a number of conclusions.

2 Bond Rating

Several categories of individuals would be interested in a model that could produce accurate estimates of bond ratings. Such a model would be of interest to firms that are considering issuing debt as it would enable them to estimate the likely return investors would require if the debt was issued, thereby providing information for pricing the bonds. The model could also be used to assess the credit-worthiness of firms that have not issued debt and hence do not already have a published bond rating. This information would be useful to bankers or other companies that are considering whether they should extend credit to that firm. Much 'rated' debt is publicly-traded on stock markets, and bond ratings are typically changed infrequently. An accurate bond-rating prediction model could indicate whether the current rating of a bond is still justified. To the extent that an individual investor could predict a bond rerating before other investors foresee it, this may provide a trading edge. In addition, the recent introduction of credit-risk derivatives allows investors to buy 'protection' against the risk of the downgrade of a bond [8]. The pricing of such derivative products requires a quality model for estimating the likelihood of a credit rating change.

Although the precise notation used by individual rating agencies to denote the creditworthiness of a bond or issuer varies, in each case the rating is primarily denoted by a 'letter'. Taking the rating structure of S&P as an example, the ratings are broken down into 10 broad classes. The highest rating is denoted AAA, and the ratings then decrease in the following order, AA, A, BBB, BB, B, CCC, CC, C, D. Ratings between AAA and BBB (inclusive) are deemed to represent 'investment grade', with lower quality ratings deemed to represent debt issues with significant speculative characteristics (junk bonds). A 'C' grade represents a case where a bankruptcy petition has been filed, and a 'D' rating represents a case where the borrower is currently in default on their financial obligations. As would be expected, the probability of default depends strongly on the initial rating which a bond receives.

An initial rating is prepared when a bond is being issued, and this rating is periodically reviewed thereafter by the rating agency. Bonds (or 'issuers') may be re-rated upwards (upgrade) or downwards (downgrade) if firm or environmental circumstances change. A re-rating of a bond below investment grade to 'junk' bond status (such bonds are colorfully termed 'a fallen angel') may trigger a significant sell-off as many institutional investors are only allowed, by external or self-imposed regulation, to hold bonds of 'investment' grade. The practical affect of a bond (or 'issuer') being assigned a lower rather than a higher rating is that its perceived riskiness in the eyes of potential investors increases, and consequently the required interest yield of the bond rises.

3   Grammatical Evolution

Grammatical Evolution (GE) is an evolutionary algorithm that can evolve computer programs in any language [1,9,10,11]. Rather than representing the programs as parse trees, as in GP [12], a linear genome representation is used. A genotype-phenotype mapping is employed such that each individual's variable length binary string, contains in its codons (groups of 8 bits) the information to select production rules from a Backus Naur Form (BNF) grammar. The grammar allows the generation of programs in an arbitrary language that are guaranteed to be syntactically correct. The user can tailor the grammar to produce solutions that are purely syntactically constrained, or they may incorporate domain knowledge by biasing the grammar to produce very specific forms of sentences.

BNF is a notation that represents a language in the form of production rules. It is comprised of a set of non-terminals that can be mapped to elements of the set of terminals, according to the production rules. An simple example BNF grammar is given below, where <expr> is the start symbol from which all programs are generated. These productions state that <expr> can be replaced with either one of <expr><op><expr> or <var>. An <op> can become either +, -, or *, and a <var> can become either x, or y.

```
<expr> ::= <expr><op><expr>  (0)
         | <var>             (1)
  <op> ::= +                 (0)
         | -                 (1)
         | *                 (2)
 <var> ::= x                 (0)
         | y                 (1)
```

The grammar is used in a generative process to construct a program by applying production rules, selected by the genome, beginning from the start symbol of the grammar. In order to select a rule in GE, the next codon value on the genome is generated and placed in the following formula:

$$Rule = Codon\ Value\ MOD\ Num.\ Rules$$

If the first codon integer value was 4, given that we have 2 rules to select from for `<expr>` as in the above example, we get $4\ MOD\ 2\ =\ 0$. `<expr>` will therefore be replaced with `<expr><op><expr>`. Beginning from the the left hand side of the genome codon integer values are generated and used to select rules from the BNF grammar, until one of the following situations arise: (a) A complete program is generated. This occurs when all the non-terminals in the expression being mapped are transformed into elements from the terminal set of the BNF grammar. (b) The end of the genome is reached, in which case the wrapping operator is invoked. This results in the return of the genome reading frame to the left hand side of the genome once again. The reading of codons will then continue unless an upper threshold representing the maximum number of wrapping events has occurred during this individuals mapping process. (c) In the event that a threshold on the number of wrapping events has occurred and the individual is still incompletely mapped, the mapping process is halted, and the individual assigned the lowest possible fitness value. A full description of GE can be found in [1].

4   Experimental Approach

The dataset consists of financial data of 791 non-financial US companies, along with their associated bond-issuer credit-rating, drawn from the S&P Compustat database. Of these companies, 57% have an investment-grade rating (AAA, AA, A, or BBB), and 43% have a junk rating. To allow time for the preparation of year-end financial statements, the filing of these statements with the Securities and Exchange Commission (S.E.C), and the development of a bond rating opinion by Standard and Poor rating agency, the bond rating of the company as at 30 April 2000, is matched with financial information drawn from their financial statements as at 31 December 1999. A subset of 600 firms was randomly sampled from the total of 791 firms, to produce two groups of 300 'investment' grade and 300 junk rated firms. The 600 firms were randomly allocated to the training set (420) or the hold-out sample (180), ensuring that each set was equally balanced between investment and non-investment grade ratings.

A total of eight financial variables were selected for inclusion in this study. The selection of these variables was guided both by prior literature in bankruptcy prediction [13,14], literature on bond rating prediction [15,5], and by preliminary statistical analysis. The financial ratios chosen during the selection process were:

i.   Current ratio
ii.   Retained earnings to total assets
iii. Interest coverage
iv.   Debt ratio

v.   Net margin
vi.   Market to book value
vii. Total assets
viii. Return on total assets

The objective in selecting a set of proto-explanatory variables is to choose financial variables that vary between companies in different bond rating classes, and where information overlaps between the variables are minimised. Comparing the means of the above ratios for the two groups of ratings, reveals a statistically significant difference at both the 5% and the 1% level, and as expected, the financial ratios in each case, for the investment ratings are stronger than those for the junk ratings. The only exception is the current ratio, which is stronger for the junk rated companies, possibly indicating a preference for these companies to hoard short-term liquidity, as their access to long-term capital markets is weak. A correlation analysis between the selected ratios indicates that most of the cross-correlations are less than $| 0.20 |$, with the exception of the debt ratio and (Retained Earnings/Total Assets) ratio pairing, which has a correlation of -0.64. The grammar adopted in this study is as follows:

```
<lc> ::= if( <expr> <relop> <expr> ) class=''Junk''; else class=''Investment Grade'';

<expr> ::= ( <expr> ) + ( <expr> ) | <coeff> * <var>

<var> ::= var3[index] | var4[index] | var5[index] | var6[index]
        | var7[index] | var8[index] | var9[index] |var10[index]
        | var11[index]

<coeff> ::= ( <coeff> ) <op> ( <coeff> ) | <float>

<op> ::= + | - | *

<float> ::= 9 | 8 | 7 | 6 | 5 | 4 | 3 | 2 | 1 | -1 | .1

<relop> ::= <=
```

where **var3** = Current Ratio, **var4** = Retained Earnings to total assest, **var5** = Interest Coverage, **var6** = Debt Ratio, **var7** = Net Margin, **var8** = Market to book value, **var9** = Total Assets, **var10** = ln (Total Assets), **var11** = Return on total assets.

5   Results

The results from our experiments are now provided. Each of the GE experiments is run for 100 generations, with variable-length, one-point crossover at a probability of 0.9, one point bit mutation at a probability of 0.01, roulette selection, and steady-state replacement. Results are reported for two population sizes (500 and 1000), and for two distinct fitness functions. To assess the stability of the results across different randomisations of the dataset between training and test data, we recut the dataset five times, maintaining an equal balance of investment and non-investment grade ratings in the resulting training and test datasets.

In our initial experiments, fitness is defined as the number of correct classifications obtained by an evolved discriminant rule. The results for the best individual of each cut of the dataset, where 30 independent runs were performed for each cut, averaged over all five randomisations of the dataset, for both the 500 and 1000 population sizes, are given in Table 1.

Table 1. Performance of the best evolved rules on their training and out-of-sample datasets, averaged over all five randomisations.

	Fitness	TP	TN	FP	FN
Train GEBOND500	0.8615	185.2	175.8	33.4	24.6
Train GEBOND1000	0.8678	183.2	180.4	28.8	26.6
Out-Sample GEBOND500	0.8560	77.6	75.8	13.6	12.2
Out-Sample GEBOND1000	0.8626	77.8	76.6	12.6	12

To assess the overall hit-ratio of the developed models (out-of-sample), Press's Q statistic [16] was calculated for each model. In all cases, the null hypothesis, that the out-of sample classification accuracies are not significantly better than those that could occur by chance alone, was rejected at the 1% level. A t-test of the hit-ratios also rejected a null hypothesis that the classification accuracies were no better than chance at the 1% level. Across all the data recuts, the best individual achieved an 87.56 (84.36)% accuracy in-sample (out-of-sample) when the population size was 500, with the best individual across all data recuts in the population=1000 case obtaining an accuracy of 87.59 (84.92)% accuracy in-sample (out-of-sample). Although the average out-of-sample accuracy obtained for population=1000 slightly exceeds that for population=500, the difference was not found to be statistically significant. A plot of the best and average fitness on each cut of the in-sample dataset, for the population=500 case, can be seen in Figure 1, and for case where population=1000 in Figure 2.

A second series of experiments were undertaken using a fitness measure that takes into consideration negative classifications. The fitness measure adopted earlier does not explicitly take into consideration the the amount of under and over-prediction represented by false negatives and false positives, respectively. A more general measure considers the correlation between the prediction and the observed reality [17]. A correlation measure indicates how much better a particular predictor is better than random predictions, and has been adopted previously in GP [18]. In the case of a binary classification problem the correlation measure, C, and the calculation of a corresponding fitness value, is given below.

$$C = \frac{(N_{tp} * N_{tn} - N_{fn} * N_{fp})}{\sqrt{(N_{tn} + N_{fn}) * (N_{tn} + N_{fp}) * (N_{tp} + N_{fn}) * (N_{tp} + N_{fp})}}$$

$$Fitness = \frac{(C + 1)}{2}$$

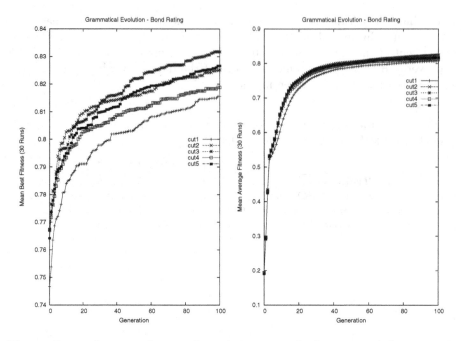

Fig. 1. Best and average fitness values of 30 runs on the five recuts of the in-sample dataset with a population size of 500.

where N_{tp}, N_{tn}, N_{fp}, N_{fn} are the number of true positives, true negatives, false positives, and false negatives respectively. A fitness value of zero means there is no correlation to the observed cases, a value of 0.5 means the classification accuracy is no better than random, and a value of 1.0 means a perfect correlation to observed cases. Results using this fitness measure for population sizes of both 500 and 1000 are provided in Table 2. Assessing the out-of-sample hit-ratio of the developed models using Press's Q statistic rejects the null hypothesis, that the out-of sample classification accuracies are not significantly better than those that could occur by chance alone, at the 1% level, however the models developed using this fitness function did not outperform those developed using the initial fitness function. As for the initial fitness function, the average classification accuracy (out-of-sample) was slightly higher for the case where population=1000 than for population=500, but the difference was not statistically significant.

Examining the structure of the best individual in the case where the initial fitness function was utilised and where population=500 shows that the evolved discriminant function had the following form:

IF $(10 + 16$ var6 -9 var4 -2 var9$) \geq 0$ THEN 'Junk' ELSE 'Investment Grade' where var6 is *Debt Ratio*, var4 is $\frac{Retained\ Earnings}{Total\ Assets}$, and var9 is *Total Assets*.

In the case where population=1000 the best evolved discriminant function had a similar form to the above:

IF $(5 + 8$ var6 -4 var4 $-$ var9$) \geq 0$ THEN 'Junk' ELSE 'Investment Grade'

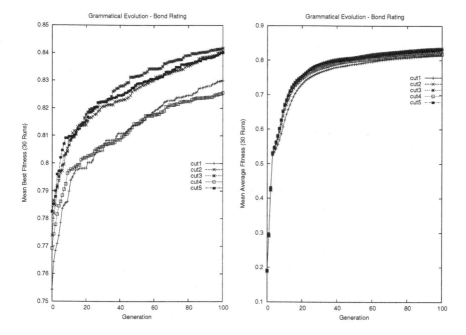

Fig. 2. Best and average fitness values of 30 runs on the five recuts of the in-sample dataset with a population size of 1000.

Table 2. Performance of the best evolved rules on their training and out-of-sample datasets, averaged over all five randomisations.

	Fitness	TP	TN	FP	FN
Train GEBOND500	0.8568	183.8	175.2	34	26
Train GEBOND1000	0.8644	187.8	174.4	34.8	22
Out-sample GEBOND500	0.8033	66	77.8	11.4	23.8
Out-sample GEBOND1000	0.8514	78.8	73.6	15.6	11

Examining the signs of the coefficients of the evolved rules does not suggest that they conflict with common financial intuition. The rules indicate that low/negative retained earnings, low/negative total assets or high levels of debt finance are symptomatic of a firm that has a junk rating. It is noted that similar risk factors have been identified in predictive models of corporate failure which utilise financial ratios as explanatory inputs [7,19]. Conversely, low levels of debt, a history of successful profitable trading, and high levels of total assets are symptomatic of firms that have an investment grade rating.

5.1   Comparison of Results

To provide a benchmark for the results obtained by GE, we compare them with the results obtained on the same recuts of the dataset, using a fully-connected, feedforward multi-layer perceptron (MLP), trained using the backpropagation algorithm. The developed networks utilised all the explanatory variables. The optimal number of hidden-layer nodes was found following experimentation on each separate data recut, and varied between two and four nodes. The classification accuracies for the networks, averaged over all five recuts is provided in Table 3.

Table 3. Performance of the MLPs on the training and out-of-sample datasets, averaged over all five randomisations.

	Fitness	TP	TN	FP	FN
Train MLP	0.8690	181.8	183.2	26.8	28.2
Out-sample MLP	0.8500	75.8	77.2	12.8	14.2

The levels of classification accuracy obtained with the MLP are competitive with earlier research, with for example [15] obtaining an out-of-sample classification accuracy of approximately 88.3%, although it is noted that the size of the dataset in this study was small. Comparing the results from the MLP with those of GE on the initial fitness function (Table 1) suggests that GE has proven competitive with an MLP methodology, in terms of producing a similar classification accuracy on the training data, and slightly out-performing the MLP out-of-sample. Benchmark results were also obtained using an LDA methodology. Utilising the same dataset recuts as GE, LDA produced results (averaged across all five recuts) of 82.74% in-sample, and 85.22% out-of-sample. Again, GE is competitive against these results in terms of classification accuracy. Comparing the results obtained by the linear classifiers (LDA and GE) against those of an MLP, suggests that strong non-linearities between the explanatory variables and the dependent variable are not present.

6   Conclusions and Future Work

The objective of this paper was to assess the utility of the GE methodology to model the corporate bond rating process, using information drawn from the financial statements of bond-issuing firms. Despite using data drawn from companies in a variety of industrial sectors, the developed models showed an impressive capability to discriminate between investment and junk rating classifications. The GE developed models also proved highly competitive with a series of MLP models developed on the same datasets. Several extensions of the methodology in this study are indicated for future work. One route is the inclusion of non-financial company and industry-level information as input variables. A related possibility would be to concentrate on building rating models for individual industrial sectors. We are also extending this study to encompass the multi-class rating prediction problem.

References

1. O'Neill M., Ryan C. (2003) *Grammatical Evolution: Evolutionary Automatic Programming in an Arbitrary Language*, Kluwer Academic Publishers.
2. Ederington, H. (1985). 'Classification models and bond ratings', *Financial Review*, 20(4):237-262.
3. Gentry, J., Whitford, D. and Newbold, P. (1988). 'Predicting industrial bond ratings with a probit model and funds flow components, *Financial Review*, 23(3):269-286.
4. Huang, Z., Chen, H., Hsu, C., Chen, W. and Wu, S. (2003). 'Credit rating analysis with support vector machines and neural networks: a market comparative study', *Decision Support Systems*, (Article in press).
5. Kamstra, M., Kennedy, P. and Suan, T.K. (2001). 'Combining Bond Rating Forecasts Using Logit', *The Financial Review* , 37:75-96.
6. Shin, K. and Han, I. (2001). 'A case-based approach using inductive indexing for corporate bond rating', *Decision Support Systems*, 32:41-52.
7. Brabazon, T., O'Neill, M., Matthews, R., and Ryan, C. (2002). Grammatical Evolution and Corporate Failure Prediction, In *Proceedings of the Genetic and Evolutionary Computation Conference (GECCO 2002)*, Spector et. al. Eds., July 9-13, 2002, pp. 1011-1019, New York: Morgan Kaufmann.
8. Altman, E. (1998). 'The importance and subtlety of credit rating migration', *Journal of Banking & Finance*, 22:1231-1247.
9. O'Neill, M. (2001). Automatic Programming in an Arbitrary Language: Evolving Programs in Grammatical Evolution. PhD thesis, University of Limerick, 2001.
10. O'Neill M., Ryan C. (2001) Grammatical Evolution, *IEEE Trans. Evolutionary Computation.* 2001.
11. Ryan C., Collins J.J., O'Neill M. (1998). Grammatical Evolution: Evolving Programs for an Arbitrary Language. *Lecture Notes in Computer Science 1391, Proceedings of the First European Workshop on Genetic Programming*, pp. 83-95, Springer-Verlag.
12. Koza, J. (1992). *Genetic Programming*, MIT Press.
13. Altman, E. (1993). *Corporate Financial Distress and Bankruptcy*, New York: John Wiley and Sons Inc.
14. Morris, R. (1997). *Early Warning Indicators of Corporate Failure: A critical review of previous research and further empirical evidence*, London: Ashgate Publishing Limited.
15. Dutta, S. and Shekhar, S. (1988). 'Bond rating: a non-conservative application of neural networks, *Proceedings of IEEE International Conference on Neural Networks*, II, 443-450.
16. Hair, J., Anderson, R., Tatham, R. and Black, W. (1998). *Multivariate Data Analysis*, Upper Saddle River, New Jersey: Prentice Hall.
17. Matthews, B.W. (1975). Comparison of the predicited and observed secondary structure of T4 phage lysozyme, *Biochemica et Biophysica Acta.*, 405:442-451.
18. Koza, J. (1994). *Genetic Programming II.* MIT Press.
19. Brabazon, T. and O'Neill, M. (2003). Anticipating Bankruptcy Reorganisation from Raw Financial Data using Grammatical Evolution, Proceedings of EvoIASP 2003, *Lecture Notes in Computer Science (2611): Applications of Evolutionary Computing*, edited by Raidl, G., Meyer, J.A., Middendorf, M., Cagnoni, S., Cardalda, J. J. R., Corne, D. W., Gottlieb, J., Guillot, A., Hart, E., Johnson, C. G., Marchiori, E. , pp. 368-378, Berlin: Springer-Verlag.

Using GAs to Create a Waveguide Model of the Oral Vocal Tract

Crispin H.V. Cooper, David M. Howard, and Andy M. Tyrrell

Intelligent Systems Group, Department of Electronics, University of York
{cc26,dh,amt}@ohm.york.ac.uk

Abstract. A Digital Waveguide Mesh is introduced as a method for acoustic modelling. Genetic Algorithms are applied to evolve the structure of a mesh to simulate the human throat and mouth, producing vowel-like sounds. The evolved shapes are compared to actual shapes adopted by the oral vocal tract during speech. The evolutionary methods are "tuned" for implementation on a new hardware device being developed under the POEtic project. Initial results given in this paper are promising.

1   Introduction

Although electronic speech synthesis has existed since the 1960s, research still continues into creating realistic, humanlike sounds. It has been shown in [1] that digital waveguide meshes (DWMs) are a promising area of research for tackling this problem. DWMs allow the creation of acoustic objects, such as a throat, simply by specifying their physical properties i.e. shape and boundary characteristics. A simulated throat can then, for example, be excited at the input (larynx) end with white noise and a whispered sound heard at the output (mouth).

A mesh that provides a realistic spoken or sung sound, will also be useful as an analysis tool for the training of singers. Ongoing projects [7] aim to produce software which can infer the shape of a singer's vocal tract from the sound they create; realistic mesh models might provide a benchmark for these applications. However, real data on the shape of the human vocal tract while in use, is not easily available. The only recorded work relates just to Russian vowels and involved high doses of X-rays [5].

As an alternative to supplying a mesh model with real data, a genetic algorithm is proposed as a means of finding a suitable shape for the mesh. This is well-suited to the problem as there is no obvious mapping between the desired output sound and the mesh shape required to create it; however it is easy to compute a fitness function by comparing the output sound to a "target" sound. Evolvable meshes are being developed as a demonstrator for the POEtic chip [4], a hardware platform designed for rapid experimentation with biologically inspired techniques.

G.R. Raidl et al. (Eds.): EvoWorkshops 2004, LNCS 3005, pp. 280–288, 2004.

The paper is structured as follows: Section 2 introduces digital waveguide meshes in more detail. Sections 3 and 4 present the work on evolving the meshes, while Sections 5 and 6 discuss the results.

2   Waveguide Meshes

Waveguide Meshes were originally described by Van Duyne and Smith in [6]. This section provides a brief introduction; detailed derivations can be found in e.g. [3].

2.1   Background

A waveguide is simply a bidirectional delay line, which is an accurate model of sound propagation in one dimension, as can be seen from the d'Alembert solution to the travelling wave equation:

$$\frac{d^2y}{dt^2} = c^2 \frac{d^2y}{dx^2} \quad \Rightarrow \quad y(x) = \psi_L(x + ct) + \psi_R(x - ct) \tag{1}$$

which shows that a 1-d wave in a medium of constant impedance can be decomposed into two separate signals travelling in opposite directions.

A two- (or higher-)dimensional space can be modelled by connecting such waveguides together in a grid. Each delay line is only one unit (sample) long, and each node on the grid necessitates a scattering junction to distribute the incoming waves as appropriate.

Various mesh topologies have been proposed, but the one used for this paper is the 2-d rectangular-grid mesh, using 4-port scattering junctions. Unlike the 1-d model, the 2-d model is not a perfect reflection of reality as sound does not propagate equally in all directions. However, a high resolution mesh can provide a good approximation.

The 2-d model has the obvious use of modelling membranes such as a drumskin. However, it also exhibits some of the properties of higher-dimensional meshes, such as the ability to contain complex standing waves - thus having a highly customisable frequency dependant response, unlike a string which for a fundamental frequency f can only stabilize at frequencies $f, 2f, 3f$ etc. Thus, a 2-d mesh can be used as an approximation to a higher-dimensional space.

2.2   Scattering Equations

The equation governing the scattering is

$$p_n^{out} = \frac{1}{2} \sum_{i=1}^{4} p_i^{in} - p_n^{in} \tag{2}$$

where p_n^{out} is the value of the nth signal leaving the junction and p_n^{in} is the nth signal arriving at the junction (as shown in Fig. 1).

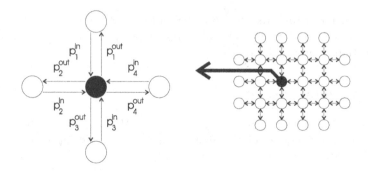

Fig. 1. A 2-d rectangular-grid mesh, showing edge nodes and the scattering equation variables for a single node

2.3   Finite Difference Formulation

Instead of calculating the value of the signal travelling in each direction, the mesh can be represented by a finite difference formulation where each node i has a pressure p_i which is updated every Δt (which depends on the wavespeed) as follows:

$$p_i(t) = \frac{1}{2} \sum_{n \in \mathcal{N}} p_n(t - \Delta t) - p_i(t - 2\Delta t) \tag{3}$$

where $\mathcal{N}$ ranges over the four neighbours of node i. Thus future mesh states can be calculated with only half the data - two values stored per junction, rather than two per connection.

2.4   Edges

At the edges of the mesh, a reflection calculation is performed. A "dummy" junction is connected as defined by

$$p^{out} = \lambda p^{in} \tag{4}$$

where λ is the user-defined coefficient of reflection of the boundary, ranging between -1 and 1. The dummy junction can be connected to all nodes on the edge of a mesh (which may be 3- or even 2-neighbour nodes). In the finite difference formulation, the dummy junctions are implemented as follows:

$$p_i(t) = (1 + \lambda)p_j(t - \Delta t) - \lambda p_i(t - 2\Delta t) \tag{5}$$

This is less efficient and less flexible (2- or 3- neighbour edge nodes cannot be specified) but necessary if the rest of the mesh is to be implemented with a finite difference model.

2.5   Sampling Rate

Equations 2 to 5 are valid for a sampling interval defined by

$$\Delta t = \frac{\Delta x}{c\sqrt{N}} \qquad (6)$$

where c is the speed of wave propagation in the material (whether modelling transverse or longitudinal waves), N is the number of dimensions and Δx is the distance between scattering junctions.

For a small object such as the human vocal tract, a high sampling rate (towards 200kHz) is chosen in order to obtain better spatial resolution in the model - even if only a low output sample rate (for example, 11kHz) is required to satisfy the Nyquist criterion for the audio output itself.

2.6   Three Dimensional Implementation

Various topologies have been successfully used for three-dimensional mesh modelling [8]. However, 3-d meshes contain many more nodes than their 2-d counterparts and therefore bring increased computational complexity. Meanwhile it has been shown in [1] that a two-dimensional mesh alone is capable of producing the effects needed (e.g. alteration of spectral content) to model the human vocal tract.

3   Evolving Waveguide Mesh Shapes

Mesh shapes were evolved to produce vowel sounds as follows.

3.1   Representation

The phenotype consists of a rectangular-grid 2-d finite difference mesh. Using a sampling rate of 44.1kHz (the audio studio standard) gives a spatial resolution of 1.1cm (from (6)), which is considered adequate but not too complex for hardware implementation. The human oral vocal tract (17cm long in the average male) is thus modelled by a mesh 16 nodes in length. The width is variable, but 9 nodes (99mm) was chosen as a maximum which is not exceeded in nature.

For simplicity, symmetry along the long axis was assumed, as was the presence of at least one normal node in the centre of the mesh (otherwise no sound would pass through). Thus, the genotype was defined to be a string of integers g_i such that at each point, the width in nodes w_i of the mesh was

$$w_i = 1 + 2g_i \qquad (7)$$

The coefficient of reflection (λ), was set to be 0.875 on all boundaries except for the mouth, where it was set to -0.875. These figures are close to those suggested in [1] but rounded to a power of two for easy hardware implementation.

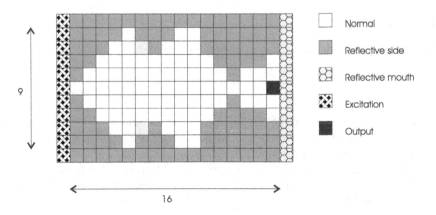

Fig. 2. Sample mesh phenotype

3.2   Fitness Evaluation

The fitness was measured by exciting the mesh at one end and comparing the spectral content of the output (at the other end) to a pre-recorded vowel sound. The excitation took the form of white noise (to simulate a whisper).

To increase the speed of calculation, the output was first downsampled to 11,025Hz. The mesh was given a period of 50 samples during which standing waves could form before the fitness was evaluated.

The spectral comparison is similar to that described in [2]. The individual being evaluated and the target sound are both normalized and transformed to the Fourier domain, where a mean absolute difference between the two spectrograms is computed (excluding DC components). Phase information is discarded.

Two minor variations on this were tried:

- a penalty was added to overly quiet sounds, this being a constant factor multiplied by the difference in peak levels of the target and individual sounds (before normalisation)
- phase information was included

However, neither of these showed better results than those derived from the original fitness function (which are shown in this paper).

3.3   Genetic Algorithm

A mutation-only genetic algorithm was implemented. Mutation changed an integer in the genome at random, and the mutation rate dropped uniformly from 100% to 0% over the first two-thirds of the run, then remained in a "single change only" mode for the remaining third. The population size was chosen to be 40. Elitism and rank were set to 5 - i.e. each generation consisted of the 5 best individuals from the previous generation followed by 35 children. The parent of each child was selected from either the best 5, or another 10 chosen at random (to prevent stagnation). Crossover was not used - the algorithm would probably run better with crossover, but adequate-sounding individuals were achieved without it. A run length of 50 generations was found sufficient; the algorithm often terminated prematurely when the maximum fitness did not improve for more than 10 generations.

4   Results

Figure 3 shows the spectral content of some evolved vowels, compared to the recorded real vowels, for meshes excited with white noise (whispers). The reader will note that they typically match markedly better at low frequencies than elsewhere. This is because the data selected are from the results which "sounded" best and the bias towards matching more in certain parts of the spectrum is thus an artefact of human selection.

For comparison, Fig. 4 shows the average spectrum of ten evolved "ah" vowels, and it can be seen that the close matching regions more evenly distributed accross the whole spectrum, but not as close in any one region as an individual. Also shown is another evolved spectrum for "ah" which appears to match as closely (overall), yet sounds inferior. All the spectra evolved were of high fitness (based on least absolute difference between spectra): thus, the close partial matching of the best sounding spectra suggests that results could be improved by using a fitness function based on psychoacoustic principles.

Figure 5 shows the average shape evolved for each vowel, measured in terms of the diameter at each point along the long axis of the vocal tract. The error bars extend to one standard deviation either side of the mean value. For comparison, the "virtual radii" ($\sqrt{\frac{area}{\pi}}$) of the corresponding human vocal tract area functions [5] are given.

5   Discussion

5.1   Spectral Content

Informal listening to the mesh's audio output suggested that the GA successfully configures the mesh to produce realistic sounding vowels. The close-matching parts of the spectra in Fig. 3, combined with the overall closeness of the average spectra in Fig. 4, also show this.

It is notable that the technique works despite the differences between the model and the real world - in particular the model is both 2-dimensional and simplified for a hardware implementation.

As noted in Sect. 4, the results could be further improved by implementing a fitness function based on psychoacoustics. Intuition suggests that this is unnecessary, as we should be able to evolve a spectrum that actually is the same as a real one, rather than just sounding the same. However psychoacoustics may be a worthwhile route to improve results when using such a simplified model.

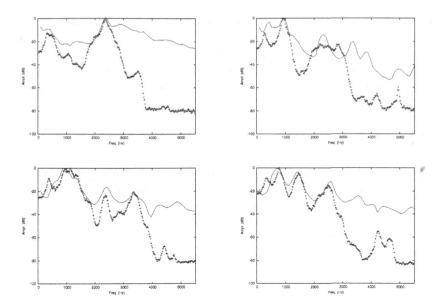

Fig. 3. The whispered "ee", "oo", "er" and "ah" vowels, as in "meet", "boot", "bird", "father" - clockwise from top left. Actual spectra shown with lines, evolved spectra with points

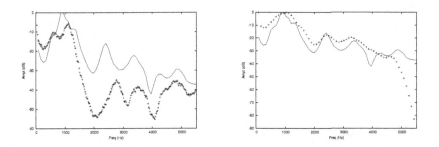

Fig. 4. LEFT: another evolved spectrum for the "ah" vowel. This has similar fitness to that shown in Fig. 3 but is audibly inferior. RIGHT: The average spectrum of ten evolved whispered "ah" vowels

5.2   Evolved Shapes

It should be noted that the standard deviations plotted on graphs of evolved shapes, are so large as to render the results (with respect to shape) insignificant. Clearly the shape of the meshes is not convergent.

In any case there is little matching between the mean evolved shapes and the real shapes. Of course, there was no guarantee that evolution would converge upon the same solution found in nature (although we might learn something in-

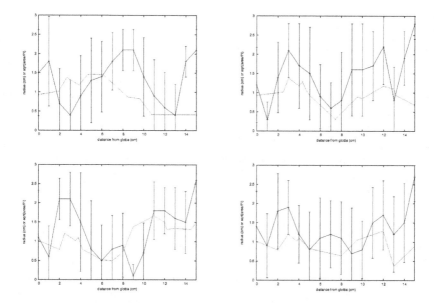

Fig. 5. Average shapes (with standard deviation) evolved for the whispered vowels "ee", "oo", "er", "ah" - clockwise from top left. The dotted line shows the actual shape formed in human throats

teresting if it did)! It is certainly not likely to here, however, given the differences between the model and reality (e.g. the 2-d vs 3-d issue).

If this is to be used as an analysis tool, convergence on shape may be possible by using a better genetic algorithm (with i.e. crossover and adaptive parameters). Evolving a "natural" shape may still be achievable by upgrading to a 3-d model and applying known biological constraints to the shapes which can be evolved. For example, the tracts could be made narrower, area variation could be restricted in certain positions and the resolution to which the area function is simulated could be increased.

5.3   Hardware Implementation

It is intended that these meshes be implemented in hardware (and further experimentation performed) on the POEtic chip, when it becomes available. The chip will contain reconfigurable hardware and a microprocessor for the running of GAs (thus, rapid evolution of meshes will be possible). The hardware (or ontogenetic tissue) can in fact reconfigure itself - thus allowing experimentation with techniques such as growth and self-repair.

As hardware will be limited, and the reflective "edge" cells are the most expensive in terms of silicon area, an experiment was conducted in which only half the number of reflecting cells were used. Alternate edge cells were implemented with the output fixed to zero (which implies $\lambda = 0$). Equally good vowels were produced through evolution, which adapted well to cope with this hack.

6   Conclusions

Digital Waveguide Meshes are a promising tool for the synthesis and analysis of speech and singing. However, real data on the shape of the human throat while in use is hard to obtain. Evolution has been shown to be an effective alternative design method for the shape of DWMs - even though the shapes are not (as yet) convergent, the sounds produced are good.

A question which should be asked from the perspective of audio synthesis is, why limit ourselves to a simulation of reality such as this? It is equally easy to simulate, for example, multidimensional meshes or nonlinear elements. While it is not obvious how to create a useful design from such components, it is possible to explore the design space by evolution.

Acknowledgements. This project is funded by the Future and Emerging Technologies programme (IST-FET) for the European Community, under grant IST-2000-28027 (POETIC). The information provided is the sole responsibility of the authors and does not reflect the Community's opinion. The Community is not responsible for any use that might be made of data appearing in this publication.

References

1. Mullen, J., Howard, D.M. and Murphy, D.T. (2003): Digital waveguide mesh modelling of the vocal tract acoustics. 2003 IEEE Workshop on Applications of Signal Processing to Audio and Acoustics, 119-122.
2. Garcia, Ricardo A. (2001): Automating the design of sound synthesis techniques using evolutionary methods. Proceedings of DAFX-01, Limerick, Ireland.
3. Murphy, D. T. (2002): Digital waveguide mesh modelling for room acoustics. PhD Thesis, University of York.
4. Tyrrell et al. (2003): POEtic tissue: an integrated architecture for bio-inspired hardware. Proceedings of ICES2003, Trondheim, Norway.
5. Childers, D. G. (1999): Speech processing and synthesis toolboxes. Wiley.
6. Van Duyne, S., Smith, J.O. (1993): The 2-d digital waveguide mesh. Proceedings of IEEE WASPAA, NY, USA, September 1993.
7. Rossiter, D.P., Howard, D.M., Downes, M. (1995): A real-time LPC-based vocal tract area display for voice development. Journal of Voice, 8, 4, 314 319.
8. Campos, G. and Howard, D.M. (2000): A paralell 3-d digital waveguide mesh model with tetrahedral topology for toom acoustic simulation. Proceedings of DAFX-00, Verona, 73-78.

Vision-Based Hand Motion Capture Using Genetic Algorithm

Jin-shi Cui and Zeng-qi Sun

State Key Laboratory of Intelligent Technology and Systems,
Department of Computer Science and Technology,
Tsinghua University, Beijing 100084, China
cuijinshi99@mails.tsinghua.edu.cn

Abstract. 3D hand motion capture plays an important role in multi-modal hu-man-computer interfaces. Existing vision-based approaches mainly include two directions: model-based optimization framework and appearance-based learn-ing approach. The main obstacle to handle with human hand motion capture is the high dimensionality associated with a full degree-of-freedom (DOF) ar-ticulated model. In this paper, a novel vision-based 3D hand motion capture al-gorithm is proposed. It views hand pose estimation and motion tracking as search problems and utilizes genetic algorithm (GA). Firstly, a learning inte-grating with optimization approach is introduced to estimate initial hand pose in 3D model based framework. And then a motion tracking method using GA-based particle filter (PF) is proposed to deal with the tracking problem in high-dimensional and multi-modal state space. Experimental results show that pres-ent approach significantly improves performance of motion tracking, especially in high-dimensional configuration space.

1 Introduction

It is an effective approach to make use of human hand movement that has abundant powers of expression as a natural human-computer interface. Some glove-based de-vices have been employed to capture full DOF human hand motion by attaching sen-sors to measure the joint angles and spatial positions of hands directly. Besides glove-based approaches, vision-based techniques provide promising alternatives to capture human hand motion. At the same time, vision systems could be very cost efficient and noninvasive. The potential applications of such systems include video coding, video surveillance, monitoring, remote control, and robots guiding.

Hand motion capture is to find the global hand posture and local finger joint con-figuration in terms of input source and known information. Input maybe a static im-age for so-called pose estimation only or an image sequences for so-called motion tracking over time. Known information maybe pre-obtained plenty of examples with specified motion parameters or a detailed internal structure, such as 3-D hand model including shape model and kinematic model. Existing vision-based hand motion capture methods include two schools of approaches: model-based optimization

G.R. Raidl et al. (Eds.): EvoWorkshops 2004, LNCS 3005, pp. 289–300, 2004.

framework and appearance-based learning approach. Detailed presentation about related work will be given in next section.

A learning integrating with optimization approach in 3-D model based framework is introduced for pose estimation and a motion-tracking scheme with an optimal filter is described in this paper. In learning process, k-nearest neighbor search gives several initial choices from pre-generated samples with known motion parameters. Then the followed GA-based optimization scheme loops over model-image silhouette/edges assignments for optimal parameter search. Such an idea would also work well in the case of other object pose estimation problem, especially for complex ones. In tracking process, a GA-based particle filter method that incorporates GA algorithm in the sequence Monte Carlo method is proposed as a solution of high-dimensional and multi-modal tracking problem.

The rest of this paper is organized as follows. Section 2 will present related approaches for vision-based hand motion capture. In Section 3, GA-based methods will be described in detail, following which we will show test results with both synthetic and real data. Section 5 concludes the paper.

2   Vision-Based Hand Motion Capture

Hand motion capture is an interesting research field that has received much attention in recent years. Many vision-based systems have been developed to capture the 3D motion of a human hand in images or video sequences [1-11].

2.1   3-D Hand Pose Estimation

Computer vision systems that estimate 3D hand pose typically do it in the context of tracking due to the necessary of both automatic initialization and recovery from tracking failure [2].

Model-Based Approach

Model-based approaches view hand pose estimation as global search of a certain likelihood surface. The likelihood is constructed from the image features response in the neighborhood of the candidate 3D model projection. They differ from each other in likelihood construction and search method. NLS (nonlinear-least-squares) is used for optimization in [3], and axes of truncated cylinders that are used to model phalanges are projected onto the image and local edges are found. Fingertip positions are measured through a similar procedure. In [4], pose estimation is performed by minimizing error of the overlap between the projected model and the silhouette image with GA and SA (simulated annealing). A two-step algorithm to estimate the hand pose is proposed in [5], first estimating the global hand pose and subsequently finding the configuration of the finger joints.

In model-based framework, high dimension of the parameter space prohibits exhaustive search. Another difficulty is that as multi-modal problems there are often multiple solutions even under an exact set of model-image assignments. So fast non-linear fitting is non-trivial only with classical optimization methods.

Appearance-Based Approach

Appearance-based approaches formulate hand pose estimation problem in a learning framework. They achieve pose estimation from a single 2D input image by learning the mapping between image features and corresponding joint configurations. Related learning algorithms include [6], where the configuration estimation is formulated as a classification problem and the system is trained with views corresponding to many different hand orientations and viewpoints. SMA (specialized mapping architecture) approach of [7] is based on regression rather than classification. The most recent learning based algorithm is described in [2], hand pose estimation is viewed as an image database indexing problem, where the closest matches for an input hand image are retrieved from a large database of synthetic hand images.

There are two factors in such learning based systems that influence the continuous and correctness of results: one is desired near-continuous sampling in high-dimensional parameter space is almost infeasible, the other is simplex feature description cannot utilize the observed information sufficiently.

2.2 3-D Hand Motion Tracking

Tracking can be viewed as a parameter estimation process over time. A typical tracking system model consists of three parts: state space model, dynamic model and measurement model. In hand tracking system, they are respectively corresponding to hand model, dynamic model for motion and image measurement.

In 3d model based framework, parameterized geometric shapes such as generalized cylinders or super-quadrics are used to approximate the homogeneous body parts. The advantage of this approach is that it can achieve equally good surface approximation with less complexity.

The human hand skeleton is composed of 27 bones. Joints between these bones will vary in the number of DOF they possess. The number of DOF at a joint is the number of axes-of-rotation at that joint. Generally used kinematic model includes base link as palm and five link chains as fingers connected to the base link through five two-DOF revolute joints. Each finger is three links connected by two one-DOF revolute joints.

Dynamic model for hand motion tracking typically uses constant position or constant velocity model.

Simple cues are used for construction of measurement model, such as silhouette, edges and fingertips. These cues provide sparse information in the image. Silhouette is insensitive to measurement ambiguity, so is robust, but affects the precision. Edge is sensitive to measurement ambiguity, but it can work in the presence of clutter. Fingertip is difficult to detect only with image processing. Optical flow [8] provides a dense cue, but is sensitive to the accumulation of errors over multiple frames. Proper combination of multiple cues will work better.

For tracking, a hierarchical method is used in [9]. They first make rough estimation from silhouette matching and later KF (Kalman Filter) with constrained covariance is used for further search. In [10], the tracker work with UKF (Unscented Kalman filter) and only 7 DOF, where observation vector is obtained by detecting edges in the neighborhood of the projected hand model. However such KF analogous methods do not adapt to the problem of non-Gaussian, high-dimensional search such as hand motion tracking. A sequential Monte Carlo tracking algorithm, based on importance sampling, produces good results in [11] with reduced dimension as seven. This method decreases the search burden to some extent, but cannot capture arbitrary natural full DOF motion.

3   Proposed Approach Using GA

3.1   Hand Motion Capture System Modeling

3D hand model with typical shape & kinematic model: State model is composed of posture (position and orientation) of hand palm and finger joint angles. If $\mathbf{x}_p = (x_1,...,x_6)$ represents posture parameter of hand palm and $\mathbf{x}_{fi}, i = 1,...,5$ represents joint angles for i^{th} finger with 4 DOF, then one configuration of hand pose can be represented with a state vector:

$$
\begin{aligned}
\mathbf{x} &= \{\mathbf{x}_p, \mathbf{x}_{f1}, \mathbf{x}_{f2}, \mathbf{x}_{f3}, \mathbf{x}_{f4}, \mathbf{x}_{f5}\} \\
&= \{x_1,...,x_6, x_7,...,x_{10}, x_{11},...,x_{14}, x_{15},...,x_{18}, x_{19},...,x_{22}, x_{23},...,x_{26}\}
\end{aligned}
\tag{1}
$$

The palm is modeled using a truncated elliptic cone, its top, bottom and side closed by three half-ellipsoids. Each finger consists of three segments of a truncated cone, one for each phalanx. They are connected by hemispheres representing the joints. The phalanges of the thumb are represented by an ellipsoid and two truncated cones. Hemispheres are used for the tips of fingers and thumb.

Physical constraint: Limited finger motion as a result of hand anatomy constraints hand articulation within the range of $[0,90]$. The motions of the DIP joint and PIP joint could be described as $\theta_{DIP} = \dfrac{2}{3}\theta_{PIP}$ from the study of biomechanics [12].

(a)   (b)

Fig. 1. 3D hand model (a) wireframe model (b) phong model

Dynamic model: Constant position model with a multi-variate Gaussian random noise is used (Equation 2). Here $N(0, \Sigma)$ represents the normal distribution and $\mathbf{x}_t$ is state model at time t.

$$\mathbf{x}_t = \mathbf{x}_{t-1} + \mathbf{B}$$

$$\mathbf{B} \sim \mathbf{N}\,(0, \Sigma) \tag{2}$$

Image cues and measurement model: In this paper, both silhouette and edges are used as measurement feature. Two kinds of similarity measurement methods are used as measurement model. One is invariant moment [7] for silhouette in learning process, and the other is chamfer distance [13] for both silhouette and edges in the whole process.

− Invariant moment: Moments are extracted features that are derived from the raw measurements and that, in 2D, can be used to achieve rotation, scale, and translation invariant. A seven-element vector can be obtained from an image as its representation. Similarity between two shapes then can be measured from calculation of the Euclidean distance between their invariant moments.

− Chamfer distance: Chamfer distance is another popular way that measures the similarity between two shapes. Chamfer distance is not rotation, scale and translation invariant, except which it is a perfect way to measure the similarity of features from two images.

Given two finite point sets $A = \{a_1, \ldots\ldots, a_p\}$ for projection of 3D model and $B = \{b_1, \ldots\ldots, b_q\}$ for image, chamfer distance is defined as follows:

$$D_{\text{chamfer}}(A, B) = \frac{1}{|A|} \sum_{a_i \in A} \min_{b_j \in B} \| a_i - b_j \|. \tag{3}$$

The function $D_{\text{chamfer}}(A, B)$ is called directed Chamfer Distance from point set A to B. It identifies the mean of the distances between each point $a \in A$ to its nearest neighbor in B. Hence, chamfer distance measures the mismatch between the two point sets and can be used as a measure for shape comparison. The function $D_{\text{chamfer}}(A, B)$ can be efficiently computed using a distance transform (DT). This transformation takes a binary feature image as input, and assigns to each pixel in the image the distance to its nearest feature. Image features constitute the point sets for computation of chamfer distance can be any feature visible in both images, e.g. edges, corners, bright spots, or areas with a certain texture. Edges and silhouette features are used here. Thus measurement model can be specified as:

$$\omega(\mathbf{x}, \mathbf{z}) = \exp-\left(\left(D_{\text{chamfer\_silhouette}} + D_{\text{chamfer\_edges}}\right) * \left(1 + \alpha_{\text{penality}}\right)\right). \tag{4}$$

Here $\mathbf{z}$ represents the input image and $\alpha_{penality}$ is a penalty coefficient, which is computed by summing violations on all joint angles and indicates a total violation of configuration parameters constraint.

3.2 Hand Pose Estimation

Our pose estimation algorithm integrates learning method in the 3D model based optimization framework. We argue that pose estimation is ultimately a high dimensional search problem, which needs efficient optimization methods, and its effectiveness also highly depends on whether the initialization process could efficiently localize multiple minima as initial estimates. Here we introduce a learning process as automatic initialization for localizing of multiple minima. Then the followed optimization schemes loop over model-image silhouette assignments and provide the optimal estimation.

In learning process, 30 typical right-hand pose configurations are used as prototypes. Each prototype is rendered from 89 different viewpoints, sampled approximately uniformly from the surface of the viewing sphere. To accommodate rotation-variant chamfer distance, 36 images are generated from each viewpoint, corresponding to 36 uniformly sampled rotations of the image plane. Overall, the database includes 96,120 images in 2,670 groups, and the number of such groups is 36. For rotation-invariant measure, such as invariant moment, 36 images in one group hold the equal measurement. Learning is implemented in two-step search. First, k-nearest neighbor search using invariant moment is performed in the database that just includes 2,670 images regardless of image rotation and 20 most probable hand configurations are filtered out. Secondly, for each choice the most probable rotation angle is determined in terms of chamfer distance. Computational time can be saved greatly in this way since the calculation of chamfer distance takes much more time than invariant moment.

In optimization process, an efficient global optimization method that can provide a global cost minimum is demanded. Here we adopt GA based algorithm for global optimization solution. Although, in general, long iterations are needed for a valid result and it often takes too much time, learning based initialization could shorten iteration time and guarantee a quicker convergence to the optimal result.

3.3 Hand Motion Tracking

Tracking can be seen as a special case of the pose estimation: an additional constraint is placed on the problem that the object pose in the previous image in a sequence is known, and the problem is to solve for them in the current image. The time between the acquisitions of images in a sequence is assumed to be small enough that certain assumptions about consistency of the scene are valid, thus providing additional constraints on the problem.

Here we introduce a novel GA-based tracking method derived from PF (particle filter). Table 1 lists the detailed description. Previous work showed that PF was an effective tool for visual tracking in non-gaussian multi-modal environments [14]. It is known that a KF will fail in this case. The kernel idea behinds PF method is using discrete particles to represent continuous probability distribution and it's likely to find a feasible solution among these particles if the dimensionality is not very high. However in high-dimensional configuration space search problem as like hand motion tracking, a large number of particles are required to achieve good representation of probability distribution, and this number grows exponentially with increasing dimensionality. In fact, conventional PF does not scale to the search problem in spaces of dimension greater than about 10 [15].

Table 1. Tracking method using GA-based particle filter

Time $k \leftarrow 0$
Initialize $\mathbf{S}_k$ from initial pose estimation result
    For $i = 1,...,N$, chromosome $\mathbf{s}_0^{(i)} = \mathbf{x}_0^{(i)} \sim p(\mathbf{x}_0)$.
Evaluate $\mathbf{S}_k$
    For $i = 1,...,N$, chromosome, $\pi_k^{(i)} = \omega(\mathbf{s}_k^{(i)}, \mathbf{z}_k)$, then π is normalized so
    that $\sum_n \pi_k^{(i)} = 1$.
Time $k \leftarrow k+1$
Begin
  Iteration layer $m \leftarrow 0$,
  For $i = 1,...,N$, $\mathbf{S}_{k-1,m}^\pi = \mathbf{S}_{k-1}^\pi + \mathbf{B}$ (dynamic model)
While (**not** termination-condition) **do**
Begin
  $m \leftarrow m+1$
  Select $\tilde{\mathbf{S}}_{k,m-1}$ from $\mathbf{S}_{k-1,m-1}$ using *Roulette-wheel* selector
  Alter $\mathbf{S}_{k,m}$ from $\tilde{\mathbf{S}}_{k,m-1}$ via crossover and mutation operators
  Evaluate $\mathbf{S}_{k,m}$

End
$\mathbf{S}_k^\pi = \mathbf{S}_{k,m}^\pi$.

Estimated optimal model configuration $\mathbf{x}_k = \sum_{i=1}^{N} \mathbf{s}_k^{(i)} \pi_k^{(i)}$.
End

GA has been proven to be a feasible method for global optimization in high-dimensional space. GA-based tracking method is motivated from both GA and PF. In each step of tracking, the particles updated from PF are treated as the initial population of GA, and the following selection, crossover, and mutation operators will draw the particles to optimized solutions. Compared with exponentially increasing number of particles in traditional PF approach, the overhead added by GA operations is much less. The state of the tracker after each layer m of a GA run is represented by a set of N weighted particles $S_{k,m}^{\pi} = \{(\mathbf{s}_{k,m}^{(1)}, \pi_{k,m}^{(1)}), ..., (\mathbf{s}_{k,m}^{(N)}, \pi_{k,m}^{(N)})\}$. Each particle contains an instance $\mathbf{s}_{k,m}^{(i)}$ of the model configuration $\mathbf{x}_k$ and a corresponding particle weighting $\pi_{k,m}^{(i)}$. An unweighted set of particles will be denoted $S_{k,m} = \{(\mathbf{s}_{k,m}^{(1)}), ..., (\mathbf{s}_{k,m}^{(N)})\}$. Then $S_k^{\pi} = \{(\mathbf{s}_k^{(1)}, \pi_k^{(1)}), ..., (\mathbf{s}_k^{(N)}, \pi_k^{(N)})\}$, $S_k = \{(\mathbf{s}_k^{(1)}), ..., (\mathbf{s}_k^{(N)})\}$.

4 Experiment Results

Experiments based on both synthetic data and real data are performed to test the feasibility of our proposed GA-based approach. The test image sequences used in experiments allow full free motion of hand (6-DOF motion of hand palm and 4-DOF joint motion of each finger). Both traditional particle filter method and our proposed GA-based approach are implemented.

4.1 Experiments on Synthetic Data

A synthetic image sequence is generated by linear interpolation between an initial and final configuration (Fig. 2). The pose estimation procedure is skipped and the initial configuration is directly used as the initial state of tracking procedure.

For GA-based approach, an evolution computation procedure with 20 generation and 100 particles (N=100, i.e., the population size is 100) is employed for each input frame. For GA parameters, the crossover probability is 0.9 and the mutation probability is 0.1. A steady state replacement policy (i.e., overlapping population) is utilized. In each generation, a new population with 50% size as original population is generated via selection, crossover, and mutation operator and replaces the worst individuals of original population.

The most time consuming operation in tracking procedure is the evaluation of similarity between hand configuration and input image, where a synthetic image is generated according to hand configuration and the distance metric is carried out to measure the similarity. The traditional particle filter method is also implemented for comparison. The particle amount is 1000 (N=1000) for impartiality since the number of similarity evaluation for each input frame in GA-based approach is also about 1000 (100 * 50% * 20). Thus the traditional PF method would take almost the same computational time as GA-based approach need for each input frame.

Fig. 3 shows the comparison of tracking performance on the same synthetic image sequence for both methods. Obviously, the proposed GA-based approach achieves a significant improvement of tracking performance under the same computational load.

Fig. 2. Initial configuration (left) and final configuration (right) of a synthetic image sequence

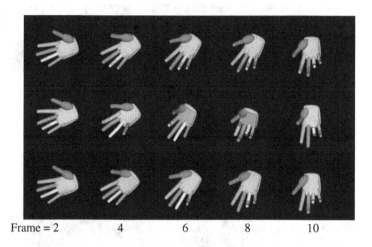

Frame = 2   4   6   8   10

Fig. 3. Tracking results on frame 1 to 10 of synthetic sequence (Frame 0 is the initial state). The first row is input synthetic images, the second row is tracking results with particle filter, and the third row is tracking results with GA-based particle filter.

4.2 Experiments on Real Data

Both a color-based approach using an adaptive skin-color model and a motion-based approach are utilized to locate the hand region in images. Experiments show that the number of sampled views impacts the learned result much more than number of sampled hand pose configurations and so we use total 3,204 viewpoints and only 30 pose configurations.

Fig. 4 shows the result of GA-based pose estimation on the first frame. Filtered out after the two-step learning process, the candidates have been rather close to the true configuration but not quite accurate. It's apparent that the final result after GA optimization improves the estimation precision significantly and nearly achieves the true configuration. Experiments also indicate that the pose estimation using only GA optimization without initialization by two-step learning process will take much more iterations to achieve a feasible solution. In conclusion, learning integrating with optimization framework could achieve a feasible result with a much quicker convergence speed.

Fig. 5 shows the result of GA-based tracking approach on the real image sequence. Results of 4 images sampled from sequence are illustrated. Traditional particle filter method is also implemented on the real image sequence but it could not give meaningful tracking results at all. In GA-based tracking approach, optimization approach is integrated to each frame step of particle filter, which will improve the performance of tracking greatly compared with conventional particle filter.

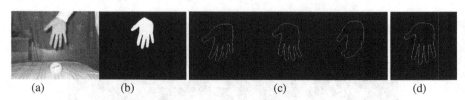

(a)   (b)   (c)   (d)

Fig. 4. Tracking initialization (GA-based pose estimation on the first frame) (a) input image (b) segmented hand region (c) 3 most likely configurations after the two-step learning process (d) final result after GA optimization

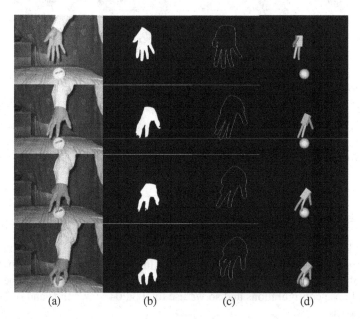

(a)   (b)   (c)   (d)

Fig. 5. Tracking results on frame 30, 45, 60, and 75 of real image sequence: (a) input image sequence (b) segmented hand region by skin colors and motion (c) tracking results using GA-based approach (only configuration of finger joint) (d) simulated dexterous hand according to tracked pose configuration and calibrated hand position in application of dexterous robot hand guiding.

5 Conclusion

In this paper, a novel vision-based hand motion capture algorithm is proposed to deal with motion tracking problem in high-dimensional configuration space. The present approach adopts a 3D model based framework with full-DOF kinematic model and an effective measurement method based on chamfer distance for both silhouette and edges. The main obstacle to handle with human hand motion capture is the high dimensionality associated with a full DOF articulated model. A novel learning integrating with optimization framework is proposed for 3-D hand pose estimation. Such an idea would also work well in the case of other object pose estimation, especially for complex ones with high-dimensional configuration space. GA-based approach is proposed as the solution of high-dimensional and multi-modal tracking problem, which can be generalized to other high-dimensional space tracking area. Experimental results show a significant improvement of tracking performance compared with traditional PF tracking methods.

In conclusion, the GA-based approach is an efficient estimation and tracking in high-dimensional configuration spaces. Our future research will focus on automatic initialization of human hand model for different user.

Acknowledgement. This work was jointly supported by the National High Technique Program (863-704-7-17), the National Key Project for Basic Research of China (Grant No: G2003cb312205), the National Science Foundation of China (Grant No: 60174018), and the National Science Foundation for Key Technical Research of China (Grant No: 90205008).

References

[1] Y. Wu and T. S. Huang. Hand modeling, analysis, and recognition. IEEE Signal Processing Magazine. 2001.

[2] V. Athitsos and S. Sclaroff. Estimating 3D hand pose from a cluttered image. In IEEE Computer Society Conference on Computer Vision and Pattern Recognition. 2003.

[3] J. Rehg. Visual Analysis of High DOF Articulated Objects with Application to Hand Tracking. PhD thesis. Electrical and Computer Eng., Carnegie Mellon University. 1995.

[4] N. Kenichi and S. Hideo. Human hand tracking from binocular image sequences. In IEEE 1996.

[5] Y. Wu and T. S. Huang. Capturing articulated human hand motion: A divide-and-conquer approach. In Proc. 7th Int. Conf. On Computer Vision, volume I, pages 606–611,Corfu, Greece, Sept. 1999.

[6] Y. Wu and T.S. Huang. View-independent recognition of hand postures. In CVPR, volume 2, pages 88–94, 2000.

[7] R. Rosales, V. Athitsos, L. Sigal, and S. Sclaroff. 3D hand pose reconstruction using specialized mappings. In ICCV, volume 1, pages 378–385, 2001.

[8] S. Lu, D. Metaxas, D. Samaras and J. Oliensis. Using multiple cues for hand tracking and model refinement. In Proceeding of IEEE Computer Society Conference on Computer Vision and Pattern Recognition 2003.

[9] N. Shimada, Y. Shirai, Y. Kuno and J. Miura. Hand gesture estimation and model refinement using monocular camera – ambiguity limitation by inequality constraints. FGR. 1998.

[10] B. Stenger, P.R.S. Mendonc and R. Cipolla. Model-based 3D tracking of an articulated hand. In Proceedings Computer Vision and Pattern Recognition, 2001.

[11] Y. Wu, J. Lin, and T. Huang. Capturing natural hand articulation. In Proceedings International Conference on Computer Vision, volume 2, pages 426–432, 2001.

[12] J. Lee and T. L. Kunii. Molde-based analysis of hand posture. In IEEE Computer Graphics and Applications, 1995.

[13] G. Borgerors. Hierarchical chamfer Matching: A parametric edge matching algorithm. IEEE Trans. On Pattern Analysis and Machine Intelligence, Vol. 10, No. 6, pp. 849-865, November 1988.

[14] M. Isard and A. Blake. CONDENSATION - conditional density propagation for visual tracking. Int. J. Computer Vision. 1998, 29(1): 5-28.

[15] D. A. Forsyth and J. Ponce. Computer Vision: A Mordern Approach. Prentice Hall, 2002.

Top-Down Evolutionary Image Segmentation Using a Hierarchical Social Metaheuristic

Abraham Duarte[1], Ángel Sánchez[1], Felipe Fernández[2], Antonio S. Montemayor[1], and Juan J. Pantrigo[1]

[1] ESCET-URJC, Campus de Móstoles, 28933, Madrid Spain
{a.duarte, an.sanchez, a.sanz, j.j.pantrigo}@escet.urjc.es
[2] Dept. Tecnología Fotónica, FI-UPM, Campus de Montegancedo, 28860, Madrid, Spain
Felipe.Fernandez@es.bosch.com

Abstract. This paper presents an application of a hierarchical social (HS) metaheuristic to region-based segmentation. The original image is modelled as a simplified image graph, which is successively partitioned into two regions, corresponding to the most significant components of the actual image, until a termination condition is met. The graph-partitioning task is solved as a variant of the min-cut problem (normalized cut) using an HS metaheuristic. The computational efficiency of the proposed algorithm for the normalized cut computation improves the performance of a standard genetic algorithm. We applied the HS approach to brightness segmentation on various synthetic and real images, with stimulating trade-off results between execution time and segmentation quality.

1 Introduction

In general, image segmentation is one of the most difficult tasks in image analysis. The problem consists in subdividing an image into its constituent regions or objects [1]. The level of subdivision depends on the specific problem being solved. The segmentation result is the labelling of the pixels in the image with a small number of labels. This partition is accomplished in such a way that the pixels belonging to homogeneous regions with respect to one or more features (i.e. brightness, texture or colour) share the same label, and regions of pixels with significantly different features have different labels. According to Ho et al [2], four objectives must be considered for developing an efficient generalized segmentation algorithm: continuous closed contours, non-oversegmentation, independence of threshold setting and short computation time.

Many segmentation approaches have been proposed in the literature [1][3][4]. Roughly speaking, they can be classified as edge-based, thresholding-based and region-based methods. Our proposed method can be considered as region-based and pursuits a high-level extraction of the image structures. As a result, the method produces a hierarchical top-down region-based decomposition of the scene. A way to

G.R. Raidl et al. (Eds.): EvoWorkshops 2004, LNCS 3005, pp. 301–311, 2004.

solve the segmentation problem is as a pixel classification task, where each pixel is assigned to a class or region by considering only local information [1]. We take into account this pixel classification approach by representing the image as a weighted graph where nodes are the pixels in the original image and the arcs together with their associated weights are defined using as local information the distance among pixels and their corresponding brightness values. An optimal bipartition that minimizes the normalized cut value for the image graph is computed. This process is successively repeated for each of the two resulting regions (image subgraphs) after bipartitioning using a binary splitting schema. The application of a hierarchical social metaheuristic to efficiently solve the normalized cut problem is the core of the proposed method.

Many optimization problems are too difficult to be solved exactly in a reasonable amount of time. Due to the complexity of these problems, efficient approximate solutions may be preferable in practical applications. Heuristic algorithms are proposed in this direction. Examples of heuristics are many local search procedures that are problem specific and do not guarantee the optimality. Metaheuristics are high-level general strategies for designing heuristics procedures [5][6][7]. The relevance of metaheuristics is reflected in their application for acceptably solving many different real-world complex problems, mainly combinatorial. Since the initial proposal of Glover about tabu search in 1986, many metaheuristics have emerged to design good general heuristics methods for solving different domain application problems. Genetic programming, GRASP, simulated annealing or ant colony optimization are other well-known examples of metaheuristics. Their relevance is reflected in the publication of many books and papers on this research area [5].

The applications of evolutionary techniques to Image Processing and Computer Vision problems have increased mainly due to the robustness of the approach [3]. Many image analysis tasks like image enhancement, feature selection and image segmentation have been effectively solved using genetic programming [8]. Among these tasks, segmentation is in general the most difficult one. Usually the standard linear segmentation methods are insufficient for a reliable object classification. The usage of some non-linear approaches like neural networks or mathematical morphology methods has provided better results [4]. However, the inherent complexity of many scenes (i.e. images with non-controlled illumination conditions or textured images) makes very difficult to achieve an optimal pixel classification into regions, due to the combinatorial nature of the task. Evolutionary image segmentation [2][8][9] has reported a good performance in relation to more classical segmentation methods. Our approach of modelling and solving image segmentation as a graph-partitioning problem is related to Shi and Malik's work [10]. They use a computational technique based on a generalized eigenvalue problem for computing the segmentation regions. Instead, we found that very acceptable results can be obtained, when applying a hierarchical social metaheuristic for image segmentation through a normalized cut solution.

2   Normalized Cut Problem

An important graph bipartition problem is the Min-Cut problem [11][12] defined for a weighted undirected graph $S = (V, E, W)$, where V is the ordered set of vertices or nodes, E is the ordered set of undirected arcs or edges and W is the ordered set of weights associated with each edge of the graph. This Min-Cut optimization problem consists in finding a bipartition G of the set of nodes of the graph: $G=(C, C')$ such that the sum of the weights of edges with endpoints in different subset is minimized. Every partition of vertices V into C and C' is usually called a cut or cutset and the sum of the weights of the edges is called the weight of the cut or *similarity* (s) between C and C'. For the considered Min-Cut optimization problem, the cut or similarity between C and C' given by

$$w(C,C') = s(C,C') = \sum_{v \in C, u \in C'} w_{vu} \tag{1}$$

is minimized. In [13] is demonstrated that the decision version of Max-Cut (dual version of Min-Cut problem) is NP-Complete. This way, we need to use approximate algorithms for finding the solution in a reasonable time. In this paper we propose a new hierarchical social (HS) metaheuristic for finding an approximate solution to a variant of the Min-Cut problem called Normalized Cut problem [10].

The Min-Cut formulation has been used to Wu and Leahy [14] as a clustering method and applied to image segmentation. These authors look for a partition of the graph into k subgraphs such that the similarity (min-cut) among subgraphs is minimized. They pointed out that although in some images the segmentation is acceptable, in general this method produces an over-segmentation because small regions are favoured. To avoid this fact, in [10] other functions that try to minimize the effect of this problem are proposed. The optimization function called min-max cut is:

$$cut(G) = \frac{\sum_{v \in C, u \in C'} w_{vu}}{\sum_{v \in C, u \in C} w_{vu}} + \frac{\sum_{v \in C, u \in C'} w_{vu}}{\sum_{v \in C', u \in C'} w_{vu}} = \frac{s(C,C')}{s(C,C)} + \frac{s(C,C')}{s(C',C')} \tag{2}$$

where the numerators of this expression are the similarity $s(C,C')$ and the denominators is the sum of the arc weights belonging to C or C', respectively. It is important to remark that in an image segmentation framework, it is necessary to minimize the similarity between C and C' (numerators of eq. 2) and maximize the similarity inside C, and inside C' (denominators of eq. 2). In this case, the sum of arcs between C and C' is minimized, and simultaneously the sums of weights inside of each subset are maximized. Reference [10] proposes an alternative cut value called *normalized cut*, which in general gives better results in image segmentation.

$$Ncut(G) = \frac{\sum_{v \in C, u \in C'} w_{vu}}{\sum_{v \in C, u \in C \cup C'} w_{vu}} + \frac{\sum_{v \in C, u \in C'} w_{vu}}{\sum_{v \in C', u \in C \cup C'} w_{vu}} = \frac{s(C,C')}{s(C,G)} + \frac{s(C,C')}{s(C',G)} \tag{3}$$

where $G=C \cup C'$. The normalized cut is characterized for maximizing the similarity inside each subset and minimizing the dissimilarity between subsets.

3   Hierarchical Social (HS) Algorithms

This section presents the general features of a new metaheuristic called hierarchical social (HS) algorithms. In order to get a more general description of this metaheuristic, the reader is referred to [15][16][17]. This metaheuristic have been successfully applied to several problems as critical circuit computation [14], scheduling with unlimited resources [17] and MAX-CUT problem [15].

HS algorithms are inspired in the hierarchical social behaviour observed in a great diversity of human organizations and biological systems. The key idea of HS algorithms consists in a simultaneous optimization of a set of feasible solutions. Each group of a society contains a feasible solution and these groups are initially randomly distributed to produce a partition of the solution space. Using evolution strategies, where each group tries to improve its objective function or competes with the neighbour groups, better solutions are obtained through the corresponding social evolution. In this social evolution, the groups with lower quality tend to disappear. As a result, the rest of group objective functions are optimized. The process typically ends with only one group that contain the best solution found.

3.1 Metaheuristic Structure

For the image segmentation problem, the feasible society is modelled by the specified undirected weighted graph $S=(V,E,W)$ also called feasible society graph. The set of individuals are modelled by nodes of the graph V and the set of feasible relations are modelled by edges E of the specified graph. The set of similarity relations are described by the weights W. Notice that the graph also models an image, where nodes model image pixels of the image and edges model the similarity between pixels.

Figure 1.a shows an example of the feasible society graph for a particular normalized cut problem.

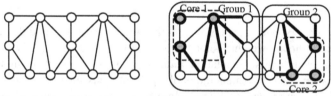

Fig. 1. (a) Feasible society graph. (b) Society partition and groups partition

The state of a society is modelled by a hierarchical policy graph [16][17]. This graph also specifies a society partition composed by a disjoint set of groups $\Pi=\{g_1,g_2,...,g_g\}$, where each individual or node is assigned to a group. Each group $g_i \subset S$ is composed by a set of individuals and active relations, which are constrained by the feasible society. The individuals of all groups cover the individuals of the whole society. Notice that each group exactly contains one solution.

The specification of the hierarchical policy graph is problem dependent. The initial society partition determines an arbitrary number of groups and assigns individuals to groups. Figure 1.b is shows a society partition example formed by two groups.

A society partition can be classified into *monopoly partition*, in which there is only one group, and *competition partition*, in which there is more than one group. The example shown in Figure 1.b shows a competition partition. Each individual of a society has two objective functions: individual objective function *f1* and the group objective function *f2* that is shared by all individuals of a group. Furthermore each group g_i is divided into two disjoint parts: core and periphery. The core determines the value of the corresponding group objective function *f2* and the periphery defines the local search region of the involved group.

In the image segmentation problem framework, the set of nodes G_i of each group g_i is divided into two disjoint parts: $G_i=(C_p,C'_i)$ where C_i represents the core or group of nodes belonging to the considered cutset and C_i' is the complementary group of nodes. The core edges are the arcs that have their endpoints in C_i and C_i'. Figure 1.b also shows an example of core for the previous considered partition. The core edges or cutset edges of each group are shown in this figure by thick lines. For each group of nodes $g_i = (C_p, C'_i)$, the group objective function $f2(i)$ is given by the corresponding normalized cut $Ncut(i)$ referred to the involved group g_i:

$$f2(i) = NCut(i) = \frac{\sum_{v \in C_i, u \in C_i'} w_{vu}}{\sum_{v \in C_i, u \in C_i \cup C_i'} w_{vu}} + \frac{\sum_{v \in C_i, u \in C_i'} w_{vu}}{\sum_{v \in C_i', u \in C_i \cup C_i'} w_{vu}} = \frac{s(C_i,C_i')}{s(C_i,g_i)} + \frac{s(C_i,C_i')}{s(C_i',g_i)} \tag{4}$$

$$\forall v \in g_i \quad f2(v,i) = f2(i) = NCut(i)$$

where $Gi=Ci \cup Ci'$ and the weights w_{vu} are supposed to be null for the edges that do not belong to the specified graph.

For each individual or node v, the individual objective function $f1(v,i)$ relative to each group $g_i = (Ci, Ci')$ is specified by a function that computes the increment in the group objective function when an individual make a movement. There are two types of movements: Intra-group movement and inter-group movement. In the intra-group movement there are to possibilities: the first one consists in a movement from C_i *to* C_i', the second one is the reverse movement $(C'_i$ *to* $C_i)$. The inter-group movement is accomplished by individual v that belong to generic group X $(X = \Pi \backslash g_i)$ that want to move from X to g_i. There are two possibilities: the first one consists in a movement form X *to* C_i, the second one consists in a movement from X *to* C'_i. The next formula shows the movement $C_i \rightarrow C'_i$.(described by the function $C\_to\_C'(v,i)$)

$$f1(v,i) = C\_to\_C'(v,i) = \frac{s(C_i,C_i') - \sigma'(i) + \sigma(i)}{s(C_i,gi) - \sigma'(i)} + \frac{s(C_i,C_i') - \sigma'(v,i) + \sigma(v,i)}{s(C_i',g_i) + \sigma(v,i)} \tag{5}$$

$$\text{where} \quad \sigma(v,i) = \sum_{u \in C_i} w_{vu} \quad \text{and} \quad \sigma'(v,i) = \sum_{u \in C_i} w_{vu}$$

This function allows to select for each individual v, the group which achieves the corresponding minimum value. The other movements $(C'_i \rightarrow C_i, X \rightarrow C_i, X \rightarrow C'_i)$ have similar functions and expressions.

The HS algorithms here considered, try to optimize one of their objective functions (*f1* or *f2*) depending on the operation phase. During an autonomous or winner phase, each group g_i aims to improve independently the group objective function *f2*. During a loser phase, each individual tries to improve the individual objective function *f1*, the original groups cohesion disappeared and the graph partition is modified in order to optimize the corresponding individual objective function. The strategy followed in a loser phase could be considered inspired in Adams Smith's "invisible hand" economic society mechanism described in his book "An Inquiry into the Nature and Causes of the Wealth of Nations".

3.2 Metaheuristic Process

The algorithm starts from a random set of feasible solutions. Additionally for each group, an initial random cutset is derived. The groups are successively transformed through a set of evolution strategies. For each group, there are two main strategies: *winner or autonomous strategy* and *loser or competition strategy*. The groups named *winner groups*, which apply the winner strategy, are that which have the lowest group objective function *f2*. The rest of groups apply loser strategy and are named *loser groups*. During optional *autonomous phases* in between competition phases, all groups behave like winner groups. These optional autonomous phases improve the capability of the search procedure.

The winner strategy can be considered as a local search procedure in which the quality of the solution contained in each group is improved by autonomously working with the individuals that belong to this group.

The loser strategy is oriented to let the interchange of individuals among groups. In this way the groups with lower quality tend to disappear because their individuals move from this group to another group with higher quality.

Winner and loser strategies are the basic search tools of HS algorithms. Individuals of loser groups, which have higher group objective functions, can change their groups during a loser strategy for improving their respective individual objective function. This way, the loser groups tend to disappear in the corresponding evolution process. Individuals of winner groups, which have lowest group objective functions, can move from the core to periphery or inversely, in order to improve the group objective function. These strategies produce dynamical groups populations, where group annexations and extinctions are possible.

3.3 High-Level Pseudo-code

The general high-level description of an HS metaheuristic for the image segmentation problem is shown in Figure 2.

The Winner Strategy is oriented to improve the normalized cut value of a group. For a given group of nodes g_i, an interchange of nodes between core and periphery

```
Procedure Hierarchical_Social_Algorithm(S)
Var
 S=(V,E,W):Initial_Society_graph;
 GS={gi}:Groups_structure;
 F1={f1}:Individuals_objective_function_structure;
 F2={f2}:Groups_objective_function_structure;
 i,k:1..Number_of_groups /*Group indices*/
Begin                               /* Begin social evolution */
 GS=Get_initial_random_partition_and_groups_structure();
 Repeat  /* group evolution*/
  Compute_F1()_and_F2(); /*Objective functions*/
  For each gi in GS
   If f2(i)=min{f2(k)∀k} Or Autonomous_phase
    Then Winner_Strategy(i) Else Loser_Strategy(i);
  End For
  Update_groups_structure(GS);
 Until termination_condition_met;      /*End of social evolution*/
 Return(GS); /* Approximate optimal solution */
End Hierarchical_Social_Algorithm
```

Fig. 2. High-level pseudo-code for Hierarchical Social Algorithms

allows to optimize the group objective function. The interchange is accomplished if there is an improvement (minimization) of the normalized cut weight of the corresponding group g_i. We allow to interchange the nodes between C_i and C'_i in parallel and simultaneously on a single iteration. The only restriction is the following: if one node v is gone out from C_i (or C'_i), none of its adjacent nodes can change their position in the same iteration. This restriction avoids node cycling in the corresponding procedure.

The winner strategy is easily specified in the pseudo-code of Figure 3, taking into account the particularization of group objective function of one generic individual v to movements $C_i \rightarrow C'_i$ and $C'_i \rightarrow C_i$ restricted to the group $gi=(C_i,C'_i)$.

```
Procedure Winner_Strategy(i)/*For Normal_Min_Cut problem*/
Var Gi=(Ci,Ci'):Nodes_partition_of_considered_group_gi;
Begin
For v = 1 to Number_of_nodes_of_considered_group_gi
   If v∈Ci and C_to_C'(v,i) < f2(v,i) Then Ci'= Ci'∪{v}; Ci= Ci\{v};
   If v∈Ci'and C'_to_C(v,i) < f2(v,i) Then Ci'= Ci'\{v}; Ci= Ci∪{v};
End For
End Winner_Strategy
```

Fig. 3. Pseudo-code of Winner Strategy

The Loser Strategy is oriented to allow group changing. The individuals that belong to groups with lower cut value can change their group in order to increase the individual objective function $f1$. Each node searches for the group that gives the best improvement in its individual objective function. Figure 4 shows the pseudo-code of Loser Strategy considering the functions $\sigma n(v,i)$ and $\sigma n'(v,i)$ previously defined (5).

```
Procedure Loser_Strategy(i) /*For Normal_Min_Cut problem*/
Var
 gi= (Ci,Ci') :Nodes_partition_of_the_considered_group_gi
 G= {g1,..gk} :Groups_partition_of_the_graph
 i,j,k:1..Number_of_groups /*Group indices*/
Begin
For v = 1 to Number_of_nodes_of_considered_group
   j = arg min {X_to_C(v,k), X_to_C'(v,k)} ,∀k} }; /*j= host group*/
   If (v∈Ci) and (j≠i) Then Ci=Ci\{v}
     Else If (v∈C'i) and (j≠i) Ci'=Ci'\{v}; /*Remove v from gi*/
   If X_to_C (v,j)< X_to_C'(v,j) Then Cj'=Cj'∪{v}
     Else Cj=Cj∪{v}; /*Add v to gj*/
End For
End Loser_Strategy
```

Fig. 4. Pseudo-code of Loser Strategy.

4   Proposed HS Brightness Image Segmentation Method

Given an image to be segmented, we first construct its simplified undirected image weighted graph $S = (V, E, W)$. This graph is defined with all the image pixels as nodes and setting the edge weights with a measure of spatial and grey level difference distances (similarity) between the corresponding endpoints. We can define the graph edge weight w_{ij} connecting the two nodes i and j by the conditional function:

$$If\ (abs(x_i - x_i) < r_x)\ Then\ w_{ij} = e^{\frac{-(I_i - I_j)^2}{\sigma_I^2}} \cdot e^{\frac{-(x_i - x_j)^2}{\sigma_x^2}}\ Else\ w_{ij} = 0 \tag{6}$$

where r_x is an experimental threshold value, I_i is the grey level intensity of one pixel i, and x_i is the spatial location this pixel. The values of σ_I, σ_x and r_x are adjusted experimentally and in general they depend on the characteristic of the image. Non-significant weighted edges, according to defined similarity criteria, are removed from the image graph. Using this graph, a high-level pseudocode of the proposed HS segmentation algorithm is described by 4 main steps in Figure 5.

```
1.  Construct the related image weighted graph as described above.

2.  Compute an approximate optimal solution for the NCut of graph using
    the proposed HS algorithm obtaining a two-region graph partition
    /*Components correspond to the most significant regions in image*/

3.  If the current partition is not an acceptable segmentation result,
    then apply step 2 to each region of the obtained bipartition.

4.  Convert the union of all intermediate graph partitions into the
    segmented image solution.
```

Fig. 5. High-level pseudo-code of HS algorithm for the segmentation problem

5 Experimental Results

The computational experiments were evaluated in a Intel Pentium 4, at 1.7 GHz, with 256 MB of RAM. All algorithms were coded by the same programmer in C++ without code optimization. We compared the performance of HS metaheuristic applied to normalized cut problem with an adapted solution for the same problem using a standard genetic [18][19] algorithm as proposed by Dolezal [11] for the Max-Cut problem. Some main details of the metaheuristics implementation are the following:

1. For the proposed *HS algorithm*, the number of groups was *nodes*/100 and number of autonomous iterations was 20.
2. For the implemented *genetic algorithm*, the initial population was 50 individuals, the maximum number of generations was 100, the probability of crossover and mutation were 0,6 and 1/*nodes*, respectively.

Both approaches were tested on several real and synthetic images. The segmentation results for two real images are respectively shown in Figures 6 and 7.

Table 1. Comparison between GA and HSA for de first NCut bipartition value for 4 images.

Image graph			Parameters			GA		HSA	
Image	Nodes	Arcs	σ^2_I	σ^2_x	r_x	NCut	Time(s)	NCut	Time(s)
Pout97x80	7760	251924	0.050	5	10	0.08921	2845	0.03149	716
Hurricane100x80	8000	1103388	0.007	15	15	0.16823	12221	0.02155	3168
Sint1_20x20	400	7414	0.030	10	4	0.08132	43	0.02886	< 1
Sint2_20x20	400	7414	0.030	10	4	0.09125	51	0.01802	< 1

Table 1 represents the comparative results between the genetic and HS algorithms for several real image (rows 1 and 2) and synthetic images (rows 3 and 4).

First and second rows of Table 1 shows the experimental results for images of figures 6 and 7. Its columns respectively represent the name and size of images, their corresponding image graphs (number of nodes and edges), the parameters that define the edges weights (σ_I, σ_x, r_x), and the results for the respective genetic and HS algorithms. For both algorithms, we show a segmentation quality result (for the first value of the *NCut*) and a computational result (execution time in seconds).

6 Conclusions

This paper has introduced an HS algorithm to efficiently solve the region-based image segmentation problem. First, the image problem has been transformed into a normalized cut problem. The HS algorithms were introduced to exploit the power of competition and cooperation among different groups in order to explore the solution space. We have experimentally shown that the proposed HS algorithms provide high quality qualitative segmentation solutions with lower computation times.

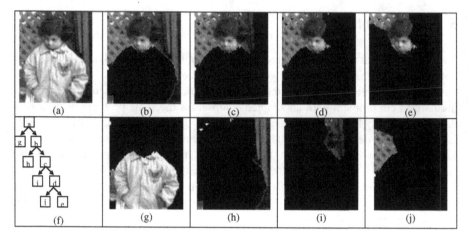

Fig. 6. Segmentation results for image *Pout*: (a) Initial image. (f) Structure of the segmentation tree. (b)..(j) Resulting segmented regions according to the segmentation tree.

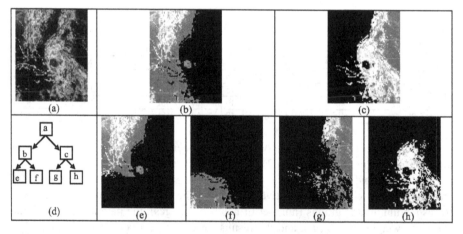

Fig. 7. Segmentation results for image *Hurricane*: (a) Initial image. (d) Structure of the segmentation tree. (b)..(h) Resulting segmented regions according to the segmentation tree.

The major advantage of using a normalized cut as group objective function is that the quality of the segmentation region is very high. However, the capability of the algorithm can be improved segmenting the image in several regions instead of two regions. In this case the normalized cut is not an adequate function, because it is not defined for several cuts. We propose as a future work the use of other group objective functions (such as K-means) in order to exploit all the potentiality of the HS metaheuristic.

References

1. R.C. Gonzalez and R. Woods, *Digital Image Processing*, 2nd Edition, Prentice Hall, 2002.
2. S.Y. Ho and K.Z. Lee, "Design and Analysis of an Efficient Evolutionary Image Segmentation Algorithm, *J. VLSI Signal Processing*, Vol 35, pp. 29-42, 2003.
3. J. R. Parker, *Algorithms for Image Processing and Computer Vision*, John Wiley, 1996.
4. M. Sonka et al. *Image Processing, Analysis and Machine Vision*, 2nd Ed., PWS, 1999.
5. F. Glover and G.A. Kochenberger (eds.), *Handbook of Metaheuristics*, Kluwer, 2002.
6. Z. Michalewicz, D.B. Fogel, *How to Solve It: Modern Heuristics*, Springer, 2nd Ed, 2000.
7. S. Voss, "Meta-heuristics: The State of the Art", A. Nareyek (ed.): *Local Search for Planning and Scheduling*, LNAI 2148, Springer, pp. 1-23, 2001.
8. R. Poli, "Genetic programming for image analysis", J. Koza (ed): *Genetic Progr.*, 1996.
9. M. Yoshimura and S. Oe, "Evolutionary Segmentation of Texture Image using Genetic Algorithms", *Pattern Recognition*, Vol. 32, pp. 2041-2054, 1999.
10. J. Shi and J. Malik, "Normalized Cuts and Image Segmentation", *IEEE Trans. Pattern Analysis and Machine Intelligence*, Vol. 22, no. 8, pp. 888-905, Aug. 2000.
11. O. Dolezal, T. Hofmeister, and H. Lefmann, H, "A comparison of approximation algorithms for the MAXCUT-problem", *Reihe CI 57/99*, Universität Dortmund, 1999.
12. P. Festa, P.M. Pardalos, M.G. Resende and C.C. Ribeiro, "Randomized Heuristics for the Max-Cut Problem", *Optimization Methods and Software*, Vol. 7, pp. 1033-1058, 2002.
13. R.M. Karp, Reducibility among Combinatorial Problems, R. Miller and J. Thatcher (eds.): *Complexity of Computer Computations*, Plenum Press, pp. 85-103, 1972.
14. Z. Wu et al, "*Optimal Graph Theoretic Approach to Data Clustering: Theory and its Application to Image Segmentation*", IEEE Trans. PAMI, V. 15, n. 11, pp. 1101-1113, 1993.
15. A. Duarte, F. Fernández, A. Sánchez, A. S. Montemayor, "A Hierarchical Social Metaheuristic for the Max-Cut Problem", To appear in Proc. of EvoCOP '04.
16. F. Fernández, A. Duarte and A. Sánchez, "A Software Pipelining Method based on a Hierarchical Social Algorithm", *Proc. 1st MISTA 2003*, pp. 382-385, 2003.
17. F. Fernández, Software Pipelining using HS Metaheuristic, *Tech. Rep. URJC*, Spain, 2003.
18. Michalewicz, *Genetic Algorithms+Data Structures=Evolution Programs*, Springer, 1996.
19. W.M. Spears, *Evolutionary Algorithms*, Springer, 1998.

Multi-objective Sensor Planning for Efficient and Accurate Object Reconstruction

Enrique Dunn and Gustavo Olague

Centro de Investigación Científica y Educación Superior de Ensenada
División de Física Aplicada, EvoVisión Lab
{edunn,olague}@cicese.mx

Abstract. A novel approach for sensor planning, which incorporates multi-objective optimization principals into the autonomous design of sensing strategies, is presented. The study addresses planning the behavior of an automated 3D inspection system, consisting of a manipulator robot in an Eye-on-Hand configuration. Task planning in this context is stated as a constrained multi-objective optimization problem, where reconstruction accuracy and robot motion efficiency are the criteria to optimize. An approach based on evolutionary computation is developed and experimental results shown. The obtained convex Pareto front of solutions confirms the conflict among objectives in our planning.

1 Introduction

Automated visual inspection is a complex task that has been addressed in different scientific communities such as computer vision, photogrammetry and robotics, see [1], [2], [3]. In fact, sensor planning is an interdisciplinary research field that can benefit from incorporating knowledge from different areas in a complementary manner. One of the challenges, in automating the decision making process for inspection systems, is the development of a sensor planner which incorporates different qualitative aspects (e.g. efficiency, accuracy, robustness) involved in a particular vision task. The literature indicates that research on this field generally studies a particular goal of the overall perception task such as minimizing sensing actions, obtaining complete coverage of interest regions or improving image quality. Consequently, despite the variety of methodologies previously proposed, the multi-objective (MO) nature of such planning has not yet been addressed. The choice of an appropriate framework is crucial to incorporate such study. For instance, approaches based on Generate and Test iterations, [4], are dependent on user expertise and interaction. Complete Enumeration is by definition inadequate for complex tasks due to its computational burden. The Synthesis approach, [5], based on the use of analytical functions, presents difficulties to incorporate the MO framework due to the complexity of obtaining an analytical multi-objective solution. Expert systems, [3], are a promising approach for MO, but concerns about the dependence on expert prior knowledge may hinder their solution quality in comparison to less heuristic based approaches. A promising alternative is the use of Simulation Techniques, [6], which using proper

G.R. Raidl et al. (Eds.): EvoWorkshops 2004, LNCS 3005, pp. 312–321, 2004.

mathematical models, allow to evaluate different application scenarios and gain insight into the studied problem. It is within this context that we present a novel approach that introduces the concept of MO optimization into the sensor planning problem. To our knowledge this is the first time that such a study has been undertaken.

This work deals with the automation of a close range photogrammetric system. We consider the use of an anthropomorphic manipulator arm equipped with a CCD camera on its end effector. The decision making process consists on designing a group of sensing actions that lead to the obtainment of a highly accurate three dimensional reconstruction. The problem is stated within the MO optimization framework. Building on previous work on sensor planning [7],[8], a solution is developed under the evolutionary computation (EC) paradigm.

The goal of this paper is two-fold. First, to describe the MO nature of the sensor planning problem for automated visual measurement tasks. Second, to present an approach based on evolutionary computation to solve such planning.

The outline of the paper is the following. Initially, a description of the sensor planning problem is presented. Then, an explanation on the MO nature of sensor planning and the aspects considered in this work is brought forth. Next, the proposed evolutionary computation approach to solve our planning problem is detailed. This is followed by experimental results. Finally, conclusions and future research guidelines are presented to end the paper.

2   Problem Statement

In the context of our automated visual inspection system, a sensor planner must explicitly specify sensing task execution. Sensing actions are carried out by a physical mechanism Q, in accordance to a set of sensing viewpoints V. Each viewpoint is a vector parametrization $V_i = [v_1, \ldots, v_s]$ which describes a single camera position (X, Y, Z), orientation angles (ω, ϕ, κ), as well as any of the configurable camera intrinsic parameters. The configuration of a manipulator consisting of r rotational joints can be represented as vector $Q = [q_1, \ldots, q_r]$. Given prior knowledge of its Denavit-Hartenberg parametrization D, this information is sufficient to determine the position and orientation of the end effector where the camera is mounted. Moreover, a viewpoint specification can be obtained by a function of the form $\Gamma(Q, D) \in \mathbb{R}^s$.

A sensing plan consists in a motion trajectory, $Q(t)$, to be followed by the manipulator which executes sensing actions at n different viewpoints V_i. In this work a viewpoint based task specification is utilized.

Definition 1. Viewpoint Based Task Specification: Obtain a set V of viewpoints $V_i \in \mathbb{R}^s$ from which to determine a time parametrized robot motion trajectory $Q(t)$ where $\forall i \in [1, 2, \ldots, n] \exists \Gamma(Q(t_i), D) = V_i$

Given some environmental description E, and depending on the chosen task T, a set of operational restrictions $g_i(\cdot) \geq 0$ for $i = 1, \ldots, m$ can be evaluated. Assuming there is parametrization of the set of V into a set of l parameters, the sensor planning problem can be stated as

Definition 2. Multi-objective Sensor Planning: Find the solution vector $x^* = [x_1^*, x_2^*, \ldots, x_l^*]^t$ which satisfies the m environmental and task defined constraints: $g_i(x, E, T) \geq 0$ $i = 1, 2 \ldots, m$; adheres to the variables bounds: $x^{(L)} \leq x_i \leq x^{(U)}$ and optimizes the vector function $f(x) = [f_1(x), \ldots, f_k(x)]^t$.

The nature of the different objective functions $f_i(x)$ and of the problem constraints $g_i(x, E, T)$, shall be given in subsequent sections of this paper. Under the previous definition, the specified constraints define the feasible region $\Omega = x \in \mathbb{R}^l$ of the decision variable space. Therefore, any point in Ω defines a feasible solution. The vector function $f(x)$ maps the set Ω into a set $\Phi = y \in \mathbb{R}^k$ that represents all possible values of the objective functions. The set of optimal solutions for a MO optimization problem consists of all decision vectors for which the corresponding objective vectors cannot be improved in any dimension without degradation of another. Mathematically, the concept is stated as follows:

Definition 3. Pareto Optimality: A point $x^* \in \Omega$ is Pareto optimal if for every $x \in \Omega$ and $I = 1, 2, \ldots, k$ either, $\forall_{i \in I}(f_i(x) = f_i(x^*))$ or, there is at least one $i \in I$ such that $f_i(x) > f_i(x^*)$.

The set of optimal task specifications vectors that satisfy such definition is known as the Pareto Optimal Set P^*. These vectors are mapped by $f(\cdot)$ to a subset on the boundary of Φ. These vectors in the objective function space are denominated Pareto Front PF^*.

3   The Multi-objective Nature of Sensor Planning

The motivation for stating sensor planning as MO is based on the characterization of a "good" sensing plan. Compliance with the task goals is an obvious requirement. However, we identify two general aspects in assessing the worthiness of a high level task specification : Solution Quality and Process Efficiency. In highly accurate 3D inspection, solution quality entails minimizing a measure of the 3D reconstruction uncertainty. On the other hand, the process efficiency can be defined in terms of the resources adjudicated to a specific task. The description of these different and usually competing aspects, as well as their integration into our sensor planning approach, is presented next.

3.1   Solution Quality: Accurate 3D Measurements

It is known in the photogrammetric and computer vision communities that viewpoint selection is a determining factor in accurate 3D reconstruction. Designing a multiple viewpoint configuration (e.g. photogrammetric network) is a complex geometrical problem. In fact, the photogrammetric network design search space is multi-modal. Therefore, for a given scenario, there exist several very different spatial distribution of viewpoints which yield similar reconstruction accuracy. In order to derive a useful criteria, an approach based on the error propagation phenomena, as presented by Olague [9], will be utilized. Relying on the implicit function theorem, the covariance matrix ΛP of a 3D reconstruction can be obtained having knowledge of: 1) the 2D image measurement uncertainty Λp and, 2) a 3D reconstruction model from 2D image data of the form $P = f(p)$. Such relationship is stated as follows.

Proposition 1. Given a random variable $p \in \mathbb{R}^m$, of Gaussian distribution, mean $E[p]$, and covariance Λp, and $P \in \mathbb{R}^n$, the random vector given by $P = f(p)$, where f is a function of class C^1, the mean of P can be approximated to a first-order Taylor expansion by $f(E[p])$ and its covariance by:

$$\Lambda P = \frac{\partial f(E[p])}{\partial p} \Lambda p \frac{\partial f(E[p])^t}{\partial p} \tag{1}$$

The 2D uncertainty Λp can be determined as a function of the incidence angle between the camera viewing direction and the surface normal of a 3D point. The function model of this phenomena in each of image axes is obtained using experimental measurements of the projectively invariant cross-ratio. The resulting model is given by the function

$$y = \beta \left(e^{\left(\frac{\alpha}{90-x}\right)} + e^{\left(\frac{\alpha}{90+x}\right)} \right) + \gamma, \tag{2}$$

where the best fit parameters are: $\alpha=79.74$, $\beta = 1.31 \times 10^{-3}$, and $\gamma = 8 \times 10^{-3}$. Once an analytical expression for the reconstruction covariance matrix is obtained, in order to derive a criteria, a metric for comparing covariance matrices needs to be adopted. For this work, the maximum element of the main diagonal of ΛP was selected as a criteria:

$$f_1(x) = \max_{i=1\ldots3} \Lambda P_{ii} \tag{3}$$

3.2   Process Efficiency: Operational Costs

In an automated iterative process, an active vision system should make optimal use of the manipulator infrastructure. This entails considerations regarding kinematic and dynamic characteristics of a task planning specification, such as: distance traveled by the manipulator, total effort required for the motion, total time required for the movement or collision risk.

Such operational costs are evaluated from a complete sensing task specification which depends on viewpoint selection V, as well as the environmental configuration E. A problem specific mapping from these descriptions into an explicit and applicable task plan is needed. We state such mapping as $S(V, E)$, which result can be generally stated as a time parametrized function of the robot joint values (e.g. configuration space), $Q(t) \in \mathbb{R}^6$ where $t \in [a, b]$ in the continuous case or $t \in [1, 2, \ldots, n]$ for the discrete one. Moreover, this general mapping $S(\cdot)$ can be adapted to consider optimal path planning, obstacle avoidance or kinematic and dynamic considerations. Since a general cost function $\Psi(\cdot) \in \mathbb{R}$ evaluates robot motion, such a function can be estimated from two robot configurations obtained at different times during task execution, which yields $\Psi(Q(t_1), Q(t_2))$. Consequently, in order to evaluate the operational cost over the entire course of task execution we have for the continuous case:

$$f_2(x) = \int_b^a \Psi(Q(t), Q(t + dt))dt, \tag{4}$$

while the discrete case yields

$$f_2(x) = \sum_{t=1}^{n-1} \Psi(Q(t), Q(t+1)). \tag{5}$$

4   Our Evolutionary Computation Approach

Evolutionary algorithms operate over multiple solutions in a concurrent manner, allowing the attainment of several different solutions at the end of a single execution run. This has lead to the design of methodologies that direct the whole population toward the Pareto optimal set. Furthermore, the stochastic nature of the EC approach has showed to be robust against the complexity of the search space, such as the one present in sensor planning [9].

4.1   Solution Representation

In this work the camera placement is restricted to an inward looking viewing sphere centered around the measured object. This simplifies the viewpoint specification, since the viewing direction is implicitly expressed as the sphere center. Moreover, by specifying a sufficient viewing distance from the object, it is possible to satisfy the focus, resolution and field of view restrictions common to viewpoint selection. In virtue of the viewing sphere model, an individual viewpoint can be expressed by its polar coordinates. Using a constant radius, the 3D position of a viewpoint can be specified by a 2D real valued vector $[\alpha, \beta]$. Given an n number of desired images, the constant length representation vector used for specifying an imaging geometry configuration is denoted as

$$x \in \mathbb{R}^{2n} \quad where \quad \alpha_i = x_{2i-1}, \beta_i = x_{2i} \quad for \quad i = 1, \ldots, n. \tag{6}$$

4.2   Constraint Handling

It is important to note that not all points on the surface of the viewing sphere are valid, nor all the possible combinations of viewpoints conform a valid network configuration. This is due to the local and global restrictions involved in our problem. A description of our camera placement search space is given in [7].

   Local restrictions are imposed to the viewpoint selection process and can be dependent upon the object studied or the working environment. The case of optical self-occlusion for complex objects limits the visibility region of some of the features on the object to a subset of the viewing sphere. In fact, it is possible for a particular viewpoint not to be able to capture any of the interest points on the object. Additionally, when considering the incorporation of a manipulator robot into the sensing task, it is necessary to also take into account kinematic restrictions. For example, a given viewpoint may not be reachable to the robot.

Global restrictions are imposed to the final task specification. In photogrammetric reconstruction this translates to data sufficiency requirements. In order to be effective, a network configuration should have a sufficient amount of redundancy in its observations. Therefore, it is possible that a certain configuration does not provide the necessary data for the triangulation of a particular object feature. This data inconsistency leads to very poor overall reconstruction due to the least squares method involved in such a process. Another type of global restrictions are the ones imposed by any specified bounds on the overall performance of the sensing task. For example: maximum displacement allowed or minimum accuracy obtained.

To incorporate the above mentioned constraints different approaches are adopted. Viewpoint selection constraints (i.e. local restrictions) are enforced using a deterministic repair mechanism. This procedure consists in:

1. Initializing an independent random number generator with a value obtained from a fixed linear combination of the α, β values corresponding to the invalid viewpoint.
2. Iteratively generate new values for α, β until a valid viewpoint is generated.
3. Locally replace such repaired values. That is, they are only used for objective function evaluation.

This enables the evolutionary algorithm to work only on valid information during the optimization process, and in turn, restrict the search space. Since the random number generator is initialized in a deterministic manner, each time that the same invalid viewpoint is repaired, the adjusted values will remain constant. Meanwhile, the 3D reconstruction data requirements (i.e. global restrictions) are enforced by means of penalty function assessment. This procedure identifies the cases when data consistency requirements are not meet and assigns an arbitrary value to the object function evaluation. This value is chosen in such a way that the violating individuals still have a possibility to contribute to the evolutionary process (i.e. $f_2(x) = 2.0$). Both of these restriction handling politics are implemented at the objective function evaluation phase, allowing a relative independence from the choice of evolutionary engine used for optimization.

4.3 Genetic Operators

The simulated binary crossover (SBX) emulates the working principle of the single point crossover operator on binary strings. From two parent solutions P_1 and P_2, it creates two children C_1 and C_2 as follows:

$$
\begin{aligned}
C_1 &= 0.5[(1+\beta)P_1 + (1-\beta)P_2] \\
C_2 &= 0.5[(1-\beta)P_1 + (1+\beta)P_2]
\end{aligned}
\quad \text{with } \beta =
\begin{cases}
(2u)^{\frac{1}{\eta_x+1}} & \text{if } u < 0.5 \\
\left(\frac{1}{2(1-u)}\right)^{\frac{1}{\eta_x+1}} & \text{otherwise.}
\end{cases}
\tag{7}
$$

The spread factor β is dependent on a random variable $u \in [0,1]$ and on an user defined nonnegative value η_x that characterizes the distribution of the

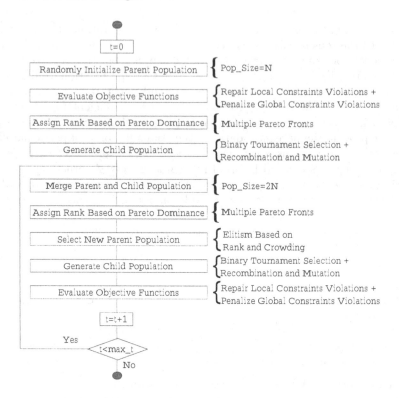

Fig. 1. Flow Diagram of our NSGA-II based approach.

children in relation to their parents. The mutation operation modifies a parent P into a child C using the boundary values $P^{(LOW)}$ and $P^{(UP)}$ of each the decision variables in the following manner:

$$C = P + (P^{(UP)} - P^{(LOW)})\delta \quad \text{with } \delta = \begin{cases} (2u)^{\frac{1}{\eta_m+1}} - 1 & \text{if } u < 0.5 \\ 1 - [2(1-u)]^{\frac{1}{\eta_m+1}} & \text{otherwise} . \end{cases} \quad (8)$$

4.4   The Evolutionary Engine

There are multiple state-of-the-art algorithms for MO optimization [10]. In this work an approach based on the NSGA-II algorithm, [11], is utilized. The main characteristics of the evolutionary engine are the use of ranking based generational elitism and the incorporation of crowding distance measures within each rank. At each iteration the Parent and Child population of the previous are joined into a temporary population. This composite population is ranked according to Pareto dominance. This iterative procedure obtains the Pareto front of the population and assigns to each of its individuals a rank value of 1. Afterward, these individuals are eliminated from consideration and a new Pareto Front is calculated from the remaining population. The elements of such "local" Pareto Front are assigned a rank value of 2. This is repeated until each individual has been ranked, increasing the rank value at each iteration. In this way, multiple "layers" or ranks of Pareto Fronts are calculated. After the ranking process has finished, all the elements of the first rank (the Pareto Front of the whole population) are assigned the same fitness. In order to promote diversity among the solutions in each rank, crowding penalties are imposed to the closely located individuals. After such penalization has been enforced on the fitness values, the process is repeated for the next rank. Special care is taken to insure that the lowest fitness found in a given rank is greater that any of the individuals on the next. This gives selective pressure to the individual with lower rank (e.g. closer to the Pareto Front of the whole population). The next population of Parents is determined by an elitist strategy that selects elements in consideration of their rank. This new Parent population generates a new Child population and the process is repeated. Figure 1 shows a high level description of our approach.

5   Experimental Results

Experimentation was carried out for the simulation of a complex three dimensional object under observation by a manipulator robot. The goal is to obtain a photogrammetric network that is optimal in terms of reconstruction accuracy and manipulator motion. It is reasonable to assume that the most efficient configuration, in terms of motion alone, will be one where the robot takes images from the same viewpoint. On the other hand, an optimal network in terms of precision exclusively, will be a well distributed set of viewpoints. Using a population of $N=100$ individuals the evolutionary algorithm was executed for a period of $t_{max} = 100$ generations. The crossover probability was $P_x = 0.8$ with a spread factor $\eta_x = 2$. The mutation probability was $P_m = 0.012$ with $\eta_m = 2$. The execution time was of 95 seconds on a Pentium 4 at 2.4 GHz. The resulting Pareto Front is illustrated in Figure 2. The horizontal axis reflects the magnitude of the 3D reconstruction uncertainty. The vertical axis illustrates the total distance traveled by the manipulator. A single point in this plot represents the function values corresponding to a given sensing specification. The asymptotic behavior on both axes, as well the convex shape of the Pareto Front, support the assumption that our sensor planning problem is indeed MO. Some of the corresponding network configurations to the set of non dominated solutions are presented in Figure 3. In the absence of prior knowledge about the real Pareto Front, it is difficult to derive conclusions on the quality of the obtained non dominated solutions in terms of convergence. However, notice how the solutions with better efficiency, Solution F in Figure 3, approach the aforementioned ideal configuration in terms of motion. On the opposite extreme of the obtained Pareto Front, Solution A in Figure 3, the most accurate configuration is similar to an optimal imaging geometry presented in [7].

6   Conclusions and Future Work

A novel MO approach to sensor planning has been presented. An EC methodology based on the NSGA-II algorithm was described, along with experimentation

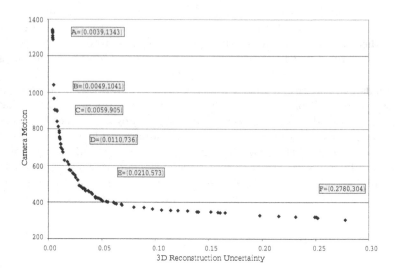

Fig. 2. Pareto Front for the case of Accuracy vs. Motion. Indicated optimal configurations are presented in Figure 3.

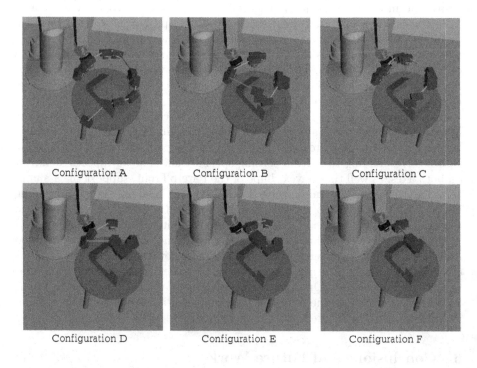

Fig. 3. Different optimal configurations. The correspondence of the presented solutions with the Pareto Front is illustrated on Figure 2.

on a simulation environment. The results comply with the assumption of conflicting objectives within the sensing task specification. Moreover, the optimal solutions found by the evolutionary algorithm form a convex Pareto Front with asymptotic behavior in each axis. The developed system is an efficient and expandable tool for the study of the MO sensor planning problem. Future research includes the implementation of our approach in a real world environment, the use of alternative optimization engines and operators, relaxing the viewpoint placement constraints and studying more complex scenarios. Particularly, the encapsulation of the crossover and mutation operators into the approach proposed in [12] is expected to improve the performance of our system.

Acknowledgments. Research funded by Contract 35267-A from CONACyT and under the LAFMI Project. First author supported by scholarship 142987 from CONACyT.

References

1. Tarabanis K.A., Allen P.K., Tsai R.Y. 1995. "A Survey of Sensor Planning in Computer Vision". IEEE Trans. on Robotics and Automation. 11(1):86-104 p.
2. Newman T., Jain A. 1995. "A Survey of Automated Visual Inspection", Computer Vision and Image Understanding 61(2):231-262.
3. Mason S. 1997. "Heuristic Reasoning Strategy for Automated Sensor Placement. Photogrammetric Engineering & Remote Sensing, 63(9):1093-1102 p.
4. Sakane S, Niepold R, Sato T, Shirai T. 1992. "Illumination Setup Planning for a Hand-eye System Based on an Environmental Model". Advanced Robotics. 6(4).
5. Tarabanis K., Tsai R., Allen P.K. 1995. "The MVP Sensor Planning System for Robotic Vision Tasks", IEEE Trans. on Robotics and Automation, 11(1).
6. Ikeuchi K., Robert J.C. 1991. "Modeling sensors detectability with the VANTAGE geometric/sensor modeler". IEEE Trans. on Robotics and Automation, Vol. 7.
7. Olague G. 2002. "Automated Photogrammetric Network Design Using Genetic Algorithms". Photogrammetric Engineering & Remote Sensing, 68(5):423-431. Awarded "2003 First Honorable Mention for the Talbert Abrams Award", by AS-PRS.
8. Dunn, E. and Olague, G. 2003. "Evolutionary Computation for Sensor Planning: The Task Distribution Plan".EURASIP Journal on Applied Signal Processing.
9. Olague G. Mohr R. 2002. "Optimal Camera Placement for Accurate Reconstruction". Pattern Recognition, 35(4):927-944 p.
10. Coello C., Van Veldhuizen D., Lamont G. 2002. "Evolutionary Algorithms for Solving Multi-Objective Problems". Kluwer Academic Publishers. New York, NY.
11. Deb K., Agrawal S., Pratab A., Meyarivan T., 2000. "A Fast Elitist Non-Dominated Sorting Algorithm for Multi Objective Optimization: NSGA-II". Proceedings of PPSN VI, Paris France. Springer. Lecture Notes in Computer Science No. 1917.
12. Olague, G., Hernández, B. and Dunn, E., 2003. "Accurate L-corner Measurement using USEF Functions and Evolutionary Algorithms". 5th European Workshop on Evolutionary Computation in Image Analysis and Signal Processing. Lecture Notes in Computer Science 2611. Springer-Verlag.

An Algorithm for Segmenting Gaseous Objects on Images

Sung-Min Kim[1] and Wonha Kim[2]

[1] Konkuk University
School of Biomedical Engineering
smkim@kku.ac.kr
[2] Kyung Hee University,
School of Electronic and Information Engineering
wonha@khu.ac.kr

Abstract. A new methodology for segmenting gaseous object images is introduced. Unlike in case of a rigid object, the edge intensity of a gaseous object varies along the object boundary (edge intensities of some pixels on a gaseous object boundary are weaker than those of small rigid objects or noise itself). Therefore, the conventional edge detectors may not adequately detect boundary-like edge pixels of gaseous objects. We develop a novel object segmenting method using fuzzy algorithm trained by the genetic algorithm. The proposed method consists of a fuzzy-based boundary detector applicable to gaseous as well as rigid objects, and concave region filling to recover object regions. This algorithm is well applicable to medical image such as breast cancer or tumor segmentation.

1 Introduction

Segmenting gaseous objects is very useful in numerous applications, for example detecting cancer or tumors on medical images, analyzing scientific data originating from climate simulation, and monitoring air pollution or mountain fires. A good example of a gaseous object is a plume (i.e. smoke rising up from a factory chimney). Although intensive research has been done on segmenting rigid objects or model-based deformable objects[1][2], few studies have been done on gaseous objects. Unlike in case of a rigid object, the edge intensity of a gaseous object varies along the object boundary. The edge intensities of some pixels on a gaseous object boundary are weaker than those of nearby small rigid objects or noise. Therefore, the conventional edge detectors, such as the Sobel, Pewitts and Canny edge detectors [3] that mainly rely on edge intensity can not adequately detect the boundary-like edge pixels of gaseous objects. We observed that a weak intensity edge pixel might belong to a boundary in the case where it belongs to the long connected edges, and that a strong intensity pixel might be a noise-like pixel in the case where it is isolated or situated on one of the short-connected edges. Based on this observation, we propose a new boundary-like edge detection rule, which is applicable to gaseous as well as rigid objects. Fig. 1 compares a conventional edge detection rule and the proposed bound-

G.R. Raidl et al. (Eds.): EvoWorkshops 2004, LNCS 3005, pp. 322–328, 2004.

ary-like edge detection rule. The conventional edge detectors declare every high intensity pixel to be an edge pixel. However, the proposed edge detector may declare low intensity edge pixels with large connectivity (the number of connected edge pixels) as boundary pixels, and declare high intensity pixels with low connectivity as non-boundary pixels. Thus, while the conventional edge detector's decision rule is a straight dotted line, as shown in Fig. 1(a), the proposed edge detector forms a nonlinear decision filter as shown in Fig. 1(b).

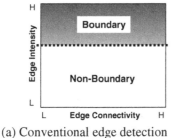
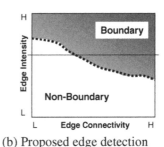

(a) Conventional edge detection   (b) Proposed edge detection

Fig. 1. Comparison of boundary edge decision rules

We propose a Fuzzy-based edge detector (FED) that uses edge connectivity as well as edge intensity. In the FED, the Fuzzy parameters are optimized through the Genetic Algorithm (GA). After detecting the boundary pixels, a concave area-filling algorithm with morphological operations is applied to reconstruct object region. The results of various simulations indicate that the proposed algorithm segments both rigid and gaseous objects reasonably well.

2   Fuzzy-Based Edge Detector (FED)

The procedure of the proposed FED is as follows:

Step 1: Apply a simple edge detector (such as the Sobel detector) with low threshold to produce all boundary candidates (edge pixels).

Step 2: Compute the edge intensity and connectivity.

Step 3: Apply the FED, in order to determine the boundary pixels.

In step 3 the input variables for the FED are the edge intensity and connectivity and the output variable is the edge confidence, which is a measure of the possibility of this being a boundary pixel. Let A_1^k, A_2^k and B^k be the fuzzy sets of the intensity, connectivity and edge confidence, respectively. For the intensity membership function, the 3 cases, *"strong"*, *"medium"* and *"weak"*, are adopted. For the connectivity membership function, *"long"*, *"medium"* and *"short"* connectivities are also used. Therefore, nine rules are finally constructed. The kth fuzzy rule is as follows:

kth Rule: If $A_1{}^k$ and $A_2{}^k$ are the *intensity* and the *connectivity*, respectively, then the edge confidence is B^k, (k=1,2...9)

For the input membership function, the triangle functions are used and the singleton memerbership funciotn is used for the output function [4]. Fig.2 and Fig.3 present the intensity and connectivity membership functions.

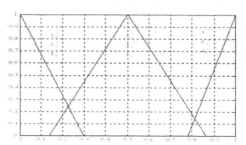

Fig. 2. Intensity membership function

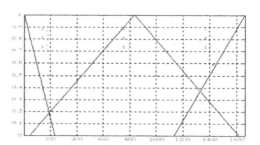

Fig. 3. Connectivity Membership function

To obtain the edge confidence, the following defuzzification function is used:

$$f(x_1,x_2) = \frac{\sum_{k=1}^{9} y^k (\prod_{i=1}^{2} \mu_{A_i^k}(x_i))}{\sum_{k=1}^{9} (\prod_{i=1}^{2} \mu_{A_i^k}(x_i))} \tag{1}$$

where x_1 and x_2 are the edge intensity and connectivity values, and y^l is the cente value of the edge confidence (B^l).

$f(x_1,x_2)$ is defuzzifier with desired edge confidence. y^k is the center of l-th edge confidence B^k. The membership function of B^k is shown in Fig. 4.

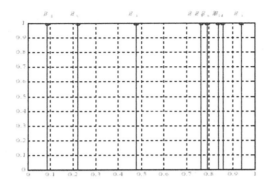

Fig. 4. Desired Edge Confidence Membership Function

3 Parameter Optimization through Genetic Algorithm (GA)

The parameters for the fuzzy membership functions are optimized through GA training[5]. Two 256x256 images that include smoke rising from a factory chimney surrounded by a mountain forest are used for the GA training. Their edge candidates are manually classified into boundary edges and non-boundary edges. The classified pixels are used to train the parameters.

GA training is performed as following steps:

Step 1: Initialize all tuning parameters (Edge intensity and connectivity.).

Step 2: Represent the tuning parameters as GA chromosomes.

Step 3: Tune the parameters on membership functions by GA operations (reproduction, crossover, mutation) so as to maximize the following fitness function.

$$Fitness = \frac{1}{\sum_{i=1}^{N_E}(1 - F_i^E)^2 + \sum_{i=1}^{N_N}(F_i^N)^2} \qquad (2)$$

where

N_E : the total number of boundary pixels,

N_N : the total number of non-boundary pixels,

F_i^E : the fuzzy reasoning result of the ith boundary pixel,

F_i^N : the fuzzy reasoning result of the ith non-boundary pixel.

Step 4: The entire steps are repeated until the fitness reaches the appropriate value.

In our case, we set GA configurations as following :

Crossover probability	0.7
Mutation probability	0.1
Population size	50
Maximum number of generation	50

The decision threshold employed to classify the "boundary pixels" and the "non-boundary pixels" can be specified in terms of the percent recognition rate, which is calculated as following :

$$\text{Recognition rate} : R_E = (C_E/N_E) \times 100,$$

where

C_E : the number of correctly decided boundary pixels.

N_E : the number of boundary pixels

In GA training, the threshold level adjusted to satisfy the appropriate recognition rate, R_E. Fig. 5 shows the desired edge characteristics.

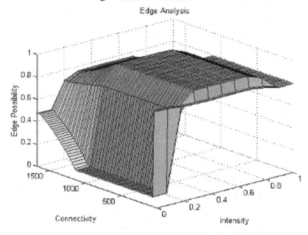

Fig. 5. Desired Edge Characteristics

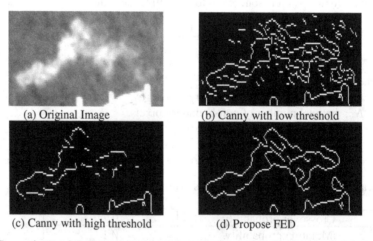

(a) Original Image   (b) Canny with low threshold

(c) Canny with high threshold   (d) Propose FED

Fig. 6. Comparisons of the boundary detection performances of the Canny edge detector and the proposed FED.

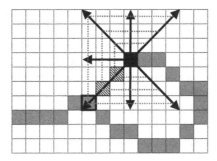

Fig. 7. Boundary construction scheme. Rectangular indicate pixels. The gray rectangulars are pixels of the detected edges. The black rectangular is an ending point. Pixels on the first line touching the edge pixel are connected so as to construct an enclosed region.

We obtain 30 representative images which include a complex background of factory and Gaseous object. Fig. 6 compares the edge detection performances of the Canny edge detector and the proposed FED. The Canny edge detector with a low threshold confuses boundary-like edges with noisy edges. On the other hand, the Canny detector with a high threshold may not be able to detect the those with a weak intensity. However, the proposed FED detects most of the gaseous boundary edges without confusing the boundary-like edges with the noisy edges. Testing with that threshold level, the desired edge confidence rate is 70%.

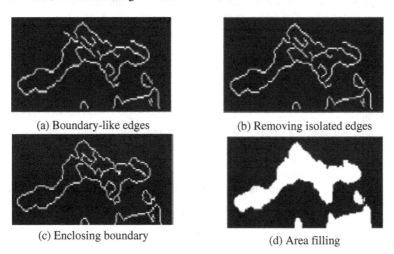

(a) Boundary-like edges   (b) Removing isolated edges

(c) Enclosing boundary   (d) Area filling

Fig. 8. Procedures of constructing object regions from unconnected edges.

4   Reconstructing Object Region from Detected Edges

When the weak edge intensity regions on a gaseous object boundary are long, the detected edges may not encompass the whole interior of an object. Thus, we need to fill the concave regions, in order to recover those regions that are not enclosed by the boundary. First, we remove the isolated lines. The lines which are connected less than 4 pixels are classified to the isolated lines. Then, we extend seven directional lines from an ending point that construct branch instead of enclosing regions. We do not extend the line whose direction is the same as the edge direction containing the ending point. We connect the first line connecting the starting ending point and already detected boundary pixel. Fig. 7 depicts the object area filling process and the objects reconstructed from the detected edges. Fig. 8 illustrates the procedure of highlighting object regions from unconnected boundaries.

5 Conclusions

In this work, we propose a Fuzzy-based edge detector (FED) that uses edge connectivity as well as edge intensity. In the FED, the Fuzzy parameters are optimized through Genetic Algorithm (GA). After detecting boundary pixels, concave area-filling algorithm with morphological operations is introduced to segment object regions. Various simulation results indicate that the proposed algorithm segments both rigid and gaseous objects reasonably well.

Acknowledgement. This study was supported by a grant of the Korea Health 21 R&D Project (02-PJ3-PG6-EV06-0002), Ministry of Health & Welfare.

References

1. J.R. Parker, "Algorithms for Image Processing and Computer Vision", John Wiley & Sons, Inc. 1997
2. A.K. Jain, `Fundamentals of Digital Image Processing', Prentice Hall, 1989.
3. L.S. Davis, "A survey of edge detection techniques", Computer Graphics and Image Processing, Vol. 4. pp. 248-270, 1975
4. L. X. Wang, "A course in fuzzy systems and control", Prentice-Hall, Inc., MA, 1997
5. D. E. Goldberg, "Genetic algorithm in search, optimization and machine learning", Addison-Wesley, MA, 1989

Evolution Strategies Approach for the Solution of an Inverse Problem in Near-Field Optics

Demetrio Macias, Alexandre Vial, and Dominique Barchiesi

Laboratoire de Nanotechnologie et d'Instrumentation Optique
Université de Technologie de Troyes,
12, rue Marie Curie, BP 2060,10010 Troyes cedex, France
{demetrio.macias,alexandre.vial,dominique.barchiesi}@utt.fr

Abstract. We propose and study two inversion procedures for the characterization of a nanostructure from near-field scattered intensity data. For this approach, the inverse problem is reformulated as a non-linear constrained optimization problem. The solution of the resultant fitness function is found through the application of the $(\mu/\rho, \lambda)$ and $(\mu/\rho + \lambda)$ strategies. The performance of the inversion algorithms is illustrated through an example and the results are discussed by means of a comparison between the methods proposed.

1 Introduction

The near-field optical microscopy has been a subject of extensive studies since the advent of the electron scanning tunnelling microscope (STM) [1] and the near-field microscope (SNOM) [2]. This new form of microscopy has been successful in demonstrating the possibility of beating the classical diffraction limit of conventional optical systems. In addition, the development of approximated solutions, i.e. perturbative approaches [3,4,5], and rigorous methods based on the numerical solution of integral equations [6,7], have lead to a better understanding of different aspects of the image formation process [8].

On the other hand, the characterization of a nanostructure from near-field data, known as the inverse problem, is more complex and less well understood. Some of the most notable works in this area are the ones conducted by Greffet *et. al.* [9] and Carminati and Greffet [10]. In the first of these references, the authors propose an inversion procedure to retrieve the topographic profile of a homogeneous sample from near-field intensity data. In Ref. [10], Carminati and Greffet explore further the inversion technique in Ref. [9] and outline a procedure to retrieve the dielectric contrast of an inhomogeneous sample. The two methods stem from the solution of an integral equation for the scattered field through a perturbative approach, under the assumption that Rayleigh's hypothesis is valid.

We propose and study an inversion procedure for the characterization of a nanostructure from near-field intensity data. Drawing on some inspiration from the procedure shown in [11], the inverse problem is reformulated as a non-linear optimization problem and its solution is searched through evolutionary

G.R. Raidl et al. (Eds.): EvoWorkshops 2004, LNCS 3005, pp. 329–338, 2004.

heuristics. The structure of this work is as follows: In Sect. 2 we formulate the direct problem and we briefly disscuss the difficulties for its solution. Sect. 3 is devoted to the description of the operational principles of the inversion procedure proposed. In Sect. 4, we illustrate through an example the performance of the method and we discuss the results obtained. Finally, in Sect. 5 we give our conclusions and final remarks.

2   Formulation of the Problem

The geometry of the system considered in the present work is depicted in Fig. 1. The region $x_3 > t$ is assumed to be the vacuum. The regions $t > x_3 > 0$ and $0 > x_3$ are filled with homogeneous and isotropic media characterized by their respective complex refractive indices n_l and n_s. A defect of width w and thickness t, with complex index of refraction n_d is embedded in the region $t > x_3 > 0$. For simplicity, the geometry is assumed to be invariant along the direction x_2 and the plane of incidence of the electromagnetic field is the x_3x_1-plane.

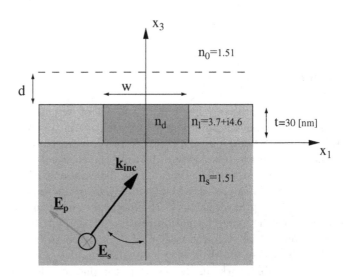

Fig. 1. Geometry of the near-field problem.

The system in Fig. 1 is illuminated in transmission from the region $x_3 < 0$, with a p- or s-polarized monochromatic plane wave at an angle of incidence θ_0. The near-field scattered intensity $I(x_1)$ is measured in the vacuum region along a line at a constant height d from the sample.

At this point, it is important to mention that the relationship between the object and its image(i.e. the near-field scattered intensity $I(x_1)$) is not trivial. It has been shown experimentally that the images obtained with a STPM/STOM set up are very sensitive to the illumination conditions (i.e. angle of incidence, polarization) and the detection distance [12]. Also, the interaction between the probe and the object leads to multiple scattering effects that play an important role in the image formation process. Furthermore, the signal detected by the optical fiber that serves as the probe tip is an image of the intensity scattered by the object and not a direct image of the object itself [13]. In order to deal with this difficulty of the direct problem, in our approach we will assume that the tip is a passive probe. That is, the multiple scattering effects bewteen the sample and the tip can be neglected [3]. Thus, the detected signal can be written as

$$I^{(p,s)}(x_1) = |E^{(p,s)}(x_1)|^2,$$ (1)

where $E^{(p,s)}(x_1)$ is the electric field scattered in the near-field of the object.

The near-field scattered intensity in Eq. (1) can be obtained through aproximated solutions, i.e. perturbative approaches [4,5] or by rigorous numerical techniques that involve the solution of integral equations [6,7]. The scattered intensity $I^{(p,s)}(x_1)$ can also be determined through the application of the Finite-Difference Time-Domain Method (FDTD) [14,15]. The success and popularity of this technique lies on the fact that it is the best established method for the direct solution of Maxwell's equations

$$\nabla \times \underline{\mathbf{E}}(\underline{\mathbf{r}}, t) = -\frac{\partial}{\partial t}\underline{\mathbf{B}}(\underline{\mathbf{r}}, t)$$ (2)

and

$$\nabla \times \underline{\mathbf{H}}(\underline{\mathbf{r}}, t) = \underline{\mathbf{J}}_{(e)}(\underline{\mathbf{r}}, t) + \frac{\partial}{\partial t}\underline{\mathbf{D}}(\underline{\mathbf{r}}, t)$$ (3)

in the space and time domains simultaneously through their representation in terms of a central finite difference form.

3 The Inversion Algorithm

In this section, we formulate the inverse problem of characterizing a nanostructure from near-field intensity data as a non-linear constrained optimization problem. It is assumed that we have access to the near-field image $I(x_1)$ generated by a sample that is illuminated with an incident field. The goal is to retrieve some parameters of the system that generated the scattering data and whose direct experimental determination is not straightforward or is not possible currently.

3.1 Definition of the Fitness Function

The near-field intensity scattered by a sample $s(\mathbf{p})$ can be written as $I(x_1|\mathbf{p})$, where $\mathbf{p}(p_1, p_2, p_3, \ldots, p_n)$ is a vector whose components are the parameters to be optimized. In the previous discussion it was mentioned that there is not a trivial relationship between the object and its image. The complexity of the inverse problem is evident. However, the direct problem can be solved numerically.

Then, the closeness of a proposed sample, $s^{(c)}(\mathbf{p}^{(c)})$, to the original one can be estimated through the discrete difference between the original image $I(x_1)$, and the image $I^{(c)}(x_1|\mathbf{p}^{(c)})$ obtained by solving the direct problem with the trial sample $s^{(c)}(\mathbf{p}^{(c)})$. The goal then would be to find a sample for which the condition $I^{(c)}(x_1|\mathbf{p}^{(c)}) = I(x_1)$ is satisfied. When this happens, one may think that the parameters of the system that generated the original image $I(x_1)$ have been retrieved.

Thus, we define our fitness(objective) function as

$$f(\mathbf{p}^{(c)}) = \int_{-\infty}^{\infty} \left[I(x_1) - I^{(c)}(x_1|\mathbf{p}^{(c)}) \right]^2 dx_1. \tag{4}$$

The Eq. (4) may be interpreted as a measure of the error between the trial and the target images.

The inverse problem can be viewed, now, as the problem of minimizing the function $f(\mathbf{p}^{(c)})$.

3.2   Representation of the Objective Variables

Usually, in an experimental set up, parameters such as the physical dimensions of a nanostructure (i.e. width, thickness, length), the detection distance at which the scattering information is measured, the angle of incidence at which the system is illuminated or the refractive indices of the sample are scalar magnitudes defined within the real domain $\mathbf{R}^{(1)}$. In addition, whatever the approach employed for the modelling of the image formation process, the numerical solution of the resultant near-field scattering equations is done in the real numbers domain. Thus, it seems natural to make use of a real representation scheme for the parameters $\mathbf{p}(p_1, p_2, p_3, \ldots, p_n)$.

3.3   Evolutionary Algorithms

A rule of thumb suggested in Ref. [16] states that *the must problem-adequate representation of individuals should be used as a starting point for the developement of an evolutionary heuristic*. With this argument in mind, we choose the Evolution Strategies as the methodology to solve the problem studied in this work.

We define the initial and the secondary populations as two sets of elements respectively represented by:

$$P_\mu^{(g)} = \{e_1^{(g)}, e_2^{(g)}, \ldots, e_\mu^{(g)}\}^T \quad \text{and} \quad \tilde{P}_\lambda^{(g)} = \{\tilde{e}_1^{(g)}, \tilde{e}_2^{(g)}, \ldots, \tilde{e}_\lambda^{(g)}\}^T, \tag{5}$$

where g is a given iteration of the algorithm, μ and λ are the sizes of the sets $P_\mu^{(g)}$ and $\tilde{P}_\lambda^{(g)}$, respectively. The elements of both populations are defined as $e_i(\mathbf{p}, \mathbf{s})$, where the components $\{p_1, p_2, p_3, \ldots, p_n\}^T$ of the n-dimensional vector $\mathbf{p}$ represent the *objective variables* to be optimized during the search process.

Each element has an associated fitness value $f(\mathbf{p})$. The vector $\mathbf{s}$ represents a set of endogenous parameters known as *strategy parameters*. The tilde in the secondary population indicates that each one of its elements has been generated through the application the genetic operators over the elements of the set $P_\mu^{(g)}$ in the initial population

3.4   Genetic Operators: Recombination and Mutation

Each element of the secondary population will be generated through the *intermediate* recombination operation that appears in Ref. [17]:

$$\langle \tilde{e}^{(g)} \rangle_\rho = \frac{1}{\rho} \sum_{l=1}^{\rho} e_l^{(g)}, \tag{6}$$

where ρ is the number of elements from the set $P_\mu^{(g)}$ to be recombinated. When $\rho = 1$, we have the canonical evolution strategy described in Ref. [18]. When $\rho \geq 2$ the recombination is known as *multiple recombination*. If $\rho = \mu$, then all the members of the population are recombinated and the resultant vector may be interpreted as the mass center of the population [17]. In the present implementation, the recombination scheme defined by Eq.(6) is also applied on the strategy parameters.

A random variation is introduced in the objective variables $\tilde{\mathbf{p}}$ and in the strategy parameters $\tilde{\mathbf{s}}$ through the self-adaptation described in Ref. [19]:

$$\tilde{\sigma}'_{l,i} = \tilde{\sigma}_{l,i} \exp\{\tau' N_l(0,1) + \tau N_i^{(1)}(0,1)\}, \tag{7}$$

$$\tilde{p}'_{l,i} = \tilde{p}_{l,i} + \tilde{\sigma}'_{l,i} N_i^{(2)}(0,1), \tag{8}$$

where $i = 1, 2, \ldots, n$ and $l = 1, 2, \ldots, \lambda$, with n and λ corresponding respectively to the number of object variables and to the number of elements in the secondary population. The strategy parameter $\tilde{\sigma}'_{l,i}$ is the mutated standard deviation for a specific element $\tilde{p}'_{l,i}$ of the secondary population. The index $j = 1, 2$ indicates that the random sequences $N^j(0,1)$ are different from each other. Finally, the exogenous parameters known as *learning rates* have the form:

$$\tau' \propto (\sqrt{2n})^{-1} \quad \text{and} \quad \tau \propto \left(\sqrt{2\sqrt{n}}\right)^{-1}. \tag{9}$$

3.5   Selection Operator

The selection operator generates, by means of a deterministic process, the set P_μ that will serve as the initial population for the next iteration $(g+1)$ of the algorithm. It must be remarked that this operator is not applied on the objective parameters, but only on the fitness values $f(\mathbf{p})$ obtained from the evaluation of the secondary population $\tilde{P}_\lambda^{(g)}$.

Employing Schwefel's notation [18], the selection schemes explored in the present work are the $(\mu/\rho, \lambda)$(or non-elitist) and the $(\mu/\rho + \lambda)$(or elitist) multi-membered evolution strategies. The definitions of the constants μ, λ and ρ correspond to the ones given in Sects. 3.3 and 3.4, respectively.

The main difference between the $(\mu/\rho, \lambda)$-ES and the $(\mu/\rho + \lambda)$-ES is that the former selects the best μ elements only from the secondary population $\tilde{P}_\lambda^{(g)}$, whereas the latter performs the selection of the best μ elements from an intermediate population $P_\mu^{(g)} \cup \tilde{P}_\lambda^{(g)}$. Whatever the selection scheme employed, the evolutionary loop is repeated until a termination criterion has been reached.

It is worth mentioning that the symbol λ is usually employed to denote the wavelength of the light in optical work. In order to avoid ambiguities in the notation, we will use the symbol λ_0 to represent for the optical wavelength.

4   Results and Discussion

In principle, the data that serves as the input for the algorithm should be measured experimentally. However, in order to evaluate the performance of the proposed algorithms, we use data obtained through the numerical solution of the direct problem by means of the FDTD method described in Ref. [15].

In the numerical experiments, the goal is to estimate the constant distance d from the sample along which the signal is measured. Also, we aim to retrieve the complex index of refraction $n_d = \Re\{n_d\} + i\Im\{n_d\}$ and the width w of the sample.

To generate the data that will serve as input for the inversion algorithm, we consider an incident monochromatic plane wave illuminating the geometry in Fig. 1 from the region $x_3 < 0$ at an angle of incidence $\theta_0 = 30°$. The wavelength of the incident field is $\lambda_0 = 0.600 \ [\mu m]$. The signal is detected in the vacuum region along a line at a constant height $x_3 = t + d$, where the thickness t is the value that appears in Fig. 1. The refractive indices corresponding to the substrate and to the thin film in which the sample is embedded are also shown in Fig. 1

The target parameters for the sample (index of refraction, width and detection distance) are respectively $n_d(\omega) = 3.9 + i2.1$, $w = \lambda_0/4$ and $d = \lambda_0/20$. We considered for the near-field calculations a sampling of $\Delta x = \frac{\lambda_0}{80}$. The intensity scattered in the near-field of the sample is depicted with a solid line in Fig. 2. The plot in Fig. 2(a) corresponds to the case when the incident field is p-polarized. The plot in Fig. 2(b) corresponds to the s polarization mode. For the strategies studied, $(\mu/\rho + \lambda)$ and $(\mu/\rho, \lambda)$, we chose $\mu = 14$ and $\lambda = 100$. These are the typically suggested values to preserve the genetic diversity through the search process and also to avoid over adaptation [18]. Also, we chose $\rho = 2$ for the recombination scheme described in Sect.3.4. The values $\tau' = 0.35$ and $\tau = 0.50$ are obtained substituting the number of objective variables $n = 4$ in Eq. (9).

In the first iteration of the algorithm, the components of the vector $\mathbf{p}$ of objective variables were generated employing random numbers uniformly distributed. In order to reduce the search space and also to avoid the unnecessary

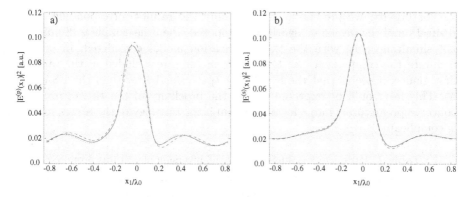

Fig. 2. Near-field images of the system depicted in Fig. 1. a) p polarization, b) s polarization. The solid line corresponds to the scattered intensity distribution obtained with the target parameters. In the two figures, the dotted line corresponds to the intensity distribution generated with the parameters estimated with the ES-$(\mu/\rho, \lambda)$, whereas the broken line corresponds to the images generated with the parameters estimated with the ES-$(\mu/\rho + \lambda)$.

evaluation of non-physical solutions, we respectively set up the largest width of the sample w and the highest detection distance d to $w_{max} = 0.2\lambda_0$ and $d_{max} = 0.2\lambda_0$. In addition, the initial ranges of variation for the real and imaginary parts of the index of refraction n_d were $n_{(min)} < \Re\{n_d\} < n_{(max)}$ and $n_{(min)} < \Im\{n_d\} < n_{(max)}$, with $n_{(min)} = 1$ and $n_{(max)} = 5$, respectively. The vector $\mathbf{s}$ of strategy parameters associated to each element of the initial population was initially defined as $\sigma_d = 0.5d_{max}$, $\sigma_w = 0.5w_{max}$, $\sigma_{n_r} = 0.5n_{(max)}$ and $\sigma_{n_i} = 0.5n_{(max)}$.

Initially, the maximum number of iterations was set to $g = 50$ and it provided the termination criterion for the search process. The computing time necessary for one realization of the $ES - (\mu/\rho, \lambda)$ was about 1.5 hours, whereas, for the $ES - (\mu/\rho + \lambda)$ was about 2.0 hours. However, through numerical experiments with the 30 initial states considered, we found that in most cases there was not a significant improvement in the fitness value after the first 15 iterations. This behavior suggested the possibility to speed up the search process through the inclusion of a threshold value in the termination criterion. Thus, if the fitness value is smaller than the threshold, the search process stops. If this condition is not fulfilled, the search process continues until the maximum number of iterations has been reached.

In order to keep the computational problem in a manageable size, the described evolution strategies were tested for their relative success by searching for the solution starting from 30 different initial states. Each random initial state consisted of (μ) vectors $\mathbf{p}(d, w, \Re\{n_d\}, \Im\{n_d\})$ and their respective associated strategy-parameters vectors $\mathbf{s}(\sigma_d, \sigma_w, \sigma_{n_r}, \sigma_{n_i})$. In all the 30 attempts the algorithms converged to a set of parameters comparable to the original one.

For brevity, we present in Table 1 only the results corresponding to one realization of the inversion algorithms proposed when the sample is illuminated, not simultaneously, with the two polarization modes considered. In order to facilitate the comparison, the target parameters are included in the table. At first glance, it seems that the ES-$(\mu/\rho, \lambda)$ performs better than the ES-$(\mu/\rho + \lambda)$. This fact could be expected due to the proclivity of the *elitist strategy* to converge prematurely into a local optimum if the topology of the fitness function is complicated.

Table 1. Parameters estimated with the inversion algorithms proposed.

p polarization				
Evolution Strategy	Detection distance d [μm]	Width w [μm]	$\Re e\{n_d(\omega)\}$	$\Im m\{n_d(\omega)\}$
$(\mu/\rho, \lambda)$	0.034	0.15	4.37	1.90
$(\mu/\rho + \lambda)$	0.047	0.12	3.74	1.75
s polarization				
Evolution Strategy	Detection distance d [μm]	Width w [μm]	$\Re e\{n_d(\omega)\}$	$\Im m\{n_d(\omega)\}$
$(\mu/\rho, \lambda)$	0.033	0.15	4.16	2.05
$(\mu/\rho + \lambda)$	0.043	0.13	4.18	1.88
Target parameters	**0.030**	**0.15**	**3.90**	**2.10**

The relative errors between the target parameters and the estimated ones are shown in Table 2. It is clear that the largest values correspond to the *elitist strategy*, with the exception of the real part of the refractive index $\Re e\{n_d\}$.

Table 2. Calculated relative errors (in percentage) for the parameters shown in Table 1.

p polarization				
Evolution Strategy	Detection distance d [μm]	Width w [μm]	$\Re e\{n_d(\omega)\}$	$\Im m\{n_d(\omega)\}$
$(\mu/\rho, \lambda)$	13.3	0.0	12.0	9.5
$(\mu/\rho + \lambda)$	56.6	20.0	4.1	16.6
s polarization				
Evolution Strategy	Detection distance d [μm]	Width w [μm]	$\Re e\{n_d(\omega)\}$	$\Im m\{n_d(\omega)\}$
$(\mu/\rho, \lambda)$	10.0	0.0	6.6	2.38
$(\mu/\rho + \lambda)$	43.3	13.3	7.1	10.47

Before we proceed further with the exposition, and in order to facilitate the comparison and the visualization of the results obtained, we consider it convenient to establish the following convention for Figs. 2 and 3. The dotted and the broken lines will be used to depict the data generated with the ES-$(\mu/\rho, \lambda)$ and the ES-$(\mu/\rho + \lambda)$, respectively.

In Figs. 3(a) and 3(b) we show the convergence behavior for the realization of the inversion procedures that generated the parameters shown in Table 1. We observe that for the two polarization modes, the lowest value of the fitness function was obtained with the ES-$(\mu/\rho, \lambda)$. This fact confirms the initial assumption that the best performance corresponded to the *non-elitist* strategy.

We present in Figs. 2(a) and 2(b) the scattered intensity distributions generated with each one of the parameters shown in Table 1. It is clear that the image depicted with the dotted line is the closest to the one corresponding to the target parameters (solid line). In spite of the closeness of each of the estimated parameters to the target ones, the results obtained clearly illustrate the sensitivity of the near-field measurements to the slightest variation of the parameters involved in the image formation process.

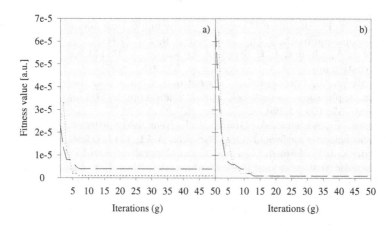

Fig. 3. Convergence behavior for the two inversion algorithms considered for a) p polarization, b) s polarization. The dotted line corresponds to the $ES - (\mu/\rho, \lambda)$ and the broken line corresponds to the $ES - (\mu/\rho + \lambda)$.

5   Final Remarks and Conclusions

We have proposed and studied an inversion procedure for the characterization of a nanostructure from near-field scattering data. Throughout the numerical experiments, we observed that the ES-$(\mu/\rho, \lambda)$ consistently retrieved the parameters of the original sample with high degree of confidence. This fact suggests that the inversion algorithm based on the *non-elitist* strategy should be the most appropriate for this particular application. Also, we found that the parameters estimated are, in most cases, located in the neighborhood of the global optimum. Thus, a further improvement could be achieved through the application of a local search method.

The success of an inversion scheme based on intensity information opens the possibility of implementing such a procedure experimentally. In principle, there are no visible restrictions for the application of the method proposed to different geometries and materials. So far, the results obtained are encouraging. However, further work is needed, not just regarding aspects related to the performance of the evolutionary strategies but also other physical aspects of the problem.

Acknowledgements. D. Macías gratefully acknowledges the financial support of "Le Ministère de la Jeunesse, de l'Education Nationale et de la Recherche through grant #1483-276.

References

1. Binning, G., Rohrer, H.: Scanning tunnelling microscopy, Helv. Phys. Acta **55**, 726, (1982).
2. Dürig, U., Pohl, D. W., Rohrer, H., Near-field optical scanning microscopy, J. Appl. Phys. **59**, 3318, (1986).
3. van Labeke, D., Barchiesi, D.: scanning tunneling optical microscopy: a theoretical macroscopic approach, J. Opt. Soc. Am. A **9**, 732, (1992).
4. Sentenac, A., Greffet, J.-J.: Study of the features of PSTM images by means of a perturbative approach, Ultramicroscopy **57**, 246, (1995).
5. van Labeke, D., Barchiesi, D.: A perturbative diffraction theory of a multilayer system: applications to near-field optical microscopy SNOM and STOM, Ultramicroscopy **57**, 196, (1995).
6. Pincemin, F., Sentenac, A., Greffet, J.-J.: Near field scattered by a dielectric rod below a dielectric surface, J. Opt. Soc. Am. A **11**, 1117, (1994).
7. Martin, O. J. F., Girard, C., Dereux, A.: Generalized Field Propagator for Electromagnetic Scattering and Light Confinement, Phys. Rev. Lett. **74**, 526, (1995).
8. Greffet, J.-J., Carminati, R.: Image formation in near field optics, Prog. Surf. Sc. **56**, 133, (1997).
9. Greffet, J.-J.,Sentenac, A., Carminati, R.: Surface profile reconstruction using near-field data, Opt. Comm. **116**, 20, (1995).
10. Carminati, R., Greffet, J.-J.: Reconstruction of the dielectric constrast profile from near-field data, Ultramicroscopy **116**, 11-16 (1995).
11. Macías, D., Olague, G., Méndez, E. R.: Surface Profile Reconstruction from Scattered Intensity Data Using Evolutionary Strategies, in *Applications of Evolutionary Computing*, S. Cagnoni *et al.*, Eds., (Springer, LNCS **2279**, Berlin), 233, (2002).
12. de Fornel, F., Adam, P. M., Salomon, L., Goudonnet, J. P., Sentenac, A., Carminati, R., Greffet, J.-J.: Analysis of image formation with a photon scanning tunneling microscope, J. Opt. Soc. Am. A **13**, 1, (1996).
13. Carminati, R., Greffet, J.-J.: Two-dimensional numerical simulation of the photon scanning tunneling microscope. Concept of transfer function, Opt. Comm. **116**, 316, (1995).
14. Yee, K. S.: Numerical solution of initial boundary value problems involving Maxwell's equations in isotropic media, IEEE Trans. Ant. Prop. **14**, 302,(1966).
15. Taflove, A., Brodwin, M. E.: Numerical solution of steady-state electromagnetic scattering problems using the time-dependent Maxwell's equations, IEEE Trans. Microwave Theory and Techniques **23**, 623, (1975).
16. Bäck, Th.: Evolution Strategies: An Alternative Evolution Computation Method, J. M. Alliot *et al.*, Eds., Artificial Evolution, Springer-Verlag, Berlin, 3, (1996).
17. H. G. Beyer, *The Theory of Evolution Strategies*, (Springer-Verlag, Berlin, 2001), p.380.
18. H. P. Schwefel, *Evolution and Optimum Seeking*, (John Wiley & Sons Inc., NY, 1995), p. 444.
19. Bäck, Th., Hammel, U., Schwefel, H.-P.: Evolutionary computation: Comments on the history and current state, IEEE Transactions on Evolutionary Computation, **1**, 3, (1997).

A Watermark Sharing Scheme to High Quality Halftone Images with Genetic Algorithms

Emi Myodo and Kiyoshi Tanaka

Dept. of Electrical and Electronic Engineering, Faculty of Engineering,
Shinshu University, 4-17-1 Wakasato, Nagano 380-8553, Japan
{myodo, ktanaka}@iplab.shinshu-u.ac.jp

Abstract. In this paper, we propose a watermark sharing scheme to binary halftone images, which is extended from an image halftoning scheme using genetic algorithms. In addition to conventional evaluation functions on gray-level precision and appropriate contrast near edges, we design and introduce an evaluation function on watermark appearance to the scheme, and generate multiple binary halftone images shared a watermark image through solution search by GA. Also, we improve the resolution of the watermark image to the same size of generated images, which contributes to increase the appearance of watermark image remarkably. Simulation results show that we can share a watermark to generated halftone images keeping high image quality, but clearly decode the embedded watermark by overlapping those images optically.

1 Introduction

In the IT (Information Technology) era, digital watermarking [1]-[3] has been earnestly developed to protect various kinds of digital contents from illegal use as a promising technique which plays a complementary role to cryptography. Contrary to cryptographic technique, which scrambles contents to a random data, digital watermark embeds certain information (ID, rights information, signature, and so on) into contents in the form that a third party cannot perceptually notice the existence of it. Thus we can use the contents as exactly same form of the original one. Also, the embedded watermark remains in the contents itself after delivery (especially after decryption), and thus it could be a firm evidence to identify the contents. These features are quite favorable in various applications.

Among various approaches of digital watermarking, a few unique watermarking schemes have recently been proposed, which generate two kinds of binary halftone images, i.e. one is to be delivered and the other to be used for verification. The watermark to be embedded is shared into these two images, and we visually decode it by overlapping them optically. A third party can never decode the embedded watermark from the delivered image without the other one which is secretly kept by the owner. This approach can be considered as a kind of visual cryptography [4]. However, we can use generated images as typical image data while [4] produces meaningless random transparencies. So far two kinds of schemes have been proposed. The first one [5] controls the pixel arrangement in

G.R. Raidl et al. (Eds.): EvoWorkshops 2004, LNCS 3005, pp. 339–348, 2004.

a cell consisting of $d \times d$ pixels to express the original gray-level of a pixel in density pattern method [6]. The generated images by this scheme are $d \times d$ times larger than the size of the original gray-level one and consequently the image resolution becomes coarser. Also, the quality of generated images is inferior because of random pixel arrangement in a cell. The second scheme [7] determines pixel values by switching two kinds of threshold matrices consisting $h \times h$ elements in ordered dithering method [6]. Although this scheme generates images whose resolution is same to the original one, the image quality is still insufficient. Also, in both conventional schemes the resolution of the watermark image is coarser than generated images. That is, just one watermark bit is embedded into $d \times d$ [5] and $h \times h$ [7] pixels, respectively.

In this paper, we propose a watermark sharing scheme to binary halftone images, which is extended from an image halftoning scheme using genetic algorithms (GAs) [8]-[10]. In addition to conventional evaluation functions on gray-level precision and appropriate contrast near edges, we design and introduce an evaluation function on watermark appearance to the scheme, and generate multiple binary halftone images shared a watermark image through solution search by GA. We can generate watermarked images whose size is same to the input original one like ordered dithering and error diffusion schemes [6] with quality higher than these traditional methods. Also, we improve the resolution of the watermark image to the same size of generated images, which contributes to increase the appearance of watermark image remarkably. We verify the performance of the proposed scheme through computer simulations. In this paper, we employ the latest halftoning algorithm using GAs, which efficiently generates halftone images with a concurrent inter-block evaluation method [10].

2   Proposed Watermark Sharing Scheme

2.1   Preparation and Individual Representation

We first prepare an original input image I and a watermark image W, both of which consist of $n_x \times n_y$ pixels. As shown in Fig. 1, we divide both images into non-overlapping blocks $D_{uv}(u = 0, 1, \cdots, n_x/r - 1, v = 0, 1, \cdots, n_y/r - 1)$ and $S_{uv}(u = 0, 1, \cdots, n_x/r - 1, v = 0, 1, \cdots, n_y/r - 1)$ consisting of $r \times r$ pixels, respectively. For each D_{uv} we prepare a population P_{uv} having a necessary number of individuals to be evolved by GA. Different from the conventional schemes [8]-[10], an individual has q pieces of 2-dimensional chromosomes $X_k(k = 1, 2, \cdots, q)$ to generate q pieces of halftone images $H_k(k = 1, 2, \cdots, q)$ shared the watermark image W. That is, we share the watermark block $S_{uv}(u = 0, 1, \cdots, n_x/r-1, v = 0, 1, \cdots, n_y/r-1)$ into $X_k(k = 1, 2, \cdots, q)$ of an individual in P_{uv} so that we can visually decode S_{uv} by overlapping $X_k(k = 1, 2, \cdots, q)$ as shown in Fig. 1. This operation (solution search by GA) is accomplished for all $D_{uv}(u = 0, 1, ..., n_x/r-1, v = 0, 1, ..., n_y/r-1)$ block by block. As an initial population $P_{uv}(0)$ of GA, we randomly generate N individuals. Precisely, the elements of the 2-dimentional chromosomes $X_k = x_k(i, j)(i, j = 0, 1, \cdots, r - 1) \in \{0, 1\}$ are randomly determined.

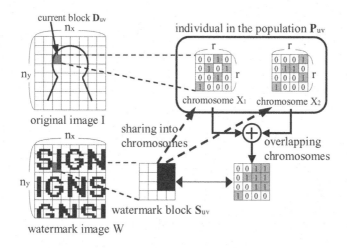

Fig. 1. Image division and individual representation

2.2 Evaluation

(i) Evaluation of image quality

We evaluate all chromosomes with two kinds of evaluation criteria. (i) One is high gray level precision (local mean gray levels close to the original image), and (ii) the other is high spatial resolution (appropriate contrast near edges) [8]. That is, the gray level precision error is first calculated by

$$E_m = \sum_{(i,j)\in D_{uv}} \frac{1}{r^2}|g(i,j) - \hat{g}(i,j)| \tag{1}$$

where $g(i,j)$ $(i,j=0,1,\cdots,r\text{-}1)$ is the gray level of the (i,j)-th pixel in the image block D_{uv}, and $\hat{g}(i,j)$ is the estimated gray level associated to the (i,j)-th pixel of the generated halftone block X_k. To obtain $\hat{g}(i,j)$ a reference region around $x_k(i,j)$ is convoluted by a gaussian filter that models the correlation among pixels. Then, the spatial resolution error to preserve the edge information is calculated by

$$E_c = \sum_{(i,j)\in D_{uv}} \frac{1}{r^2}|G(i,j) - B(i,j)| \tag{2}$$

$$G(i,j) = g(i,j) - \bar{g}(i,j)$$

$$B(i,j) = (x_k(i,j) - \frac{1}{2})R$$

where $G(i,j)$ is the difference between the gray level $g(i,j)$ of the (i,j)-th pixel in the input image block D_{uv} and its neighboring local mean value $\bar{g}(i,j)$, and R is a gray level numbers of the input image. Here we normalize E_m and E_c by

$$E'_m = \frac{E_m - E_m^{min}}{E_m^{max} - E_m^{min}} \tag{3}$$

$$E'_c = \frac{E_c - E_c^{min}}{E_c^{max} - E_c^{min}} \qquad (4)$$

where E_m^{max}, E_m^{min}, E_c^{max} and E_c^{min} are maximum and minimum values for E_m and E_c, respectively. These normalized errors are combined into one single error on image quality as

$$E_q = \alpha_m E'_m + \alpha_c E'_c \qquad (5)$$

where α_m and α_c are weighting parameters of E'_m and E'_c, respectively ($\alpha_m + \alpha_c = 1$). We evaluate individuals with the average error for q pieces of chromosomes $X_k(k = 1, 2, \cdots, q)$ in an individual.

(ii) Evaluation of watermark appearance

In addition to the image quality error, we design the evaluation function on watermark appearance. The conventional schemes [5],[7] basically explore the change of gray-level in local image region by overlapping images. Here we show an example allocating eight black pixels in the image block consisting of 4×4 pixels in Fig. 2. If we generate two image blocks having a same pixel pattern like Fig. 2(a), no gray-level change in the block by overlapping them (8/16 is kept in this case). On the other hand, if we generate two image blocks having a different pixel pattern each other like Fig. 2(b), the gray-level changes by overlapping (8/16 to 16/16 in this case). Moreover, bigger change means more noticeable in visual decoding process. Also, we need to consider the color of $(i, j) - th$ pixel when we overlap q pieces of chromosomes. If at least one element of $x_k(i, j)(k = 1, 2, \cdots, q)$ is 1 (black), the overlapped pixel color becomes 1. In other word, if all $x_k(i, j)(k = 1, 2, \cdots, q) = 0$ (white), the overlapped pixel color becomes 0.

While conventional schemes [5],[7] embed only one watermark bit into each image block, the proposed scheme does one watermark block into it. To realize this, we separate the watermark block $S_{uv} = s(i, j)(i, j = 0, 1, \cdots, r - 1)$ into two regions, i.e. S_0 consisting of only white pixels ($s(i, j) = 0$) and S_1 consisting of only black ones ($s(i, j) = 1$) as shown in Fig. 3. In this scheme, we use S_{uv} as a mask for watermark embedding. The gray level should change in S_1 region while no need to change in S_0 by overlapping. Therefore, in order to clearly decode the shared watermark block S_{uv}, we should increase the density of pixels whose color by overlapping is 1 in S_1. We count such pixels in the image block by

$$c_w = \sum_{(i,j)\in S_1} \delta(i, j) \qquad (6)$$

where

$$\delta(i, j) = \begin{cases} 1 & if \ (\bigcup_{k=1}^{q} x_k(i, j) = 1) \\ 0 & else. \end{cases} \qquad (7)$$

Also, we should consider the available black pixel numbers m in S_1 of the current image block to show the watermark block S_{uv}. m is obtained by

$$m = min\{pq, n_s\} \qquad (8)$$

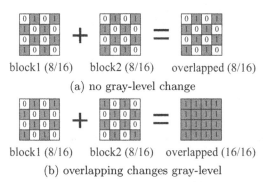

block1 (8/16)   block2 (8/16)   overlapped (8/16)

(a) no gray-level change

block1 (8/16)   block2 (8/16)   overlapped (16/16)

(b) overlapping changes gray-level

Fig. 2. Black pixel allocation in a block

where p denotes a dot density in S_1 region consisting of n_s pixels, which is determined from the balance between the gray-level precision and appropriate contrast near edges. By using c_w and m, we calculate the error on watermark appearance by

$$E_w = \frac{|m - c_w|}{m}, \tag{9}$$

where $m \neq 0$ and $E_w = 0$ for $m = 0$. By considering m we can suppress to appear unpleasant noise caused by watermark embedding in output images especially when the gray-level of the image block is low.

Finally we combine both image quality and watermark errors by

$$E = \alpha_q E_q + \alpha_w E_w \tag{10}$$

where α_q and α_w are weighting parameters for both errors ($\alpha_q + \alpha_w = 1$). Fitness is assigned by

$$F = E_{max} - E \tag{11}$$

where E_{max} is the error associated with the worst individual in a population. The GA is used to find the optimum compromise between image quality and watermark appearance with the above fitness functions.

2.3   Genetic Operators

After parents selection, we randomly determine one chromosome's index number $z(1 \leq z \leq q)$ and apply 2-dimensional crossover between chromosomes having the same index number z in both parent individuals. Then we apply mutation to the recombined chromosome. As we mentioned in **2.2**, the gray level should change in S_1 region but no need to change in S_0 in the overlapped block. Therefore, we apply masking to the generated chromosomes $X_k(k = 1, 2, \cdots, q)$ by using the watermark block S_{uv}. That is, as shown in Fig. 4, pixel pattern of

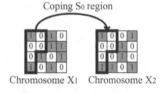

Coping S_0 region

Chromosome X1   Chromosome X2

Fig. 3. An example of watermark block, which is used as a mask for watermark embedding

Fig. 4. An example of masking by using the pixel pattern of S_0 region in Fig. 3

S_0 region in a chromosome randomly selected is copied to other chromosome's S_0 region within the individual. In this way we can change gray-level only in S_1 region while keeping on solution search by GA. Since there are q pieces of chromosomes having constraints between them to visually decode the shared watermark by overlapping, in general the evolution of individuals tends to be delayed to achieve similar image quality attained by conventional schemes [8]-[10] including no watermark. In this work, we increase evaluation numbers to obtain high quality images by repeating the above procedure.

3   Simulation Results and Discussion

3.1   Experimental Setup

We use two kinds of benchmark images, Lenna and Girl (256×256 pixels, 256 gray-levels) from SIDBA and a same-size watermark image (256×256 pixels, bi-level) to be shared into $q = 2$ pieces of generated halftone images. We set the size of image block as $r \times r = 4 \times 4$ similar to [10]. As genetic parameters, we set crossover ratio to $P_c = 1.0$, mutation ratio $P_m = 0.0625 (= 1/r^2)$. Also we employ (μ, λ) proportional selection and set the population size to $(\mu, \lambda) = (4, 8)$ (4 parent individuals and 8 offspring). We fix the weights in Eq.(5) to $\alpha_m = 0.4$ and $\alpha_c = 0.6$, but vary the ones between image quality and watermark density, α_q and α_w, to conduct some experiments. The generation numbers to terminate run is set to $G = 30$. However, as mentioned in **2.3**, we spend about $2q^2$ times more evaluations than [10] (Total evaluation numbers becomes $T \approx 870$ for $q = 2$ and $G = 30$).

3.2   Effects of the Weight α_w

First we define the watermark density. For all S_1 regions, we sum up all available black pixel numbers m of Eq.(8) by

$$M_1 = \sum_{\{S_1\}} m, \tag{12}$$

which is the total black pixel numbers in the output image available to show the black pixels $(s(i,j) = 1)$ in a watermark image W. On the other hand, we can count up the actual black pixel numbers c_w in Eq.(6) by overlapping for the entire image by

$$\hat{M}_1 = \sum_{\{S_1\}} c_w. \tag{13}$$

By using M_1 and $\hat{M}_1$ we can define the watermark density as

$$\phi_w = \frac{\hat{M}_1}{M_1}, \tag{14}$$

which could be an indicator of watermark appearance on the overlapped image. That is, it becomes easier (clearer) to visually decode the embedded watermark image as ϕ_w approaches to 1. We show the result on watermark density ϕ_w as we increase α_w in Fig. 5. We can see that ϕ_w converges to 1 as we increase the weight α_w. Next, we show the result on image quality error E_q as we increase the weight α_w in Fig. 6. We can see that the error gradually increases by increasing the ratio of α_w for α_q. The image quality of output images gradually deteriorates as well. Thus we should determine the weighting parameters α_q and α_w by considering the trade-off between image quality and watermark appearance. We show generated watermarked halftone images (one is for verification and another one for delivery) and the overlapped one to visually decode the shared watermark by conventional [7] and proposed schemes in Fig. 7. We can see that the proposed scheme produces remarkably higher quality watermarked halftone images than conventional schemes [5],[7]. Also, we can see the improvement of resolution of the watermark image appeared on the overlapped image.

3.3   Transition of Solution Search by GA

We show the transition of image quality error over evaluation numbers in Fig. 8, where we set $\alpha_w = 0.1$. Two kinds of dotted lines are reference values on image quality that can be achieved with $T = 40,000$ evaluations using 200 parent population by a simple GA [8]. We can achieve fairly higher image quality than the reference value in early stage of evolution. However, it gradually becomes hard to achieve the reference value in early stage as we increase α_w, while we can attain the value by spending more evaluations.

3.4   Watermark Robustness against Attacks

Here we discuss about security aspect of the proposed scheme. We can expect some attacks by a third party to the delivered image such as adding random noise, overwriting characters, cropping, local pixel modification, and so on. In the following experiments, we set the weighting coefficient $\alpha_w = 0.1$. First we show the watermark density ϕ_w and image quality error E_q against random

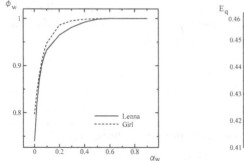

Fig. 5. Watermark density ϕ_w for α_w **Fig. 6.** Image quality error E_q for α_w

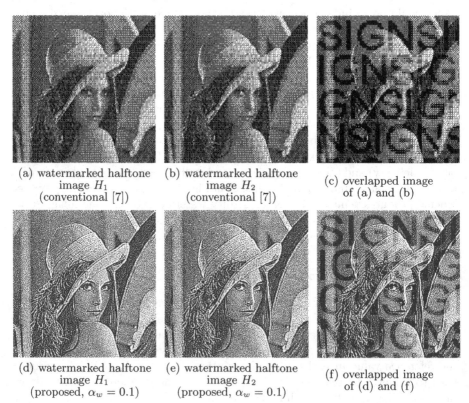

(a) watermarked halftone image H_1 (conventional [7])

(b) watermarked halftone image H_2 (conventional [7])

(c) overlapped image of (a) and (b)

(d) watermarked halftone image H_1 (proposed, $\alpha_w = 0.1$)

(e) watermarked halftone image H_2 (proposed, $\alpha_w = 0.1$)

(f) overlapped image of (d) and (f)

Fig. 7. An example of generated images (Lenna)

noise in Fig. 9. Also, we show the decoded watermark image against adding 5% random noise in Fig. 10(a). From these results the embedded watermark image W can be robustly decoded while deteriorating not only watermark appearance but also image quality. Against overwriting characters on the image, we can

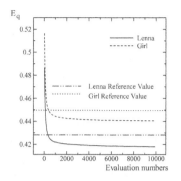

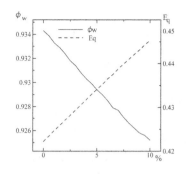

Fig. 8. Transition of image quality error E_q over evaluation numbers

Fig. 9. Watermark density ϕ_w and image quality error E_q against adding random noise ($\alpha_w = 0.1$)

(a) against 5% random noise ($\phi_w = 0.9294$)

(b) against cropping

(c) against local pixel modification ($\phi_w = 0.8933$)

Fig. 10. Decoded watermark images against attacks

clearly decode W while disappearing a part of W by overwritten characters. Against cropping, we can decode the partial watermark image included in the cropped region of delivered image after synchronizing the base position (corner address (x_0, y_0)) of the cropped image on the verification image as shown in Fig. 10(b), where we specified (x_0, y_0) by using auto-correlation function.

Because a third party can never expect the watermark information to be shared in multiple pieces of images, it is quite difficult for him/her to remove it without serious degradation of image quality. As a local pixel modification, we replaced neighbor pixels having relatively small contrast. We show the decoded watermark against this attack in Fig. 10(c). As we can see that this attack causes serious damage not only to the embedded watermark but also to the generated halftone image. As another attack, there is a possibility to generate a similar halftone image including no watermark or a different watermark image from the delivered image. Since a third party cannot use the original gray-level image to generate halftone images, the realization of this attack depends on the accuracy of estimation. However, in general it would be a very difficult task to precisely estimate the original gray level image from the generated binary image. Thus we can consider that the possibility to successfully acheive this attack is low. This scheme can be used for both hardcopy and softcopy images, and from the above results and discussion we can say that the proposed scheme is fairly robust against possible attacks.

4   Conclusions

In this paper we have proposed a watermark sharing scheme to binary halftone images using GAs, and verified its performance. Also, we have improved the resolution of the watermark image to the same size of generated images. We have shown that we can share a watermark image to generated halftone images keeping high image quality by using proper parameters, but clearly decode the embedded watermark by overlapping these images optically. Also, we have shown the proposed scheme is fairly robust against possible attacks.

As future works, we should extend this scheme to multi-level and color halftoning techniques, and develop some application systems using this scheme.

References

1. K. Matsui, *Fundamentals of Digital Watermark*, Morikita Publishing, 1998 (in Japanese).
2. S. Katzenbeisser, F. A. P. Petitcolas, *Information Hiding: Techniques for Steganography and Digital Watermarking*, Artech House, 2000.
3. I. J. Cox, M. L. Miller, and J. A. Bloom, *Digital Watermarking*, Morgan Kaufmann, 2000.
4. M. Noar, A. Shamir, "Visual Cryptography", *Proc. Eurocrypt'94*, pp.1-12, 1994.
5. K. Oka, Y. Nakamura and K. Matsui, "Embedding Signature into a Hardcopy Image Using a Micro-Patterns", *IEICE Trans.*, Vol.J79-D-II, No.9, pp.1624-1626, 1996 (in Japanese).
6. Robert Ulichney, *Digital Halftoning*, MIT Press, 1987.
7. K. Oka, Y. Nakamura and K. Matsui, "Embedding Signature into a Hardcopy of Dithered Image", *IEICE Trans.*, Vol.J80-D-II, No.3, pp.820-823, 1997 (in Japanese).
8. N. Kobayashi and H. Saito, "Halftoning Technique Using Genetic Algorithm", *Proc. IEEE ICASSP'94*, Vol.5, pp.105-108, 1994.
9. H. Aguirre, K. Tanaka and T. Sugimura, "Accelerated Halftoning Technique Using Improved Genetic Algorithm with Tiny Populations", *Proc. IEEE Intl. Conf. Systems, Man, and Cybernetics*, pp.905-910, 1999.
10. E. Myodo, H. Aguirre and K. Tanaka, "Improved Image Halftoning Technique Using GAs with Concurrent Inter-block Evaluation", *Proc. 2003 Genetic and Evolutionary Computation Conference, LNCS, Springer*, Vol.2724, pp.2251-2262, 2003.

Using Genetic Programming for Character Discrimination in Damaged Documents

Daniel Rivero, Juan R. Rabuñal, Julián Dorado, and Alejandro Pazos

Univ. A Coruña, Fac. Informatica, Campus Elviña, 15071, A Coruña, Spain
danielrc@mail2.udc.es, {juanra, julian, apazos}@udc.es

Abstract. This paper presents an application of Genetic Programming (GP) to solve one problem in the field of image processing. This problem is the recovery of a deteriorated old document from the damages caused by centuries. This document was affected by many aggresive agents, mainly by the humidity caused by a wrong storage during many years. This makes this problem particularly hard and unaffordable by other image processing techniques. Recent works have shown how Genetic Algorithms is a technique suitable for this task, but in this paper it will be shown how to obtain better results with GP.

1 Introduction

Old documents suffer the effect of time. Manipulation, humidity and wrong storage affect them and make them difficult to read. Moreover, the more manipulated and read they are, the more deteriorated they get. As they are unique, i.e. they were written in a time when there was no press; this problem makes them even more valuable. Thus, their restoration is needed for the conservation of the ancient knowledge they contain. In many cases much of this knowledge is completely lost, so there is the need to recover their information while it is still available.

These documents have been affected by many agents which make many parts very difficult to decipher, reaching the point that only an expert is able to read them. Some other parts are so damaged that their information is completely lost.

The recovery of these documents is a huge work that involves many steps. These steps include noise filtering, character recognition, and so on; all of them in the field of image filtering [1][2]. This paper focuses on the first step: the discrimination between letters and paper in these damaged documents. Page images of old manuscripts use to be terribly dirty and considerable large in size. To overcome this problem, a new effective method is proposed in this paper for separating characters from noisy background, since conventional threshold selection techniques are inadequate to cope with the image where the gray levels of the characters can be overlapped by the background.

To solve this problem, GP [3] is used to develop a filter for character discrimination. GP makes a process of automatic program generation by means of a process based on Darwin's evolution theory [4]. In this process, after subsequent generations, new individuals of a population are produced from old ones by means of crossover, copy and mutation operations [5][6]. Each individual is a solution of the

G.R. Raidl et al. (Eds.): EvoWorkshops 2004, LNCS 3005, pp. 349–358, 2004.
© Springer-Verlag Berlin Heidelberg 2004

problem. This process will give as result an individual representing a filter which, from a damaged document as an input, will return a new document containing just the original writing.

GP has been very used in the field of signal processing. Its ability of returning mathematical functions has made it a proper tool in this field, with many different applications, like signal modeling or filter design [7][8]. But it has also shown that can be successfully applied to many different image processing problems like image analysis [9][10] or object detection [11]. A variant of GP, Sub-Machine-Code GP (SMCGP) [12][13] has also been used successfully in this field, in applications like design of low-level vision algorithms. This was successfully applied in a plate detection and character recognition approach [14][15][16][17].

2   Description of the Problem

In this particular problem GP will be use to develop a filter. The objective is, from an initial deteriorated image, to get another image representing just the original writing. The desired filter must be able to discriminate the original letters from the paper, even in some parts where this document is too damaged and deteriorated.

A representative part of this document is shown on Fig. 1. Here we can see that in some parts it is very damaged, due to humidity or ink, and in some other parts the information is completely lost. This can happen either because bents caused by wrong storage of the document or because it is broken.

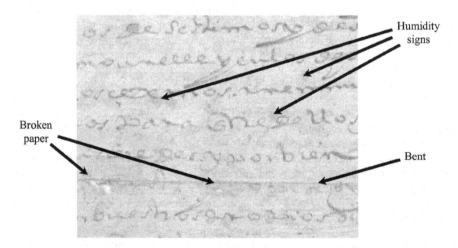

Fig. 1. Part of the document.

There are two methods to detect characters in a text. The first one consists in making a comparison with other characters taken as examples, like ANNs do. The second one consists in selecting the characters by taking as a basis some of their characteristics, like color or shape.

In the first way there are some works done with oriental alphabets. These alphabets have a very high number of characters in comparison with Latin alphabet. In those alphabets it is necessary that characters are extracted more clearly because it is more difficult to recognize them.

The second solution can be divided into two classes: the ones that detect the border of the characters and select those pixels that are inside the character, and those that try to recognise the pixels from the characters by comparing them with their neighbourhood. The first technique was used in the work by Wen Hwang and Hu Chang titled "Character Extraction from Documents Using Wavelet Maxima" [18]. Some relevant works in the second technique are the work titled "Character Extraction from Noisy Background from an Automatic Reference System" [19] and, more recently, the work titled "Old Text Reconstruction: An Artificial Intelligence Approach" [20]. These two works make a selection of pixels by looking at their colour, neighbourhood and the document to determine if they are characters or not.

But the most recent work done in this field is [21]. That paper presents a solution to the problem presented here with GAs. The authors of that paper worked with the same document, so it is a good reference for comparing the results obtained with GP and GAs. The work described in that paper is very similar to the one presented here. The difference is the method used: GAs in [21] and GP here.

3   GP Configuration

In this work, GP is used to solve the described problem. The aim of using GP is to develop a filter which can do the transformation from an original image into another one that only has the text. This filter will be a matrix with a size of M x M.

This window will be applied to an input image that will be a part of the document to be restored. For this purpose, an expert is asked to manually restore one of the most damaged parts of the document, the same part used in [21]. Therefore, the restored image is also the same as in the previous work. The resulting window from GP should be able to return this restored image from the original damaged part, as shown on Fig. 2.

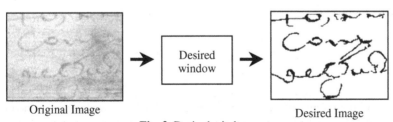

Original Image   Desired Image

Fig. 2. Desired window.

To develop this window, GP is used to evolve an equation that will be transformed into a 2-dimensional window. This transformation is done by using this expression to compute all of the points of the matrix in the following way:

$$W(i, j) = F\left(\sqrt{\left(i - 1 - \frac{M-1}{2}\right)^2 + \left(j - 1 - \frac{M-1}{2}\right)^2} \right) \tag{1}$$

where W(i,j) is the point at location (i,j) of a window of size M x M (i and j take values between 1 and M), and F(x) is the expression evolved by GP. Note that M will always be an odd number, so the expression (M-1)/2 will always return an integer number, which will be the half the size of the window. More graphically, this transformation can be seen on Fig. 3.

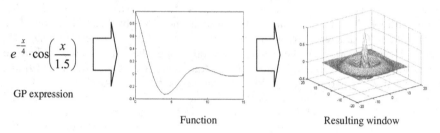

$$e^{-\frac{x}{4}} \cdot \cos\left(\frac{x}{1.5}\right)$$

GP expression   Function   Resulting window

Fig. 3. Example of a 31 x 31 window.

To get this expression, many different terminal and function sets were tried, and the best results were obtained with the following parameters:

Table 1. Terminal and function sets

Function set		+, -, *, %, sin, cos, exp
Terminal set	**Constants**	[-5, 5],
	Variables	X

Different fitness functions were tried, including those that direct evolution towards a good trade-off between sensitivity and specifity [17]. This fitness function did not work properly so, the one described in [21] was used. This fitness function returns the mean value of the distances between each value of the pixels of the desired restored image and their correspondent from the output image. Let o(i,j) be the pixel value of the output image at position (i,j). Let O(i,j) be the pixel value of the desired image at position (i,j). Let N_1 be the number of rows and N_2 be the number of columns of the original, output and desired image, the fitness function is the following:

$$f = \frac{1}{N_1 \cdot N_2} \sum_{i=1}^{N_1} \sum_{j=1}^{N_2} |O(i,j) - o(i.j)| \qquad (2)$$

The whole process can be seen on Fig. 4.

This initial configuration has been modified in this way: when loading the original image, its color attributes are inverted. In a color image, every pixel has three different color values (one for each color), all of them between the values of 0 (no color) and 255 (most intensity of the color). The inversion done consists in taking these values as 255 – original value, so 0 will be the most intensity of color and 255 the absence of color. This process is done due to the fact that the effect of the multiplication convolution operations in the filtering process is higher in those pixels with higher values. Therefore, to remark the text, it is better to have highest values (closer to 255) rather than lower ones (closer to 0), which would be the normal case.

Text pixels, darker, are normally closer to 0 than paper pixels, which are brighter and closer to 255. With this transformation dark pixels (text) will have a value closer to 255.

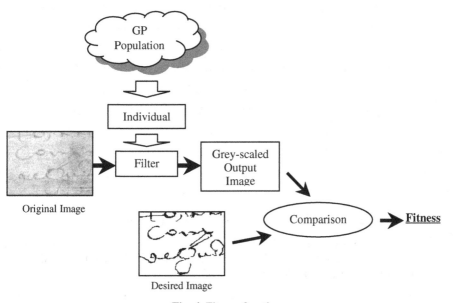

Fig. 4. Fitness function.

4   Results

Different trials with different parameter configurations were carried out. The configuration that worked best is the following:

- Selection Algorithm: Roulette.
- 2-point crossover.
- Mutation rate: 5 %.
- Crossover rate: 90 %
- Population: 500 individuals.

As done in [21], the main effort was to determine which window size is better. In that paper, results shown that the best window sizes were 13 and 15. In this particular problem, different executions with sizes between 9 and 23 were done, with 20 independent runs for each window size. Fig. 5 draws a comparison between the results obtained with these sizes. This graph seems to show that the best window sizes, with this fitness function, are 15 and 17, although the fitness values are not very different.

In this graph it can be seen that, in order to obtain good results, it is necessary to take a window size of at least 13. With a smaller size, the system does not get enough information of the environment to classify a pixel either as a character or background. As happened with GAs in [21], lower window sizes get a few noisily image but the text is slightly visible.

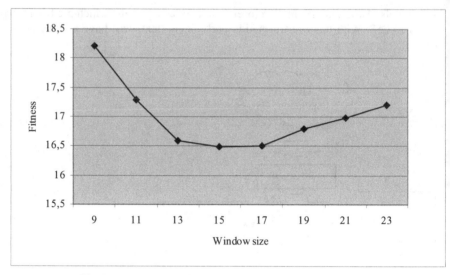

Fig. 5. Fitness values obtained for different window sizes.

The comparison between the results obtained with GAs [21] and GP can be seen on Table 2. It is observable that the results obtained with GP are much better than with GAs. The fitness of the original image is 71.165.

Table 2. Fitness values with GAs and GP

		Fitness	
		GA	GP
Window Size	11	23.845	17.290
	13	23.534	16.598
	15	23.489	16.486
	17	23.653	16.498

Fig. 6 shows some examples of the output images, corresponding to the input shown on Fig. 1. The images on Fig. 6 are also compared with the output images obtained with GAs.

As can be seen on Fig. 6, the images obtained with GP are clearer than the ones obtained with GAs, but some information has been lost. To solve this problem, there can be applied some image processing techniques in order to obtain a more readable text, as done in [21]. This time these techniques will be applied to the original document and the resulting image is used as input to the GP windows. As results, a very clear and readable text is obtained. The techniques used are based on the work with groups of pixels and on the use of thresholds for deciding whether a pixel is part of a letter or not. These techniques are extensively described in [20].

Fig. 7 shows the resulting images obtained using these processing techniques and GP, applied to the original document. The processed images are compared with the best ones obtained with GAs.

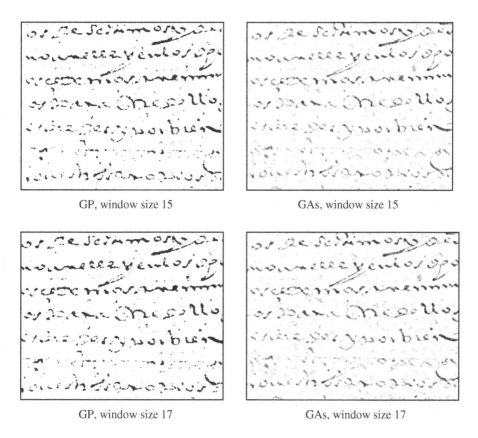

Fig. 6. Resulting images with window sizes of 15 and 17

This time, the image obtained with GP and window size 17 is much clearer and readable than the ones obtained with GAs. This image shows the wanted result: a document with black letters and white background. In this document there is still a part which could not be recovered, because the text was lost due to a bent.

5   Conclusions

This paper shows how to apply GP to solve a problem in the field of image processing. This problem consists in discriminate between text and paper in a document deteriorated by time. As result, the document obtained has just the original text. However, some areas of the original document were so damaged (in some of them the paper was even broken) that the information on that areas could not be recovered.

GP is a powerful tool for image processing tasks. In this paper it is applied to discriminate between text and noisy background, and the results show how GP can be succesfully adapted to solve it.

An important point in this work is the comparison between the results obtained with GP and the ones with GAs, described in [21]. The fitness of the expressions obtained with GP is better than the fitness of the windows obtained with GAs, and the quality of images obtained with GP is much better.

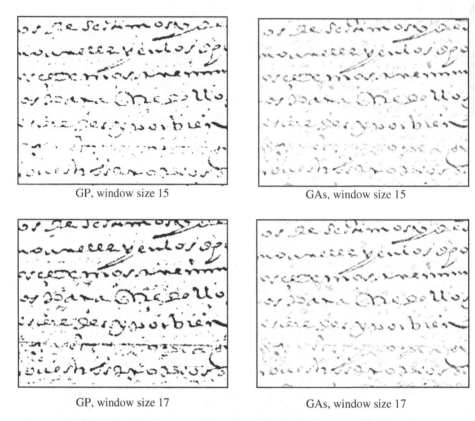

GP, window size 15   GAs, window size 15

GP, window size 17   GAs, window size 17

Fig. 7. Resulting images mixing GAs, GP and the clearing techniques

As done in the previous work with GAs, the results obtained with GP are mixed with some image processing techniques. These techniques improve the results obtained with GP. Thus, different image processing techniques can be mixed in order to obtain better results. Before the GP process, the use of other image processing techniques helps to produce a more readable and visible text.

6   Future Works

This paper is the continuation of the work described in [21]. Here, a different technique is used to solve the same problem. A future work could be to use other techniques, such as Artificial Neural Networks (ANNs), and compare the results to choose the best tool.

For the development of this work only one document was processed, so another future work could be to study the possibility of obtaining a more general set of windows for restoring a complete set of documents.

Once the resulting images are obtained, the restoration process goes on in other directions. One of them could be the detection of a piece of text that is a letter, the recognition of that letter or the translation of text. These tasks are particularly hard, because it is necessary to recognize old text, and old writing is very different than today's. There is also a great difference in documents written in different centuries, so this problem becomes really difficult. However, OCR techniques have proved to have good results at text recognition.

References

1. Castleman, K. R.: Digital Image Processing. Prentice-Hall (1996)
2. Russ, J. C.: The Image Processing Handbook (third edition). CRC Press LLC (1999)
3. Koza, J.: Genetic Programming. On the Programming of Computers by means of Natural Selection, The MIT Press, Cambridge, Massachusetts, USA, (1992)
4. Darwin, C.: On the Origin of Species by means of Natural Selection or the Preservation of Favoured Races in the Struggle for Life. Cambridge University Press, Cambridge, UK, sixth edition, (1864), originally published in 1859.
5. Fuchs, M.: Crossover Versus Mutation: An Empirical and Theoretical Case Study, 3rd Annual Conference on Genetic Programming, Morgan-Kauffman, (1998)
6. Luke, S. & Spector, L.: A Revised Comparison of Crossover and Mutation in Genetic Programming. 3rd Annual Conference on Genetic Programming, Morgan-Kauffman, (1998)
7. Dorado, J., Rabuñal, J. R., Puertas, J., Santos, A., Rivero, D.: Prediction and Modelling of the Flor of a Typical Urban Basin Through Genetic Programming. Applications of Evolutionary Computing, Proceedings of EvoWorshops 2002: EvoCOP, AvoIASP, EvoSTIM/EvoPLAN. (2002)
8. Rabuñal J.R., Dorado J., Puertas J., Pazos A., Santos A., Rivero D.: Prediction and Modelling of the Rainfall-Runoff Transformation of a Typical Urban Basin using ANN and GP. Applied Artificial Intelligence. (2003)
9. Howard,D., Roberts, S. C.: A Staged Genetic Programming Strategy for Image Analysis, Proceedings of the Genetic and Evolutionary Computation Conference. Vol. 2. (1999) 1047-1052
10. Quintana, M. I., Poli, R., Claridge, C.: On Two Approaches to Image Processing Algorithm Design for Binary Images Using GP. Applications of Evolutionary Computing, Proceedings of EvoWorkshops2003: EvoBIO, EvoCOP, EvoIASP, EvoMUSART, EvoROB, and EvoSTIM (2003)
11. Howard, D., Roberts, S. C.: The Boru Data Crawler for Object Detection Tasks in Machine Vision, Applications of Evolutionary Computing, Proceedings of EvoWorkshops2002: EvoCOP, EvoIASP, EvoSTim/EvoPLAN, (2002) 222-232
12. Poli, R., Langdon, W.B.: Sub-machine-code Genetic Programming. In L. Spector, U.M.O'Reilly W.B.Langdon and P.J.Angeline, editors, Advances in Genetic Programming 3, MIT Press , chapter 13 (1999) 301-323
13. Poli, R.: Sub-Machine-code GP: New results and extensions. In Poli, R., Nordin, P., Langdon, W.B., Fogarty T.C. eds.: Genetic Programming. Proceedings of EuroGP'99. Volume 1598 of LNCS., Goteborg, Sweden, Springer-Verlag (1999) 65-82
14. Adorni, G., Cagnoni, S., Gori, M., Mordonini, M.: Efficient low-resolution character recognition using sub-machine-code genetic programming. In: WILF 2001. (2002)

15. Adorni, G., Cagnoni, S., Mordonini, M.: Efficient low-level vision program design using sub-machine-code genetic programming. Workshop sulla Percezione e Visione nelle Macchine, available at citeseer.nj.nec.com/539182.html (2002)
16. Adorni, G., Cagnoni, S.: Design of explicitly or implicitly parallel low-resolution character recognition algorithms by means of genetic programming. In Roy, R., Koppen, M., Ovaska, S., Furuhashi, T., Hoffmann, F. (eds.), Soft Computing and Industry: Recent Applications, (Proc. 6th Online Conference on Soft Computing). Springer (2002) 387-398
17. Quintana, M.I., Poli, R., Claridge, E.: On Two Approaches to Image Processing Algorithm Design for Binary Images Using GP. Applications of Evolutionary Computing, Proceedings of EvoWorkshops2003: EvoBIO, EvoCOP, EvoIASP, EvoMUSART, EvoROB, and EvoSTIM (2003) 422-431
18. Hwang, W., Chang, H.: Character Extraction from Documents using Wavelet Maxima, Image and Vision Computing. Volume 16, Issue 5 (1998) 307-315
19. Negishi, H., Kato, J., Hase, H., Watanabe, T.: Character Extraction from Noisy Background for an Automatic Reference System, Proceedings of the Fifth International Conference on Document Analysis and Recognition, Bangalore, India, 20-22 September (1999)
20. Vidal, R.: Old Text Reconstruction: An Artificial Intelligence Approach, Graduate Thesis, Facultad de Informática, Universidade da Coruña (1999)
21. Rivero, D., Vidal, R., Dorado, J., Rabuñal, J. R., Pazos, A.: Restoration of Old Documents with Genetic Algorithms. Applications of Evolutionary Computing, Proceedings of EvoWorkshops2003: EvoBIO, EvoCOP, EvoIASP, EvoMUSART, EvoROB, and EvoSTIM (2003)

Evolutionary Algorithm-Based Local Structure Modeling for Improved Active Shape Model*

Jeongho Shin, Hyunjong Ki, Vivek Maik, Jinyoung Kang, Junghoon Jung, and
Joonki Paik

Image Processing and Intelligent Systems Lab.
Department of Image Engineering,
Graduate School of Advanced Imaging Science, Multimedia, and Film,
Chung-Ang University,
221 Huksuk-Dong, Tongjak-Ku, Seoul 156-756, Korea,
paikj@cau.ac.kr, http://ipis.cau.ac.kr

Abstract. An evolutionary algorithm-based robust local structure modeling technique is proposed to improve the performance of the active shape model (ASM). The proposed algorithm can extract boundary of an object under adverse condition, such as noisy corruption, occlusions, and shadow effect. The principle idea of the evolutionary algorithm is to find the global minimum of an objective function by evolving from a large set of populations rather than a single solution which may cause a local minimum. The proposed algorithm has been tested for various images including a sequence of human motion to demonstrate the improved performance of object tracking based on the evolutionary ASM.

1 Introduction

Among various model-based shape analysis approaches we propose evolutionary algorithms to improve the performance of active shape model (ASM), which manipulates a model to describe the shape and location of a target in a sequence of images. ASM-based approach includes two steps: The first describes how to build statistical models of shape and appearance, and the second describes how these models can be used to interpret new images. This approach offers potential solutions to a variety of practical applications, particularly in the areas of robotics, medical imaging, and video processing technology [1,2,3,4].

Evolutionary algorithms [6,7] depend on Darwin's theory of survival of the fittest. The mechanism solely depends on evolution of the fittest individual, which will replace the parent. The major difference between Evolutionary algorithms and other similar algorithms is that Evolutionary algorithms evolve not from a single source of point but from population of solutions.

In this paper, we propose an evolutionary algorithm-based robust local structure modeling technique to improve the performance of the ASM. The proposed

---

* This work was supported in part Korean Ministry of Science and Technology under the National Research Lab. Project and in part by Korean Ministry of Education under Brain Korea 21 Project.

G.R. Raidl et al. (Eds.): EvoWorkshops 2004, LNCS 3005, pp. 359–368, 2004.
© Springer-Verlag Berlin Heidelberg 2004

technique is based on evolutionary algorithms which can be classified as stochastic search methods.

The paper is organized as follows. A brief review of basic theory of ASM is given in Sec. 2. In Sec. 3 the proposed evolutionary algorithm for local structure modeling and fitting is proposed. Experimental results and conclusions are given in Secs. 4 and 5, respectively.

2   Basic Theory of ASM

This section briefly reviews the ASM algorithm for a boundary-based segmentation. ASM is constrained by the measured shape variations from the training set, and is attracted to edges of the target object at the same time.

2.1   Landmark Points (LPs)

If a shape is described n points in d dimensions we represent the shape by an nd element vector formed by concatenating the elements of the individual point position vectors. In a two-dimensional image, we represent n LPs by a $2n$-dimensional vector as

$$\mathbf{x} = [x_1, \cdots, x_n, y_1, \cdots, y_n]^T. \tag{1}$$

The number of LPs should be determined based on a specific application. For instance in order to locate and track human object, only the position and size of an object are of interest. Therefore, small number of LPs are enough for efficient and fast tracking. However, if we want to model a human face, hand or any other specific structure of human body we need to use a sufficient number of LPs [2].

2.2   Alignment of the Training Set

ASM modeling method works by examining the statistics of the co-ordinates of the labeled points over the training sets. In order to compare equivalent points

---

Algorithm 1 Alignment of the Training Set.

1. Translate each example so that center of gravity is at the origin.
2. Choose one example as an initial estimate of the mean shape and scale so that $|\bar{\mathbf{x}}| = 1$.
3. Record the first estimate as $\bar{\mathbf{x}}_0$ to define the default reference frame.
4. Align all the shapes with the current estimate of the mean shape.
5. Re-estimate mean from the aligned shapes.
6. Apply constraints on the current estimate of the mean by aligning it with $\bar{\mathbf{x}}_0$ and scaling so that $|\bar{\mathbf{x}}| = 1$.
7. If not converged, return to step 4. (convergence declared if the estimate of the mean does not change significantly after iteration)

---

from different shapes, they must be aligned in the same way with respect to a set of axes. Otherwise any statistics derived would be meaningless. We achieve the required alignment by scaling, rotating and translating the training shapes so that they correspond as closely as possible. We aim to minimize the weighted sum of squares of distances between equivalent points on different shapes [5]. Simple iterative method for this approach is summarized in Algorithm 1.

2.3   Shape Modeling Using Principle Component Analysis (PCA)

Suppose we have m shapes in the training set. The PCA algorithm can be summarized as:

Algorithm 2 PCA.

1. Compute the mean of the aligned training set,

$$\bar{\mathbf{x}} = \frac{1}{m} \sum_{i=1}^{m} \mathbf{x}_i. \tag{2}$$

2. Compute the covariance matrix, C, of the training set,

$$C = \frac{1}{m-1} \sum_{i=1}^{m} (\mathbf{x}_i - \bar{\mathbf{x}})(\mathbf{x}_i - \bar{\mathbf{x}})^T. \tag{3}$$

3. Compute the eigenvectors, ϕ_i, and eigenvalues, λ_i, of C, Sort the eigenvalues and eigenvectors from largest to smallest eigenvalues.
4. Compute the total variance (sum of eigenvalues),

$$V_T = \sum_{i=1}^{2n} \lambda_i. \tag{4}$$

5. Choose the first t eigenvalues such that their sum captures at least a large fraction, f_v of the total variation in the training set,

$$\sum_{i=1}^{t} \lambda_i \geq f_v V_T, \tag{5}$$

   where f_v defines the proportion of the total variation one wishes to explain (i.e., 0.98 for 98% of the variation in the training set)
6. Model any new sample $\mathbf{x}$ as
$$\mathbf{x} = \bar{\mathbf{x}} + \Phi b, \tag{6}$$
   where the column of Φ are the first t eigenvectors corresponding to the largest t eigenvalues.

The eigenvectors of the matrix Φ define the axes of a new t-dimensional vector space to which we can transform our aligned training vectors, $\mathbf{x}_i$. The elements of b define the extent of the shape along the axes formed by the corresponding eigenvectors.

2.4   Local Structure Modeling and Fitting

To find a new set of candidate LPs, we look along profiles normal to the model boundary through each model point. If we expect the model boundary to correspond to an edge, we can simply locate the strongest edge (including orientation if known) along the profile.

The new location can update each model point. However, model points are not always placed on the strongest edge in the local region - they may represent a weaker secondary edge or some other image structures. The best approach is to learn, from the training set, what to look for in the target image. Here we will discuss how to utilize the gray level (not only shape) information in the training set of images to find such desirable movements. To the end we examine the gray level information around each LP in all the training set of images. The gray-level appearance model training process is as follows:

Algorithm 3 Gray-Level Appearance Model Training.

1. For each LP, sample the gray-level profile (k pixels on either side of the LP) along the normal to the boundary that passes through that LP. Take the derivative of the profile and normalize it by the absolute sum of the element values. This results in a $2k + 1$ length vector, g_j, for each LP.
2. Calculate the covariance, S_j, of all derivative profiles, g_j, for a given LP across all images in the training set.
3. Calculate the mean derivative profile, $\bar{g}_j$, by averaging all the profiles for an LP across all images in the training set.
4. Create the gray-level component for the KP as an objective function of the form

$$f(g_j) = (g_j - \bar{g}_j)^T S_j^{-1} (g_j - \bar{g}_j), \qquad (7)$$

where g_j is, in a testing (not training) mode, the derivative profile from a candidate LP in a new test image.

---

3   Evolutionary Algorithm for Local Structure Modeling and Fitting

In this section evolutionary algorithms are applied to ASM-based boundary segmentation algorithm. Evolutionary algorithms are stochastic search methods, which incorporate aspects of natural selection or survival of the fittest. In other words, an evolutionary algorithm maintains a population of structures (usually randomly generated initially), and it evolves according to rules of selection, crossover, mutation and survival, referred to as genetic operators. A shared "environment" determines the fitness or performance of each individual in the population. The fittest individual is more likely to be selected for reproduction (retention or duplication), while crossover and mutation modify those individuals, yielding potentially superior ones.

As summarized in Sec. 2, the basic algorithm of ASM consists of four steps: (i) assignment of LPs, (ii) alignment of the training set, (iii) shape modeling using PCA, and (iv) local structure modeling and fitting. In order to apply evolutionary algorithms to the existing ASM, we use the proposed evolutionary algorithms to be presented in this section, instead of using the existing local structure modeling and fitting. Starting from an initial population of feasible shapes, the ASM evolves throughout mutation and crossover operations that induce gradually better solutions. The selection is performed by evaluating the fitness of the solutions. We will present the main components of the evolutionary algorithm for ASM in the remaining of this section.

3.1   Initial Population

In order to start the evolutionary algorithm, we first generate an initial population of shapes at random. The initial population can be generated under assumption that any feasible shape should be near the boundary of a target object. In our algorithm the initial population can be obtained by generating random shapes between magnified and reduced versions of the given shape. Here both shapes should be aligned on their centroid. There can be various ways to get a new shape between the both shapes. For example, draw n radial lines across each LP of the smaller shape from the centroid with equi-spaced angles. Take a random initial LP on each radial line. On the other hand, take a random initial LP on each line between the corresponding LPs. As a result, the initial population can be created, which usually consists of a large number of shapes, and the number of shapes depends on the application. The better is the initial population, the easier and faster is the search for the optimal shape.

3.2   Crossover and Mutation

Crossover in biological terms refers to the blending of chromosomes from the parents to produce new chromosomes for the offspring. The analogy carries over to crossover in evolutionary algorithms. The evolutionary algorithm selects two shapes at random from the mating pool. The shapes selected may be different or identical, it does not matter. Once randomly you choose one location and then produce new shapes by swapping all LPs on the corresponding location.

Mutation randomly changes a LP of the shape of the population from time to time. As the result of reproduction and crossover operations, some local configurations of LPs in shapes of the population can be totally lost. Mutation protects evolutionary algorithms against such irrecoverable loss of good solution features.

3.3   Fitness and Selection

An evolutionary algorithm performs a selection process in which the "most fit" member of the population survives, and the "least fit" member is eliminated. As a result, the selected shapes are allowed to mate at random, creating offsprings which are subject to crossover and mutation with constant probabilities. The evaluation of the fitness depends on the value of the objective function. In the proposed ASM-based algorithm, the selection criterion describes how close it is from the optimal boundary. In this paper we use the cumulative local intensity differences to evaluate the fitness.

The proposed evolutionary local structure modeling and fitting algorithm is summarized as follows:

Algorithm 4 Evolutionary Local Structure Modeling and Fitting.

---

1. Given a shape from the $i - 1$th frame, denoted as $\mathbf{x}_{i-1}$, generate both magnified and reduced versions of $\mathbf{x}_{i-1}$ by 20%, denoted as $\mathbf{x}_{i-1}^R$ and $\mathbf{x}_{i-1}^M$, respectively. Align both shapes on the centroid of $\mathbf{x}_{i-1}$.
2. Draw n radial lines from the centroid with equi-spaced angles. (n represents the number of LPs of the shape.)
3. On each radial line, take a random initial LP in the range bounded by $\mathbf{x}_{i-1}^R$ and $\mathbf{x}_{i-1}^M$. Repeat this step until the initial population size becomes N.
4. Mutation: Choose an LP from the first shape, and perform mutation on it. Repeat this step for all N shapes.
5. Crossover: Randomly choose a pair of shapes, and choose one location and swap LPs on the corresponding location. Repeat this step N times.
6. Among $3N$ shapes, produced by steps 3, 4, and 5, choose N best shapes based on a fitting criterion.
7. Repeat steps 3 to 6 until the best fitted shape converges to the desired one.

---

4   Experimental Results

In this section we evaluate and analyze the proposed evolutionary algorithm for several applications of boundary extraction including local structure modeling in the ASM framework.

4.1   Evolutionary Algorithm for Boundary Extraction

We used a 25dB zero-mean Gaussian noisy image to evaluate performance of the proposed evolutionary algorithm for boundary extraction. Fig. 1 shows experimental results using a synthetic bumpy image and its noisy version. The latter image was simulated using 25dB zero-mean Gaussian noise. For the experiment 1,000 initial populations were generated and 1,000 iterations were performed. The more complicated a shape becomes, the more number of initial populations and iterations are needed.

4.2   Evolutionary Algorithm for Local Structure Fitting in the ASM Framework

In this experiment we compare the performance of the proposed evolutionary algorithm for local structure modeling in the ASM framework with the existing algorithm that minimizes the Mahalanobis distance. The set of input images was captured using a SONY 3-CCD DCR-TRV900 video camera with size 640×480. In order to analyze the effect of an environment and noise, an indoor image with simple background, an outdoor image with complicated back-ground, and

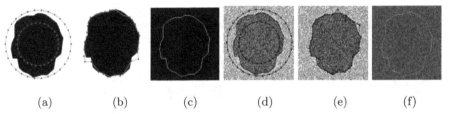

(a)   (b)   (c)   (d)   (e)   (f)

Fig. 1. Experimental results using a bumpy shape: (a) the original shape, (b) the detected contour of the original shape, (c) the gradient image of the original shape, (d) a bumpy shape with 25dB zero-mean Gaussian noise, (e) the detected contour of the noisy shape, and (f) the gradient image of the noise shape.

their noisy versions were used. For all experiments 500 initial populations were generated and 100 iterations were performed. Fig. 2 shows experimental results of local structure modeling followed by the PCA algorithm in the ASM framework. As shown in both noise-free and noisy gradients in Figs. 2b and 2d, the final results seem acceptable. We computed an objective measure of boundary fitting performance by using the manually assigned set of land-mark points.

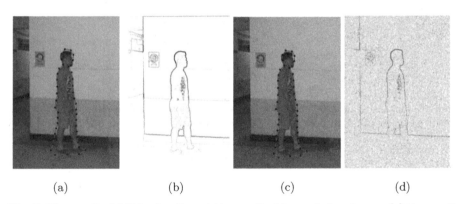

(a)   (b)   (c)   (d)

Fig. 2. The result of ASM using the existing method for an indoor image: (a) the result of ASM for an indoor image, (b) its gradient, (c) the result of ASM for a noisy indoor image, and (d) its gradient.

Fig. 3 shows experimental results using the proposed evolutionary algorithm that replaces the local structure modeling part in the ASM framework. In Fig. 3a the largest and smallest shapes represent the 120% and 80% versions of the mean shape, respectively. The former defines the outer boundary and the latter defines the inner boundary of the possible location of an initial population. The experiment shows that the proposed evolutionary algorithm also works very well for both noise-free and noisy inputs.

Fig. 4 shows experimental results of the existing local structure modeling followed by the PCA algorithm for an outdoor image with complicated background. As shown in the gradient image (Fig. 4b) the neighborhood of the man's right foot does not give a clear boundary, so the modeling accuracy becomes low

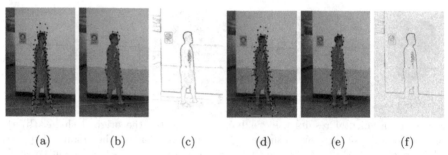

(a)   (b)   (c)   (d)   (e)   (f)

Fig. 3. Experimental results using the proposed evolutionary algorithm: (a) the original input image, (b) the detected contour followed by the PCA algorithm, (c) the gradient of the original image, (d) the input image with noise, (e) the detected contour of the noisy input, and (f) the gradient of the noisy image.

(a)   (b)   (c)   (d)

Fig. 4. The result of ASM using the existing method for an outdoor image: (a) the result of ASM for an outdoor image, (b) its gradient, (c) the result of ASM for a noisy outdoor image, and (d) its gradient.

in the region. When we added 20dB Gaussian noise, the performance became significantly worse, as shown in Figs. 4c and 4d.

Table 1. Mean-squred error of the fitted shapes using the existing and the proposed methods for indoor and outdoor images.

	Indoor image		Outdoor image	
Noise (dB)	Existing method	Proposed method	Existing method	Proposed method
45	258.15031	233.14784	402.59731	395.40541
35	270.55701	268.07845	432.37504	323.44104
25	270.38621	260.48063	448.95266	390.76600
15	320.75391	293.66130	495.20887	352.76822

Fig. 5 shows experimental results of the proposed evolutionary algorithm for an outdoor image. Compared with the result of the existing method shown in

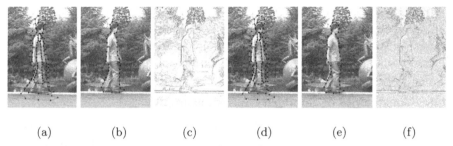

(a)   (b)   (c)   (d)   (e)   (f)

Fig. 5. Experimental results using the proposed evolutionary algorithm: (a) the original outdoor image, (b) the detected contour followed by the PCA algorithm, (c) the gradient of the original image, (d) the input image with noise, (e) the detected contour of the noisy input, and (f) the gradient of the noisy image.

(a)   (b)   (c)   (d)   (e)   (f)   (g)   (h)

Fig. 6. Object tracking results of multiple image frames: (a) 1st frame, (b) 7th frame, (c) 12th frame, (d) 20th frame, (e) 35th frame, (f) 50th frame, (g) 62th frame, and (h) 81th frame

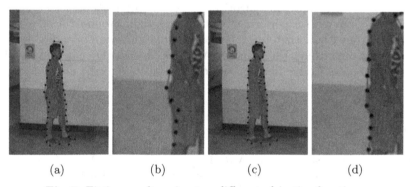

(a)   (b)   (c)   (d)

Fig. 7. Fitting results using two different objective functions.

Fig. 4, the proposed algorithm provides significantly improved fitting result even with a complicated background. Moreover, the propose algorithm still works very well with the noisy image.

4.3   Evolutionary Algorithm for Tracking in Image Sequences

If we provide an accurately estimated initial population, the evolutionary algorithm can be used for tracking an object in image sequences. Because the difference of objects between adjacent frames is very small, the estimated shape in the $i-1$th frame is almost the optimal initial guess for the ith frame. For this reason using the magnified and reduced versions of the shape from the $i-1$th frame can provide a feasible region of the initial location. Fig. 6 shows experimental results of tracking a human body of multiple frames.

4.4 Constraints of Similarity in Adjacent LPs

In this subsection we provide experimental results using an additional constraint that minimizes the intensity difference between adjacent LPs. The resulting objective function for fitting measure can be expressed as:

$$\sum_i [\{I(j) - I(j+1)\}^2 + \{I(j) - I(j-1)\}^2], \tag{8}$$

where $I(j)$ represents intensity value of the jth LP. Fig. 7a shows the result by minimizing an objective function of gradient only, and Fig. 7c shows the result by minimizing an objective function of gradient with the similarity constraint. Figs. 7b and 7d show the magnified versions of Figs. 7a and 7c for clearer comparison of the two objective functions.

5   Conclusions

We proposed an evolutionary algorithm-based robust local structure modeling technique to improve the performance of the ASM. The proposed ASM algorithm can efficiently extract the object boundary from an image or video. By using evolutionary algorithms, the proposed ASM-based algorithm can find the global minimum of an objective function, which is insensitive to the noise, occlusions, and shadow effect.

References

1. Maik, V.: Active Shape Model: A Review. Technical Report Image Processing and Intel-ligent Systems Lab. Chung-Ang University TR-IPIS-03-04 (2003)
2. Koschan, A., Kang, S., Paik, J., Abidi, B., Abidi, M.: Color active shape models for track-ing non-rigid objects. Pattern Recognition Letters **24** (2003) 1751-1765
3. Cootes, T. F., Taylor, C. J., Cooper, D., Graham, J.: Active Shape Models - Their Training and Application. Computer Vision and Image Understanding **61** (1995) 38–59
4. Blake, A., Isard, M.: Active Contours. Springer-Verlag (1998)
5. Goodall, C.: Procrustes methods in the statistical analysis of shapes. Journal of the Royal Statistical Society **53** (1991) 285–339
6. Goldberg, D.: Genetic Algorithms in Search, Opitimization and Machine Learning. Addision-Wesley (1989)
7. Sonka, M., Hlavac, V., Boyle, R.: Image Processing, Analysis, and Machine Vision. PWS Publishing (1999)

Multiclass Object Classification Using Genetic Programming

Mengjie Zhang and Will Smart

School of Mathematical and Computing Sciences
Victoria University of Wellington,
P. O. Box 600, Wellington, New Zealand,
{mengjie,smartwill}@mcs.vuw.ac.nz

Abstract. We describe an approach to the use of genetic programming for multiclass object classification problems. Rather than using fixed static thresholds as boundaries to distinguish between different classes, this approach introduces two methods of classification where the boundaries between different classes can be dynamically determined during the evolutionary process. The two methods are centred dynamic class boundary determination and slotted dynamic class boundary determination. The two methods are tested on four object classification problems of increasing difficulty and are compared with the commonly used static class boundary determination method. The results suggest that, while the static class boundary determination method works well on relatively easy object classification problems, the two dynamic class boundary determination methods outperform the static method for more difficult multiple class object classification problems.

1 Introduction

Classification tasks arise in a very wide range of applications, such as detecting faces from video images, recognising words in streams of speech, diagnosing medical conditions from the output of medical tests, and detecting fraudulent credit card transactions [1,2]. In many cases, people (possibly highly trained experts) are able to perform the classification task well, but there is either a shortage of such experts, or the cost of people is too high. Given the amount of data that needs to be classified, automated classification systems are highly desirable. However, creating automated classification systems that have sufficient accuracy and reliability turns out to be very difficult.

GP research has considered a variety of kinds of classifier programs, using different program representations, including decision tree classifiers and classification rule sets [3]. Recently, a new form of classifier representation – numeric expression classifiers – has been developed using GP [4,5,6,7]. In these years, this form has become the "standard form" of GP and has been successfully applied to some real world classification problems such as detecting and recognising particular classes of objects in images [5,6,8,9], demonstrating the potential of GP as a general method for classification problems.

G.R. Raidl et al. (Eds.): EvoWorkshops 2004, LNCS 3005, pp. 369–378, 2004.
© Springer-Verlag Berlin Heidelberg 2004

Numeric expression GP classifiers model a solution to a classification problem in the form of a mathematical expression, using a set of arithmetic and mathematical operators, possibly combined with conditional/logic operators such as the "if-then-else" structures commonly used in computer programs.

The output of a numeric expression GP classifier is a numeric value that is typically translated into a class label. For the simple binary classification case, this translation can be based on the sign of the numeric value [5,6,10,11]; for multi-class problems, finding the appropriate boundary values to separate the different classes is more difficult. The simplest approach – fixing the boundary values at manually chosen points – often results in unnecessarily complex programs and could lead to poor performance and very long training times [4,7,9].

The goal of this paper is to develop better classification strategies in GP for multi-class object classification problems. The main focus is on the translation of the numeric output of a genetic program classifier into class labels. Rather than using manually pre-defined boundary values, we will consider new methods which allow each genetic program to use a set of dynamically determined class boundaries. We will compare the dynamic methods with the current static (manually defined) method on a number of image classification problems of increasing difficulty.

2   The GP Approach for Object Classification

In this approach, we used the numeric expression based tree-structure to represent genetic programs. The ramped half-and-half method was used for generating the programs in the initial population and for the mutation operator. The proportional selection mechanism and the reproduction, crossover and mutation operators were used in the learning and evolutionary process.

2.1   Terminals

For object classification problems, terminals generally correspond to image features. In this approach, we used pixel level, domain independent statistical features (referred to as pixel statistics) as terminals and we expect the GP evolutionary process can automatically select features that are relevant to a particular domain to construct good genetic programs.

Four pixel statistics are used in this approach: the average intensity of the whole object cutout image, the variance of intensity of the whole object cutout image, the average intensity of the central local region, and the variance of intensity of the central local region. Since the range of these four features are quite different, we linearly normalised these feature values into the range [-1, 1] based on all object image examples to be classified.

In addition, we also used some constants as terminals. These constants are randomly generated using a uniform distribution. To be consistent with the feature terminals, we also set the range of the constants as [-1, 1].

2.2   Functions

In the function set, the four standard arithmetic and a conditional operation were used to form the function set:

$$FuncSet = \{+, -, *, /, if\} \tag{1}$$

The $+$, $-$, and $*$ operators have their usual meanings — addition, subtraction and multiplication, while $/$ represents "protected" division which is the usual division operator except that a divide by zero gives a result of zero. Each of these functions takes two arguments. The if function takes three arguments. The first argument, which can be any expression, constitutes the condition. If the first argument is negative, the if function returns its second argument; otherwise, it returns its third argument.

Table 1. Parameters used for GP training for the four datasets.

Parameter Kinds	Parameter Names	Shape1	shape2	coin1	coin2
Search Parameters	population-size	300	300	300	500
	initial-max-depth	3	3	3	3
	max-depth	5	5	6	6
	max-generations	50	50	50	50
	object-size	16×16	16×16	70×70	70×70
Genetic Parameters	reproduction-rate	20%	20%	20%	20%
	cross-rate	50%	50%	50%	50%
	mutation-rate	30%	30%	30%	30%
	cross-term	15%	15%	15%	15%
	cross-func	85%	85%	85%	85%

2.3   Fitness Function

We used classification accuracy on the training set of object cutout images as the fitness function. The classification accuracy of a genetic program classifier refers to the number of object cutout images that are correctly classified by the genetic program classifier as a proportion of the total number of object images in the training set. According to this design, the best fitness is 100%, meaning that all object images have been correctly recognised without any missing objects or any false alarms for any class.

To calculate the classification accuracy of a genetic program, one needs to determine how to translate the program output to a class label. This is described in section 3.

2.4   Parameters and Termination Criteria

The parameter values used in this approach are shown in table 1.

In this approach, the learning/evolutionary process is terminated when one of the following conditions is met:

- The classification problem has been solved on the training set, that is, all objects of interest in the training set have been correctly classified without any missing objects or false alarms for any class.
- The number of generations reaches the pre-defined number, *max-generations*.

3   Translation Rules in Classification

As mentioned earlier, each evolved genetic program has a numeric output value, which needs to be translated into class labels. The methods which perform this translation are referred to as *class translation rules* in this paper.

This section briefly describes the static class boundary determination method for multi-class classification commonly used in many approaches, then details the two new class translation rules: centred dynamic class boundary determination and slotted dynamic class boundary determination.

3.1   Static Class Boundary Determination

Introduced in [6,7], the static class boundary determination (SCBD) method has been used in many approaches to classification problems with three or more classes. In this method, two or more pre-defined thresholds/boundaries are applied to the numeric output value of the genetic program and the ranges/regions between these boundaries are linearly translated into different classes. This method is simple because these regions are set by the fixed boundaries at the beginning of evolution and remain constant during evolution.

If there are n classes in a classification task, these classes are sequentially assigned n regions along the numeric output value space from some negative numbers to positive numbers by $n-1$ thresholds/boundaries. Class 1 is allocated to the region with all numbers less than the first boundary, class 2 is allocated to all numbers between the first and the second boundaries and class n to the region with all numbers greater than the last boundary $n-1$, as shown in equation 2.

$$\text{Class} = \begin{cases} \text{class 1}, & v \leq T_1 \\ \text{class 2}, & T_1 < v \leq T_2 \\ \text{class 3}, & T_2 < v \leq T_3 \\ \cdots & \cdots \\ \text{class i}, & T_{i-1} < v \leq T_i \\ \cdots & \cdots \\ \text{class n}, & v > T_{n-1} \end{cases} \tag{2}$$

In this equation, n refers to the number of object classes, v is the output value of the evolved program, and T_1, T_2, T_{n-1} are static, pre-defined class boundaries.

3.2   Centred Dynamic Class Boundary Determination

The first new method is the Centred Dynamic Class Boundary Determination (CDCBD), where the class boundaries are dynamically determined by calculating the centre of the program output value for each class. The algorithm is presented as follows.

Step 1. Initialise the class boundaries as certain pre-defined values and evaluate each genetic program in the population to obtain the program output value and the class for each training example based on the SCBD method.

Step 2. For each class c, calculate the centre of the class according to equation 3:

$$\text{Center}_c = \frac{\displaystyle\sum_{p=1}^{M} \sum_{\mu_c=1}^{L} \text{ProgOut}_{p\mu_c}}{M \times L} \tag{3}$$

where M is the number of programs in the population and p is the index, L is the number of training examples for class c and μ_c is the index, $\text{ProgOut}_{p\mu_c}$ is the output value of the pth program on training example μ_c for class c.

Step 3. Calculate the boundary between every two classes by taking the middle point of the two adjacent class centres. If the region for a class is too small, extend it to 1.0.

Step 4. Perform classification based on the new boundaries and equation 2.

3.3   Slotted Dynamic Class Boundary Determination

The second new class translation rule is Slotted Dynamic Class Boundary Determination (SDCBD). In this method, the output value of a program is split into certain slots. When a large number of slots are used, a large amount of computation would be required. In our experiment, we used 200 slots derived from the range of [-25, 25] with a step of 0.25. Since the input features (terminals) are scaled into [-1, 1], the range [-25, 25] is usually sufficient to represent the program output. Each slot will be assigned to a value for each class.

In the first step, this method evaluates each genetic program in the population to obtain the program output value (`ProgOut`) and the initial class label for each training example based on the SCBD method.

In the second step, the method calculates the slot values for each class (`Array[slot][class]`) based on the program output value. The algorithm for this step is as follows:

```
FOR each slot and each class
   Array[slot][class] = 0
FOR each training example X {
   FOR each program p {
      ProgOut = execute program p with X as input
      IF ProgOut > 25 THEN ProgOut = 25
      IF ProgOut < -25 THEN ProgOut = -25
      slot = trunc((ProgOut + 25) / 0.25)
      Array[slot][class] += 1
   }
}
```

In the third step, this method dynamically determines to which class each slot belongs by simply taking the class with the largest value at the slot. However, in case a slot does not hold any positive value, that is, no programs produce any output at that slot for any training examples, then this slot will be assigned to the class of the nearest neighbouring slot.

While the two new methods could be applied to every generation of the evolutionary process, we applied them to the training examples every five generations to keep balance between evolution and class boundary determination.

3.4 Characteristics of the Dynamic Methods

Compared with the SCBD method, these two new methods have the following characteristics:

- The optimal boundaries for every two different classes or the optimal slot values for each class can be dynamically determined during the evolutionary process.
- Class labels do not have to fit into the predefined sequential regions. The optimal regions for each class in the program output space can be automatically determined in the evolutionary process. For example, class 3 can be set in between class 1 and class 2 if necessary.

4   Image Data Sets

We used four image databases in two groups with object classification problems of increasing difficulty in the experiments. Example images are shown in figure 1.

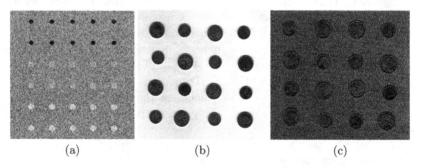

(a)   (b)   (c)

Fig. 1. Example images from Shape (a), Coin1 (b) and Coin2 (c)

4.1   Computer Generated Shape Datasets

The first group of images (figure 1 (a)) was generated to give well defined objects against a noisy background. The pixels of the objects were produced using a Gaussian generator with different means and variances for each class. Four classes of 711 small objects were cut out from those images to form the classification data. The four classes are: black circles, light grey squares, white circles, and the grey noisy background.

Two different data sets, *shape1* and *shape2* were constructed from this group of images. While set shape1 arranges the four classes in an ordinary order based on the intensities, set shape2 is out of this order.

4.2 NZ Coin Datasets

The second group of images has two NZ coin data sets. The first data set (*coin1*, figure 1 (b)) consists of scanned 5 cent and 10 cent New Zealand coins. There are five classes of 480 object cutouts: 5 cent heads, 5 cent tails, 10 cent heads and 10 cent tails, and a relatively uniform background. These images were scanned with a very low resolution of 75pt and the coins were located in different positions with random orientations. Compared with the *shape* data set, this set of objects (heads versus tails for either 5 cent or 10 cent coins) are more difficult to distinguish and it has more classes. The second data set (*coin2*, figure 1 (c)) also consists of five classes of object cutouts, but the background is highly clustered, which makes the classification problems much harder. Even human eyes cannot perfectly distinguish these objects.

The objects in each of the these data sets were equally split into three separate data sets: one third for the training set used directly for learning the genetic program classifiers, one third for the validation set for controlling overfitting, and one third for the test set for measuring the performance of the learned program classifiers.

5 Results and Discussion

This section presents a series of results of the two new dynamic class boundary determination methods on the four data sets in the shape and coin image groups. These results are compared with those for the static class boundary method. For all experiments, we run 10 times and the average results were presented.

5.1 Shape Data Sets

Table 2 shows the results of the three methods on the two shape data sets. The first line shows that for the Shape1 data set with 4 classes, the SCBD method achieved an average accuracy of 99.90% of 10 runs on the test set and the average number of generations of the 10 runs spent on the training process was 9.2.

Table 2. Results on the shape data sets.

Data set	Classes	Method	Gens	Accuracy
Shape1	4	SCBD	9.2	99.90%
		CDCBD	17.0	99.69%
		SDCBD	35.0	98.59%
Shape2	4	SCBD	50.0	96.87%
		CDCBD	26.5	99.67%
		SDCBD	43.5	98.46%

For the Shape1 data set, all the three classification methods obtained nearly ideal results, reflecting the fact that this classification problem is relatively easy. In particular, the SCBD method achieved the best performance.

For the Shape2 data set, the two new dynamic methods gave very good results. However, the static SCBD method produced a much worse performance in both classification accuracy and training time[1] than the two new dynamic methods because the classes in this data set were arranged arbitrary rather than in an ordinary order. This suggests that while the SCBD method could perform well on relatively easy classification problems with the classes arranged in an ordinary order, this method is not very appropriate for multi-class object classification problems with a randomly arranged order of classes. The two new dynamic methods, however, should be applied in this case. In addition, for these relatively easy classification problems, the CDCBD method seemed to be more effective and more efficient than the SDCBD method.

5.2   Coin Data Sets

Table 3 shows the results of the three methods on the two coin data sets. For these more difficult datasets, both the two dynamic methods achieved better results than the static method. In particular, the SDCBD was clearly superior to the CDCBD method, suggesting that the SDCBD method is more effective than the CDCBD for these difficult classification problems.

Table 3. Results on the coin data sets.

Data set	Classes	Method	Gens	Accuracy
Coin1	5	SCBD	50	82.94%
		CDCBD	48.4	85.46%
		SDCBD	48.5	89.44%
Coin2	5	SCBD	50	72.78%
		CDCBD	50	76.48%
		SDCBD	49.3	84.50%

5.3   Summary and Discussion

In summary, the results suggest that the SCBD method could perform well on relatively easy object classification problems if the classes were arranged in their ordinary order (such as Shape1), but would perform badly when the classes were out of this order (as in Shape2) or when the classification problems became more difficult (such as Coin1 and Coin2). This is mainly because a high degree of non-linearity is required to map the class regions on the program output to the object features in these situations.

The performances of all the three methods on the Coin1 and Coin2 data sets were worse than the two shape data sets, reflecting the fact that the classification problems in these two data sets are more difficult than in the two shape

---

[1] Note that the dynamic boundary determination process takes a bit time time. However, since we apply the dynamic methods once every five generations and the computation cost of the two dynamic methods is quite low, the average time spent on each generation can be still considered similar.

data sets. Because these problems were harder, more features might need to be selected, extracted and added to the terminal set. Also more powerful functions might also need to be applied in order to obtain good performance. However, the investigation of these developments is beyond the goal and the scope of this paper. We leave this for the future work.

In terms of the two dynamic methods, the CDCBD method performed better for the relatively easy datasets, while the SDCBD method performed better for the relatively difficult datasets.

6 Conclusions

The goal of this paper was to investigate and explore dynamic class boundary determination methods as class translation rules in genetic programming for multi-class object classification problems, and to determine whether the new dynamic methods could outperform the static method for relatively difficult problems. Two new classification methods, CDCBD and SDCBD, were developed and implemented where the class boundaries were dynamically determined during the evolutionary process.

The results on the four object classification problems in two groups of images showed that the static method, SCBD, performed very well on the relatively easy object classification problems where the classes were arranged in their ordinary order, but performed less well when the classes were arranged in an arbitrary order. While the two dynamic methods, CDCBD and SDCBD, also performed very well on the relatively easy object classification problems, they generally took longer training times. However, the two new dynamic methods performed much better than the static SCBD method for the relatively difficult object classification problems.

As expected, the performance on the four image data sets deteriorated as the degree of difficulty of the object classification problems was increased.

These results suggest that, for relatively easy object classification problems with classes in an ordinary order, both the static method (SCBD) and the two dynamic methods (CDCBD and SDCBD) can be applied, but the static method SCBD is recommended if training time is a critical factor. For other situations, the two dynamic methods are recommended.

Although developed for image/object classification problems, these two dynamic methods are also expected to be applied to general classification problems.

For future work, we will investigate whether the performance on the relatively difficult coin data sets can be improved if more features are added to the terminal set. We will also investigate the influence related to the fitness between different programs in the two dynamic methods. It would be also interesting to investigate the power and reliability of the two new methods on even more difficult, real-world image classification problems such as face recognition problems and satellite image detection problems, and compare the performance with other long-term established methods such as decision trees and neural networks.

References

1. J. Eggermont, A. E. Eiben, and J. I. van Hemert. A comparison of genetic programming variants for data classification. In *Proceedings of the Third Symposium on Intelligent Data Analysis (IDA-99), LNCS 1642*. Dpringer-Verlag, 1999.
2. Helen Gray. Genetic programming for classification of medical data. In John R. Koza, editor, *Late Breaking Papers at the 1997 Genetic Programming Conference*, pages 291–297. Standford University, 1997.
3. John R. Koza. *Genetic Programming II: Automatic Discovery of Reusable Programs*. Cambridge, Mass. : MIT Press, London, England, 1994.
4. Thomas Loveard and Victor Ciesielski. Representing classification problems in genetic programming. In *Proceedings of the Congress on Evolutionary Computation*, volume 2, pages 1070–1077, COEX, World Trade Center, 159 Samseong-dong, Gangnam-gu, Seoul, Korea, 27-30 May 2001. IEEE Press.
5. Andy Song, Vic Ciesielski, and Hugh Williams. Texture classifiers generated by genetic programming. In David B. Fogel, Mohamed A. El-Sharkawi, Xin Yao, Garry Greenwood, Hitoshi Iba, Paul Marrow, and Mark Shackleton, editors, *Proceedings of the 2002 Congress on Evolutionary Computation CEC2002*, pages 243–248. IEEE Press, 2002.
6. Walter Alden Tackett. Genetic programming for feature discovery and image discrimination. In Stephanie Forrest, editor, *Proceedings of the 5th International Conference on Genetic Algorithms, ICGA-93*, pages 303–309, University of Illinois at Urbana-Champaign, 17-21 July 1993. Morgan Kaufmann.
7. Mengjie Zhang and Victor Ciesielski. Genetic programming for multiple class object detection. In Norman Foo, editor, *Proceedings of the 12th Australian Joint Conference on Artificial Intelligence (AI'99)*, pages 180–192, Sydney, Australia, December 1999. Springer-Verlag Berlin Heidelberg. Lecture Notes in Artificial Intelligence (LNAI Volume 1747).
8. Mengjie Zhang, Peter Andreae, and Mark Pritchard. Pixel statistics and false alarm area in genetic programming for object detection. In Stefano Cagnoni, editor, *Applications of Evolutionary Computing, Lecture Notes in Computer Science, LNCS Vol. 2611*, pages 455–466. Springer-Verlag, 2003.
9. Mengjie Zhang, Victor Ciesielski, and Peter Andreae. A domain independent window-approach to multiclass object detection using genetic programming. *EURASIP Journal on Signal Processing, Special Issue on Genetic and Evolutionary Computation for Signal Processing and Image Analysis*, 2003(8):841–859, 2003.
10. Daniel Howard, Simon C. Roberts, and Richard Brankin. Target detection in SAR imagery by genetic programming. *Advances in Engineering Software*, 30:303–311, 1999.
11. Jamie R. Sherrah, Robert E. Bogner, and Abdesselam Bouzerdoum. The evolutionary pre-processor: Automatic feature extraction for supervised classification using genetic programming. In John R. Koza, Kalyanmoy Deb, Marco Dorigo, David B. Fogel, Max Garzon, Hitoshi Iba, and Rick L. Riolo, editors, *Genetic Programming 1997: Proceedings of the Second Annual Conference*, pages 304–312, Stanford University, CA, USA, 13-16 July 1997. Morgan Kaufmann.

Program Size and Pixel Statistics in Genetic Programming for Object Detection

Mengjie Zhang and Urvesh Bhowan

School of Mathematical and Computing Sciences
Victoria University of Wellington,
P. O. Box 600, Wellington, New Zealand,
{mengjie,urvesh}@mcs.vuw.ac.nz

Abstract. This paper describes an approach to the use of genetic programming for object detection problems. In this approach, local region pixel statistics are used to form three terminal sets. The function set is constructed by the four standard arithmetic operators and a conditional operator. A multi-objective fitness function is constructed based on detection rate, false alarm rate, false alarm area and program size. This approach is applied to three object detection problems of increasing difficulty. The results suggest that the concentric circular pixel statistics are more effective than the square features for the coin detection problems. The fitness function with program size is more effective and more efficient for these object detection problems and the evolved genetic programs using this fitness function are much shorter and easier to interpret.

1   Introduction

Object detection tasks arise in a very wide range of applications, such as detecting faces from video images, finding tumors in a database of x-ray images, and detecting cyclones in a database of satellite images. Since the 1990s, there have been a number of reports on the use of genetic programming (GP) in object detection and classification [1,2,3,4,5,6,7,8,9]. Typically, simple image features or high level features based on the whole objects (or the whole sliding windows) are used to form terminals, and the four arithmetic operations form the function set. However, the GP systems with the global pixel statistics for object detection often results in many false alarms. The main reason is that those global features are position and rotation invariant and not effective for object localisation. In this paper, we investigates three domain independent terminal sets based on pixel statistics of local regions from the whole object or the whole sliding window.

The main objective of a detection system is to achieve a high detection rate and a low false alarm rate, so that fitness functions in genetic programming for object detection are often based on detection rate and false alarm rate or similar measures [10]. A problem with such fitness functions is that the sizes of evolved genetic programs are usually quite large and often have a large amount

G.R. Raidl et al. (Eds.): EvoWorkshops 2004, LNCS 3005, pp. 379–388, 2004.
© Springer-Verlag Berlin Heidelberg 2004

of redundancy, which could make the genetic search very slow and very hard to find good solutions.

The overall goal of this paper is to develop a GP based approach to object detection problems. Specifically, we investigate two developments. The first is to explore the effectiveness of local region pixel statistics in the terminal sets. The second is to explore the effect on the evolutionary process of an additional measure, *program size*, in the fitness function.

The rest of the paper is organised as follows. Section 2 describes the main aspects of this approach. Section 3 describes the three image data sets and section 4 presents the experimental results. Section 5 draws the conclusions and gives future directions.

2   The Approach

This approach has a learning process and a testing procedure. In the learning process, the evolved genetic programs use a square input field which is large enough to contain each of the objects of interest. The programs are applied, in a moving window fashion, to the entire images in the training set to detect the objects of interest. In the test procedure, the best evolved genetic program obtained in the learning process is applied to the entire images in the test set to measure object detection performance.

In this system, we used tree structures to represent genetic programs. The ramped half-and-half method [11,12] was used for generating the programs in the initial population and for the mutation operator. The proportional selection mechanism and the reproduction, crossover and mutation operators [10,12] were used in the learning process.

2.1   Terminal Sets

Instead of using global features of an entire input image window only, we consider a number of local regions from which pixel statistics will be computed. In this approach, we investigated three sets of terminals based on different local regions.

Terminal Set I — Whole Window and Central Pixel Statistics. This terminal set only consists of four pixel statistics: the mean and standard deviation of the whole window, and the mean and standard deviation of the central local region, as shown in figure 1 (a). Since the centres of the objects are used to represent the object themselves, we hypothesised the central region is important. The motivation of this set is to investigate whether a very simple set like this can do a good enough job or not.

Terminal Sets II — Local Square Region Pixel Statistics. This terminal set was constructed by the means and standard deviations computed from a series of concentric local square regions centred in the input image window, as shown in figure 1 (b). For each input image window, four such regions were formed and eight features were constructed. The motivation here is to investigate whether this group of local square region features can do a better job than the first terminal set.

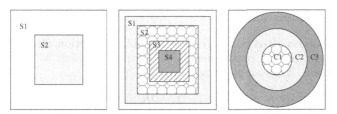

Fig. 1. Terminals. (a) Terminal set I; (b) Terminal set II; (c) Terminal set III.

Terminal Sets III — Local Circular Region Pixel Statistics. This terminal set was constructed by the means and standard deviations computed from a series of concentric circular regions centred in the input image window, as shown in figure 1 (c). For each input image window, three such regions were formed and six features were constructed. The motivation here is to investigate whether the circular local region pixel statistics are more effective than the square features.

2.2 Function Sets

In the function set, the four standard arithmetic operators and a conditional operator were used to form the non-terminal nodes:

$$FuncSet = \{+, -, *, /, if\}$$

The $+$, $-$, and $*$ operators have their usual meanings — addition, subtraction and multiplication, while $/$ represents "protected" division which is the usual division operator except that a divide by zero gives a result of zero. Each of these functions takes two arguments. The *if* function takes three arguments. The first argument, which can be any expression, constitutes the condition. If the first argument is positive, the *if* function returns its second argument; otherwise, it returns its third argument.

2.3 Object Classification Strategy

The output of a genetic program in a standard GP system is a floating point number. In this approach, we used the *program classification map*, as shown in equation 1, to perform multiple class object detection problems [8,10]. Based on the output of an evolved genetic program, this map can identify which class of the object located in the current input field belongs to. In this map, m refers to the number of object classes of interest, v is the output value of the evolved program and T is a constant defined by the user, which plays a role of a threshold.

$$Class = \begin{cases} background, & v \leq 0 \\ class\ 1, & 0 < v \leq T \\ class\ 2, & T < v \leq 2T \\ \cdots & \cdots \\ class\ i, & (i-1) \times T < v \leq i \times T \\ \cdots & \cdots \\ class\ m, & v > (m-1) \times T \end{cases} \tag{1}$$

2.4 Fitness Function

The goal of object detection is to achieve a high detection rate and a low false alarm rate. In genetic programming, this typically needs a "multi-objective" fitness function. An example fitness function [9] is:

$$fitness(DR, FAR) = K_1 * (1 - DR) + K_2 * FAR + K_3 * FAA \qquad (2)$$

where DR is the Detection Rate (the number of small objects correctly reported by a detection system as a percentage of the total number of actual objects in the images), FAR is the False Alarm Rate (also called *false alarms per object*, the number of non-objects incorrectly reported as objects by a detection system as a percentage of the total number of actual objects in the images), and FAA is the False Alarm Area (the number of false alarm pixels which are not object centres but are incorrectly reported as object centres before clustering). The parameters K_1, K_2 and K_3 reflect the relative importance between the DR, the FAR, and the FAA.

A problem of using this fitness function is that some evolved genetic programs are very long. When a short program and a long program produce the same detection rate and the same false alarm rate, the GP system will randomly choose one for reproduction, mutation or crossover during the evolutionary process. If the long programs are selected, the evolution for the rest of the learning process will be slow. In addition, such long programs are usually very difficult to interpret. This is mainly because this fitness function does not include any hints about the sizes of programs.

In this approach, we consider the effect of *program size* in the fitness function. The new fitness of a genetic program is calculated as follows.

1. Apply the program as a moving $n \times n$ window template (n is the size of the input image window) to each of the training images and obtain the output value of the program at each possible window position. Label each window position with the 'detected' object according to the object classification strategy. Call this data structure a detection map.
2. Find the centres of *objects of interest only* by the clustering algorithm:
   – Scan the detection map for an object of interest. When one is found, mark this point as the centre of the object and skip pixels in $n/2 \times n/2$ square to right and below this point. Continue this process until the whole detection map is scanned.
3. Match these detected objects with the known locations of each of the desired true objects and their classes.
4. Calculate the detection rate DR, the false alarm rate FAR, and the false alarm area FAA of the evolved program.
5. Count the size of the program by adding the number of terminals and the number of functions in the program.
6. Compute the fitness of the program according to equation 3.

$$fitness = K1 \cdot (1 - DR) + K2 \cdot FAR + K3 \cdot FAA + K4 \cdot ProgSize \qquad (3)$$

where $K1, K2, K3$, and $K4$ are constant weights which reflect the relative importance between detection rate, false alarm rate, false alarm area, and program size.

Table 1. Parameters used for GP training for the three databases.

Parameter Kind	Parameter Name	Shape	Coin1	Coin2
	population-size	800	1000	1600
Search	initial-max-depth	2	2	5
	max-depth	6	7	8
Parameters	max-generations	50	150	200
	input-size	20×20	82×82	62×62
	reproduction-rate	2%	2%	2%
Genetic	cross-rate	72%	70%	70%
Parameters	mutation-rate	28%	28%	28%
	T	100	80	80
Fitness	K1	5000	5000	5000
	K2	100	100	100
Parameters	K3	10	10	10
	K4	1	1	1

2.5   Parameters and Termination Criteria

The important parameter values used in this approach are shown in table 1. In this approach, the learning/evolutionary process is terminated when one of the following conditions is met:

- The detection problem has been solved on the training set, that is, all objects in each class of interest in the training set have been correctly detected with no false alarms.
- The number of generations reaches the pre-defined number, *max-generations*.

3   Image Data Sets

We used three data sets in the experiments. Example images are given in figure 2. These data sets provide object detection problems of increasing difficulty. Data set 1 (Shape) was generated to give well defined objects against a uniform background. The pixels of the objects were generated using a Gaussian generator with different means and variances for different classes. There are two classes of small objects of interest in this data set: circles and squares. Data set 2 (Coin1) was intended to be somewhat harder and consists of scanned images of New Zealand coins. There are two object classes of interest: the 5 cent coins and 10 cent coins. Each class has either tail side up or head side up and accordingly has a greater variance than data set 1. The objects in each class have a similar size but are located at arbitrary positions and with different rotations. Data set 3

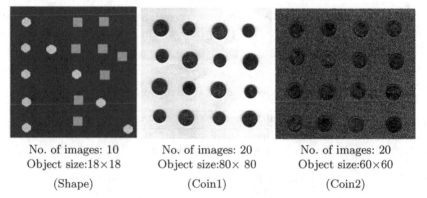

No. of images: 10   No. of images: 20   No. of images: 20
Object size:18×18   Object size:80× 80   Object size:60×60

(Shape)   (Coin1)   (Coin2)

Fig. 2. Object Detection Problems.

(Coin2) also contains two object classes of interest, but the detection task is significantly more difficult. The task is to detect the head side and the tail side of New Zealand 5 cents from a highly cluttered background. This detection task is very difficult and even human eyes could not detect those objects perfectly.

In the experiments, we used one, three, and five images as the training set and used five, ten and ten images as the test set for the *shape, coin1,* and *coin2* data sets, respectively.

4   Results

This section describes the detection results. For all cases, the experiments were repeated 10 times and the average results on the *test set* were presented.

4.1   Data Set I — Shape

The detection results using the three terminal sets and the two fitness functions are shown in table 2. The GP system using each of the three terminal sets and each of the two fitness function produced ideal result, that is, all the objects of interest were correctly detected from the large images in the test set without producing any false alarms. This reflects the fact that the detection problem in this data set is relatively easy. However, the genetic program detectors evolved by the evolutionary learning process were quite different if different fitness functions were used. We now analyse the evolved genetic programs.

Table 2. Object detection results for the *shape* data set.

Shape Data Set		Object Classes	
		circles	squares
Best Detection Rate(%)		100	100
False Alarm	Term set I	0	0
Rate (%)	Term set II	0	0
	Term set III	0	0

Genetic Program vs Fitness Function. To analyse the effect of program size in fitness function, we use the second terminal set as an example for this discussion. Other two terminal sets have a similar pattern.

To make a fair comparison, we did 20 experimental runs by using each of the two fitness functions and chose the best 40 evolved genetic program detectors trained using each fitness function. The average program size and a typical evolved genetic program trained with each fitness function are shown in figure 3.

```
                        Fitness function I

Average program size: 62
Sample Program:
(/ (+ (* (/ (/F8 T) (+ T F1)) (+ (+ T F2) (if F7 T F8)))
      (if (- (* T F4) F5) (- (+ F6 T) (* T F7)) (/ (- T F8) (- F1 T)))
      )
   (+ (if (/ (/ F2 T) (* T F3)) (+ (if T F4 F7) (- T F5))
         (* (/ F1 F6) (+ F7 T))) (* (/ T (+ T T)) (/ T (/ T F4))))
)
-----------------------------------------------------------------
                        Fitness function II

Average program size: 24
Sample program:
  (/ (if (/ (- F7 T) F7) F8 (* (- F7 F3) F2)) (/ F7 F7))
```

Fig. 3. Program size, sample programs and fitness function

As can be seen from figure 3, the size of evolved genetic program detectors obtained using the second fitness function is much shorter than using the first. This not only had the training time greatly reduced, but also made the program detector much easier to interpret. For example, the program detector obtained using the second fitness function in figure 3 can be simplified as

(if (- F7 T) F5 (* (- F7 F3) F2))

where F3, F5 and F7 are the means of the central regions S2, S3, and S4 (see figure 1b) of a detected object window, respectively, F2 is the standard deviation of the largest region, and T is a predefend threshold. This program can be translated into the following rule:

if (F7 > T) then ProgOut = F5; else ProgOut = (F7 - F3) * F2;

If the sweeping window is over the background only, F7 would be smaller than the threshold (100 here), the program would execute the "else" part. Since F7 is equal to F3 in this case, the program output will be zero. According to the classification strategy — object classification map, this case would be correctly classified as *background*. If the input window contains a portion of an object of interest and some background, F7 would be smaller than F3, which resulted in a negative program output, corresponding to class *background*. If F7 is greater than the threshold T, then the input window must contain an object of interest, either for *class1* or for *class2*, depending the value of F5.

While this program detector can be relatively easily interpreted and understood, the programs obtained using the first fitness function are generally hard to interpret due to the length of the program and lack of good building blocks.

4.2 Data Set II — Coin1

Since the second fitness function was proved to be better than the first, we only applied the second fitness function to this and the next data sets. The results for detecting 5 cent coins and 10 cent coins from a relatively uniform background are shown in table 3.

Table 3. Object detection results for the *coin1* data set.

Coin1 Data Set		coin10	coin05	overall
Best Detection Rate(%)		100	100	100
False Alarm	Term set I	0	20.83	10.42
Rate (%)	Term set II	0	12.5	6.25
	Term set III	0	0	0

According to table 3, every terminal set correctly detected all the objects of interest for each class. The false alarm rates produced by the three sets were, however, quite different. While terminal set III gave the ideal performance, terminal set II produced fewer false alarms than set I, indicating that only four pixel statistics from the whole window and a single central region are not sufficient for the detection problems in this data set. In addition, terminal sets I and II took much longer training time than set III. This suggests that the detection problems in this data set are more difficult than in the first data set, and the terminal set III is the best suited to these detection problems.

4.3 Data Set III — Coin2

As can be seen from table 4, none of the three terminal sets gave the ideal results, reflecting the difficulty of the object detection problems in this data set. While all the three terminal sets correctly detected all objects of interest in all images, they produced different false alarm rates. The first terminal set resulted in 68.5% false alarm rate. In particular, it produced 100% false alarm rate for detecting the tails. This indicates that four features only, two from the whole window and two from the local central region of the window, are not sufficient at all for this difficult detection problem. The false alarm rate was improved to 50% by using more local square region features in terminal set II. The third terminal set, with the local circular region features, produced the best results. The overall false alarm rate was decreased to 39.28%, which suggests that concentric local circular region pixel statistics perform better than local square region features.

This is probably because the local circular regions captured more knowledge from the coins.

Table 4. Object detection results for the *coin2* data set.

Coin2 Data Set		Object Classes		
		tails	heads	overall
Best Detection Rate(%)		100	100	100
False Alarm	Term set I	100	30.7	68.5
Rate (%)	Term set II	87.5	12.5	50
	Term set III	55.35	23.21	39.28

It is interesting to note that in each case, the false alarm rate for the tails was always higher than for heads. After a careful check and analysis from the object centres detected by the system, it was observed that all false alarms for the tails were generated along the borders of some objects of the heads. None of the centres of class *heads* were reported as false alarms for class *tails* — it was only the input windows with half of some objects in class heads and a bit more than half window of background that were incorrectly reported as tails.

5 Conclusions

The goal of this paper was to investigate the effectiveness of different local region pixel statistics and the effect of program size in fitness functions for object detection using genetic programming. The approach was tested on three object detection problems of increasing difficulty and achieved good results.

We developed three different terminal sets based on low level, statistical image features. Our results suggest that, in genetic programming for object detection problems, input terminals should include sufficient local region pixel statistics, and that the pixel statistics computed from local circular regions are more effective than square regions for these coin detection problems.

We modified the fitness function by including a measure called program size. The inclusion of program size in the fitness function resulted in shorter and better genetic program detectors. This not only reduced the search space and accordingly saved computation time, but also made the genetic program much easier to interpret and accordingly improved the comprehensibility of the evolved programs.

For future work, we will investigate whether the performance on the highly cluttered coin data sets can be improved if more features are added to the terminal set, if the fitness parameters $K2$ and $K3$ are increased, and if a better classification strategy is applied. We will also investigate whether the approach can perform well on more difficult object detection problems and compare this approach with other long term established methods such as neural networks and decision trees.

References

1. Walter Alden Tackett. Genetic programming for feature discovery and image discrimination. In Stephanie Forrest, editor, *Proceedings of the 5th International Conference on Genetic Algorithms, ICGA-93*, pages 303–309, University of Illinois at Urbana-Champaign, 17-21 July 1993. Morgan Kaufmann.
2. Karl Benson. Evolving finite state machines with embedded genetic programming for automatic target detection within SAR imagery. In *Proceedings of the 2000 Congress on Evolutionary Computation CEC00*, pages 1543–1549, La Jolla Marriott Hotel La Jolla, California, USA, 6-9 July 2000. IEEE Press.
3. Daniel Howard, Simon C. Roberts, and Conor Ryan. The boru data crawler for object detection tasks in machine vision. In Stefano Cagnoni, Jens Gottlieb, Emma Hart, Martin Middendorf, and G"unther Raidl, editors, *Applications of Evolutionary Computing, Proceedings of EvoWorkshops2002: EvoCOP, EvoIASP, EvoSTim*, volume 2279 of *LNCS*, pages 220–230, Kinsale, Ireland, 3-4 April 2002. Springer-Verlag.
4. Michael Patrick Johnson, Pattie Maes, and Trevor Darrell. Evolving visual routines. In Rodney A. Brooks and Pattie Maes, editors, *ARTIFICIAL LIFE IV, Proceedings of the fourth International Workshop on the Synthesis and Simulation of Living Systems*, pages 198–209, MIT, Cambridge, MA, USA, 6-8 July 1994. MIT Press.
5. R. Poli. Genetic programming for image analysis. In John R. Koza, David E. Goldberg, David B. Fogel, and Rick L. Riolo, editors, *Genetic Programming 1996: Proceedings of the First Annual Conference*, pages 363–368, Stanford University, CA, USA, 28-31 July 1996. MIT Press.
6. Andy Song, Thomas Loveard, and Victor Ciesielski:. Towards genetic programming for texture classification. In *Proceedings of the 14th Australian Joint Conference on Artificial Intelligence*, pages 461–472. Springer Verlag, 2001.
7. A Teredesai, E Ratzlaf, J Subrahmonia, and V Govindaraju. On-line digit recognition using off-line features. In *Indian Conference on Computer Vision, Graphics and Image Processing*, 2002.
8. Mengjie Zhang and Victor Ciesielski. Genetic programming for multiple class object detection. In Norman Foo, editor, *Proceedings of the 12th Australian Joint Conference on Artificial Intelligence (AI'99)*, pages 180–192, Sydney, Australia, December 1999. Springer-Verlag Berlin Heidelberg. Lecture Notes in Artificial Intelligence (LNAI Volume 1747).
9. Mengjie Zhang, Peter Andreae, and Mark Pritchard. Pixel statistics and false alarm area in genetic programming for object detection. In Stefano Cagnoni, editor, *Applications of Evolutionary Computing, Lecture Notes in Computer Science, LNCS Vol. 2611*, pages 455–466. Springer-Verlag, 2003.
10. Mengjie Zhang, Victor Ciesielski, and Peter Andreae. A domain independent window-approach to multiclass object detection using genetic programming. *EURASIP Journal on Signal Processing, Special Issue on Genetic and Evolutionary Computation for Signal Processing and Image Analysis*, 2003(8):841–859, 2003.
11. John R. Koza. *Genetic Programming II: Automatic Discovery of Reusable Programs*. Cambridge, Mass. : MIT Press, London, England, 1994.
12. Wolfgang Banzhaf, Peter Nordin, Robert E. Keller, and Frank D. Francone. *Genetic Programming: An Introduction on the Automatic Evolution of computer programs and its Applications*. San Francisco, Calif. : Morgan Kaufmann Publishers; Heidelburg : Dpunkt-verlag, 1998. Subject: Genetic programming (Computer science); ISBN: 1-55860-510-X.

Intrinsic Evolvable Hardware in Digital Filter Design

Yang Zhang, Stephen L. Smith, and Andy M. Tyrrell

Department of Electronics
The University of York
York, UK, YO10 5DD
{yz110, sls5, amt}@ohm.york.ac.uk

Abstract. This paper presents the application of Intrinsic Evolvable Hardware to real-world combinational circuit synthesis, as an alternative to conventional approaches. The evolutionary technique employs Cartesian Genetic Programming at a functional level by devising compact evolutionary processing elements and an external genetic reconfiguration unit. The experimental results conclude that in terms of computational effort, filtered image signal and implementation cost, the evolution outperforms convention approaches in most cases.

1 Introduction

Evolvable hardware (EHW) is a new method of circuit design, applying techniques derived from Evolutionary Computation (EC), such as Genetic Algorithms (GAs) and Genetic Programming (GP), to hardware design and synthesis.

EHW is usually implemented on Programmable Logic Devices (PLDs), such as Field Programmable Gate Arrays (FPGAs) and Reconfigurable Processing Units (RPUs). Early PLDs contained a collection of digital logic modules whose interconnections could be programmed, and thus genetic representations were used to encode the block connections. However, these PLDs were limited by slow programming cycles and limited programming times. Subsequently, FPGAs were developed, which offered finer granularity and allowed evolution of more complicated EHW circuit design. Although FPGAs overcame the PLDs programming problem by loading their configuration from SRAM, they are not fail-safe. Most of the design systems currently used are RPUs, which offer the high density and reconfigurability of SRAM-based FPGAs but with an open, fail-safe architecture.

EHW can be classified into Intrinsic Evolvable Hardware and Extrinsic Evolvable Hardware. Extrinsic EHW is simulated and evaluated in software and only the elite chromosome is downloaded to the hardware device in each generation, whereas in Intrinsic EHW, the hardware is configured directly for each chromosome. Thus, intrinsic EHW is reconfigured for each member of the population in each generation. Extrinsic EHW has an advantage over Intrinsic EHW in that its implementation is easier, whereas Intrinsic EHW research is often limited by the restriction of the hard-

G.R. Raidl et al. (Eds.): EvoWorkshops 2004, LNCS 3005, pp. 389–398, 2004.

ware. Therefore, most EHW experiments have been carried out using Extrinsic EHW. However, Intrinsic EHW performs more accurately in the real world environment and unpredictable situations, such as system adaptation and optimization. Intrinsic EHW is also more tolerant of inaccuracy within a particular simulation environment.

A broad and disparate range of applications of evolutionary computation in image processing may be found in literature, including the use of genetic algorithms in the segmentation of medical resonance imaging scans [1], a genetic program that performs edge detection on one-dimensional signals [2], the evolution of genetic programs to detect edges in petrographic images [3], and the evolution of spatial masks to detect edges within gray scale images [4]. It is worth mentioning that Sekanina [5][6][7] has achieved evolutionary design of digital image filters with virtual reconfigurable circuits. In [8], Cartesian Genetic Programming (CGP) was extended to a functional level. Instead of CLBs and 1-bit interconnection wires, Configurable Functional Blocks (CFBs) and 8-bit data-paths are utilized, making a considerable improvement. Digital image processing operations, such as image smoothing, edge detection, and image compression, have been carried out in an extrinsic EHW environment, which exhibits the potential of EHW in digital image operator design.

This paper proposes a novel configurable architecture, inspired by Cartesian Genetic Programming, dedicated for implementing high performance digital filters on a custom Xilinx Virtex FPGA xcv1000, together with a flexible and local interconnect hierarchy. Providing high reconfigurability and realization of a given circuit specification, this highly parallel architecture scales linearly with the filter complexity. It is reconfigured by an external Genetic Processing Unit (GPU).

Evolutionary computation can be successfully applied to small cells that outperform human designs, but the challenge of intrinsically evolving more complex combinational circuit still remains open. Section 2 of this paper introduces the application of intrinsic EHW in both gate-level and complex digital circuit design. For the EHW hardware implementation, there are two distinct phases, the evolutionary design phase and the execution phase, which are described in sections 3 and 4 respectively. The experimental results in section 5 reveal that this evolutionary design of digital image filter outperforms conventional approaches. An interesting conclusion is then drawn in section 6.

2   Complex Digital Circuit Design Employing Intrinsic EHW

As described above, evolutionary computation is able to improve or even replace human design of combinational circuits. However, this is usually achieved either through a computational effort that involves the sampling of a large number of individuals and the evolution of a great number of generations, or by devising new evolutionary techniques. For the latter, a sensible combination of the reconfigurable primitives and the evolutionary operators is essential to the success of intrinsic EHW design. The work in this paper employs intrinsic EHW by devising an array of compact processing elements and an external genetic reconfiguration unit, which outperforms human design in terms of computational effort and implementation cost.

We approached the problem using Cartesian Genetic Programming, which proved to be successful, not only in logic level evolution of three-bit adders, but also in functional level design of digital image filters. In terms of image filter evolution that employs at least nine 8-bit inputs (for a 3×3 neighborhood) and one 8-bit output, it is almost impossible to achieve the 72 inputs and 8 outputs required in a conventional CGP architecture. We adopted the extended CGP architecture [5] and adapted it for our own purpose, as shown in fig.1. The Processing Elements (PEs) are indexed from the top left (index 9), row-wise, and then column-wise finishing with the output PE. The two inputs of every PE can be connected to one of the outputs from the previous l columns (if the level-back parameter is l).

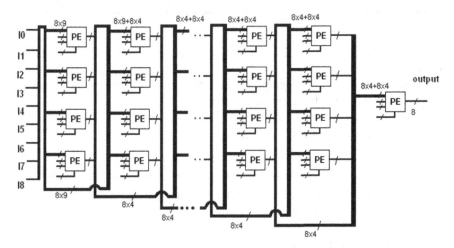

Fig. 1. The Cartesian Genetic Programming Reconfigurable Architecture

Since we are employing an intrinsic EHW processor design, we choose the most convenient application to evolve image filters for certain types of noise. Grayscale images of 256×256 pixels (8 bits/pixel) are considered in this paper. As with the conventional approach, a square neighbourhood of 3×3, centered on the target pixel, is defined and applied at $I0 \sim I8$. Every PE executes a function from table 1.

Chromosomes are encoded into linear integer strings in triplets, such as shown in fig. 2, which is a description of a 4×6 CGP architecture.

A 'steady-state' GA is employed, which suffices and aids the intrinsic hardware implementation. The initial population of 16 is generated randomly. The individual with the highest fitness is chosen as the parent and its mutated versions provide the

```
273  863  341  172  053  1211  1342  10 111  923  3 131  13 181
16 153  11 172  · · ·  23 174  21 232  24 281  25 272  22 261  29 324
```

Fig. 2. The chromosome encoded in an integer string

Table 1. Function codes

Code	Function	Code	Function
F0: 0000	X >> 1	F8: 1000	(X+Y+1) >> 1
F1: 0001	X >> 2	F9: 1001	X & 0x0F
F2: 0010	~ X	F10: 1010	X & 0xF0
F3: 0011	X & Y	F11: 1011	X	0x0F
F4: 0100	X	Y	F12: 1100	X	0x F0
F5: 0101	X ^ Y	F13: 1101	(X&0x0F)	(Y&0xF0)
F6: 0110	X + Y	F14: 1110	(X&0x0F) ^ (Y&0xF0)
F7: 0111	(X+Y) >> 1	F15: 1111	(X&0x0F) & (Y&0xF0)

new population. Previous experiments suggest that an adaptive mutation rate works best for hardware evolution [10]. In the case of the intrinsic evolution of image filters, an adaptive mutation rate was employed and the number of genes to be mutated was decided accordingly by this adaptive description:

$$num = c + p \times Ngenes \times (1 - norm\_fit)$$

$$norm\_fit = fitness / (255 \times (H-2) \times (W-2))$$

Where c and p are parameters set by experiment and experience. Here c is set to be 4 and p is set to be $(0,1)$. *Ngenes* is the number of genes in every individual.

For image filter design, usually two fitness functions are used, of which one is PSNR (Picture Signal Noise Ratio) and the other is MDPP (Mean Difference Per Pixel).

$$PSNR: fitness = 10 \times \lg \sqrt{S/N}$$

$$MDPP: fitness = 255 \times (H-2) \times (W-2) - \sum_{i=1}^{254} \sum_{j=1}^{254} orig(i, j) - crpt(i, j)$$

For the sake of the generality and adaptability of this work, both fitness functions have been employed in the software simulation, but only the MDPP fitness function was implemented in hardware evolution, as it is computationally easier for hardware calculation and implementation. The image size used was 256×256, and subsequently, only an area of 254×254 pixels could be chosen for 3×3 neighborhood processing.

3 The Evolvable Hardware Design Phase

3.1 Overview

The EHW CGP structure is implemented in a Xilinx Virtex xcv1000 FPGA. As fig.1 shows, the genotype layer contains the genetic information for evolution, which consists essentially of Processing Elements (PEs). Every PE cell is made up of two input multiplexers, one Functional Block (FB) and necessary interconnections. The FB contains a compact, and possibly redundant representation of the functions, one of which is to be chosen as the active function for this PE cell.

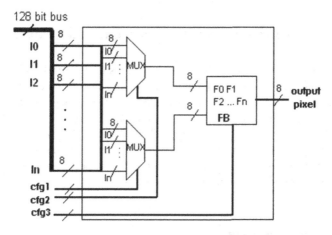

Fig. 3. The Architecture of the Processing Element (PE)

3.2 Actual Implementation

The evolutionary circuit operates nine 8-bit inputs and one 8-bit output. For each PE, the, multiplexer inputs will be the outputs from the previous two columns. Accordingly, both cfg1 and cfg2 should not exceed the number of the multiplexer inputs. The cfg3 input should be the binary representation of the number of functions in store. The fewer the functions, the faster is the evolution. Experience has shown that only functions F5, F7, F8 and F13 were exploited in the final best evolved best circuits. Further functions can be excluded but this is dependant on the resource requirements, as there is a trade-off between the functionality and the complexity of the hardware structure.

3.3 Synthesis Report

The main feature of this chip, the 128-bit bus from the memory pre-fetch circuitry, is evident. It supplies the PE array with a new 3×3 mask frame for every clock cycle. The entire kernel, therefore, is loaded in a single clock cycle; in each subsequent cycle, a 3×3 block is brought in from the larger image until the last pixel and its neighborhood. Each PE is allotted 8 bits of the 128-bit bus, so they are directly supplied with data individually. A 32-bit output bus for each column is another feature of this device. The output buses from the previous two columns are prepared for the configuration of the PEs. The functional configuration bus makes this structure compact as it only requires 2 bits for each PE. 254×254 clock cycles are required to download masks for evaluation for the whole image. The compact architecture requires 23 to 41 slices for each PE on a Xilinx Virtex xcv1000 FPGA.

4   The Intrinsic Evolvable Hardware Execution Phase

The execution phase, namely the Genetic Processing Unit (GPU), is realized by the hardware implementation of a Genetic Algorithm. Due to pipelining, parallelization and no function call overhead, a hardware GA yields a significant speedup over a software implementation [11], which is especially useful for real-time applications. While FPGAs are not as fast as typical Application Specific Integrated Circuits (ASICs), they still hold a great speed advantage over functions executing in software. In fact, a speedup of 1 to 2 orders of magnitude has been observed when frequently used software routines have been implemented on FPGAs.

4.1   The GPU Components

The GPU system consists of seven modules, as shown in fig. 4:

Interface Memory (IM): This is the central control unit. It responds to the start-up signal from the front end by asking the Input Buffer to download input data, and signals the front end to shut down when the evolution is accomplished. The initial population is produced by the Random Number Generator (RNG), read and stored in the IM without being initially evaluated.

Input Buffer (IB): The IB communicates with the front end at the request of the IM and reads in the original and distorted images, the mutation rate, and the RNG seed.

Random Number Generator (RNG): The RNG reads the seed from the IB. After the seed is loaded, the RNG module employs linear cellular automata (CA) to generate a sequence of pseudorandom bit strings. The CA uses 10 cells that change their states according to the rule 90 and rule 150 by Wolfram [12]. It generates the initial chromosomes for the IM. At the request of the Mutation module (MUT), it sends out mutation points, the genes to be mutated and the possible mutated genes.

Mutation (MUT): For each chromosome, it reads and uses the parameters from the RNG and IM. The adaptive mutation rate is employed. Chromosomes are sent back to the IM for further processing.

Evaluation (CGP): This is the core of EHW. It reads chromosomes from the IM and configures the CGP hardware structure. For each chromosome, or each potential circuit, the distorted bitmap is applied for evaluation.

Fitness Calculation (SEL): MDPP fitness function is used to calculate the MDPP. The best chromosome is sent back to the IM.

Output Buffer (OB): The evolution is shut down when a specific number of generations is reached. The OB will output the best chromosome and the filtered image.

4.2 The GPU Hardware Architecture

The GPU modules were designed to correlate well with the CGP operations, be simple and easily scalable, and have interfaces that facilitate parallelization. They were also designed to operate concurrently, yielding a coarse-grained pipeline. The Interface Memory (IM) acts as the main control unit during start-up and shutdown and communicates with the front end. After start-up and shutdown, control is distributed. All modules operate autonomously and asynchronously. The basic functionality of the GPU architecture is as follows.

1. The front end signals the IM that the evolution is to start; the IM accepts the request, asks for the parameters from the front end and stores them into the IB.

2. After loading the parameters, the IM notifies the CGP, the MUT and the RNG. Each of these modules requires its user specified parameters from the IB.

3. The initial population is randomly generated by the RNG and stored in the IM for evaluation and evolution.

4. The IM starts the pipeline by requesting the CGP to download the chromosomes and then the CGP passes them onto the SEL to calculate and store their fitness.

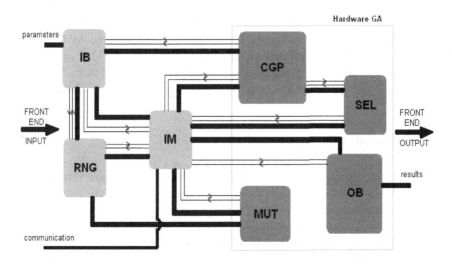

Fig. 4. The GPU Hardware Architecture

5. The SEL selects the best individual and sends it back to the IM.

6. When the IM receives all the chromosomes, ready for the next generation, it signals the MUT to start mutation.

7. The genes to undergo mutation are sent to the MUT by the IM, and the MUT mutates them within a set range and return them to the IM.

8. The CGP is working concurrently with the MUT.

This continues until the IM determines that the current GPU run is finished; it shuts down and signals the front end to read the final population back from the OB.

4.3   The Inter-module Communications

The modules in fig. 4 communicate via a simple asynchronous handshaking protocol similar to asynchronous bus protocols used in computer architectures shown in fig. 5. The chromosome communication among modules is through one 256-bit bus and accomplished in one clock cycle.

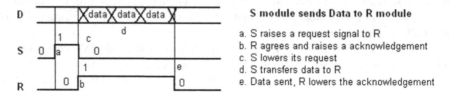

S module sends Data to R module

a. S raises a request signal to R
b. R agrees and raises a acknowledgement
c. S lowers its request
d. S transfers data to R
e. Data sent, R lowers the acknowledgement

Fig. 5. The Inter-module Handshaking Protocol

4.4   Synthesis Report

When HGA starts up, the IB reads in the bitmap image within 256×256 clock cycles. The IM takes $16 \times (3 \times 4 \times 6)$ clock cycles to generate the initial population. While the CGP is evaluating the chromosomes (254×254 clock cycles) the MUT executes reproduction ($16 \times 10 \times 7$ clock cycles). The whole GPU uses 50.72% of the Xilinx Virtex FPGA xcv 1000 (6322 slices), of which the CGP takes 1322 slices. This allows more complex CGP evolution and permits processing chromosomes in parallel.

5   Experimental Results

We designed the experiments using additive noise distorted bitmaps. Gaussian noise and uniform noise are both additive noise, which is independent of the image itself. In many cases, additive noise is evenly distributed over the frequency domain, whereas an image contains mostly low frequency information. Hence, the noise is dominant for high frequencies and can be suppressed by low-pass filters. This can be done either with a frequency filter or with a spatial filter. Generally, a spatial filter is preferable in evolvable hardware applications, as it is computationally cheaper than a frequency filter. In both noise categories, we used the bitmap of Lena as the target image at different distortion levels for the generality of the EHW architecture. All results were compared with the filtered results from the conventional image filters, such as gaussian, median and mean filters.

Fig 6.1 is the original Lena bitmap. Fig 6.2 is the Lena bitmap distorted by Gaussian noise with mean 0 and $\sigma = 16$. Fig 6.3 is the resulting image filtered by the EHW filter. Fig 6.4, 6.5 and 6.6 results from Median filter, Mean filter and Gaussian filter respectively. The MDPP is 15734299, 16040034, 16039677, 16017517 and 159980366 from Fig 6.2 to 6.6.

Fig 6.1. Original Lena bmp

Fig 6.2. Distorted by Gaussian Noise ($\sigma = 16$)

Fig 6.3. Filtered by the EHW filter

Fig 6.4. Filtered by the Median filter

Fig 6.5. Filtered by the Mean filter

Fig 6.6. Filtered by the Gaussian filter

6 Conclusion

The paper has presented a novel approach to combinational digital circuit design based on the technique of Intrinsic Evolvable Hardware. General-purpose image filters lack the flexibility and adaptability for un-modeled noise types. The EHW architecture evolves filters for certain types of noise without *a priori* information. In most industrial applications where design time and labour are of importance, this approach is preferable. The EHW approach employs fewer hardware slices, thus is a computationally cheaper alternative and for certain types of noise, the evolved filters outperform conventional filters.

References

1. R. Poli: Genetic Programming for Image Analysis. Genetic Programming: Proceedings of the First Annual Conference (1996) 363-368
2. C. Harris and B. Buxton: Evolving Edge Detectors. Research Note RN/96/3. University College London, Department of Computer Science (1996)
3. B. Ross, F. Feuten and D. Yashkir: Edge Detection of Petrographic Images Using Genetic Programming. Brock Computer Science Technical Reports, Brock University, Ontario, Canada CS-00-01 (2000)
4. S. Smith, D. Crouch and A. Tyrrell: Evolving Image Processing Operations for an Evolvable Hardware Environment. Evolvable Systems: From Biology to Hardware. Fifth International Conference, ICES 2003, 332-343
5. L. Sekanina: Virtual Reconfigurable Circuits for Real-World Applications of Evolvable Hardware. Evolvable Systems: From Biology to Hardware. Fifth International Conference, ICES 2003, 186-198
6. L. Sekanina, V. Drabek: Automatic Design of Image Operators Using Evolvable Hardware. Fifth IEEE Design and Diagnostic of Electronic Circuits and Systems DDECS'02, 132-139
7. L. Sekanina. Image Filter Design with Evolvable Hardware. Applications of Evolutionary Computing – Proceedings of the 4th Workshop on Evolutionary Computation in Image Analysis and Signal Processing EvoIASP'02, LNCS 2279 Springer-Verlag, Berlin (2002), 255-266
8. J. F. Miller, D. Job, and V. K. Vassilev: Principles in the Evolutionary Design of Digital Circuits – Part I. Journal of Genetic Programming and Evolvable Machines, Vol. 1, No. 1, 2000, pp. 8-35.
9. T. Back, F. Hoffimeister and H. P. Schwefel (1991): A Survey of Evolutionary Strategies. Proceedings of the 4th International Conference on Genetic Algorithms. pp. 2-9, San Fransisco, CA: Morgan Kaufmann
10. R. Krohling, Y. Zhou and A. Tyrrell: Evolving FPGA-based robot controller using an evolutionary algorithm. 1st International Conference on Artificial Immune Systems, Canterbury, Sep 2003
11. Stephen D. Scott, Sharad Seth and Ashok Samal: A Synthesis VHDL Coding of a Genetic Algorithm. Technical Report UNL-CSE-97-009, 1997
12. S. Wolfram: University and Complexity in Cellular Automata. Physica, 10: 1-35

Swarm Granulator

Tim Blackwell[1] and Michael Young[2]

[1]Department of Computing, [2]Department of Music,
Goldsmiths College, University of London, New Cross, London SE14 6NW, U.K.
{tim.blackwell, michael.young}@gold.ac.uk

Abstract. This paper describes a Swarm Granulator, a new application of particle swarms to sound synthesis. Granulation, an established technique in sound synthesis, depends on many parameters which are non-intuitive and hard to control from a human perspective. It is proposed here that a particle swarm can organize these parameters and produce musically interesting and novel timbres. A crucial element of the system is the self-organization of grain parameters around attractors which themselves represent musical events and textures in an external environment. This means that Swarm Granulator is interactive, and not merely reactive.

1 Introduction

Swarms, flocks, herds and shoals are natural systems that are remarkable in many ways, not least for their properties of self-organization. Killer bees chase and swarm around an unfortunate 'target', and termites exploit stigmergy (response at a later time to local environmental modification) and build elaborate nests. Starlings, fruit bats and herring all congregate in large numbers, developing spatio-temporal organization over large distances and long time-scales. It has been realized that spontaneous organization can develop without central control, but from interactions and a degree of positive and negative feedback [7].

Freely improvised music differs from composed music, or even music that accepts improvisation within an agreed structure (exemplified by some genres of jazz), by the degree of uncertainty that surrounds a performance. The performers (and indeed the audience) may have little idea of how the music will proceed before it starts [2]. Making improvised music is a social experience; social processes take precedence over traditional Western concepts like form and structure [8]. Such music is created spontaneously through the process of "becoming situated" [1] in which performers assume and cast roles, recognize and pursue shared goals and explore forms of interaction. Structure emerges as a consequence of these behaviors, (that is, from the 'bottom up'); players contribute musical material and interact with one another, establish relationships that are, to use Berry's terminology, complementary, counteractive or co-functioning (that is, relationships which are also evident in composed music) [3]. It is frequently the case therefore that 'free' improvisation can evolve structures, at least at a local level, creating the illusion of certainty, as if there actually is a

G.R. Raidl et al. (Eds.): EvoWorkshops 2004, LNCS 3005, pp. 399–408, 2004.

conductor or a script. It has been proposed that self-organization is one mechanism for furthering the generation of spontaneous musical structure [6]; the computer intervenes and contributes to these collaborative processes.

It has already been demonstrated that a virtual swarm of particles can develop musically interesting 'improvisations' [4]. In Swarm Music, the particles move in a physical space. Particle positions are mapped onto sound-event parameters (such as event duration, loudness and pitch) and the swarm-like shape generated by the particles corresponds to a melody and, importantly, to an expressive performance of this melody. The result sounds improvisational rather than compositional because the fluctuations in the swarm shape produce ever-changing melodic and rhythmic variations. In this view, the organization of notes in a melody can arise from the (self) organization of particles in sound-event space.

However, Swarm Music is also interactive in the sense that it can both respond to, and initiate, changes in the musical environment. (A purely reactive system would only respond.) Following the inspiration from nature, the interaction is implemented as a series of targets or attractors, which represent modifications to the local environment. These attractors are parameterizations of musical events produced by human performers and by other swarms [4]. As the swarms organize around these attractors, musical ideas are generated which influence the improvisations of the musicians, leading to further attractor placements. Musical structure is generated stigmergetically by modifications to the environment of sound-event space.

Swarm Music is a MIDI-based system. It only provides sound-events; it does not specify how the events should actually sound. MIDI, like Western notation, is limited to the confines of the pitch-rhythm "lattice" [13]. The "lattice" represents music's conceptual confinement to the traditional hierarchy of musical 'notes', phrases, fixed instrumentation and so on. Pitch and duration are emphasized at the expense of the many other characteristics of a sound event, particularly timbre and its morphology. Musicians are acutely aware of these characteristics; a considerable part of their training is after all spent at developing instrumental control, and much of the expressive quality of music arises from timbral manipulations. Unsurprisingly, it is a key feature of freely improvised music, where the focus is often on expressive gesture, texture and the exploration of timbre. These concerns are shared by composers working with electronics and computers; there is a widely accepted aesthetic which rejects the pitch-based "lattice" as the only basis for musical organization.

It is pertinent, then, to consider if swarming can be used to develop music which explores these characteristics, and if self-organization can be used to relate timbres, (and even gestures and textures) to the impetus offered by external sounds. Artificial instruments can be constructed using various synthesis techniques [9]. The most appealing technique from a swarm perspective is granular synthesis because this technique provides a direct metaphor. Sound grains are packets of sound of very short duration; the asynchronous superposition of many of these grains produces a rich mass or 'cloud' of sound, whose characteristics are determined by a wide range of parameters [10]. It is tempting therefore to map the grains to particles, and the cloud to a swarm. Evolution of the cloud will be influenced by the attractors which themselves are a parameterization of the external sound events to which the system has access. There are many ways an external sound could be parameterized as attractors in the physical space of the swarm, and many ways that particle positions can be interpreted as grain parameters. The next section explains the issues involved, and an interpretive model of interaction is presented in section 3. Section 4, which is an overview of the system, explains how the analysis of sections 2 and 3 is integrated in the final design. A brief evaluation concludes the paper.

2 Organizational Levels

The structural parameters of music, and their complex interrelations, form the basis of whole areas of scholarly endeavor. In this paper we can only briefly outline a working method for the swarm granulator. Music, whether composed or improvised, can be conceived in terms of a hierarchy of parameters, or organizational levels in which some properties (such as pitch, duration and timbre) are considered the most fundamental, and many others, (such as melody, harmony, rhythm, instrumentation) are accepted as complex, conceptual and historically/culturally specific [3].

One useful approach to understanding organizational level is based on perceptual and relative time scales [10]. The timescale closest to our immediate experience of sound is the sound-event (ministructural) level, a timescale around 0.1 to 10 seconds.

The granular process works at the grain-event (microstructural) level. Grains are measured in milliseconds; heard individually they may appear as clicks (that is, on the verge of timbral perception) or as longer fragments of recognizable source sound. We may on occasion consciously perceive that a sound comprises discreet events, but nevertheless it is not easily possible to measure the granular properties of a given sound.

The third relevant timescale is the mesostructural level; the level at which sound-events are experienced in relation to one another, rather than individually, as in the musical phrase, a melody or rhythmic pattern. Mesostructure can be considered as divisions of a higher level, that of musical form (the macrostructural level), or as a product of the lower sound event level. The interface between the sound-event and mesostructure is extremely hard to determine, especially outside the context of a given musical style. In fact in both free improvisation and electoacoustic composition, the alleged separation between these levels is itself explored and questioned, necessitating a alternative vocabulary characterized by terms such as "sound mass" and "cloud" [10].

The essential difficulty faced in the design of Swarm Granulator is the decision about parameterization of the external sound, since this can occur at any level, and may even involve several levels. Most transparently, grain-event parameters could be extracted by wavelet analysis. The entire system would then be unified at this level, and it would be very interesting to explore self-organization upwards through the levels, from grains to notes, and from notes into form. (Swarm Music is a unified system, working entirely at the sound-event level.) It is not clear if wavelet analysis is a real-time technique; parameterization at the note-level is used in Swarm Granulator.

3 Interpretation

Interactive processes in musical improvisation are undoubtedly highly complex, functioning across different timescales/structural levels and subject to all manner of social and cultural influences, just as computer processes are subject to programming decisions. A simple model known as *interpretation* has been proposed in Swarm Music [4, 5]. Interpretation is a crucial function in Swarm Music and Swarm Granulator.

Figure 1 depicts interaction between two systems (human or silicon-based) A and B. System A (system B) is listening to an audio stream Y (stream X) emanating from B (system A). A (B) is also producing an audio stream X (Y). This picture, however, hides much. Human systems will be quite selective about which parts of the audio environment they will use to inform their own output, and this is desirable for silicon improvisers too. Interactivity merely implies that A is *influenced* by B, although A's musical output will depend on many personal, hidden variables h_A which are unaffected by what he/she/it hears.

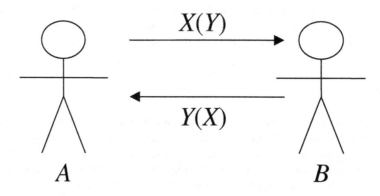

Fig. 1. A Simple Illustration of Interaction

The Swarm Music and Swarm Granulator systems both comprise attractors and swarms of virtual particles moving in a physical space. The attractors are parameterizations of the input stream, and the particle motions lead to parameterization of the external stream, whether at the note-level (Swarm Music) or at the grain-level (Swarm Granulator). The particles move autonomously, but they will respond to any attractors in their nearby environment, so that external events *influence* the swarm. Interpretation refers to the level-dependent rules for attractor placement, and on how the particle positions are used to modulate the output. In other words, interpretation is at the heart of system interaction.

A 'interprets' or attaches level-dependent meaning to the input Y in some way; this can be represented symbolically as P: $Y \rightarrow p$ where p represents some of the information which can be inferred from Y. If A decides to interact with B, then A must adjust her/his/its output in some way using this information, although this may not happen immediately, and the influence may be weak. In other words, A must memorize recent information p, and A can be quite selective about what elements of p to use. This process will be represented as $F(h, p)$: $x \rightarrow q$ where $F(h, p)$ is an internal process, dependent on hidden parameters h, that prepares output information q from internal states x. This formulation emphasizes that output is generated from internal processes which may depend only weakly on p, and can even continue in the absence of p. Finally, q modulates the output stream, which in Swarm Granulator is a stream of sound grains, using an algorithm Q, Q: $q \rightarrow X$.

4 System Overview

4.1 Swarming

Particle swarms ultimately derive from the virtual flocks of Reynolds' original animations [11], but the flapping animated 'boids' are replaced with structure-less point-particles in an N-dimensional 'physical' space. The particles change their positions by the application of simple forces or accelerations. In Reynolds original work, the accelerations are spring-like attractions towards the centre of mass of neighboring particles, a collision avoiding acceleration and a velocity matching term.

The particle swarm used in Swarm Granulator builds on the experience gained from Swarm Music. Particles are not stateless, but have a number of parameters which determine their interactions. A particle is specified by the set $\{x, v, p\}$ where $x = (x_1, \ldots x_N)$ and $v = (v_1, \ldots v_N)$ are the particle position and velocity and p is the particle attractor (an N-dimensional vector). Five scalar parameters $\{c\}$ determine the dynamics of each particle in the swarm; v_{clamp} is a clamping or limiting speed, q and m are for particle charge and mass, d_{core} is a small distance used to shape the inter-particle repulsion and d_{limit} is a perception limit. This perception limit is an extension of the perception limit for charged swarms, which was only relevant for the computation of inter-particle repulsion; a particle at x is only aware of other particles and attractors within a box $B_{limit}(x) = [-d_{limit}, d_{limit}]^N$ centered on x. These dynamical parameters $\{c\}$ determine particle motion, and hence ultimately sound output, independently of where (if anywhere) the attractors are, and correspond to the hidden parameters discussed in section 3. The swarm position x_{swarm} and swarm attractor p_{swarm} are defined to lie at the centroids of the particle positions and particle attractors respectively.

The particle dynamics are a set of update rules. These have been simplified from the rules used in Swarm Music and from other particle swarms. In particular, the spring constants determining the strengths of the attractions have been set at unity. This is because the parameter with the dominating effect on output is v_{clamp} [5].

The particle update rules for particle k, $k = 1, 2...M$ are given in Equations (1) – (5). Components of vectors along any direction are projected out by scalar products with the unit vectors e_i, $i = 1...N$. Equation (1) calculates the accelerations which are added to the velocity at iteration t-1 to form the updated velocity at iteration t, (2). The updated velocity is then added to the position (3). The linear spring-like attractions to swarm and attractor centers are preceded by a delta function, defined by equation (4), which ensures that these calculations are only applied if $x_{swarm, \, t-1}$ and $p_{swarm, \tau}$ are in the box $B_{limit}(x)$. The attractor is updated in real time τ and runs as a separate process to the particle update thread.

Equation (5) is a Coulomb repulsion between particles that are within the perception limit of each other, and is equal to a constant for separations less than the d_{core} and given by the inverse square law otherwise. Equation (5) sums up terms $a_{k,l, \, t-1}$ which are the Coulomb repulsions between particle l and k, and equation (6) shows the calculation of a component of this term.

The Coulomb repulsion differs from the particle dynamics used in [5] because the spatial dimensions are decoupled. The update rules are merely N copies of a one dimensional dynamical system. Previously, the components were coupled through the Coulomb repulsion which was a function of the Euclidean distance $|r|$ between particles. Dimensional coupling can still take place in Swarm Granulator, but it must be handled by the interpretative functions.

$$
\begin{aligned}
A_{k,t} \quad &= \quad m_k^{-1} \, [\, \delta(x_{swarm, \, t-1}, x_{k, \, t-1})(x_{swarm, \, t-1} - x_{k, \, t-1}) \\
&\quad + \delta(p_{swarm, \, \flat} \, x_{k, \, t-1})(p_{swarm, \tau} - x_{k, \, t-1}) \\
&\quad + a_{k, \, t-1}\,] \tag{1}
\end{aligned}
$$

$$
v_{k,t} \quad = \quad v_{k, \, t-1} + A_{k, \, t} \tag{2}
$$

$$
x_{k, \, t} \quad = \quad x_{k, \, t-1} + v_{k, \, t} \tag{3}
$$

$$
\delta(y, x) \quad = \quad 1 \text{ if } y_{k, \, t-1} \in B_{limit}(x_k) \tag{4}
$$
$$
 0, \text{ otherwise}
$$

$$
a_{k, \, t-1} \quad = \quad \sum_{l=1, l \neq k}^{M} a_{k,l,t-1} \delta(x_k, x_l) \tag{5}
$$

$$
a_{k,l,t-1} \quad = \quad \frac{Q_l Q_k}{|x_{core}|^2} \frac{x_{k,t-1} - x_{l,t-1}}{|x_{k,t-1} - x_{l,t-1}|}, \quad |x_k - x_l| < d_{core} \tag{6}
$$

$$
\phantom{a_{k,l,t-1}} \quad = \quad \frac{Q_l Q_k}{|x_{k,t-1} - x_{l,t-1}|^2} \frac{x_{k,t-1} - x_{l,t-1}}{|x_{k,t-1} - x_{l,t-1}|}, \quad \text{otherwise.}
$$

4.2 Interpreter and Swarmer

This interpretive model forms the basis of Swarm Granulator which is comprised of two systems running on different computers, an interpreter and a swarmer. The interpreter is responsible for the listening and modulating functions P and Q, and the swarmer implements F. A diagrammatic overview is shown in Figure 2.

P parses the input stream into a series of *N*-dimensional parameters p_τ (no level implied). The p_τ's are sent to the swarmer where they are stored in a buffer. They are stored here for a holding time (which depends on the buffer size and the rate of flow of information into the buffer) after which they are placed in the physical space of the swarm as attractors. The buffer is a simple implementation of a memory and is important for stigmergetic interactions which are not instantaneous.

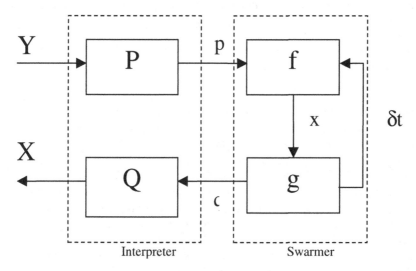

Fig. 2. Block view of Swarm Granulator

The swarmer splits *F* into two processes, *f* and *g*. *f* is a particle update function and *g* is a function which determines timing. Each particle *k* in the swarmer, *k* = 1…*M*, is updated in turn in a continuous loop. Immediately after particle *k* has been updated, the swarmer pauses for a time interval δt_i. The index *i* is a counter which is incremented by one at each particle update. The particle update can be expressed formally as

$$x_i \quad = \quad F(x_{i\text{-}M}\ldots x_{i\text{-}1}, \{p_\tau\}, \{c\}) \tag{7}$$

where *M* is the swarm size. Equation (7) is a formal statement of the rules (1) - (6) where x_i is the position of particle *k* at iteration *t*. Particle velocities do not appear in the swarming function *f* because they can always be constructed from the x_i using $v_{k,t}$ = $x_{k,t}$ - $x_{k,t\text{-}1}$ $v_i = x_i$ - $x_{i\text{-}M}$. Equation (7) shows that the swarm can be replaced by a state machine whose current state x_i depends on its *M* previous states $x_{i\text{-}M}\ldots x_{i\text{-}1}$ and is influenced by the inputs $\{p_i\}$ and parameters $\{c\}$.

A second function *g* extracts event information δt_i and $\delta t_{i,\,event}$ from x_i where δt_i is the time between successive events and $\delta t_{i,\,event}$ is the duration of this event. The output from the swarmer is a stream of 'event' parameters (no level implied) q_0, q_1, q_2… at real times T, T+δt_0, T+δt_1, … Two components of q_i contain timing information and the remaining *N*-2 components are real numbers.

The interpreter receives q_i and prepares output using Q. From the perspective of the interpreter, the swarmer merely transforms the input parameterization into modulating numbers $q = gf(p)$. The job of the interpreter is to listen at some structural level (P) and respond at the same or different level (Q). The interpretation can be 'transparent' with $P = Q^{-1}$ (and this is the case in Swarm Music which operates at a single level) but this is not the only option. All that matters is that the interpretative functions P and Q are *transparent enough* for interacting humans to grasp and use during performance (a similar point applies for human-human interaction).

4.3 Granulator

The overall system has three modules; interpreter, swarmer and the granulator which is the actual sound engine. In granulation, or granular synthesis, grains are generated by multiplying an envelope (window) of given amplitude, duration and shape with a waveform. The simplest approach would be to employ a Gaussian envelope and sine tone waveform of a given frequency. Other envelope shapes are feasible, as are more complex waveforms (for example, derived from sampled audio, as in our case). Synthesis is achieved by iterating grains either synchronously or asynchronously. The result is a stream of sound with potentially very diverse timbral characteristics. Many grain-event level parameters affect these perceptual features; the diverse approaches to this technique are explored in detail by Roads [10].

The granulator is implemented using Max/MSP, with objects from a 'granular toolkit' [20]. In our current implantation, the interpretative function P operates at the sound-event level and Q operates at the grain-event level, and a transparent mapping is made from extracted parameters to grains. Specifically, P extracts four sound-event parameters: pitch, amplitude, duration and duration between successive sound-events. Q uses q to determine grain-event pitch, amplitude, duration, time between successive grains, and grain attack and decay time. The swarmer, therefore, operates in $N = 6$ dimensional physical space; attractor components in the dimensions representing grain attack and decay times are fixed. The grains are shaped with a Hanning window and the point of entry in the buffer of continuously sampled audio is set by the operator.

Three simultaneous grain streams are used. This means that there are three swarmers, each with different parameter settings $\{c\}$ (which can be altered by the operator) sending parameter streams to three granulators. The granulators and interpreters are implemented on a 500 MHz Apple G4 and the swarmers, written in Java, run on a 1.7GHz pc. The two machines communicate using our own implementation of the Open Sound Control protocol for Ethernet communication [21].

5   Evaluation and Future Developments

Swarm Granulator, which is still essentially a prototype of a more complete system, was nevertheless 'tested' at two recent events. These two performances of Swarm

Granulator have both involved interactions between the granulator and live musicians. The first event was at the Modular 2003 meeting, London College of Music and Media, Sept 11 2003, with the classical singer Robin Higgins. The second event was part of Big Blip, the Brighton (U.K.) Arts-Science festival, Oct 11th 2003, with L.E.G., an improvising ensemble comprising Mette Bille (voice), Panos Ghikas (violin) and Johannes von Weiszacker (cello). Some excerpts from the second performance are available on a website [17].

Each concert comprised a single spontaneously improvised performance, undertaken with minimal preparation (a technical sound check). The performances lasted a little over ten minutes. Ultimately the performances can only be evaluated subjectively, that is, according to personal aesthetic criteria, but they demonstrated that the Swarm Granulator is sustainable under real-life performance conditions. Two reactions follow:

It was a really successful performance. Although I work in algorithmic composition it is rare indeed that I experience a system with genuine musicality, so it's always exiting when that happens. Andrew Gartland-Jones, Big Blip organizer.

The effect on the listener was one of fascination; surprisingly musical. Howard Moscovitz, performer at Modular 2003 [15].

We can also gain some insight into the experience of the performers through discussion.

-Did your contribution feel valued...did the machine support your contribution?
Panos Ghikas: *My contribution did feel valued. I felt the resulting sound was very interesting because the 'machine' complimented my 'real' sound.*
-To what extent did you feel 'directed' by the swarm machine?
PG: *I felt there was a sense of 'direction' as strong as the one that can be felt during 'human-only' improvisation.*
-To what extent did you feel you controlled/influenced the machine?
PG: *The extent of influence I felt was varied but mostly strong.*
- Did the machine give you ideas?
PG: *Yes, mainly structurally.*
- Was this a new musical experience?...in what way?
PG: *I am not sure if it was a new musical experience but it was the most impressive musical interaction I have experienced with a 'machine'!*

Also these comments from Mette Bille:
"The free improvisation with the ensemble and [Swarm Granulator] worked fine, it was great that you could record some of the playing and then send it back as an extra element to play with or against. I didn't find any problems with the program as an extra element as it was easy to hear what was happening. So generally it was just a question of tuning in [to] each other as musicians...I thought [it] worked well."

These comments do not in themselves verify the system but they do motivate further work with Swarm Granulator. Future developments will concern parameter extraction and mapping and an investigation of how equations (1) – (6) relate to the actual sound produced. Our current approach to parameter mapping is essentially one-to-one and at two levels. Although it is arguable that literal parameter mirroring is neither necessary nor desirable, it is desirable to integrate further characteristics of the sound event level (e.g. timbre) and some elements of the meso-level (such as changes in dynamics, rhythmic or pitch-based patterns). It should be borne in mind that parameter mapping is a creative process in any context, and the exploration of parameter relationships in improvised performance constitutes an intrinsic element of the live, creative and quasi-social process. In other words, all we need to do is to be consistent, since the musicians will establish mappings intuitively or aurally by experiment.

References

1. Bastien, D. and Hostager T.: Cooperation as Communicative Accomplishment: A Symbolic Interaction Analysis of an Improvised Jazz Concert. Communication Studies 43 (1992)
2. Bailey D.: Improvisation: its Nature and Practice in Music. The British Library Sound Archive. London (1992)
3. Berry, W.: Structural Functions in Music. New Jersey: Prentice-Hall (1976)
4. Blackwell, T.M.: Swarm Music. MSc dissertation, University College London. (2001)
5. Blackwell, T.M.: Musical Interaction with a Multi-Swarm. In: AISB (2003)
6. Blackwell, T.M.: Swarms and Self-Organized Music. Newsletter of the Society for Artificial Intelligence and Simulation of Behavior. (2003)
7. Bonabeau E., Dorigo M. and Theraulaz T.: From Natural to Artificial Swarm Intelligence. Oxford University Press, New York (1999).
8. Lewis G.: Interacting with Latter-Day Musical Automata. Contemporary Music Review 18 (1999) 1
9. Miranda E.: Computer Sound Synthesis for the Electronic Musician. Focal Press (1998)
10. Roads C.: Microsound. MIT press, Cambridge (2002)
11. Reynolds C. Flocks, Herds, and Schools: A Distributed Behavioral Model, in Computer Graphics. SIGGRAPH '87 Conference Proceedings. 21(4) (1987) 25-34
12. Rovan, J. Wanderley, M. Dubnov, S. and Depalle P.: Instrumental gestural mapping strategies as expressivity determinants in computer music performance. In: Proceedings of the Kansei - The Technology of Emotion Workshop. Genova, Italy, (1997)
13. Wishart, T. Audible Design. Orpheus the Pantomine Ltd (1994)
14. http://www.crca.ucsd.edu/~msp
15. http://www.electro-music.com/article.php?t=473
16. http://www.nathanwolek.com
17. http://www.timblackwell.com

Aesthetic Video Filter Evolution in an Interactive Real-Time Framework

Matthew Lewis

The Advanced Computing Center for the Arts and Design (ACCAD)
The Ohio State University, Columbus OH 43212, USA
lewis.239@osu.edu,
http://www.accad.ohio-state.edu/~mlewis/

Abstract. A data-flow network-based interactive evolutionary design framework is presented which will provide a testbed for the development and exploration of a diverse range of visual artistic design spaces. The domain of real-time layered video filters is focused on as the primary example. The system supports both real-time video streams and prerecorded video. Issues of stylistic signature, GA vs. GP-based approaches, rapid tuning of fitness distributions, and desirable traits of generic evolutionary design systems are discussed.

1 Introduction

Artists and designers increasingly rely on an incredible array of complicated software which often takes years of study to learn. Simultaneously, the explosion of the Web, blogs, customizable online games, and social networking software have created an environment in which individuals who are not professional artists or designers are creating vast amounts of digital content to the best of their abilities with the authoring software that is available to them.

While these early days of consumer generated digital design have been focused primarily on the generation and manipulation of text and images, the creation of expressive 3D graphics, interactive experiences, and manipulated streaming video are feasible in terms of cost, bandwidth, and processing power. Accessibility remains elusive however due to the complexity of interfaces, concepts, and representations.

The ideal digital content authoring interface for most people would behave with the omniscience of science-fiction: "Computer? Create an Irish pub. No, more 19th-century. Yes, that's more like it." While such intelligent software is problematic for numerous reasons, interactive evolutionary design (IED) systems attempt just this approach ("I like those, show me more like them ... ") albeit in extremely limited domains. This paper will describe a new framework being developed to enable rapid prototyping of IED-based digital content design interfaces and representations. After the primary system is described, an initial example design space of real-time digital video filter evolution will be discussed in depth.

G.R. Raidl et al. (Eds.): EvoWorkshops 2004, LNCS 3005, pp. 409–418, 2004.

What are the needs of a system such as the one outlined above? If the system is to be successfully used has a testbed for experimentation in different domains requiring different approaches, then representational flexibility and system modularity are both key. We would like to be able to easily modify the interface as appropriate for different problem spaces.

Perhaps just as important in an academic environment, we would like to enable non-programmer meta designers to quickly develop solution spaces in novel domains. Finally, a development environment in which the predominant visual design qualities defining a solution space can be quickly and frequently tuned and (re)evaluated without resorting to laborious and fatiguing chores like recompilation is an absolute necessity.

While it has been common over the past decade for individual researchers to program IED systems for specific problem domain, it is rare to find more generic systems for visual design space representation. One of the likely factors is the substantial task of authoring a wide range of graphics primitives and corresponding manipulation routines.

The last few years have seen a monumental drop in the cost of digital content development software that is readily extensible via integrated scripting languages, SDKs, and user-friendly data-flow network programming interfaces. While such software a few years ago was roughly the same price as an automobile, such features are now accessible commercially for hundreds of dollars, or even for free in open source software.

By creating IED frameworks within the context of extensible digital content development software, the processing, representation, communication, and interface capabilities of such systems can be harnessed. This in turn can provide easy access to the authoring power of the software, without requiring users to completely comprehend the intricacies of the systems' interfaces, processing concepts, and representations. The creation of design spaces within this context provides a valuable educational opportunity for those learning about a specific problem domain. Finally, advanced designers can readily craft, explore, and refine massive solution spaces, using them generatively to rapidly produce large numbers of alternative designs.

2   Background

The evolutionary design systems used for creating and manipulating images are far too numerous to survey here (see [1][2][3].) The majority of image generation and animation systems (e.g., [4][5][6][7]) are variants on the techniques pioneered by Sims [8]. Most such software, in addition to producing images and animations, supports still image manipulation as well. In general however, these systems do not operate in real-time on streams of images and most often the generate-and-select cycle is tuned to maximize the resolution possible in the time that the user is willing to wait for a new population.

There have been few generic systems for visual IED. Rowley's software combined a toolkit for displaying and judging image based individuals, with a mod-

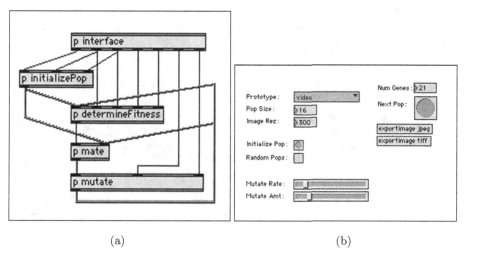

(a)   (b)

Fig. 1. The primary system patch and the evolution controls

ular system for mutating and crossbreeding expression based representations such as fractal images [9]. Pontecorvo was developing software primarily for consumer product design [10][11]. Lewis's generic system used data flow networks for solution spaces and genetic algorithm representations [12].

Perhaps most interestingly, Todd and Latham created a generic evolutionary design system called *PC Mutator* capable of interfacing with external existing Windows-based design software such as paint programs. Once parametric models were built (e.g., for designing cartoon faces), *PC Mutator* sent commands to external applications to create populations. The external application generated images of the individuals, which were then passed back to *PC Mutator* for display. Subjective fitness determination, mutation and crossover take place in *PC Mutator* [13][14].

3   Interactive Evolution Framework

Max and MSP have for years been among the cornerstones of computer music performance and composition software [15][16]. A little over a year ago, Max was formally extended to fully support a range of visual domains in an extremely well integrated fashion, via a set of objects called Jitter [15]. Jitter is at its core an extensible library for matrix manipulation. The matrix data in question might include images, video, sound, sensors, text, or anything which can be mapped into an N-dimensional numerical form.

The Max and Jitter environment is not a turn-key digital content authoring environment, but rather can be viewed as a toolkit for constructing such systems. Applications constructed within the Max/Jitter framework, once refined can be

Fig. 2. Initial populations

packaged and distributed as standalone software. While the user can certainly extend the system via an SDK, the primary development approach is via a dataflow network programming paradigm. Figure 1(a) shows the top level network or "patch" (also "patcher") for the system described below. With information flowing downward, the data path from the interface and the initial population, into an iterative cycle of fitness determination, mating, and mutation, can clearly be viewed. The encapsulation of details in sub-patches makes it easy for those learning about the system to quickly understand the architecture of the system, and eventually extend and modify the process. Furthermore, the system can be modified on-the-fly, with no stopping/compiling/linking/etc. The primary evolution interface can be seen in 1(b) showing the a typical range of controls for things such as mutation rate and amount, population initialization, and so on.

Design Domains. Designs produced using a given IED system invariably show a strong *signature* [17]. Signature, in this context, refers to the lack of visual diversity and generality in the designs produced (e.g., the polar coordinate remapping appearing in many of the individuals in the left initial population in figure 2.) Most work produced using a given IED implementation shares extremely strong visual characteristics, identifying the work as having been produced by that system, regardless of user. Ideally sufficiently general design spaces containing all possible desirable solutions could be created, with a broad distribution of high fitness regions to make satisfactory convergence certain. However, this is much easier said than done.

Solution space authors must constantly weigh convergence speed and fitness against generality and signature. While a given representation might contain an image of the Mona Lisa [18], it's extremely unlikely that a user of the system using a low-level representation (e.g., a simple math expression hierarchy) will discover it in any reasonable amount of time interactively. As will be discussed below, basing our system on an easily extensible genetic algorithms approach allows for precise remapping of specific genes into "more desirable" value distributions for phenotype parameters.

Representation. The framework used in this system relies on a fixed length vector of genes representing normalized parameter values. This is to be contrasted with the genetic programming approach involving hierarchical graphs of variables, constants, and functions, more typically used for evolving imagery. Several authors have commented on the comparative difficulty of controlling GP-based systems interactively. Margaret Boden claims Sims' system "can not be used to explore or refine an image space in a systematic way [19]." Todd and Latham question whether structure-based mating and mutation "...gives enough control for artistic applications [20]." While the space of possibilities is generally more vast, practical convergence remains a serious issue. Musgrave puts it best when he says that GP-based systems "tend to be simultaneously more chaotic, hard to control, and creative [21]."

Architecture. Choosing a software development environment such as Max and Jitter for infrastructure support means a framework capable of supporting real-time 3D graphics, networking, interaction, image creation, particle systems, lighting, and of course, video. Since video processing is one of Jitter's primary strengths, it was an appropriate initial design domain to address. (The significant demand recently from the students and faculty in our departments of theater, dance, and fine art for real-time, data driven video manipulation capabilities for performance and installation has provided additional incentive.)

The initial GA framework was developed and tested using a very simple solution space for evolving color palettes, nearly identical to the one shown in [12]. Most IED systems which evolve populations of static or unchanging individuals in this manner can render and display each phenotype, requiring only that the genotype and image (or polygons, animation, etc.) be stored for each population. This "generate and forget" paradigm is impractical in domains requiring each individual to remain active during fitness evaluation, such as in the video filtering domain described below.

Once the user selects the fittest individuals (by clicking on them), they form the mating pool. Random pairings are then mated to form a new population of offspring. Though uniform crossover was primarily used, and only the selected individuals are mated, the modularity of the patches make it trivial to switch to single-point crossover, allow selected individuals to survive with some percentage chance, etc. These sort of modifications can even be made on-the-fly in the running system.

4   Video Filter Space

For the real-time video processing design space, a flexible "processing layer" approach was used. A single processing layer consists of a bank of different possible

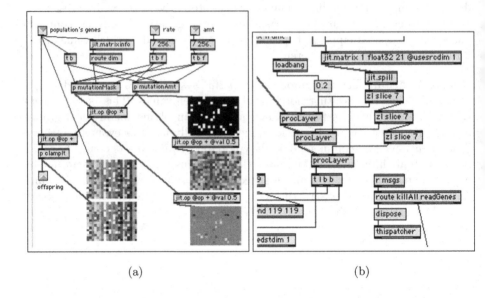

(a)   (b)

Fig. 3. The mutation patch on the left illustrates the mutation process. In the patch excerpt on the right, the matrix in the upper right holds the 21 genes for one individual. These are sliced off seven at a time for use by each of three video processing layers.

video filters. Nineteen were used for the work discussed in this paper. Each filter has one or more continuous parameters (three on average) and many have several different modes, each of which yields different visual results. Some examples of classes of video filters include adjustments to brightness, contrast, saturation, and hue, various spacial remappings, resamplings, and transformations, the addition of different types of noise, stochastic pixel position transformations, edge detection, thresholding, and feedback. The hierarchical patch-based nature of the software makes it simple to extend this by dropping in any new processing filters as desired.

Phenotypes are produced by slicing off blocks of g genes (currently $g = 7$) and passing them to a sequence of processing layer objects (figure 3(b)). In each layer, the first gene of each block functions as a "choice" gene determining which filter each layer will use. The remaining $g - 1$ genes in each layer function as "activation" and "parameter" genes, determining which filter modes are used and with what intensity or setting, respectively. Three layers of filters (21 genes) were used for the images in this paper.

Since different filtering processes' modes have different visual "strengths", the different filter modes can be manually assigned individual activation thresholds. For a filtering mode to activate, the value of its activation gene must exceed the assigned threshold value. This is one means by which individual formal visual qualities of the solution space can be controlled by the meta designer, increasing or decreasing specific stylistic signatures.

Any attempts to correlate Euclidean distance in the genotypic space with a continuous visual/perceptual difference requires careful remapping of normalized gene values into often nonlinear filter parameter ranges. Perlin's bias and gain functions can be used to intuitively push and pull normalized gene values towards or away from extremes [22]. Even a simple function remapping genes' lower and upper domains ($[0.0, 0.5]$ and $[0.5, 1.0]$) into $[low, default]$ and $[default, max]$ ranges respectively can be enormously useful, as well as simple to adjust on-the-fly as solution spaces are refined.

The use of the single filter-choice gene in each layer produces local minima since an individual filtering layer can only transition from its current filter to either neighboring filter. A simple extension to address this will be the use of two or three genes controlling filter choice. In a two or three dimensional filter space, a filter could mutate into one of its eight or twenty-six neighbors, respectively.

The mutation sub-patch in figure 3(a) shows the generation of the mutation mask (upper right) which is applied to random mutation values (middle right) to produce final gene mutations (lower right). In the matrix images within the patch, pixel rows represent individuals, and columns are individual genes. Interactive sliders allow the user to control the percentage of the population's genes that are mutated, as well as the amount they are mutated.

Note that a mutation mask should be used to control the visual step size in individual dimensions by scaling the applied mutation amplitude differently for selected genes, specifically in this case for the very sensitive filter selection gene within each of the processing layers.

Results. The benefits of a real-time architecture become particularly evident when the user is suddenly able to probe the *behavior* of the individuals in a population via the interactive feedback loop. The "credit assignment" problem of determining what components were responsible for the fitness of an individual is often implicitly addressed in IED via experience, e.g., a user might discover they should breed individuals which appear to compose *mod* and *fbm* functions which often lead in interesting directions, but perhaps not choose the ones with attractive high frequency aliasing which will probably turn to mush in another generation, etc. In a real-time system however the user finds they can often use more information about the visual robustness of a given solution, instead of waiting until the next population is produced only to find their choice was sitting atop a tiny fitness peak.

Figure 4 shows a set of sample converging solution populations, as well as three frames of one population's behavior over time. The images shown were recorded with the system running on a 1ghz G4 laptop at about 6-10fps sampling a live video feed at 160x120 resolution. It is expected that a dual 2.0ghz G5 should allow faster frame rates, higher resolutions, and additional layers. Note that while *live* video (from a FireWire camera) is being discussed, the system can just as easily display and process looping digital video clips, or arbitrary other DV or analog video sources (with the use of an inexpensive analog-to-DV converter) such as video tapes, live television, teleconferencing, etc.

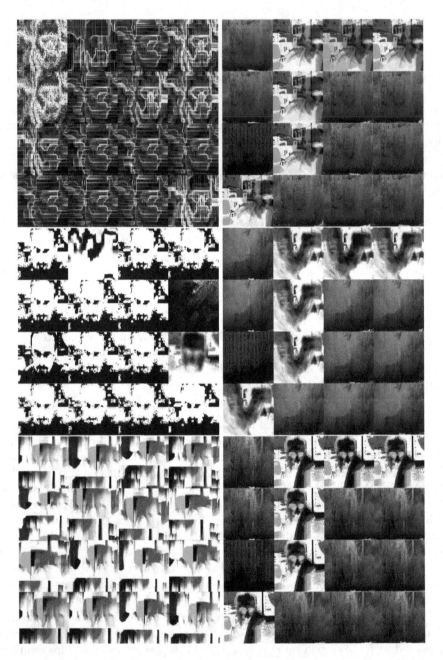

Fig. 4. The left column shows several converging populations, while the right column shows several frames of the same population's behavior over time.

5   Conclusion

As the approach begun here is extended, it is hoped that an extremely flexible system can be produced which will allow artists and designers (both professional and aspiring) to create expressive digital content using a simple interactive evolution paradigm. Usage of data-flow network authoring and real-time systems should aid in the rapid development of solution spaces by non-computer scientists.

In the near future we are looking forward to investigating the wide range of interactive data domains which this software allows one to represent including combinations of shapes, images, geometry, particles, lighting, materials, motion, environmental sensors, networking, text ... we've only just begun to explore the potential spaces to which evolution-based techniques could be applied within this framework. In addition to expanding the range of domains, one of the next extensions will be to explore interface options to make the fitness evaluation resolution more interactively dynamic using OpenGL-based zoomable user interface (ZUI) approaches.

Within the video manipulation domain, currently only sequential processing filters have been used. Additional processing power should allow for the addition of compositing operators to parametrically combine two video filter sequences in different ways. Also a library of interchangeable patches giving different options for mating and fitness evaluation needs to be developed. There are many options for extracting and extending the genetic representation so that new domains can be more rapidly created from older ones via shared sub-patches. Ideally, the transition between different filters would be more more continuous, with the center of a filter's region of genetic space mapping to a full activation of the effect which then fades in strength as it transitions into regions of neighboring filters (within one filter layer.)

Educationally, this system will serve as a tool for our art and design students to explore spaces of design options (literally and metaphorically), as well as encourage them to seriously consider *how* they explore these spaces of possibilities, by allowing them to explicitly attempt to design and refine them.

The promise of interactive evolutionary design is the creation of software based on the encouragement of exploration of many ways of seeing, as well as the critical examination of current and future possibilities. The merging of art, design, and technology in this new paradigm in order to represent, study, and harness diversity interestingly mirrors the corresponding need for its increased appreciation in the larger world.

References

1. Bentley, P.J.: Evolutionary Design by Computers. Morgan Kaufmann (1999)
2. Lewis, M.: Visual aesthetic evolutionary design links.
   http://www.accad.ohio-state.edu/~mlewis/aed.html (2003)

3. Takagi, H.: Interactive Evolutionary Computation: Fusion of the Capabilities of EC Optimization and Human Evaluation. Proceedings of the IEEE **89** (2001) 1275–1296
4. Greenfield, G.:   Mathematical building blocks for evolving expressions.   In: BRIDGES: Mathematical Connections in Art, Music and Science July 28-31. (2000)
5. Musgrave, F.K.: Genetic programming, genetic art. http://www.wizardnet.com/musgrave/mutatis.html (2003)
6. Rooke, S.: The Evolutionary Art of Steven Rooke. http://www.azstarnet.com/~srooke/ (2001)
7. Unemi, T.: SBART2.4: Breeding 2D CG Images and Movies, and Creating a type of Collage. In: The Third International Conference on Knowledge-based Intelligent Information Engineering Systems, Adelaide, Australia, August, Geneva, Switzerland (1999) 288–291
8. Sims, K.: Artificial evolution for computer graphics. ACM Computer Graphics **25** (1991) 319–328
9. Rowley, T.: A toolkit for visual genetic programming. Technical Report GCG-74, The Geometry Center, University of Minnesota (1994)
10. Emergent Design: Emergent Design. http://www.emergent-design.com (2000)
11. Pontecorvo, M.S.: Designing the undesigned: Emergence as a tool for design. In: Proceedings of Generative Art 1998, Milan, Italy. (1998)
12. Lewis, M.: Aesthetic evolutionary design with data flow networks. In: Proceedings of Generative Art 2000, Milan, Italy. (2000)
13. Todd, S.: Personal communication (2000)
14. Todd, S., Latham, W.: The mutation and growth of art by computers. In Bentley, P.J., ed.: Evolutionary Design by Computers. Morgan Kaufmann (1999) 221–250
15. Cycling '74.: Max/MSP and Jitter software. http://www.cycling74.com (2003)
16. Winkler, T.: Composing Interactive Music: Techniques and Ideas Using Max. MIT Press, Cambridge, MA (1998)
17. Rowbottom, A.: Evolutionary art and form. In Bentley, P.J., ed.: Evolutionary Design by Computers. Morgan Kaufmann (1999) 261–277
18. Whitelaw, M.: Breeding aesthetic objects: Art and artificial evolution. In Bentley, P.J., Corne, D., eds.: Proceedings of the AISB'99 Symposium on Creative Evolutionary Systems (CES). Morgan Kaufmann (1999)
19. Boden, M.A.: Agents and creativity. Communications of the ACM **37** (1994) 117–121
20. Todd, S., Latham, W.: Evolutionary Art and Computers. Academic Press (1992)
21. Musgrave, F.K.: Genetic textures. In Ebert, D., ed.: Texturing and Modeling: a Procedural Approach. Academic Press (1998) 373–384
22. Perlin, K.:   Noise, hypertexture, antialiasing, and gestures.   In Ebert, D., ed.: Texturing and Modeling: a Procedural Approach. Academic Press (1998) 209–274

Generative Art: Fuzzy Polygon Clipping in Program Generated Line Oriented Drawings

Hans E. Dehlinger

Universität Kassel, Kunsthochschule, Menzelstr.15, D34132 Kassel
dehling@uni-kassel.de

Abstract. The paper addresses aspects of Generative Art with a focus on algo-rithmically generated drawings of high density, executed on pen-plotters. Spe-cial attention is given to the concept of fuzzy clipping, extending the classical approaches to the clipping of line drawings. Strategies for fuzzy clipping are discussed and illustrated. The generating program is regarded as a personal ve-hicle designed for experiments of an artist. It supports the pursued intentions on the basis of defined preferences. The universe of hand-generated drawings is compared to the universe of program-generated drawings. It is argued that the richness of the universe of program generated drawings reveals aesthetic prop-erties, which rival those of the universe of hand drawings. Examples of gener-ated drawings are used to demonstrate the range of variety in the output of the generator.

1 The Line as a Basic Element of Drawings

The drawings we talk about are line-oriented, because the line may be regarded as a basic element of artistic expression, and consequently, artists have made use of it from the beginning of art. The line as such, is of a specific fascination. It starts in a point and it ends in a point. Described from a geometrical point of view, both points have similar properties. From an artist's point of view, they do not. In statu nascendi the beginning point seems to be more important. It is placed with more conscious-ness, from it the line evolves, and where it ends may not yet be decided. The decision where to start seems to come easier. While the line is evolving, the space for its pos-sible development is expanding. For the algorithmic generation of lines it therefore makes sense to pay special attention to the starting points. The drawings discussed here will all be based on polygonal lines, and the definition of those polygons will follow some personal preferences. This is intended, because it will make the resulting drawings identifiable and "unique" in a sense. The "personally shaped polygon" has been deliberately designed for the use of a single artist. Other artists working with algorithmic generation like Verostko [1] and Herbért [2] for example also use very personally defined lines base on their design of the generative code. For the process of the drawing with w program using polygons, parameters are defined, as for in-stance: Starting points, the number of points from which lines will emerge, the num-ber of segments of a polygon, the angle of diversion for segments, the length of seg-

G.R. Raidl et al. (Eds.): EvoWorkshops 2004, LNCS 3005, pp. 419–426, 2004.

ments etc. Although individual lines can be treated, it is interesting for the production of drawings to generate a great number of lines, say for example 20 000. "At one blow". A point-cloud is defined for this purpose from which the lines emerge. If one follows a concept, which I choose to call "Generative Minimalism" [3], then, entire drawings may emerge "at one blow". One example of such a drawing with the title tree_11 [4], is given in Fig. 4. Outside the image plane a dense point-cloud is located, from which the lines emerge, which generated tree_11. The parameter, which determines the direction of the first segment of each produced polygon, is set to force all polygons to develop with their first segment into the same direction, thus forming the stem of tree_11. With these settings, only one command "generate" is needed to trigger the generation of the entire drawing. It is an interesting argument to postulate a relation between the "strength" of the generated image and the generative rules applied. A recommendation for the design of a generator in line with "Generative Minimalism" could be:

On input, apply a minimum set of rules to generate output.

Besides the generation of lines, lines can be manipulated after generation. Among the many possible of such manipulations, polygon clipping, which will be addressed next, is especially interesting.

2 Polygon Clipping

Through clipping, arbitrary shapes within a drawing can be cleared of lines passing through it. The clipping line then is the borderline between clipped and unclipped regions. Clipping is a well-established computer specific operation (as are: scaling, moving, rotating and so on). These operations have, which is interesting to note, been used by artists long before computers came into existence. Descriptions of production processes of Renaissance painters give many hints in this direction. There are a number of clipping algorithms that can be used to clip lines. Probably one of the most commonly used ones is the Sutherland-Hodgman clipping algorithm [5]. Classical clipping refers to clipping, which aims at a perfect and clean fitted cut along the clipping line as shown in Fig. 1. This is of course, what is needed in most practical cases such as technical drawings, CAD, clipping against a window or clipping a viewport etc.

2.1 Fuzzy Clipping

In art, we do not have to accept the strictness of a clean fitted cut along the clipping line as the only mode of clipping. On the contrary, dropping this objective will give rise to some interesting questions. With fuzzy clipping, a number of strategies become available, which may be preferable to the artist and support his intentions. In fuzzy clipping, rules are defined which allow a certain number of lines to escape clipping. Such rules can be based on various assumptions. Some cases of interest are discussed and illustrated in the following sections.

2.2 Starting Point on Clipping-Line

To derive a rule for a first type of fuzzy clipping, a focus on the starting points of the polygons is suggested, and all polygons with a starting point located precisely on the clipping line are singled out. In technical drawings and also in drawings of low density, few such polygons may exist, but in the drawings under discussion here, there may be many. The suggested rule for fuzzy clipping, using the property of the staring point is:

Clip all polygons except those, which originate precisely on the clipping line.

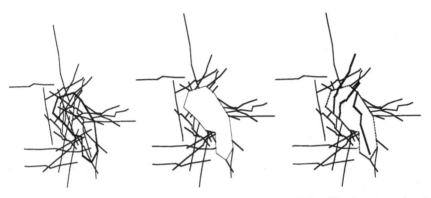

Fig. 1. Left: Lines and an area surrounded by a clipping-line. Middle: Clipping along the clipping-line with a "clean" cut. This figure resembles the classical case of clipping. Right: Surviving lines after a fuzzy clipping operation based on the property of starting points.

2.3 Recognize Offset Region to Clipping-Line

This strategy comes close to thinning out a region of the drawing. In Fig 2 the inner square is offset to form a clipping region. The rule applied is:

Eliminate all end-segments of poly-lines found within the offset area.

The fuzzy clipping here is determined by the geometric location of the end-segments of poly-lines in the drawing. If the condition is fulfilled, the entire end-segment will be removed from the drawing, no matter how far it will extend beyond the clipping line. Other, more relaxed or more restrictive clipping-rules in the same spirit may be formulated:

- Eliminate all end-segments of poly-lines extending towards the outside (inside) of the offset area.
- Eliminate all poly-lines for which an end-segment is entirely located within the offset area.

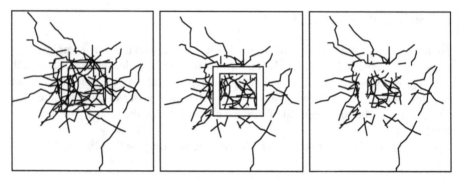

Fig. 2. Left: Drawing with clip-area formed by an offset of the inner square. Middle: Fuzzy clipping of end-segments of polygons located in clipping area. Right: Resulting drawing

2.4 Layers of Clipping-Lines

In clipping poly-lines using layered clipping-lines (areas), a logical rule is applied. Clipping in those cases is considered a "not draw" rule. Applying the rule repeatedly will result in command chains like: "not not draw" which amounts to "draw", as illustrated in Fig 3.

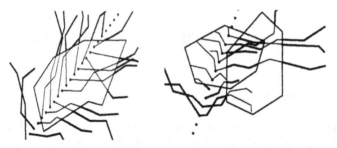

Fig. 3.   Left: One clipping-line, the standard case. Right: Two overlapping clipping-lines. In the overlapping area the (not(not draw)) rule will result in a draw command.

2.5 A Measure for the Number of Surviving Lines

Consider c, with $0 \leq c \leq 1$ to be a fuzzy measure for the number of lines, which will survive the execution of a clipping operation. For c = 0, no clipping will be performed; for c = 1, the classical clipping operation will be performed and all lines affected will be clipped. Since clipping is a sequential operation, a counting mechanism is used to determine, which of the affected lines will be allowed to survive. Again, such a mode of clipping may be useless for drawings with technical content; it seems nonetheless interesting in the context under discussion here.

Some details of artwork with employed clipping strategies are shown in Fig. 4.

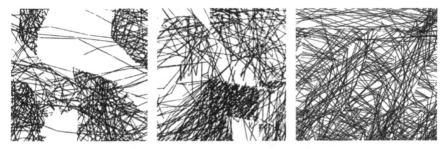

Fig. 4. Examples of clipping from generated drawings

3   Characteristics of Algorithmic Drawings

Sometimes artists decide to subject themselves to self-imposed restrictions that run close to what is understood by a "program" in information technology. Sentences like: "draw a tree with short, violent strokes", "use only vertical strokes of same length", "go to and fro along a contour", etc., are examples for such "programs". When we formulate rules for drawing by hand with increasing sharpness, we move towards algorithmic drawing. To write a generator producing drawings one has to be explicit. Even if it is decided to make use of random processes, it is necessary to specify how, where in the procedural chain and for what purpose they will be employed.

Fig. 5. Left: Generated drawing (detail). Right: tree_11 2001 / 1994

3.1 Hand versus Machine

There is a universe of drawings which may be generated by algorithms running on machines, let us call it the "M-Universe", which seems to be similarly opulent as the one generated by the human hand, the "H-Universe". The drawings from this machine-universe are unique in their own right. They are totally different from those of the universe of the hand and they can be characterized by a set of distinct features. Drawings do not jump into existence in one single "shot" like photographs do. There is always a more or less sequential process about them, regardless of whether they are produced by hand or by a machine. Neither hand nor machine can withdraw from this sequentiality. In order to recognize differences it is interesting to compare the production processes of both the hand and the machine.

Fig. 6. Example of generated drawing [6]

3.2 Hand-Drawing versus Machine Drawing

Obviously the abilities and the limitations of the human hand - or rather of the hand of the artist - are of importance. A hand-made drawing comes to life through a personal expression, roughly comparable to the one of handwriting. Some characteristics of these drawings are: Usually no line equals the other. Only through enormous concentration is it possible to draw identical lines. Even within a very narrow "program" there are innumerable opportunities of faint deviations, which may become overriding and significant as a whole. The position of the pen to the paper, the speed of drawing, pushing, rubbing etc., the pressure differences, the mechanics and the motoricity of the hand generate wide spheres of expression, indescribable in geometrical terms. The hand that draws lines operates under the constant control of the eye, hereby allowing a direct feedback. The spectrum of this feedback may begin with the rational control over every single stroke and may end with a totally subdued perception of all activity. The hand gets tired.

Among the characteristics, which apply to the machine drawing are the following: The machine is indefatigable, exact, fast. It works with constant regularity. Its so-and-so many-thousandth line is performed under absolutely the same conditions as its first line. Irregularities, if they occur, are due to mechanical shortcomings and failures like the tearing up of the paper or the lack of absorptive capacity of the paper, dried-up pen and so forth. It is, by the way, due to the mechanical shortcomings, pen plotters have become obsolete for technical applications. For machine-generated drawings, the pen-pressure, drawing speed, the position of the pen to the paper are always the same. An algorithm guides the pencil. This algorithm is followed blindly until it comes to an end.

These characteristics are, of course, exactly what we expect from a machine when it is used for CAD, for example. An artist, however, may find it more interesting to push the machine to its mechanical limits or even beyond. It then may behave very different, and mechanical failures may become a wanted side effect. As a last feature specific to the machine drawings we may state: Only when the last line has been drawn, can the result be inspected. The machine itself does not perform a judgement of the result.

3.3 Semantics

The meaning hidden in the generated drawings can be detected only gradually or in a subtle, indirect, or covert way. Of special interest to the artist is the possibility of generating a series of images, which may, for example, engage the observer to decipher a story or a tale by following a sequential chain. Such an arrangement allows the viewer to find an individual perspective to a given theme. Fanciful interpretations are stimulated and expressly permitted. Familiar shapes appear as a provocation, when they are altered through intellectual transformations to such an extent, that their clarity is completely obscured. A shape may appear only after long-term contemplation and then in a snap or not at all. It is a challenge to find a rule (or rules), which may be applied repeatedly, and which explain intellectually the process of the destruction of the unequivocal, order it mentally, and process it algorithmically. The repeated application of random processes is such rule. It is admittedly rather general. And yet, even here, there are many different paths that can be taken. A process applying a random action only once within a sequence of other actions, is different from a process applying a sequence of random actions in very large numbers.

References

1. http://www.verostko.com/
2. Hebèrt, J. P., Santa Barbara, CA; see also: http://dam.org/hebert/
3. Dehlinger, H. E.: Minimal Generative Principles for Large Scale Drawings: An Experimental Approach and its Results. In: Proceedings of GA'99: Generative Art'99, 2nd International Conference. Generative Design Lab of Politecnico di Milano (1999)
4. Dehlinger, H. E.: tree_11. 2001 / 1994, ACM SIGGRAPH Travelling Art Show (2003)
5. See for example: Foley, J. D., van Dam, A., Feiner, S. F., Hughes, J. F.: Computer Graphics, Principles and Practice. Addison-Wesley Publ. Comp. Reading, Massachusetts, second edition, (1990)
6. Dehlinger, H. E.: Tier nach links. 45 cm / 54 cm, plotterdrawing, pencil on paper

Tilings of Sequences of Co-evolved Images

Gary Greenfield

Mathematics & Computer Science
University of Richmond
Richmond VA 23173, USA
ggreenfi@richmond.edu
http://www.mathcs.richmond.edu/~ggreenfi/

Abstract. Sims' well-known technique for using evolving expressions to generate abstract images is paired with a co-evolutionary hosts and parasites fitness scheme to instantiate an evolutionary simulation. An added twist is that image populations are completely replaced after each generation. The goal is to identify evolutionary epochs where significant aesthetic themes emerge so that sequences of maximally fit images can be culled. Culled sequences are used to construct tilings. The technique yields abstract tilings where the interplay between creation, competition, and cooperation of visual themes combine to produce some surprising aesthetic results.

1 Introduction

In Sims' method for aesthetic image generation known as evolving expressions [17] each image phenotype is generated from an (algebraic) expression genotype. The user, viewing the entire population of phenotypes, interactively assigns aesthetic fitness values to phenotypes so that mating and mutation of the genotypes of the most fit individuals can take place in accordance with the rules of the underlying artificial genetics. Sims' method has spawned a cottage industry. Efforts which are of interest include those of Rooke [8] [24], Greenfield [5], Unemi [23], McGuire [12], Ibrahim [9], Musgrave [14], Bedwell and Ebert [2], and Mount [13]. Further examples are described by Rowbottom [16]. Undoubtedly there are more examples of which we are unaware. Image generation using an interactive genetic algorithm also plays a key role in several other evolutionary image generation techniques [3] [22] [10] [21].

This paper considers abstract aesthetic images that are tilings constructed from an evolutionary sequence of co-evolved images. The rationale for doing so comes in response to the question, *How* do evolved images that are proffered as evolutionary art actually arise? The reason this is a difficult question to answer is twofold. First, because an evolutionary run typically considers several thousand images, out of necessity one usually examines the entire image population only at fixed, widely spaced intervals. Second, because the goal is to obtain the highest rated aesthetic image, elitism is usually employed to ensure that the most promising aesthetic images evolved to date are never discarded and always

G.R. Raidl et al. (Eds.): EvoWorkshops 2004, LNCS 3005, pp. 427–436, 2004.

remain in the breeding pool. In this paper, instead of using elitism, the entire image population is replaced after every generation. The result is that image evolution is more fluid, roiling, and tumultuous. Visualization techniques are required to identify evolutionary windows, or *epochs*, where promising aesthetic evolutionary explorations are taking place. These windows furnish sequences of highest-rated aesthetic images that are then used to construct tilings. The tilings show the emergence, interaction, and competition occurring between thematic elements during the epoch selected. They are of aesthetic interest in their own right.

It must be emphasized at the outset that the co-evolutionary mechanism used here to "automate" the evolution of aesthetic images is specific to two-dimensional imagery. In general, the problem of using computational methods to make aesthetic decisions appears to be a difficult one. This is evidenced by a paucity of literature on the subject (but see, for example, [11] [19] [20]). Work on this problem that is related to the Sims' method is surveyed below.

Baluja, Pommerleau, and Jochem were first to attempt to *fully* automate Sims' evolving expressions [1]. They used neural nets. According to the authors, the results were "somewhat disappointing" and "mixed and very difficult to quantify." Rooke (unpublished) also attempted to automate Sims' evolving expressions method, but using a different experimental design. Rooke co-evolved a *population* of art critics, which he called "image commentators," to perform aesthetic evaluations based on statistics obtained from each image. Interestingly enough, these critics were also populations of evolving expressions, albeit expressions packed with location finding primitives for isolating sub-regions of the image and for statistically analyzing these sub-regions. In the end, Rooke judged his art critics to have been capable of learning his aesthetics, but once more they seemed incapable of using this knowledge to explore new areas of image space [15]. Greenfield [5] adopted yet a different approach by employing populations of critics — in this case mindless digital convolution filters — to act as "irritants" for steering evolution toward imagery with a high degree of entropy. This was accomplished by giving the digital filters an elementary but harsh survival task: "predict" pre-selected image pixel values based on neighboring pixel values. This paper also uses digital filters, but alters the repopulation strategy after each generation.

2 Description of the Co-evolutionary Simulation

An image genotype is defined to be a symbolic expression tree E represented in postfix form. The leaves of the tree are chosen from a set consisting of constants whose values range from 0.000 to 0.999 in increments of 0.001 together with two independent variables. The constants are denoted by $C0$ - $C999$, and the variables by $V0$ and $V1$. The internal nodes are chosen from sets of unary and binary primitives. A unary primitive is a function from the unit interval to itself, and a binary primitive is a function from the unit square to the unit interval. The five unary primitives are written as $U0$ - $U4$ and the fifteen binary primitives as

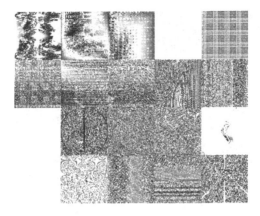

Fig. 1. A 4 × 5 mosaic from an uninteresting run.

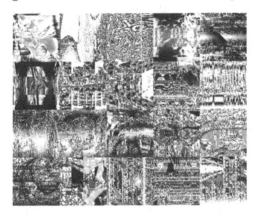

Fig. 2. A 4 × 5 mosaic from an interesting run.

Fig. 3. Detail from the mosaic of Figure 2. On the left the most fit image at generation #250 and on the right the most fit image from generation #300.

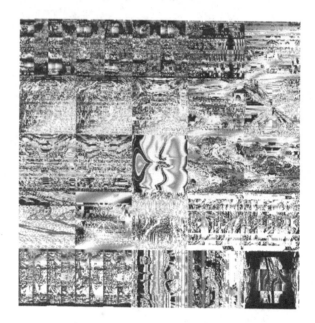

Fig. 4. The 5×5 tiling resulting from the epoch bracketed by the images in Figure 3.

$B0$ - $B14$. Explicit descriptions for this set of primitives may be found in [6]. An image phenotype is defined by using a left to right stack evaluation algorithm which assigns to the expression E at a point $(V0, V1)$ of the unit square the value $E(V0, V1)$ in the unit interval. For aesthetic evaluation purposes, image phenotypes are resolved at 100×100 pixels. For display purposes, higher resolutions are used. Pixels are always colored using a gray scale defined via a linear ramp from black to white obtained by resolving the unit interval into 256 values.

The rationale underlying the co-evolution scheme rests on the premise that aesthetically interesting images have visual anomalies. To identify such anomalies, digital convolution filters are passed over small portions of the image, and the image is rewarded if the convolved portion is significantly *different* than the original portion, otherwise the filter is rewarded. Since co-evolution is at work, this establishes a relative, as opposed to absolute, measure of aesthetic fitness. Alternatively, one could say the filter is parasitic upon the host image with its survivability determined by how well it is able to blend with the host, while the survivability of the host image is determined by how well it is able to repel the parasite by making it visible as a blemish. The fitness formulation being used promotes the evolution of images with significant entropy, whence the image style is very "noisy." The required technical details follow.

Given a 100×100 host image, with phenotypic values $h_{i,j}$ in the interval $[0, 1]$, at location L extract a 10×10 patch $p_{i,j}$ where $1 \leq i, j \leq 10$. A parasite genotype is defined to be a 3×3 matrix of integers $(f_{i,j})$ where $0 \leq i, j \leq 2$ whose values are restricted to lie in the interval $[-P_{\max}, P_{\max}]$. The results presented in this paper use $P_{\max} = 8$. The neighborhood of the patch is the 12×12 region of the

Fig. 5. Bracketing images for an epoch from generations #300 to #350 together with the tiling that resulted.

image consisting of the original patch surrounded by a one pixel wide border. Pass the convolution filter of the parasite genotype over the neighborhood to obtain the convolved patch $v_{i,j}$ defined by

$$v_{i,j} = \frac{\sum_{r=0}^{2} \sum_{c=0}^{2} p_{i+(r-1),j+(c-1)} f_{i+(r-1),j+(c-1)}}{S},$$

where

$$S = 1 + |\sum_{i,j} f_{i,j}|.$$

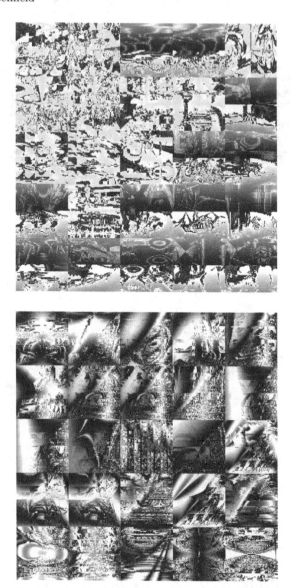

Fig. 6. Two tilings from epochs where images were culled every other generation.

To calculate the host's fitness set

$$h_{\text{fitness}} = \sum_{i,j} \delta_{i,j} \, ,$$

where

$$\delta_{i,j} = \begin{cases} 1 \text{ if } |v_{i,j} - p_{i,j}| > \varepsilon \, , \\ 0 \text{ otherwise} \, , \end{cases}$$

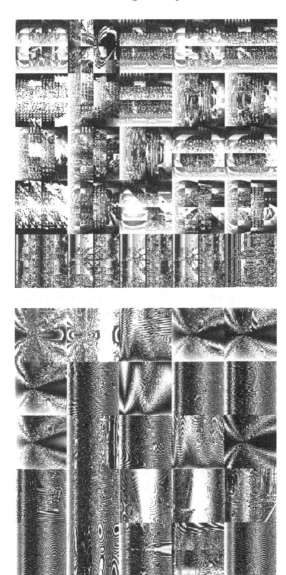

Fig. 7. Two tilings from epochs where images were culled every generation.

and ε is the host's *exposure* threshold. The results presented here use $\varepsilon = 0.05$. Since the patch is 10×10, define the parasite's fitness to be

$$p_{\text{fitness}} = 100 - h_{\text{fitness}}.$$

When *multiple* parasites are attached to a host, each at a different location, host fitness is the average fitness taken over all parasites. The subtlety here is that in some sense a parasite can never win the fitness battle. This is because a parasite's attempt to predict the value of a pixel it is centered upon by simply "doing nothing" is thwarted by the weighting factor S and the threshold ε. To help compensate for this inequity, hill-climbing is used between host generations so that parasites have an opportunity to keep pace with their more capable evolving hosts. The genetic operators used for evolving expressions are straightforward. The genetic operators used for evolving filters are omitted here for lack of relevance. All images shown were co-evolved using two parasite locations that were pseudorandomly generated at the start of each evolutionary run. Image population size was fixed at thirty and co-evolutionary runs lasted for either 500 or 1000 host generations. Image populations were completely replaced after each host generation by first forming a breeding pool consisting of the fifteen top rated images from the current generation. Second, fifteen matings were performed by randomly choosing two distinct individuals from the breeding pool for each mating. Finally, crossover plus mutation was used in order to contribute two individuals from each mating to the next generation. In contrast, only one-sixth of the parasite population for each location was replaced after each generation. Parasite replacement was egalitarian, meaning a randomly selected surviving parasite was cloned and mutated to serve as a replacement. As indicated previously, twenty-five *parasite* generations worth of hill-climbing took place between each host generation in order to allow parasites to better cope with the complete replacement strategy used for the host population.

3   Identifying Aesthetic Epochs during Co-evolution

To identify epochs of evolutionary interest that occurred during simulation runs, *mosaics* were constructed using twenty hosts culled from the image population. The twenty images culled were the top-ranked images in the host population after every twenty-five (respectively fifty) generations of an evolutionary run that lasted for five hundred (respectively one thousand) host generations. The resulting 4×5 mosaic was then examined to see if there were *consecutive* images that were aesthetically interesting indicating that significant evolutionary events probably occurred during the intervening generations. Because evolution was under the control of a pseudorandom number generator, the co-evolutionary run could then be repeated and the most fit host from every one (respectively two) generations could be culled during the twenty-five (respectively fifty) generation epoch identified with the aid of the mosaic. From this culled sequence a 5×5 *tiling* was constructed.

As the mosaic in Figure 1 demonstrates, most evolutionary runs did not yield aesthetically promising imagery. Figure 2 gives an example of a mosaic that did exhibit aesthetic potential. Figure 3 gives enlarged detail of two successive images from that mosaic that were selected to bracket a window of aesthetic interest and Figure 4 shows the resulting tiling.

In Figure 5 a tiling from another run together with the two images that bracket this epoch are shown. This tiling shows how hyperactive image evolution was during this epoch. In fact, this tiling is too overwhelming to be of aesthetic

interest. Omitting both accompanying mosaics and bracketing images for reasons of space, and with due consideration given to the fact that the tilings are reduced in size from their normal 7" × 7" resolution, Figure 6 and Figure 7 exhibit four tilings selected from the best aesthetic tilings that were obtained. They show the emergence and exploration of visual themes interspersed with the novelty of occasional "accidentals." At full resolution these tilings have a hypnotic effect.

4   Summary and Conclusion

Examples of abstract tilings were exhibited. They allowed us to observe the emergence of thematic elements and experience the nuances of aesthetically driven evolution. Future work needs to consider how to quantify the success ratio of such computational techniques and how well they generalize to other types of imagery.

References

1. Baluja, S., D. Pomerleau, and T. Jochem, Towards automated artificial evolution for computer-generated images, *Connection Science*, **6** (1994), 325–354.
2. Bedwell, E., and D. Ebert, Artificial evolution for implicit surfaces, *Conference Abstracts and Applications, Computer Graphics Annual Conference Series, 1998*, Association for Computing Machinery, New York, NY, 1998, 261.
3. Dawkins, R., The evolution of evolvability, *Artificial Life*, C. Langton (ed.), Addison-Wesley, Reading, MA, 1989, 201–220.
4. Graf, J., and W. Banzhaf, Interactive evolution of images, *Genetic Programming IV: Proceedings of the Fourth Annual Conference on Evolutionary Programming*, J. McDonnell et al (eds.), MIT Press, 1995, 53–65.
5. Greenfield, G., Art and artificial life — a coevolutionary approach, *Artificial Life VII Conference Proceedings*, M. Bedau et al (eds.), MIT Press, Cambridge, MA, 2000, 529–536.
6. Greenfield, G., Mathematical building blocks for evolving expressions, *2000 Bridges Conference Proceedings*, R. Sarhangi, (ed.), Central Plain Book Manufacturing, Winfield, KS, 2000, 61–70.
7. Hillis, D., Co-evolving parasites improves simulated evolution as an optimization procedure, *Artificial Life II*, C. Langton et al (eds.), Addison-Wesley, Reading, MA, 1991, 313–324.
8. Hitchcock, N., Painting pictures through time, *Computer Artist*, December/January 1996, 9.
9. Ibrahim, A., GenShade, *Ph.D. Dissertation*, Texas A&M University, 1998.
10. Lewis, M., Creating continuous design spaces using interactive genetic algorithms with layered, correlated, pattern functions, *Ph.D. Dissertation*, Ohio State University, 2001.
11. Machado, P. and A. Cardoso, Computing aesthetics, in *Proceedings XIV-th Brazilian Symposium on Artificial Intelligence SBIA'98, Porto Allegre, Brazil*, F. Oleiveira (ed.), Springer-Verlag, LNAI Series, New York, NY, 1998, 219–229.
12. McGuire, F., The origins of sculpture: evolutionary 3D design, *IEEE Computer Graphics & Applications*, January, 1993, 9–12.

13. Mount, J., http://mzlabs.com/gart/g4.html.
14. Musgrave, K., http://www.wizardnet.com/musgrave/mutatis.html.
15. Rooke, S., Personal communication.
16. Rowbottom, A., Evolutionary art and form, in *Evolutionary Design by Computers*, P. Bentley (ed.), Morgan Kaufmann Publishers, San Francisco, CA, 1999, 261–277.
17. Sims, K., Artificial evolution for computer graphics, *Computer Graphics*, **25** (1991), 319–328.
18. Sims, K., Interactive evolution of dynamical systems, *Toward a Practice of Autonomous Systems: Proceedings of the First European Conference on Artificial Life*, MIT Press, 1991, 171–178.
19. Sprott, J., The computer artist and art critic, *Fractal Horizons*, C. Pickover (ed.), 1996, 77–115.
20. Staudek, T., Computer-aided aesthetic evaluation of visual patterns, *ISAMA/Bridges 2003 Conference Proceedings*, J. Barrallo et al (eds.), University of Granada, Granada, Spain, 2003, 143–150.
21. Thomas, D., Aesthetic selection of developmental art forms, *Artificial Live VIII Conference Proceedings*, R. Standish et al (eds.), MIT Press, Cambridge, MA, 2003, 157–163.
22. Todd, S., and W. Latham, *Evolutionary Art and Computers*, Academic Press, San Diego, CA 1992.
23. Unemi, T., SBART 2.4: an IEC tool for creating two-dimensional images, movies, and collages, *Leonardo*, **35** (2002) 189–192.
24. Voss, D., Sex is best, *WIRED*, December, 1995, 156–157.

Adaptive Critics for Evolutionary Artists

Penousal Machado[1], Juan Romero[2], María Luisa Santos[2],
Amílcar Cardoso[1], and Bill Manaris[3]

[1] Centre for Informatics and Systems of the University of Coimbra, 3030 Coimbra, Portugal
{machado, amilcar}@dei.uc.pt
[2] Creative Computer Line, RNASA Lab. Faculty of Computer Science, University of Coruña,
Spain
jj@udc.es, infmsa01@ucv.udc.es
[3] Computer Science Department, College of Charleston, Charleston, SC 29424, USA
manaris@cs.cofc.edu

Abstract. We focus on the development of artificial art critics. These systems analyze artworks, extracting relevant features, and produce an evaluation of the perceived pieces. The ability to perform aesthetic judgments is a desirable characteristic in an evolutionary artificial artist. As such, the inclusion of artificial art critics in these systems may improve their artistic abilities. We propose artificial art critics for the domains of music and visual arts, presenting a comprehensive set of experiments in author identification tasks. The experimental results show the viability and potential of our approach.

1 Introduction

The artistic process depends on the ability to perform aesthetic judgments, to be inspired by the works of other artists, and to act as a critic of one's own work. These factors depend on the artist's ability to see and listen. Modelling this capacity of the artist is an important step in the creation of an artificial artist. After all, an artist is also, and foremost, a viewer and listener. This view contrasts with the vast majority of the evolutionary computation systems for artwork generation (for a survey see, e.g., [1]), which tend to be completely blind/deaf to the outside world.

According to our view, the creation of a genuine evolutionary artificial artist requires the development of an Artificial Art Critic (AAC) – a system that is able to "perceive" an artwork, and perform an evaluation of the piece. The idea is to use the evaluations produced by the AAC to guide the evolutionary process.

In [2] we presented a general framework for the development of AACs. This framework consists of: an architecture, comprising a *feature extractor* and an *evaluator*; and a multi-stage validation methodology. The first stage includes identification tasks, such as the identification of the author or style of a given piece. This allows the objective, and meaningful, assessment of the AACs, providing a solid basis for their development. The later stages incorporate more subjective criteria, and include testing the AACs in a hybrid society of humans and artificial agents.

Following this set of ideas, we developed AACs for the musical and visual arts domains and conducted a broad set of experiments in the task of author identification.

G.R. Raidl et al. (Eds.): EvoWorkshops 2004, LNCS 3005, pp. 437–446, 2004.

2 System Description

The developed AACs are composed by two modules: a feature extractor and an evaluator. The feature extractor is static and domain specific. It is responsible for the perception of the artwork, generating as output a set of measurements that reflect relevant characteristics of the artwork. These measurements serve as input to the evaluator, which assesses the artwork according to a specific criterion defined by the user. The evaluator is an adaptive system, in our case implemented by means of an Artificial Neural Network. In the next sections we describe the modules used in the construction of the AACs. Namely, the musical and visual art feature extractors (section 2.1 and 2.2) and the adaptive evaluator (section 2.3).

2.1 Musical Feature Extractor

The musical feature extractor is similar to the one presented in [3]. It employs a series of Zipf's law [4] based metrics to extract features from music pieces encoded in MIDI format. Zipf distributions have been discovered in a wide range of phenomena including music. For instance, in [5] presents a study of 220 pieces of various music styles (baroque, classical, romantic, twelve-tone, jazz, rock, DNA strings, and aleatory music) discovering several Zipf distributions.

We use a total of 40 metrics, in addition to the number of notes of the piece. Each of the 40 metrics produces two real numbers:

1. The *slope* of the trendline of event frequencies plotted on a log-log, rank-frequency format; this number ranges from 0 to $-\infty$, with -1 denoting a Zipf distribution; and
2. The strength of the linear correlation, R^2, of the trendline; this ranges from 0 to 1, with 1 denoting a perfect fit.

The metrics used in the feature extractor can be divided into three types:

– Global metrics provide useful statistical information about the piece as a whole. There are seven metrics of this type: pitch, pitch-relative-to-octave, duration×pitch, duration×pitch-relative-to-octave, melodic interval, harmonic interval and melodic-harmonic interval.
– Structural metrics measure the equilibrium of higher orders of pitch change. Currently, we capture six orders of change. The first-order metric measures the equilibrium of changes between melodic intervals. The second-order metric measures the equilibrium of changes between first-order intervals, and so on.
– Fractal metrics measure the fractal dimension of each of the previous metrics. These metrics apply a given metric recursively at different levels of resolution within a piece. By successively subdividing a piece into parts, the lack of local balance can be exposed. Like the other metrics, fractal metrics produce a slope and a mean-square error value. The slope is equivalent to the fractal dimension of the given metric. The partitioning process stops when we reach phrases with less than five notes.

2.2 Visual Art Feature Extractor

The feature extractor presented herein is based on the notion that the complexity of an image is an important feature for the assessment of its aesthetical proprieties. This view is supported by a variety of studies (e.g. [6, 7])

In [8] the authors propose the use of complexity estimates to assess the aesthetical value of images, pointing the difference between complexity of the visual stimulus and complexity of the image perception task. The employed image and complexity estimates are based on the quality of jpeg and fractal image compression. A method for assigning aesthetic value according to these estimates is also presented. The approach was tested using a psychological test [9] designed to estimate the level in which an individual recognizes and reacts to basic principles of aesthetic order, achieving surprisingly good results. More recently, the same approach was used as part of an evolutionary art tool to assign fitness values to images and to filter images that are unquestionably bad [10]. Additionally, an image similarity metric based on these estimates is also presented.

The feature extractor proposed in this paper includes two types of complexity estimates: jpeg and fractal. To obtain these estimates we apply jpeg and fractal compression. The complexity of a given image is the ratio between the root mean square error resulting from its compression and the compression rate.

To better characterize the images, we vary the quality of the encoding by setting limits to the maximum error per pixel, and thus the amount of detail kept. This results in three complexity estimates for each compression technique.

After calculating these estimates for the whole image, the image is split into its Hue (H), Saturation (S) and Lightness (L) channels. We proceed by calculating the previously described estimates for each of the channels. Additionally we also calculate, for each channel: the average value; the standard deviation; the slope of the trendline of the Zipf distribution and root mean square error.

This process yields a total of 33 metrics, six for the whole image and nine for each of the three channels[1].

These global measurements can be misleading. For instance, the complexity of an image with three blank quadrants and a highly complex one can be similar to the complexity of an image with detail in all its quadrants. To get a better grasp of the distribution of these features by the different regions of the painting, we partition the image in five regions of the same size: the four quadrants, and an overlapping central rectangle. We apply to each region the previously described metrics. This yields a total of 198 measurements (33 for the entire image and 165 for the partitions). This number may seem too high but we prefer to use all the measurements for these initial experiments and to cut in a latter stage the ones that prove less meaningful.

2.3 Evaluator Module

The evaluator module is an adaptive system that uses the measurements made by the feature extractor as an input, and produces, as output, an evaluation of the artwork. Being an adaptive module, the evaluator can adjust its behavior in order to perform different tasks. In this paper we focus in the task of author identification. Taking into

---

[1] Fractal image compression is not applied to the image as a whole since it would be redundant.

account that we selected artists of different styles and movements to train and test our system, this task is, to some extent, also a style identification task.

From an architectural point of view, the adaptive evaluator consists of a feedforward ANN with one hidden layer. We use: standard backpropagation, with a learning rate of 0.2 and a momentum of 0, as learning function; the logistic function, as neuron activation function; and identity, as the output function. These settings remain unchanged throughout all the tests. The measurements made by the feature extractors are normalized between -1 and 1, before being fed to the network.

The number of measurements produced by the feature extractor determines the number of neurons of the input layer. Accordingly, the number of units in this layer is different for the two domains (music and visual arts). In the initial experiments in the musical domain we use an input layer composed by 81 neurons. In the visual arts domain, the input layer size is 198. In subsequent experiments we eliminate some of the inputs of the ANN, to assess the relevance of the different measurements. We conducted several preliminary experiments, varying the number of neurons of the hidden layer. In the experimental results presented in this paper we use hidden layers with 6 and 12 neurons, since these configurations gave the best overall results. The number of neurons of the output layer is equal to the number of authors considered for the test. In order to build, train and test the ANN we use SNNS[2].

3   Experimental Results

In order to train and test the ANNs we collected a significant amount of musical scores and artworks. We use a total of 741 scores, from a wide variety of music styles (e.g. prelude, fuga, toccata, mazurka, opera ...). These scores were composed by five different authors, namely: Scarlatti (50 scores), Purcell (75), Bach (149), Chopin (291) and Debussy (176). We use a total of 802 different artworks, belonging to six different painters: 98 from Goya, 153 from Monet, 93 from Gauguin, 122 from Van Gogh, 81 from Kandinsky, and 255 from Picasso.

The training sets are constructed by randomly selecting a percentage (75% or 85%) of the available pieces. The test sets comprise the remaining ones.

3.1 Musical Domain

In this section we present some of the results achieved in a series of experiments in the musical domain. Due to space restrictions it is impossible to present all the performed experimentation.

Experiment 1. The aim of this experiment is to check the efficiency of the network in distinguishing between two authors (Scarlatti and Purcell) who belong to the same musical period (Baroque).

---

[2] Stuttgart Neural Network Simulator (http://www-ra.informatik.uni-tuebingen.de/SNNS/).

We used two different network architectures: 81-6-2 and 81-12-2. An output of (1,0) indicates a Scarlatti score, while (0,1) indicates a Purcell score. Table 1 summarizes the results of this experiment.

The experimental results show that the ANN is able to learn and generalize. The success rate on the test set varies between 100% and 90%, which corresponds to zero to four errors of identification (Table 1). As expected, using a training set with 85% of the scores yields better results. The results attained using 10000 learning cycles are globally worse than those achieved using a smaller number of cycles. This can be explained by the over-specialization of the network, which hinders its generalization abilities.

Table 1. Scarlatti vs. Purcell, two authors belonging to the same musical period

Train Set	Test Patterns	Architecture	Cycles	Errors	Success Rate	MSE Train	Test
85%	19	81-6-2	10000	1	94.8%	0.00003	0.00003
			3000	0	100%	0.00021	0.00987
		81-12-2	10000	1	94.8%	0.00003	0.08408
			4000	1	94.8%	0.00020	0.06573
70%	37	81-6-2	10000	5	86.5%	0.00006	0.00023
			2000	4	90%	0.00023	0.17713
		81-12-2	10000	4	90%	0.00005	0.18011
			2000	3	92%	0.00026	0.12819

Experiment 2. The goal of this experiment is to distinguish between two composers that belong to different musical periods: Chopin (Romanticism) and Debussy (French Impressionism).

The architecture is identical to the one used in the previous experiment. In this case an output of (1,0) indicates a Chopin score, while (0,1) indicates a Debussy score. The results of this experiment are summarized in table 2.

Table 2. Chopin vs. Debussy, authors from different musical periods

Train Set	Test Patterns	Architecture	Cycles	Errors	Success Rate	MSE Train	Test
85%	70	81-6-2	10000	0	100%	0.00001	0.00395
			3000	0	100%	0.00003	0.00358
		81-12-2	10000	0	100%	0.00001	0.00318
			3000	0	100%	0.00004	0.00205
70%	140	81-6-2	10000	1	99.3%	0.00001	0.01529
			4000	1	99.3%	0.00002	0.01356
		81-12-2	10000	1	99.3%	0.00001	0.01460
			5000	2	98.6%	0.00004	0.01848

As in the previous experiment, smaller training sets lead to a decrease of performance. However, in the current experiment the degradation of performance is minimal.

In this experiment the use of 10000 learning cycles appears to be adequate, there are no signs of over-fitting.

The results are clearly superior to the ones attained in experiment 1. There are two, possibly concurrent, explanations for the improvement of performance:

- The authors used in this experiment belong to different musical periods, which may make their discrimination easier;
- The number of musical scores available for the training (and testing) of the ANN is significantly larger, which may give a better coverage of the pieces created by the authors.

Experiment 3. The object of this experiment is the discrimination between three authors of three different musical periods: Baroque, Romanticism and French Impressionism. In this case the output layer is composed by three neurons. The output is interpreted as follows: (1,0,0) for a Purcell piece; (0,1,0) for Chopin; and (0,0,1) for Debussy.

Even though the composers belong to different schools, the success rates attained in this experiment are worse than the ones achieved in experiment 2. This is explained by the higher difficulty of the task, and also by the already noted difficulty in correctly identifying Purcell scores.

Experiment 4. The task in this experiment is discriminating between Bach compositions and works of other artists, namely: Scarlatti, Purcell, Chopin and Debussy. As before we use two output neurons, with an output of (1,0) indicating a Bach score, and an output of (0,1) indicating a composition made by other author.

The experimental results presented in table 4 show that this proved to be an easy task, which is undoubtedly due to the pronounced and highly recognizable style of this prolific composer.

Experiment 5. The goal of this experiment is to check the efficiency of the network in distinguishing between the five considered composers. Accordingly the output layer is composed by five neurons. Since this was the more complete experiment performed we conducted a more exhaustive analysis, identifying the most relevant features for author recognition.

Table 3. Purcell vs. Chopin vs. Debussy, three authors of different musical periods

Train Set	Test Patterns	Architecture	Cycles	Errors	Success Rate	MSE Train	MSE Test
85%	82	81-6-3	10000	5	94%	0.00438	0.11285
			4000	6	92.7%	0.00452	0.11363
		81-12-3	10000	4	95.2%	0.00219	0.10078
			5000	4	95.2%	0.00005	0.10461
70%	162	81-6-3	10000	10	93.9%	0.00001	0.10437
			3000	10	93.9%	0.00257	0.11973
		81-12-3	10000	7	95.7%	0.00001	0.07450
			5000	8	95.1%	0.00002	0.07708

Table 4. Experiment in order to recognize Bach from other composers

Train Set	Test Patterns	Architecture	Cycles	Errors	Success Rate	MSE Train	Test
85%	106	81-6-2	10000	1	99.1%	0.00001	0.00997
			4000	0	100%	0.00316	0.00361
		81-12-2	10000	0	100%	0.00001	0.00413
			4000	0	100%	0.00315	0.00006
70%	217	81-6-2	10000	0	100%	0.00381	0.00246
			4000	1	99.6%	0.00382	0.00897
		81-12-2	10000	1	99.6%	0.00381	0.00288
			4000	1	99.6%	0.00382	0.00698

In order to assess the importance of each metric used in this experiment, we estimate the contribution of each metric for the output of the network. This is attained by calculating the sum of the absolute values of the weights between each input neuron and the neurons of the hidden layer. The reason for this procedure is the fact that the learning capacity of the biological neurons resides in their synapse, i.e. the intensity of their connections. In ANNs, the weights tag these connections with a value, which is related to the relevance of the associated neuron.

Table 5. Experiment with the five composers

Train Set	Test Patterns	Architecture	Cycles	Errors	Success Rate	MSE Train	Test
85%	106	81-6-5	10000	6	94.4%	0.00005	0.07000
			4000	6	94.4%	0.00325	0.10905
		30-6-5	10000	7	93.4%	0.00319	0.12876
		15-6-5	10000	15	85.9%	0.01131	0.26105
		81-12-5	10000	6	94.4%	0.00313	0.11006
			4000	5	95.3%	0.00321	0.10201
		30-12-5	10000	10	90.6%	0.00348	0.12835
		15-12-5	10000	13	87.8%	0.00955	0.25258
70%	217	81-6-5	10000	11	95%	0.00386	0.09076
			4000	11	95%	0.00199	0.10651
		30-6-5	10000	14	93.6%	0.00386	0.10837
		15-6-5	10000	23	89.5%	0.02518	0.19658
		81-12-5	10000	14	93.6%	0.00194	0.14195
			4000	11	95%	0.00388	0.09459
		30-12-5	10000	11	95%	0.00195	0.08771
		15-12-5	10000	29	86.7%	0.02110	0.23455

According to this criterion for determining the importance of the features, we selected the 30 most relevant ones. We conducted several tests in which the input for the ANN was composed, only, by this set of features.

The experimental results (see table 5) indicate that these features are sufficient for the discrimination between the five authors. Therefore, we further reduced the set of input, conducting tests with the 15 most relevant features. The experimental results show a performance degradation. Using the 15 most relevant features yields an average success rate of 87.5%, using 30 yields an average success rate of 93.2%.

The analysis of the errors made by the ANN when identifying the test set patterns allows us to determine the most recognizable composers, and also the most challenging ones. As the results from experiment 4 led to believe, Bach was the most recognizable author. The most difficult author to recognize was Debussy. His works were often classified as scores of Chopin. Considering the remarkable influence of Chopin on composers such as Liszt, Wagner, Tchaikovsky, and especially Debussy, (melodic clashes, ambiguous chords, delayed or surprising cadences, remote or sliding modulations, unresolved dominant 7ths…) this does not come as a surprise.

An overall analysis of the results of the AAC in the different experiments reveals that they are coherent to the results that could be expected from a human. This reinforces the idea that the proposed feature extractor and evaluator are well suited to the task of identification.

3.2   Visual Arts Domain

Due to space restriction we only present the experimental results for the task of discrimination between six authors. The considered authors (with the exception of Gauguin and Van Gogh, which are usually considered Post-Impressionists) belong to different art movements. However, they all produced several works that are not within the style of the movement to which they are usually connected. Picasso, for instance, is usually associated with cubism; nevertheless he created a vast amount of non-cubist artworks. We faced two possible approaches for the collection of the artworks: using only the artworks that are more characteristic of a give painter; use a, hopefully, representative set of all the artworks produced by a given artist.

We chose the second approach. This choice was motivated by the following reasons: we needed a large set of training and test images; using only the most characteristic artworks may induce a bias, making the experiment artificially simple; the use of a more heterogeneous set of images increases the difficulty of the classification task.

The architecture of the ANN is similar to the used in the previous experiments. In this case the input layer is composed by 198 neurons. The number of neurons in the input layer was subsequently decreased to 148, 124, and finally to 99 neurons, in an attempt to identify the most relevant features.

To select the most relevant features we took into consideration the weights of the ANN using the configuration that yields the best results (198-12-6). The criterion used for the pruning of the input layer was the same as the one described in experiment 5.

An analysis of the results presented in table 6, shows that the success rates achieved using the 198 measurements are similar to the ones attained using, only, the 99 most relevant ones. In fact, for some configurations the deletion of the inputs yields higher success rates. This indicates that those features are of small or no relevance. The use of non relevant features during the training stage usually hinders the generalization abilities of the ANNs.

Table 6. Experiment with the six painters

Train Set	Test Patterns	Architecture	Cycles	Errors	Success Rate	MSE Train	MSE Test
85%	120	198-6-6	10000	9	92.5%	0.00589	0.13879
		198-12-6	10000	4	96.7%	0.00299	0.09533
		148-12-6	10000	6	95%	0.00002	0.08357
		124-12-6	10000	6	95%	0.00297	0.06601
		99-12-6	10000	8	93.4%	0.00737	0.12137
70%	241	198-6-6	10000	22	90.9%	0.00537	0.15199
		198-12-6	10000	17	93%	0.00359	0.15364
		148-12-6	10000	14	94.2%	0.00182	0.12319
		124-12-6	10000	16	93.4%	0.00361	0.11943
		99-12-6	10000	14	94.2%	0.00360	0.09729

An analysis of the errors made by the ANN in the classification of the test set instances, shows that the most recognizable painter is Gauguin, whereas Goya was the most difficult to identify. The total classification errors were distributed as follows: 4.3% while classifying Gauguin artworks; 8.5% on Van Gogh pieces; 9.4% on Monet; 10.1% on Picasso; 30.4% on Kandinsky; and 37.3% on Goya.

The difficulties in correctly identifying Goya's paintings were unexpected. An analysis of the artworks used in the training and testing of the ANN, indicates that the training instances do not provide a good coverage of the types of artwork produced by this author. Additionally, some of the paintings of this 18th century author were restored, which may pose further problems. The difficulties in the identification of Kandisnky's paintings can be explained by the heterogeneity of the Kandinsky's works included in the training and test set.

4 Conclusions and Future Work

In this paper we described the development of AACs for the domains of music and visual arts. The AACs follow a common architecture, and are composed by a feature extractor and an evaluator module. To validate our approach we tested their performance in several identification tasks.

The experimental results show that the proposed AACs are well-suited for these tasks, and that the extracted features are sufficient for the characterization of the pieces. Moreover, the analysis of the results allowed the identification of the most relevant features for the identification task, which is of key importance for the further development of our system.

The architecture used in the development of the AACs enables, the easy incorporation of additional features without damaging the performance, and the adaptation to other art domains.

Future research directions include: the further development of the feature extractor modules; assessing the performance of the system on a wider variety of tasks, including the aesthetic evaluation of the pieces; and the incorporation of the developed AACs in an evolutionary art system.

Research in the area of evolutionary artists is still on embryonic stage. The construction of AACs is an important step in the design of a true evolutionary artificial artist, and potentially in the better understanding of the artistic and creative process.

References

1. Johnson, C., Romero, J.: Genetic Algorithms in Visual Art and Music. In: Leonardo. MIT Press. Cambridge MA, Vol. 35, (2), (2002) 175-184
2. Romero, J., Machado, P., Santos, A., Cardoso, A.: On the Development of Critics in Evolutionary Computation Systems. In: Lecture Notes in Computer Science, Applications of Evolutionary Computing. LNCS 2611, Springer-Verlag, (2003) 559- 569
3. Manaris, B., Purewal, T. and McCormick, C.: Progress Towards Recognizing and Classifying Beautiful Music with Computers. In: Proceedings of EEE SoutheastCon, Columbia, SC. (2002) 52–57
4. Zipf, G.K.: Human Behavior and the Principle of Least Effort. New York: Hafner Publishing Company, (1949)
5. Manaris, B., Vaughan, D., Wagner, C., Romero, J., and Davis, R.: Evolutionary Music and the Zipf-Mandelbrot Law: Developing Fitness Functions for Pleasant Music. In: Lecture Notes in Computer Science, Applications of Evolutionary Computing. LNCS 2611, Springer-Verlag, (2003) 522–534
6. Arnheim, R.: Entropy and Art. University of California Press (1971)
7. Taylor, R. P., Micolich, A. P., and Jonas, D.: Fractal Analysis of Pollock's Drip Paintings. In: Nature (1999) 399–422
8. Machado, P., and Cardoso, A.: Computing Aesthetics. In: Oliveira, F., ed., Proceedings of the XIVth Brazilian Symposium on Artificial Intelligence SBIA'98. Porto Alegre, Brazil, Springer-Verlag, LNAI Series, (1998) 219-229
9. Graves, M.: Design Judgement Test Manual. The Psychological Corporation, New York, (1948).
10. Machado, P., and Cardoso, A.: All the truth about NEvAr. In: Bentley, P., Corne, D., eds., Applied Intelligence, Special issue on Creative Systems. Vol. 16, Nr. 2, Kluwer Academic Publishers (2002) 101–119

Automated Aesthetic Selection of Evolutionary Art by Distance Based Classification of Genomes and Phenomes Using the Universal Similarity Metric

Nils Svangård and Peter Nordin

Chalmers University of Technology
Complex Systems Group
SE-41296 Gothenburg, Sweden
nils@svangard.org, nordin@fy.chalmers.se

Abstract. In this paper we present a new technique for automatically approximating the aesthetic fitness of evolutionary art. Instead of assigning fitness values to images interactively, we use the Universal Similarity Metric to predict how interesting new images are to the observer based on a library of aesthetic images. In order to approximate the Information Distance, and find the images most similar to the training set, we use a combination of zip-compression, for genomes, and jpeg-compression of the final images. We evaluated the prediction accuracy of our system by letting the user label a new set of images and then compare that to what our system classifies as the most aesthetically pleasing images. Our experiments indicate that the Universal Similarity Metric can successfully be used to classify what images and genomes are aesthetically pleasing, and that it can clearly distinguish between "ugly" and "pretty" images with an accuracy better than the random baseline.

1 Introduction

The idea of Evolutionary Art as we know it today probably started around 1987 when Richard Dawkins introduced a program called "The Blind Watchmaker." This program evolved branch like stick figures, with an underlying genome, through repeated cycles of mutations and selections [1]. Later, in 1991, Karl Sims pioneered the technique of evolving color raster images, and animations, using genetic programming with LISP expressions as both the genome and the runtime algorithm [2]. This technique has later been followed by many other "genetic artists", where Steven Rooke is probably one of the most well known [3].

Throughout the history of evolutionary art, most systems have been interactive and required human input to assign fitness values to the genomes in more or less elaborate ways. The most common way is to simply rate or select the images that looks the best, but other more elaborate systems that for example time how long users view the picture as a measure for how interesting they were also exist. Even though there has

G.R. Raidl et al. (Eds.): EvoWorkshops 2004, LNCS 3005, pp. 447–456, 2004.
© Springer-Verlag Berlin Heidelberg 2004

always existed an interest to build models that can generalize and "understand" what makes an image visually interesting, little research has been done in this area since aesthetic selection process is very complex and not really well understood. Apart from just being useful for speeding up the interactive process of evolutionary art, an aesthetic selection model could also be applied on other problems, such as for example predicting whether certain advertisements or illustrations will be visually appealing, and if so to what group of people they are most interesting.

The question about how aesthetic selection work is in hot debate, and has been for hundreds of years, but recently there have appeared a number of interesting theories, and computer models using machine learning, explaining how it might work. One of the most popular way to approach this problem seem to be using prior knowledge of images and genomes that produce visually interesting images. Since most genetic artists usually work with a large quantity of genomes that looks good to seed new runs, there exist plenty of such information. Unfortunately there's no given method to assign aesthetic fitness values to genomes based on this information, and most techniques for classification, such as artificial neural networks or statistical analysis, usually requires expert knowledge about the features of the problem and does not provide any universal method for solving this problem.

In previous research there have been several, more or less successful, attempts to solve this problem. In [4], Shumeet Baluja et al, trained a set of artificial neural networks with low resolution images as input in order to predict whether an image looks good or not. Another similar setup was also used by Rob Saunders and John Gero in [5]. Penousal Machado et al have made other attempts using more "expert knowledge." In one experiment they used the root mean square error to compare the aesthetics of images (with little success) [6], but they later refined this approach using the ration between Image Complexity and Processing Complexity (which was approximated using jpeg and fractal compression respectively) with much better results [6,7]. Recently they have also tried an approach using feature extraction and artificial neural networks for music classification [8].

However, there are new general techniques that require no expert knowledge that seem promising; recently there have been great advances in the mathematical theory of similarity where a new universal metric for calculating the similarity of any two objects has emerged. Instead of requiring detailed knowledge about the objects and problem to compute the similarity, this metric can detect all similarities between the objects that any other effective metrics could detect. This metric was developed in [9-11] and is based on the "information distance" described in [12] and [13]. Roughly speaking, two objects are said to be similar if we can significantly compress one given the information in the other, the idea being that if two objects are more similar then we can more easily describe one given the other. In this context, compression is based on the ideal mathematical notion of Kolmogorov complexity, which unfortunately is not effectively computable, but can be approximated with good results using standard compression algorithms.

The idea we present in this paper is to use the universal similarity metric to compute how similar unknown genomes are to the prior knowledge of aesthetically pleasing genomes. Unlike Penousal Machado et al, which also use compression as a measure of aesthetics but reduce every image into a single scalar feature before comparing them [7], our approach compare "all possible" features of the images simultaneously. We will use the similarity metrics to evaluate both how the genomes (that generates the images) and the phenomes (the final images) can be used to guess how aesthetically pleasing any given image is. (As a side note this can be compared to the old and new school of medicine, where the old school diagnosed the person being ill, i.e. the phenome, and the new school that diagnose the human genome directly.) The genomes will be encoded as text strings and then compressed with a standard binary zip-compressor. The images will be analyzed using both JPEG compression and LZW (which is lossless). Using JPEG to compress the images is particularly interesting, compared to using a standard binary compressor, since it is designed to exploit known limitations of the human eye, notably the fact that small color changes are perceived less accurately than small changes in brightness. Thus, JPEG is intended for compressing images that will be looked at by humans, which is exactly what we try to model.

This paper is organized as follows; the first section will give a brief introduction to evolutionary art followed by a section that give a detailed introduction to Kolmogorov complexity and the universal similarity metric. Finally, we discuss our implementation and experiments as well as an analysis of our results.

2 Evolutionary Art

Like Karl Sims and Steven Rooke, we use symbolic expressions as genotypes to generate the images evolutionary with Genetic Programming [2]. These expressions are in fact equations that calculate the color for each pair of pixel coordinates (x,y) in the final image. The functional set contains standard mathematical functions, vector transformation, procedural noise generators and other image processing operators. These expressions can then be mutated, evolved and evaluated like in any other genetic programming system.

Since the main focus of this paper is aesthetic selection and the theory behind it, we will not go into further detail about how the evolutionary art systems function. However, it should be noted that unlike previous systems, we do not use the expressions to evaluate individual pixels, but instead we evaluate vectors of pixels (i.e. the whole image). The motivation behind this approach was that it is very computationally expensive to evaluate an expression for every pixel in a large image, and with this vector-based approach we can use the SIMD architecture of modern computers to calculate several pixels in parallel using sub-machine genetic programming [14,15]. The only disadvantage as we see it is that it introduces some minor limitations on the flexibility of the expressions, but on the other hand we can evaluate up to 16 pixels at the same cost as one in the other systems, which is a great advantage.

3 Aesthetic Selection

Most systems for generating evolutionary art require human input to assign fitness to the genomes. Since, to the best of our knowledge, there is no universally accepted model for how human aesthetic selection works, we have to fall back on using prior knowledge to approximate this measure. There are several different ways this could be accomplished though; for example using neural networks [4], statistical analysis or expert knowledge [7], but these methods usually require either rough simplifications and assumptions to be made, or an extraction of aesthetic features from the images [8]. However, since the introduction of the universal similarity metric there is a very powerful tool that can be applied to this tasks without any prior knowledge about aesthetics and which conforms to the principle of Occam's Razor; "Less is more."

3.1 Kolmogorov Complexity

Given an object, x, that can be encoded as a string over a finite alphabet (e.g. the binary alphabet), the Kolmogorov complexity, $K(x)$, is the length of the shortest compressed binary version from which x can be fully reproduced. Here "shortest" means the minimum taken over every possible decompression program, both real and imaginary. In fact, there does not even have to be a program that can compress the original object to the compressed form, but if there is one so much the better.

Technically the definition of Kolmogorov complexity is as follows: First, we fix a syntax for expressing all computable functions. The usual form is as an enumeration of all Turing machines, but an enumeration of all syntactically correct programs in some universal programming language like Java, Lisp or C is also possible. Then we define the Kolmogorov complexity of a finite binary string as the length of the shortest Turing machine that can generate it in our chosen syntax. Which syntax we use is not important, but we have to use the same syntax in all calculations. With this definition, the Kolmogorov complexity of any finite string will be a definite positive integer.

Even though Kolmogorov complexity is defined in terms of a particular machine model, it is actually machine-independent up to an additive constant. This means it is asymptotically universal and absolute through Church's thesis, and from the ability that universal machines can simulate one another and execute any effective process. The Kolmogorov complexity of an object can then be seen as an absolute and objective quantification of the amount of information it contains.

So $K(x)$ gives the length of the ultimately compressed version x^* of x which can be thought of as the amount of information, in number of bits, contained in the string. Similarly, $K(x|y)$ is the minimal number of bits required to reconstruct x given y. In a way $K(x)$ expressed the minimum amount of information required to communicate x when the sender and receiver has no knowledge where x comes from. For more information on individual information content, see [12].

3.2 The Similarity Metric

As mentioned our approach is based on a new and very general similarity distance that can categorize objects depending on how much information they share. In mathematics, there are many different types of distances, but they are usually required to be 'metric' in order to avoid undesired effects. A metric is a distance function, $D(\cdot,\cdot)$, that assigns a non-negative distance, $D(a,b)$, to any two objects a and b under the following conditions:

1. $D(a,b) = 0$ only when $a = b$
2. $D(a,b) = D(b,a)$ (symmetry)
3. $D(a,b) \leq D(a,c)+D(c,b)$ (triangle inequality)

In [11] a new theoretical approach to a wide class of similarity metrics was proposed: the "normalized information distance." This distance is a metric and universal in the sense that this single metric uncovers all similarities simultaneously that the any metric in the class uncovers separately. This could be understood in the sense that if two objects are similar (that is, close) according to a particular feature described by a particular metric, they are also similar in the sense of the normalized information distance metric, which justifies calling the latter *the* similarity metric. Oblivious to the problem area concerned, simply using the distance according to the similarity metric can be used to automatically classify objects of any kind.

Mathematically the similarity metric is defined as the distance of any pair of objects, x and y, where

$$d(x,y)=\frac{\max\{K(x|y),K(y|x)\}}{\max\{K(x),K(y)\}} \tag{1}$$

It is clear that $d(x,y)$ is symmetric and in [11] it is shown to be metric. It is also universal in the sense that every metric expressing some similarity that can be computed from the objects concerned is comprised in $d(x,y)$.

To compute the conditional measure, $K(x|y)$, we use a sophisticated theorem from [12] known as the "symmetry of algorithmic information":

$$K(x|y)\approx K(xy)-K(x) \tag{2}$$

So in order to compute the conditional complexity, $K(x|y)$, we can just take the difference of the unconditional complexities, $K(xy)$ and $K(x)$, which allows us to easily approximate $K(x|y)$ for any pair of objects.

3.3 Distance Based Classification

Given a pool of genomes with unknown aesthetic fitness, and a group of genomes that we known are attractive to the user, we have to figure out which of the new genomes the user will find most interesting. In order to do this we have to figure out which genome (or phenome) shares the most information with the library of prior knowledge using the similarity metric. There are several ways this can be done, but the three basic methods we considered where:

1. The minimum distance to any genome in the library
2. The average distance to all genomes in the library
3. The distance to a concatenation of all genomes in the library

We rejected the first idea quickly since it would essentially mean that the system just try to mimic any genome in the library, and we believed it would not add much creativity to the system.

The second idea makes more sense since it considers all known information, but unlike the third method, it does not consider it simultaneously. However, since it is less computationally expensive, we still find it worth investigating.

The third method we believe is the best and most creative since it considers all knowledge in the library simultaneously. The concatenation process simply works by taking all genomes (or phenomes) and creating a new object that is the combination of all such objects with a separator token between them. The genomes will simply be concatenated into a long string while the images will be lined up, one after the other, in a larger image.

4 Method

The application that evolves images has a very simple user interface where it displays nine candidate images from the internal population. The user then picks the image he, or she, finds most interesting. Then the application displays nine other images and this procedure is repeated. Every other step the application will replace the internal population with the children and mutations of the two images the user selected, and the evolution progresses.

Since aesthetic selection is probably as far from an objective system you can get, there is no given way to measure how well our method really work. However, we wanted to get some statistical indication on the predictive power of our system so we decided to test the classification accuracy of our system by letting the user label a new set of images and then having our system trying to predict which were the most interesting images.

First, we let our test subject use our application to evolve some images (s)he find interesting. During evolution, we will store all images classified as interesting in the library of aesthetically pleasing images. When a reasonable amount of images has been selected, we start to use our method for aesthetic selection. Two new images are generated and the user has to pick the one he finds most interesting in a similar manner as before. Simultaneously we let our system process the images and predict which is most interesting, and with the users choice as a label we can evaluate the classification accuracy of our system on this binary classification task.

Genomes are encoded in text form, and then compressed using LZ77 (a.k.a. Lempel-Ziv, used in gzip). Initially we considered using bzip2 for genome compression since it can usually compress files significantly better than gzip, but initial tests showed that that for small files such as genomes (which are only about 100-200 bytes in length) gzip performed better. The images will be compressed using either JPEG (with compression set to max) or as TIFF with LZW compression (which is lossless). Just like the LZ77 algorithm both the JPEG and TIFF-compression "learns as they go along" so they can successfully be used with our concatenated representation of the image library. One drawback with JPEG is that it is lossy, and the approximation of Kolmogorov complexity requires the compression algorithm to be able to completely reproduce the object. However, this only manifests itself as a linear error term in the model, which we think is a reasonable cost.

This sum up to a total of six different flavors of the universal similarity metric we test to analyze the aesthetic values of the genomes and images. To summarize, on the genomes we test two flavors:

1. Shortest distance to any genome in library (LZ77 compression)
2. Shortest distance to concatenated genome library (LZ77 compression)

and on the phenomes (images) four:

1. Shortest distance to any phenome in the library (JPEG, lossy)
2. Shortest distance to the concatenated phenome library (JPEG, lossy)
3. Shortest distance to any phenome in the library (LZW, lossless)
4. Shortest distance to the concatenated phenome library (LZW, lossless)

Out of these six methods we believe the that the methods using concatenations of the genome or phenome library will perform best, in particular when the phenomes are compressed using JPEG since it's got a much higher level of compression and understanding of images. Selection using phenomes could probably generalize better than genome selection too since it analyzes the result and ignores introns in the genome that does not affect the final image.

5   Results

We used a library of 50 genomes that we had previously classified as aesthetically pleasing images, and then we evaluated the different methods on 100 new images that we labeled manually and compared to the systems aesthetical prediction (see Table 1).

Table 1. The average accuracy of the aesthetic fitness system for the different methods

Method	Accuracy
Concatenated genomes	65%
Average genome distance	59%
Concatenated phenomes (lossy)	75%
Average phenome distance (lossy)	34%
Concatenated phenomes distance (lossless)	54%
Average phenome distance (lossless)	34%

When we look at these values, we clearly see that two of the methods stand out as being the best – selection using the concatenated genomes and selection using the average lossless distance to the phenomes. In our hypothesis, we believed that the concatenated genome and (lossy) phenome methods would be the best, which seem to agree quite well with our results. All these methods perform better than both the theoretical random baseline. We also see that the average phenome distances stands out as the worst methods, performing worse than the random baseline.

When we experimented with the aesthetic selection process for completely automated evolution we noted that it performed best when images were not looking very much alike. If the images were very similar in appearance, the system had a hard time predicting which image the user would select, but many times the human decision was very ambiguous in these cases too. So we argue that not even two human observers would have problems guessing which images the other user would find most interesting we didn't perform any statistical tests to validate this hypothesis yet though.

It should also be noted that out of these methods the phenome classification is much slower than genome classification since it not only requires the genomes to be evaluated into images, but also requires a larger amount of data to be compressed, which makes them an interesting candidate even though they did not perform as well as the JPEG classifier. The LZ77 compression algorithm doesn't work very well with short strings either, which probably affects the performance negatively so we might see better performance if we used some other kind compression algorithm better suited to this type of data instead.

6 Future Work

One of the first extensions to this system that springs to mind is completely automatic evolution without any user interaction (short of observing the final image). Therefore, instead of letting the user choose which image to pick as parents as the next generation, we would take those that our aesthetic system believes the user would have picked. However, initial tests with automatic evolution using our aesthetic fitness measure did not work that well after many generations since it had a hard time when the images looked alike, so it requires more work.

In addition to this, one interesting extension would be to use a large library of photographs instead of evolutionary produced images. In this case, we could only use phenome selection since there are no genomes for the photographs. Otherwise, using a larger library of evolutionary images could probably improve the quality of aesthetic decisions too. In a similar way, it would also be interesting to apply it on evolving other kind of art, for example music, and make more rigorous tests with different kinds of users (with or without artistic background, color blindness, et.c.).

Finally, we think it would be interesting to combine information about both the genome and the phenome into a single aesthetic measure, in hope of getting the best of both worlds. This could be as simple as just averaging the two measures, but some other more elaborate scheme might perform even better.

7 Conclusion

Our experiments indicate that the universal similarity metric can be used to successfully pick images and genomes that humans finds aesthetically pleasing. Even though the accuracy of he classifier is not perfect, it can clearly distinguish between "ugly" and "pretty" images, and performs significantly better than the random baseline. However, it does not perform as well when all the candidate images are very similar, but on the other hand, neither did our human test subject.

The best method seems to be the one using the JPEG information distance between the candidate phenome and the concatenation of all phenomes in the library. Second best is the method using the information distance between the candidate genome and a concatenation of all genomes in the library which not only perform very well, it is also much faster than corresponding method with selection on phenomes. Finally we believe that a combination of both genome and phenome selection could bring out the best of both worlds and probably perform better than either method separately, but this is left for future experiments to investigate.

References

1. Dawkins, R.: The Blind Watchmaker, Harlow Logman (1986)
2. Sims, K.: Artificial Evolution for Computer Graphics, in 1991 ACM SIGGRAPH Proceedings, Computer Graphics 25(4) (1991)
3. Rooke, S.: Eons of Genetically Evolved Algorithmic Images, Creative Evolutionary Systems, Morgan Kaufmann Publishers (2002), 339-365
4. Baluja, S., Pomerlau, D. and Todd, J.: Towards Automated Artificial Evolution for Computer-Generated Images. Connection Science, 6 (1994), 325-354
5. Saunders, R. and Gero J. S.: Artificial Creativity: A Synthetic Approach to the Study of Creative Behaviour, in J. S. Gero (ed.), Proceedings of the Fifth Conference on Computational and Cognitive Models of Creative Design, Key Centre of Design Com-putting and Cognition. (2001)
6. Machado, P. and Cardoso, A.: NEvAr – The Assessment of an Evolutionary Art Tool. In: Wiggins, G. (Ed.). Proceedings of the AISB00 Symposium on Creative & Cultural Aspects and Applications of AI & Cognitive Science, Birmingham, UK (2000)

7. Machado, P., Cardoso, A.: Computing Aesthetics. In: Oliveira, F. (Ed.), Procs. XIVth Brazilian Symposium on Artificial Intelligence SBIA'98, Porto Alegre, Brazil, Springer-Verlag, LNAI Series (1998), 219-229, ISBN 3-540-65190-X

8. Machado, P.,. Romero, J,. Manaris, B,. Santos, A., and Cardoso, A., "Power to the Critics – A Framework for the Development of Artificial Critics," in Proceedings of 3rd Workshop on Creative Systems, 18th International Joint Conference on Artificial Intelligence (IJCAI 2003), Acapulco, Mexico (2003), 55-64

9. Li, M., Badger, J. H., Chen, X., Kwong, S., Kearney, P., Zhang, H.: An information-based sequence distance and its application to whole mitochondrial genome phylogeny, Bioinformatics, 17:2(2001), 149-154

10. Li, M., Vitányi, P.: Algorithmic Complexity, International Encyclopedia of the Social & Behavioral Sciences, Smelser, N, Baltes, P., Eds., Pergamon, Oxford (2001/2002), 376-382

11. Li., M., Chen, X., Li, X., Ma, B., Vitányi, P.: The Similarity Metric, in proceedings at the 14th ACM-SIAM Symposium on Discrete Algorithms (2003)

12. Li, M., Vitányi, P.: An Introduction To Kolmogorov Complexity and its Applications, Springer-Verlag, New York, 2nd Edition (1997)

13. Bennet, C., Gács, P., Li, M., Vitányi, P., Zurek, W.: Information Distance, IEEE Transactions on Information Theory, 44:4(1998), 1407-1423

14. Riccardo, P., Langdon, W. B.: Submachine-code Genetic Programming, Technical Report CSRP-98-18, University of Birmingham, School of Computer Science (1998)

15. Svangård, N., Nordin, P., Lloyd, S.: Parallel Evolution of Trading Strategies Based on Binary Classification using Sub-Machine-Code Genetic Programming, in proceedings at the 4th Asia-Pacific Conference on Simulated Evolution and Learning, 2002 (SEAL'02)

Improvisational Media Space:
Architecture and Strategies for Evolution

Paul Nemirovsky and Rebecca Luger-Guillaume

MIT Media Laboratory, 20 Ames St., Cambridge, MA, USA 02139
{pauln, beccalg}@media.mit.edu

Abstract. This paper presents the current state in an ongoing development of the Emonic Environment (EE): a real-time improvisational system employing evolutionary principles for the mutation of media space. We position the associated problems in the context of user interaction, provide eight principles essential for creating an improvisational media environment, follow with a description of how the EE implements these principles, and conclude with a description of the evolutionary algorithms' functionality.

1 Introduction

These days, a desktop PC is capable of real-time recording, processing, and playback of audiovisual media. It can exchange sounds and images with remote users, or access vast and readily available databases online. With this wealth of information around, how can a computer help us in structuring it, perusing and organizing the media into something that is novel and *uniquely ours*? Furthermore, how can that assistance be provided in real-time and with no precise planning / guidance given by the user? To address this problem, in section II, we propose integrating the power of an *editor* and the ease-of-use of a *browser* into a new media interaction paradigm, based on the principles of non-idiomatic improvisation[1]. We posit that these principles can provide us with a powerful framework for addressing the problem. In section III, we present an up-to-date version of the principles (initially proposed in [1]). In order to exemplify the new paradigm, in section IV, we present the Emonic Environment, a system that makes computer-assisted construction and navigation of media space possible. While improvisation offers a general theoretical framework, to implement this framework, a method is needed. In section V, we argue that genetic algorithms are appropriate for the task and describe the problems encountered in their implementation within the EE.

---

[1] Not following one fixed aesthetic idiom, such as a particular music style.

G.R. Raidl et al. (Eds.): EvoWorkshops 2004, LNCS 3005, pp. 457–466, 2004.

2 Beyond Editor and Browser

Today's world of computer interaction largely remains a cold and impersonal affair: a participant directs input to a computer, which blindly and mechanically responds in the exact way it was programmed. The types of input and response vary dramatically, with two prevalent paradigms emerging: the editor and the browser.

The editor paradigm forces us to regard any creative exploration in terms of individual components: notes of a sonata, files of the peer-to-peer, shots of a movie, articles of a newspaper. The computer is passive; it is capable of responding to a fixed set of commands by performing a fixed set of functions, but provides no inspiration. As humans, we are expected to know precisely when and how to activate functions and produce results. That view is limiting, for it does not prompt further learning and limits us to what we already know and understand. Furthermore, we frequently struggle to describe our experience in creating and perceiving music, stories, or films in terms of individual components; a higher-level, structural view is required.

Such a view is provided by the browser paradigm, located at the opposite end of the interactive spectrum. The browser paradigm regards the computer as a black box, guided by a set of algorithms hidden from human view. The user is relegated to controlling a high-level space to the extent defined by the browser's rules, with no ability to affect the internals of the ongoing processes or dynamically change the structures of what is being browsed.

This editor / browser dichotomy negates what is special about human interaction: the ability to dynamically switch between high- and low-level views of the process being explored; to think structurally. Looking at the creative process as a type of search, both paradigms can be said to assume that the participants have and are aware of a fixed objective, even before the search begins. As a result of non-structural thinking and an implied search objective, we are denied further learning or creativity.

As researchers further realize the value of improvisational creativity, we see a growing effort to combine evolution and improvisation. Projects such as Voyager [2], Galapagos [3], ChaOs [4], and Swarm Music [5], while not necessarily explicitly improvisational, present media spaces that incorporate evolutionary change and user feedback. We attempt to further expand this area of research by creating a playground for building non-idiomatic improvisational media environments that allow their users to move freely on the editor/browser axis while providing both computer-influenced and human-driven evolution in an improvisational context.

3 Improvisational Principles

The EE is inspired by the ideas of non-idiomatic improvisation and experimental music tradition [6]. In this section, we present our reading of these ideas formulated as 8 principles upon which the EE is built. We focus on aspects that deal with the nature of the performance, the type of audience interaction, and the role of evolution as a vehicle for exploring the media space.

1. Dynamic nature of improvisational structures. Structural representations used in the course of improvisation are incorporated, modified, and purged dynamically to satisfy the improviser's changing focus (as affected by both aesthetic criteria and

stimuli from the outside environment). We implement this principle by constantly initiating and accounting for change in the system's state through the evolutionary process that is able to adjust to the incoming new stimuli.

2. Changing, multi-leveled focus. An improviser thinks about what he is doing at different levels of abstraction simultaneously. Continuously switching between the macro- and micro-levels, he attends to the minute details at one moment, only to switch to structural development (e.g., a climax) a second later. We implement this principle by providing a visualization of the EE's underlying multi-layered architecture, allowing the participants to switch focus between particular elements and a higher-level structural view of the system's activity.

3. Diversity of types. Improvisation is a result of interrelating multiple perceptual inputs and memories; an improvisation resulting in a video 'output' is nevertheless an improvisation that includes auditory, tactile, and other formative content. We implement this principle by allowing users of the EE to interact with sampled and generated sound, video, and photographs (work on incorporating text is ongoing).

4. Relevance of context. An improviser's decision-making is rooted in the totality of his perception of the moment. In other words, improvisation is not formed in a vacuum; it incorporates and reflects the environment in which it is created. We implement this principle by providing an interface to which a variety of sensors (e.g. temperature, motion) can be connected, affecting the ongoing evolutionary process[2].

5. Process, not artifact production, as the goal. An improviser, unlike a feature-film cinematographer, a Western composer or a product designer, is not concerned with a final production – a movie, a sonata, a pop song, or a chair. While improvisation might be recorded and, as such, seen as a fixed construct, improvisation is the process of exploration, contextualizing and interrelating memories and perceptions. The improviser weaves together an array of 'sketches,' which gain their relevance and meaning only as the improvisation unfolds. We implement this principle by ensuring that each interaction with the EE is unique. The traditional notion of recording is absent in the EE. Instead, states of the system are saved and, if restored, will evolve to a different configuration given the currently active evolutionary processes.

6. Absence of a static plan. The process of improvisational creation cannot be (should not be) thought of in terms of planning – or as a result of planning. Instead, the act of improvisation might be more aptly described as one of exploration and continuous evolution of multiple planning possibilities. An improviser is expected to be far less concerned with playing perfectly to a specification than with breaking new ground and learning from unintended mistakes and unexpected successes. This principle is implemented in the EE by the mere nature of the evolutionary process, which is adaptive by definition.

7. Distributed responsibility and control. In an improvisational performance, no fixed contract specifying responsibilities of control (i.e., a balance of power) exists between the performers. The criteria that define the degree to which each party assumes creative control over different aspects of the ongoing improvisation are set dynamically, according to implicit and explicit negotiations between performers. Giving up part of the control frees the improviser from preoccupation with creating

---

[2] This aspect of the system has recently been explored at an installation of the EE at the Centre Pompidou (Paris, 2003-4) as part of the Non-Standard Architectures exhibition.

a perfect finalized product resulting in lower costs of experimentation. We implement this principle in two ways: First, the evolutionary process plays a role of a co-improviser, sharing control with the participant. Second, the networked nature of the EE allows multiple participants to share the control of the ongoing performance with the evolution as the mediator.

8. Audience as a participant. From the passive audience of the linear storytelling to the nearly equally passive audience of the multiple-choice "interactive" environments, a strict giver / taker dichotomy has been enforced between the consumer (the audience) and the producer (the performer). In the context of improvisation, however, such a distinction is obsolete; anyone can co-improvise, so long as the effect of his activity is seen or heard in some way by the other performers. Similarly, even when not actively participating in the act of media creation, the audience is not to be regarded as passive but as a part of the improvisational circle. The implementation of this principle is evident in the participant interaction within the EE; by merely browsing (observing), the participant affects the ongoing evolution, thus, blurring the distinction between an audience and a creator.

4 The Emonic Environment

Our research interest lies in exploring situations of co-improvisation: a scenario in which the participants and the system are symbiotically contributing to a shared performance. The system described in this section – the Emonic Environment (EE) – is our attempt at creating an improvisational framework that lets its participants control media experiences through both direct input and ongoing evolutionary processes. The EE integrates component-centric precision and process-centric structural control into a single environment for improvisational media exploration in time and space.

The EE consists of 3 interconnected networks: Perceptual, Structural, and Mediated. Perceptual and Structural networks exist as independent entities. The Perceptual network is a media-processing engine that determines how media is generated, modified, and played back (e.g., speed, volume, pattern). It is populated with *emons*[3] of various types, each having an array of properties that can be connected in numerous ways. On a higher level, the Structural network, revolving mainly around the concept of stimulation changes over time, provides a structure of control through a neural net populated with *nodes*. The Structural network is concerned solely with change of its elements' activities. It is a purely abstract system for controlling objects, without which its control is utterly meaningless. Connections between the elements in the two networks are utilized to establish chains of control throughout the EE.

In order to relate the activity within the Structural network and the media processing of the Perceptual network, an auxiliary network, the Mediator, is provided. Together, the three networks form an evolving environment for improvisational interaction. Every action of a participant is based upon the following evolutionary capabilities of the environment: individual properties of the objects can be adjusted,

---

[3] Emon: functional media-processing primitive; combined together, emons form an inter-connected structure for generation, modification and presentation of media.

the system can be set to evolve into another system, and the participant can choose to contribute feedback reflecting on the ongoing evolutionary process. The three networks all operate in real time and in a balance determined by a participant, making the environment 'come alive.' Let's look at the individual components of the system[4], and then proceed to a larger-frame picture of the networks and their functionality.

Master Tempo Emon. In any system comprising multiple, separable parts, a uniform measurement of time must exist, acting as the beating heart by which the entire environment can live. The conductor of an orchestra, the sun, the heart, for example, all provide a basis from which the rest of the environment can determine its course of action. The Master Tempo acts as the emon that provides the pulse to be used by other elements of the Perceptual network as a synchronization reference. On each of its beats, it fires signals to all of the directly connected emons, thus, prompting a reaction within the rest of the system.

The Master Tempo can be adjusted dynamically. A slower tempo may result in a network in which numerous actions occur within each beat, while a faster tempo may contribute to a fast-paced but less intricate network. Changing the Master Tempo can have an effect on the entire attitude of an environment.

Tempo Emon. Tempo emons, although dependent on a supplied beat, have the power to break up their parent tempo into smaller, more distinct bits of time. Through nesting Tempo emons, the participant becomes able to create complex polyrhythmic temporal structures without having to understand concepts of music theory and composition dealing with time. As a result, the Perceptual network becomes capable of processing events in an asynchronous manner.

Additionally, Tempo emons can introduce a time delay, propagating a beat slightly offset from the original tempo. The offset property of a Tempo emon controls the amount of time that separates notification of an incoming beat and its further propagation. Such time variance can be utilized to create an echo or stagger effect.

Filter Emon. No system is complete without the ability to ignore the directives provided by others. Such 'resistance' of an element within a system can be formalized using the concept of a mask or filter. The Filter emon implements a mutable pattern of resistance, propagating events at its own discretion. This action can be thought of as denying stimulation to the emons connected to it in accordance with the given mask.

A filter consists of a binary array signaling which events the filter should and should not propagate. The filter operates in a circular fashion, looping through the array in synch with the input events it is filtering. Filters can be used to further enhance the media performance by allowing for variation in frequency of the output. For example, instead of a simple, repetitive chain of events playing an audio sample every beat, the filter allows for a structured but not monotonous repetition. Filters can be modified by changing either the entire pattern or individual bits of the mask.

---

[4] Additionally, the more advanced users can utilize the provided architecture to expand the amount of available control by building new processing components.

Audio Playback Emon. Each Audio Playback emon controls how a given audio element, be it participant-recorded or retrieved from a database, can be played back. The playback is activated by receiving a beat from a connected time source (e.g., Tempo or Filter). Audio Playback emons constitute the audible body of the environment, each having adjustable properties of volume, start and stop cue points within the sample, playback direction, time and pitch shift, audio file location, and more, all of which can be modified in real-time.

Each Audio Playback emon can store a sequence of volumes to process at each playback occasion. Subsequently, fades and crossfades can be performed, allowing different samples to become prominent at different times.

Start and stop cues serve to define additional boundaries within the audio sample. Consider an audio sample with a middle section that fits 'well' in a given network, but, the participant does not want to clutter the overall output with the rest of the sample. Instead of permanently changing the sample, start and stop cue points can be added to indicate which portions of the sample should be played. As the network evolves, the participant might decide that the rest of the audio sample fits the new network state better, thus, requiring a simple change of cues. Similarly, as a network evolves on its own, the portion of an audio sample being played can be changed to create a different sound without modifying the source file.

Furthermore, the participant may desire to play multiple sections of the same audio file. Two implementations of this functionality have been designed utilizing a system of multiple start and stop cues: (1) a mask that preserves the length of the sample in its playback, introducing silence in the masked-out portions of the sample, or (2) a selective mask that plays only the desired portions, skipping over the masked-out spots.

Additional variance in an audio sample's character can be achieved by changing the playback direction or time and pitch shift. Each of these properties adds to the repertoire of the environment.

Master Output Emon. One of the key improvisational principles is the importance of context (surrounding events) in the course of improvisation. The Master Output emon is one way to express this concept by controlling the spatial placement of sound. While it may be intriguing to have a network of intricately connected Tempo, Filter, and Audio Playback emons that result in a one-dimensional audio output, spatializing the participants' audio space can bring the EE closer to the contextual world of the participant. A person standing in one part of the room may hear a certain output and choose to modify the tempo he hears, while a participant on the other side of the room may hear a combination of other outputs and change what audio samples are playing.

How is this separation of outputs achieved? The Master Output emon allows us to connect Audio Playback emons to specific audio outputs. By dynamically changing the connections between Audio Playback and Master Output emons, we control the spatial presence of audio in particular areas. Mutation of this balance results in shifting or rotating of sound around a room for a fully encompassing atmosphere.

The type of output the Master Output provides is defined automatically dependent on the type of the incoming emon; in this way, the Master Output is capable of controlling color of lighting in a room, streaming video over the net, delivering commands to cell phones, and more.

Perceptual Network. All the emons interact through the Perceptual network, a network that has connections that define the character of *what* and *how* we hear (unlike the Structural network, described below, which defines *when* and *why* we hear). By combining multiple Tempo, Filter, and Audio Playback emons, a Perceptual network can be built to taste, both visually and aurally. The relations in the network are the foundation of how the system works: originating from a single, repetitive beat; propagating through tempo adjusters to become faster or off-beat; propagating again through filters which alter the overall pattern of emons' processing; and finally ending with a disjoint collage of signals being provided to audio samples and output into our physical environment.

Structural Network. On a different level, unaware of emon activity, nodes of the Structural network are entwined to create a net similar to that of neurons. The nodes each possess an independent activation level, its value continuously decaying. They communicate by sending stimuli, which can originate at any point in the network. When a node is triggered, implying that its activation level is beyond a propagation threshold, it sends stimuli of proportional strength to all connected nodes. The growth and decay of nodes' activation levels are always due to outside stimulation.

Mediator. How can we invoke change in the Perceptual network activity? By using the Mediator, we couple the control of the Structural network with the Perceptual network's processing. The Mediator is notified every time a Structural *node* passes a threshold and maps this information to a property of a Perceptual *emon*. The Mediator insulates each network and allows for their independence, making it possible to replace either network with a different type of controller or media system if desired. In separating these two different layers of processing, the participants are allowed to balance their focus between control levels throughout their performance.

To implement this layered construct, we designed nodal and emonic *tokens*. The nodal tokens specify two properties: the activation level at which a notification will occur and the direction of change in the activation level at the time of the token's notification (e.g., activation level rising/decreasing past 0.5). The emonic tokens correspond to specific properties of an emon and instructions for its change. Two forms of emonic tokens exist: relative and direct. A relative token can refer to toggling a value, such as a digit in a filter, or in/decreasing a value, such as a tempo. A direct token corresponds to setting a property to a set value, such as a filename or a tempo. Participants have control over which, if any, tokens are connected through the Mediator. These mediated connections can also change through mutation, leading to a complex system where transparent changes imperatively affect the overall state.

5 Evolutionary Methods for Effecting Change

From the principles stated in section III, it should be clear that the aim of the EE is not generating system actions predictable in their behavior (for no behavior is universally good or bad), but, rather making the EE capable of adaptation to unforeseen changes within the media space. GAs allow us to make the EE capable of adaptation. Furthermore, the very integration of component-centric precision and process-centric structural control exemplified in the EE is made possible by utilizing GAs. Evolution serves as our instrument for effecting change within the media space, affording flexibility in the interaction possible with the system, and potentially leading the participants to unforeseen and emergent spaces for media creation and consumption.

5.1 GAs: Implementation and Its Challenges

In the following sections we will address two questions: (1) what are the individuals that populate the evolutionary space, and (2) what constitutes a 'good' fitness function, given the idiomatically unconstrained media space?

The first question is the easiest to answer: the individuals are all the different system properties. For the Perceptual layer, these properties are emon-type specific (e.g., the Offset of Tempo emons). For the Structural layer, these are the properties of the nodes. For the Mediated layer, these are the token sets' mappings. There are also overall system properties as well as a possibility of creating macro-properties consisting of two or more properties from different layers.

The second question is much more involved and has no simple answer. In the EE, we think about evolution in terms of the system as a whole progressing from one state to another. Where is the evolution going at any given point? This is defined by the user, who selects a state toward which the evolution will progress. We call these attractor states *magnets*. The progress of evolution thus depends on human input and principles of evaluation rather than on survival.

In order to define a magnet, we need to define a representation of the system's state; that is, a function that defines what is relevant about a given state, so that given that representation we can decide whether two states are similar.

Each individual is mutated in order to reach a desired *magnet*. As the evolutionary process takes place, the environment learns which types of mutations are preferred for that particular evolution and combines the mutations that bring us closer to a magnet with the participants' preferences.

In order to judge which mutations are better than others and to make sure those are more likely to occur, we need to be able to evaluate the distance in parametric space of an environment to a state described by a magnet. We can do that by determining the fitness of the current state, and then proceeding to evolve randomly by a distance of one mutation at a time. This concept of trial and error makes the environment learn which mutations are more desirable. After each mutation, an evaluation will occur to determine if the current state is closer to the magnet. This process of mutation and evaluation continues until the current environment and the magnet are within a reasonable distance from each other.

The fitness of an environment is represented through a numeric representation, or a *checksum*. This checksum is reflective of the individuals present in the current state and is calculated uniformly. By weighting each individual on a different scale, we can derive a checksum that represents a given state, then used in comparing two states to each other. In addition to the basic weights of each property, a participant can weigh which mutations he personally prefers to occur more often. These combined weights shape the overall evolution so that it continuously tries to balance the participant's desires and the direction suggested by a magnet.

Mutations available within the EE are component-specific. For example for nodes there are Add-Node, Change-DecayRate and more; for Tempo emon, there is SetBeat, and SetPhase. General system properties, such as the number of mutations per minute are themselves subjects to the evolution. Currently there are about 60 different types of mutations available within the system.

In order to check the distance between two states we need to have a method for checksum comparison. There are two factors that influence a mutation's worth: (1) the overall direction of change, and (2) the rate of change. A combination of the two factors can be used to reflect the desirability of any mutation.

The direction of change is an obvious factor: if the difference between the current and the magnet checksums has decreased, the mutation is favorable. The rate of change is less obvious: consider filling an empty glass with water. If we were to begin by first adding single teaspoons at a time, it would take an absurd amount of teaspoons to fill the glass. However, if we were to start by adding a cup of water at a time until the glass is almost full, and then continue by adding a teaspoon at a time so the glass does not overflow, the method would be more efficient. In the case of the EE, performing a mutation that only moves the state slightly closer to the magnet is not considered as valuable as a mutation that moves the state closer in more appropriately-sized steps. Because of the scaling factors, each property change affects the checksum differently, thus resulting in mutation probabilities reflective of the desirability of the change. Each time a mutation occurs due to its having the best-predicted probability, its fitness is reevaluated to reflect the new resulting state. In this way, the EE learns about its progress and attempts different mutations in order to step closer to the magnet's checksum.

5.2 Multiple Magnets

No real life example exists where one influence single-handedly defines the evolution of an object or environment. In our context, we want to have the possibility of creating a divergent sequence of states. This becomes possible if we change the current state of the environment in multiple directions at once. While placing a single magnet in the EE influences, over a period of time, mutation of the current state, bringing its characteristics closer to those of the magnet, placing multiple magnets should have a similar effect, but with an inherent competition between themselves.

To do so, we employ an evolutionary process that takes into account that a given mutation will bring the environment closer to one magnet, while farther away from another. Active magnets are each assigned equivalent initial weights. After each mutation, the evolutionary process evaluates the distance between the mutation performed and the state defined by the magnet with the current most probable weight. Magnets are chosen in a roulette fashion with the probabilities of picking each magnet defined by its weight within the EE. As the evolution progresses, the participants dynamically alter the weights assigned to the magnets, thus, shaping the path taken by the evolutionary process. In doing so, we can account for multiple influences on the current state. The concept of multiple magnets enables us to determine if a given mutation contributes to obtaining a better balance between the currently active magnets. This balancing act reflects the nature of improvisation – a process of continuous flux.

6 Conclusion

This paper is a progress report. We have focused on the implementation, showing how principles of non-idiomatic improvisation help us in shaping a real-time evolutionary system for improvisation. We have shown how evolving a media space can be possible through multi-layered control architecture and magnet-based strategies for evolution.

We hope to continue exploring improvisational landscapes, bringing about new strategies for evolving media spaces and applying these to facilitate creation, modification, search, exchange, and performance in the domains of digital media.

Acknowledgements. The authors thank Glorianna Davenport, Ariadna Quattoni and Tammy Gilson for their ideas and help.

References

1. Nemirovsky, P. and Watson, R.: Genetic Improvisation Model: a framework for real-time performance environments. In Proceedings of EuroGP2003, Essex, UK (2003)
2. Lewis, G.: Interacting with latter-day musical automata. Contemporary Music Review. **18**(3) (1999) p. 99-112.
3. Sims, K.: *Galapagos*. Information online at: http://www.genarts.com/galapagos (1993)
4. Miranda, E. R.: On the Origins and Evolution of Music in Virtual Worlds. In Bentley, P. and D. Corne (eds.): Creative Evolutionary Systems. San Francisco, CA. Academic Press (2002)
5. Blackwell, T.M. and Bentley, P.J.: Improvised Music with Swarms. Proceedings of Congress on Evolutionary Computation, CEC-2002 (2002)

The Virtual Ecosystem as Generative Electronic Art

Alan Dorin

Center for Electronic Media Art
School of Computer Science and Software Engineering
Monash University, Clayton, Australia 3800
http://www.csse.monash.edu.au/~aland
aland@csse.monash.edu.au

Abstract. This paper proposes four desirable attributes of processes to be applied in generative electronic art. By example, it then demonstrates that the virtual ecosystem in its entirety is a process with many of these desirable attributes. The paper contrasts this process with the use of cellular automata. It outlines a number of generative artworks with which the author has been involved that utilize the virtual ecosystem, and discusses their pros and cons in the context of generative art. The paper suggests means by which the application of the four desirable attributes may extend the creative possibilities for these works.

1 Introduction

This paper explores the application of virtual ecosystems to the task of creating dynamic works of electronic art with and without user intervention. While it has been claimed that aesthetic selection has seen its heyday as a mode of audience interaction in the art world [1], the virtual ecosystem treated as a whole shows as yet un-harnessed potential for a number of reasons including:

- It demonstrates complex dynamics over fine and coarse timescales;
- Its may explore large search spaces independently of human input;
- It has the potential for user-events to influence its behaviour;
- It has the potential to allow artist-laid constraints on the search spaces.

Research such as Yaeger's seminal *PolyWorld* virtual ecosystem [2], provides a model for the material discussed here. Whilst *Polyworld* is not intended to be a work of art, it does in fact exhibit many characteristics, such as those listed above, which make it of relevance to generative artists.

The term *generative art*, refers to an art form in which a process (physical, chemical, conceptual or other), acting to some extent outside the control of the artist, is responsible for the production of the artwork, or actually constitutes the artwork [3]. Exhibitions such as *Cybernetic Serendipity* (1968) and the performances of the *Scratch Orchestra* (c.1970) set the stage for process-based art in the late twentieth century. Computer simulation has brought the concept out of its roots in performance art, physical and mechanical sculpture, into the virtual/representational realm.

G.R. Raidl et al. (Eds.): EvoWorkshops 2004, LNCS 3005, pp. 467–476, 2004.
© Springer-Verlag Berlin Heidelberg 2004

One significant aspect of the generative process as it appears in art is its ability to provide novelty and complexity greater than that which may, in practice, be specified by hand. This tendency towards novelty may be tempered by the wishes of the artist, so that some degree of control may be maintained over the aesthetic outcomes of the process. Electronic, computer-based generative art permits an extremely broad range of possibilities for the artist, since it has become possible to set in motion processes outside the realms of physics and chemistry.

Additionally, some new-media artists aim to involve the viewer of the work in the generative process, perhaps without completely undermining their own aesthetic decisions. In the case of the *digital* ecosystem, this may be through direct aesthetic selection as introduced by Dawkins [4] and widely utilized since, or indirectly by allowing the user to influence the virtual environment and the behaviour of the creatures which inhabit it. Certainly digital evolution is far more practical as a process for human manipulation than its biological counterpart.

A number of works have been constructed which utilize the digital ecosystem as a generative system with variable degrees of success. The ideas in the list above will be explored here in this context. In particular, the works discussed include:

- *Listening Sky*: (Fig. 1) an interactive sonic virtual reality environment in which the evolving inhabitants move across the surface of a globe singing to one another and passing their songs onto their offspring [5];
- *Meniscus*: (Fig. 2) an interactive work in which virtual invertebrates mate and swim. The invertebrates are visualized as a series of connected discs with tufts of cilia-like hair. Humans may vary the space by adjusting the depth and agitation of the water to suit the different creatures that evolve. The creatures have preferred depths and certain levels of agitation they find favourable for breeding [6];
- *Eden*: (Fig. 3) a sonic and visual composition in which an evolving population of creatures roam a space of virtual plants and minerals. The creatures communicate their whereabouts and the location of resources to one another audibly. As they produce offspring adapted to their environment, musical patterns emerge for mating calls, food indicators etc. Humans indirectly alter the conditions in the virtual environment by moving in a physical space monitored by infrared sensors [7,8];
- *Autumn Squares*: (Fig. 1) a textural, tapestry-like video work in which populations of coloured rectangles roam a two-dimensional grid. The grid is representative of the paths through any human construction (a city, an office building), the rectangles (people who populate the construction) wander down its paths meeting and avoiding one another depending on the kind of "boxes" they are/fit into. Rectangle communities form fanning, intermingling clusters of colour in an evolving visual field [9].

Before delving into the application of the evolutionary process to art-making, it is worth remarking that *any* process may be harnessed for electronic generative art: from the repetitive cycle of a square wave to the population explosion of an email-spread virus. Its characteristics may reflect those listed above, or they may not. This is entirely up to the artist. This paper does not presume to dictate desirable traits suitable for all artists, only to be outlining some areas the author thinks worthy of exploration.

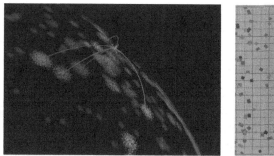
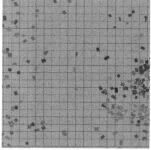

Fig. 1. Berry, Dorin, Rungsarityotin: Left, Liste*ning Sky* (2001) Listener probes indicted by arcs [5]. Right, Dorin, *Autumn Leaves* (2000) [9]

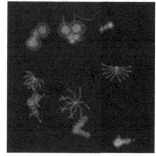

Fig. 2. Dorin: *Meniscus* (2003). Left: Interactive Installation. Right: detail [6]

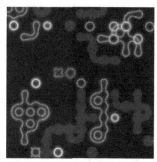

Fig. 3. McCormack: *Eden* (2001). Left: Interactive Installation. Right: detail [7]

2   A Brief Look at an Alternative: Cellular Automata

Prior to investigating the evolutionary process in the context of the desirable traits listed above, cellular automata (CA) will be discussed to see how the evolutionary algorithm shapes up against an example of the competition. A cursory summary does not do justice to the potential of these systems but such a discussion is outside the scope of this paper.

The CA grid has been applied for sometime as a process for generating music (e.g. [10]) and visual art (e.g. [11]). As indicated by Wolfram [12], such a system may fall into one of a handful of different basins of attraction. In its "interesting" state, a CA continually undergoes change into novel and complex spatial patterns. Unfortunately for artists, CA rules which reliably generate this outcome are scarce. Hence, effective CA's such as Conway's *Game of Life* [13] have been utilized countless times (e.g. [14,15]).

Despite attempts (including aesthetic evolution [16]) to overcome CA rule-set's brittleness and the difficulty of specifying rules which generate interesting behaviour, this remains a difficult process for an artist with specific aims that fall outside the possibilities for well-known rule-sets. However, two notable aspects in the favour of CA's include: simple modes for user interaction (e.g. by changing the states of cells in the grid the audience may influence the outcome); a beautiful and engaging display of complex shapes and patterns which, whilst being difficult for the audience or artist to "mould", is nevertheless rich for all of its autonomy.

Unfortunately for an artist hoping to achieve a temporal, dynamic work which explores new territory as it operates, cellular automata are not of much use unless additional rules are implemented to bump them out of boring cycles or fixed points. There are examples of CA rule sets which generate distinct sets of behaviour, the *Demon* CA for example [17], however once settled into their final dynamic state, there is no significant qualitative change in their behaviour. We shall see in the following section that this tendency towards repetition is more easily overcome in a digital evolutionary process.

3   Evolution, Generative Art, and the Audience's Perspective

Amongst the desirable attributes of a generative algorithm listed above is its ability to vary over time in a controlled manner. This drift needs to occur within constraints specified by the artist, and yet be tempered by sufficient autonomy that the work is able to generate outcomes which exhibit some degree of novelty for the audience. Novelty to the creator of the work may also be desirable (see section 4) and is subject to substantial research by those studying artificial life [18].

The evolutionary process as a whole is interesting in this context because the aesthetic experience of the audience is not being provided by a single frozen visual outcome (or even a set of such instances) from a programmer-specified process. Instead, the development occurs before the senses of the viewer who is engaged by the sub-processes as they explore novel possibilities for "survival" within the various spatial and temporal regions initiated by the programmer.

3.1   Generating Novelty

The works *Autumn Squares* and *Meniscus* are conceptually similar in many respects. In each, the intended outcome is a pleasing visual field orchestrated by the changes in a population of individuals as it evolves before the gallery visitor. Sound plays an important but nevertheless secondary role in *Meniscus*. *Autumn Squares* was conceived as a silent work.

Within *Autumns Squares*, a number of distinct phases are presented to a viewer. Similar phases appear in *Meniscus*. These mimic those of any dynamical system (including the CA) outlined by Wolfram [12]. Firstly, *Autumn Squares* is initialized with a random population of creatures of various colours and dimensions. The visual spectacle is somewhat chaotic as each of the creatures quickly orients itself, takes stock of its surroundings and sets about chasing or fleeing its neighbours. After this transient stage, the creatures start to find attractive mates and begin reproducing. The more successful creatures have distinct sizes and colouration that gradually dominate the population. From here on, the system settles down to form colonies of creatures of particular colours, sizes, and in various locations and then, unlike a CA, enters a state of "drift".

Creatures occasionally wander from their place of birth to encounter creatures of other colonies. Sometimes they settle down and start their own colony passing on the successful traits inherited from their parents. Alternatively, the creatures may chase one another across the grid, leaving a coloured trail of offspring as they go. Sometimes the creatures die in the wasteland between colonies.

The most attractive feature of this work is its gradual drift in colour and density over extended periods of time. Consequently, on the one hand, in order to grasp the gradual pace of the evolutionary process, the audience needs to approach the work over a period of at least a few hours. On the other hand, due to the simple geometric forms of the creatures and their environment, the work does not change significantly over the periods required to view it. Even after a week the *kind* of patterns that appear will not have changed. This was intentional on the part of the artist who had in mind to explore the ongoing processes of human interaction in a bustling metropolis where only the surface/fashions change whilst life continues much as it always has. *Autumn Squares* is therefore something of a self-contradiction for the audience: it is an ever-changing work that remains the same — there is something of the *organism* in the work. Its unique identity is preserved despite its continual renewal.

Whilst the minimalist design of *Autumn Squares* does not appeal to everybody, in practice, watching it for any length of time brings about a sensation like that experienced when gazing into a fire, at a metamorphosing cloud, or at waves lapping against a rocky outcrop. These simple, hypnotic processes fascinate the artist and do in fact form the major influence for his artistic practice.

The work *Meniscus* swaps some of the limitations of *Autumn Squares* for limitations of its own. Nevertheless, it makes up for these with a far more broad exploration of. the visual space than its predecessor. The creatures paddling beneath the user-adjustable water level in this work are visual impressions of invertebrate pond-life. Their body-plans, complete with wriggling cilia and tails, their colouration, locomotive cycles and behaviour are all subject to the pressures of evolution.

The success of a creature in *Meniscus* is based on its ability to encounter suitable mates, give birth to offspring using its limited supply of energy, and find a satisfactory depth and level of water agitation in which to swim. Since the audience may indirectly alter the behaviour of the creatures by adjusting the water level and agitation interactively, aesthetic selection also plays a role.

Gallery visitors may also reinitialize the evolutionary process of *Meniscus* with a wall-mounted control. This allows the work to run through the same sequence of visually diverse states outlined above for *Autumn Squares* — an initial flurry of activity, settling to a few distinct communities of creatures at various locations in the space, and finally a gentle genetic drift.

At several scales there are aspects of the *Meniscus* environment for an audience to explore. At the macro-level these include an individual creature's appearance and the changes in its form as it moves. Over time, creatures respond differently to the movement and level of the water surface. Additionally, the group behaviour of creatures varies — some prefer to cluster together, others remain aloof. Over much longer periods of time, various populations of creatures emerge and fall extinct. New populations appear in various locations under the surface and, as was the case in *Autumn Squares*, creatures from different communities may interbreed to start new families.

3.2 User Incomprehension of the Generative Process

Perhaps through its presentation as a video projection with no user input, perhaps also due to its visual simplicity, *Autumn Squares* seems to avoid the problem of "user incomprehension". In fact, due to its lack of interaction with the audience in the click-and-play sense, there is no "user" for the work, only a "passive" audience. The experiences of this author indicate that *Meniscus* and works where the user feels they have to *do* something, tend to demand of the them "Learn how this works and how to use it correctly".

In practice viewers of *Meniscus* fail to grasp exactly how it functions. The fact that digital evolution is occurring remains a mystery to most. It *is* difficult to see creatures reproducing as they move so rapidly that the trio of parents and child are apart before the user has noticed their conjunction. There is therefore no easy way to identify parents and offspring and to make the connection between a child's visual and behavioural traits and those of its parents.

Whilst the controls for altering the water level and reinitializing the population are clearly understood, the *significance* of these actions eludes most gallery visitors. The idea that they are not simply replaying a pre-rendered sequence of events triggered by a controller-click also seems to be incomprehensible to the audience. Does this matter?

As indicated above, perhaps because of the presence of the control device, the audience mentally makes the shift from passive observer to "user" and therefore feels compelled to "understand" how the work operates and control its behaviour. The questions they ask about the work (which are not those the artist wished to raise), and their frustration at failing to "understand" its "function", may be a direct consequence of this. The works which overcome this hurdle seem to be those in which the level of interaction with the audience is extremely simple and immediate. The *Mimetic Starfish* of Brown [19] being a good example. Perhaps as audiences become better educated about electronic generative art such difficulties will become a thing of the past. Perhaps the artist just needs to think more carefully about the interaction design or make the decision not to worry about this aspect of public exhibition at all.

Even without the comprehension of an audience, *Meniscus* explores some fascinating areas of the visual space dictated by (and of interest to) the artist. The most frequent positive response to the work overheard by the artist has been "beautiful". A not altogether unsatisfactory outcome, even given the audience's lack of comprehension and trigger-happy approach to operating the controls.

The work *Eden* is also problematic from the audience's perspective. Relying as it does on invisible sensors placed around the room, the work caused the audience to ponder if and how they were controlling the creatures' behaviour. It was seemingly difficult for the audience to sit back and just enjoy the environment without trying to figure out how it worked. In comparison to *Meniscus* however, *Eden*'s presentation in an environment dedicated to this one work was far more engaging for the audience than the presentation of the former work. *Meniscus* was competing for attention in a space of about twenty other interactive works, thereby establishing user expectations for a click-and-play style of interaction which was not satisfied.

As with *Meniscus*, *Eden*'s evolutionary process was not immediately obvious. Creatures were not visually different to their parents, the differences lay in their behaviour and sonic performance. Since the sounds were not easily tied to a particular creature in a well-populated world (the inherent problems of presenting numerous sound sources through stereo audio output devices), even this complex cue of the evolutionary process was difficult to interpret.

In light of the above discussion, the author's experience has been that whilst it is possible to provide engaging and novel outcomes utilizing complete evolutionary systems, the artist must be careful about the way in which the works are presented if the intention is to make the evolutionary process clear. Since the idea of all of the software discussed above was to create a generative artwork, and not a didactic visualization, this may of course be completely irrelevant to the artists, something which is explored in the following section.

4 Constraining and Guiding Evolution, the Artist's Perspective

From an artist's perspective, it is important to control the range of freedom offered to the evolutionary process. The decisions made will influence the aesthetic outcome perhaps even more significantly then the action of the algorithm itself. This is true especially since at this stage in our implementation of digital evolutionary systems, the degree of novelty and the emergence of complexity, (particularly where an organism's relationship to its environment is concerned) is severely limited [20].

In the case of a digital evolutionary system, clearly, the rules laid down by the programmer will dictate the way in which the environment unfolds. For example, if the programmer writes code in which flat-shaded, cubic creatures skim over a Cartesian plane, there is no potential for the software to make the leap into producing translucent, spline-based forms roaming a spherical-polar space. The initial creative input of the programmer has dictated the aesthetic state-space to be explored upfront. If flexibility and novelty are required, the programmer must generalize to provide sufficient scope for the evolutionary algorithm to play its part.

In early versions of *Meniscus*, creatures the artist considered unattractive or insufficiently invertebrate-like frequently appeared in the environment after initialization. In many cases they came to dominate the population. For example some of these undesirables were much too large for the display, or their hairstyles were messy and unnaturally geometric. Since the idea of the work, like that of *Autumn Squares*, was to create a pleasing visual field, this was objectionable to say the least.

To reduce the likelihood of such creatures appearing in the work, the artist first bred a database of attractive forms using interactive aesthetic evolution. When a user initializes a population of creatures in the completed *Meniscus* environment, the software, instead of randomly generating creatures from scratch, chooses two parents from the database and breeds a population of their children. Hence, although the creatures vary sufficiently for visual interest and to allow the evolutionary process to take hold, there is only a slim chance unattractive forms may arise.

The work *Eden* has as its major outcome a sonic environment produced by the communication of the creatures that populate the ecosystem. In designing the sounds for such a work, the artist may elect to provide primitive elements of varying degrees of complexity, allowing the evolutionary process to shape the sonic environment from the ground up, or giving it "high-level" audio on which to operate. Such a decision is akin to that made by a graphics programmer utilizing a genetic algorithm to synthesize 3D models. In graphics the choices lie between having as primitives control points and edges or, say, spheres and cuboids.

Within *Eden* there is a mixture of high-level and low level audio events which, when the environment is heard in its entirety, produce a meandering and often surprising composition. It is the aleatory nature of these compositions which provide their novelty. The changes in soundscape are generated by the gradual movement of the population through the genetic landscape in search of successful strategies for seeking food and mates. As was the case in *Meniscus*, the careful consideration of the sensual primitive elements upon which the evolutionary process acts determine to a large extent the success of the work as a whole.

In contrast, the work *Listening Sky*, utilizes sonic-elements far more simple than those of *Eden*. Instead of allowing the listener to hear the entire ecosystem simultaneously, a "listener" is suspended above the *Listening Sky* globe (Fig. 1). This listener sends probes to the surface and eavesdrops on the sonic activities of its inhabitants, transferring them to the audio hardware for the audience. The software system which underlies this work is the same engine upon which *Autumn Squares* is based. Hence as in the earlier work, communities of breeding creatures tend to cluster together in particular zones. This ensures the sonic environment of *Listening Sky* at a particular locality is coherent in terms of its tonal and timbral properties. The soundscape, whilst it utilizes low-level elements, is nevertheless engaging and encourages exploration by the audience.

As far as the artist is concerned, all of the above works aim to produce complexity (not just in the phenotypes, but in their interaction) from the simplicity of the genotypes. None of the works above reaches the kind of sophistication or self-determination of *The Game of Life*'s self-assembling structures, and so in this regard, the evolutionary algorithm currently falls behind. Where it excels however is in its potential as a process for generating ongoing change, even if the phenotypes are not the most complex processes we have yet engineered on a computer.

5   Conclusions

The digital ecosystem settles into a state where it drifts through an aesthetic space which may be defined carefully by the artist and may be influenced in various ways by the audience. The ecosystem (viewed as a single entity) falls short in its ability to create the dynamic complexity and novelty exhibited by a CA in full flight. The best the algorithm is able to manage is a drift through the evolutionary landscape, exploring the possibilities it holds —a significant and desirable feature. The variation within a well-defined landscape may provide ample scope for change, particularly where the environment requires of its virtual inhabitants continual adaptation. For the future, artists might examine the digital ecosystem with a mind to using it *somehow* to generate the kind of complexity and autonomy exhibited by a CA. A truly open-ended evolutionary system would be a boon for the generative artist keen to develop works which expanded not only our general understanding of biology, but made specific contributions to our understanding of aesthetics and creativity.

References

1. Dorin, A.: Aesthetic Fitness and Artificial Evolution for the Selection of Imagery from The Mythical Infinite Library. Advances in Artificial Life, Proc. 6th Euro. Conf. on Artificial Life, Kelemen & Sosik (eds), Prague, Springer Verlag (2001) 659-668
2. Yaeger, L.: Computational Genetics, Physiology, Metabolism, Neural Systems, Learning, Vision and Behavior or Polyworld: Life in a New Context. Proc. Artificial Life III, SFI Studies in the Sciences of Complexity, Langton (ed), Addison-Wesley (1994) 263-298
3. Dorin, A. & McCormack, J.: First Iteration: A Conference on Generative Computational Processes in the Electronic Arts. Leonardo, Vol. 34, No. 3, MIT Press, (2001)
4. Dawkins, R.: The Evolution of Evolvability. Artificial Life, SFI Studies in the Sciences of Complexity, Langton (ed.), Addison-Wesley (1989) 201-220
5. Berry, R., Rungsarityotin, W., Dorin, A., Dahlstedt, P., Haw, C.: Unfinished Symphonies - songs of 3 1/2 worlds. In Artificial Life Models for Musical Applications, Bilotta et al (eds), ECAL 2001 Prague, Editoriale Bios (2001) 51-64
6. Dorin, A.: Meniscus. In Experimenta: House of Tomorrow Catalogue, Taylor (ed.), Experimenta Media Arts, Australia, (2003) p32
7. McCormack, J.: Evolving Sonic Ecosystems. In Adamatzky (ed), Int. J. Systems & Cybernetics - Kybernetes, Emerald, UK, Vol. 32, Issue 1/2 (2003) 184-202
8. McCormack, J.: Eden: an evolutionary sonic ecosystem, Advances in Artificial Life, Proc. 6th Euro. Conf. on Artificial Life, Kelemen & Sosik (eds), Prague, Springer Verlag (2001) 133-142
9. Dorin, A.: Software Sketches, SIAL Colloquium, Spatial Information Architecture Laboratory, RMIT University, Australia, Sept (2002)
10. Beyls, P.: The Musical Universe of Cellular Automata. In Wells, T. and D. Butler (eds), Proceedings of the 1989 International Computer Music Conference, International Computer Music Association, San Francisco (1989) 34-41
11. Whitelaw, M.: Morphogenetics: generative processes in the work of Driessens and Verstappen. In Digital Creativity, Brown (ed.) Vol 14. No. 1 (2003) 43-53
12. Wolfram, S.: Universality and Complexity in Cellular Automata. In Physica 10D, North-Holland (1984) 1-35
13. Gardner, M.: Mathematical Games: The Fantastic Combinations of John Conway's New Solitaire Game 'Life'. Scientific American, 223(4), 1970, 120-123
14. Dorin, A.: Liquiprism: Generating Polyrhythms with Cellular Automata. Proceedings of the 8th International Conference on Auditory Display, Nakatsu & Kawahara (eds), Advanced Telecommunications Research International (ATR), Japan, (2002) 447-451
15. Miranda, E.R.: On the Evolution of Music in a Society of Self-taught Digital Creatures. In Digital Creativity, Brown (ed.) Vol 14. No. 1 (2003) 29-42
16. Sims, K.: Interactive Evolution of Dynamical Systems. In Proc. 1st Euro. Conf. on Artificial Life, Varela & Bourgine (eds), MIT Press (1992) 171-178
17. Dewdney, A.K.: Computer Recreations: A Cellular Universe of Debris, Droplets, Defects and Demons. Scientific American, Aug (1989) 102-105

18. Bedau, M.A., McCaskill, J.S., Packard, N.H., Rasmussesen, S., Adami, C., Green, D.G., Ikegami, T., Kaneko, K., Ray, T.S.: Open Problems in Artificial Life. Artificial Life, Vol. 6, No. 4, MIT Press (2000) 363-376
19. Brown, R.: Mimetic Starfish. Exhibited at Millennium Dome, UK (2000)
20. Taylor, T.: Creativity in Evolution: Individuals, Interactions & Environments. Creative Evolutionary Systems, Bentley & Corne (eds), Academic Press (2002) 79-108

Aesthetic Evolution of L-Systems Revisited

Jon McCormack

Centre for Electronic Media Art,
School of Computer Science and Software Engineering
Monash University, Clayton 3800, Australia
jonmc@csse.monash.edu.au
http://www.csse.monash.edu.au/~jonmc

Abstract. Methods for evolving Lindenmayer systems (L-systems) have been discussed in the literature for more than 10 years. This paper revisits one of the first published methods on the application of interactive evolution of L-systems for creative purposes, using aesthetic selection. An epilogue surveys the techniques and applications of evolutionary L-system methods since the original publication by the author in 1993. Conclusions are drawn about the utility and difficulties associated with evolving L-system productions, and aesthetic evolution in general, particularly with application to design and creative process.

1 Introduction

L-systems are a well-established collection of mathematical formalisms that have found application to the modeling of biological phenomena, particularly visual models of herbaceous (non-woody) plants. They were originally devised by the biologist Lindenmayer in 1968 as a mathematical formalism for modeling multicellular organisms [1]. The use of L-systems in visual modeling has produced an inspiring variety of detailed and realistic computer graphic models of plants [2]. The richness and complexity of the images created has interested a number of biologists, artists and designers, who seek to exploit the power of generative systems to study complex and novel structures.

Aesthetic evolution (also known as *interactive evolution, artificial evolution,* or *aesthetic selection*), was first described by Richard Dawkins in his book, *The Blind Watchmaker* [3]. Dawkins evolved two-dimensional, insect-like shapes composed of lines with a designated bilateral symmetry. The technique demonstrated that human users could evolve structures based on aesthetic preference. That is, they could exploit the searching power of evolution to find designs that satisfied *subjective* criteria.

This paper looks at the integration of evolutionary techniques with L-systems for the purposes of generative modeling. The application of aesthetic evolution to L-systems was first described by the author just over ten years ago [4]. The techniques developed in this paper for the purposes of creating a generative, evolutionary modeling system, based on L-systems are revisited here.

G.R. Raidl et al. (Eds.): EvoWorkshops 2004, LNCS 3005, pp. 477–488, 2004.

An 'epilogue' looks at developments in evolution and L-systems that have followed over the last ten years and draws some conclusions on common pitfalls and
problems associated with using L-systems as a basis for evolutionary art and design.

1.1 L-Systems

In the 35 years since their initial development, L-systems have undergone a wide
variety of formal analysis, enhancements, variations and extensions. Particular types
of L-systems have been developed for specific modeling problems.

Fundamentally, L-systems are iterative symbol re-writing systems, where strings of
symbols are replaced *in parallel* according to a set of rules, known as *productions*.
For detailed descriptions, the reader is referred to [2, 5, 6]. The key types of L-
systems considered here are variants of *context-free* L-systems (0L-systems): *deterministic, stochastic, parametric* and *timed*.

1.2 Turtle Interpretation of Derived Strings

The developmental strings generated by L-systems can be interpreted using a 'turtle'
[7], which moves around in space and can draw and instance various geometric objects as instructed, thus creating a geometric model, possibly time-varying in the case
of timed L-systems. Symbols from the L-system alphabet are interpreted by the turtle
in order from left to right in the derivation string. Two special commands, usually
represented by the square parenthesis symbols '[' and ']', push and pop (respectively)
the current turtle position onto a stack, thus enabling the turtle to construct branching
structures. Further details can be found in [2]. More complex turtle interpretations
permit the construction of detailed geometric models, utilizing constructs such as
generalized cylinders [8]. Parametric L-systems associate real-valued parameters with
symbols, and can be used to control continuously varying qualities of the turtle interpretation.

2 Aesthetic Evolution of L-Systems

Following the primary work in aesthetic evolution by Dawkins, Todd and Latham
used the idea to interactively evolve CSG-based forms with their *Mutator* software
[9].

Building on these works, Sims describes the use of interactive evolution for computer graphics purposes, using it to evolve morphogenic plant-like structures from
parameter sets; images and solid textures generated from mathematical functions and
expressions [10]; dynamic systems of cellular automata [11], and procedural surfaces
[12]. In the case of plant-like structures, a series of parameters describing 'fractal
limits, branching factors, scaling, stochastic contributions, etc.' were used to describe
the model, in a similar manner to algorithms described by de Reffye [13]. These pa-

rameters were used to generate three-dimensional tree structures consisting of connected line segments. More advanced geometry was constructed from the segmented models (using cylinders for example) as a post-processing operation. Growth parameters were also incorporated into the model, allowing animations to be produced [14].

Chen and Lienhardt describe a system to evolve surface forms based on combinatorial maps and deformations [15]. This work began with the goal of modeling plant leaves [16] and general developmental models for computer graphics. The work is significant as it allowed the development of structures with varying topology over time (i.e. temporal development was achieved by switching between a sequence of modular maps).

The work described in [4] was the first published example where interactive evolution had been applied to L-system grammars. The evolution of expression trees is similar to the genetic programming techniques of Koza, who evolved lisp s-expressions, to solve a variety of programming problems [17, 18]. The remainder of Section 2 refers to the evolutionary L-system techniques developed in [4].

2.1   Interactive Aesthetic Evolution

Like all generative systems, a *genotype* is used to generate a *phenotype*. In the case of L-systems, the genotype is an L-system, the phenotype the geometric model it generates when a derivation of a certain length or time is generated and interpreted. In an aesthetic evolutionary system, the user selects phenotypes to undergo the standard genetic operations of mutation and crossover. By repeating this process, the user may select for aesthetic or subjective traits in the phenotypes and thus incrementally search for genotypes that satisfy implicit fitness criteria.

The *germinal genotype* is the first parent from which offspring are mutated. A library of existing L-systems is available for the user to select from to begin the evolutionary process. It is also possible to evolve 'from scratch', i.e. with only implicitly defined identity productions in the germinal genotype.

Following the evolutionary process, the user has the option of saving the mutated genotype in the library. Alternatively, the phenotype (three-dimensional geometric data, shading and lighting information) can be exported to software or hardware based rendering systems for further visualization and processing.

2.1.1 Mutation of L-Systems

In order for the structure and form of an L-system-generated model to change, its productions and module parameters must be changed. Small changes in genotype are usually preferred so as not to completely alter the form on which it is based. However, even simple mutation of productions can cause radical changes in the resultant phenotype (e.g. see Section 3.4.2). Thus, the user interface to the system described in [4] allows detailed control of more than 30 different mutation probabilities, careful adjustment of which allows a good deal of creative control throughout the mutation/selection process.

The principal components of an L-system grammar to which mutation can be applied are: *(i)* Mutation of rules (productions) and successor sequences; *(ii)* Mutation of parameters and parametric expressions; *(iii)* Mutation of development functions and symbol ages. Details on these specific mutations can be found in [4, 8].

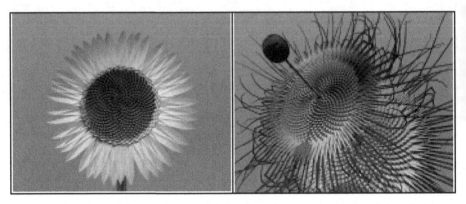

Fig. 1. Original form (left, a sunflower) and the form after many generations of aesthetic evolution (right)

2.2 Example

The figure above shows an example of a model evolved from a more conventional form (a sunflower), highlighting the ability of aesthetic selection to search for novel design spaces. Notice how the patterns of phyllotaxis present in the original model are preserved and replicated in the evolved model. If the L-system incorporates a time component (*timed L-systems*), the resultant phenotypes may have time-varying properties, which can be visualized in an animation[1].

3   Epilogue: Other Work in Evolving L-Systems

This section surveys other work in evolving L-systems and the uses of aesthetic selection over the last ten years.

3.1   More Recent Work in Evolving L-Systems

Jacob presents an evolutionary technique for parameter-less, bracketed D0L-systems using a hierarchical, typed, expression system, similar to Koza's genetic programming method [19-21]. An initial population is created from a pre-defined pool of structures, as opposed to a collection of terminal nodes and operators. His system

---

[1] Time based models can be difficult to evolve by aesthetic selection, because each phenotype must be generated over some time-period, slowing the selection process down.

does not use aesthetic selection, rather defines explicit fitness functions to rank phenotypes at each generation. A fitness function described seeks to maximize the tree end-points to lie outside a cube of given dimensions. Ochoa describes a similar technique to evolve parameter-less, bracketed D0L-systems, using genetic programming techniques [22]. She defines mutation and crossover operations achieved by string manipulation of rules. The genetic algorithm used a steady-state selection [23], with only 1/5 of the population replaced at each generation. The fitness function in this case was based on previous studies by Niklas, oriented to the synthesis of realistic tree topologies [24]. Fitness criteria included positive phototropism, a balanced bilateral symmetry, light-gathering ability, structural stability and proportion of branching points. The results were limited to simple two-dimensional structures composed of lines.

Mock also describes a system to evolve parameter-less D0L-systems using similar techniques to Ochoa [25]. He uses interactive evolution techniques to select phenotypes for mutation and crossover operations, with special criteria to avoid generating strings with unbalanced bracketing. This is achieved by selecting groups of strings for crossover within sets of bracket pairs ('[' and ']') or without any bracket symbols at all. He also describes experiments with simple automated fitness criteria to evolve simple plant-like structures to volumetric or proportional criteria.

Extending the techniques of Ochoa and Mock, Kókai, Tóth, and Ványi describe a procedure for evolving parametric D0L-systems to fit an existing morphological description [26]. They began with a tree description and were able to evolve a parametric D0L-system to describe it. In the case of this method, the object of maximum fitness must exist, although some attempt can be made to evolve towards a minimal description (i.e. remove redundancy) using D0L-systems that still adequately describes the model under consideration.

Traxler and Gervautz also describe a technique to evolve parametric D0L-systems, based on a previously developed method that combines CSG operations with parametric D0L-systems [27, 28]. Their technique for evolution of L-systems is based on that of [10] and restricts genetic operators to the numeric parameters of letters. Hence, topological changes cannot be achieved by evolution.

Similarly, Curry describes a system to evolve parametric L-systems using aesthetic selection using seven floating-point numbers in the genotype, representing parameters to a fixed L-system [29]. These parameters control qualities such as branch trajectories and child branch lengths. Mutation and crossover operations are provided, but since the L-system itself is not evolved (only the parameters to specific symbols), the range of structures possible is limited to specific tree-like models.

Hornby and Pollack [30] also evolved parametric D0L-systems to generate 'virtual creatures', similar to those of Sims [31, 32]. Their models were composed of segments connected together via fixed and articulated joints. The strings generated by the L-system were interpreted by turtle commands representing construction operations. These articulated structures are subject to a 'quasi-dynamic simulator' to provide physical constraints and give some realism to the physical simulation. For the mutation genetic operators, they apply special constraints in string creation and replacement to ensure correct bracket closure. They also define simple crossover operations for letters with multiple productions. Fitness functions were set to maximize the distance traveled by the creature's centre of mass.

Bian Runqiang and colleagues describe a method for automating the inference of L-systems to particular tree species [33]. To avoid the problems associated with random mutation and specification of individual production successors, they use a 'repair mechanism' to correct genotypes before fitness evaluation. The repair mechanism divides symbols into subsets, largely based on their turtle interpretation. Only certain combinations of successor strings from each subset have plausible semantics in the context of tree generation, hence there is a need for some form of constraint in the ordering and number of symbols generated in the successor. Strings are modified by the repair mechanism to correct strings with inappropriate syntax. This could be considered as a wider analysis of the bracketing problem, adding the problem of redundancy (i.e. strings such as '[-]' have no effect on the generated phenotype).

Other applications of evolutionary programming and L-systems include architectural structures [34, 35], tables [36], and neural networks [37].

3.2   Observations Regarding Evolution and L-Systems

Surveying the algorithms and applications described in the previous section, a number of key points can be made regarding the evolution of L-systems.

Most authors limit themselves to evolving D0L-systems, as these are suited to the most general evolutionary methods. Context sensitive, stochastic and timed L-systems are more difficult to devise evolutionary representations suited to genetic operations.

Inevitably, due to the operation of bracketed L-systems, measures must be put in place to ensure mutation or crossover operations maintain the bracket balance. This is usually achieved by *(i)* limiting mutations to exclude changing brackets; *(ii)* selecting crossover points and sub-string groups of successor symbols to lie within bracketed pairs; *(iii)* modifying the string to eliminate mismatches and redundancy.

Explicit fitness functions seem difficult to define with any degree of generality. In most cases, the criteria for fitness are simplistic or limited to highly specific domains (such as trees with certain volumetric or topological properties). Not surprisingly, most of the evolutionary applications of L-systems are confined to the application to which L-systems are most commonly deployed: the description of branching tree structures and herbaceous plants. The work presented in [4] remains one of the few applications of L-system evolution to the more general modeling of animated form. Aesthetic selection remains the broadest form of fitness criteria, but this generality comes at a cost. This issue is examined more closely in Section 3.4.

3.3   Work in Aesthetic Evolution

Since the earlier publications (listed in Section 2), the use of aesthetic evolution has been adopted for a variety of purposes. These include the work of Steven Rooke, who evolved images generated from mathematical expressions, based on the work of Karl Sims [38]. Rooke used a larger set of functions and included a number of 'fractal' algorithms in his set of base functions. Graff and Banzhaf used similar techniques to also evolve images, extending the domain to include three-dimensional, voxel images as well [39].

Ventrella generated animated figures by aesthetic evolution using a pre-determined topology [40, 41]. He used a 'qualitative' physics model as a constraint for the system. Evolved forms had to fit within the constraints of this ad-hoc physics system and the topology permitted by the software design.

Bullhak evolved musical patterns and structures [42], presenting the user with a small selection of beat-based music clips generated using an evolvable finite state automata (FSA) based system.

Other applications of aesthetic selection include line drawings [43], sculptural 'art' formed by distorted surfaces of revolution [44], and architectural applications [45, 46].

3.4 Aesthetic Evolution and Subjectivity

Typically, genetic algorithms evolve towards finding maxima in fitness, where fitness is some criteria that can be evaluated for each phenotype of the population. Conventional systems define an explicit fitness function that can be machine evaluated for every phenotype at each generation [23].

Regardless of the system or form being evolved, aesthetic selection relies on the user to explicitly select phenotypes at each generation. Users typically evolve to some subjective criteria — often described as 'beautiful', 'strange', or 'interesting' — criteria that prove difficult to quantify or express in a machine representable form (hence the use of the technique in the first place).

Whitelaw looks at modern-day successors to Latham and Sims who use artificial evolution techniques, principally for creative purposes [47]. He contrasts the work of Steven Rooke with that of Dutch artists Driessens and Verstappen. He sees the work of Rooke following a direct lineage from the methods pioneered by Dawkins, Latham and Todd, and Sims. Driessens and Verstappen however, *subvert* the evolutionary process. Typically, genetic algorithms search vast spaces, too large or difficult to be searched by other techniques. In terms of impetus, the artist must first construct the potential for such a space to be vast by adding complexity, usually in the form of a variety of operators and functions (as in the case of Rooke's images for example).

Rather than looking for this expansive landscape in their art, Driessens and Verstappen define deliberately simplistic representations and automate the fitness criteria offering many variations of basic thematic structures, such as recursive cuboids [48] or visually organic tuboid structures, reminiscent of some of the biologist Haeckel's drawings [49]. Here, the aesthetic selection process becomes one of parody, whereby the machine-defined fitness function produces phenotypes of endless variety, but aesthetic banality. The process of evolution itself becomes the primary focus of artistic exploration, rather than the results that the process produces.

Dorin criticizes the concept of aesthetic evolution from a creative perspective. He argues that the process of selection is limiting, likening it to 'pigeon breeding' and that the real artistic merits lie in the development of the model that is being mutated, rather than the aesthetic selection of phenotypes generated by that model [50].

3.4.1 Difficulties with Aesthetic Evolution

In terms of being an efficient search technique, aesthetic evolution has two significant problems:

(i) The number of phenotypes that can be evaluated at each generation is limited by both screen area (in the case of visual representation) and the ability of people to perform subjective comparisons on large numbers of objects (simultaneously comparing 16 different phenotypes is relatively easy, comparing 10,000 would be significantly more difficult).

(ii) The subjective comparison process, even for a small number of phenotypes, is slow and forms a bottleneck in the evolutionary process. Human users may take hours to evaluate many successive generations that in an automated system could be performed in a matter of seconds.

What we would like is a system that combines the ability to subjectively evolve towards phenotypes that people find 'interesting' without the bottleneck and selection problems inherent in aesthetic evolution. This problem is addressed (in a certain context) in [51] where the actions of the audience of the artwork are used to control the evolutionary process implicitly based on the interest they shown in the artwork. In [52] Saunders and Gero evolve artificial agents that attempt to exhibit 'creative' behavior by generation and evaluation of novelty between agents, illustrating possible strategies for creative evolution in an artificial context.

3.4.2 Dependency Relationships

One particular difficulty[2] when evolving L-systems is the way sets of productions may become 'hidden' for many generations only to resurface some time latter. This is due to dependency relationships and the dynamic nature of the grammar. For example, consider the following set of productions in a D0L-system, the first four derivations, and a new version of the L-system following a single mutation:

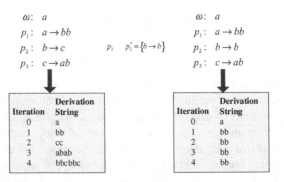

If the current derivation string does not contain the symbol *c*, p_3 will not be called upon, yet the production continues to exist as part of the system. Some time latter, a

---

[2] Or perhaps benefit, depending on the results required.

successor may again mutate to include c, which means that the particular production (p_3 in this case — or a mutated variation) will again come into play. More complex dependencies (such as a single production that 'bridges' two groups of rules) means that a single mutation of the successor in a production can cause major changes in the resultant phenotype.

3.5 The Inference Problem

As was observed by Prusinkiewicz and Lindenmayer et. al.:

Random modification of productions gives little insight into the relationship between L-systems and the figures they generate. [2, page 11]

The *inference problem* — inferring an L-system from the observation of an existing developmental process — remains difficult. Recent attempts give some insight into how the problem may be automated by genetic algorithms [33], in the application of tree generation. However, as a number of the systems described in this paper indicate, under limited circumstances the synthesis of models that could *never* be observed occurring naturally (or perhaps even explicitly designed) is possible using aesthetic evolution techniques. Aesthetic selection is a solution to the problem of creative exploration. Certain inferences may be implicitly solved by this technique, but this says nothing about the relationship between representation and model explicitly, other than that the model generates the representation. That is a problem, it seems, which needs addressing via other techniques.

4 Conclusions

Generative modeling with L-systems and aesthetic evolution are two powerful methods for creative synthesis. Combining two powerful synthesis techniques does not necessarily result in a new technique with twice the capabilities of its component parts. After more than ten years of research and development, difficulties remain in developing fitness evaluation criteria that can really exploit the representational power of L-systems. Aesthetic evolution is yet to find a worthy successor.

The real problem that remains to be addressed in any automated evolutionary technique used for creative purposes is one of *novelty*. How can artificial systems be constructed so that they can autonomously generate genuinely novel structures — not just one particular 'style', set of similar variants, or canned combination of existing techniques.

From an artistic perspective, it remains a challenge to those who use and design evolutionary creative systems to address this problem, since in critical terms many have argued that those art works which subvert or parody the aesthetic and evolutionary selection processes are of more critical importance than those that use such techniques simply as creative search systems. This is the research challenge that needs to be addressed in the coming decade.

References

1. Lindenmayer, A.: Mathematical Models for Cellular Interactions in Development, Parts I and II. Journal of Theoretical Biology, Vol. 18 (1968) 280-315
2. Prusinkiewicz, P. and Lindenmayer, A.: The algorithmic beauty of plants. The virtual laboratory. Springer-Verlag, New York (1990)
3. Dawkins, R.: The Blind Watchmaker. Longman Scientific & Technical, Essex, UK (1986)
4. McCormack, J.: Interactive Evolution of L-System Grammars for Computer Graphics Modelling. In: Bossomaier, T., (ed.): Complex Systems: from Biology to Computation, ISO Press, Amsterdam (1993) 118-130
5. Salomaa, A.: Formal Languages. Academic Press, New York, NY (1973)
6. Rozenberg, G. and Salomaa, A.: The Mathematical Theory of L-systems. Academic Press, New York (1980)
7. Abelson, H. and DiSessa, A.A.: Turtle geometry: the computer as a medium for exploring mathematics. The MIT Press series in artificial intelligence. MIT Press, Cambridge, Mass. (1982)
8. McCormack, J.: The Application of L-systems and Developmental Models to Computer Art, Animation, and Music Synthesis. Ph.D. Thesis, School of Computer Science and Software Engineering, Monash University, Clayton (2003)
9. Todd, S. and Latham, W.: Mutator: a subjective Human Interface for Evolution of Computer Sculptures. Technical Report, 248, IBM United Kingdom Scientific Centre (1991)
10. Sims, K.: Artificial Evolution for Computer Graphics. Proceedings of SIGGRAPH '91 (Las Vegas, Nevada, July 28 - August 2, 1991) In: Computer Graphics, Vol. 25, 4, ACM SIGGRAPH, New York (1991) 319-328
11. Sims, K.: Interactive evolution of dynamical systems. In: First European Conference on Artificial Life, Paris, MIT Press (1991)
12. Sims, K.: Interactive Evolution of Equations for Procedural Models. The Visual Computer, Vol. 9 (1993) 466-476
13. de Reffye, P., et al.: Plant Models Faithful to Botanical Structure and Development. Proceedings of SIGGRAPH '88 (Atlanta, Georgia, August 1-5, 1988) In: Computer Graphics, Vol. 22, 4, ACM SIGGRAPH, New York (1988) 151-158
14. Sims, K.: Panspermia. In: SIGGRAPH Video Review, ACM SIGGRAPH, New York (1990)
15. Chen, X. and Lienhardt, P.: Modelling and Programming Evolutions of Surfaces. Computer Graphics Forum, Vol. 11, 5 (1992) 323-341
16. Lienhardt, P.: Free-Form Surfaces Modeling by Evolution Simulation. In: Proceedings of Eurographics '88, Nice, France (1988)
17. Koza, J.R.: Genetic Programming: A Paradigm for Genetically Breeding Populations of Computer Programs to Solve Problems. Technical Report, STAN-CS-90-1314, June 1990, Stanford University Computer Science Department (1990)
18. Koza, J.R.: Genetic programming: on the programming of computers by means of natural selection. Complex adaptive systems. MIT Press, Cambridge, Mass. (1992)
19. Jacob, C.: Genetic L-System Programming. In: Männer, R., (ed.): Parallel Problem Solving from Nature III, Springer-Verlag, Berlin (1994) 334-343
20. Jacob, C.: Genetic L-System Programming: Breeding and Evolving Artificial Flowers with Mathematica. In: IMS '95 First International Mathematica Symposium, Southampton, UK, Computational Mechanics Publications (1995)

21. Jacob, C.: Evolving Evolution Programs: Genetic Programming and L-Systems. In: Riolo, R.L., (ed.): Genetic Programming 1996: Proceedings of the First Annual Conference, MIT Press, Cambridge, MA (1996) 28-31

22. Ochoa, G.: On Genetic Algorithms and Lindenmayer Systems. In: PPSN IV, Amsterdam, Springer-Verlag (1998)

23. Mitchell, M.: Introduction to Genetic Algorithms. Complex adaptive systems. MIT Press, Cambridge, MA (1996)

24. Niklas, K.J.: Computer Simulations of Early Land Plant Branching Morphologies: canalization of patterns during evolution? Paleobiology, Vol. 8, 3 (1982) 196-210

25. Mock, K.J.: Wildwood: The Evolution of L-systems Plants for Virtual Environments. In: International Conference on Evolutionary Computing '98, Anchorage, Alaska, IEEE-Press (1998)

26. Kókai, G., Tóth, Z., and Ványi, R.: Evolving Artificial Trees Described by Parametric L-systems. Proceedings of the First Canadian Workshop on Soft Computing, Edmonton, Alberta, Canada (1999) 1722-1728

27. Gervautz, M. and Traxler, C.: Representation and Realistic Rendering of Natural Phenomena with Cyclic CSG-Graphs. Technical Report, TR-186-2-94-19, Institute of Computer Graphics and Algorithms, Vienna University of Technology (1994)

28. Traxler, C. and Gervautz, M.: Using Genetic Algorithms to Improve the Visual Quality of Fractal Plants Generated with CSG-PL-Systems. Research Report, TR-186-2-96-04, Institute of Computer Graphics and Algorithms, Vienna University of Technology (1996)

29. Curry, R.: On the Evolution of Parametric L-systems. Technical Report, 1999-644-07, 9 November 1999, Department of Computer Science, University of Calgary (1999)

30. Hornby, G.S. and Pollack, J.B.: Evolving L-systems to generate virtual creatures. Computers & Graphics, Vol. 26, 6 (2001) 1041-1048

31. Sims, K.: Evolving 3D Morphology and Behavior by Competition. In: Proceedings of Artificial Life IV, MIT Press (1994)

32. Sims, K.: Evolving Virtual Creatures. Proceedings of SIGGRAPH 94 (Orlando, Florida, July 24-29, 1994) In: Computer Graphics, ACM SIGGRAPH (1994) 15-22

33. Runqiang, B., et al.: Derivation of L-system Models from Measurements of Biological Branching Structures Using Genetic Algorithms. In: Ali, M., (ed.): IEA/AIE 2002, Lecture Notes in Artificial Intelligence 2358, Springer-Verlag, Berlin (2002)

34. Coates, P.: Using Genetic Programming and L-systems to explore 3D Design Worlds. In: Junge, R., (ed.): CAADFutures '97, Kluwer Academic Publishers, Netherlands (1997)

35. Coates, P., Broughton, T., and Jackson, H.: Exploring Three-dimensional Design Worlds using Lindenmayer systems and Genetic Programming. In: Bentley, P.J., (ed.): Evolutionary Design by Computers, Morgan Kaufmann, London, UK (1999) Chapter 14

36. Hornby, G.S. and Pollack, J.B.: The Advantages of generative grammatical encodings for physical design. Congress on Evolutionary Computation (2001) 600-607

37. Kitano, H.: Designing neural networks using genetic algorithms with graph generation system. Complex Systems, Vol. 4, 4 (1990) 461-476

38. Rooke, S.: Eons of Genetically Evolved Algorithmic Images. In: Corne, D.W., (ed.): Creative Evolutionary Systems, Academic Press, London (2002) 339-365

39. Graf, J. and Banzhaf, W.: Interactive Evolution of Images. In: Fogel, D.B., (ed.): Evolutionary Programming IV: Proceedings of the Fourth Annual Conference on Evolutionary Programming (1995) 53-65

40. Ventrella, J.: Eukaryotic virtual reality. In: ISEA '95: International Symposium on Electronic Art, Montréal, Canada (1995)

41. Ventrella, J.: Disney Meets Darwin — The Evolution of Funny Animated Figures. In: Computer Animation '95, Montréal, IEEE (1995)

42. Bulhak, A.: Evolving Automata for Dynamic Rearrangement of Sampled Rhythm Loops. In: McCormack, J., (ed.): First Iteration: a conference on generative systems in the electronic arts, CEMA, Melbourne, Australia (1999) 46-54

43. Baker, E. and Seltzer, M.I.: Evolving Line Drawings. Graphics Interface '94, Banff, Canada (1994) 91-100

44. Tabuada, P., et al.: 3D Artificial Art by Genetic Algorithms. In: Workshop on Evolutionary Design at Artificial Intelligence in Design - AID' 98 (1998)

45. Rosenman, M.A.: The Generation of Form Using an Evolutionary Approach. In: Michalewicz, Z., (ed.): Evolutionary Algorithms in Engineering Applications, Springer-Verlag, Southampton and Berlin (1997) 69-85

46. Soddu, C.: Argenia, a Natural Generative Design. In: Generative Art '98, Milano, Italy (1998)

47. Whitelaw, M.: Breeding Aesthetic Objects: Art and Artificial Evolution. In: Corne, D.W., (ed.): Creative Evolutionary Systems, Academic Press, London (2002) 129-145

48. Driessens, E. and Verstappen, M.: Not Not (Artist's home page). website. http://www.xs4all.nl/%7Enotnot/ (Accessed: 7 October 2001)

49. Haeckel, E.: Art Forms in Nature: The Prints of Ernst Haeckel. Prestel-Verlag, Munich (1998)

50. Dorin, A.: Aesthetic Fitness and Artificial Evolution for the Selection of Imagery from The Mythical Infinite Library. In: Advances in Artificial Life, Proceedings of the 6th European Conference on Artificial Life, Prague, Springer-Verlag (2001)

51. McCormack, J.: Evolving for the Audience. International Journal of Design Computing, Vol. 4, Special Issue on Designing Virtual Worlds (2002)

52. Saunders, R. and Gero, J.S.: Artificial Creativity: A Synthetic Approach to the Study of Creative Behaviour. In: Gero, J.S., (ed.): Proceedings of the Fifth Conference on Computational and Cognitive Models of Creative Design, Key Centre of Design Computing and Cognition, Sydney (2001)

Multi-swarm Optimization in Dynamic Environments

Tim Blackwell[1] and Jürgen Branke[2]

[1] Department of Computing, Goldsmiths College, University of London
New Cross, London SE14 6NW, U.K.
t.blackwell@gold.ac.uk

[2] Institute AIFB, University of Karlsruhe,
D-76128 Karlsruhe, Germany
branke@aifb.uni-karlsruhe.de

Abstract. Many real-world problems are dynamic, requiring an optimization algorithm which is able to continuously track a changing optimum over time. In this paper, we present new variants of Particle Swarm Optimization (PSO) specifically designed to work well in dynamic environments. The main idea is to extend the single population PSO and Charged Particle Swarm Optimization (CPSO) methods by constructing interacting multi-swarms. In addition, a new algorithmic variant, which broadens the implicit atomic analogy of CPSO to a quantum model, is introduced. The multi-swarm algorithms are tested on a multi-modal dynamic function – the moving peaks benchmark – and results are compared to the single population approach of PSO and CPSO, and to results obtained by a state-of-the-art evolutionary algorithm, namely self-organizing scouts (SOS). We show that our multi-swarm optimizer significantly outperforms single population PSO on this problem, and that multi-quantum swarms are superior to multi-charged swarms and SOS.

1 Introduction

Particle Swarm Optimization (PSO) is now established as an efficient optimization algorithm for static functions in a variety of contexts [18]. PSO is a population based technique, similar in some respects to evolutionary algorithms, except that potential solutions (particles) move, rather than evolve, through the search space. The rules, or particle dynamics, which govern this movement, are inspired by models of swarming and flocking [17]. Each particle has a position and a velocity, and experiences linear spring-like attractions towards two attractors:

1. The best position attained by that particle so far (particle attractor), and
2. The best of the particle attractors (swarm attractor),

where best is in relation to evaluation of an objective function at that position. The swarm attractor therefore enables information sharing between particles, whilst the particle attractors serve as individual particle memories.

The optimization process is iterative. In each iteration, the acceleration vectors of all the particles are updated based on the position of the corresponding attractors.

G.R. Raidl et al. (Eds.): EvoWorkshops 2004, LNCS 3005, pp. 489–500, 2004.
© Springer-Verlag Berlin Heidelberg 2004

Then, this acceleration is added the velocity vector, after which the velocity is 'constricted' so that the particles progressively slow down, and this new velocity is used to move the individual from the current to the new position. The constriction factor acts like friction, slowing the particles, so that finer exploration is achieved.

While most of the optimization problems discussed in the scientific literature are static, many real-world problems change over time, i.e. they are dynamic. In those cases, the optimization algorithm has to track a moving optimum as closely as possible, rather than just finding a single good solution. It has been argued [9] that evolutionary algorithms (EAs) may be a particularly suitable candidate for that type of problems. Recently, the application of PSO to dynamic problems has been explored [18, 15, 12, 1].

Although similar to EAs, PSO needs to be adapted for optimal results on dynamic optimization problems. This is due to diversity loss and linear collapse. If the swarm is converging, the attractors will be close to the optimum position and the swarm will be shrinking at a rate determined by the constriction factor and by the local environment at the optimum. For functions with spherical symmetric local neighborhoods, a theoretical analysis and an experimental verification suggest that the shrinkage (and hence diversity loss) is scale invariant [3, 4, 5]. If the optimum shifts within the collapsing swarm, then re-optimization will be efficient. However, if the optimum shift is significantly far from the swarm, the low velocities of the particles will inhibit tracking, and the swarm can even oscillate about a false attractor and along a line perpendicular to the true optimum (linear collapse) [2].

Various adaptations to PSO have been suggested. Hu and Eberhart [15] list a number of these, which all involve randomization of the entire, or part of, the swarm. This is either in response to function change, or at some pre-determined interval. Function change can be detected by a re-evaluation of the objective function at one or several of the attractors. These techniques are somewhat arbitrary, and suffer from the fact that randomization implies loss of information gathered during the search so far. As an alternative adaptation, Blackwell and Bentley [2] introduced charged swarms with the aim to maintain diversity throughout the run. In charged PSO (CPSO), mutually repelling particles orbit a nucleus of neutral particles. This nucleus is, in fact, a conventional PSO swarm. The picture is reminiscent of classical pictures of the atom [2], although the orbits are chaotic rather than elliptical. The idea is that the charged subswarm maintains population diversity, at least within the spatial extent of the charged orbits, so that function change can be quickly (and automatically) registered, and the swarm can adapt. Meanwhile the neutral swarm can continue to explore the neighborhood of the optimum in increasing detail. CPSO has been applied to a number of uni- and bi-modal test functions of high change frequency and spatial severity, and has been shown to work well, outperforming conventional PSO [1].

In the area of EAs, multi-population approaches like the self-organizing scouts developed by Branke [9] have shown to give excellent results. The goal there is to have a number of sub-populations watching over the best local optima. For that purpose, a part of the population is split off when a local optimum is discovered, and remains close to this optimum for further exploration. The remainder of the population continues to search for new local optima, and the process is repeated if any more local optima are found. This technique is expected to work well for a class of dynamic functions consisting of several peaks, where the dynamism is expressed by small changes to the peaks' locations, heights and widths. These have been argued to be more representative of real world problems [8]. To track the optimum in such an environment, the algorithm has to be able to follow a moving peak, and to jump to another peak when the peak heights change in a way that makes a previously non-optimal peak the highest peak.

Inspired by self-organizing scouts, we investigate here whether a multi-population version of CPSO (multi-CPSO) might also be beneficial in dynamic environments. Again, the underlying idea is to place a CPSO swarm on each local optimum in a multi-modal environment. Whilst the neutral sub-swarms continue to optimize, the surrounding charged particles maintain enough diversity to track dynamic changes in location of the covered peaks.

There has been some work on parallel niching PSO sub-swarms for static problems [11]. The approach of the authors in [11] is to create a 2 particle sub-swarm from a particle and its nearest spatial neighbor, if the variance in that particle's fitness is less than a threshold. Sub-swarms may merge, and they also absorb particles from the main swarm. The nichePSO was able to optimize successfully some static multi-modal benchmark functions, but is not adaptable to the dynamic problem in an obvious way. This is because the algorithm, as the authors point out, depends on a very uniform distribution of particles in the search space, and on a training phase.

The multi-swarm approach developed here has already been proposed in a non-optimization context [6]. Two multi-swarm models are proposed here. One of these, multi-CPSO, is a multi-population version of CPSO. The other, multi-Quantum Swarm Optimization (multi-QSO) uses quantum swarms, which are based on a quantum rather than classical picture of an atom. This is proposed here in order to cure some deficiencies in CPSO (see below) and for comparative purposes.

This paper continues with an explanation of multi-swarm algorithms. Then, an experiment to test multi-swarms on the moving peaks benchmark is described and results are presented. The results are discussed and conclusions are drawn in the final section.

2   Swarm Algorithms

2.1   General Considerations

Multi-PSO swarms do not immediately generalize, since the swarms do not interact (i.e. the dynamics governing the position and velocity updates of a particle in a particular swarm are specified by parameters belonging to that swarm only). Multi-PSO's may interact if swarms have access to attractors from other swarms; however, this reduces to a single swarm with different information sharing topologies [16].

A multi-swarm is, however, easily constructed as combination of CPSO swarms. Multiple CPSO swarms will interact since charged particles repel charged particles from any swarm, including their own. However a few difficulties are apparent and these will now be discussed.

It is hoped that the repulsions between the charged swarms will enable explorations of different regions of the search space by different swarms. However, since the neutral particles do not repel, a situation may arise where the attractors from a number of swarms are on a single peak. This might be remedied by implementing repulsions between neutral particles from different swarms, but this would not prevent an equilibrium arising where a number of swarms surround a single peak and the attractions to the swarm attractors are in balance with the inter-swarm repulsions. In such a case, no single swarm would be able to move closer to the peak and optimization would cease.

In order to prevent this, we use a simple competition between swarms that are close to each other. The winner is the swarm with the best function value at its swarm attractor. The loser is expelled, and the winner remains. Swarms can be considered to be close to each other when their swarm attractors are within an 'exclusion radius' r_{excl}. Although a force law could be used for the expulsion suffered by the loser, a simple randomization of the swarm in the search space is considered in this paper.

A further difficulty is that CPSO is difficult to control, in the sense that the spatial extent of the charged swarm is unpredictable due to the chaotic nature of the orbits [5]. This might have drawbacks in multi-CPSO where it is desired to find swarms on and around localized optima. Another problem is that CPSO suffers from $O(N^2)$ complexity, arising from the Coulomb repulsion. It is probable that the success of CPSO over PSO in the dynamic context is due to the increased diversity around the contracting PSO swarm, rather than due to charged particles finding better solutions within the contracting nucleus. If this is true, then the exact dynamics are not important as long as diversity is maintained. In which case, simple randomization of the charged particles in a region surrounding the neutral swarm may be sufficient, negating the need for expensive $O(N^2)$ computations. This is the basis of the quantum swarm.

The quantum swarm, which builds on the atomic picture of CPSO, uses a quantum analogy for the dynamics of the charged particles. In the quantum model of the atom, the orbiting electrons are replaced by a 'quantum cloud'. This cloud is actually a probability distribution governing where the electron will be found upon measurement. The electron does not follow a classical trajectory in between 'measurements'. The probability distribution depends on the energy (and various other quantum numbers) of the electron. For example, electron positions in the lowest energy state of the hydrogen atom are distributed according to $p(r)\, dr = (\text{const})r^2 e^{-2r}$ [14].

Quantum Swarm Optimization (QSO) is therefore a hybrid technique, since the contracting nucleus of the PSO sub-swarm follows deterministic dynamics whereas the enveloping charged cloud follows stochastic dynamics. By stretching the quantum analogy still further, a 'measurement' corresponds to a function evaluation. At this point the charged particles are randomized within a ball of radius r_{cloud} centered on the swarm attractor. This provides a very simple update rule and corresponds to a uniform (and very unphysical) probability distribution. The velocity of the charged particle is irrelevant (it is indeterminate in the quantum picture) and the charged particles are not repelled from other charged particles or attracted to any attractor. However, any good location that they do find by virtue of their random positioning around the swarm attractor may still be useful to the neutral swarm due to information sharing.

The multi-QSO is therefore an assembly of QSO swarms. The only interaction between these swarms occurs when swarms collide and the exclusion principle is applied.

2.2 Proposed Algorithm

After initialization, the proposed multi-swarm algorithm iterates a main loop with four stages: Test for function change, particle update, attractor update and exclusion. These stages are described below.

INITIALIZE. Randomize positions and velocities of each particle in search space, set all attractors to randomized particle positions, set swarm attractor to particle attractor 1 and set all stored function values to function floor.
REPEAT.
    FOR EACH swarm n
    // Test for Change.
    Evaluate function at swarm attractor of swarm n.
    IF new value is different from last iteration **THEN**
        Re-evaluate function values at each particle attractor.
        Update swarm attractor.
        Store function values.
    FOR EACH particle k of swarm n
    //Update Particle
    Apply equations (1) – (7) to particle k of swarm n.
    //Update Attractor.
    Evaluate function at updated position and store value.
    IF new value better than particle attractor value **THEN**
        Particle attractor k := position and value of particle k.
    IF new value better than swarm attractor value **THEN**
        Swarm attractor := position and value of particle k.
    FOR EACH swarm $m \neq n$
    //Exclusion.
    IF swarm attractor p_n is within r_{excl} of p_m **THEN**
        Randomize the swarm with the worse swarm attractor value.
        (re-set particle attractors, evaluate f at each new position, store these
        values, and set attractor of swarm to the position of its best particle).
UNTIL number of function evaluations performed > max

For updating particle k in swarm n, the following equations are used:

1. For neutral particles:

$$v_{nk} = \chi[\, v_{nk} + c_1\, \varepsilon\, (p_n - x_{nk}) + c_2 \varepsilon\, (p_{nk} - x_{nk})] \tag{1}$$

$$x_{nk} = x_{nk} + v_{nk} \tag{2}$$

2. For charged particles in QSO:

$$x_{nk} \in B_n(r) \tag{3}$$

3. For charged particles in CPSO:

$$v_{nk} = \chi[\, v_{nk} + c_1\, \varepsilon\, (p_n - x_{nk}) + c_2 \varepsilon\, (p_{nk} - x_{nk})] + a^+_{nk} \tag{4}$$

$$x_{nk} = x_{nk} + v_{nk} \tag{5}$$

$$a^+_{nk} = \sum_{m=1}^{M} \sum_{l=1}^{N_m^+} a_{nk,ml}\,(1 - \delta_{nk,ml}) \qquad \delta_{nk,ml} = \begin{cases} 1 & nk = ml \\ 0 & \text{otherwise} \end{cases} \tag{6}$$

where

$$a_{nk,ml} = \begin{cases} \dfrac{Q_{ml}Q_{nk}}{|x_{core}|^2}\dfrac{x_{nk} - x_{core}}{|x_{nk} - x_{core}|} & |x_{nk} - x_{ml}| < r_{core} \\[2ex] 0 & |x_{nk} - x_{ml}| > r_{\lim it} \\[2ex] \displaystyle\sum_{m=1}^{M}\sum_{l=1}^{N_m^+}\dfrac{Q_{ml}Q_{nk}}{|x_{nk} - x_{ml}|^3}(x_{nk} - x_{ml}) & \text{otherwise} \end{cases} \tag{7}$$

In these equations, x_{nk}, v_{nk}, p_{nk} are d-dimensional position, velocity and attractor vectors of particle k from swarm n. The PSO parameters are the spring constants $c_{1,2}$, and the constriction factor $\chi < 1$. ε is a random number drawn from a uniform distribution.

The stored function values f_{nk} arise from evaluations $f(p_{nk})$ at time t and, with $g(n)$ as the index of the best attractor (the swarm attractor), $f_{ng(n)} = \max\{\, f_{nk}\}$. The test for change therefore compares $f_{ng(n)}$ with $f(p_{ng(n)})$.

A convenient representation of the multi-swarm *configuration* is $M(N_n + N_n^+)$ where N_n and N_n^+ are the numbers of neutral and charged particles in swarm n and M as the number of swarms in the multi-swarm. $M(N_n + N_n^+)$ also evaluates to the total number of particles. From an information-theoretic viewpoint, swarm n is actually the data set $S_n = \{x_{nk}, v_{nk}, p_{nk}, f_{nk}, g(n)\,\}$, $k = 1,\ldots, N_n + N_n^+$.

The multi-swarm is therefore a colony of M interacting swarms. Neutral particles in any swarm always follow a pure PSO position and velocity update rule. Charged classical particles obey the neutral dynamics, but are also mutually repelled from other charged particles in any swarm. A charged quantum particle, on the other hand, does not follow a classical rule and, upon measurement (a function evaluation), is to be found in a d-dimensional ball $B_n(r_{cloud})$ of radius r_{cloud} centered on $p_{ng(n)}$.

3   Experiments

The experiment was designed to investigate the effect of different multi-swarm configurations on the optimization of a dynamic benchmark function. In order to compare the multi-swarms with the results of evolutionary techniques reported in [8], population size N was fixed at 100 particles. Many different configurations of 100 particles are possible. The number of swarms, M, can range from 1 (where the multi-swarms reduce to PSO, CPSO and QSO) to 100 (where the concept of a swarm is lost, and the model becomes a 'gas' of interacting particles). However it is expected that optimal configurations will lie in between these extremes. As far as possible, symmetrical configurations of 2 to 50 swarms were tested, along with the extremes. The effects of different near-symmetrical configurations was also tested for $M = 6$ and 7 multi-swarms.

Table 1. PSO and CPSO Parameters.

$c_{1,2}$	κ	r_{core}	r_{limit}	r_{cloud}	Q_{nk}	r_{excl}
2.05	0.729843788	1.0	10.0	10.0	1.0	10.0

The parameter settings for all algorithms were fixed at standard values (cf. [13] for PSO and [2, 1] for CPSO) and are listed in Table 1. The standard PSO parameters $c_{1,2}$ and κ have been well tested by many authors and have been shown to lead to convergence for non-interacting particles, and for interacting particles close to symmetric optima [3, 4]. The single QSO parameter, the exclusion radius r_{cloud}, was set to the perception limit of the equivalent CPSO. This choice was made for comparative purposes: the intention is that charged particles can move freely in a hypersphere of radius $r_{cloud} = r_{limit}$ (although there are large fluctuations in CPSO). The final parameter in both algorithms is the exclusion radius r_{excl}. It would be important to study the dependence of the algorithms on this free parameter, but in this study r_{excl} is fixed at a value chosen to be commensurate with the peak width (between 1 and 12) and the charged swarm size (10). It can be conjectured that a much larger values of r_{excl} would lead to one swarm covering many peaks, and a much smaller value would lead to many swarms trying to optimize the same peak.

For performance evaluation, we used the publicly available moving peaks benchmark [10] which consists of a number of peaks, moving around in the search space, while also changing heights and width. The benchmarks parameter settings correspond to the Scenario 2 as specified on the benchmark web site [10]. The search space has five dimensions $[0, 100]^5$ with 10 peaks. Peak heights can vary randomly in the interval [30, 70], width can vary within [1, 12]. Scenario 2 specifies a family of benchmark function since the initial location, height and width of the peaks, and their subsequent development is determined by a pseudorandom number generator. Furthermore, some of the parameters of Scenario 2 are only defined to within a range of values. Of these, the following choices were made to facilitate comparisons with the experiments of reference a [7]: Change severity vlength = 1.0, correlation lambda = 0.0, and peak change frequency = 5000.

Each experiment consists of a particular function instance and initial particle distribution. The termination condition for each experiment is 500000 function evaluations. The experimental conditions are altered by changing the random seed of the benchmark generator and the initial positions and velocities of the particles. The primary performance measure is the offline error [7] which is recorded for each experiment and then averaged, for each algorithm, over 50 experiments with different random seeds (which also means different instances of the class of benchmark problems). This measure is always greater or equal to zero and would be zero for perfect optimization. The results for the offline error are tabulated in Table 2, together with the standard error. The configurations marked by a star in this table have 98 rather than 100 particles. For easier comparison, the data is also visualized in Fig. 1.

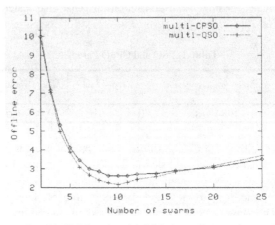

Fig. 1. Performance of multi-CPSO and multi-QSO depending on the number of swarms.

4 Discussion

In the limiting case of a single swarm, configurations 1(100+0) and 1(50+50), the multi-swarm models reduce to the three single particle swarm algorithms, PSO, CPSO and QSO. The PSO is marginally superior, with an offline error of 16.5076. The slightly better performance of the swarm with the smallest diversity is presumably due to its better optimization on a single peak. Clearly, the dynamics of the peak function is too severe for the two simple diversification measures (charged and quantum sub-swarms) to be effective. The very similar offline errors of the single swarm algorithms is quite curious, and to gain insight into this phenomenon, animations of the particle motions were viewed in two dimensional slices through the 5 dimensional space. These animations revealed that in each case the single swarm becomes attracted to, and remains on, a single peak, irrespective of whether this is the maximum peak. Interestingly, the offline error for the single swarms is comparable to the results for a standard EA of the same population size, and for the same experimental conditions, cf. Fig. 4 of [7]. The standard EA and the EA with memory have offline errors > 18 so the single swarm algorithms are performing better than these evolutionary techniques, although neither is particularly good.

However, when the standard EA is augmented with a diversification strategy, the offline error is considerably improved, with a best result of approx. 4.6 for the self-organizing scouts model. The effect of replacing the single swarm with increasingly numerous multi-swarms can be seen by reading down Table 2. The offline error dips below 4.6 at 5 swarms and rises above 4.6 for $M > 25$, demonstrating that multi-

Table 2. Mean offline error ± standard error for multi-CPSO/QSO and various configurations of 100 particles.

Number of Swarms, M	Configuration $M(N_n + N_n^+)$	multi-CPSO	multi-QSO
1	1(100+0)	16.51 ± 0.56 (PSO)	16.51 ±0.56 (PSO)
	1(50+50)	16.72 ± 0.54 (CPSO)	16.99 ±0.51(QSO)
2	2(25 + 25)	9.98 ± 0.35	10.33 ± 0.33
3	3(17+16)*	7.15 ± 0.27	7.04 ± 0.27
4	4(13 + 12)	5.32 ± 0.18	4.97 ± 0.18
5	5(10 + 10)	4.12 ± 0.15	3.89 ± 0.15
6	4(8+8)+2(8+10)	3.45 ± 0.14	3.09 ± 0.10
	4(8+8)+2(10+8)	3.45 ± 0.14	3.05 ± 0.10
	4(8+8) + 2(9+9)	3.42 ± 0.12	3.11 ± 0.10
7	6(7+7) + 1(9+7)	3.03 ± 0.12	2.74 ± 0.10
	6(7+7) + 1(7+9)	3.07 ± 0.12	2.74 ± 0.10
	6(7+7) + 1(8+8)	3.06 ± 0.11	2.65 ± 0.08
	7(7+7)*	3.00 ± 0.12	2.66 ± 0.11
8	7(6+6)+1(8+8)	2.85 ± 0.11	2.38 ± 0.07
9	8(6+5)+1(6+6)	2.62 ± 0.11	2.25 ± 0.07
10	10(5+5)	2.63 ± 0.10	2.16 ± 0.06
11	10(5+4)+1(5+5)	2.62 ± 0.09	2.27 ± 0.06
12	11(4+4)+1(6+6)	2.72 ± 0.11	2.44 ± 0.07
14	14(4+3)*	2.73 ± 0.09	2.57 ± 0.07
16	14(3+3)+2(4+4)	2.90 ± 0.10	2.82 ± 0.07
20	20(3+2)	3.06 ± 0.08	3.16 ± 0.07
25	25(2+2)	3.50 ± 0.10	3.69 ± 0.08
50	50(1+1)	16.07 ± 0.39	5.72 ± 0.15
100	100(1+0)	44.33 ± 1.57	44.33 ± 1.57
100	100(0+1)	44.34 ± 1.58	8.44 ± 0.17

swarms perform very well when compared to diversity-enhanced EA's in this environment. The best result (2.1566) is for the 10 swarm multi-QSO.

The optimum configurations for multi-CPSO and multi-QSO are 11 and 10 swarms respectively. This is comparable to the maximum number of peaks in the dynamic function. (Although a ten peak scenario is chosen, it is possible that a lower peak may move under a higher peak, thus effectively removing one of the local maxima.) This result is consistent with the motivating picture of each swarm shadowing a peak.

The multi-QSO performs better than the equivalent multi-CPSO for most configurations. The suspicion that the Coulomb dynamics are not important for adding diversity to a neutral swarm seems to be supported by this set of experiments. It is known that the Coulomb force is responsible for some very large fluctuations in the charged

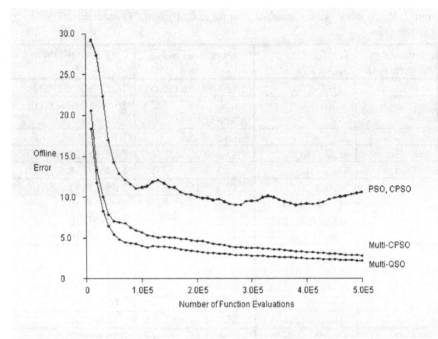

Fig. 2. Convergence plot for the offline error over time. Multi-CPSO and Multi-QSO use the 10(50+50) configuration, respectively.

swarm size [4, 5]. On the other hand, the quantum cloud approach of QSO means that the diversity increasing sub-population is concentrated close to the optimum discovered by the neutral swarm. These results suggest that this strategy is more efficient, presumably because it is less wasteful; the quantum particles are always close to where they will be needed at peak change.

As the number of swarms increases away from the optimum number of 10 swarms towards the extreme configurations 20(3+2) and 25(2+2), the two algorithms converge in terms of performance. Two and three particle neutral swarms are the smallest for which the PSO algorithm makes any sense and the performance of each neutral swarm is at its lowest. When there are many more swarms than peaks, it is expected that 'free' swarms (i.e. those that are not associated with peaks) will be constantly 'patrolling' the search space. This is because patrolling swarms will be attracted to peaks, but will be expelled by any swarms which are already optimizing that peak. If this picture is correct then diversity lies in the multi-swarm as a whole, and the single swarm diversity of CPSO or QSO is of lesser importance. Once more, this conjecture was explored qualitatively by observing animations, and this picture was observed to be broadly correct.

The 100(1+0) and 100(0+1) configurations are very distorted and the concept of a swarm is lost. In the 100(1+0) model, every particle is neutral and feels an acceleration towards its best position. The model could be viewed as 100 independent local optimizers, or a single non-interacting gas of free particles since there is no information sharing amongst the particles. Unsurprisingly, the offline error for multi-CPSO and multi-MSO is very poor (and identical, because there are no charged particles) and worse than single swarms. However, in the 100(0+1) configuration, each particle is charged and although there is no information sharing, there will be interactions (in multi-CPSO) since each particle is repelled from every other. The difference this makes to the offline error is however very small. But, if every free particle is a quantum particle with an updated position in the cloud surrounding its best position, the offline error is reduced from 44.3 to 8.4, a stunning performance considering the simplicity of the model and the results of the standard EA (offline error ~19).

The results for the $M = 6$ and 7 configurations suggest that small differences to N_n and N_n^+ make little difference. The most symmetrical configurations, 4(8+8) + 2(9+9) and 7(7+7) are slightly better.

Figure 2 shows the evolution of the offline error over time (starting at evaluation 10000 for clarity). As can be seen, the multi-PSO outperforms the single population PSO or CPSO right from the beginning.

5 Conclusions

This paper has proposed two multi-swarm generalizations of particle swarms and compared their performance on a benchmark dynamic multi-modal environment. The first of these models, multi-CPSO, is an assembly of charged particle swarm optimizers. It is already known that surrounding a neutral or conventional PSO sub-swarm with an orbiting sub-swarm of mutually repelling particles increases swarm diversity. This improves pure PSO results in dynamic optimization of uni- and bi-modal functions of high severity [1,2,4,5]. The results presented here suggest that in a multi-modal environment a multi-CPSO is preferable to a single swarm, and that the optimum number of swarms is commensurate with the number of optima.

The second model, multi-QSO, was introduced to see if the particular dynamics (inverse square repulsions) of the charged particles in the CPSO are important, or whether a diversity increasing measure would by itself be sufficient. The results tend to suggest the latter. In QSO, the charged particles are simply randomized within a hyper-sphere centered on the swarm attractor at each update, and multi-QSO outperforms multi-CPSO for almost every configuration, and has the best overall result. A further advantage of QSO is that it is scaleable, being of linear complexity.

A comparison has also been made to experiments applying evolutionary techniques to the same environment [7]. Single swarm PSO and CPSO are broadly comparable (in fact slightly better) with an EA and a memory-enhanced EA optimization. However, the multi-swarms manage to at least halve the offline error of the diversity enhanced multi-population EA's (which represent the best evolutionary approach found in these experiments).

While the reported experiments are very encouraging, future tests should examine the sensitivity to parameter settings and also look at benchmark problems with other characteristics, e.g. where the number of peaks is significantly higher than the number of particles. Furthermore, it would be worthwhile to develop self-adaptation mechanisms for the number of swarms and the exclusion radius r_{excl}.

References

1. Blackwell, T.M.: Swarms in Dynamic Environments. Proc Genetic and Evolutionary Computation Conference (2003) 1-12
2. Blackwell, T.M. and Bentley, P.J.: Dynamic search with charged swarms. Proc Genetic and Evolutionary Computation Conference (2002) 19-26
3. Blackwell, T.M.: Particle Swarms and Population Diversity I: Analysis. GECCO Workshop on Evolutionary Algorithms for Dynamic Optimization Problems (2003) 103-107
4. Blackwell, T.M.: Particle Swarms and Population Diversity II: Experiments. GECCO Workshop on Evolutionary Algorithms for Dynamic Optimization Problems (2003) 108-112
5. Blackwell, T.M.: Particle Swarms and Population Diversity. Soft Computing (submitted)
6. Blackwell, T.M.: Swarm Music: Improvised Music with Multi-Swarms. Proc. AISB '03 Symposium on Artificial Intelligence and Creativity in Arts and Science (2003) 41-49
7. Branke, J. and Schmeck H.: Designing Evolutionary Algorithms for Dynamic Optimization Problems. S. Tsutsui and A. Ghosh, editors, Theory and Application of Evolutionary Computation: Recent Trends. Springer (2002) 239-262.
8. Branke, J.: Memory Enhanced EA for Changing Optimization Problems. Congress on Evolutionary Computation CEC'99. 3 (1999) 1875-1882.
9. Branke, J.: Evolutionary optimization in dynamic environments. Kluwer (2001)
10. Branke, J.: The moving peaks benchmark website. Online, http://www.aifb.uni-karlsruhe.de/~jbr/MovPeaks
11. Brits, R., Engelbrecht, A.P., van den Bergh, F.: A Niching Particle Swarm Optimizer. Fourth Asia-Pacific Conference on Simulated Evolution and Learning. Singapore (2002) 692-696
12. Carlisle, A. and Dozier, G.: Adapting Particle Swarm Optimization to Dynamic Environments. Proc of Int Conference on Artificial Intelligence. (2000) 429-434
13. Clerc, M. and Kennedy, J.: The Particle Swarm: Explosion, Stability and Convergence in a Multi-Dimensional Complex Space. IEEE Transactions on Evolutionary Computation. 6 (2002) 158-73
14. French, A.P. and Taylor, E.F.: An Introduction to Quantum Physics. W.W. Norton and Company (1978)
15. Hu, X. and Eberhart, R.C.: Adaptive particle swarm optimisation: detection and response to dynamic systems. Proc Congress on Evolutionary Computation (2002) 1666-1670.
16. Kennedy, J. ad Mendes, R.: Population Structure and Particle Swarm Performance. Congress on Evolutionary Computation (2002) 1671-1676
17. Kennedy, J. and Eberhart, R.C.: Particle Swarm Optimization. Proceedings of the 1995 IEEE International Conference on Neural Networks. IV (1995) 1942-1948.
18. Parsopoulos, K.E. and Vrahatis, M.N.: Recent Approaches to Global Optimization Problems through ParticleSwarm Optimization. Natural Computing 1 (2002) 235-306

Evolutionary Algorithms for Stochastic Arc Routing Problems

Gérard Fleury[1], Philippe Lacomme[2], and Christian Prins[3]**

[1] Université Blaise Pascal / LMA
24 Avenue des Landais, F–63177 Aubière Cedex, France
fleury@math.univ-bpclermont.fr
[2] Université Blaise Pascal / LIMOS
BP 10125, F–63177 Aubière Cedex, France
lacomme@isima.fr
[3] Université de Technologie de Troyes / LOSI
12 Rue Marie Curie, BP 2060, F–10010 Troyes Cedex, France
prins@utt.fr

Abstract. The Capacitated Arc Routing Problem (CARP) is a combinatorial optimization problem in which vehicles with limited capacity must treat a set of arcs in a network, to minimize the total cost of the trips. The SCARP is a stochastic version with random demands on the arcs. The management rules used for instance in waste collection enable to derive mathematical expressions for objectives like the expected total cost. A memetic algorithm (MA) for the SCARP is proposed and compared with two deterministic versions based on average demands. All solutions are evaluated by simulation, to see how they are affected by random fluctuations of demands. This evaluation confirms the expected cost computed by the MA and shows its ability to provide robust solutions, without significant enlargement of the cost of planned trips.

1 Introduction – Arc Routing and Waste Collection

The *Capacitated Arc Routing Problem* (CARP) is defined on an undirected network $G = (V, E)$, with a set V of n nodes and a set E of m edges. A fleet of identical vehicles of capacity W is based at a depot node. Each edge e can be traversed any number of times, each time with a cost c_e, and has a non-negative demand q_e. All costs and demands are integers. The τ edges with non-zero demands, called *required edges* or *tasks*, require service by a vehicle. The goal is to determine a set of vehicle trips (routes) of minimum total cost, such that each trip starts and ends at the depot, each required edge is serviced by one single trip, and the total demand handled by any vehicle does not exceed W.

The CARP is $\mathcal{NP}$-hard and exact methods are still limited to small instances with at most 25 edges [14]. Hence, larger instances must be solved in practice with heuristics. Among fast constructive methods, one can cite for instance Path-Scanning [6], Augment-Merge [7] and Ulusoy's splitting technique

---

** Corresponding author

G.R. Raidl et al. (Eds.): EvoWorkshops 2004, LNCS 3005, pp. 501–512, 2004.

[16]. Metaheuristics available are very recent and include tabu search methods [8,9], guided local search [3] and memetic algorithms [10,11]. All these heuristics can be evaluated thanks to very good lower bounds [1,2].

The most important application of this deterministic CARP (DCARP) is urban refuse collection. In reality, this problem is a *Stochastic CARP* (SCARP), because the amount of waste in a street (edge) is a random variable. In practice, the trips are computed in advance from average demands and must remain stable over a long period, e.g. one year, otherwise the residents could forget to output their waste containers on time. Hence, the objective of the SCARP is to design planned trips whose the expected total cost on the field is minimized.

To the best of our knowledge, the SCARP has been investigated only by Fleury *et al.* [5]. These authors use simulation to evaluate *a posteriori* how solutions computed by heuristics for the DCARP are affected by random demand fluctuations. Their goal is to select heuristics that can be executed with average demands in the planning phase, while providing robust solutions on the field.

In this paper, the most efficient solution method for the DCARP, the MA of [11], is extended to compute *a priori* a robust solution for the SCARP. The concept of robust GA is not new. For instance, Tsutsui and Gosh [15] and Branke [4] have proposed different modifications to make the standard GA more robust and tested them on continuous functions of several variables. Our contribution is a) to study the stochastic version of a classical combinatorial problem (the CARP), b) to propose a memetic algorithm for the SCARP and c) to use an accurate approximation of the expected total cost to guide the MA, instead of resorting to simulation or noising techniques to evaluate chromosomes.

The SCARP is similar to the *Stochastic Vehicle Routing Problem* (SVRP), in which nodes must be serviced instead of arcs. However, methods for the SVRP [12] are not used to solve the SCARP because the network conversion triples the number of nodes. Moreover, no memetic algorithm (and even no basic GA) is available for the SVRP. Hence, this paper describes the first evolutionary algorithm ever proposed for a stochastic capacitated routing problem.

The remainder of this paper is structured as follows. Section 2 recalls the MA for the DCARP [11]. Section 3 is devoted to a mathematical analysis of SCARP solutions, made possible by the management rules used in waste collection. This analysis enables relatively simple modifications in the MA, to produce robust solutions to the SCARP. The resulting algorithm is compared with two versions of the original MA on standard DCARP instances in Section 4.

2   A Memetic Algorithm for the DCARP

A memetic algorithm is a GA hybridized with a local search procedure, see for instance Moscato [13] for a tutorial. This section recalls the MA proposed by Lacomme *et al.* [11] for the DCARP. It is called DMA (like *Deterministic MA*) in the sequel. This algorithm is adapted in Section 3 to solve the SCARP.

2.1   Chromosomes and Evaluation

A chromosome is an ordered list of the τ tasks, in which each task may appear as one of its two directions. Implicit shortest paths are assumed between successive tasks. The chromosome does not include trip delimiters and can be viewed as a giant tour for an uncapacitated vehicle. A procedure *Split* optimally partitions (subject to the sequence) the giant tour into feasible trips. The guiding function of the memetic algorithm is the total cost of the resulting DCARP solution.

Figure 1 illustrates *Split* on a giant tour (a, b, c, d, e) with $\tau = 5$ tasks, with demands in brackets. Thin lines represent shortest paths, not detailed. The dashed ones represent possible returns to the depot. *Split* builds an auxiliary graph with $\tau + 1$ nodes, indexed from 0 onwards, in which each possible trip is modeled as one arc $(i - 1, j)$, weighted by the trip cost. A shortest path from node 0 to node τ in that graph (bold arrows) can be computed in $O(\tau^2)$ using Bellman's algorithm. It indicates the optimal splitting, here 3 trips with a total cost 141.

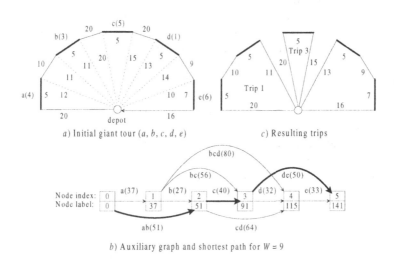

a) Initial giant tour (a, b, c, d, e) c) Resulting trips

b) Auxiliary graph and shortest path for $W = 9$

Fig. 1. Principle of Split

Note that the encoding is *valid*, i.e. there exists one optimal chromosome. Indeed, consider one optimal DCARP solution and build a chromosome by concatenating the lists of tasks of each trip: *Split* will retrieve the optimal solution when applied to this chromosome.

2.2   Other DMA Ingredients

DMA works with a small population *Pop* of nc chromosomes (typically $nc = 30$). The initial population comprises three good solutions computed by fast DCARP heuristics already cited in the introduction: Path-Scanning (PS), Augment-Merge (AM) and Ulusoy's heuristic (UH), completed by random permutations. Clones (identical chromosomes) are forbidden. In practice, a stronger condition is imposed: at any time, *Pop* must contain solutions with distinct costs.

At each iteration, two parents are selected by binary tournament and reproduce according to a slightly modified version of the classical order crossover (OX). The only modification is that OX must recognize the same edge when it finds the two possible service directions in the parents. One child is randomly selected, the other is discarded.

The mutation is replaced by a local search procedure *LS*, called with a fixed probability p_m, which works on the individual routes computed by *Split* instead of the giant tour. The moves include the removal of one or two consecutive tasks from a route, with reinsertion at another position, the exchange of two tasks, and 2-opt moves. All moves may involve one or two routes and the two traversal directions of an edge are tested in the reinsertions. Each iteration scans all these moves to perform the first improving move. *LS* stops when no more improvement can be found. The trips are then concatenated into a chromosome, which is re-evaluated by *Split* because this brings sometimes a further improvement.

The resulting child replaces one of the $nc/2$ worst chromosomes, randomly chosen in the population and such that no clone is created. DMA stops after a given number of iterations ni, after a stabilization period of ns iterations without improving the best solution or when reaching a lower bound LB.

When the lower bound is not reached in this main phase, nr short restarts are performed with an intensified local search (rate $p_{mr} > p_m$). Each restart begins with a special procedure which replaces ncr chromosomes by new ones ($ncr < nc$), while preserving the best solution. It stops when the lower bound is achieved or after a given number of iterations nir ($nir < ni$).

Algorithm 1 summarizes the main phase of DMA. $h(C)$ denotes the evaluation of chromosome C, i.e. the cost of the DCARP solution (set of trips) computed by *Split*. The restarts have the same structure. Compared to Moscato's general MA template [13], the local search is not applied to the initial population, it is not systematically applied to children, and there is no mutation operator (solutions with distinct costs ensure a sufficient diversity).

3   Analysis of the Stochastic CARP

3.1   Additional Notation

For any planned solution x (set of trips), θ_{xj} denotes the j-th trip of x, $h(x)$ the deterministic cost (total cost of the edges traversed by the trips), and $t(x)$ the number of trips. $H(x)$ and $T(x)$ represent the random variables corresponding to $h(x)$ and $t(x)$ when the average demands q_e are replaced by random quantities Q_e. For a given realization ω of random demands, the planned cost and number of trips are denoted by $H(x,\omega)$ and $T(x,\omega)$. For any random variable $F(x)$, $\overline{F(x)}$, $var[F(x)]$ and $\sigma[F(x)]$ respectively denote in the sequel the expectation, the variance and the standard deviation.

Algorithm 1 – Overview of DMA structure

1: run the DCARP heuristics PS, AM and UH
2: convert solutions into chromosomes by concatenating their trips
3: $Pop \leftarrow \{\text{resulting chromosomes}\}$
4: complete Pop using random chromosomes with distinct costs
5: sort Pop in increasing cost order
6: $cni, cns \leftarrow 0$
7: **repeat**
8:     $cni \leftarrow cni + 1$
9:     select two parents P_1, P_2 by binary tournament
10:     apply crossover OX to P_1, P_2 and choose one child C at random
11:     evaluate C with *Split*
12:     **if** $random < p_m$ **then**
13:         improve C by the local search procedure LS
14:     **end if**
15:     draw k at random between $\lfloor nc/2 \rfloor$ and nc included
16:     **if** $(Pop \setminus \{Pop(k)\}) \cup \{C\}$ contains no duplicate cost **then**
17:         $Pop(k) \leftarrow C$
18:         **if** $h(C) < h(Pop(1))$ **then**
19:             $cns \leftarrow 0$
20:         **else**
21:             $cns \leftarrow cns + 1$
22:         **end if**
23:         shift $Pop(k)$ to keep Pop sorted
24:     **end if**
25: **until** $(cni = ni)$ or $(cns = ns)$ or $(h(Pop(1)) = LB)$

3.2   Vehicle Management Rules

In waste collection, a DCARP with average demands $q_e = \overline{Q_e}$ must be solved to inform the residents about the planned trips and to prevent drivers from improvizing their own trips. When the deterministic solution x is implemented, extra-costs are induced when a vehicle is filled earlier than expected: it must go to the depot, unload its waste, and come back to continue its planned trip.

There are several reasons for using this simple policy: calling another vehicle may be impossible due to lack of communication systems, the other trucks can not come because all trips are performed in parallel, the driver is the only one to know the sector, etc. Therefore, the cost $h(x)$ computed from average demands becomes a random variable $H(x)$ and the SCARP generally consists of minimizing $\overline{H(x)}$, the expected cost of x. For any solution x, note that $h(x)$ is the best possible value of $H(x)$.

Figure 2 shows (left) a DCARP solution x with $t(x) = 2$ trips, a vehicle capacity $W = 9$, and average demands in brackets. Other numbers represent costs. The total cost is then $h(x) = 241$. On the field, the driver must face a realization ω of the random variables (right). The cost of the first trip is not affected but the second trip is split into trips 2' and 2". Finally, $H(x,\omega) = 284$ and $T(x,\omega) = 3$. The deviation to the planned solution is 43 (+17.8%).

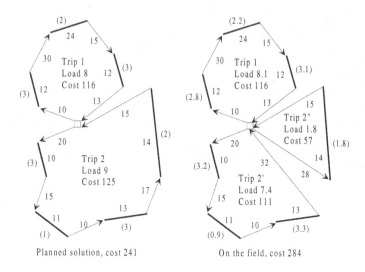

Fig. 2. Modification of a planned solution on the field

3.3   Random Edge Demands

In practice, the random demand Q_e on edge e results from a large number of small and independent demands, such as containers or plastic bags. The central limit theorem holds and Q_e may be modelled as a *Gaussian random variable* $N(q_e, \sigma_e^2)$, with two restrictions: the demand can not be negative nor exceed vehicle capacity W. Q_e is truncated to avoid these abnormal values. In general, the expectation q_e of Q_e is well-known, but not its variance. In the sequel, a standard deviation $\sigma_e = k \cdot q_e$ is assumed, where k is a positive constant.

It is also assumed that the average demand per street is small compared to W, so the probability for one single edge to fill a vehicle is negligible. Moreover, we do not consider situations where demands become dependent, for instance a global increase of waste production after a feast like Christmas. Finally, the quantities to collect can be modelled by independent truncated Gaussian random variables $N(q_e, k^2 \cdot q_e^2)$.

3.4   Probability of Trip Interruption

Thanks to independent demands and management rules, the perturbation of a DCARP solution x may be evaluated trip per trip. For any trip θ_{xj}, the total amount collected is $\sum_{e \in \theta_{xj}} q_e \leq W$. For the SCARP, the probability to report a trip interruption is $p_j = P(\sum_{e \in \theta_{xj}} Q_e > W)$. Since $\sum_{e \in \theta_{xj}} Q_e$ is a Gaussian random variable with expectation $\sum_{e \in \theta_{xj}} q_e$ and variance $k^2 \cdot \sum_{e \in \theta_{xj}} q_e^2$, p_j can be expressed by Equation 1, where ϕ is the cumulative probability of $N(0,1)$, i.e. $\phi(x) = \frac{1}{\sqrt{2\pi}} \int_{-\infty}^{x} e^{-\frac{t^2}{2}} dt$.

$$p_j = 1 - \phi \left(\frac{W - \sum_{e \in \theta_{xj}} q_e}{k \cdot \sqrt{\sum_{e \in \theta_{xj}} q_e^2}} \right) \tag{1}$$

3.5 Simplified Expressions

Although more general expressions can be derived, two other assumptions are done to simplify the presentation in the sequel: a) since the average demand of each edge is small in front of vehicle capacity, it seems reasonable to assume that a trip can not be interrupted several times, and we assume it is true with probability 1, b) in a robust solution, a trip is seldom interrupted and, when it is, this occurs with high probability just before the last task.

Knowing the p_j and according to assumption a), the expected number of trips simply is $\overline{T(x)} = t(x) + \sum_{j=1}^{t(x)} p_j$. Let s_j denote the cost to go from the last but one edge of θ_{xj} to the depot, unload the waste, and go back to collect the last edge. Under the previous assumptions, with probability $1 - p_j$, the trip cost is $C_j = \sum_{e \in \theta_{xj}} c_e$ and, with probability p_j, it is $C_j = \sum_{e \in \theta_{xj}} c_e + s_j$. Other expressions can easily be derived:

1. the expected cost of trip θ_{xj}: $\overline{C_j} = \sum_{e \in \theta_{xj}} c_e + s_j \cdot p_j$
2. its variance: $var[C_j] = s_j^2 \cdot (p_j - p_j^2)$
3. the deterministic cost of solution x: $h(x) = \sum_{j=1}^{t(x)} \sum_{e \in \theta_{xj}} c_e$
4. its stochastic cost: $H(x) = \sum_{j=1}^{t(x)} C_j$
5. its expected cost: $\overline{H(x)} = \sum_{j=1}^{t(x)} \overline{C_j} = h(x) + \sum_{j=1}^{t(x)} s_j \cdot p_j$
6. the variance of the cost: $var[H(x)] = \sum_{j=1}^{t(x)} s_j^2 \cdot (p_j - p_j^2)$

3.6 Objective Functions for the SCARP and Modifications of DMA

The expected total cost $\overline{H(x)}$ and the expected number of trips $\overline{T(x)}$ are good candidates for minimization, because they can be compared with $h(x)$ and $t(x)$, the best possible values obtained by solving the DCARP. Composite objectives can be considered as well to avoid excessive standard deviations, for instance $\overline{H(x)} + \rho \cdot \sigma[H(x)]$, with a given positive penalty ρ.

Thanks to the analytical expressions derived for all these stochastic objectives, DMA can be modified in a relatively simple way to solve the SCARP, by using the new objective when evaluating initial solutions, sorting the population, selecting parents by binary tournament and determining the chromosome to be replaced. When evaluating a chromosome, *Split* is still used to compute a partition into trips (a solution) x and its deterministic cost $h(x)$, but the new objective is immediately evaluated afterwards. The local search must be adapted too, to perform only the moves that decrease the new objective. The MA modified in this way is called *Stochastic MA* or *SMA*.

4 Computational Evaluation

4.1 Algorithms Tested and Benchmark Instances

The original DMA (Algorithm 1) and a more robust version in which a slack $\mu = 10\%$ is booked in each vehicle are first evaluated. The SMA is tested with two objectives: the expected cost $\overline{H(x)}$ and the composite function $\overline{K(x)} = \overline{H(x)} + \rho \cdot \sigma[H(x)]$, with $\rho = 10$ (if H were Gaussian, this would give too much weight to the variance, but H is *not* Gaussian, for $H = h$ with high probability and $H \geq h$). All demands are independent truncated Gaussian random variables $N(q_e, k^2 \cdot q_e^2)$, as explained in 3.3. Here $k = 10\%$. This respectively gives four algorithms MA1, MA2, MA3 and MA4, with solutions x_1, x_2, x_3 and x_4.

All algorithms are implemented in Delphi 6 and tested on 23 classical CARP instances, called *gdb* files [7], on a 1.8 GHz Pentium IV PC (Windows 2000). These files are numbered from 1 to 25 but instances 8-9 contain inconsistencies and are never used. The deterministic demands q_e in the files are interpreted as mean demands by MA3 and MA4. The parameters for the four MAs (see 2.2) are: $nc = 30$, $p_m = 0.1$, $ni = 20000$, $ns = 6000$, $nr = 20$, $p_{mr} = 0.2$, $ncr = 7$ and $nir = 2000$. All MAs may also stop when reaching a lower bound. Results for larger instances are also available but are not presented due to lack of space.

The detailed results are given in tables 2 to 5, which indicate first the file name, the number of nodes n, the number of tasks m, the best-known lower bound LB for the deterministic cost [2], the deterministic cost $h(x)$ and the number of trips $t(x)$ found by the MA. x is evaluated by simulation. One trial ω draws a random demand on each edge and computes $H(x, \omega)$ and $T(x, \omega)$. The following estimators for $a = 1000$ trials are reported: the average cost $\overline{H(x, a)}$, the average number of trips $\overline{T(x, a)}$, the percentage of trials with interrupted trips $p(x, a)$, the standard deviations of the cost $s_H(x, a)$ and of the number of trips $s_T(x, a)$. They respectively approximate $\overline{H(x)}$, $\overline{T(x)}$, $P(T(x) > t(x))$, $\sigma[H(x)]$ and $\sigma[T(x)]$. The last column gives the running time in seconds.

Table 1. Summary of results

Method	$\dfrac{H(x,a)-h(x)}{h(x)}$	$\dfrac{T(x,a)-t(x)}{t(x)}$	$p(x,a)$	$s_H(x,a)$	$s_T(x,a)$	Time	$\dfrac{s_H(x,a)}{H(x,a)}$	$\dfrac{H(x,a)-H(x_1,a)}{H(x_1,a)}$
MA1	8.05%	22.68%	70.00%	16.08	0.84	2.83s	5.15%	--
MA2	0.06%	0.11%	1.06%	1.33	0.07	1.32s	0.40%	-3.20%
MA3	1.17%	5.91%	24.94%	4.05	0.34	18.05s	1.40%	-4.50%
MA4	0.00%	0.06%	0.46%	0.21	0.03	24.99s	0.08%	-2.29%

Table 1 provides a synthesis with the following averages on the 23 files: the deviations of the expected cost and number of trips to the deterministic values, then $p(x, a)$, $s_H(x, a)$, $s_T(x, a)$ and the running time. The table is completed by a *robustness estimator* $s_H(x, a)/\overline{H(x, a)}$, approximating the variability $\sigma[H(x)]/\overline{H(x)}$), and by the expected cost saved (compared to MA1) $(\overline{H(x, a)} - \overline{H(x_1, a)})/\overline{H(x_1, a)}$.

4.2   Results of MA1 – Deterministic MA, No Capacity Restriction

The results are detailed in Table 2. From a deterministic point of view, they are excellent since 21 instances out of 23 are solved to optimality (asterisks). According to the synthetic results of Table 1, MA1 is very fast (it reaches LB very quickly). However, planned solutions undergo on the field an extra-cost of 8.05% and the probability of interrupted trips is 70%. In fact, most solutions have nearly full vehicles and are sensitive to augmented demands. This is confirmed by the average robustness of 5.15%.

Table 2. Results of MA1 on gdb instances

File	n	m	LB	$h(x_1)$	$t(x_1)$	$\overline{H(x_1,a)}$	$\overline{T(x_1,a)}$	$p(x_1,a)$	$s_H(x_1,a)$	$s_T(x_1,a)$	Time
gdb1	12	22	316	316*	5	351.23	5.82	66.20	31.17	0.68	0.01
gdb2	12	26	339	339*	6	389.50	8.08	94.20	28.06	1.10	0.39
gdb3	12	22	275	275*	5	292.82	5.81	64.40	15.34	0.70	0.03
gdb4	11	19	287	287*	4	320.93	5.24	79.70	23.58	0.86	0.01
gdb5	13	26	377	377*	6	443.17	8.09	92.70	37.67	1.12	0.13
gdb6	12	22	298	298*	5	335.00	6.25	79.40	27.98	0.86	0.13
gdb7	12	22	325	325*	5	354.67	5.82	65.00	25.27	0.70	0.00
gdb10	27	46	344	350	10	385.10	11.99	92.30	21.19	1.09	0.60
gdb11	27	51	303	303*	10	362.98	13.58	99.30	24.58	1.40	6.16
gdb12	12	25	275	275*	4	286.29	4.43	43.00	13.12	0.50	0.05
gdb13	22	45	395	395*	5	412.21	5.67	58.90	15.63	0.62	1.14
gdb14	13	23	448	458	7	511.76	8.18	78.20	39.93	0.85	0.05
gdb15	10	28	536	536*	6	584.81	8.81	97.60	24.71	1.21	6.53
gdb16	7	21	100	100*	5	102.45	5.47	40.30	3.74	0.63	0.01
gdb17	7	21	58	58*	4	58.06	4.03	2.90	0.34	0.17	0.00
gdb18	8	28	127	127*	5	134.46	6.63	88.50	5.23	0.94	0.03
gdb19	8	28	91	91*	6	91.22	6.11	11.10	0.63	0.31	0.01
gdb20	9	36	164	164*	5	167.02	5.30	28.70	4.91	0.49	0.09
gdb21	8	11	55	55*	3	60.50	3.69	59.20	5.78	0.64	0.00
gdb22	11	22	121	121*	4	129.40	5.74	91.00	5.39	0.95	0.27
gdb23	11	33	156	156*	6	164.59	7.69	90.20	5.37	0.95	0.12
gdb24	11	44	200	200*	8	205.82	9.64	87.90	3.63	1.02	3.02
gdb25	11	55	233	233*	10	248.73	13.79	99.30	6.69	1.50	46.29

4.3   Results of MA2 – Deterministic MA with Capacity Restriction

Table 3 lists the results for MA2. Vehicle capacity, reduced by 10% in the MA, is reset to its nominal value in the simulation. Table 1 shows that this simple technique increases the deterministic cost but provides robust solutions: on the field, the average increase in cost is 0.06% only, and the probability of trip interruptions is 1.06%. The average robustness (5.15% for MA1) drops here to 0.4%. Compared to MA1, the expected cost is 3.20% smaller. A drawback of this method is the difficulty to find the optimal percentage of vehicle capacity μ that must remain unused in the planned solution x_2: the MA should be executed once for each value tested. A slack of 10% gives good results on gdb instances but it could be different for other benchmarks.

Table 3. Results of MA2 on *gdb* instances

File	n	m	LB	$h(x_2)$	$t(x_2)$	$\overline{H(x_2,a)}$	$\overline{T(x_2,a)}$	$p(x_2,a)$	$s_H(x_2,a)$	$s_T(x_2,a)$	Time
gdb1	12	22	316	337	6	337.0	6.0	0.0	0.0	0.0	0.01
gdb2	12	26	339	359	7	359.0	7.0	0.0	0.0	0.0	1.98
gdb3	12	22	275	296	6	296.0	6.0	0.0	0.0	0.0	0.01
gdb4	11	19	287	313	5	313.0	5.0	0.0	0.0	0.0	0.05
gdb5	13	26	377	409	7	409.0	7.0	0.0	0.0	0.0	0.02
gdb6	12	22	298	324	6	324.0	6.0	0.0	0.0	0.0	0.02
gdb7	12	22	325	351	6	351.0	6.0	0.0	0.0	0.0	0.01
gdb10	27	46	344	370	11	371.6	11.1	6.8	6.3	0.3	16.65
gdb11	27	51	303	331	12	331.9	12.1	4.7	4.6	0.2	6.04
gdb12	12	25	275	283	5	283.1	5.0	0.7	1.3	0.1	0.01
gdb13	22	45	395	403	6	403.0	6.0	0.0	0.0	0.0	0.26
gdb14	13	23	448	478	8	480.2	8.0	4.0	12.1	0.2	0.12
gdb15	10	28	536	544	7	544.2	7.0	1.0	2.6	0.1	0.47
gdb16	7	21	100	100*	5	100.1	5.0	0.5	0.7	0.1	0.22
gdb17	7	21	58	58*	4	58.0	4.0	0.1	0.1	0.0	0.02
gdb18	8	28	127	129	6	129.0	6.0	0.7	0.3	0.1	0.04
gdb19	8	28	91	91*	6	91.0	6.0	0.0	0.0	0.0	0.01
gdb20	9	36	164	164*	5	164.0	5.0	0.4	0.5	0.1	0.13
gdb21	8	11	55	63	4	63.0	4.0	0.0	0.0	0.0	0.00
gdb22	11	22	121	123	5	123.1	5.0	0.5	0.7	0.1	0.03
gdb23	11	33	156	158	7	158.1	7.0	1.2	0.4	0.1	0.04
gdb24	11	44	200	202	9	202.1	9.0	2.7	0.6	0.2	2.62
gdb25	11	55	233	237	12	237.0	12.0	1.0	0.3	0.1	1.46

4.4 Results of MA3 – Stochastic MA to Minimize $\overline{H(x_3)}$

Table 4 provides the detailed results for MA3, the algorithm aimed at minimizing the expected total cost. Like Table 5, it contains a new column (rank 7) with the expected cost computed by the MA for the best solution. The accuracy of the MA is confirmed by simulation: we computed the average error $|\overline{H(x_3,a)} - \overline{H(x_3)}|/\overline{H(x_3)}$ and found 0.21%. Compared to MA1 (see Table 1), the expected cost is 4.50% smaller on average. However, the algorithm is less robust than MA2: its average robustness is 1.4% vs 0.4%. This can be explained by the fact that the variance is not taken care of. The algorithm is also slower than its deterministic counterparts, because chromosome evaluations are computed using real numbers, while all costs are integers in MA1 and MA2: the convergence takes longer and each call to the local search performs more neighborhood explorations.

4.5 Results of MA4 – Stochastic MA to Minimize $\overline{K(x_4)}$

The results for the objective $\overline{K(x_4)}$ are listed in Table 5. If we compute the average error $\overline{K(x_4)} = \overline{H(x_4)} + \rho \cdot \sigma[H(x_4)]$ between the expected costs computed by the MA and by simulation, we get a significant value of 0.8%, but remember that MA4 minimizes the composite function, not the expected cost alone. For instance, for *gdb*10, the error on the expected cost is $(388.1 - 372.1)/372.1 = 4.3\%$) but the composite function value found by the MA (not included in the table) is in fact 388.0.

Compared to MA1 (see Table 1, the expected total cost is decreased by 2.29%. Even if MA2 does better in that respect (-4.50%), the planned solutions of MA4

Table 4. Results of MA3 on *gdb* instances

File	n	m	LB	$h(x_3)$	$t(x_3)$	$\overline{H(x_3)}$	$\overline{H(x_3,a)}$	$\overline{T(x_3,a)}$	$p(x_3,a)$	$s_H(x_3,a)$	$s_T(x_3,a)$	Time
gdb1	12	22	316	323	5	334.0	331.6	5.8	61.6	8.0	0.7	8.4
gdb2	12	26	339	345	6	356.0	354.4	6.9	66.8	8.0	0.7	4.6
gdb3	12	22	275	279	5	291.5	289.5	5.8	66.0	9.3	0.7	3.4
gdb4	11	19	287	313	5	313.0	313.0	5.0	0.0	0.0	0.0	40.8
gdb5	13	26	377	395	6	406.0	403.8	6.8	64.0	7.8	0.7	3.6
gdb6	12	22	298	312	5	323.0	321.2	5.8	65.2	8.1	0.7	7.1
gdb7	12	22	325	325*	5	342.0	339.1	5.8	66.6	13.4	0.7	0.8
gdb10	27	46	344	358	12	362.6	361.9	12.2	20.0	8.5	0.4	90.3
gdb11	27	51	303	317	11	320.0	320.1	11.2	15.7	7.6	0.4	48.4
gdb12	12	25	275	275*	4	279.2	278.6	4.4	43.4	4.3	0.5	6.3
gdb13	22	45	395	395*	5	395.0	395.1	5.0	0.6	0.9	0.1	9.4
gdb14	13	23	448	478	8	479.8	479.3	8.0	3.0	8.1	0.2	21.8
gdb15	10	28	536	544	7	544.2	544.2	7.0	1.0	2.5	0.1	41.0
gdb16	7	21	100	100*	5	100.0	100.0	5.0	0.5	0.4	0.1	4.0
gdb17	7	21	58	58*	4	58.0	58.0	4.0	0.9	0.2	0.1	0.1
gdb18	8	28	127	129	6	129.0	129.0	6.0	0.7	0.4	0.1	1.6
gdb19	8	28	91	91*	6	91.0	91.0	6.0	0.1	0.1	0.0	0.1
gdb20	9	36	164	164*	5	164.0	164.0	5.0	0.3	0.5	0.1	2.2
gdb21	8	11	55	55*	3	57.4	57.2	3.7	58.1	2.7	0.6	0.1
gdb22	11	22	121	123	5	123.0	123.0	5.0	0.5	0.3	0.1	1.5
gdb23	11	33	156	158	7	158.0	158.0	7.0	1.1	0.2	0.1	1.8
gdb24	11	44	200	202	9	202.1	202.1	9.0	3.9	0.5	0.2	25.2
gdb25	11	55	233	235	11	235.9	235.8	11.4	33.7	1.3	0.6	92.1

Table 5. Results of MA4 on *gdb* instances

File	n	m	LB	$h(x_4)$	$t(x_4)$	$\overline{H(x_4)}$	$\overline{H(x_4,a)}$	$\overline{T(x_4,a)}$	$p(x_4,a)$	$s_H(x_4,a)$	$s_T(x_4,a)$	Time
gdb1	12	22	316	337	6	337.0	337.0	6.0	0.0	0.0	0.0	0.6
gdb2	12	26	339	366	7	366.0	366.0	7.0	0.0	0.0	0.0	6.7
gdb3	12	22	275	296	6	296.0	296.0	6.0	0.0	0.0	0.0	1.2
gdb4	11	19	287	313	5	313.0	313.0	5.0	0.0	0.0	0.0	4.1
gdb5	13	26	377	409	7	409.0	409.0	7.0	0.0	0.0	0.0	2.6
gdb6	12	22	298	324	6	324.0	324.0	6.0	0.0	0.0	0.0	0.2
gdb7	12	22	325	351	6	351.0	351.0	6.0	0.0	0.0	0.0	11.7
gdb10	27	46	344	388	13	372.1	388.1	13.0	0.4	1.6	0.1	74.8
gdb11	27	51	303	335	12	326.3	335.1	12.0	0.5	1.2	0.1	159.4
gdb12	12	25	275	283	5	283.0	283.0	5.0	0.0	0.0	0.0	2.0
gdb13	22	45	395	403	6	396.0	403.0	6.0	0.1	0.7	0.0	4.7
gdb14	13	23	448	534	8	534.0	534.0	8.0	4.1	0.0	0.2	0.5
gdb15	10	28	536	552	8	552.0	552.0	8.0	0.0	0.0	0.0	14.6
gdb16	7	21	100	102	9	96.6	102.0	5.0	4.0	0.5	0.2	29.0
gdb17	7	21	58	58*	4	58.0	58.0	4.0	0.0	0.0	0.0	0.5
gdb18	8	28	127	129	6	129.0	129.0	6.0	0.0	0.0	0.0	6.8
gdb19	8	28	91	91*	5	91.0	91.0	5.0	0.0	0.0	0.0	0.3
gdb20	9	36	164	164*	5	161.5	164.0	5.0	0.1	0.3	0.0	0.3
gdb21	8	11	55	63	4	63.0	63.0	4.0	0.0	0.0	0.0	0.0
gdb22	11	22	121	123	5	123.0	123.0	5.0	0.0	0.0	0.0	1.4
gdb23	11	33	156	158	7	154.6	158.0	7.0	0.2	0.3	0.0	14.6
gdb24	11	44	200	202	9	201.1	202.0	9.0	0.2	0.1	0.0	86.5
gdb25	11	55	233	238	12	237.1	238.0	12.0	0.9	0.1	0.1	152.4

are practically not affected on the field: less than 0.01% for the total cost and 0.46% for the number of trips. The robustness estimator is also excellent: 0.08%. For the reasons already explained for MA3, the average running time is increased compared to the deterministic versions, but remains reasonable: 25 seconds. Hence, MA4 represents the best compromise between cost and robustness.

5   Conclusion

In many applications of the CARP, demands are random variables. The management rules used for instance in waste collection make possible mathematical expressions for several stochastic criteria like the expected total cost. The most efficient metaheuristic published for the CARP, a memetic algorithm, can easily be adapted to handle these new criteria. The validity of the approach is confirmed by simulation: the stochastic MA is more robust than simpler techniques like keeping a slack in each vehicle, provided the objective function takes the variance into account (MA4 version).

References

1. A. Amberg and S. Voß. A hierarchical relaxations lower bound for the Capacitated Arc Routing Problem. In R.H. Sprague (Hrsg.), editor, *35th Annual Hawaii Int. Conf. on Systems Sciences*, pages DTIST02:1–10, Piscataway, 2002. IEEE.
2. J.M. Belenguer and E. Benavent. A cutting plane algorithm for the Capacitated Arc Routing Problem. *Computers and Operations Research*, 30(5):705–728, 2003.
3. P. Beullens, L. Muyldermans, D. Cattrysse, and D. Van Oudheusden. A guided local search heuristic for the Capacitated Arc Routing Problem. *European Journal of Operational Research*, 147(3):629–643, 2003.
4. J. Branke. Creating robust solutions by means of evolutionary algorithms. In A.E. Eiben et al., editor, *Parallel Problem Solving from Nature V*, Lecture Notes in Computer Science 1498, pages 119–128. Springer, 1998.
5. G. Fleury, P. Lacomme, C. Prins, and W. Ramdane-Chérif. Improving robustness of solutions to arc routing problems. *J. Oper. Res. Soc.*, 2004. To appear.
6. B.L. Golden, J.S. DeArmon, and E.K. Baker. Computational experiments with algorithms for a class of routing problems. *Comp. Oper. Res.*, 10(1):47–59, 1983.
7. B.L. Golden and R.T. Wong. Capacitated arc routing problems. *Networks*, 11:305–315, 1981.
8. P. Greistorfer. A tabu-scatter search metaheuristic for the arc routing problem. *Computers and Industrial Engineering*, 44(2):249–266, 2003.
9. A. Hertz, G. Laporte, and M. Mittaz. A tabu search heuristic for the Capacitated Arc Routing Problem. *Operations Research*, 48(1):129–135, 2000.
10. P. Lacomme, C. Prins, and W. Ramdane-Chérif. A genetic algorithm for the CARP and its extensions. In E.J.W. Boers et al., editor, *Applications of evolutionnary computing–EvoWorkshops 2001*, Lecture Notes in Computer Science 2037, pages 473–483. Springer, 2001.
11. P. Lacomme, C. Prins, and W. Ramdane-Chérif. Competitive memetic algorithms for arc routing problems. *Annals of Operations Research*, 2004. To appear.
12. G. Laporte M. Gendreau and R. Séguin. Stochastic vehicle routing. *European Journal of Operational Research*, 88:3–12, 1996.
13. P. Moscato. Memetic algorithms: a short introduction. In D. Corne et al., editor, *New ideas in optimization*, pages 219–234. McGraw-Hill, 1999.
14. Y. Saruwatari R. Hirabayashi and N. Nishida. Tour construction algorithm for the carp. *Asia-Pacific Journal of Oper. Res.*, 9:155–175, 1992.
15. S. Tsutsui and A. Gosh. Genetic algorithms with a robust solution searching scheme. *IEEE Transactions on Evolutionary Computations*, 1:201–208, 1997.
16. G. Ulusoy. The fleet size and mix problem for capacitated arc routing. *European Journal of Operational Research*, 22:329–337, 1985.

A Hierarchical Particle Swarm Optimizer for Dynamic Optimization Problems

Stefan Janson and Martin Middendorf

Parallel Computing and Complex Systems Group
Department of Computer Science, University of Leipzig
Augustusplatz 10/11, D-04109 Leipzig, Germany
{janson,middendorf}@informatik.uni-leipzig.de

Abstract. Particle Swarm Optimization (PSO) methods for dynamic function optimization are studied in this paper. We compare dynamic variants of standard PSO and Hierarchical PSO (H-PSO) on different dynamic benchmark functions. Moreover, a new type of hierarchical PSO, called Partitioned H-PSO (PH-PSO), is proposed. In this algorithm the hierarchy is partitioned into several sub-swarms for a limited number of generations after a change occurred. Different methods for determining the time when to rejoin the hierarchy and how to handle the topmost sub-swarm are discussed. The test results show that H-PSO performs significantly better than PSO on all test functions and that the PH-PSO algorithms often perform best on multimodal functions where changes are not too severe.

1 Introduction

Particle Swarm Optimization (PSO) is a population based method for function optimization [14]. In PSO a swarm of individuals, also called particles, iteratively explores a multidimensional search space. Each particle "flies" through the search space according to its velocity vector. In every iteration the velocity vector is adjusted so that prior personal successful positions (cognitive aspect) and the best position found by particles within a specific neighborhood (social aspect) act as attractors.

A hierarchical version of PSO (H-PSO) has been proposed in [13]. In H-PSO all particles are arranged in a tree that forms the hierarchy so that each node of the tree contains exactly one particle. A particle is influenced by its own best position so far and by the best position of the particle that is directly above in the hierarchy. In order to give the best particles in the swarm a high influence particles move up and down the hierarchy. If a particle at a child node has found a solution that is better than the best so far solution of the particle at the parent node both particles are exchanged. An advantage of H-PSO is that it offers a dynamic neighborhood but due to the fixed tree structure the neighborhood does not have to be computed. It was shown that H-PSO outperformed the standard PSO on several of the standard (static) test functions and that the dynamic nature of the hierarchy does not hinder the subtrees to specialize to different

G.R. Raidl et al. (Eds.): EvoWorkshops 2004, LNCS 3005, pp. 513–524, 2004.

regions of the search space. This and the ability of H-PSO to react to changes of the environment by adapting its hierarchy makes H-PSO potentially attractive for dynamic environments.

In this paper we study H-PSO for dynamic functions. We also propose a variant of H-PSO, called Partitioned H-PSO (PH-PSO), that is especially suited for dynamic function optimization. In PH-PSO the swarm is partitioned into sub-swarms after a change of the environment has been detected. The sub-swarms then search for a limited number of iterations independently for a new optimum. After a certain number of iterations the sub-swarms are reunited. We study also a method where the time for reunification is variable and is determined depending on the optimization behavior after the partitioning. The variants of H-PSO and PH-PSO are compared with standard PSO on several benchmark test functions. All algorithms also use some random individuals after a change, as has been shown to be useful in dynamic environments (e.g., [12]).

The paper is organized as follows. An overview over existing approaches to use PSO for dynamic functions is given in section 1.1. The PSO method and the H-PSO are explained in Section 2. The PH-PSO algorithm is introduced in Section 3. The experiments are described in section 4 and results are discussed in Section 5. Conclusions are given in Section 6.

1.1   Overview of PSO for Dynamic Functions

Carlisle and Dozier studied several variants of a PSO algorithm for dynamic environments. One approach was to let the particles periodically replace their previous best position by the current position. This approach was compared with a variant where the replacements are triggered by detecting when the environment has changed is studied in [6]. For the detection a fixed point in the search space was reevaluated regularly. A similar method where the global best point was used for reevaluation was proposed in [11]. In a variant a set of random points was used for reevaluation to increase the probability to cope with local changes that may not be detected everywhere [7,9]. Moreover, the previous best position is exchanged by the current position only when the current position is better, both (re)evaluated after the change. In [15] it was shown that the standard PSO can cope with dynamic functions that were rotated regularly by random angles and where random noise is added to the function values.

In [12] several detection and response methods are compared for a dynamic parabolic test function. The test function is always changed with various severities once a certain goal value is reached. A detection method (reevaluation of the best and the second best position) notices the change and a respective response method is applied and the number of steps counted, until the goal is reached again. As a result of a comparison of several response methods it is suggested to re-randomize a portion (10%) of the swarm and to reset the global best value of the rest of the swarm to their actual value.

A so called charged particle swarm optimizer (CPSO) was proposed in [1] where the idea is to use particles that, in analogy with electrostatics, have a "charge". The charge imposes a repulsion force between particles and thus hinders the swarm to collapse. In [2] the charged CPSO is compared to the regular

PSO on different dynamic environments and it was shown that CPSO performs better in extreme dynamic environments due to its increased diversity.

2 PSO and H-PSO

In this section we describe the PSO and H-PSO algorithms. PSO is an iterative method that is based on the search behavior of a swarm of m particles in a multidimensional search space (see also [14]). In each iteration the velocities and positions of the particles are updated. For each particle i its velocity vector v_i is updated according to Formula 1. The inertia weight $w > 0$ controls the influence of the previous velocity. The current position of the particle is denoted by x_i. Parameter $c_1 > 0$ controls the impact of the personal best position so far y_i, i.e. the position where the particle found the smallest function value so far — assuming that the objective function has to be minimized. Parameter c_2 determines the impact of the best position that has been found so far by any of the particles in the respective neighborhood $\hat{y}_i$. Here we use the so called gbest neighborhood were all particles are in the neighborhood. Random values r_1 and r_2 are drawn with uniform probability from $[0, 1]$.

After velocity update the particles move with their new velocity to their new positions 2. Then for each particle i the objective function f is evaluated at its new position. If $f(x_i(t + 1)) < f(y_i)$ the personal best position y_i is updated accordingly, i.e. y_i is set to $x_i(t + 1)$.

$$v_i(t + 1) = w \cdot v_i(t) + c_1 \cdot r_1 \cdot (y_i - x_i) + c_2 \cdot r_2 \cdot (\hat{y}_i - x_i) \qquad (1)$$

$$x_i(t + 1) = x_i(t) + v_i(t + 1) \qquad (2)$$

In H-PSO all particles are arranged in a hierarchy that defines the neighborhood structure (see [13]). Each particle is neighbored to itself and the parent in the hierarchy. Hierarchies where the underlying topology is a (nearly) regular tree so that all inner nodes have the same out-degree and only the inner nodes on the deepest level might have a smaller out-degree have been studied in [13]. Then, the maximum difference between the out-degrees of inner nodes on the deepest level is at most one. Hence, the hierarchy is determined by the *height* h, the *degree* d, i.e. the maximum (out)degree of the inner nodes, and the *total number of nodes* m of the corresponding tree.

In order to give the best individuals in the swarm a high influence particles move up and down the hierarchy. In every iteration after the evaluations of the objective function at the particles actual positions the new positions of the particles within the hierarchy are determined as follows. For every particle j in a node of the tree its own best solution is compared to the best solution found by the particles in the child nodes. If the best of these particles, particle i, is better ($f(y_i) < f(y_j)$) particles i and j swap their places within the hierarchy. These comparisons are performed starting from the top of the hierarchy and proceeding breadth-first down the topology. Observe, that the top down approach implies that in one iteration an individual can move down several levels in the hierarchy but can move up at most one level. Thus, the current global best particle will be on top of the hierarchy after at most h steps – unless, a better solution was found meanwhile.

For the update of the velocities in H-PSO a particle is influenced by its own so far best position and by the best position of the individual that is directly above it in the hierarchy. This means that for particle i the value of $\hat{y}_i$ in Formula 1 equals y_j when j is the particle in the parent node of particle i. Only when particle i is in the root H-PSO uses $\hat{y}_i = y_i$. Same as in PSO in H-PSO after the particle's velocities are updated and after they have moved, the objective function is evaluated at the new position. If the function value is better than that of the personal so far best position, the new position is stored in y_i.

2.1   Detection and Response for Dynamic Environments

In order to use PSO and H-PSO for dynamic environments both algorithms are tested in this paper with integrated methods for the detection of a change and for responding to a change. The change of the environment is detected by re-evaluating the position $\hat{y}$ of gbest at every iteration ([11]). If the function value $f(\hat{y})$ does not match the remembered global best value, a change is detected and the respective response method is initiated. This *changed-gbest* detection method works fine for the considered optimization functions, where a change in the environment can be detected at any location.

The response method that is used here and that has been recommended in [12] is to re-randomize a portion of the swarm and resetting the rest. Therefore the particles to be randomized get a new location and velocity assigned and forget their personal best position. This new location x_i' is randomly chosen from $[X_{min}, X_{max}]^n$ and moved along with the gbest position, $x_i = x_i' + \hat{y}$. This is done in order to follow the optimum and to not cancel the previous search effort. This is especially necessary for a linear optimum move, where the optimum quickly leaves the initial search space. For the Moving Peaks benchmark the re-randomized location x_i' is just taken from $[X_{min}, X_{max}]^n$, because the peaks never leave the initial search space. The reset particles forget their personal best location setting $y_i := x_i$.

In the rest of this paper PSO and H-PSO denote the corresponding algorithms that include the described change detection and response method.

3   Partitioned H-PSO

In this section we introduce a variant of H-PSO that is called Partitioned H-PSO (PH-PSO) and is designed for dynamic environments. PH-PSO uses the described changed-gbest method to detect a change of the environment. After a change has been detected the hierarchy is partitioned into a set of sub-hierarchies or sub-swarms. These swarms continue to search for the optimum independently. This way the sub-swarm can spread out, after a change in the environment occurred. In order to enforce the spread out one or a few individuals in each sub-swarm are re-randomized.

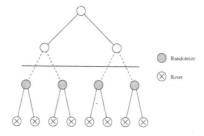

Fig. 1. Schema of PH-PSO with $h = 4, d = 2$ and $h_{div} = 2$

The partitioning is done by splitting the hierarchy at a certain height h_{div} which means that afterwards no swaps of individuals are permitted between level h_{div} and $h_{div} - 1$ — where the root is on level 0 (see Figure 1). The top sub-swarm containing the current best individuals is not changed, only the function values at personal best positions $f(y_i)$ are updated. Thus a certain memory of the function before the change is preserved, which can be helpful in situations where the change is not too severe. All the lower $d^{h_{div}}$ sub-swarms are re-randomized by initializing the top individuals on level h_{div} with a random position and velocity and resetting their personal best position. The lower particles also forget their personal best position. After the splitting all sub-swarms are seeking independently for a certain number of iterations. The sub-swarms are rejoined by reintroducing the connections of the hierarchy that have been cut. The hierarchical compare operation ensures that the rejoined sub-swarms get rearranged soon within the full hierarchy according to their respective fitness.

In a variant called adaptive PH-PSO (PH-PSO-*adaptive* or PH-PSO-a) the number of iterations that the division of the swarm is kept is determined according to a certain criterion that depends on the optimization behavior. In order to differ between PH-PSO-a and the PH-PSO algorithm where the rejoining is done after a fixed number of iterations the latter is also denoted by PH-PSO-*temp* or PH-PSO-t. To determine, when a new promising region of the search space is found by a sub-swarm, it is observed which sub-swarm contains the current gbest particle of the entire swarm. If a sub-swarm contained this particle for 5 (not necessarily consecutive) iterations the swarm is joined again.

For environments with severe changes where it might not make sense to use the memory function of the upper sub-swarm we also studied variants where the upper sub-swarm is handled in the same way as the other sub-swarms. These no-memory variants of the algorithms are denoted PH-PSO-*temp-noMem* and PH-PSO-*adaptive-noMem*.

4   Experiments

We tested PSO, H-PSO and PH-PSO on different dynamic optimization functions each with various severities. For all test functions after every 100 iterations the environment changes.

4.1   Test Functions and Parameter Values

The considered optimization functions are either unimodal (a single local and global optimum) or multimodal (several local optima). As a unimodal function we used the parabolic function $f_1(x) = \sum_{i=1}^{n} x_i^2$ of dimension $n = 10$. A change of the environment is done by moving the function in every dimension by adding a severity value s (for the tests we used $s = 0.1$, $s = 1$, and $s = 10$). Value s is called the severity parameter. Since function f_1 has a single moving optimum the function is called Moving Goal.

The following two multimodal functions were used for the other experiments. The Dynamic Rastrigin function $f_2(x) = \sum_{i=1}^{n}(x_i^2 - 10\cos(2\pi x_i) + 10)$ of dimension $n = 10$ which is moved by adding or subtracting the same random value in every dimension, at every change of the environment. The random value that is added for a change is randomly chosen from an exponential distribution, $F(x) = 1 - e^{-\lambda x}$, with parameter λ. As severity parameter the mean value is used, i.e., $s = E(x) = 1/\lambda$ (for the test we used $s = 0.005$, $s = 0.05$, and $s = 0.1$). The chosen random number is either added or subtracted for all dimensions alike – the choice whether to add or subtract is done randomly with equal probabilities. For each test run a different random seed was used.

As a second multimodal function Branke's Moving Peaks benchmark [5] was used for the experiments. This benchmark creates a number p of peaks with variable height and width. These peaks are moved by a vector of fixed length in a random direction and randomly change their height H_i and width W_i. The returned function value is the maximum of all peak functions $f_3(x) = \max_{i=1,...,p}\{H_i(t)/(1 + W_i(t) \cdot \sum_{j=1}^{n}(x_j - X_j(t))^2)\}$ evaluated at the current position. Thus not only the optimum position but also the optimum value changes. As parameter values for the Moving Peaks benchmark dimension $n = 5$ is used. The number of peaks used is $p = 50$. The random height of each peak is chosen uniformly in $[30.0, 70.0]$ (initially 50.0 for all the peaks) and the random width is chosen uniformly in $[1.0, 12.0]$. The length of the random move vector is the severity parameter (values $s = 0.1$ and $s = 3.0$ were used for the tests). The random seed for the environment change is 1 for all runs.

For the Moving Goal and the Dynamic Rastrigin experiment, that are both minimization problems, the offline performance has to be minimized which is defined as $\frac{1}{t}\sum_{i=1}^{t}(f(\hat{y}, t))$. Since the Moving Peaks benchmark varies the optimum location and value we measured the deviation of the value of the currently best individual from the optimum value, instead of measuring the actual function value of the best individual. For this case the offline error at iteration t is defined as $\frac{1}{t}\sum_{i=1}^{t}(f(opt, t) - f(\hat{y}, t))$. The offline error has to be minimized in the Moving Peaks benchmark.

4.2   Algorithm Parameters

The PSO algorithm and H-PSO variants use the common parameters for $w = 0.729$ and $c_1 = c_2 = 1.494$ (see [16]). The velocity vector v is restricted in each dimension d to $|v_d| \leq v_{max} = X_{max}$. The particles initial positions are randomly selected from $[X_{min}, X_{max}]^n$ for dimension n of the search space where these intervals are $[-50, 50]^n$ for Moving Goal, $[-5.12; 5.12]^n$ for Dynamic Rastrigin, and $[0; 100]^n$ for Moving Peaks. During the search the particles are not restricted to this particular space. Recall, that after a dynamic change of the function the randomized particles are placed within $[X_{min} + \hat{y}, X_{max} + \hat{y}]^n$ for the Moving Goal and the Dynamic Rastrigin experiment, see Subsection 2.1.

4.3   Swarm Parameters

For the experiments we used a swarm size of $m = 30$ for the Moving Goal and the Dynamic Rastrigin function and $m = 40$ for the Moving Peaks benchmark. To determine the structure of the hierarchy parameter values $h = 2, d = 5$ were used for the swarms of size 30 and parameter values $h = 4, d = 3$ otherwise. The hierarchy of H-PSO with size 30 is slightly irregular, with 5 particles below the root particle and 5 successors for each of these, except for the last one with only 4 successors. Thus this hierarchy has three levels, but the height is still $h = 2$. This is done in order to keep the commonly used swarm size of 30.

The PH-PSO algorithm re-randomizes the top individuals of the $d^{h_{div}}$ lower sub-swarms, see 1. The number of randomized individuals is thus 5 for $m = 30$ and 8 for $m = 40$. For comparison we also tested PSO and H-PSO with the same number of re-randomized particles in addition to a portion of 10% of the population as recommended in [12]. PSO always performed better in our experiments with the higher number of re-randomized particles. For some tests with a high severity the H-PSO performed slightly better with the smaller number of 10% re-randomized individuals. Nevertheless, the results for the case with 10% re-randomized individuals are omitted in the results section for comparability.

4.4   Significance

All results are averages over 50 test runs. For testing the significance of the results the Wilcoxon Rank Sum Test was used to compare the results for two algorithms after a fixed number of generations. The results of the 50 test runs for two algorithms form two independent samples. For the results values X and Y of the two algorithms their distributions, F_X and F_Y, are compared using the Null-Hypothesis $H_0 : F_X = F_Y$ and the one-sided alternative $H_1 : F_X < F_Y$. Only if the probability of the Null-Hypothesis $P(H_0)$ is at most 0.01 it is rejected and the alternative Hypothesis is accepted. We use the following notation: "H-PSO < PSO" denotes the case that the results of H-PSO are significantly better than for PSO, "H-PSO $\approx$ PSO" denotes the case that the results of H-PSO are not significantly better than for PSO (analogous notations are used for other pairs of algorithms).

5   Results

In this section we describe the results of PSO, H-PSO, and PH-PSO on the three dynamic test functions.

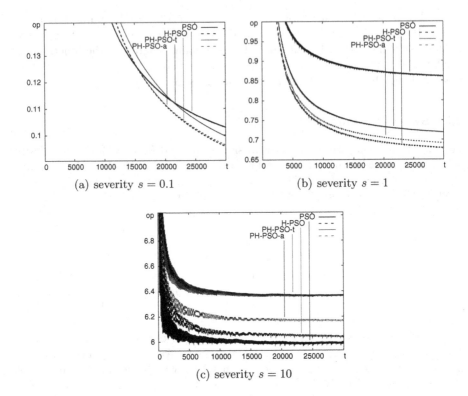

Fig. 2. Moving Goal: Offline performance (op) of PSO, H-PSO, PH-PSO-t, and PH-PSO-a with different severities, significance at $t = 30000$:
a) (H-PSO $\approx$ PH-PSO-*adaptive*) < PH-PSO-temp < PSO, b) H-PSO < PH-PSO-*adaptive* < PH-PSO-*temp* < PSO, c) PSO < H-PSO < PH-PSO-*adaptive* < PH-PSO-*temp*

5.1   Moving Goal

The results show that the Moving Goal function is significantly better tracked by the hierarchical H-PSO and PH-PSO algorithms than by PSO for short and medium severities (see Figure 2). Only for a small number of iterations the offline performance of PSO is better. The best performance for a larger number of iterations is obtained by H-PSO and PH-PSO-*adaptive* performs better than PH-PSO-*temp*. This is probably due to the fact that there is not much to be gained by enforcing a divided exploration of the changed environment, since there is only one local optimum (unimodal). The adaptive PH-PSO-*adaptive* reunites the swarm earlier than PH-PSO-*temp* and profits earlier from the collective search. For high severity ($s = 10$) the PSO algorithm performs slightly better better than H-PSO and much better than the PH-PSO algorithms. Observe, that in this case the obtained qualities are much worse than for the medium and small severities.

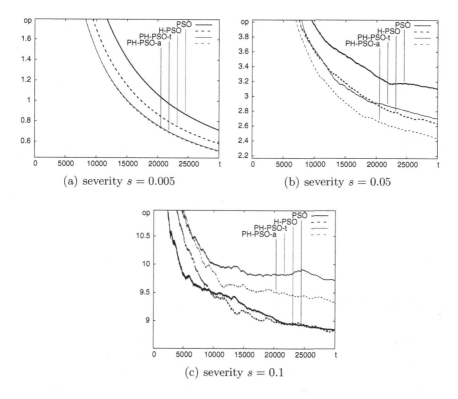

(a) severity $s = 0.005$ (b) severity $s = 0.05$

(c) severity $s = 0.1$

Fig. 3. Dynamic Rastrigin: Offline performance (op) of PSO, H-PSO, PH-PSO-t, and PH-PSO-a for different severities, significance at $t = 30000$:
a) (PH-PSO-*adaptive* $\approx$ DH-PSO-*temp* $\approx$ H-PSO) $<$ PSO, b) PH-PSO-*adaptive* $<$ PH-PSO-*temp* $<$ PSO; H-PSO $<$ PSO ; PH-PSO-*adaptive* $\approx$ H-PSO ; H-PSO $\approx$ PH-PSO-*temp*, c) (H-PSO $\approx$ PSO) $<$ (PH-PSO-*adaptive* $\approx$ PH-PSO-*temp*)

5.2 Dynamic Rastrigin

The multimodal Rastrigin function is solved best by the two PH-PSO variants for small and medium severity (see Figure 3). PH-PSO-*adaptive* is significantly better than PH-PSO-*temp* for the medium severity $s = 0.05$ and both are similar for small severity. This is different from the results for the unimodal function where H-PSO performed better than the PH-PSO variants. This indicates that the partition of the swarm into independent sub-swarms is advantageous in more complex dynamic situations where it is more difficult to find the location of the new optimum. Similar as for the unimodal test function for high severity PSO and H-PSO perform equally well and significantly better than the PH-PSO algorithms. For this case the obtained quality is much worse than for the smaller severities. The results indicate that it might be most important to move fast into the region of the optimum which can in general be done better by one large swarm than by several small ones.

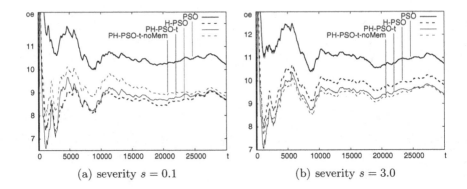

(a) severity $s = 0.1$ (b) severity $s = 3.0$

Fig. 4. Moving Peaks benchmark: Offline error (oe) of PSO, H-PSO, PH-PSO-t, and PH-PSO-a for with different severities, significance at $t = 30000$:
a) (H-PSO $\approx$ PH-PSO-*temp* $\approx$ PH-PSO-*temp-noMem*) $<$ PSO, b) (PH-PSO-*temp* $\approx$ PH-PSO-*temp-noMem*) $<$ H-PSO $<$ PSO

5.3   Moving Peaks Benchmark

The moving peak benchmark has different characteristics than the multimodal Rastrigin function because the height of the peaks change. This has the effect that the position of the optimal peak can change very fast. Hence it not clear whether the use of the uppermost sub-swarm as a memory in the PH-PSO is an advantage and therefore the no-memory versions were also tested. The hierarchical H-PSO and PH-PSO algorithms gave much better results than PSO (see Figure 4). Since PH-PSO-*temp* gave better results than PH-PSO-*adaptive* we show only the results for PH-PSO-*temp*. For high severity ($s = 3.0$) PH-PSO-*temp* is also significantly better than H-PSO. The results show that PH-PSO-*temp-noMem* can profit from the additional sub-swarm, if the top sub-swarm is also re-randomized, and from the enforced division lasting longer than for the PH-PSO-*adaptive-noMem*. This can be explained by the fact that Moving Peaks provides an environment with severe changes in optimum location and value.

In order to estimate the influence of the memory, i.e. the top sub-swarm, in PH-PSO-*adaptive-noMem* we counted the number of times that the topmost swarm is responsible for rejoining the swarm because it contained the gbest particle 5 times. Recall that the tests for Moving Peaks worked with a swarm of size $m = 40$ where all of the 10 sub-swarms are identically shaped — one particle guiding three others. The top sub-swarm is used in 10.5% of the cases for $s = 0.1$ and in 3.71% for $s = 3$. This shows that the sub-swarm with memory is slightly better than a randomized sub-swarm for small severity ($s = 0.1$) but clearly worse for high severity ($s = 3$). This is reflected by the fact that PH-PSO-*temp* is for most iterations better than PH-PSO-*temp-noMem* for small severity and worse for high severity (see Figure 4).

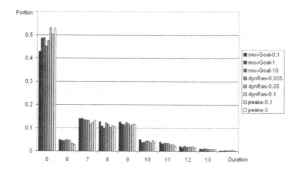

Fig. 5. Average duration (number of iterations) of division after a change of the environment of PH-PSO-*adaptive* for the different test functions

5.4   Further Results

To find out whether the time of division (more exactly the number of iterations the sub-swarm work independently after a change) for PH-PSO-*adaptive* differs during a run of the algorithm or for the different test problems these times were measured. We call the iterations where the sub-swarms work independently a division interval. Figure 5 shows the distribution of the measured length of the division intervals over the 50 test runs for each test problem and severity value. Recall, that the minimal length of a division interval is 5.

It is interesting that all distributions are very similar with an average division interval length of about 7. The most significant difference between the distributions is that for each of the three test problems the relative number of division intervals of length 5 increases with the severity of the problem. This indicates that for smaller severities several of the sub-swarms find good solutions and it takes some iterations until one of these sub-swarms has had the best solutions for 5 iterations. This is a further indication that PH-PSO-*adaptive* works well for dynamic problems with smaller severities.

6   Conclusion

A new type of hierarchical PSO, called Partitioned Hierarchical PSO (PH-PSO), that is designed for dynamic function optimization has been proposed. In this algorithm particles are arranged in a dynamic hierarchy. The hierarchy is partitioned into several sub-swarm for a limited number of generations after a change occurred. Different methods for determining the time when to rejoin the hierarchy and how to handle the topmost sub-swarm have been studied. The PH-PSO algorithms were compared with dynamic variants of standard Particle Swarm Optimization (PSO) and dynamic variants of the Hierarchical PSO (H-PSO) on several dynamic test functions. The test results show that H-PSO performs significantly better than PSO on all test functions (except Moving Goal for $s = 10.0$ and Dynamic Rastrigin for $s = 0.1$) and that the PH-PSO algorithms often perform best on multimodal functions where changes are not too severe.

References

1. T. M. Blackwell, P. J. Bentley: Dynamic Search With Charged Swarms. Proceedings of GECCO-2002, Morgan Kaufmann Publishers, 19–26 (2002).
2. T. M. Blackwell: Swarms in Dynamic Environments. Proceedings of the Genetic and Evolutionary Computation Conference (GECCO 2003), 1-12 (2003).
3. T. M. Blackwell: Particle Swarms and Population Diversity I : Analysis. Proceedings of the Bird of a Feather Workshops (in EvoDOP2003), Genetic and Evolutionary Computation Conference, 103–107, AAAI, (2003).
4. T. M. Blackwell: Particle Swarms and Population Diversity II : Experiments. Proceedings of the Bird of a Feather Workshops, Genetic and Evolutionary Computation Conference (in EvoDOP2003), AAAI, 108–112 (2003).
5. J. Branke: Memory Enhanced Evolutionary Algorithms for Changing Optimization Problems. Proc. of CEC 1999, IEEE Press, 1875–1882 (1999).
6. A. Carlisle, G. Dozier: Adapting Particle Swarm Optimization to Dynamic Environments. Proceedings of the International Conference on Artificial Intelligence (2000).
7. A. Carlisle and G. Dozier: Tracking Changing Extrema with Particle Swarm Optimizer. Technical Report CSSE01-08, Auburn University, (2001).
8. A. Carlisle: Applying the Particle Swarm Optimizer to Non-Stationary Environments. PhD Dissertation, Auburn University, (2002).
9. A. Carlisle, G. Dozier: Tracking Changing Extrema with Adaptive Particle Swarm Optimizer. ISSCI, 2002 World Automation Congress, Orlando, USA,)2002).
10. R. C. Eberhart, Y. Shi: Tracking and Optimizing Dynamic Systems with Particle Swarms. Proceedings of the 2001 Congress on Evolutionary Computation (CEC2001), IEEE Press, 94–100 (2001).
11. X. Hu, R. Eberhart: Tracking dynamic systems with PSO: where's the cheese. Proceedings of the Workshop on Particle Swarm Optimization, Purdue School of Engineering, Indinapolis, USA, (2001).
12. X. Hu, R. Eberhart: Adaptive Particle Swarm Optimization: Detection and Response to Dynamic Systems. Proceedings of the 2002 Congress on Evolutionary Computation (CEC2002), IEEE Press, 1666–1670 (2002).
13. S. Janson and M. Middendorf: A Hierarchical Particle Swarm Optimizer. Proc. Congress on Evolutionary Computation (CEC-2003), IEEE Press, 770–776, (2003).
14. J. Kennedy, R. C. Eberhart: Particle Swarm Optimization. IEEE International Conference on Neural Networks (ICNN'95), 1942–1947 (1995).
15. K. Parsopoulos, M. Vrahatis: Particle Swarm Optimizer in Noisy and Continuously Changing Environments. In M.H. Hamza (Ed.), Artificial Intelligence and Soft Computing, IASTED/ACTA Press, 289–294, (2001).
16. I.C. Trelea: The particle swarm optimization algorithm: convergence analysis and parameter selection. Information Processing Letters, 85(6):317–325 (2003).

Constructing Dynamic Optimization Test Problems Using the Multi-objective Optimization Concept

Yaochu Jin and Bernhard Sendhoff

Honda Research Institute Europe
63073 Offenbach/Main, Germany
yaochu.jin@honda-ri.de

Abstract. Dynamic optimization using evolutionary algorithms is receiving increasing interests. However, typical test functions for comparing the performance of various dynamic optimization algorithms still lack. This paper suggests a method for constructing dynamic optimization test problems using multi-objective optimization (MOO) concepts. By aggregating different objectives of an MOO problem and changing the weights dynamically, we are able to construct dynamic single objective and multi-objective test problems systematically. The proposed method is computationally efficient, easily tunable and functionally powerful. This is mainly due to the fact that the proposed method associates dynamic optimization with multi-objective optimization and thus the rich MOO test problems can easily be adapted to dynamic optimization test functions.

1 Introduction

Solving dynamic optimization problems using evolutionary algorithms has received increasing interest in the recent years [4]. One of the important reasons for this increasing interest is that many real-world optimization problems are not stationary. To solve dynamic optimization problems, the optimizer, e.g. an evolutionary algorithm, must be able to adapt itself during optimization to track the moving optimum (peak).

Generally, three measures can be taken to enhance the ability of evolutionary algorithms for tracking a moving optimum:

1. Maintain population diversity by inserting randomly generated individuals [14], niching [7], or reformulating the fitness function considering the age of individuals [12] or the entropy of the population [20].
2. Memorize the past using redundant coding [13,9], explicit memory [22,19], or multiple populations [26,24,5,23].
3. Adapt the strategy parameters of the evolutionary algorithms [8,15]. However, conventional self-adaptation can have negative influences if no particular attention is paid to the dynamics of the optima [2,25].

G.R. Raidl et al. (Eds.): EvoWorkshops 2004, LNCS 3005, pp. 525–536, 2004.
© Springer-Verlag Berlin Heidelberg 2004

To benchmark different algorithms for dynamic optimization, it is thus necessary to have a number of test functions. So far, there is a relatively small number of test functions available, most of which are very specific [4]. Not much work has been done to generate dynamic optimization test problems with a few exceptions for single objective optimization [21,3] and multi-objective optimization [11]. As pointed out in [21,3], a feasible dynamic optimization test problem generator should be easy to implement, computationally efficient, and flexible enough to change the type of dynamics of the optimum. In addition, the properties of the moving optimum should be known to evaluate the performance of various algorithms for solving dynamic problems.

This paper proposes a novel method for constructing dynamic optimization test problems by borrowing concepts from multi-objective optimization. The basic idea is to construct dynamic optimization problems by aggregating different stationary objectives using dynamically changing weights, which is directly inspired from the dynamic weighted aggregation method for solving multi-objective optimization problems [16,17].

2   Types of Dynamic Problems

In most typical dynamic optimization problems, the location of the optimum moves deterministically or stochastically during optimization. Other cases in which the representation or constraints are changed during optimization, such as dynamic scheduling problems [4] will not be considered in this paper. In general, dynamic optimization problems with a moving optimum can be divided into the following types:

1. The optimum moves linearly in parameter space over time. (MP1)
2. The optimum moves nonlinearly in parameter space over time. (MP2)
3. The optimum oscillates periodically among a given number of points in parameter space deterministically. (MP3)
4. The optimum moves randomly in the parameter space. (MP4)

It should be pointed out that for problem types $MP1$ and $MP2$, the changes can also be periodic. Besides, depending on the speed of changes, changes may occur generation-wise or within a generation [6]. In the former case, the optimum is supposed to be static within one generation, in other words, the objective function for each individual is the same. In the latter case, the objective function for each individual can be different.

3   MOO-Based Dynamic Test Problems Generator

3.1   Multi-objective Optimization and Dynamic Weighted Aggregation

Consider the following multi-objective optimization problem:

$$\min_{x \in S}(f_1(x), ..., f_m(x)), \qquad (1)$$

subject to the following inequality and equality constraints:

$$g_i(\boldsymbol{x}) \geq 0, i = 1, ..., p \tag{2}$$

$$h_j(\boldsymbol{x}) = 0, j = 1, ..., q \tag{3}$$

where $\boldsymbol{x}$ is the design vector, S is the set of all feasible solutions, m is the number of objectives, p and q are the number of inequality and equality constraints.

A traditional and conceptually straightforward way of solving the MOO problem in equation (1) is to aggregate the objectives into a single scalar function and then to minimize the aggregated function:

$$\min F(\boldsymbol{x}) = \sum_{i=1}^{m} w_i f_i(\boldsymbol{x}), \tag{4}$$

where $0 \leq w_i \leq 1, i = 1, ..., m$, and $\sum_{i=1}^{m} w_i = 1$. In this way, an MOO problem is reduced to a single objective one when the weights are fixed.

The conventional weighted aggregation (CWA) formulation of the MOO has many important features. First, for every Pareto-optimal solution of a convex problem, there exists a positive weight such that this solution is an optimum of $F(\boldsymbol{x})$. However, multiple runs have to be conducted to obtain multiple solutions. Second, solutions located in the concave region of the Pareto front can not be obtained. Third, for a set of evenly distributed weights, the obtained Pareto optimal solutions may or may not distribute evenly in parameter space [1]. If evenly distributed Pareto solutions are obtained, the MOO problem is termed as *uniform*. Otherwise, it is called *non-uniform*.

These features are often known as the main drawback of the CWA approach to MOO. However, it has also been shown that these weaknesses can be fixed if the weights are changed dynamically during optimization using evolutionary algorithms, which is termed as the dynamic weighted aggregation (DWA) method [16,17,18]

3.2   Generating Dynamic Single Objective Test Problems

Inspired from the DWA method for solving MOO problems, we find that changing the weights in equation (4) also provides a very efficient approach to generating dynamic optimization test problems. For simplicity, we assume the number of objective is 2, thus equation (4) becomes:

$$F(\boldsymbol{x}) = w f_1(\boldsymbol{x}) + (1 - w) f_2(\boldsymbol{x}), \tag{5}$$

where $0 \leq w \leq 1$. Obviously, by changing the weight w, we can construct all dynamic optimization problems discussed in Section 2. It should be pointed out that we are discussing the movement of the optimum in the parameter space.

---

[1] We are more concerned with the movement of the optimum in parameter space in generating dynamic problems. Therefore, the uniformity in this paper refers to the distribution of the Pareto optimal solutions in parameter space.

1. If w changes linearly and if the MOO problem has a uniform and convex Pareto front, the optimum of $F(x)$ moves linearly. (MP1)
2. If w changes linearly, and if the Pareto front of the MOO problem is non-uniform but convex, the optimum of $F(x)$ moves nonlinearly. (MP2)
3. If w changes nonlinearly, and if the Pareto front of the MOO problem is uniform but convex, the optimum of $F(x)$ moves nonlinearly. (MP2)
4. If w switches between a few fixed values periodically and if the Pareto front is convex, the optimum of $F(x)$ oscillates among the different points. If the Pareto front is concave, the optimum oscillates between two different points, which are the minimum of f_1 and f_2 respectively. (MP3)
5. If the weights changes randomly, and if the Pareto front is convex, then the optimum of $F(x)$ moves randomly. (MP4)

A few additional remarks can be made on the above method for generating dynamic optimization test problems. First, both the peak location and the peak height may be changeable. Second, if the weight changes periodically, the optimum of $F(x)$ also moves periodically. The speed of the movement can be adjusted by the change speed of w. Third, the change can be made generation by generation, or within a generation. In the latter case, the optimum moves before one generation is finished. Finally, the above method can be easily extended to generating dynamic multi-objective optimization problems. For example, given a stationary three-objective problem, it is possible to generate a two-objective problem with a moving Pareto front.

3.3   Generating Dynamic Multi-objective Test Problems

The method for generating dynamic single objective optimization based on dynamic weighted aggregation can easily be extended to generating dynamic multi-objective optimization test problems. Consider the following three-objective optimization problem:

$$\text{minimize } (f_1, f_2, f_3). \tag{6}$$

Reformulate the above three-objective optimization test function as follows:

$$\text{minimize } (F_1, F_2) \tag{7}$$
$$F_1 \;=\; wf_1 + (1 - w)f_2,$$
$$F_2 \;=\; wf_1 + (1 - w)f_3,$$

where $0 \le w \le 1$. Obviously, the two-objective optimization problem in equation (7) has a moving Pareto front when the weight changes. We can show that the solutions of the two-objective MOO problem in equation (7) with a fixed weight is a subset of the solutions of the three-objective MOO problem in equation (6). To verify this, we aggregate the two objectives of the dynamic MOO problem in equation (7):

$$F = vF_1 + (1 - v)F_2 \tag{8}$$
$$= wf_1 + v(1 - w)f_2 + (1 - v)(1 - w)f_3, \tag{9}$$

where $0 \le v \le 1$. It can easily be seen that for $0 \le v, w \le 1$, the weight for each objective in equation (9) is between 0 and 1 and the sum of the three weights always equals 1:

$$w + v(1 - w) + (1 - v)(1 - w) = 1, \tag{10}$$

which means that the optimization task in equation (9) is a weighted aggregation of the original three-objective optimization problem in equation (6).

3.4   Illustrative Examples

To illustrate the idea of generating dynamic optimization test problems using the aggregation concept in MOO, we consider the following convex and uniform MOO problem:

$$f_1 = \frac{1}{n} \sum_{i=1}^{n} x_i^2, \tag{11}$$

$$f_2 = \frac{1}{n} \sum_{i=1}^{n} (x_i - 2)^2. \tag{12}$$

By aggregating the two objectives, we have:

$$F(\boldsymbol{x}) = w \sum_{i=1}^{n} x_i^2 + (1.0 - w)(\sum_{i=1}^{n} (x_i - 2)^2), \tag{13}$$

where $0 \le w \le 1$. Thus, various dynamic single objective problems can be generated. If w is changes in the following form:

$$w(t) = -0.01t + 1, \ 0 \le t \le 100, \tag{14}$$

then the location of the optimum of equation (13) moves linearly in parameter space as well as in objective space, see Fig. 1 for $n = 2$.

If we change the weight w nonlinearly:

$$w(t) = -0.0001t^2 + 1, \ 0 \le t \le 100. \tag{15}$$

The optimum of $F(\boldsymbol{x})$ in equation (13) will move nonlinearly, as shown in Fig. 2.

Similarly, if the weight w is changed randomly in every 10 generations, the optimum of $F(\boldsymbol{x})$ jumps randomly, refer to Fig. 3 for $n = 2$.

To illustrate how to generate a moving Pareto front, we take the following widely used three-objective optimization problem as an example:

$$f_1 = x_1^2 + (x_2 - 1)^2, \tag{16}$$
$$f_2 = x_1^2 + (x_2 + 1)^2 + 1, \tag{17}$$
$$f_3 = (x_1 - 1)^2 + x_2^2 + 2, \tag{18}$$
$$\text{subject to:} \quad -2 \le x_1, x_2 \le 2. \tag{19}$$

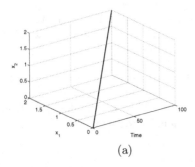

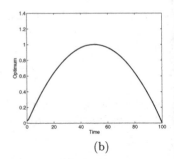

(a)   (b)

Fig. 1. The optimum moves linearly with time. (a) Peak location, (b) peak height.

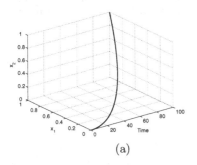

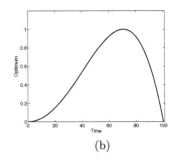

(a)   (b)

Fig. 2. The optimum moves nonlinearly with time. (a) Peak location, (b) peak height.

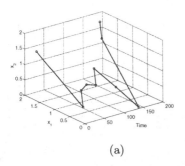

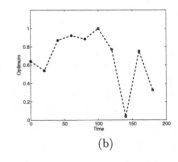

(a)   (b)

Fig. 3. The peak moves randomly in every 10 generations. (a) Peak location, (b) Peak height.

The Pareto front of this MOO test function is a convex surface. Reformulating the above MOO problem as shown in equation (7), and changing the weight w, a moving Pareto front can be obtained, see for example in Fig. 4, where w changes from 0.3 to 0.5 and to 0.7.

The above examples illustrate how dynamic single objective and multi-objective optimization test functions can be generated by combining multiple objectives. From the above examples, we can conclude that the proposed approach

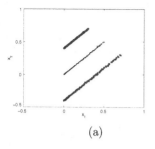

(a)

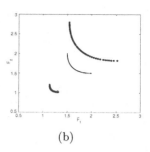

(b)

Fig. 4. A dynamic MOO problem. (a) Parameter space, (b) objective space.

to generating dynamic test problems is efficient, tunable and capable of generating various number of dynamic optimization problems considering the rich test problems proposed for multi-objective optimization [10].

3.5 Discussions

Many concerns may arise with regard to the proposed methods for generating dynamic test problems. First, is it possible to know the exact trajectory of the moving optimum? The answer is yes, if the Pareto front of the original MOO test problem is known. For any given time instant t, weights can be determined if the trajectory of the weights is defined. Then, the location of the optimum can be obtained for given weights, as shown in the examples. Second, how to control the complexity of a test problem? Generally, the dynamic problem constructed from a MOO test problem has similar features in ruggedness and deceptiveness. However, the dynamic problem may become more complex than the original MOO problem. It has been found that a uni-modal concave MOO problem will be changed into a multi-modal single objective optimization problem by aggregating different objectives. Third, what does the proposed method contribute to the research field given the existing methods for generating test functions, such as the moving peak function in [4]? Obviously, the moving peak function is more advantageous in specifying the properties of the test problems. However, the proposed method reflects more closely what happens in a class of real-world applications, where the problem that has the dominating influence changes over time Last but not the least, the proposed method discloses inherent relationships multi-objective optimization and dynamic optimization.

4   Behavior of Evolution Strategies in Dynamic Optimization

In this section, we present a few preliminary results on the behavior of evolution strategies (ES) in tracking different types of moving optima generated using the proposed method. Previous studies on the behavior of evolution strategies in tracking dynamic optima can be found in [2,25,1].

The standard evolution strategy and the ES with the covariance matrix adaptation have been considered. The parent and offspring population sizes are 15 and 100 respectively and the initial step-sizes are all set to 0.1. Neither recombination nor elitism has been adopted.

The behavior of the evolution strategies in tracking a linearly moving optimum of the test problem defined in equation (13) is shown in Fig. 5, where dimension n is set to 20. The optimum moves from one end to the other in 100 generations and then moves back. It can be seen that both evolutionary algorithms work well in tracking slowly moving optimum and the ES-CMA outperforms the standard ES in that it can track the moving optimum more closely. When the optimum moves faster, optimum tracking becomes difficult. To show this, we change the weight in equation (13) so that the optimum first moves from one end to the other in 10 generations, then moves back in the next 10 generations and finally keeps static. The tracking results are presented in Fig. 6. We see that neither the ES nor the ES-CMA is able to track the moving optimum closely. We also notice that the tracking speed of the ES-CMA is much faster, but the "overshoot" is also larger.

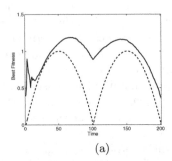
(a)

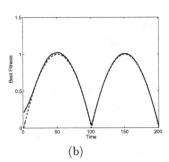
(b)

Fig. 5. Tracking a slowly moving optimum. The dashed line denotes the height of the moving optimum and the solid line the tracking result. (a) ES, (b) ES-CMA.

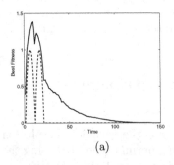
(a)

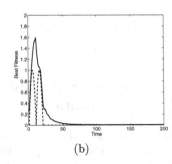
(b)

Fig. 6. Tracking a rapidly moving optimum. The dashed line denotes the height of the moving optimum and the solid line the tracking result. (a) ES, (b) ES-CMA.

It is believed to be more critical for evolutionary algorithms to track a jumping optimum after the algorithm has converged. In order to investigate the behavior of evolution strategies in tracking a jumping optimum more clearly, we modify the dynamic test function in equation (13) slightly so that not only the peak location but also the peak height will change when the weight changes:

$$F(\boldsymbol{x}) = w \sum_{i=1}^{n} x_i^2 + (1.0 - w)(\sum_{i=1}^{n}(x_i - 2)^2 + 1). \tag{20}$$

The weight is switched between 0.2 and 0.8 in every 50 generations. When the weight changes from 0.2 to 0.8, the location of the optimum of the function (20) moves from $(1.6, 1.6)$ to $(0.4, 0.4)$ in parameter space and its height changes from 1.44 to 0.84.

The tracking performance of the standard ES for $n = 3$ is shown in Fig. 7(a). It can be seen that the ES fails to track the optimum and gets stuck in a local minimum. If we look at the step-sizes, it is obvious that one of the step-sizes converges to zero and fails to adapt itself to the changing environment, refer to Fig. 7(b).

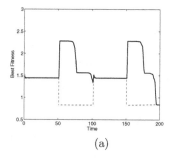
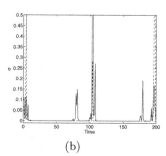

(a)   (b)

Fig. 7. Tracking a jumping optimum using the standard ES. (a) Best fitness, (b) step-sizes.

To solve this problem, the step-sizes are checked during optimization and they are reset once they are smaller than a given threshold. In this work, the threshold is set to 0.0005. By doing this, the ES tracks the jumping optimum properly because the step-sizes are able to adapt, see Fig. 8(b).

Similar results have been obtained for the ES-CMA. Again, step-size checking is important for the ES-CMA to track the jumping optimum, refer to Fig. 9 and Fig. 10 respectively. Compared with the ES case, the ES-CMA gets fully stuck when no step-size checking is implemented. This is due to the fact that all step-sizes are converged to zero and cannot recover when the environment changes, refer to Fig 9(b). In contrast, the step-sizes adapt properly with checking, see Fig. 10(b).

From the previous results, it appears that the ES-CMA tracks continuously moving optima faster than the standard ES. However, when the optimum jumps

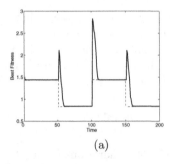 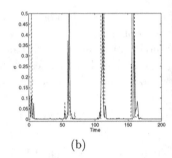

(a)   (b)

Fig. 8. Tracking a jumping optimum using the standard ES with step-size checking. (a) Best fitness, (b) step-sizes.

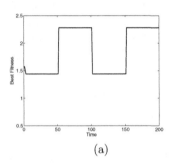 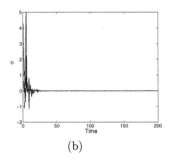

(a)   (b)

Fig. 9. Tracking a jumping optimum using the ES-CMA. (a) Best fitness, (b) step-sizes.

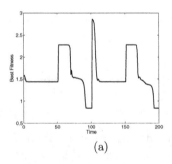 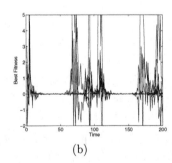

(a)   (b)

Fig. 10. Tracking a jumping optimum using the ES-CMA with step-size checking. (a) Best fitness, (b) step-sizes.

randomly, the standard ES shows better performance than the ES-CMA, even after step-size checking is introduced in the ES-CMA. This might be attributed to the fact that self-adaptation in ES-CMA needs history information. If the optimum jumps significantly over time, the mechanism of self-adaptation may fail to work properly.

5 Conclusions

The main purpose of this paper is to propose a computationally efficient, easily tunable and functionally capable dynamic optimization test problem generator using multi-objective optimization concepts. One of the major merit of the proposed approach is that it provides an easy way of taking advantage of the rich test problems available in multi-objective optimization. Furthermore, it brings us to consider the inherent connections between multi-objective optimization, multi-modal optimization and dynamic optimization, for all of which population diversity plays a key role.

Acknowledgement. The authors would like to thank Prof. E. Körner for his support.

References

1. D. Arnold and H.-G. Beyer. Random dynamic optimum tracking with evolution strategies. In *Parallel Problem Solving from Nature*, volume VII, pages 3–12, 2002.
2. T. Bäck. On the behavior of evolutionary algorithms in dynamic environments. In *IEEE Congress on Evolutionary Computation*, pages 446–451, 1998.
3. J. Branke. Memory enhanced evolutionary algorithms for changing optimization problems. In *Proceedings of the 1999 Congress on Evolutionary Computation*, pages 1875–1882. IEEE, 1999.
4. J. Branke. *Evolutionary Optimization in Dynamic Environments*. Kluwer Academic Publisher, Boston, 2002.
5. J. Branke, T. Kaußler, C. Schmidt, and H. Schmeck. A multi-population approach to dynamic optimization problems. In *Adaptive Computing in Design and Manufacturing*, pages 299–307. Springer, 2000.
6. J. Branke and W. Wang. Theoretical analysis of simple evolution strategies in quickly changing environments. In *Proceedings of Genetic and Evolutionary Computation Conference*, LNCS 2723, pages 537–548. Springer, 2003.
7. W. Cedeno and V.R.Vemuri. On the use of niching for dynamic landscapes. In *International Conference on Evolutionary Computation*, pages 361–366. IEEE, 1997.
8. H.G. Cobb and J.J. Grefensttee. Genetic algorithms for tracking changing environments. In *Proc. of 5th Int. Conf. on Genetic Algorithms*, pages 523–530, 1993.
9. D. Dasgupta and D.R. McGregor. Nonstationary function optimization using structured genetic algorithms. In *Parallel Problem Solving from Nature*, pages 145–154. Elsevier, 1992.
10. K. Deb, A. Pratap, and T. Meyarivan. Constrained test problems for multi-objective evolutionary optimization. In *Proc. of the 1st Int. Conf. on Evolutionary Multi-criterion Optimization*, LNCS 1993, pages 284–298, Berlin, 2001. Springer.
11. M. Farina, K. Deb, and P. Amato. Dynamic multi-objective optimization problems: Test cases, approximation, and applications. In *Proceedings of Genetic and Evolutionary Computation Conference*, LNCS 2632, pages 311–326. Springer, 2003.
12. A. Ghosh, S. Tsutsui, and H. Tanaka. Function optimization in nonstationary environment using steady state genetic algorithms with aging individuals. In *Proceedings of IEEE Congress on Evolutionary Computation*, pages 666–671, 1998.

13. D.E. Goldberg and R.E. Smith. Nonstationary function optimization using genetic algorithms with dominance and diploidy. In *Proceedings of the 2nd International Conference on Genetic Algorithms*, pages 59–68, 1987.
14. J.J. Grefenstette. Genetic algorithms for changing environments. In *Parallel Problem Solving from Nature*, 2, pages 137–144. Springer, 1992.
15. J.J. Grefenstette. Evolvability in dynamic fitness landscapes: A genetic algorithm approach. In *IEEE Congress on Evolutionary Computation*, pages 2031–2038, 1999.
16. Y. Jin, T. Okabe, and B. Sendhoff. Adapting weighted aggregation for multiobjective evolution strategies. In *Proc. of 1st Int. Conf. on Evolutionary Multi-Criterion Optimization*, LNCS 1993, pages 96–110. Springer, 2001.
17. Y. Jin, M. Olhofer, and B. Sendhoff. Evolutionary dynamic weighted aggregation for multiobjective optimization: Why does it work and how? In *Genetic and Evolutionary Computation Conference*, pages 1042–1049, San Francisco, CA, 2001.
18. Y. Jin and B. Sendhoff. Connectedness, regularity and the success of local search in evolutionary multiobjective optimization. In *Proceedings of the 2003 Congress on Evolutionary Computation*, pages 1910–1917. IEEE, 2003.
19. N. Mori, S. Imanishi, H. Kita, and Y. Nishikawa. Adaptation to a changing environment by means of memory based thermodynamical genetic algorithm. In *Proc. of the 7th Int. Conference on Genetic Algorithms*, pages 299–306, 1997.
20. N. Mori, H. Kita, and Y. Nishikawa. Adaptation to a changing environment by means of the feedback themodynamic genetic algorithms. In *Pallel Problem Solving from Nature*, volume V, pages 149–158, 1998.
21. R.W. Morrison and K.A. De Jong. A test problem generator for non-stationary environments. In *Proceedings of the 1999 Congress on Evolutionary Computation*, pages 2047–2053. IEEE, 1999.
22. C.L. Ramsey and J.J. Grefenstette. Case-based initialization of genetic algorithms. In *Proc. of the 5th Int. Conf. on Genetic Algorithms*, pages 84–91, 1993.
23. Y. Sano and M. Yamaguchi H.Kita, H. Kaji. Optimization of dynamic fitness function by means of genetic algorithm using sub-populations. In *4th Asia-Pasific Conference on Simulated Evolution and Learning*, pages 706–711, 2002.
24. R.K. Ursem. Multinational GAs: Multimodal optimization techniques in dynamic environments. In *Proceedings of the Genetic and Evolutionary Computation Conference*, pages 19–26. Morgan Kaufmann, 2000.
25. K. Weicker and N. Weicker. On evolution strategy optimization in dynamic environments. In *IEEE Congress on Evolutionary Computation*, pages 2039–2046, 1999.
26. M. Wineberg and F. Oppacher. Enhancing the GA's ability to cope with dynamic environments. In *Proceedings of Genetic and Evolutionary Computation Conference*, pages 3–10. Morgan Kaufmann, 2000.

Competitive Goal Coordination in Automatic Parking

Darío Maravall[1], Javier de Lope[1], and Miguel Ángel Patricio[2]

[1] Department of Artificial Intelligence
Faculty of Computer Science
Universidad Politécnica de Madrid
Campus de Montegancedo, 28660 Madrid, Spain
{dmaravall,jdlope}@fi.upm.es
[2] Department of Computer Science
Universidad Carlos III de Madrid
mpatricio@inf.uc3m.es

Abstract. This paper addresses the problem of automatic parking by a back-wheel drive vehicle, using a biomimetic model based on direct coupling between vehicle perceptions and actions. The proposed automatic parking solution leads to a dynamic multiobjective optimization problem that cannot be dealt with analytically. A genetic algorithm is therefore used. The paper ends with a discussion of the results of computer simulations.

1 Introduction

We have previously developed a biomimetic approach thanks to which we have been able to solve specific manipulation and locomotion problems in both articulated mechanisms[1,2] and wheeled vehicles [3,4].

In this paper, we address the problem of automatically parking a back-wheel drive vehicle and put forward a solution based on the above-mentioned biomimetic approach. In particular, we analyze the problem of dynamically coordinating contradictory goals, such as positioning and heading, in automatic parking. We use a genetic algorithm to solve this multicriteria optimization problem.

The remainder of the paper is organized as follows. The biomimetic approach that we advocate for the design of autonomous robots is very briefly outlined in the next section. This approach has two noteworthy properties. First, the controller does not need to know the agent or robot kinematics or dynamics and, second, neither does it call for *a priori* knowledge of the spatial distribution or map of the working environment. Thanks to these two features, very simple designs can be obtained without prior knowledge being injected into the robot controller. This approach is then tailored to the case of automatic car parking, and we go on to address the specific question mentioned above of coordinating contradictory criteria, proposing a solution based on genetic algorithms. Finally,

G.R. Raidl et al. (Eds.): EvoWorkshops 2004, LNCS 3005, pp. 537–548, 2004.
© Springer-Verlag Berlin Heidelberg 2004

we present and discuss the results of simulation, as a previous step to implementing the approach in an automated vehicle, a task on which we are now working.

2 Biomimetic Approach for Sensory and Motor Coordination in Autonomous Robots

The design and development of increasingly more autonomous robots has been tackled with both conventional control techniques [5,6], including a strong adaptive and learning component, and techniques based on the use, primarily, of artificial neural nets [7,8] and fuzzy logic [9]. Generically, it can be said that conventional analytical methods are based on formal and aprioristic representations or models of the environment, as well as an exact knowledge of robot dynamics and kinematics. The respective controllers are obtained as a result of rigorous mathematical developments. The design of fuzzy controllers, on the other hand, is based on the use of approximate reasoning rules and linguistic sensory and action variables. In this case, the analytical developments of the conventional methods are transformed into processes of control rule conversion into *if-then* type rules on linguistic variables. The process of designing the control rules and, particularly, of tuning the membership functions of the linguistic variables involved is usually very complex and tricky. To optimize this process, recourse is sometimes taken to complementary techniques aimed at overcoming the inherent rigidity of fuzzy control: especially, neural nets and genetic algorithms [10]. The key to controller design in methods based on artificial neural networks lies in the supervised learning of the appropriate actions for each situation that the robot will encounter. Neural methods simplify the design process appreciably, although they have the important drawback of needing an exhaustive set of training examples to rule out the serious problems of generalization that tend to plague neural networks.

As mentioned above, we have been employing a method that is based on the *perception-decision-action* cycle and is capable of solving control problems in autonomous robots, without the need to inject control or approximate reasoning rules (as in the case of fuzzy controllers) or for supervised solutions (as in the case of neural nets). The method does not even need prior knowledge of the kinematic and dynamic equations of the actual robot.

The idea underpinning the method is to optimize the measurable behavior indexes using appropriate sensors. The optimization is solved by means of heuristic techniques, which makes the robot controller highly flexible and very simple. In the manner that living beings solve their physical control problems, like manipulation and locomotion, the robot develops a behavior strategy based on the perception of its environment, embodied as behavior indexes and aimed at improving (optimizing) the evolution of the above-mentioned behavior indexes. It does all this following the known *perception-decision-action* cycle.

The tailoring of this biomimetic approach to the parking problem is illustrated in Fig. 1.

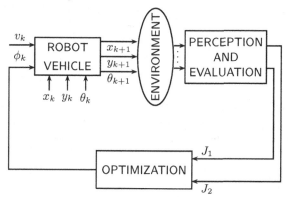

Fig. 1. Conceptual diagram of the biomimetic model

The robot vehicle considered in this paper is a conventional back-wheel drive car, whose dynamic equations can be modeled, for the low-speed range typical of parking maneuvers, as:

$$\dot{x}(t) = v(t) \cos \theta(t)$$
$$\dot{y}(t) = v(t) \sin \theta(t) \tag{1}$$
$$\dot{\theta}(t) = v(t)/L \tan \phi(t)$$

where (x, y) are the coordinates for the point of application of the force of traction on the vehicle; θ is the heading of the vehicle on the plane on which it is moving; v is its speed; L is the distance between the front and back axles, and the variable ϕ is the direction of the driving wheels with respect to the vehicle heading θ. Obviously, (v, ϕ) are the robot control variables and (x, y, θ) are its state variables. The discrete version of (1) is:

$$x_{k+1} = x_k + v_k \cos \theta_k$$
$$y_{k+1} = y_k + v_k \sin \theta_k$$
$$\theta_{k+1} = \theta_k + v_k/L \tan \phi_k \tag{2}$$
$$|\phi_k| < \phi_{\max}$$

where $\phi_{\max}$ is the maximum angle that can be applied to the direction of the driving wheels.

In the case of automatic parking, there are two behavior indexes of interest: J_1 and J_2. These two indexes quantify the goal that the robot should park in the final position (x_d, y_d) and the goal that the robot should park in line with the parking space direction, θ_d, respectively. Hence:

$$J_1 = \tfrac{1}{2} \left[(x - x_d)^2 + (y - y_d)^2 \right]$$
$$J_2 = \tfrac{1}{2} (\theta - \theta_d)^2 \tag{3}$$

Supposing that the vehicle maneuvers at constant speed, the other available control variable, ϕ, should minimize both indexes:

$$\dot{\phi}(t) = -\mu_1 \frac{\partial J_1}{\partial \phi} - \mu_2 \frac{\partial J_2}{\partial \phi} \tag{4}$$

where μ_1 and μ_2 weight the importance of each goal. The discrete version of (4) is:

$$\phi_{k+1} = \phi_k - \mu_1 \left.\frac{\partial J_1}{\partial \phi}\right|_{\phi(k)} - \mu_2 \left.\frac{\partial J_2}{\partial \phi}\right|_{\phi(k)} \tag{5}$$

Equations (4) and (5) raise an important practical problem, which is what we might refer to as the relationship between the *distal* sensory information scale (given by the gradients or changes of the behavior indexes ΔJ_1 and ΔJ_2) and the *proximal* actions scale (given by the gradients of the control actions $\Delta\phi_k = \phi_k - \phi_{k-1}$ or $\Delta\phi_{k+1} = \phi_{k+1} - \phi_k$).

A practical way of solving this scale problem is to establish a tabular relationship between the distal levels and the proximal levels. In particular, the range of robot actions (speed v and steering wheel turn ϕ) can be distributed on a discrete scale of values. In view of the practical importance of the distal/proximal relationship (which in living beings takes a lot of learning), one open line of research is to develop flexible diagrams to quantify this relationship, where fuzzy linguistic variables or even genetic algorithms could play a role in adequate tuning. In this paper, however, we have not addressed this problem and have used a range of just three steering wheel action values: $+10°$, $0°$, $-10°$, depending on whether the ratios of the distal and proximal gradients are positive, zero or negative, respectively. We have achieved good results with this small scale of actions.

3   Multicriteria Optimization

Set out in the terms described in the preceding section, automatic parking can be considered as a standard multicriteria optimization problem, where the agent control actions (in this case, the direction of the steering wheel, because the robot is moving at constant speed) should simultaneously minimize the two indexes that appear in expressions (3) to (5). As any driver will have found in practice, the dynamic coordination of these indexes in a parking maneuver is an extremely complex control problem, as, in nonholonomic vehicles, any slip in the combination of the actions suggested by the approach and heading indexes may be disastrous for the parking maneuver.

Apart from the fact that our working methods in autonomous robot design, including the one we are concerned with here, are based on the strategic goal of minimizing the inherent rigidity of analytical control methods and, consequently, our working methods are motivated by an exploration of the potential of biological function-inspired heuristic procedures, analytical methods do not appear to be able to successfully tackle the simultaneous optimization of goals J_1 and J_2 anyway. Thus, taking the simplest case, where the magnitude of the steering wheel control actions, ϕ, is small, we have that:

$$\dot{\theta}(t) = \frac{v(t)}{L}\tan\phi(t) \approx \frac{v(t)}{L}\phi(t) \tag{6}$$

In this case, the optimization of J_2 can be assured by a simple PD control:

$$\phi^2(t) = K_p \left[\theta(t) - \theta_d\right] + K_d \dot{\theta}(t) \tag{7}$$

where the superindex 2 refers to the fact that it is a control path aimed at minimizing index J_2. After substituting the control law (7) in (6), we would get:

$$\dot{\theta}(t) = \frac{v(t)}{L} K_p \left[\theta(t) - \theta_d\right] + \frac{v(t)}{L} K_d \dot{\theta}(t) \tag{8}$$

and, hence, the vehicle would rapidly converge towards the desired final heading. As far as the minimization of the other index is concerned, let us first express this index as an explicit function of the control variable $\phi(t)$:

$$J_1 = \frac{1}{2} \left[\int_{t_0}^{t_f} \cos\left[\frac{v(t)}{L}\phi(t) \right] \cdot t - x_d \right]^2 +$$

$$\frac{1}{2} \left[\int_{t_0}^{t_f} \sin\left[\frac{v(t)}{L}\phi(t) \right] \cdot t - y_d \right]^2 \tag{9}$$

Although more complex than the heading index, due to its non-linear dependence on the control variable, the optimization of J_1 can be tackled using analytical procedures to find a control path $\phi^1(t)$ that makes J_1 tend to zero. But the key question is the dynamic coordination of the two control paths $\phi^1(t)$, which minimizes J_1, and $\phi^2(t)$, which minimizes J_2. That is, the key is to find the coordination function:

$$\phi(t) = f\left[\phi^1(t), \phi^2(t)\right] \tag{10}$$

that assures the correct execution of the parking maneuver. A simple approach to the problem of goal coordination would be to formulate it in linear terms as:

$$\phi(t) = \omega_1(t)\phi^1(t) + \omega_2(t)\phi^2(t) \tag{11}$$

where $\omega_1(t)$ and $\omega_2(t)$ dynamically designate the instantaneous weight to be assigned to each goal.

The difficulty with the problem of dynamically coordinating contradictory goals, at least in the automatic parking problem, lies in the fact that the weight coefficients depend primarily on the relative positions of the robot $(x(t), y(t), \theta(t))$ and the parking space as opposed to time. This means that the analytical approach to optimizing the weight coefficients $\omega_1(t)$ and $\omega_2(t)$ further complicates the already complex analytical processing required to output control laws $\phi^1(t)$ and $\phi^2(t)$ separately.

Finally, appealing to the reader's intuition, we would like to stress that the dynamic coordination of the optimization paths of the two indexes J_1 and J_2 is a hypersensitive issue. Just imagine a driver giving more priority to heading than to approach instructions when he is far away from the parking space or doing just the opposite, and giving more priority to the approach goal, when he is near to the space: the respective paths would be disastrous. Note, also, the additional difficulty of having to formalize the linguistic terms near and far.

In sum, we believe that a problem that is as complex to address using analytical procedures as the dynamic coordination of opposing goals in automatic parking is a natural candidate for being tackled by evolutionary heuristic techniques, which is what the remainder of the paper deals with.

4   Goal Coordination with Genetic Algorithms

The dynamic nature of the problem of coordinating contradictory goals in automatic parking should again be underlined. Therefore, the parameters or variables coded in the genotype of the genetic algorithm that is to be designed to solve this problem must forcibly match the appropriate dynamic behaviors. In this respect, direct genetic encoding of the weighting coefficients ω_1 and ω_2 is not an option, as, being dynamic values that depend, at all times, on the relative position and heading of the vehicle with respect to the parking space, they cannot be represented as static genes.

One possibility would be to address the problem of dynamic coordination by a neural network that optimized the combination of the control actions generated by each goal in real time. However, this alternative would necessitate a battery of optimal paths that would allow supervised neural net learning, which contravenes the basic idea that we set out at the start of this paper of designing a totally autonomous solution that required the designer to inject no more information than some generic behavior goals.

Therefore, taking into account that our genetic algorithm has to solve a dynamic multicriteria optimization problem, let us consider how a human driver performs the automatic parking operation to see if we can find any clues as to how to define the appropriate parameters and variables so that a genetic algorithm can solve the coordination problem.

Very briefly, we find that parking operations obey the following two basic rules:

1. If the vehicle is *far* from the target, then priority should be given to the approach goal (index J_1).
2. If the vehicle is *near* to the target, then priority should be given to the heading goal (index J_2).

Note the ambiguity of the linguistic terms far and near. If we take the simplest case of linear coordination:

$$\phi(t) = \omega_1(t)\phi^1(t) + \omega_2(t)\phi^2(t) \tag{12}$$

then these two basic rules of parking goal coordination can be simply formalized as shown in Fig.2, which resembles the standard membership functions used in fuzzy subset theory.

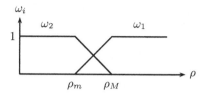

Fig. 2. Basic goal coordination rules

This graph, where ρ is the distance of the vehicle from the target or parking space, is straightforward to interpret. Supposing that the curves of the coefficients are symmetric, the two parameters that determine the coordination dynamics are ρ_m and ρ_M. Thus, it would now be feasible to think of applying a genetic algorithm to optimize the choice of these parameters for dynamically coordinating the goals, that is,

$$\omega_1 = f_1(\rho_m, \rho_M) \; ; \; \omega_2 = f_2(\rho_m, \rho_M) \tag{13}$$

A practical problem here is that undesired situations may materialize, if the genetic algorithm search is confined to the parameters ρ_m and ρ_M, which somehow determine the concepts of far and near in the implementation of the two basic parking rules. Specifically, once the vehicle has entered the region of attraction of coefficient ω_2 (that is, when it is *near* to the target), it will park parallel to, but not inside the space, if it reached this region by "connecting" with the straight line defined by the prolongation of the direction of the space. Such situations could be ruled out by allowing both goals to have some influence in the region of attraction of near and far, as shown in Fig. 3.

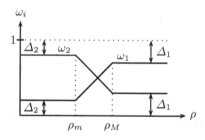

Fig. 3. Rules with region of attraction influence

In this case, the genetic algorithm would be responsible for optimizing the additional parameters Δ_1 and Δ_2, apart from ρ_m and ρ_M.

Looking again at how humans park, we find that one very efficient maneuver, provided there are no obstacles, is to approach, in almost any direction, an area close to the position and direction of the space, as shown in Fig. 4. As of then priority, albeit not absolute, is given to heading and, when the vehicle is aligned with the space, the approach goal takes maximum, but again not exclusive, priority.

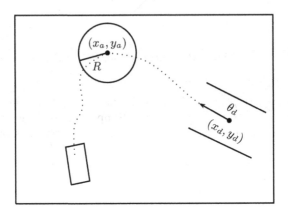

Fig. 4. Illustration of the third method described in the text

Let us take a qualitative look at the execution of this maneuver.

Phase 1. Transfer region approach.

This phase can be performed, in principle, without concern for the heading goal J_2. However, the position of the vehicle in this transfer region should be as aligned as possible with respect to the direction of the space.

Phase 2. Alignment with the direction of the space.

Once it is positioned in the transfer or subtarget region, the vehicle gives maximum, but not exclusive, priority to the heading goal. Obviously, the more aligned it is, the smoother the maneuver will be.

Phase 3. Parking space approach according to the desired heading.

After alignment with the direction of the space, the vehicle's only concern will be to reduce its distance to the space (maximum priority of index J_1). To prevent possible losses of alignment, goal J_2 should retain some, albeit a very weak, influence.

5   Experimental Results

The experiments were conducted using the University of Sheffield's Genetic Algorithm Toolbox for Matlab [11]. For all cases, a 20-bit resolution binary coding was used for the parameters processed; the parameter ranges depend on the variables to be optimized.

The stochastic universal sampling method was used to select individuals. The crossover probability used is 0.7; the mutation probability is set proportionally to the size of the population, and is never over 0.02. Additionally, elitism from generation to generation is used. Hence, 90% of the individuals of each new population are created by means of the selection and crossover operators and 10% of the best individuals of each generation are added directly to the new population.

Quality is determined by rewarding the individuals that simultaneously minimize the two indexes J_1 and J_2, that is, the closer an individual is to the position and direction defined as the target, at the end of the path, the better this individual is. Additionally, individuals who manage to reach the target along a shorter path are also considered better, although the weighting of this factor is lower.

A measure of the number of changes of vehicle heading, that is, the number of operations effected on the steering wheel along the path causing the vehicle to modify its heading instructions (brusque changes from right to left and vice versa) was also used in some experiments. However, this index appears to be somehow included in the shortest path index, and was, therefore, not used in the final experiments.

The experiments were actually designed by defining a set of initial and final vehicle position and heading pairs that would cover the different relative situations between the source and target. Each individual generated in the evolutionary process was simulated with these initial and final conditions to thus determine its problem-solving quality.

As explained in the previous section, the first parking method is based on evolving parameters ρ_m and ρ_M (Fig.2) that denote the distance to the target and determine whether the position index $(\rho > \rho_M)$, the heading index $(\rho < \rho_m)$ or a combination of the two $(\rho_m \leq \rho \leq \rho_M)$ should be used.

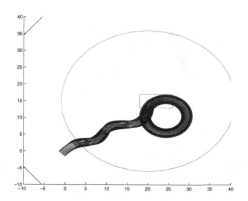

Fig. 5. Erroneous parking evolving ρ_m and ρ_M

For this method, the parameters ρ_m and ρ_M were initially left to evolve freely, which encouraged situations where the fittest individuals had a ρ_m greater than the distance at which they were positioned at the start. In other words, only the heading index was taken into account in parking, which led to executions such as the one shown in Fig. 5. The area denoted by the internal circumference represents the region in which $\rho < \rho_m$, and the external circumference starting at $(-10, -5)$ and $(-10, 35)$ matches the region $\rho > \rho_M$.

After detecting this erroneous behavior, the parameters ρ_m and ρ_M were forced to evolve so that the initial distance between the vehicle and the target fell within the subintervals they determine. Fig. 6 shows the path followed by one of the individuals included in this procedure.

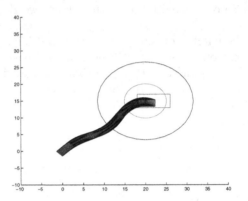

Fig. 6. Successful parking evolving ρ_m and ρ_M

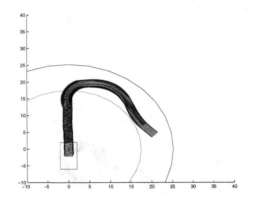

Fig. 7. Parking by evolving ρ_m, ρ_M, Δ_1 and Δ_2

Apart from evolving parameters ρ_m and ρ_M, the second parking strategy also considers Δ_1 and Δ_2 (Fig. 3), which, as mentioned above, means that both the position and the heading indexes are taken into account at all times.

The results obtained are more or less equivalent to the results of the first parking procedure, although, as four parameters had to be tuned in this case, the number of individuals in each population had to be doubled (80 as compared to 40 used in the experiments with the first procedure) and convergence to the best solution was also much slower (at least 100 generations were needed to

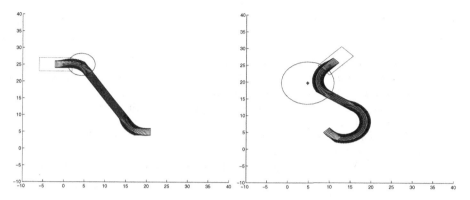

Fig. 8. (a) Parking with subtarget and (b) parking in a tricky situation

reach the first correct solution). Fig. 7 shows the path achieved by the fittest individual.

In the third and last parking method, the parameters evolved are distances from the goal to the subtarget and radius of the subtarget region depicted in Fig. 4. Fig. 8a shows one of the parking paths achieved using this procedure.

The parking paths using this method are much better and more natural than those achieved with the other two. As an illustration, Fig. 8b shows a relatively tricky situation that calls for a complicated and successful parking maneuver.

6   Conclusions

We have presented a solution for conventional nonholonomic vehicle automatic parking. The proposed solution is based on a biomimetic approach that can be used to design extremely simple and robust autonomous robot control systems, as the designer has to inject only the robotic system goals. This approach means, therefore, that the use of dynamic and kinematic robot models and even the aprioristic formal descriptions of their working environments can be ignored. Tailoring this approach to the case of automatic parking leads to a problem of dynamic antagonistic goal coordination, which, owing to its complexity and instability, cannot be dealt with using analytical methods. Therefore, this multicriteria optimization problem has been formalized to be tackled by genetic algorithms. Three automatic parking strategies have been designed, and the results obtained using genetic algorithms have been presented.

Acknowledgements. This work has been partially funded by the Spanish Ministry of Science and Technology, project DPI2002-04064-C05-05.

References

1. D. Maravall, J. de Lope, "A Bio-Inspired Robotic Mechanism for Autonomous Locomotion in Unconventional Environments", C. Zhou, D. Maravall, D. Ruan (eds.), *Autonomous Robotic Systems: Soft Computing and Hard Computing Methodologies and Applications*, Physica-Verlag, Heidelberg, 2003, pp. 263–292.
2. D. Maravall, J. de Lope, "A Reinforcement Learning Method for Dynamic Obstacle Avoidance in Robotic Mechanisms", D. Ruan, P. D'Hondt, E.E. Kerre (eds.), *Computational Intelligent Systems for Applied Research*, World Scientific, Singapore, 2002, pp. 485–494.
3. J. de Lope, D. Maravall, "Integration of Reactive Utilitarian Navigation and Topological Modeling", C. Zhou, D. Maravall, D. Ruan (eds.), *Autonomous Robotic Systems: Soft Computing and Hard Computing Methodologies and Applications*, Physica-Verlag, Heidelberg, 2003, pp. 103–139.
4. D. Maravall, J. de Lope, "Integration of Potential Field Theory and Sensory-based Search in Autonomous Navigation", *15th IFAC World Congress, International Federation of Automatic Control*, Barcelona, 2002.
5. J.-P. Laumond, P.E. Jacobs, M. Taix., R.M. Murray, "A motion planner for nonholonomic mobile robots", *IEEE Trans. on Robotics and Automation*, 10(5), 1996, pp. 577–593.
6. I.E. Paromtchik, C. Laugier, "Motion generation and control for parking an autonomous vehicle", *Proc. IEEE Int. Conf. on Robotics and Automation*, Minneapolis, 1996, pp. 3117–3122.
7. S.G. Kong, B. Kosko, "Comparison of fuzzy and neural track backer-upper control systems", B. Kosko (ed.), *Neural Networks and Fuzzy Systems*, Prentice-Hall, Englewood Cliffs, 1992, pp. 339–361.
8. D. Gu, H. Hu, "Neural predictive control for a car-like mobile robot", *Robotics and Autonomous Systems*, 39, 2002, pp. 73–86.
9. M. Hitchings, L. Vlacic, V. Kecman, "Fuzzy control", L. Vlacic, M. Parent, F. Harashima (eds.), *Intelligent Vehicle Technologies*, Butterworth&Heinemann, Oxford, 2001, pp. 289–331.
10. O. Cordón, F. Herrera, F. Hoffmann, L. Magdalena, *Genetic Fuzzy Systems*, World Scientific, Singapore, 2001.
11. A. Chipperfield, P. Fleming, H. Pohlheim, C. Fonseca, *Genetic Algorithm Toolbox for Matlab*, Department of Automatic Control and Systems Engineering, University of Sheffield, 1994.

Evolutionary Bayesian Network Dynamic Planner for Game RISK

James Vaccaro[1,2] and Clark Guest[1]

[1]University of California San Diego
9500 Gilman Dr., La Jolla, CA 92093
{jvaccaro, cguest}@ece.ucsd.edu
[2]Lockheed Martin Information Assurance
4770 Eastgate Mall, San Diego, CA 92121
{jvaccaro}@orincon.com

Abstract. Many artificial intelligence problems are susceptible to a goal-directed solution. For some problems, such as dynamic planning and execution, a goal-directed approach may be the only option. Using information available about a desirable state or a measure of acceptability of possible future states, a goal-directed approach determines routes or plans to reach these desirable states. These problems can be categorized as game problems. One such game is RISK. RISK is complex, multi-scaled, and provides a good application for testing a variety of goal-directed approaches. A goal-directed hybrid evolutionary program that plays the RISK game effectively has been developed. This approach advances an understanding of: (1) how to use Bayesian probability to prune combinatorial explosive planning spaces; (2) how to incorporate temporal planning cost in an objective function; and (3) provides a procedure for mapping a problem (i.e., data and knowledge) into a dynamic planning and execution framework.

1 Introduction

This paper concentrates on the automation problem of *dynamic planning and execution* (DP&E). The term *planning* is used to refer to all decision making about future actions within the constraints of a problem. This includes *what* actions to take, the order or *when* to take them, *where* to take them and by *whom*. Planning involves the generation of a sequence of actions that transform an initial situation into a more desirable situation as defined by a set of goals. The term *execution* is defined as carrying out a plan. Execution is coupled with planning, because what is predicted to happen and what actually happens are often different. The term *dynamic* refers to adapting to changes in the environment, either during the planning or execution phases. The planning systems of concern here are ones with the following requirements:

- State-space representation
- Finite set of available actions
- Known state transitions (possibly stochastic)
- Finite set of measurable goals

G.R. Raidl et al. (Eds.): EvoWorkshops 2004, LNCS 3005, pp. 549–560, 2004.

2 Related Work

Given the general criteria above, there are several approaches to tackling the dynamic planning and execution problem. When making plans with dynamically changing circumstances, one must be able to adjust plans on the fly to ensure that the best possible final situations can be achieved. These DP&E problems are often game problems, such as chess, checkers or backgammon. Games such as chess are deterministic problems in the sense that they do not possess elements of chance imposed by rolling dice. These game problems have been solved to a certain extent through rule-based approaches with decision tree architectures [1], such as is used in the chess-playing computer, Deep Blue [2]. The techniques used in chess, which are a combination of minimax [3] and rules, cannot solve most DP&E problems, because the elements of chance and variable plan lengths make DP&E an intractable problem under this method. Games such as backgammon however, do include stochastic elements and have been solved to a certain extent through a goal-directed temporal difference Reinforcement Learning (RL) approach. Through competing against itself, a Neural Network (NN) can be trained over the course of many games [4]. DP&E however, is different in the sense that the number of combinatorial behaviors at any given moment is astronomically higher, and finding the best set of behaviors is not a matter of learning over many trials, but instead, of pursuing goals in the face of a changing environment. Checkers has been solved to a great extent as well by applying a NN. With evolutionary learning a more effective player evolves over many trials of playing the game [5]. Even though evolving a NN over many trials does provide a good exploration of the space, it has not yet been proven effective over problems where the input and output combinations are far greater than checkers.

For DP&E problems one cannot focus solely on any one technique to solve the problem well. Having some deterministic capabilities such as chess solving solutions, a reward feedback mechanism such as those used in backgammon, and the exploration capabilities as used in the checkers' solution provide a better overall approach than applying any of these techniques individually. On the one hand, using learning techniques such as RL provide a well-defined formalized methodology for converging on a solution [6], while adaptation techniques, such as evolutionary computation (EC), can be argued to explore large spaces more efficiently [7]. These approaches have been used on discrete rules through Dynamic Programming (DP) [6], on decision trees and NNs through reinforcement learning [4] [8] [9], on sequential tasks with Monte Carlo (MC) methods and on some practical real-world problems with EC or genetic algorithms [10] [11].

The advantages of discrete rule systems are that they incorporate a priori knowledge directly and are deterministic and tractable. The disadvantages of discrete rule systems are that they require expert-knowledge, can only handle domain specific problems, grow exponentially with available choices, cannot generalize, and do not account for uncertainty.The advantages of Monte Carlo methods are that they require no a priori knowledge, require only sample transitions and are non-deterministic yet tractable. The disadvantages of Monte Carlo methods are that they require much exploration, their convergence properties are not well-defined and they cannot handle associative tasks well.The advantages of DP methods are that they guarantee convergence, handle stochastic problems and are deterministic and tractable. The disadvantages of DP methods are that they require perfect model of environment, grow exponentially, and can handle only domain specific problems well. The advantages of RL methods are that they balance both depth and breadth search, handle incremental learning well, handle stochastic problems well, are deterministic and tractable and can incorporate a temporal difference (λ) factor that links rewards over time. The limitations of RL methods are that they do not scale well for large problems, which thus require a Temporal Difference NN (TDNN) to functionally approximate the value function, and this in turn requires many examples for training. TDNNs have worked well on the backgammon problem where there is only one starting state and continual playing of the game guarantees a winner for training purposes [9]. For DP&E problems there is no guarantee that a winning situation can be reached in a finite time interval and thus training a winner will be difficult. In addition, λ performs a weighted average over rewards and thus large valleys of high cost areas will outweigh a sudden overall positive outcome, as seen in RISK.The advantages of EC methods are that they quickly search large combinatorial spaces, have an expert-defined evaluated state space to measure the quality of achievable states, handle stochastic problems well and are tractable [12]. The limitations of EC methods are that they do not learn long-term from previously explored options, require expert knowledge in the form of prioritized goals (fitness function), require exploitation and exploration parameters that are domain specific [13] and do not take into account state transition probabilities, thus becoming overly optimistic.

3 New Approach

The approach presented here addresses three deficiencies of existing methods. First, in many games, the number of possible moves to consider grows beyond available computational resources. Our approach recognizes that for games in which elements of chance exist, not all branches of the decision tree are equally probable. A technique we call Bayesian Guided Evolutionary Computation (BGEC) is used to prune improbable branches. The threshold for pruning can be adjusted to maintain computational tractability.

Another symptom of broad and deep decision trees is that the planning process can go on for indefinite periods of time. Some approaches arbitrarily limit planning time to a fixed duration, but this is a blind, inflexible approach. A technique called Temporally Aware Planning Termination (TAPT) is used in our algorithm to provide flexible limits on planning time. The real time used to improve upon a plan is included as a penalty on plan fitness. When modifications to the plan fail to overcome the increasing time penalty, planning is terminated.

A side effect of BGEC and TAPT is that sometimes the execution of a plan takes an improbable turn. Outcomes may be considerably better or considerably worse that expected. For such circumstances, Success Moderated Execution (SME) is introduced. The step-by-step outcome of plan execution is compared with the predicted probability of that outcome. The probability of completing the original plan is recomputed. If that probability falls below a threshold, the existing plan is discarded and the planning process is reinitiated, perhaps in an abbreviated form.

BGEC and TAPT are techniques to control proliferating branches of decision trees. In future papers we will quantify the degree to which they are successful. SME compensates for the incomplete thoroughness introduced by BGEC and TAPT. Future papers will also demonstrate its effectiveness in restoring plans that are coming off the track.

The new DP&E approach taken here is three algorithmic steps: (1) taking the *current* state and *projecting* actions and resulting states into the future; (2) *selecting* the best expected plan based on the resulting state and probability of successful completion; and (3) *executing* the best plan action by action as long as probability of plan success remains high, otherwise form a new plan (go back to step 1). Each step has been improved in a novel way:

1. Bayesian Guided Evolutionary Computation (BGEC)
2. Temporally Aware Planning Termination (TAPT)
3. Success Moderated Execution (SME)

BGEC is an approach where a Bayesian Network autonomously prunes traditional evolutionary computation outcomes at each step. When planning, all possibilities need to be considered, but often times the number of possibilities explodes exponentially as a function of plan length. To counter this, a Bayesian Network is used to chain individual state transition probabilities. This was simply done by multiplying the probability of all previous outcomes (A) by the conditional probability that an event occurred (i.e., $Pr(A,B) = Pr(A) \, Pr(B/A)$). The sum of all probable events adds to one and the most probable outcome or expected state is the weighted average of all possibilities. This new probability density function (outcome-probability pairs) is then stored at the new transition node and further actions from this state can take into account the new probability density function, thus reducing the computation required for multiple chained dependent actions.

TAPT is an approach where the computational resources required to develop a plan are balanced with the needs of the user and the quality of the plan. The more generations, offspring, and selections used will create a higher quality plan, but the higher the parameters, the slower the evolutionary algorithm. All the while the opponents are waiting to take their turn. To counter this, time is measured for each plan developed to determine the best change in reward vs. EC parameters. Preliminary results have shown that 8 offspring, 8 selections and 10 generations usual provide an excellent plan. However, this can take up to several minutes to calculate using Matlab and this is entirely too long a delay when playing against human opponents. To offset the waiting time, the evolutionary algorithm now performs one generation per move while RISK is executing. This gives a slight hesitation between moves, but could save in long waiting periods. Also factored into the TAPT is how often the execution fails. All these temporal factors are currently being measured and the best combination will be learned in a future version.

SME is an approach where the Bayesian calculations are used again. This time, however, only the successful outcomes for each independent *campaign* are considered. A *campaign* is by definition a connected series of operations designed to bring about a particular result. The leaf nodes of each campaign are a set of possible outcomes that represent the successful completion of that campaign. By summing all the probabilities associated with successful outcomes for each leaf node, one has the success probability for that campaign. Then by multiplying all leaf nodes for all independent campaigns, one has a true probability of success for all independent campaigns together. This probability of success ($Pr(su)$) needs to fall within the guidelines placed by the user (threshold η) so that the plans generated meet that criterion ($Pr(su) > $ η). In addition, this criterion is also integrated into the execution function to determine whether the plan will succeed or not, based on the realization of implementing the plan iteratively. Each realized state is projected into the future to find the expected outcome and if the expected outcome has a probability of success less than the threshold (default value 0.5), a new plan is reinitiated from this realized state.

In summary, the BGEC, TAPT and SME provide five advantages: (1) the Bayesian probability metric prunes back the combinatorial explosion and focuses computational effort on the most probable outcomes; (2) the selection process recognizes the cost associated with planning and balances the benefit of additional planning against the cost of delayed execution; (3) moderated execution follows the selected plan only while it remains a probable success and reinitiates planning when it is not; (4) each stage of the process is adaptable to changes in goals; and (5) since the process directly responds to the goals, plan justification is directly traceable.

4   Application Areas

This new approach can be used for a wide variety of applications:
- Business Decision Support
- Investment Portfolio Management
- Battle Planning and Wargaming
- Intelligent Gaming Opponents for Training and Entertainment
- Autonomous Vehicle Navigation
- Personal Time Planner and Scheduler

To apply this approach to other problems four domain specific tasks must be accomplished first: (1) develop a model of the environment taking into account all pertinent states; (2) develop a function that provides a finite set of possible actions for each state (e.g., rules); (3) calculate outcome probabilities for each action for stochastic applications; and (4) develop a goal-based state evaluation function.

4.1   RISK Application

RISK is a game where many AI techniques can be tested prior to deployment in real-world war games. RISK incorporates the principles of war, is a top-down scalable model, and provides a good application for testing a variety of goal-directed AI approaches, such as DP, [6] RL, [3] [4] [6] EC [10] [11] [12] [13] and others [1] [2] [3]. RISK has much of the top-level decision-making structure of DP&E for command and control with the probability of rolling dice and turning in cards provides stochastic environmental effects. By integrating a goal-directed hybrid approach, one can develop a program that plays the RISK game effectively and move one step closer to solving more difficult real-world AI problems.

We have developed a DP&E program for the game RISK that incorporates the elements of planning and execution together [14]. The game RISK is not the real world and therefore some restrictions were placed on the problems this technique was geared to solve. For the RISK problem, as for many DP&E problems, a bounded state-space representation is warranted. However, the number of possible states within this representation is very high (over 10^{100}). As in many problems, applying a given action to a similar state does not always give the same result, thus there are stochastic state transitions. The space of concern is a partially observable Markov decision process [15], because the rolling of the dice and other opponents' moves are not known a priori. Progress can be measured in the game RISK, as in many other applications, because of the quantifiable attributes associated with any given state (e.g., number of troops). As in many DP&E problems, there is a finite set of behaviors and tasks of varying length. A summary of RISK problem characteristics is as follows:

- Discrete bounded state-space representation
- State transitions are stochastic in nature
- Partially observable Markov decision process
- Goal progress is measurable, and not just at the end state
- Many alternative behaviors, and for each, many more possible resulting states
- Variable length set of behaviors
- Multi-phase process with different types of behaviors, states and goals

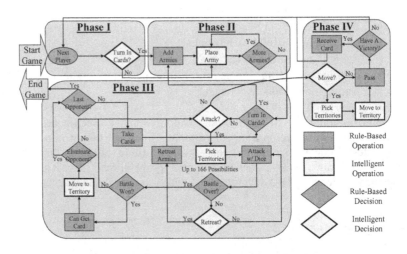

Fig. 1. RISK: Flowchart of Player's Turn

To solve a problem such as RISK one must first understand the nature and the complexity of the problem. Generally speaking, the game of RISK is a multiple player strategic game where players take turns at trying to conquer the world (see http://www.centralconnector.com/GAMES/RISK.htm for detailed RISK rules). Each turn is composed of reinforcing troops, battling opponents and moving forces. Every player has to follow the rules and procedures shown in Figure 1. The shaded shapes represent decisions imposed by the rules of the game while the transparent shapes represent intelligent decisions made by a player. The diamond-shape boxes represent yes/no decisions while the rectangular boxes represent decisions that have multiple choices. Using the model in Figure 1, which represents the rules of the game for one turn, one can measure the successes, failures and all possible outcomes of allocation, battle and move strategies.

4.2 Algorithm

```
Loop Games
  Loop Turns
    Loop Generations (1)
      Loop Selections
        Loop Offspring
          Generate Mutated Plans
      Add Parents
      Loop Selections
        Loop Offspring
          Loop Phases
            Generate Recombined Plans
      Add Parents
      Select Best Plans (Pareto Peaks)
    Loop Execute Plan
      Evaluate after each roll
      If Plan is deemed unsuccessful
        Go To 1
        Otherwise Continue
Tune Objective Weighting
```

The player up is dependent on the rules of the game [Appendix A: eqn. 1]. The actions available to take are a function of the rules of the game and the current state [Appendix A: eqn. 2]. Actions are randomly selected including a no action possibility, all with equal probability [Appendix A: eqn. 3]. As long as an action is selected the plan is continually projected, otherwise the current plan is terminated and proceeds to the next plan. Each plan can be a set of interdependent campaigns, note that for any independent action, increment the number of campaigns employed, otherwise continue along an existing campaign. Each action taken produces a set of n outcome-probability pairs that are a function of the rules of the game placed on the current state and set of actions projected [Appendix A: eqn. 4]. All outcome probabilities are calculated using the Bayesian theorem $Pr(A,B) = Pr(A) \, Pr(B/A)$. To keep the method from expanding exponentially, like outcomes are combined and their probabilities are added. Outcome-probability pairs can be ranked from worst case to best (i.e., increasing reward) and categorized from inconsequential (probability that an action was not possible based on previous action outcomes) to failures (action tried but failed) and successes (action tried and succeeded). For instance, the total success probability is the sum of all successful outcome probabilities. These three combined probability regions sum to one. Next from this list of possible outcomes an expected outcome is selected. The expected outcome is a function of the current state, set of actions and rules of the game along with a speculation heuristic that picks the expected values [Appendix A: eqn. 5]. The current projected actions and expected outcomes with success probabilities makeup the entire projected plan. The final set of plans are evaluated via a fitness function that equals the weighted multi-objective reward function for the final expected state minus the reward function of the initial state times the product of success probabilities of all expected campaigns with the reward function of the initial state re-added [Appendix A: eqn. 6]. This provides a better measure than just having a traditional fitness function that does not take into account success probability.

5   Results/Benefits

Admittedly, these are initial results. They are intended to show that the three techniques can play a role in a process to produce plans within constrained computational resources. Without these techniques, the explosion of the Risk decision tree would have made a standard evolutionary planning process intractable. In future papers we will quantify the benefit bestowed by each technique.

Results have been achieved in three major areas: (1) for the BGEC, adapting the weights for all the objectives in the evaluation function provide a better overall strategy and can handle a wider range of situations, (2) for the TAPT, monitoring the computational resources provides insight into situational dependencies so that evolutionary parameters can be adjusted to terminate the process sooner, and (3) for the SME, including the probability of success in the fitness function is less likely to require re-evolving when the plan is executed, thus saving computational resources and producing a more stable and successful plan.

BGEC is greatly dependent on the user-defined set of objectives laid out a priori and five plausible objectives for RISK are shown in Figure 2. These five objectives were chosen to be important factors for measuring the quality of a plan through the use of playing the RISK II game by Hasbro (http://www.searchamateur.com/corkboard/Risk.html). In an offline manner, BGEC was run against the Hasbro RISK game to determine the best weightings. Given the time required to play offline (two hours per game), only about 20 games were played to determine quality weightings, where the BGEC won more than half the games against multiple opponents. It was determined that not all of these objectives are of equal importance and weighting them is situational dependent. For instance, if one only used objective 1, no battles would be fought because one would not risk losing any troops on a turn to gain objective 2, reinforcements. Conversely if one only used the reinforcement objective then one would fight to the end, thus so weakening that the player may not last to next turn. Balancing these objectives is a concern and the only true way to converge on the best weightings is with 'trial and error' of playing the game. Thus far, the best weightings are shown in Figure 2 in the right column. Future versions of BGEC will learn these weightings from playing the game against itself.

For TAPT to be effective, knowledge on what processes are running and how much computer time they take is required. At the most rudimentary level, computational time is calculated based on modules used in nine distinct areas: (1) a one time setup, (2) enforcement of rules to provide possible actions, (3) choice of a random action, (4) Bayesian calculations for state transition probabilities, (5)

Objectives	Reward Values	Weighted
1. Maximize Overall Strength (OS)	$\dfrac{\text{Individual Force}}{\text{Total Forces}}$	0.45
2. Maximize Expected Reinforcements (ER)	$\dfrac{\text{Individual Reinforcements}}{\text{Total Reinforcements}}$	0.33
3. Minimize No. of Defensive Fronts (DF)	$1 - \dfrac{\dfrac{\text{Individual Frontal Regions}}{\text{Individual Total Regions}}}{\dfrac{\text{Total Frontal Regions}}{\text{Total Regions}}}$	0.02
4. Maximize Strength of Fronts (SF)	$\dfrac{\text{Individual Frontal Forces}}{\text{Total Individual Forces}}$	0.05
5. Maximize Logistical Support (LS)	$\dfrac{\dfrac{\text{Individual Frontal Forces}}{\text{Individual Support Forces}}}{\dfrac{\text{Total Frontal Forces}}{\text{Total Support Forces}}}$	0.15

Fig. 2. Expert-Defined Evaluation Function

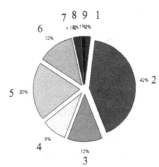

Fig. 3a. Computational Resources Used for Simple Plan   **Fig. 3b.** Computational Resources Used for Complex Plan

fitness function calculations, (6) plan storage, (7) add parents to increase selection pool, (8) selection of the best plans and (9) clip the best plans at their Pareto peaks. Figure 3 shows two different temporal resource situations, 3a shows how the resources are used on a simple situation in the game while 3b shows how the resources are used in a much more complex situation (takeovers are involved). Numbers 1-9 in the pie charts correspond to the resource areas described above. Note that areas 1 and 2 are independent of the evolutionary parameters chosen and in both circumstances require an appreciable amount of resources. Also note that areas 4 and 9 increase appreciably for complex plans, because many battles require more Bayesian calculations and more takeovers increases the phase number and thus increases the number of plans that require clipping during recombination. For example, the number of phases in a turn could grow to as high as 16 with the possibility of 7 takeovers in a given turn and given 8 selections and 8 offspring gives up to 8 x 8 x 16 possible recombined plans in a given generation, thus shifting the burden of processing to modules such as the Bayesian battle outcomes (i.e., 4) and clipping these plans at their Pareto peaks (i.e., 9). Monitoring of temporal processes at this level allows one to adapt the evolutionary parameters based on the situation. Further research is necessary in making this objective automatic.

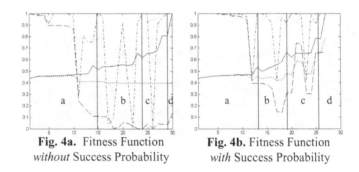

Fig. 4a. Fitness Function
without Success Probability

Fig. 4b. Fitness Function
with Success Probability

The SME provides a way to re-evolve plans when the probability of success ($Pr(su)$) falls below a threshold. Thus, when multiple campaigns are incorporated in a plan, applying the probability of success in the fitness function creates a better overall plan. The best way to see this is with an example. Consider a strategic point in the game where one player has the possibility of taking over four players in a single turn and winning the game. In this instance, the other players have enough cards to take control of the game if the current player does not take advantage of the current situation. Figure 4a and 4b illustrate four underlying components that discern the difference in success of two plans. Figure 4a represents the plan without the probability of success included, while 4b uses the probability of success. The x-axis represents each move, while the y-axis either represents probability or fitness. The solid lines in both figures represent the measure of the evaluation function (Figure 2) without probability of success, the dot-dashed line represents individual action success probabilities, the dashed lines represent the overall probability of success based on multiplying independent campaigns, while the dotted line represents the overall fitness function value if the probability of success were included. The most notable feature from figure 4a and b are the overall probability of success (dashed lines). For the simple fitness function case, the overall success probability is 14%, while for the case where the probability of success was included the competition drove the probability of success to 66%. Thus, including the probability of success gives a far better chance of taking over all four opponents in this turn and will probably not require a re-evolving of the turn plan. Both results were calculated using selections equal to 8, offspring equal to 8, and generations equal to 10. For more detail on the battle sequence, see posted website: http://www.viewtap.com/risk.

6 Future Work

The near-term plans are to evaluate the developed algorithm in two ways: winning percentage and planning time performance. The game of RISK will be the challenging problem used where DP&E novelty and significance can be proven empirically. Currently, the algorithm is equipped to play against itself and many game trials will be run to determine the best evolutionary parameters and the best weighting parameters. Also, the algorithm will be available to play against human players, however, the program is written in a Matlab environment and players currently require a Matlab license. Plans are underway to convert the program into a Java version such as the open-source version found on the web (http://prdownloads. sourceforge.net/javarisk/JRiskv2_0.92.jar?use_mirror=cesnet). This open source version uses a more traditional cost-based algorithm that may give the Evolutionary Bayesian Network some competition. Thus, the *JRisk* program will be integrated into the current design and play against Evolutionary Bayesian Network.

These results will provide quantitative measures to: (1) better characterize how parameter choices within the algorithm affect the computational resources required such as time and memory; (2) see if there is a point where training the Evolutionary Bayesian Network can better compete with other algorithms and human players, if so, how many training games and how much time were necessary; (3) human players currently have the right to limit the time the algorithm has to converge on a solution. At what point, if any, does the game player outplay a human player?

This approach advances understanding as to: (1) how to use Bayesian probability to prune combinatorial explosive planning spaces; (2) how to incorporate temporal planning cost in an objective function; and (3) a procedure for mapping a problem (i.e., data and knowledge) into the dynamic planning and execution framework.

The work accomplished thus far lays a strong foundation for future work. More specifically, incorporating learning into the current adaptable approach can further improve action selections, the environmental model and the multi-objective evaluation function. Also, the temporal costs in learning (training) can be factored into the overall planning process. Other questions that may be answerable are: what factors matter in how long a plan is retained? What affect does the incorporation of re-planning cost in the objective function have? How does a user-defined time constraint affect the winning performance? We will also work to establish a foundation for determining the efficiency of an algorithm for exploring planning spaces.

References

1. T. Taipale, S. Pieska, & J. Riekki, "Dynamic planning based control of autonomous machine," *Proceedings on Real-Time Systems*, 1991, pp. 120-126.
2. R. Levinson, F. H. Hsu, J. Schaeffe, T. A. Marsland, & D. E. Wilkins, "The role of chess in artificial-intelligence research," *ICCA Journal*, V. 14, N. 3, 1991, pp. 153-161.
3. H.J. van den Herik, J. W.H.M. Uiterwijk & J. van Rijswijck, "Games solved: now and in the future," *Artificial Intelligence V. 134*, 2002, pp. 277-311.
4. G. Tesauro, "Temporal difference learning and TD-Gammon," *Communications of the ACM*, V. 38, N. 3, 1995, pp. 58-68.
5. K. Chellapilla and D.B. Fogel, "Anaconda defeats Hoyle 6-0: a case study competing an evolved checkers program against commercially available software," *Proceedings of the 2000 Congress on Evolutionary Computation*, IEEE Press, Piscataway, NJ, 2000, pp. 857-863.
6. R. S. Sutton & A. Barto, *Introduction to Reinforcement Learning*, MIT Press / Bradford Books, Cambridge, MA, 1998.

7. D.B. Fogel "The advantages of evolutionary computation," *Bio-Computing and Emergent Computation* 1997, D. Lundh, B. Olsson, and A. Narayanan (eds.), Sköve, Sweden, World Scientific Press, Singapore, pp. 1-11.
8. Aluizo F. R. Araujo & Arthur P.S. Braga, "Reward-penalty reinforcement learning scheme for planning and reactive behavior," *IEEE International Conference on Systems, Man and Cybernetics*, V. 2, 1998, pp. 1485-1490.
9. G. Tesauro, "Programming backgammon using self-teaching neural nets," *Artificial Intelligence*, V. *134*, 2002, pp. 181-199.
10. K. P. Dahal, G. M. Burt, J. R. McDonald, & A. Moyes, "A case study of scheduling storage tanks using a hybrid genetic algorithm," *IEEE Transactions on Evolutionary Computation*, V. 5, N. 3, June 2001, pp. 283-294.
11. V. William Porto, "Using evolutionary programming to optimize the allocation of surveillance assets," *Lecture Notes in Computer Science*, V. *1585*, 1999, pp. 215-222.
12. J. B. Zydallis, "Explicit building-block multiobjective genetic algorithms: theory, analysis and development", *Dissertation: Air Force Institute of Technology*, March 2003.
13. D. H. Wolpert and W. G. Macready, "No free lunch theorems for optimization", *IEEE Transactions on Evolutionary Computation, 1(1)*, April 1997, pp. 67-82.
14. R. Barrufi & M. Milano, "Planning and execution in dynamic environments," *Lecture Notes in Computer Science*, V. *2175*, 2001, pp. 382-387.
15. M.L. Littman, "Value-function reinforcement learning in Markov games," *Journal of Cognitive Systems Research*, V. 2, 2001, pp. 55-66.

Appendix: Algorithm Equations

$$u = R(\mathbf{E}) \tag{1}$$

$$A = R(\mathbf{E}, S_{p,\lambda}') \tag{2}$$

$$A_{p,\lambda+1}' = \text{randselect}[\mathbf{A}, \text{Null}] \tag{3}$$

$$R(\mathbf{E}, S_{p,\lambda}', A_{p,\lambda+1}') = \{o_1, \Pr(o_1), o_2, \Pr(o_2), o_3, \Pr(o_3), \ldots, o_n, \Pr(o_n)\} \tag{4}$$

$$S_{p,\lambda+1}' = R(\mathbf{E}, S_{p,\lambda}', A_{p,\lambda+1}', \eta) \tag{5}$$

$$F_p' = ((M(S_p') - M(S_0)) \bullet W) \, \Pi \upsilon + M(S_0) \tag{6}$$

E = Game Environment: Multiple Arrays
R = Rules of Game: Multiple Functions
A = Set of Actions Available
S_0 = Current or Original State
λ = length of a plan
p = Plan
$S_{p,\lambda}'$ = Projected State: plan p at length λ
$A_{p,\lambda+1}'$ = Projected Action: plan p at step $\lambda+1$
η = Speculation Heuristic: Scalar Constant
M = Objectives Evaluation Function
φ = Objectives (five shown in Figure 2)

ψ = Number of Players (3 to 8 for RISK)
W = φ by ψ Weighted Objective Matrix
o_n = Outcome n
$\Pr(o_n)$ = Probability of Outcome n
υ = Set of Success Probabilities
F_p' = Projected fitness of plan p

Author Index

Lecture Notes in Computer Science

For information about Vols. 1–2879

please contact your bookseller or Springer-Verlag

Vol. 2941: M. Wirsing, A. Knapp, S. Balsamo (Eds.), Radical Innovations of Software and Systems Engineering in the Future. X, 359 pages. 2004.

Vol. 2940: C. Lucena, A. Garcia, A. Romanovsky, J. Castro, P.S. Alencar (Eds.), Software Engineering for Multi-Agent Systems II. XII, 279 pages. 2004.

Vol. 2939: T. Kalker, I.J. Cox, Y.M. Ro (Eds.), Digital Watermarking. XII, 602 pages. 2004.

Vol. 2937: B. Steffen, G. Levi (Eds.), Verification, Model Checking, and Abstract Interpretation. XI, 325 pages. 2004.

Vol. 2934: G. Lindemann, D. Moldt, M. Paolucci (Eds.), Regulated Agent-Based Social Systems. X, 301 pages. 2004. (Subseries LNAI).

Vol. 2930: F. Winkler (Ed.), Automated Deduction in Geometry. VII, 231 pages. 2004. (Subseries LNAI).

Vol. 2926: L. van Elst, V. Dignum, A. Abecker (Eds.), Agent-Mediated Knowledge Management. XI, 428 pages. 2004. (Subseries LNAI).

Vol. 2923: V. Lifschitz, I. Niemelä (Eds.), Logic Programming and Nonmonotonic Reasoning. IX, 365 pages. 2004. (Subseries LNAI).

Vol. 2919: E. Giunchiglia, A. Tacchella (Eds.), Theory and Applications of Satisfiability Testing. XI, 530 pages. 2004.

Vol. 2917: E. Quintarelli, Model-Checking Based Data Retrieval. XVI, 134 pages. 2004.

Vol. 2916: C. Palamidessi (Ed.), Logic Programming. XII, 520 pages. 2003.

Vol. 2915: A. Camurri, G. Volpe (Eds.), Gesture-Based Communication in Human-Computer Interaction. XIII, 558 pages. 2004. (Subseries LNAI).

Vol. 2914: P.K. Pandya, J. Radhakrishnan (Eds.), FST TCS 2003: Foundations of Software Technology and Theoretical Computer Science. XIII, 446 pages. 2003.

Vol. 2913: T.M. Pinkston, V.K. Prasanna (Eds.), High Performance Computing - HiPC 2003. XX, 512 pages. 2003. (Subseries LNAI).

Vol. 2911: T.M.T. Sembok, H.B. Zaman, H. Chen, S.R. Urs, S.H. Myaeng (Eds.), Digital Libraries: Technology and Management of Indigenous Knowledge for Global Access. XX, 703 pages. 2003.

Vol. 2910: M.E. Orlowska, S. Weerawarana, M.M.P. Papazoglou, J. Yang (Eds.), Service-Oriented Computing - ICSOC 2003. XIV, 576 pages. 2003.

Vol. 2909: R. Solis-Oba, K. Jansen (Eds.), Approximation and Online Algorithms. VIII, 269 pages. 2004.

Vol. 2908: K. Chae, M. Yung (Eds.), Information Security Applications. XII, 506 pages. 2004.

Vol. 2907: I. Lirkov, S. Margenov, J. Wasniewski, P. Yalamov (Eds.), Large-Scale Scientific Computing. XI, 490 pages. 2004.

Vol. 2906: T. Ibaraki, N. Katoh, H. Ono (Eds.), Algorithms and Computation. XVII, 748 pages. 2003.

Vol. 2905: A. Sanfeliu, J. Ruiz-Shulcloper (Eds.), Progress in Pattern Recognition, Speech and Image Analysis. XVII, 693 pages. 2003.

Vol. 2904: T. Johansson, S. Maitra (Eds.), Progress in Cryptology - INDOCRYPT 2003. XI, 431 pages. 2003.

Vol. 2903: T.D. Gedeon, L.C.C. Fung (Eds.), AI 2003: Advances in Artificial Intelligence. XVI, 1075 pages. 2003. (Subseries LNAI).

Vol. 2902: F.M. Pires, S.P. Abreu (Eds.), Progress in Artificial Intelligence. XV, 504 pages. 2003. (Subseries LNAI).

Vol. 2901: F. Bry, N. Henze, J. Ma luszyński (Eds.), Principles and Practice of Semantic Web Reasoning. X, 209 pages. 2003.

Vol. 2900: M. Bidoit, P.D. Mosses (Eds.), Casl User Manual. XIII, 240 pages. 2004.

Vol. 2899: G. Ventre, R. Canonico (Eds.), Interactive Multimedia on Next Generation Networks. XIV, 420 pages. 2003.

Vol. 2898: K.G. Paterson (Ed.), Cryptography and Coding. IX, 385 pages. 2003.

Vol. 2897: O. Balet, G. Subsol, P. Torguet (Eds.), Virtual Storytelling. XI, 240 pages. 2003.

Vol. 2896: V.A. Saraswat (Ed.), Advances in Computing Science – ASIAN 2003. VIII, 305 pages. 2003.

Vol. 2895: A. Ohori (Ed.), Programming Languages and Systems. XIII, 427 pages. 2003.

Vol. 2894: C.S. Laih (Ed.), Advances in Cryptology - ASIACRYPT 2003. XIII, 543 pages. 2003.

Vol. 2893: J.-B. Stefani, I. Demeure, D. Hagimont (Eds.), Distributed Applications and Interoperable Systems. XIII, 311 pages. 2003.

Vol. 2892: F. Dau, The Logic System of Concept Graphs with Negation. XI, 213 pages. 2003. (Subseries LNAI).

Vol. 2891: J. Lee, M. Barley (Eds.), Intelligent Agents and Multi-Agent Systems. X, 215 pages. 2003. (Subseries LNAI).

Vol. 2890: M. Broy, A.V. Zamulin (Eds.), Perspectives of System Informatics. XV, 572 pages. 2003.

Vol. 2889: R. Meersman, Z. Tari (Eds.), On The Move to Meaningful Internet Systems 2003: OTM 2003 Workshops. XIX, 1071 pages. 2003.

Vol. 2888: R. Meersman, Z. Tari, D.C. Schmidt (Eds.), On The Move to Meaningful Internet Systems 2003: CoopIS, DOA, and ODBASE. XXI, 1546 pages. 2003.

Vol. 2887: T. Johansson (Ed.), Fast Software Encryption. IX, 397 pages. 2003.

Vol. 2886: I. Nyström, G. Sanniti di Baja, S. Svensson (Eds.), Discrete Geometry for Computer Imagery. XII, 556 pages. 2003.

Vol. 2885: J.S. Dong, J. Woodcock (Eds.), Formal Methods and Software Engineering. XI, 683 pages. 2003.

Vol. 2884: E. Najm, U. Nestmann, P. Stevens (Eds.), Formal Methods for Open Object-Based Distributed Systems. X, 293 pages. 2003.

Vol. 2883: J. Schaeffer, M. Müller, Y. Björnsson (Eds.), Computers and Games. XI, 431 pages. 2003.

Vol. 2882: D. Veit, Matchmaking in Electronic Markets. XV, 180 pages. 2003. (Subseries LNAI).

Vol. 2881: E. Horlait, T. Magedanz, R.H. Glitho (Eds.), Mobile Agents for Telecommunication Applications. IX, 297 pages. 2003.

Vol. 2880: H.L. Bodlaender (Ed.), Graph-Theoretic Concepts in Computer Science. XI, 386 pages. 2003.